Reinventing Foreign Aid

edited by William Easterly

foreword by Nancy Birdsall

sponsored by the Center for Global Development

The MIT Press
Cambridge, Massachusetts
London, England

MIT Press books may be purchased at special quantity discounts for business or sales promotional use. For information, please e-mail special_sales@mitpress.mit.edu or write to Special Sales Department, The MIT Press, 55 Hayward Street, Cambridge, MA 02142.

This book was set in Times New Roman on 3B2 by Asco Typesetters, Hong Kong and was printed and bound in the United States of America.

Library of Congress Cataloging-in-Publication Data

Reinventing foreign aid / edited by William Easterly ; foreword by Nancy Birdsall.
  p. cm.
Includes bibliographical references and index.
ISBN 978-0-262-05090-6 (hardcover : alk. paper) — ISBN 978-0-262-55066-6 (pbk. : alk. paper)
1. Economic assistance—Developing countries—Evaluation. 2. Economic development projects—Developing countries—Evaluation. I. Easterly, William Russell.
HC60.R353   2007
338.9109172′4—dc22   2007013993

10 9 8 7 6 5 4 3 2

Contents

Foreword

Foreign aid in 2005 was higher than ever before in history, at around $100 billion. Not only that, but it attracted an unprecedented amount of attention from the media and from politicians in 2005 and 2006. Such unlikely companions as George W. Bush and Bono, Tony Blair and Bob Geldof, Bill Clinton and Brad Pitt, Jeffrey Sachs and Angelina Jolie, Bill Gates and Kofi Annan, all turned their attention to the problems of poor countries and the potential for well-intentioned people from rich countries to help address those problems by increasing aid flows.

Yet at the same time that foreign aid was attaining unprecedented amounts of funding and attention, the long-standing debate about what foreign aid could, should, or would do grew fiercer and more contentious than it had been in years.

At the Center for Global Development, we are dedicated to the idea that the rich world can do better for the poor world through more development-friendly approaches to trade, migration, security and other policies, and most obviously through more effective deployment of foreign aid. We believe the debate about foreign aid has and will contribute to the hard struggle to make foreign aid work better for the world's poor. Bill Easterly, one of the center's first senior fellows in 2001–2002 and now a nonresident fellow, has made an outstanding (and controversial) contribution to that debate in the past decade, including the 2005 publication of his best-seller (for a development book!) *The White Man's Burden: Why the West's Efforts to Aid the Rest Have Done So Much Ill and So Little Good.*

Now in this book, he has brought together leading scholars and practitioners in the field of foreign aid to address all sides of the debate in which he has been already a major player. The chapter authors do not necessarily agree with him or with each other. They bring diverse perspectives, arguments, styles, and methodologies. What they share is a firm commitment to ideas and evidence—to bringing useful knowledge and experience to bear on the challenge of making foreign aid effective. Hardly anyone in this book, including myself (or, for that matter, outside this book), is satisfied with the past performance of foreign aid agencies. Yet progress in public policy does happen. It happens, among other means, through improved knowledge and through the process of open intellectual debate. At the Center for Global Development, we are pleased to bring this book to readers in the hope that there will be more and faster progress in reinventing foreign aid.

Nancy Birdsall
President, Center for Global Development

Reinventing Foreign Aid

1 Introduction: Can't Take It Anymore?

William Easterly

Foreign aid is in the headlines more than ever before in its sixty-year history, and it has big ambitions. Such diverse scholars as George Clooney, Penelope Cruz, Alicia Keyes, Jay-Z, Will Smith, Stevie Wonder, Elton John, Paul McCartney, Salma Hayek, Brad Pitt, Mariah Carey, Bono, and Angelina Jolie have appeared in public events or in the media calling for an increase in foreign aid to poor countries. The objective of "the biggest ever antipoverty movement" was to "Make Poverty History."

Strong claims are made about the potential of aid in many current aid agency documents. The UNDP makes a general statement: "International aid is one of the most effective weapons in the war against poverty." However, at the same time, discontent with the existing aid system is also remarkably universal, including some of the same authors who make strong claims for aid. For example, the very next sentence in the UNDP report just cited seems to contradict the previous statement that the aid weapon is effective: "Today, that weapon is underused, inefficiently targeted and in need of repair."[1] (UNDP 2005, p. 2).

Similarly the UN Millennium Project also makes the link from expert plans to foreign aid: "Poverty in the poorest countries can be dramatically reduced only if developing countries put well designed and well implemented plans in place to reduce poverty—and only if rich countries match their efforts with substantial increases in support."[2] However, much later in the same report, we learn that "many national strategies will require significant international support. But the international system is ill equipped to provide it because of a shortage of supportive rules, effective institutional arrangements, and above all resolve to translate commitments to action."[3] To show how universal this bipolarity is, the Department for International Development (DFID) states, "Aid works. Aid helps reduce poverty by increasing economic growth, improving governance and increasing access to public services." But again, toward the end of the same report, we have the seemingly contradictory statement: "But some parts of the international system have become either too complicated and inefficient or simply do not work at all. They must change."[4]

This bipolarity of "aid does work already and will work in the future, but aid is also not working" sometimes leads to remarkably penitential statements by the aid agencies themselves. For example, the international financial institutions—the World Bank and International Monetary Fund (IMF)— issued a report in 2006 in which a sentence in the opening paragraph of the executive summary states: "International financial institutions still emphasize loans and reports rather than development outcomes."[5]

The mixture of grandiose expectations for future aid with frustration about existing aid captures well the current, muddled climate of opinion about what foreign aid is doing, will do, can do, or should do. Although many aspects of foreign aid are hotly debated, one view that seems to command almost universal assent from observers of the aid system (including from the aid agencies themselves about their own operations) is that the current aid system is not working very well.

Despite this dissatisfaction with the current system, all of the main political actors in the rich countries seem to agree on increasing the volume of aid. (They also talk about ways to improve the aid system, but progress on that appears inherently more problematic than increasing aid spending.) The World Bank and IMF in their *Global Monitoring Report 2006* say, "Donors are delivering more assistance, and the prospects for scaling up aid have brightened. At their summit in Gleneagles, the Group of Eight (G-8) leaders pledged to increase aid to Africa by $25 billion a year by 2010—more than doubling assistance to the region—and Development Assistance Committee (DAC) members have agreed to expand aid to all developing countries by about $50 billion."[6]

After stagnating in the 1990s, total foreign aid has indeed increased sharply in the new millennium (figure 1.1).[7] Hence, it is more important than ever before to think about how aid can effectively help the poorest people in the world.

In section 1.1, I sketch some of the larger issues in the foreign aid debate, which many of the authors of the chapters in this book are grappling with (although not necessarily in agreement with my take on the debate). Just as these chapters span the range from academic journal style to nontechnical opinion pieces, this introduction is not intended so much to be a scholarly contribution as it is to provoke debate and highlight the opposing points of view. Section 1.1 is frankly polemical, a style that I chose to reflect the dissatisfaction that I and others feel with a dysfunctional business that is supposed to be benefiting the most desperate people in the world (although not all of us are in agreement on diagnoses or cures). I then give a summary of the rest of the chapters in section 1.2.

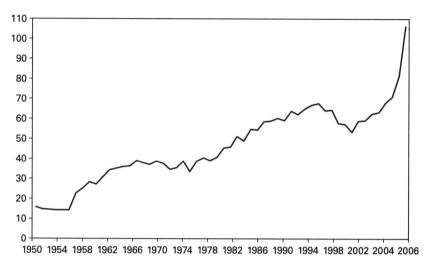

Figure 1.1
Total foreign aid from OECD countries in 2005 US$ billion, 1950–2005

1.1 Comprehensive Planning versus Piecemeal Searching in Foreign Aid

The nature of man is intricate; the objects of society are of the greatest complexity: and therefore no simple disposition or direction of power can be suitable either to man's nature or to the quality of his affairs.
—Edmund Burke (1790)

All of the major aid agencies are now engaged in an exercise to achieve what are known as the Millennium Development Goals (MDGs) by the year 2015. As the United Nations Development Program explains, "Five years ago, at the start of the new millennium, the world's governments united to make a remarkable promise to the victims of global poverty. Meeting at the United Nations, they signed the Millennium declaration—a solemn pledge 'to free our fellow men, women and children from the abject and dehumanizing conditions of extreme poverty.'"[8]

Jeffrey Sachs presents the aim of his recommendations as to "help foster economic systems that spread the benefits of science, technology to all parts of the world; Help foster international cooperation to secure a perpetual peace; Help promote science and technology, grounded in human rationality, to fuel the continued prospect of improving the human condition. This agenda is broad and bold, as it has been for two centuries, but many of its sweetest fruits are just within our reach."[9]

U.K. Secretary of State for International Development Hilary Benn in a DFID white paper in 2006 agreed that "today...—for the first time—[the human family] has the capacity to make sure that every one of its members is lifted out of poverty. What people want and need is enough food to eat and water to drink. A roof over their heads, a job, a school for their children, and medicine and care when they are sick. The chance to live in peace, without fear of violence or war. And the opportunity to realise the potential in each and every one of us.... It is up to us to accept that responsibility and do what needs to be done."[10]

These statements could be just inspirational rhetoric, and these campaigns do talk about specific, feasible tasks. However, an important part of the field of economic development has always been influenced by utopian ideals, which in turn seem to influence the approach to foreign aid (as they do for the UNDP, DFID, and Sachs). "Economic development" is sometimes presented as something like a teleological philosophy of history, in which all countries are destined to attain the goal of development, meaning industrialization and a high mass standard of living, not to mention peace and democracy. In this view, economic development is something like the other teleological philosophies of history, like Hegelianism and Marxism. The teleological worldview goes all the way back at least to Aristotle, who talked about a Final Cause that was more fundamental than the proximate causes of events. The Final Cause was the goal or destiny toward which the object was progressing. In this worldview, the future causes the present, so the destiny of development causes all countries (if not already developed) to be developing. Unfortunately, like all other teleological theories, the claims of this approach to economic development are nontestable and nonfalsifiable. (You can test hypotheses about the past but not about the future.)

A curious paradox of the teleological philosophies of history is that they give great importance to vigorous action by a small chosen group of actors to achieve what is predestined to happen anyway. Hegel talked about "world-historical individuals," Marxists talked about the revolutionary vanguard of the working class, and economic development has a prominent role for development experts, who come with a plan of government actions to promote development. The Make Poverty History campaign urges its members to "take action now to pressure politicians and decision makers to help make poverty history."[11]

Discussions of world poverty often begin with a question something like, "What must we do"? Lenin may have helped launch this twentieth-century fad with his 1902 pamphlet, "What Is to Be Done?" in which he looked for the intelligentsia to find the answers for the masses. He reprints an 1874 quote from Engels: "It is the specified duty of the leaders to gain an ever-clearer understanding of the theoretical problems, to free themselves more and more from the influence of traditional phrases inherited from the old conception of the world. The task of the leaders will be to bring understanding, thus acquired and clarified to the working masses, to spread it with increased enthusiasm."[12]

Sachs says, "I have gradually come to understand through my scientific research and on the ground advisory work the awesome power in our generation's hands to end the massive suffering of the extreme poor." Sachs boldly states that "success in ending the poverty trap will be much easier than it appears."[13]

DFID puts it a little less eloquently: "There needs to be rapid progress on the commitments made by developing countries and the international community to provide peace and security, encourage economic growth, and invest in the most important public services."[14]

Like the teleological view of development, the impact of development experts is presented in a way that makes it nonfalsifiable: if a past group of experts did not achieve development, they were bad experts, whereas now we have good experts. Or there has been progress in knowledge or technology such that the latest generation of experts can now for the first time eliminate poverty: "The practical solutions exist. . . . And for the first time, the cost is utterly affordable."[15] As Hilary Benn said in the DFID report quoted above, world poverty can now be ended "for the first time." This claim of a brand new opportunity to reduce poverty at an "utterly affordable" cost is important, because otherwise one wonders why previous development experts did not already achieve the easy solutions promised by the current experts to world poverty and its attendant miseries.

The expert plans are to be financed by foreign aid. Thus, the UNDP places aid at the center of achieving the promise of attaining the MDGs: "If donor countries are serious about tackling global poverty, reducing inequality and securing a safer and more prosperous future for their own citizens, they need to set their sights firmly on the target of delivering 0.5% of their national income in aid by 2010 and 0.7% by 2015."[16]

DFID concurs that to finance peace, economic growth, and public services, "Additional resources will be essential for this. We must, therefore, ensure that the international community delivers the US$50 billion increase in aid promised by 2010."[17]

1.1.1 Two Alternative Philosophies of Foreign Aid

The response of this introduction to the statements I have quoted is frankly polemical, a word that is often given a negative connotation. This introduction argues that polemics is useful in aid debates, because too often the aid policy-making community tolerates approaches that go against common sense and basic economics.

For example, the utopian expectations of what foreign aid should do often create an unfortunate approach to aid. Seventeen years after the fall of the Berlin Wall, there is only one major area of the world in which something that sounds a lot like central planning is still seen as a way to achieve prosperity: countries that receive foreign aid. Behind the aid wall that divides poor countries from rich, the aid community is awash in plans, strategies, and frameworks to meet the very real needs of the world's poor. These exercises make sense only in a central planning mentality in which the answer to the tragedies of poverty is a large bureaucratic apparatus to dictate quantities of different development goods and services by administrative fiat.[18] The planning mind-set is in turn linked to previously discredited theories, such as that poverty is due to a "poverty trap," which can be alleviated only by a large inflow of aid from rich country to poor country governments to fill a "financing gap" for poor countries (I examine this idea yet again below). The aid inflow is, of course, administered by this same planning apparatus.

This is bad news for the world's poor, as historically poverty has not been ended by central planners. It is ended by "searchers," both economic and political, who explore solutions by trial and error, have a way to get feedback on the ones that work, and then expand the ones that work, all of this in an unplanned, spontaneous way. Examples of searchers are firms in private markets and democratically accountable politicians.

What are some of the characteristics of planners and searchers? In foreign aid, the planners set out a predetermined big goal, like ending world poverty, to be solved. They also determine a big plan to reach the big goal and throw an endless supply of resources and a large administrative apparatus at that big goal.

The searcher is more humble about how little she knows about other people's problems. Searchers do not set predetermined problems and do not have big plans; they are just on the lookout for favorable opportunities to solve problems—any problem no matter how big or small, whose solution will benefit themselves or others. Searchers must learn enough about each little problem to solve it, which means they must get feedback from the people affected by the problem and what they need to fix it.

A planner thinks he already knows the answers; he thinks of poverty as a technical engineering problem that his answers will solve. As the UN Millennium Project put it in 2005, "Throughout, we stress that the specific technologies for achieving the [Millennium Development] Goals are known. What is needed is to apply them at scale."[19]

A searcher admits she does not know the answers in advance; she believes that poverty is a complicated tangle of political, social, historical, institutional, and technological factors. A searcher only hopes to find answers to individual problems of the world's poor by trial-and-error experimentation.

Planners conceive the key to progress on poverty as a grand international effort at collective action. Sachs says in the opening pages of *The End of Poverty*: "Although introductory economics textbooks preach individualism and decentralized markets, our safety and prosperity depend at least as much on collective decisions to fight disease, promote good science and widespread education, provide critical infrastructure, and act in unison to help the poorest of the poor.... Collective action, through effective government provision of health, education, infrastructure, as well as foreign assistance when needed, underpins economic success."[20] He says that each poor country should have five plans, such as an "Investment Plan, which shows the size, timing, and costs of the required investments" and a "Financial Plan to fund the Investment Plan, including the calculation of the Millennium Development Goals Financing Gap, the portion of financial needs the donors will have to fill."[21]

U.N. secretary-general from Kofi Annan, uses the collective action *we*: "We will have time to reach the Millennium Development Goals—worldwide and in most, or even all, individual countries—but only if we break with business as usual. We cannot win overnight. Success will require sustained action across the entire decade between now and the deadline. It takes time to train the teachers, nurses and engineers; to build the roads, schools and hospitals; to grow the small and large businesses able to create the jobs and income needed. So we must start now. And we must more than double global development assistance over the next few years. Nothing less will help to achieve the Goals."[22] Annan uses *grow* as an active verb applied to business—something that "we must start now." To the UN, collective action will create jobs and income, as opposed to the decentralized efforts of individual entrepreneurs and firms operating in free markets.

Insofar as the MDG campaign mentions private entrepreneurs, they are "partners" subject to "our" resolve: "We resolve further:... To develop and implement strategies that give young people everywhere a real chance to find decent and productive work.... To develop strong partnerships with the private sector and with civil society organizations in pursuit of development and poverty eradication."[23]

For their part, the IMF and World Bank are fervent advocates of free markets for prosperity, not statist strategizing, but some unlucky countries are so poor that they face the requirement to do statist strategizing anyway. This is in the form of what is called a poverty reduction strategy paper (PRSP). The preparation of the PRSP requires planning that would overwhelm the most so-phisticated government bureaucracy anywhere, much less the underskilled and underpaid government workers in the poorest countries: "The sector ministries prepare medium-term strategic plans that set out the sector's key objectives, to-gether with their associated outcomes, outputs, and expenditure forecasts (with-in the limits agreed upon by the Cabinet). These plans should consider the costs of both ongoing and new programs. Ideally, spending should be presented by program and spending category with financing needs for salaries, operations and maintenance, and investment clearly distinguished."[24] If they have any time left after all this planning (not to mention time left after their meeting with the hundreds of donor missions that arrive every year to check up on the plan), they can also come up with a plan for those same donors: "an external assistance strategy in the context of the PRSP process that explicitly identifies the priority sectors and programs for donor financing.... More detailed exter-nal assistance strategies can then be developed for key areas through sectoral working groups in which representatives of major donors and line agencies participate.... Agreeing on financing priorities for individual donors within the framework of a global external assistance strategy, rather than through bi-lateral agreements."[25]

The World Bank and IMF further affirmed in the 2006 *Global Monitoring Report* a commitment to "accountability for achieving results by 'Implement-ing the results agenda,'" in which they will draw "on MDB [multilateral devel-opment bank] frameworks and action plans to implement managing for development results (MfDR)." MfDR is summed up in a 2006 *MfDR Source-book*, prepared by the Organization for Economic Cooperation and Develop-ment (OECD) and the World Bank, which again places its faith in planning:

At the national level (see Part 2), MfDR is used in the planning and implementation of results-based national plans, budgets, and antipoverty strategies. International agencies may support this process with technical assistance.[26]

In sector programs and projects (see Part 3), partner countries and development agencies use MfDR in planning assistance programs or individual projects that are based on country outcomes and priorities defined in national or sector development plans.

Of course, the failure to meet planning goals could occur because the goals were too optimistic or depend on factors beyond the control of the UN, IMF, and the World Bank. Far from absolving the aid community, however, this only raises the question of why so much energy is devoted to a campaign (the MDGs) that does not create any positive incentives for any actors because it is overpromising on things that the actors cannot control. The World Bank itself cautions poor countries against setting targets in the PRSPs that are too optimistic for exactly this reason: "Most often [the PRSP targets] are overambitious; they are technically and fiscally unattainable, which defeats their role as effective incentives to action."[27] The same PRSP Sourcebook of the World Bank also warns, "It must be possible to disentangle the effects of poor performance by the implementing actors from the effects of external shocks."[28] The MDGs endorsed by the Bank fail both of the tests suggested by the Bank.

Even a group one might have expected to shy away from central planning—American private businesspeople—have shown surprising sympathy for it in foreign aid: "All 191 member states of the United Nations have agreed to eradicate extreme poverty and address the many other burdens facing the very poor through the Millennium Development Goals. Once a country has formulated a national development strategy, external donors and NGOs can then contribute their resources and expertise in support of the country's priorities" (noted a consortium of Seattle-area private businessmen known as the Initiative for Global Development).[29]

Of course, in between the extremes of central planning and anarchic searching, all human activities involve some degree of planning. Corporations operating in the free market have corporate plans and planning departments, and they coordinate their activities with these plans rather than with market mechanisms. Larger-scale projects are likely to involve more planning rather than small-scale projects. However, this kind of planning is not the same as the large-P Plans to end world poverty.

First, there is a difference between discovering what works (or what sells, to follow the corporate analogy) and then scaling up the discovery. Scaling up can be done by replicating a set of routine actions once the search for what works has found the right set of routine actions. Hence, scaling up often does involve some little-p planning. Discovering what works, however, can never be planned. Since the large-P Plans operate in many areas where there is not a good track record or knowledge base on what works (as the chapters in this book make clear), they are prematurely scaling up things about which there is no grounds to think they will work (or worse, scaling up things that have a demonstrated track record of failure).

Some of the (not very common) aid successes scaled up a discovery that did involve some small-p planning. For example, the vaccination campaigns of the World Health Organization (WHO), which successfully lowered infant mortality, certainly had some top-down planning. The success stemmed from finding that a combination vaccination package could be effectively administered (which was not automatic—perhaps it was due to the observability and ease of monitoring vaccinations and the simpler link between inputs and outcomes) and then scaled up campaign style to cover large numbers of children.[30] This kind of success may have unfortunately led aid agencies to a stronger belief in the power of planning than was applicable in most other situations.

Second, although a large project like a dam or electric plant involves some planning, it takes place on purely engineering grounds. Ending world poverty is not an engineering problem (or even a vaccination problem); it presents many variables of human behavior as well as technical complexity.

Nevertheless, the aid agencies often seem to have in mind the kind of engineering problem that a dam poses when designing Planning solutions to the problems of poverty. They seem to assume a Leontief production function between aid inputs and development outcomes that lends itself to detailed planning (and makes it possible to come up with precise estimates for costs of attaining plan targets): "The starting point is for donors and aid recipients to agree on a financial needs assessment that identifies the aid requirements for achieving the MDGs. Donors then need to provide predictable, multiyear funding to cover these requirements, and developing countries need to implement the reforms that will optimize returns to aid."[31]

The UN Millennium Project even talks about planning the growth rate, using a mechanical relationship joining aid, public investment, and growth: "By entering the projected public investments from the needs assessment into the macroeconomic framework, planners can assess whether the resulting growth rate is consistent with achieving the poverty target using country-specific poverty-growth elasticities and incremental capital-output ratios. Any major discrepancies between projected investment needs can be adapted to prepare an MDG consistent scenario."[32]

The World Bank has pursued a similar exercise of "costing the MDGs," which then become the basis for recommendations about aid volume. Devarajan et al. report an attempt to derive aid needs for the MDGs based on the costs of inputs to the health and education outcomes covered by the MDGs.[33] There are two problems: first, the technology is seldom so simple as to know the precise "input requirement" for a particular output, and there is no reason to suppose that unit costs are constant as volume varies. Second, even if it were possible to overcome the first problem, it is one thing to estimate the cost of providing a health service as being, say, $1 per drug dose, and a completely different thing to assume that an additional $1 of foreign aid will result in a drug dose being given to a sick patient. Unwilling to stop themselves from being good economists, Devarajan et al. themselves state that they see no reason to believe their own calculations: "Empirical evidence from developing countries suggests only a weak link between public spending on education and school enrollments, or between health expenditures and mortality or disease."[34]

Unfortunately, many health problems in foreign aid are more difficult than the vaccination example I gave (and even this success story has stalled, with only partial coverage of, for example, African children against measles). The authors whom Devarajan et al. cite for this weak link, Deon Filmer, Jeffrey Hammer, and Lant Pritchett (also World Bank researchers—Pritchett and Woolcock have a similar discussion in this book), point out such stories as the results of a survey at government health centers in the Mutasa district of Tanzania. In the survey, new mothers reported what they least liked about their birthing experiences assisted by government nurses. The poor expectant mothers were "ridiculed by nurses for not having baby clothes (22 percent)... and nurses hit mothers during delivery (13 percent)."[35] Because of the insistence on working through governments, aid funds get lost in patronage-swollen national health bureaucracies, not to mention international health bureaucracies. In countries where corruption is as endemic as any other disease, health officials often sell aid-financed drugs on the black market. Studies in Guinea, Cameroon, Uganda, and Tanzania estimated that 30 to 70 percent of government drugs disappeared before reaching any patients. In one low-income country, a crusading journalist accused the Ministry of Health of misappropriating $50 million in aid funds. The ministry issued an astonishing rebuttal: the journalist had irresponsibly implied the $50 million went AWOL in a single year, whereas they had actually misappropriated the $50 million over a three-year period.

The same belief in aid service costing implying aid service delivery appears in the Millennium Project's Investing in Development, Sachs's *The End of Poverty*, and the earlier report of the Commission on Macroeconomics and Health.[36] Each of these exercises has elaborate costing exercises based on unit costs of multitudinous inputs, but each fails to address the issue of who will be motivated to deliver these inputs to the poor in such a way that they produce better outcomes. Devarajan et al. cite the Commission on Macroeconomics and Health's estimates as support for the estimates in their chapter, estimates based on the same flawed methodology that their chapter disqualifies on evidentiary grounds.[37]

The UN Millennium Project also suffers from the first problem: that planners do not really know the precise technology that translates inputs into outputs. The participants in the Millennium Project themselves know this obvious point—"it is often difficult to precisely quantify the link between coverage of interventions and MDG outcomes"—yet insist in the same sentence that somehow "national MDG planning involves mapping interventions to MDG outcomes."[38]

The UN Millennium Project participants are also savvy enough to know that "on balance, it can be difficult to predict the direction of change for marginal costs—let alone its magnitude—as coverage increases." Yet two pages earlier, the same authors are able to state that costs of meeting the MDGs follow from this simple formula:

[Population size] × [percentage of population reached] × [number of

interventions per person or household] × [unit cost of the intervention][39]

A key characteristic of the planners is that they decide on the nature of the foreign aid intervention in advance. They think they know both the technical fix and the manner of its implementation. To quote from Pritchett and Woolcock in chapter 5 in this book: on public service delivery, the planners opt for a preconceived solution:

That is, development activities (in general, and those supported by development agencies in particular) have almost uniformly attempted to remedy problems of "inadequate services" (in infrastructure, education, health, law enforcement, regulation) by calling upon a centralized bureaucracy to supply a top-down and uniform public service. These decisions to "skip straight to Weber" were historical, social, and political processes whereby the interactions between citizens, the state, and providers were simply overlooked. The solution was a coherent approach to service delivery in which a universal need was met by a technical (supply) solution, and then implemented by an impersonal, rules-driven, provider. That is, "need as the problem, supply as the solution, civil service as the instrument" became the standard organizational algorithm for solving public services concerns.

An even deeper problem is that plans can never have enough information about little problems since they are overwhelmed with the information requirements for hundreds of problems in hundreds of locales required to reach the big targets such as the MDGs. For a big plan involving myriads of intended beneficiaries, planners in the West have no way to use the knowledge of the poor people themselves about their own needs and problems. There is no way they can gather enough information to know which of the interventions has the highest payoffs in a given locale or even if a particular intervention has a high payoff or zero payoff.

A more subtle point is that development research itself may be hampered because the high social importance of human poverty is often taken as predetermining the research questions to be asked. Research in the natural sciences, in contrast, does not start with a predetermined research agenda, and so researchers can look for those questions that they can opportunistically solve. The first approach is more appealing morally, although Thomas Kuhn in *The*

Structure of Scientific Revolutions suggests that this difference in approach helps explain why progress in the natural sciences is faster than progress in the social sciences.[40]

F. A. Hayek presciently noted more than sixty years ago how the complexity of knowledge made planning impossible. A representative quote is:

> The interaction of individuals, possessing different knowledge and different views, is what constitutes the life of thought. The growth of reason is a social process based on the existence of such differences. It is of essence that its results cannot be predicted, that we cannot know which views will assist this growth and which will not—in short, that this growth cannot be governed by any views which we now possess without at the same time limiting it. To "plan" or "organize" the growth of mind, or for that matter, progress in general, is a contradiction in terms. The tragedy of collectivist thought is that, while it starts out to make reason supreme, it ends by destroying reason because it misconceives the process on which the growth of reason depends. Individualism is thus an attitude of humility before this social process and of tolerance to other opinions and is the exact opposite of that intellectual hubris which is at the root of the demand for comprehensive direction of the social process.[41]

The debate between planners and searchers in Western assistance is the latest installment in a long-standing philosophical divide in Western intellectual history about social change. The great philosopher of science Karl Popper described it eloquently as "utopian social engineering" versus "piecemeal democratic reform" (see chapter 19 in this book by John McMilllan on the hubris of utopian social engineering): "The piecemeal engineer knows, like Socrates, how little he knows. He knows that we can learn only from our mistakes. Accordingly, he will make his way, step by step, carefully comparing the results expected with the results achieved, and always on the look-out for the unavoidable unwanted consequences of any reform; and he will avoid undertaking reforms of a complexity and scope which makes it impossible for him to disentangle causes and effects, and to know what he is really doing. Holistic or Utopian social engineering, as opposed to piecemeal social engineering...aims at remodeling the "whole of society" in accordance with a definite plan or blueprint."[42]

The missing elements in big plans, it can never be stressed enough, are feedback and accountability. Many chapters in this book (see, for example, chapters 6, 9, and 10 by, respectively, Reinikka, Martens, and Svensson) note the peculiar characteristic of foreign aid that distinguishes it from either commercial markets or democratic politics. In markets, the consumer is giving his own money to suppliers, who strive to satisfy his needs. In the domestic politics of democracies, the people who vote are the same ones who receive the services. In foreign aid, this feedback and accountability loop is broken: the rich people who give the money or vote for foreign aid are not the ones receiving aid services. The poor have no way of registering their satisfaction or dissatisfaction with aid services by how they spend or how they vote. The bottom line is that aid agencies have more of an incentive to please the rich than the poor.

Alas, the planners are repeating the mistakes of history, just as my critique here is repeating criticisms that were made even at the time of the first development planners. As the blog AdamSmithee.com noted in response to Easterly (2006), the planner versus searcher debate goes back a long way.[43] S. Herbert Frankel, in the *Quarterly Journal of Economics* of August 1952, commented on the United Nations Primer for Development published in 1951: "It is... precisely because the authors of the report see economic development primarily as an intellectual or artistic exercise by leaders and governments that they fail to do justice to their examination of existing realities in underdeveloped countries.... Development depends not on the abstract national goals of, and the more or less enforced decisions by, a cadre of planners, but on the piecemeal adaptation of individuals to goals which emerge but slowly and become clearer only as those individuals work with the means at their disposal; and as they themselves become aware, in the process of doing, of what can and ought to be done."[44]

The planners have the rhetorical advantage of promising great things, the end of poverty. The only thing the planners have against them is that plans do not work.

1.1.2 Evaluating the Need for Big Plans

Another reason that planners dominate the debate on foreign aid is that poor countries are supposed to need a "big push" of foreign aid to get out of a "poverty trap."[45] This taps in well to the planners' affection for emphasizing resource transfers and implementing aid programs from the top. As Jeffrey Sachs explains in *The End of Poverty*, "When people are... utterly destitute, they need their entire income, or more, just to survive. There is no margin of income above survival that can be invested for the future. This is the main reason why the poorest of the poor are most prone to becoming trapped with low or negative economic growth rates. They are too poor to save for the future and thereby accumulate the capital that could pull them out of their current misery."[46]

Simple tests provide no support for either the low-income poverty trap or a role for aid in escaping it. Easterly divides the poorest quintile of countries at the beginning of each period in two between the half with the highest aid and the other half with the lowest.[47] There is no significant difference in growth rates between the two groups, despite average aid as percentage of GDP being two to five times larger in the top group. The low-aid countries in the poorest quintile had no trouble registering positive growth for the whole period 1950–2001 and in the period 1950–1975. The bottom quintile (like the middle and second to bottom quintiles) had worse growth in more recent periods, possibly consistent with a poverty trap. However, this was the period in which the poorest countries had much higher aid, which should have made a poverty trap less likely according to the standard narrative. While possibly reflecting reverse causality from poor growth to higher aid, the stylized facts are not consistent with a low-income poverty trap due to insufficient aid.

To be sure, there were individual poor countries that failed to grow among the poorest countries. Chad had zero growth from 1950 to 2001, and Zaire/Democratic Republic of the Congo had negative per capita growth over this period. However, the stagnant economies were offset by such success stories as Botswana, which was the fourth poorest in 1950 but increased its income by a factor of thirteen by 2001. Lesotho was the fifth poorest in 1950 but increased its income by a factor of five over the half-century. Other subsequent success stories that were among the poorest in 1950 are China and India.

Other scholars have also failed to find any evidence for a "poverty trap." Aart Kraay and Claudio Raddatz studied the saving rate and found that saving does not behave the way the poverty trap requires at low income. The reasons countries stay poor must lie elsewhere.[48]

Poor countries do have lower growth rates relative to rich countries in some time periods, and so there is evidence of divergence between poorest and richest. This is not the same as the absolute poverty trap hypothesized above, but it is still of interest to ask why there is divergence. The UN Millennium Project and Jeffrey Sachs argue that it is the poverty trap rather than bad government that explains poor growth of low-income countries and the failure to make progress toward the MDGs. Sachs says, "The claim that Africa's corruption is the basic source of the problem [the poverty trap] does not withstand practical experience or serious scrutiny."[49] Likewise the Millennium Project says, "Many reasonably well governed countries are too poor to make the investments to climb the first steps of the ladder."[50]

The case for planners is even weaker if they must deal with the complexities of bad government, as many chapters in this book document. Jeffrey Sachs worries in *The End of Poverty*: "If the poor are poor because ... their governments are corrupt, how could global cooperation help?"[51] Unfortunately, whether governments of poor countries are corrupt must be determined by evidence, not by the writer's chosen advocacy campaign.

The search for the elusive "well-governed low-income countries" casts a broad net. The Millennium Project report lists sixty-three poor countries that are "potentially well governed," and thus potentially eligible for a massive increase in foreign aid. The list includes five of the seven countries singled out by Transparency International in October 2004 as the most corrupt in the world: Azerbaijan, Bangladesh, Chad, Nigeria, and Paraguay. The list of "potentially well-governed" countries also includes fifteen governments that Freedom House classifies as "not free." Such dictators as Paul Biya of Cameroon, Hun Sen of Cambodia, and Ilham Aliyev of Azerbaijan are on the list. President Aliyev of Azerbaijan scored a double as most autocratic and most corrupt since he was "elected" to succeed his autocratic father in 2003.[52]

Although convinced that bad government was not the problem, the UN report did rule out aid to the four most awful rulers in the world. The report identifies these four governments—Belarus, Myanmar, North Korea, and Zimbabwe—as beyond the pale. This is a pretty small number for bad governments of the world. Even a dictator like the late Saparmurat Niyazov of Turkmenistan, who so terrorized his country that he renamed the months of the year after himself and his late mother, did not get into the UN bad despots club.

The UN seems desperately to want to deny the existence of bad government because it threatens another cherished model of traditional aid delivery, which this book will examine critically: the government-to-government aid model. In this view, the altruistic rich country government (either directly or through multilateral organizations) gives money to an altruistic poor country government, which implements aid projects to benefit the poor in the poor country.

Actually if the UN Millennium Project report about escaping the well-governed poverty trap had looked in its own country studies, it would have found interesting clues to this result, such as the following vignette on Cambodian schoolteachers: "Many supplement their income by soliciting bribes from students, including the sale of examination questions and answers. . . . The end result is a high dropout rate."[53]

Another camp of planners has a variant on the UN model of overlooking bad government. This other camp (associated with the U.S. government, World Bank, and IMF) says governments of poor countries are bad and the West should get tough with the bad governments—force them to change in return for aid. This contrasts with the UN/Sachs camps that says these governments are not so bad and should be free to determine their own development strategies. However, this artificially restricts the debate. It may be true that governments of poor countries are bad, and it may be just as true that Western attempts to change them have been fruitless.

Again evidence should decide the debate. The hypothesis is so straightforward as to lend itself to a test of bad government against the poverty trap as a story for poor economic growth in low income countries. Easterly runs a horse race between initial income and various measures of quality of institutions.[54] There was divergence between 1960 and 2002. This does not contradict the evidence on lack of an absolute poverty trap over 1960 to 2001 presented earlier, since the predicted growth rate of the lowest-income group in the regression below is still significantly above zero. Both the following statements are true: (1) we can reject that the coefficient of growth from 1960 to 2002 on initial income is zero (unconditionally, it is positive), and (2) we cannot reject the hypothesis that the poorest quintile had the same growth as the top four-fifths of the sample. We could still detect a tendency toward absolute divergence with the help of the middle-income and high-income observations, even though we cannot detect abnormally low growth of the bottom quintile over the past four decades.

A robustness check on these results would be to consider whether there might be interaction effects such that the payoff to better government may depend on income, or vice versa. To consider such a possibility, Easterly does some simple nonparametric tests. The exercise divides the sample into upper and lower halves of good government (according to the various measures) and upper and lower halves of initial income, and then considers average per capita growth in the four groups: low income and poor government, low income and good government, high income and poor government, and high income and good government.[55] Figure 1.2 illustrates the results.

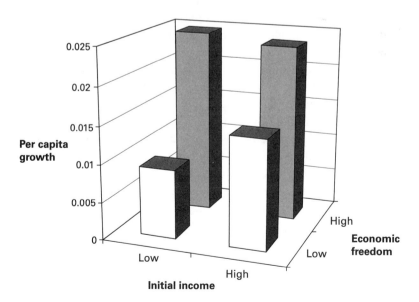

Figure 1.2
Economics growth, economic freedom, and initial income, 1950–2002

Economic growth increases with more economic freedom over 1960 to 2002 at both low and high income (the differences are statistically significant at the 5 precent level). Growth increases with more income at low economic freedom (but the difference is not statistically significant even at the 10 percent level) but decreases slightly at high economic freedom.

Of course, the largest question is whether aid raises economic growth. There is a vast and inconclusive literature on aid and growth (for a dissenting view that argues for clearly positive growth effects of aid, see chapter 16 by Radelet and Levine in this book). The literature suffers from such unrestricted specifications and endless iteration among these specifications that virtually any result on aid and growth is possible, and indeed virtually all possible results have already been presented in the literature: aid effects are conditional on good policies, they are not conditional on good policies; aid has a positive effect on growth, aid has no effect on growth; aid has a linear effect on growth, aid has a quadratic effect on growth; only certain types of aid matter, all types of aid are equivalent. Growth regressions in general have been criticized on the grounds of data mining and specification searching, since there are more right-hand-side variables that have been identified as empirical determinants of growth than there are degrees of freedom in the sample.[56] The aid and growth literature seems like a particularly egregious example of this problem (interestingly Durlauf, Johnson, and Temple did not even list aid as one of the right-hand-side variables that had been shown to determine growth).

What makes the big plan debate so contentious is that it is not easy to evaluate the effect of big plans. No identification strategy with such a deeply endogenous variable as aid is going to convince everyone, and indeed the regression wars on foreign aid and growth show no sign of ending any time soon. It is perhaps never going to be possible to have a natural experiment in aggregate data that conclusively resolves the effect of aid on growth. Far from being a defense of the big plan approach to aid, however, this is an argument against it. Why would anyone recommend a public policy to be pursued on a large scale without knowing whether its effects are going to be positive or negative?

As far as disentangling the different things that worked even if a big plan does work, this is pretty much hopeless. Doing everything at once is not a good search strategy for finding out what works to promote development.

1.1.3   How Searchers Handle Uncertainty Better Than Planners

What the planning vision always misses is that success is rare and failure is common. Economic success is always very uneven and unpredictable, across almost any possible unit of analysis one might consider.[57] The decentralized search for success is one big reason that free markets outperformed central planning. It is seldom known in advance what will succeed. Many thousands of searchers mount myriads of different trials as to what will please consumers. A free market system gives rapid feedback as to which products are succeeding and which are not, and searchers adjust accordingly. Activities that succeed attract more financing and more factors of production so that they can be scaled up enormously; activities that fail to please consumers are discontinued. Planners do not have a search and feedback mentality; they implement a preconceived notion of what will work and keep implementing it whether it is working or not.

Economic success stories are often unexpected and unpredicted. MP3 players were invented several years ago and seemed to offer great promise as a great new way for music lovers to listen to large amounts of their favorite music. Despite this promise, none of the early players caught consumers' fancy. The Apple Corporation was known mainly for its failures in the PC market. It was a surprise when Apple suddenly found a huge hit in the iPod, which as of March 2006 had 78 percent of the market for MP3 players. So far Apple has sold 50 million iPods. The matching iTunes program of selling songs online to put on iPod accounts for 87 percent of the legal music downloads in the United States.[58]

Histories of large firms are full of accidental discoveries of big hits. 3M today is a $20 billion corporation. It started in 1904 with a failed attempt to mine corundum (3M stands for Minnesota Mining and Manufacturing). It then adapted to the failure by using the grit from its failed mine to make sandpaper. It was more successful when it tinkered to get a waterproof sandpaper. Its breakthrough product arrived by accident more than two decades later, discovered again by accident and by tinkering to find waterproof packaging tape that became an iconic consumer product: Scotch tape.[59]

Johnson and Johnson, a $50 billion corporation today, was founded in 1886. It produced a wide array of medical products such as medical plasters. In 1890, it started including a can of talc in shipments of its other products, in response to the request of a doctor for something to treat skin irritation from the plasters. To its surprise, the customers started requesting that they send just the talc. Thus was born another iconic consumer product of the twentieth century: Johnson's Baby Powder. Another happy accident came along in 1920 when an employee stitched together surgical tape and a small piece of gauze for his wife, who kept cutting herself in the kitchen, giving the world the Band-Aid.[60]

Another easily observable example of the rarity of big hits is the Hollywood movie. Over the years 2000–2005, the top-grossing 5 percent of all movies released accounted for nearly half of total box office gross revenues over that period. Of course, the flip side of these success stories are the much more numerous product failures—the bottom-grossing half of movies released from 2000 to 2005 accounted for a mere 0.4 percent of box office gross. This does not even take into account the numerous movie projects that never even get accepted by Hollywood studios.

Predicting what is going to be a hit in the movies is famously difficult. As William Goldman wrote in his classic *Adventures in the Screen Trade*, "Nobody knows anything. Why did Paramount say yes [to *Raiders of the Lost Ark*]? Because nobody knows anything. And why did all the other studios say no? Because nobody knows anything. And why did Universal, the mightiest studio of all, pass on Star Wars?...Because nobody, nobody—not now, not ever—knows the least goddamn thing about what is or isn't going to work at the box office."[61]

Uneven product success is closely related to uneven firm success. Just 0.3 percent of firms in the United States accounted for 65 percent of all firm sales in 2002.[62] Firm size is well known to follow what is known as Zipf's law, also known as a power law, in which the log of the size is a negative linear function of the frequency of this size occurring (or, equivalently, the rank). Power laws have generated a lot of hype; for the purposes of this chapter, it is enough to point out how large-scale success is rare, while failure is common. In other words, the frequency distribution of firms (or whatever other unit we are interested in) has a fat and long right-hand-side tail, of which there are many special cases such as a log-normal distribution and a power law (Pareto distribution).[63] In other words, most of the distribution is concentrated at some mediocre level; then there are a small number of firms that are just totally off the charts (way above what something like a standard bell curve would predict).

Of course, one reason that some large firms are so large is that they have been able to make the execution of a successful business formula routine, so that it can replicated at low cost by inexpensive (not heavily trained) workers subject to managerial oversight. To return to the theme of the first section of this chapter, this is corporate "planning" at work, but only after the search for the right formula was successful. McDonalds could grow enormous using minimum-wage high school graduates following simple instructions to prepare meals. However, even this kind of planning is subject to competition from searchers, continually changing the environment and always threatening to make existing corporate plans obsolete. McDonalds has lost market share as other searchers have discovered Americans' increasing desire for low-fat alternatives to Big Macs.

Maybe this is why, even though large firms dominate the marketplace, it is not so easy to be a large firm. Of the world's largest one hundred companies in 1912, some, like Procter & Gamble and British Petroleum, were many times larger in 1995. However, they were the exception, as 1912's big 100 firms also included such dinosaurs as Central Leather and Cudhay Packing in the United States. Only 19 of the top 100 in 1912 were still in the top 100 in 1995, and 48 of 1912's big 100 had disappeared altogether by 1995.[64]

This unpredictable behavior has given rise to pseudoscience even worse than development pseudoscience. Business books lay out the secrets for success of a few large companies celebrated by the author, only to see the firms fall on hard times after the book is published. Business writers celebrated Enron for its innovative approach right up to the last minute.[65] Even the most successful business gurus have their embarrassments: Tom Peters' and Robert Waterman's 1982 mega-best seller, *In Search of Excellence*, included among its celebrated companies some that would later go bankrupt, such as Atari, Wang, and Delta. This generation's guru is Jim Collins, who coauthored the 1994 *Built to Last* (3.5 million sold over its first ten years) and followed up with another big hit in 2001 in *Good to Great*. The magazine *Fast Company* concluded in 2004 that about half of the companies identified as built to last in 1994 have since stumbled badly (among them are Motorola, Ford, Sony, Walt Disney, Boeing, Nordstrom, and Merck) and would not meet the criteria for a 2004 *Built to Last* list. In fact, Jim Collins's own *Good to Great* suggested in 2001 that Merck was now second rate and identified a new pharmaceutical success story: Abbott Laboratories.[66]

Another from an inexhaustible list of such examples is Harvard Business School strategy guru Michael Porter. As late as 1990, Porter was celebrating Digital Equipment Corporation (DEC), which was destroyed by the competition from personal computers a mere two years later.[67]

Such business books have no predictive power because they are based on slippery propositions that cannot be tested or falsified (what Collins calls a "law of physics" is "preserve the core, but stimulate progress"—in other words, a business should both change and not change).[68] You could say the best-selling business authors do meet the market test themselves, but so do astrologers.

The difficulty of achieving and maintaining success is not peculiar to large firms. Every year, about 10 percent of existing firms of all sizes go out of business. Not that it is so easy to start a new firm to replace the ones that go out of business. More than half of new firms fail within four years of their founding in the United States.[69] With so much uncertainty even in an economy with well-developed institutions, infrastructure, and technology, imagine how much riskier is the world of foreign aid and economic development.

1.1.4   The Strategy of Search

What is the best way to handle this uncertainty? A mathematical example may help illustrate this. Suppose an aid agent tries to execute a comprehensive plan that has n components that each must work for the plan to be successful (this is the strongest version of complementarity, one of the traditional arguments for the big push). The components are such things as agricultural productivity, health, education, housing, sanitation, clean water, roads, and electricity. For each of these areas, an intervention is designed. If each component i has a probability of p_i of working, then the probability p_s that the n-component comprehensive plan will work is:

$$p_s = p_{1j}p_{2j}p_{3j}, \ldots, p_{nj}. \tag{1.1}$$

It is of course more realistic to have a separate p_i for each component i, but let us assume that the probabilities are equal to illustrate how the number of components lowers probability of success of comprehensive plans:

$$p_s = p^n. \tag{1.2}$$

If the number of components is 10, then even with a probability of each component succeeding as high as .85, the overall probability of success of the comprehensive intervention is only .20. If the number of components is 20, the probability of success is only .04.

There is plenty of reason to think that the number of interventions has to be large for a comprehensive plan. Each of the components above has multiple subcomponents, which in turn have subcomponents. For example, attaining good health requires dealing with AIDS, malaria, tuberculosis, infant diarrhea, and other maladies, all of which have separate interventions. Dealing with malaria requires interventions like medicines for those who have malaria, and for prevention such measures as indoor spraying, bed nets, and drainage of standing water. Dispensing bed nets in turn will be successful if funding is available for the net, if the net is designed correctly (e.g., impregnated with insecticide, easy to use), if each intermediary along the way between manufacturer and consumer passes along the net (through an administrative or commercial transaction), if the consumer is successfully educated on the importance of sleeping under the net every night, and on a number of other idiosyncratic details that cannot even be anticipated.

It is little wonder, therefore, that in an attempt to be comprehensive, the UN Millennium Project listed 449 separate interventions to achieve the MDGs. For this number, even a probability of success of each intervention of 99 percent would yield an overall success probability for the comprehensive plan of 1 percent. This is the ultimate revenge of complementarity: the same strong complementarity that big push advocates say requires a comprehensive plan also makes it unlikely that the comprehensive plan will work.

But suppose you search among m possible interventions and are content to find one that works, which you will then scale up. The reason that development is possible at all is that there are not only complementarities among inputs to development outcomes; there is also the possibility of substitution. Suppose that the m interventions are perfect substitutes for each other for your particular objective. If the objective is general—perhaps, "Find something that works to help a lot of poor people at a feasible cost," which would be typical of the open-minded searchers' approach to aid—then indeed many possible interventions are perfect substitutes. (This is the same principle that makes businesspeople successful searchers: they have the general objective of profits and can search among many possible products for one that delivers a profit. See Duggan 2003 on this point.)[70] The point of this section would be embarrassingly simple if it were not so widely violated in practice: setting a fixed intermediate goal to a more general good is counterproductive, since the chances of success are so much higher if you are willing to accept any intermediate step to the general good.

For example, chapters 2 and 3 by, respectively, Banerjee and He and by Duflo and Kremer in this book give many examples of interventions that have been found to work to alleviate poverty and can be scaled up with the limits of politically feasible aid budgets: remedial teaching, uniforms and textbooks, schooling vouchers, monetary rewards to parents for sending children to school, iron supplements, albendazole (deworming), iodine supplements, condom provision, improving management of sexually transmitted diseases, voluntary counseling and testing for HIV prevention, prophylaxis for opportunistic infections, short-course zidovudine regime, spraying for malaria, fertilizer, vaccines for various illnesses, school meals, and putting a second teacher in the classroom.

The probability that at least one intervention will work when searching among m interventions is:

$$p_s = 1 - (1 - p_1)(1 - p_2)(1 - p_3)\ldots(1 - p_m). \tag{1.3}$$

For purely illustrative purposes, suppose that all the p's are equal (of course, this does not make any sense since search would be pointless if all interventions have the same probability of success; we will say for the moment that the searchers do not know this until they try each one). With this, equation 1.3 simplifies to

$$p_s = 1 - (1 - p)^m. \tag{1.4}$$

With perfect substitutability, the power of multiplication works for us rather than against us. With a probability of success of each intervention of .85, you need to try only three different interventions to get a probability of .99 of success (because only one has to succeed). If the success probability for each intervention was as low as .5, then it would be enough to experiment with seven different interventions to reach a probability of .99 for success; a success probability of a miserable 0.2 would still require a less than herculean nineteen different experiments to attain .99 probability of at least one success.

Note that the power of searching compared to planning holds even when we consider the probabilities of one step being executed successfully as the same between comprehensive planning and decentralized searching. In reality, incentives for completing an intervention (presumably raising its probability of success) are more difficult to implement with planning than with searching. Moreover, the bureaucracy of planning could itself create a longer list of necessary conditions for success than with decentralized searching. For example, bureaucracies create rules that officials must sign off on different steps for a task to proceed. The risk that a careless or unmotivated official will not sign off on an otherwise successful task adds to the risk of failure.

Having multiple searches for what works may sound like a lot to a planner, who thinks in terms of a top-down bureaucratic hierarchy. However, the great thing about searching is that it can be totally decentralized. A myriad of searchers are available in the field to look for what works for each piece of the puzzle. The aid system just has to be designed so that it rewards successful searches and scales them up to achieve widespread benefits for the poor.

1.1.5 Conclusion

The comprehensive ambitions of the planners have misfired badly, crowding out more sensible and pragmatic approaches that are humble about their own limitations. The world's poor will mostly determine their own fate by their own home-grown institutions and initiatives, as much historical and contemporary evidence suggests.

In the meantime, however, the efforts of the rich world to help the poor could benefit from a lot more piecemeal searching and a lot less comprehensive planning. The 2006 Nobel Peace Prize was a contest between a searcher (Mohammad Yunus) and a planner (Bono). Maybe Yunus's award is a good omen for a more constructive approach to the tragic problems of the world's poor. The many constructive insights in this book are a good start.

1.2   How to Reinvent Aid

None of the chapter authors are claiming that their ideas will achieve the end of poverty. They just take on specific problems and propose hard-headed solutions. In this section, I weave together some of their conclusions and debates. My goal is more to stimulate a reading of the chapters and suggest how they fit together than to be a comprehensive summary of each chapter. Note, however, that not all the authors necessarily agree with each other (or with me). Rather, the value of this book is that it offers an airing of different viewpoints by some of the leading scholars in the field.

The chapters in part I discuss evaluation of aid interventions.

Abhijit Banerjee and Rumin He give examples in chapter 2 of interventions that have been verified as cost-effective uses of foreign aid (using the methodology discussed by in the following chapter by Duflo and Kremer): deworming; dietary supplements like those for iron, vitamin A, and iodine; education in using condoms and treating other sexually transmitted diseases to slow the spread of AIDS; indoor spraying to control malaria; fertilizer subsidies; vaccination; and urban water provision. None of these are keys to development according to some utopian scheme; they are modest interventions, but they make people's lives better. Banerjee and He also note many problems on the way to getting these interventions to the poor. Although they identified these interventions as effective through a careful scientific methodology, the donors themselves do not subject themselves to independent evaluation. They lament the lack of evaluation as one of the key weaknesses of aid agencies.

Duflo and Kremer in chapter 3 discuss the methodology of randomized controlled trials (RCTs) to evaluate aid interventions. They argue, "There is scope for considerably expanding their use, although they must necessarily remain a small fraction of all evaluations." The RCT is a welcome introduction of the scientific method into foreign aid and development, an area where wishful thinking, politically motivated conclusions, and pseudoscience have perhaps been more predominant than in other areas of economics. The RCTs are not a panacea, and they are not applicable to all areas of foreign aid and development, but they have already made a great contribution to the field of economic development.

The World Bank has recently endorsed the idea of RCTs on a very small scale with its Impact Evaluation group.[71] These are used to evaluate which interventions work (a noble purpose), though not for holding the bank itself or any of its units accountable for results. The bank fails to specify any consequences it might have, for example, in managerial or staff rewards for good performance.

Chapter 4 by Lant Pritchett discusses the political economy of why rigorous evaluation is so rare in foreign aid, either for knowing what works or for accountability purposes. Even purely altruistic advocates for particular interventions and particular objectives have an incentive to do just enough to persuade the public to allocate funds to the program, without risking a possibly negative rigorous evaluation. Log-rolling coalitions of single-issue advocates can form, all agreeing that "I won't demand rigorous evaluation of your program, if you don't demand it of mine." Pritchett goes into much more precise detail about how political incentives kill off rigorous evaluation. As with all other political economy analyses, it is hard to say what would break the logjam. Perhaps a more informed and more demanding public can force agencies to do evaluation anyway?[72]

The chapters in part II address the Gordian knot of the state. Foreign aid has struggled mightily with the question of how to deal with the government in the aid recipient country. The central dilemma is that donors want to give money to states led by what the donors think is a good government, yet at the same time they believe that the "country" (always meaning the government) should "own" its homemade approach to development. There is an inescapable contradiction between the donors' imposition of conditions on what it takes to be a good government and the logical implication of "ownership" that the "country" will decide on its own what is a good government. The donor agencies paper over this contradiction with euphemisms or simply present contradictory statements side by side in the same donor report. For example, DFID's 2006 white paper is about "making governance work for the poor." There is some ill-defined way in which "we [the donors] need to help governments and citizens make politics work for the poor," putting "support for good governance at the centre of what we do." DFID sternly lectures poor country governments that "unless governance improves, poor people will continue to suffer from a lack of security, public services and economic opportunities." Yet the same report also takes the opposite approach: "If developing countries are to lead their own development, they [meaning the governments] must have more authority to ensure that the international development system responds to their needs."[73]

The more intellectually consistent researchers in this book struggle with these same questions. Are donors bound to give aid through the recipient state out of respect for its sovereignty? (This was the traditional idea that still binds the World Bank and IMF, for example.) Or should they bypass dysfunctional, often corrupt, states and try to get the aid directly to poor people? Or would such bypassing undermine and retard the political development of the state in the poor country? Or are donors currently making the state worse—more corrupt, more bureaucratic, more accountable to donors than to their own citizens—with their current practices? There is no easy answer and no consensus on these questions by the authors of the chapters in part II, but plenty of dazzling insights.

Pritchett and Woolcock in chapter 5 have a tour d'horizon of the difficult issues facing state delivery of public services in poor countries. They draw an effective double dichotomy between discretionary versus nondiscretionary and transaction-intensive versus nontransaction-intensive activities. Areas that are discretionary but not transaction intensive can be handled with "ten smart people." Areas that are nondiscretionary but transaction intensive can be handled with a nearly automated procedure that can handle the large volume of transactions (see the discussion of corporate planning above). The problem with most public services is that they are both discretionary and transaction intensive (think of nurse-patient and teacher-student interactions, for example). In the authors' words, they "are intrinsically incompatible with the logic and imperatives of large-scale, routinized, administrative control." They document failures in rural water supply (where 50 percent of standpipes administered by the central government broke down due to lack of maintenance), irrigation, schooling, family planning, agricultural extension, and health care (where patients often bypassed public clinics for private and traditional healers). When the failure of public institutions in all these areas was recognized, donors sent "experts" from rich country bureaucratic environments to redesign poor country bureaucratic institutions (the authors note that this is "like sending a cab driver to design a car").

Pritchett and Woolcock document three other failed remedies, which they refer to as intensification (do the same, just try harder), amputation (privatize even if there is a market failure or political expectation of government responsibility that created the need for the public service in the first place), and policy reform (which fails to recognize that "policies" are not transaction intensive and are not hardest to change).

The current proposals for reform after these three failures now take us up to eight different choices: (1) supplier autonomy (public sector reform II), (2) single-sector participatory, (3) contracting out, (4) decentralization to states or provinces, (5) decentralization to localities or municipalities, (6) demand-side financing, (7) social funds, and (8) community-driven development. They see "no theoretical or empirical basis for making any claims about what the 'right' solution is for any sector in any country that has not itself tried the alternatives." They conclude more constructively that "if the incessant quest for *the* solution is in fact the problem, development professionals need to help create the conditions under which genuine experiments to discern the most appropriate local solutions to local problems can be nurtured and sustained." (In terms of section 1.1 of this introduction, Pritchett and Woolcock recommend searching rather than planning.)

Chapter 6 takes on the issue of whether donors should bypass the government to deliver public services directly or work with the government. Reinikka sides clearly with the second, joining those concerned about aid agencies' undermining the local state by interfering in the relationship between the state and the service providers. She points out that having aid donors deal directly with the latter can destroy the relationship of accountability between the state and the service providers that work for it. This is an important consideration in the three dozen developing countries where aid provides more than 40 percent of the country's total public spending. Sometimes donors even set up parallel project units that are accountable only to the donors and drain off local professionals (in Kenya, for example, "a World Bank agricultural project paid eight local staff between $3,000 and $6,000 a month, many times the $250 available to a senior economist in the civil service.")

Reinikka would prefer that donors work within the local state, aligning their support with what it is doing. Measures to improve citizen voice and feedback to the state are more constructive than having the donors themselves force conditions down the throat of the state. But she notes that the "unintended negative effects of donor behavior" are a long-standing problem, in part explained by the donors' having other objectives besides reducing poverty.

Chapter 8, by Moss, Pettersson, and Van de Walle, has a much less benign view of how the aid system interacts with governments in poor countries. These authors see aid as often reinforcing the patrimonial, patronage-driven, rent-seeking state in Africa, "where some countries have now entered into their third and fourth decades of receiving substantial volumes of aid." In their own words:

Projects provide for the allocation of all sorts of discretionary goods to be politicized and patrimonialized, including expensive four-wheel drive cars, scholarships, decisions over where to place schools and roads, and so on. The common practice of paying cash "sitting fees" for civil servants attending donor-funded workshops, where the daily rates can exceed regular monthly salaries, even turns training into a rent to be distributed. . . . Aid dependence thus leads to a situation in which bureaucrats are often not rewarded for focusing on their core developmental functions but rather on getting money from donors.

They see a long history of aid agency attempts at improving governance, with little sign of progress: "The World Bank alone provided Africa with 70 civil service reform projects between 1987 and 1997."

The authors then give voice to a long-standing worry about aid: that it makes government officials much more responsive to aid agencies than to their own citizens: "If donors are providing the majority of public finance and governments are primarily accountable to those external agencies, then it may simply not be possible to also expect a credible social contract to develop between the state and its citizens. Using the current terminology, aid may undercut the very principles the aid industry intends to promote: ownership, accountability, and participation." Large aid flows can result in a reduction in governmental accountability because governing elites no longer need to ensure the support of their publics and the assent of their legislatures when they do not need to raise revenues from the local economy, as long as they keep the donors happy and willing to provide alternative sources of funding.

Aid may actually lead to a decrease in the country ownership the donors say they are promoting. Moss, Pettersson, and Van de Walle note that African leaders typically enjoy high longevity in office despite chronically poor economic performance. The African state is characterized by strong presidential rule, with weak legislatures and civil society and few participatory checks on the executive. Since donors play such an important role in governmental functions, the government can blame the donors for poor public service delivery (while the donors of course blame the government). The authors are sufficiently chastened by their review of the historical record that they close by suggesting that the extra public dollars now being proposed for traditional development assistance might well be better spent for other types of assistance that in the long run would have a greater impact on the development of the region.

Kremer and Miguel in chapter 7 also take a less sanguine view of the viability of aid working through governments. They note the stubborn persistence in the aid community of the notion of sustainability of projects, meaning that aid projects should be taken over by local or national governments, or at least some locally organized user committee. This is inspired more by the appealing dogmas of the self-help gospel than any appreciation of aid or political incentives. In reality, sustainability has been an illusion, as recipient governments or local groups seldom take over aid projects and so projects are not sustained. The consequences are unhappy. In one large water project in western Kenya, "43 percent of borehole wells were useless ten years after the shift from external donor support for water-well maintenance to the training of local maintenance committees."

Kremer and Miguel study the case of deworming drugs to analyze different methods commonly put forward to promote sustainability. They point out one common problem: most of the benefits of taking drugs against highly contagious worm infections accrue to others rather than to the individual. Hence, it is not so surprising that interventions that rely on strong individual incentives (e.g., user fees or education of individuals on the need for the drugs) fail in their study. Peer pressure could solve collective action problems created through externalities, perhaps leading to another path to sustainability. However, Kremer and Miguel also rigorously study peer effects on using the drugs and find them to be negative. They conclude that a good that has external benefits to others should be subsidized indefinitely. Locally funded governments would be best suited to provide a good with local externalities, like deworming drugs, but local governments in Africa are weak and do not raise their own revenue from local communities. Donors may or may not want to fund a public good that needs indefinite financial support, but there is no reason that they should keep chasing the illusory hope that temporary funding will ensure that a public good will be permanently sustainable.

Part III takes a step back to look at what aid agencies are supposed to do and what they actually do. In chapter 9, Martens asks the sensible question: Why does delivery of money have to be tied to implementation of programs and projects by the same agency? His answer is that aid agencies are intermediaries between the wishes of donors and the wishes of recipients. First, the donor may have other interests to accommodate besides meeting the needs of recipients, such as donor country foreign policy or commercial interests: "For instance, a bilateral aid agency may approve the delivery of water pumps to a village in the recipient country. Such a project satisfies the preferences of all donor interest groups: genuine wealth transfers and empowerment of (water-carrying) women, profits for commercial water pump suppliers and consultants involved in the project, visibility for the donor government, political goodwill from the influential village politician in support of the political interests of the donor country."

Second, the donor agencies must deal with the nonalignment of donor and recipient preferences, because the recipients may be engaged in behavior of which the donor does not approve. The donors invest heavily in project management and monitoring and put conditions on aid to make sure the "right" recipient behavior takes place, although they seldom put it in these terms (citing instead their allegedly greater managerial and policy expertise).

Multilateral agencies are sometimes favored instead of bilateral agencies for aid delivery because they can realize economies of scale and scope for information gathering (such as for conditionality), and they can internalize externalities from aid-industry public goods that would be underprovided by each bilateral aid agency. This is the theory, at least; whether it works in practice will be considered more here.

Martens closes with a bracing dose of common sense on the current state of aid:

So far, there has been very little debate in the aid community on the merits of various types of agencies and aid instruments. This is partially due to the fact that the aid community has apparently rallied in recent years around the single objective of poverty reduction, with the implicit assumption that all donors, recipients, agencies and actors in the aid delivery process are motivated only by that same objective.... This is not only unrealistic but also unhelpful to understand the incentives that play a role in the aid delivery process and the comparative advantages of different types of aid agencies.

Martens is searching not only for which aid interventions work but also which types of aid agencies are best suited to carry out those interventions.

Svensson, in chapter 10, emphasizes the broken feedback loop between aid recipients in the poor country and taxpayers in the rich country who fund aid. This creates incentives in the aid agencies to emphasize things easily observable to the rich country public like volume of aid and to underemphasize getting (less observable) results with those funds.[74] (Another interesting example of this emphasis on observability is that a natural disaster heavily covered by the news media gets much more aid than a similar disaster less well covered. Earthquakes are better covered than famines, so a famine would have to have 40,000 times as many deaths as an earthquake to get equivalent news coverage and aid.)

Svensson suggests some practical measures to enhance visibility of results and get client feedback, backed up by field experience. A study that Svensson coauthored (with Reinikka, who contributed chapter 6 to this book) found that only 13 percent of aid and domestically funded central government grants to local schools were actually reaching the schools. The study prompted the government to start publishing the amounts of the grants in the newspapers, where they could be monitored by parents. After this program began, the schools started receiving 80 percent of their intended grants.

Other features of the emphasis on observable volumes of aid require different solutions. Since the country or sector allocation of the aid budget is made by a central unit in the aid agency, and then the disbursement decision is made by a lower-level department, the latter has an incentive to always spend the budget. This lowers the credibility of threats to withhold disbursements unless aid conditions are met. The recipients hence have little incentive to observe conditions, explaining the empirical record on how conditions are often violated. Svensson proposes an alternative: to have "aid tournaments," in which the aid budget is allocated to a pool of countries and then disbursed only to the best-performing countries in the pool.

Next, Knack and Rahman note in chapter 11 the well-known problem of donor fragmentation, in which a large number of donors each have a small share of the total aid inflow into a country. In a typical African country, some thirty official donors and several dozen international nongovernmental organizations (NGOs) provide aid through over a thousand distinct projects and several hundred resident foreign experts."[75] Echoing Reinikka's concern about undermining government, Knack and Rahman give an example from Niger where several ex-government ministers left governments to set up local NGOs that received aid funding that otherwise would have gone to their former ministries. Knack and Rahman show that both a higher level of total aid and higher donor fragmentation are associated with worsening bureaucratic quality in aid recipient governments from 1982 to 2000, where bureaucratic quality measures "autonomy from political pressure," "strength and expertise to govern without drastic changes in policy or interruptions in government services" when governments change, and "established mechanisms for recruiting and training." While donors complain about the low quality of bureaucracy in poor countries, the results of Knack and Rahman suggest that donors themselves are partly to blame. The authors recommend holding aid agencies to account for "how each donor proliferates aid across recipients and sector."

Part IV considers two notable actors in the foreign aid arena: the International Monetary Fund and the World Bank. The IMF does not consider itself an aid agency and is not usually classified as such by others. It is seen instead as a bail-out lender for countries with economic crises. However, this conventional classification has eroded to the point of collapse because the IMF is a notorious repeat lender to low-income countries, much of whose debt was later forgiven, and so de facto was an aid provider to these countries. The World Bank does consider itself an aid agency, but exactly what kind of aid agency it should be has been much debated over time.

Vreeland finds in chapter 12 that IMF lending lowers economic growth in the loan recipients, a finding that is consistent with several other recent studies. Even less econometrically ambitious studies prior to Vreeland and the other recent literature has found a zero effect of IMF lending on growth. The finding of negative or zero growth effects of IMF lending echoes the findings on overall aid (the emphasis on negative results in the literature so far is stronger with IMF lending than with aid). So the question becomes, Why do countries borrow from the IMF if it lowers their growth, not to mention that it was politically unpopular anyway? Vreeland's answer is sobering and controversial:

Governments enter into IMF programs under bad economic circumstances. Their choice is not usually between good and bad economic performance, but between bad performance on their own—without the IMF—or worse performance under a program sponsored by the IMF. . . . By bringing in the IMF, governments gain political leverage—via conditionality—to help push through unpopular policies. For some constituencies, these policies dampen the effects of bad economic performance by redistributing income upward and thus rewarding elites. If the distributional consequences are strong enough, key groups can be made better off even though growth is hurt. But IMF programs doubly hurt the less well off in society: total output growth is lowered, and income is shifted away from them.

While the IMF claims to be apolitical (as all aid donors always do), to Vreeland it is clearly a political actor: "Yet the moment the IMF demands [some conditions to be met], it has entered into domestic politics. The influence of the IMF can be used as leverage to push through policies that favor some at the expense of others; the IMF should not pretend otherwise." This portrait does not leave one sanguine about the current status quo of IMF lending and aid.

Morduch in chapter 13 has a complementary analysis about the World Bank's claim to be a neutral actor, this time in the realm of knowledge about development. One problem is the bank's universalist approach, celebrating "best practices" that are alleged to apply everywhere. This leads to complaints such as that the bank pays "little attention to local needs or ideas," or to "local circumstances," or to "alternative perspectives." Even the bank's dissemination of its knowledge is criticized as too focused on the government and to "top-down."

Then there is the problem that the World Bank faces organizational incentives to be too favorable about a particular paradigm, even when evidence contradicts it. Morduch quotes a bank official with one such example, a review of a structural adjustment loan to Zambia in 1990:

Projects and programs of technical cooperation are developed within the governing sets of assumptions or paradigms, and must comply with them, even in situations where the staff and the client know that the prevailing paradigm is highly unreliable, if not downright wrong. The phenomenon is quite striking in the field of economic adjustment where an operation containing a few important measures is expected to return an entire economy to a strong growth path within a miraculously short timeframe, despite a backlog of decades of economic mismanagement. When, as might be expected, the operation by itself fails to achieve the promised economic growth, reports are written assigning reasons for the shortfall. Ironically, the one cause that such evaluation reports are not allowed to discover is frequently the real reason—namely a faulty paradigm.

Morduch further analyzes how a priori attachment to questionable paradigms can even create poor incentives for data collection: "People with strong positions (either for careerist or ideological reasons) may actively work to discourage data collection that could undermine their credibility." More generally, when the World Bank takes public positions on economic policies in its operations, then its role of disinterested repository of evidence for and against these policies is not going to be credible. This is deeply problematic, as it tarnishes the reputational mechanism by which users—whose lack of resources to independently collect and verify knowledge created the need for the "knowledge bank" in the first place—could know what knowledge to accept as reliable.

Morduch gives an example of the "knowledge bank" misfiring on the issue of microcredit. The World Bank put forward as a best practice the idea that microfinance should be commercially self-sustaining (also endorsed enthusiastically by the U.S. Agency for International Development (USAID). Morduch points out this view turned out to be both theoretically and empirically problematic. Theoretically, this creates obvious incentives for microlenders to drift to richer clients, contradicting the original objective of reaching the poor. Empirically it was not clear that the real world fit the ideal of commercially viable microlending. (Morduch's magisterial book on the subject points out that many microcredit schemes rely on donor subsidies.) Nor were data collected to test the socioeconomic benefits of microlending (the universal standard for judging success of microlending was the repayment rate, hardly a clear measure of success at helping the poor.) The advocates for the "best practice" did not collect data that could be used to test these purely empirical questions—to such a notorious extent that the U.S. Congress passed a law in 2004 to force USAID to collect the data!

The final part of this book looks at various new and imaginative proposals for distributing aid.

Michael Kremer advocates in chapter 15 that aid resources be used to make an advance purchase commitment (APC) for vaccines against diseases such as malaria, AIDS, and tuberculosis. There is a global market incentive to do medical research on diseases that afflict those who will pay the most for the drugs: the rich. Infectious and parasitic diseases account for only 3 percent of the disease burden of the rich but one-third of the disease burden in poor countries. The result is as predicted: there is little research into drugs for such diseases. An APC would have donors guarantee to purchase X million doses of a vaccine for, say, malaria for a price of Y, giving private drug companies the incentive to do research on a malaria vaccine. The advantage of this pull mechanism for research is that money will be spent only on success. If the drug companies fail to find a cure, the initiative will have cost nothing. If the drug companies succeed, millions of lives will be saved. Since vaccine delivery has been more successful than many other aspects of foreign aid, since it is readily monitorable and needs to be delivered only once to each patient, a new vaccine will bypass those parts of the foreign aid system that are not working well.

Levine and Radelet discuss in chapter 16 some new mechanisms in aid that have already started: the Millennium Challenge Account (MCA) of the United States, the Global Fund against AIDS, TB, and Malaria (GFATM), and the Global Alliance on Vaccines and Immunizations (GAVI).

The MCA seeks to untie the Gordian knot of the state by seeking to screen out "bad" governments and then allow the "good" governments to determine their own programs. In practice, neither part works as well as in theory: (1) it is not so easy to find a group of sixteen or so countries that unambiguously have good government compared to the muddle in the middle, and (2) the MCA cannot bring itself to fully relinquish influence over the design of the programs. The MCA does place greater emphasis on evaluation and monitoring of results than existing aid programs, but it is operating on such a broad canvas that it is not clear how to measure its impact on outcomes that depend on many other factors.

GFATM was a notable advance in specializing in three diseases on which there is broad consensus that there could be high payoff to focused action. It also promised to be performance based, although the methodology for this still remains unclear. Its approach to the "bad state–good state" problem was to leave it up to each country to come up with a participatory country coordinating mechanism (CCM) to administer the funds, and it did not screen out any but the most egregiously "bad" states like North Korea. It still remains unclear how participatory the CCMs are, and all of these actions by the Global Fund have generated some controversy that has yet to be resolved.

GAVI is also noteworthy for taking a focused, performance-based approach to one set of interventions that are low cost and high benefit. As Levine and Radelet explain, "GAVI provides an incentive for expanded coverage by, first, ceasing funding if and when coverage declines or fails to increase at an acceptable rate; and, second, rewarding coverage increases with a one-time transfer of $20 per additional fully-immunized child." GAVI has already cut off some poor performers. It has been less successful in catalyzing supportive funding for immunization, and prices of new drugs have not fallen as quickly as GAVI expected.

All three new agencies have lean headquarters staff and hence begin to address the concerns about excessive bureaucracy in foreign aid. Nevertheless, the creation of three new agencies has itself added to the bureaucratic tangle of actors operating in foreign aid. As the authors note, "The United Nations is replete with specialized agencies that began with the promise of a narrow focus, clear objectives, a smaller bureaucracy, and more effective support for development." Whether these three agencies will follow the fate of the now ineffective bureaucratized agencies at the UN or represent promising new approaches that put competitive pressure on existing aid agencies is something that will be closely watched by aid observers in coming years.

In chapter 17, Whittle and Kuraishi are clearly negative on the existing aid bureaucracy. They condemn the current approach to aid in a manner similar to (and which helped inspire) the planners versus searchers dichotomy already discussed: "Efforts in international development are conducted largely by unwieldy bureaucracies that centrally plan economies of developing countries, by making large-scale choices. If the international aid regime were a national economy, one thing is clear: the World Bank and IMF would be after it to reform.... Top-down and agency-driven approaches translate into projects that are not responsive to the needs of local communities, tend to serve the priorities and perspectives of so-called aid experts rather than the aid recipients, and lead to inefficient results." They suggest that the free market is a good metaphor (and possible inspiration) for how the aid system could work better. A free market rates borrowers and lenders. Could an aid marketplace develop ratings for aid donors and aid recipients? Markets feature entry and exit. Could an aid marketplace attract new promising entrants and close down poorly performing incumbents? Markets create competitive pressure to innovate. Could an aid marketplace force donors to innovate?

Unfortunately, there has not existed any "market square" where aid participants could meet. Whittle and Kuraishi are trying to change this both intellectually and physically. They have created a Web-based NGO, globalgiving.com, a sort of eBay approach to foreign aid. However, chapter 17 is about more than their own efforts. They suggest network theory as another market-type inspiration for foreign aid, where individuals in social networks spontaneously develop an emergent order without any top-down direction (the Internet being the current fashionable example).

How could this happen in foreign aid? This is clearly blue-sky territory where there has been little experimentation in foreign aid. But Whittle and Kuraishi suggest brainstorming based on precedents such as the American tradition of self-organizing community groups to meet local collective needs, the principle that decentralized choices outperform centralized decision making, the self-organization of cities (à la Jane Jacobs and Paul Krugman), and the agglomeration economies demonstrated by self-forming clusters like Silicon Valley.

To make this practical, an aid marketplace would have to face the problem of creating trust among participants. Decentralized monitoring, checking each participant's identity and past history, and each participant's concern for his or her reputation in a market where there are repeated transactions make these issues potentially tractable, although far from easy or straightforward to solve.

What other mechanisms could create markets in foreign aid? Easterly (2006, 2002, 2001) proposed the idea of "aid vouchers":[76] "Another market-oriented step would be for the common pool [of aid money] to issue vouchers to poor individuals or communities, who could exchange them for development services at any aid agency, NGO, or domestic government agency. These service providers would in turn redeem the vouchers for cash out of the common pool. Aid agencies would be forced to compete to attract aid vouchers (and thus money) for their budgets."[77] This idea was too poorly articulated, too crazy, or too threatening to the aid establishment to attract much support. Yet frustration with the existing bureaucratic, top-down, planner-dominated aid system is growing. UK Conservative leader David Cameron endorsed the idea of experimenting with vouchers in a speech on June 29, 2006: "One idea we will investigate, based on our belief in trusting people—and our instinctive dislike of top-down solutions—is aid vouchers. Aid vouchers, put directly in the hands of poor communities, would be redeemable for development services of any kind with an aid agency or supplier of their choice. The vouchers could be converted into cash by the aid agencies. For the first time, poor people themselves would be the masters, and aid agencies would have a direct and clear incentive to deliver effective services. Such an innovation would help show us what the poor really want—and who is most effective in meeting their needs."[78]

Chapter 18 by Hoffman is also very much informed by the examples of market mechanisms that reduce poverty. Hoffman wonders why so little aid actually goes to stimulate enterprise development, when private enterprise is well established as the means by which most people have historically escaped poverty. He points out that the aid system is "overwhelmingly focused on what local government, donors, or the other battalions of aid actors and NGOs need to do first to achieve the Millennium Development Goals.... 'What to do' about enterprise usually comes way down the list."

The second defect of the aid system, according to Hoffman, is its inability to think like a business. Business thinking would include risk assessment, knowing what the target "customer" wants, setting out precisely how the project is going to help meet those wants at lowest cost, and how many customers (in our case, pro-poor enterprises or poor people) are going to be measurably better off at the end of the project.

Hoffman suggests consequence accountability of donors to recipients similar to that which exists from a start-up firm to an investor, a corporate manager to shareholders, and businesses to customers. He calls for "business DNA" to make its way down the foreign aid supply chain, first with the donors themselves, and says that business DNA should be transferred to enterprises in poor countries. Unfortunately, aid workers have little business experience and little business DNA to transfer. Oddly enough, even private corporations that have corporate social responsibility (CSR) departments operating in poor countries show little appreciation for the business principles that should be applied to aid. It is as if private corporations want to imitate aid agencies, while it should be the other way around.

An example of Hoffman's desired approach is a recent experiment to market cleaner indoor stoves to poor families in India. Smoky stoves are a leading source of indoor air pollution, which causes respiratory infections, leading to around 2 million deaths globally. The traditional approach was to design the perfect stove with little regard for costs or customer wants, only to see it rejected by the poor or fail to attain any significant scale. The recent experiment test-marketed stoves with the customers and kept costs down. The pilot successfully sold 65,000 stoves, and the objective now is to scale up dramatically.

Part VI of this book looks at the big picture in the aid system. Like Hoffman, McMillan in chapter 19 also uses the market as inspiration in his chapter. His concern is with the big-bang and shock therapy approach to economic reform often advocated by Jeffrey Sachs, the IMF, World Bank, and other aid agencies. He believes that comprehensive reform to all economic policies is just as misguided as trying to do all aid interventions at once: "Acknowledging our ignorance means moving step by step rather than betting everything on a comprehensive blueprint.... The whole point of the market economy, after all, is that it handles, better than any more centralized alternative, the unforeseen and the unforeseeable. If we could plan the reforms, we could have planned the economy."

McMillan contrasts piecemeal reform with utopian social engineering à la Popper. China is an example of the success of the first, Russia an example of the failure of the second. China achieved some easy gains by replacing collective farming with individual farming; it then moved to village enterprises, which competed with each other and could expand the scale of success using their powers of taxation. The reform process has since moved on, and village enterprises are no longer a good model for the next phase of growth in China, not to mention for other countries with very different circumstances. To McMillan, there is no room in policy reform for aid experts who apply universal blueprints; policy reform in each country should be intentionally experimental (searching rather than planning again). His most important advice to would-be aid experts on reforming other countries' policies is, "Avoid hubris."

Birdsall in chapter 20 analyzes the "sins" of the donors, some of them related to the emphasis on observable aid spending. Another version of the pressure to spend is the reluctance to stop spending even when conditions become supremely unpromising: donors exit far less than they should. Pressure to spend the budget also leads to overemphasis on short-run outputs (or, worse, short-run inputs) and scandalously little emphasis on long-run results.

Even when the donors find something that has a long-run dimension, like the MDGs for 2015, these seem designed more for short-term publicity than for rewarding good long-run performance. For example, Burkina Faso is projected to raise net primary enrollment from its current level of 35 percent to 59 percent by 2015. The UNDP describes this projected performance as "off-track" to meet the MDG of universal primary enrollment by 2015, even though Burkina Faso's performance would far outpace the historical performance of the United States over the same range.

A related sin that comes from aid agencies' desire to "be seen" is the proliferation of projects, countries, and sectors within each aid agency's portfolio, presumably because each additional project, country, and sector in which an aid agency is involved attracts additional observers. The consequence is the thicket of huge numbers of donors and projects with which even the smallest country must cope. One solution that Birdsall advocates is to pool donor funds at the country level, but this proposal has met stiff political resistance.

Another sin of the donors is the obfuscation that has surrounded the issue of ownership of development policies. Birdsall notes that "the misguided imposition of policy conditions morphed into the misguided imposition of participation. The prevailing approach to participation, as demanded by donors, has been narrow and apolitical. In practical terms, it has relied mostly on engagement of civil society groups in discussions of proposed government programs (including the PRSPs...) Members of minority groups and the truly poor are often excluded from apparently open discussions, reflecting the reality that participatory efforts alone are unlikely to alter the prevailing distribution of power and influence."

Donors' desire to show individual observable efforts has also led them to overemphasize countries as the receiving unit and to underemphasize global public goods, such as research on tropical agriculture and diseases.

The greatest sin of the donors emphasized by Birdsall is as easy to state and to solve as it is difficult to overcome the political resistance: the almost complete lack of independent evaluations of aid (as noted also in chapter 2 by Banerjee and He and chapter 3 by Duflo and Kremer), so that donors are both ignorant of their impact and unaccountable for that impact. Groups on the left, right, and center have called for an independent entity to do aid evaluation, Birdsall notes, and this could be easily funded by a small proportional contribution from each donor.

1.3 Conclusion

"Avoiding hubris" and "independent evaluation" is a fitting way to end this introduction. Focusing on specific feasible tasks and holding the aid actors responsible for whether they achieve them is a no-brainer, except for the absence of these simple principles in today's foreign aid system. The talented explorers of the aid domain in this book offer much good sense and much hope for the future, even if they do not strive for the headline-grabbing and utopian promises of making poverty history anytime soon. To the extent that outsiders can assist the poor in their search for prosperity, the chapters in this book offer a promising set of ways to go forward.

Notes

1. *Human Development Report 2005: International Cooperation at a Crossroads: Aid, Trade and Security in an Unequal World* (New York: United Nations Development Program, 2005), p. 7.

2. United Nations Millennium Project, *Investing in Development: A Practical Plan to Achieve the Millennium Development Goals* (New York: United Nations, 2005), p. 4.

3. Ibid., p. 193.

4. Department for International Development, *Eliminating World Poverty: Making Governance Work for the Poor* (London: Department for International Development, 2006), p. 13.

5. World Bank and International Monetary Fund, *Global Monitoring Report 2006: Millennium Development Goals: Strengthening Mutual Accountability, Aid, Trade, and Governance* (Washington, D.C.: World Bank and International Monetary Fund, 2006), p. xvii.

6. Ibid.

7. Some NGOs such as Oxfam have pointed out that the 2005 number was inflated by large-scale debt relief, which counts as aid. They argue that debt relief is not true aid, for example, because it writes off debt that is not being serviced anyway and should not be included. This is a paradoxical position, as the same NGOs (such as Oxfam) campaigned for debt relief under the argument that debt was strangling poor countries, so it is not clear why debt relief should not counted as a boon to poor countries.

8. Human Development Report 2005. *Crossroads*, p. 1.

9. Jeffrey Sachs, *The End of Poverty: Economic Possibilities for Our Time* (New York: Penguin USA, 2005), 352.

10. Department for International Development, *Eliminating World Poverty*, p. iii.

11. http://www.makepovertyhistory.org/.

12. V. I. Lenin, *What Is to Be Done? Burning Questions of Our Movement* (New York: International Publishers, 1943), p. 80.

13. Sachs, *End of Poverty*, 2, 289.

14. Department for International Development, *Eliminating World Poverty*, 18–19.

15. United Nations Millennium Project, *Investing in Development*, 2.

16. Lenin, *What Has to be Done?*, p. 76.

17. Department for International Development, *Eliminating World Poverty*, 19.

18. William Duggan of Columbia University suggested the Aid Wall comparison to the Berlin Wall to me in private conversation. The chapter 17 by Whittle and Kuraishi in this book also inspired the central planning metaphor.

19. UN Millennium Project, *Investing in Development*, 2.

20. Sachs, *End of Poverty*, 2–3.

21. Ibid., 273.

22. http://www.un.org/millenniumgoals/. July 6, 2005.

23. UN General Assembly, 55th Session. *UN Millennium Declaration* (A/RES/55/2). September 8, 2000.

24. Jeni Klugman, ed., *Poverty Reduction Strategy Paper Sourcebook* (Washington, D.C.: World Bank, 2002).

25. Ibid.

26. http://www.mfdr.org/Sourcebook/1stEdition/MfDRSourcebook-Feb-16-2006.pdf. Organization for Economic Cooperation and Development and World Bank, *Managing for Development Results Principles in Action: Sourcebook on Emerging Good Practice*. p. 4. February 16, 2006.

27. Luc Christiaensen, Christopher Scott, and Quentin Wodon, "Development Targets and Costs," in Klugman, ed., *Poverty Reduction Strategy Paper Sourcebook*, 132.

28. Ibid.

29. http://igdleaders.org/policy/documents/IGDDevelopmentGuide_000.pdf. Initiative for Global Development, *The IGD Development Guide: A Business Approach to Ending Extreme Global Poverty*, p. 7.

30. See Ruth Revine, *Millions Saved: Proven Successes in Global Health* (Washington: Center for Global Development, 2007), for a description of the successful vaccination campaigns.

31. Human Development Report 2005. *Crossroads*, 77.

32. UN Millennium Project, *Preparing National Strategies to Meet the Millennium Development Goals: A Handbook* (New York: United Nations, 2005), p. 130.

33. Shantayanan Devarajan et al., "Goals for Development: History, Prospects and Costs," *World Bank Discussion Paper* No. 2819 (Washington, D.C.: World Bank, 2002).

34. The research they cite is Deon Filmer, "A Note on Public Spending and Health and Education Outcomes" (Washington, D.C.: World Bank, 1999) (processed), and Deon Filmer, Jeffrey S. Hammer, and Lant H. Pritchett, "Weak Links in the Chain: A Diagnosis of Health Policy in Poor Countries," *World Bank Research Observer* 15(2000): 199–224.

35. Filmer, Hammer, and Pritchett, "Weak Links in the Chain," pp. 199–224.

36. UN Millennium Project, *Investing in Development*; Sachs, *End of Poverty*; Jeffrey Sachs, *Macroeconomics and Health: Investing in Health for Economic Development* (Geneva: World Health Organization, 2001).

37. Shantayanan Devarajan, et al., "Goals for Development."

38. UN Millennium Project, *Preparing National Strategies*, 45–46.

39. Ibid., 48, 50.

40. This discussion and the citation of Kuhn is based on William Duggan, *The Art of What Works: How Success Really Happens* (New York: McGraw-Hill, 2003) 234.

41. F. A. Hayek, *The Road to Serfdom* (Chicago: University of Chicago Press, 1944), 181.

42. Karl Popper, *The Poverty of Historicism* (London: Routledge, 2002), p. 61.

43. William Easterly, *The White Man's Burden: Why the West's Efforts to Aid the Rest Have Done So Much Ill and So Little Good* (New York: Penguin Press, 2006).

44. http://adamsmithee.blogs.com/blog/ (posted May 19, 2006).

45. This section is based on William Easterly, "Reliving the 50s: The Big Push, Poverty Traps, and Takeoffs in Economic Development," *Journal of Development Economics* 11, 4 (December 2006): 289–318.

46. Sachs, *End of Poverty*, 56–57.

47. This involved some data construction, since the World Development Indicators (WDI) have complete data on aid for the bottom quintile (the few aid observations missing can usually be interpreted as representing zero aid) but not on GDP. I used the Maddison per capita gross domestic product (GDP) numbers and population numbers to impute GDP for missing observations in WDI. Since the Maddison numbers are purchasing power parity (PPP), I used GDP in nominal dollars and PPP for that country in the year for which both were available in WDI closest to the sample period to convert the imputed Maddison number from PPP to nominal dollars.

48. Aart Kraay and Claudio Raddatz, "Poverty Traps, Aid, and Growth," mimeo., World Bank, January 2005, and Bryan Graham and and Jonathan Temple, "Rich Nations, Poor Nations: How Much Can Multiple Equilibria Explain?" mimeo., Harvard University, 2004.

49. Sachs, *End of Poverty*, 191.

50. UN Millennium Project Report, *Investing in Development: A Practical Plan to Achieve the Millennium Development Goals: Main Report*, 34.

51. Sachs, *End of Poverty*, 226.

52. http://www.underreported.com/modules.php?op=modload&name=News&file=article&-sid=1241.

53. UN Millennium Project Report, *Millennium Development Goals Needs Assessment* (January 2005), 119.

54. Easterly, "Reliving the 50s."

55. Ibid.

56. Durlauf, Johnson, and Jonathan Temple, "Rich Nations, Poor Nations."

57. A thoughtful and entertaining discussion of this theme is in Virginia Postrel, *The Future and Its Enemies: The Growing Conflict over Creativity, Enterprise, and Progress* (New York: Touchstone, 1998). She stresses a dichotomy between stasis and dynamism that is related to the dichotomy here between planning and searching. Another great book on unpredictable success is Paul Ormerod, *Why Most Things Fail: Evolution, Extinction, and Economics* (New York: Pantheon Books, 2005).

58. http://www.macnn.com/articles/06/04/20/apples.music.business/.

59. Jim Collins, *Built to Last* (New York: Harper Collins Publishers, 1994), p. 153.

60. Ibid., 141.

61. Malcolm Gladwell, "The Formula," *New Yorker*, 16 October 2006, 138.

62. U.S. Small Business Administration, Office for Advocacy, http://www.sba.gov/advo/research/data.html.

63. Lada A. Adamic, *Zipf, Power-laws, and Pareto—A Ranking Tutorial* (Palo Alto, Calif.: Information Dynamics Lab, HP Labs, 2004), is a helpful primer on power laws.

64. Paul Ormerod, *Why Most Things Fail: Evolution, Extinction, and Economics* (New York: Pantheon Books, 2005).

65. Ibid.

66. Tom Peters and Robert Waterman, *In Search of Excellence* (New York: Harper & Row, 1982); Jim Collins, *Built to Last* (New York: Harper Collins, 1994) and *Good to Great* (New York: Harper Collins, 2001). Jennifer Reingold and Ryan Underwood, "Was *Built to Last* Built to Last?" *Fast Company* 88 (November 2004): 103.

67. Michael Porter, *The Competitive Advantage of Nations* (New York: Free Press, 1990).

68. http://www.fastcompany.com/magazine/88/built-to-last-collins.html, Ryan Underwood, "Built to Last: The True Test of Timeless Companies: Interview with Jim Collins," *Fast Company* 88 (November 2004).

69. Amy E. Knaup, "Survival and Longevity in the Business Employment Dynamics Database," *Monthly Labor Review* 128:5 (May 2005): 50–56; Brian Headd, "Redefining Business Success: Distinguishing between Closure and Failure," *Small Business Economics* 21:1 (August 2003): 51–61.

70. David H. Autor and Mark G. Duggan, 2003. "The Rise In The Disability Rolls And The Decline In Unemployment," *The Quarterly Journal of Economics* 118(1): 157–205.

71. http://web.worldbank.org/WBSITE/EXTERNAL/TOPICS/EXTPOVERTY/EXTISPMA/ 0,,menuPK:384336~pagePK:149018~piPK:149093~theSitePK:384329,00.html.

72. For one attempt to mobilize political change and for further analysis, see *Report of the Evaluation Gap Working Group, When Will We Ever Learn? Improving Lives through Impact Evaluation* (Washington, D.C.: Center for Global Development, May 2006). William D. Savedoff, Ruth Levine, Nancy Birdsall Co-Chairs.

73. Department for International Development, *Eliminating World Poverty*, 10, 21, 78.

74. For an extended treatment of this theme for general audiences, see Easterly, *White Man's Burden* (2006).

75. Nicolas Van de Walle, *African Economies and the Politics of Permanent Crisis* (Cambridge: Cambridge University Press, 1991), 58.

76. William Easterly, *The Elusive Quest for Growth: Economists' Adventures and Misadventures in the Tropics* (Cambridge: MIT Press, 2001); "The Cartel of Good Intentions: The Problem of Bureaucracy in Foreign Aid," *Foreign Policy* 131 (July–August 2002): 40–49; *White Man's Burden* (2006).

77. Easterly, "Cartel of Good Intentions," 48.

78. David Cameron, Speech at Oxford Town Hall, U.K. 29 June 2006.

I THE POWER OF SCIENTIFIC EVALUATION—AND WHY ISN'T IT DONE MORE OFTEN?

2 Making Aid Work

Abhijit V. Banerjee and Ruimin He

One would think that giving away money ought to be easy. After all, there are so many who need it so badly, and we have a pretty good idea of where they are. Yet, rather remarkably, we seem to have arrived at a point where more or less everyone agrees that aid giving is not working the way it ought to.

Part of the problem is that most people are not actually giving away money—or rather, while they often give away money, the ultimate recipients do not get it as a straight gift of money. Somewhere along the chain, a non-governmental organization (NGO) or a government is responsible for turning this money into schools, or hospitals, or roads, or whatever else the people are supposed to get.

2.1 What Makes Giving Away Money Hard?

The bias against just giving people money stems in part from the feeling that the best use of the money may not be to spend it on consumption. This is plausible, and indeed likely: there is some relatively convincing evidence that many people do not invest as much in their businesses and their children's human capital as the rewards to such investment seem to warrant. What is less clear is why people could not be relied on to make the right investments on their own—in which case it would be enough to hand them the money. One possible reason may have to do with the lack of self-control. It may be too tempting, especially for poor people, to spend the money on something they need right away. The incompleteness of the intrafamily contract is another reason not to trust the family with the money: parents may put too little weight on improving their children's earning capacity because they do not expect to share in their children's prosperity. And, of course, people may not know what is good for them.

There was a time when many of these kinds of arguments could not be made among respectable economists. They were seen as a transgression against the freedom of the individual, and bad economics to boot. Now the pendulum has swung in the other direction: it is an item of faith in the development community that no one should be giving away money. It is not clear what, if any, evidence lies behind this shared conviction. Certainly no one has done the experiment of showering large gifts of money on poor people in poor countries and then following them to see what they do with the money and what happens afterward.

A very different kind of argument for giving people goods rather than money comes from the fear that if you are seen handing out money, even those who have enough of their own may want to pretend to be needy. The advantage of providing public services rather than money is that the nonpoor may not want them enough to make it worth their while to simulate poverty. The very rich in the United States, after all, choose to pay for their children to go to private schools, even though their children are entitled to go to public schools at no charge, simply because they feel that the public education system is not quite up to the standards to which they aspire. This saves the government the cost of finding teachers for these extra children. But these parents do not hesitate to claim any tax deductions that they may be entitled to, which suggests that if the government was giving away money instead of schooling, the rich would be in the queue with everyone else.

It is, however, not at all obvious that one cannot give away money without opening the floodgates. After all, the rich value their time: making it necessary to queue up in order to collect the money should discourage those who really do not need it.

The broader point here is not to deny that giving away money has significant disadvantages, but to emphasize that we know very little about how serious these disadvantages might be. In particular, are these costs necessarily large enough to outweigh the significant costs of trying to give away anything other than money?

2.2   Delivering Goods and Services to the Poor

If you do not want to give away money but still think it is worth trying to help the poor, you would have to give them things: roads, schools, banks, hospitals, fertilizer. Giving away things is more work than giving away money for the simple reason that someone needs to produce them: roads have to be built, teachers hired and trained, fertilizer produced, and hospitals kept in good repair. It would be simple if it were just a matter of paying for the roads, fertilizer, and the other things, but that is just the first step. Then we would have to make sure that the roads are built to the required standards, the teachers teach, the fertilizer gets to the right people, the process of delivery is not subverted by corruption or bureaucratic incompetence.

What is perhaps even more difficult is to be reasonably confident that the money is being spent on things that are really worth getting, in the usual sense of being at least as good as any other way of spending the same amount of money. After all, to take one popular example, there are many ways to spend money on promoting education: build more buildings, hire more teachers, provide free textbooks, distribute free uniforms, put flip charts in classrooms, set up computer labs in every school, provide a bonus for teachers who teach well, serve hot meals in school, and much more. Indeed every one of the interventions listed here (and many more) has been tried somewhere in the world in the past few years. This diversity in part reflects differing needs, but often it is just ignorance. Lacking a clear sense of what works, well-meaning donors will choose what their intuition suggests, even though it may be very different from what the donor next door believes. Both seem to believe that they are right.

There is also no guarantee that it makes sense to spend the money on directly promoting education. The fact that people are not getting an education on their own might reflect the lack of jobs for those who have an education. Pushing out more graduates who will not find jobs either may actually be counterproductive, because it might reinforce the lack of faith in the value of education. The best way to promote education may be to create jobs. Or we may even want to look beyond education. Perhaps one should invest in health and leave education to private initiative—or forget about both and go for fertilizers. How should we decide where to go?

It is no surprise that the process of helping the poor by giving them access to goods and services is fraught with difficulty. There needs to be a system for picking the right project and a system for making sure that the project is carried out as it should be, and for figuring out how much people are getting out of it and whether it continues to be what they need or want.

For this, donors need to get involved in the process of decision making and delivery at the ground level, though the exact nature of the involvement can vary substantially. The actual production of the good is usually contracted out, though even this is not always the case. Both the process of delivery and its impact have to be assessed, though once again there is a choice between doing it yourself and contracting it out. And the broader strategy needs to be worked out, based, one presumes, on knowledge of the situation on the ground. This might mean consulting local experts. Even carrying out some new research as a prelude to the intervention is not out of the question.

In all of this, the donor will typically work with one or more local organizations, be it government departments or NGOs. Some of these local partners may have their own sources of funding, which will allow the donor to leverage its resources.

Whatever the exact strategy, whether the donor does the monitoring or preliminary research, or whether these are contracted out, they involve substantial expenditures over and above the direct cost of delivering the good (or service) to the ultimate beneficiaries. To get a sense of how large these expenses might be, we note that between the years 1996 and 2001, the World Bank administrative budget averaged US$1,401 million per year (World Bank 2001, appendix 5; World Bank 2003b, appendix 1), while the total World Bank International Bank for Reconstruction and Development (IBRD) and International Development Association (IDA) loans per year (World Bank 2000b, 10, World Bank 2002b, 26) averaged US$15,615 million and US$6,154 million respectively. The Operations Evaluation Department of the World Bank calculates ex post economic rate of returns for the projects that it evaluates (World Bank 2002a, statistical appendix table 12), but only for certain sectors.[1] It finds that the median revised (ex post) economic rate of return for both the IBRD and IDA/blend lending operations for fiscal years 1996–2001 exits (the date that the project leaves the World Bank's active portfolios) was about 20 percent. The aggregate economic return on the bank's portfolio was 20 percent of $15.615 billion plus $6.154 billion, or about $4.400 billion. It follows that the benefits from World Bank lending are lower by almost a third because of administrative costs.

As we will discuss, we should not expect to entirely avoid these costs by switching to donating money rather than goods. For now, however, the relevant point is that these costs are large.

2.3   Evaluating Donor Effectiveness

Given everything that they spend on the design and management of aid projects, are donors getting what they hoped for? The short answer is that we do not know. Part of the problem is data: As table 2.A.1 in the appendix shows, most of the larger public donor organizations (as opposed to private foundations) do evaluate their projects, but they usually stop short of a summary quantitative assessment of the social impact of the project, such as a rate of return. Of the donors listed in this appendix, only the World Bank reports rates of returns, and then only for certain sectors; education, health, and nutrition, for example, are left out. This reflects, in part, doubts about whether it makes sense to try to reduce the many dimensions of a project outcome to a single rate of return. In part, it also reflects the inherent difficulties of coming up with a rate of return: How do you come up with the right counterfactual that tells you what would have happened in the absence of the project?

What some of these donors do instead is to assess overall project performance combining both process evaluation ("the right number of schools were built") and impact evaluation ("the children's test scores improved") on a set scale such as satisfactory/unsatisfactory or successful/unsuccessful (table 2.A.1).[2] However, this evaluation is often carried out by those who are also involved in the implementation of the program, making it somewhat hard to know what to make of the results. Finally, many of these organizations do not allow the public access to their assessments. Of the eight organizations listed in table 2.A.1, only the World Bank and the Asian Development Bank (ADB) have their projects assessed by a formally independent organization, report project level assessments on a set scale, and allow the public access to the assessment results.[3] These are the only two, therefore, that offer the possibility of delving deeper.

This is far from ideal. The World Bank is not just any donor organization: it is probably the most visible organization of this class, with all the constraints that come from being in the public eye. It is formally responsible to those who provide its financing, which are the governments of a handful of rich countries. Moreover, it gives only loans (albeit on very attractive terms). It is also an organization that attracts and employs many of the best minds thinking about development today. Perhaps most important, it sees itself as a leader in the efforts to promote development in the world. This probably means that its projects need to be evaluated not just in terms of what they directly achieve but also in terms of how they shape efforts outside the bank to promote development. In a previous paper, we (Banerjee and He 2003) try to evaluate the bank's achievement as a leader and conclude that there is no evidence that others are following its lead. But we also argue that the bank is ideally placed to take this leadership role and that it is important that it does so, which obviously implies that we must take it seriously in evaluating the bank's performance.

The ADB is also quite special, being the one multilateral funding organization that has close ties with the Japanese government. We may expect it to have been influenced by the Japanese government's rather distinct view of economic policy.

Given that the World Bank and ADB evaluations are on different scales and the evaluators have potentially different standards, there is no point in trying to compare these two organizations directly. One could, of course, take their assessments at face value. In 2002, the Operations Evaluation Department (OED) of the World Bank wrote that "at the project level, the outcomes of Bank-financed projects continue to improve," and more than 60 percent of all projects evaluated each year since 1990 have had satisfactory outcomes (World Bank 2003a, xii); while the ADB wrote that the proportion of successful projects or programs (by year of completion) has been more than 50 percent since 1997 and has been trending upward since 1989 (Asian Development Bank 2003, 37).

The problem is that we do not really know what to make of the scale they use. What does it, at some absolute level, mean to say that the World Bank's OED feels that the project was satisfactory? How much of this assessment reflects, for example, what they expected (which we do not know) rather than some objective that we all share? Clearly there are many who would join Bill Easterly in his reluctant conclusion that the last fifty years of aid giving by the bank (which for many years employed Easterly) has achieved relatively little (Easterly 2001, 2003). It seems safer, therefore, not to put too much weight on how the OED (or its equivalent elsewhere) feels about the project and to focus on how assessments vary across different projects or sets of projects for the same organization.

World Bank or ADB projects vary considerably in the degree of their involvement, as measured by the share of the project financed by these organizations. If we assume that putting more money into the project reflects a greater commitment to the cause, we can use this ratio as a measure of the bank's priorities.

What can we say about the World Bank's priorities? For each project approved (i.e., launched) between 1994 and 2001, the World Bank reports the share of World Bank funding in total funding for that project.[4] For the period 1987–2001, we also have the evaluation of projects by sector,[5] averaged over three-year periods (1987–1990, 1990–1993, 1994–1997, and 1998–2001).[6] We label these four periods 1, 2, 3, and 4. We then regress the share of World Bank funding in a particular project approved in period t on the average evaluation in period $t - 2$ of the sector that it belongs to [*Prevperf*], and the improvement of its evaluation between $t - 1$ and $t - 2$ [*Diffperf*]. We control for fixed differences across sectors, countries, and periods and cluster errors by sector.

The results in column 1 of table 2.1 show that when a sector's performance improves, projects in that sector get a higher fraction of their financing from the bank (the *DiffPerf* coefficient is positive). But it also helps to start at a low base (conditional on the same degree of improvement, projects in sectors that started with a worse record get more money: the coefficient on *Prevperf* is negative), which immediately implies that if two sectors have shown the same improvement, the one that is doing worse will get more money from the bank.

A similar pattern emerges when we look at the total amount of money allocated to each sector. For four sectors—agriculture, finance, technical assis-

Table 2.1
OLS regressions on project selection

	World Bank (1)	ADB (including multisector/others) (2)	ADB (excluding multisector/others) (3)
PrevPerf	−.002553*	−.006767*	.0004253
	[.0011]	[.0033]	[.0047]
DiffPerf	.001852*	−.004361*	−.001184
	[.00051]	[.0014]	[.0020]
N	1513	519	468
Adjusted R^2	.29	.33	.39

Note: Dependent variable: percentage of individual project that is funded by the World Bank. Significant at the 5 percent level of significance. Robust standard errors reported.

Table 2.2
Cross-sectional panel regressions on project selection

	World Bank (1)	ADB (2)
$Log(expenditure_{t-1})$	.7677*	.1523
	[.028]	[.18]
$Outcome_{t-1}$	−.002256	.000925
	[.0026]	[.0089]
$Outcome_t - outcome_{t-1}$	.001594*	−.0004837
	[.00075]	[.0073]
Number of observations	16	45
Number of groups	4	7

Note: Dependent variable: $Log(expenditure_t)$.
*Significant at the 5 percent level of significance. Robust standard errors reported.

tance, and water and sanitation[7]—the World Bank provides data from 1974, when data start, to 1993[8] for every block of three years (with the exception of 1992–1993) on the sector outcome measured by OED evaluation,[9] and the log of total expenditure on that sector.[10] Using this data set, we regress using the Arellano-Bond linear dynamic panel data estimator [log($expenditure_t$)], on [log($expenditure_{t-1}$)], [$outcome_{t-1}$], and [$outcome_t-outcome_{t-1}$], correcting for period and sector effects. The results are shown in column 1 of table 2.2. They show that increased spending for a particular sector is associated with an improving trend in sector performance over the immediate past. Once again, having started from a lower initial level of performance helps, but the coefficient is not significant in this case.[11]

When we do the same exercise for the ADB, we get very different results. Both past performance and improvement in performance seems to have a negative impact on the allocation of its funding (column 2 of table 2.1). However this result is very sensitive to the inclusion of the "Multisector/Others" sector, where there were only two evaluations between 1986 and 1989 (both successful). Once this sector is dropped, the past level and the improvement in the level become insignificant (column 3 of table 2.1). All that matters then are fixed cross-country differences and perhaps cross-sector differences.[12]

The results for the ADB seem consistent with the view that its priorities are largely set by high-level decisions and are not particularly subject to any short-term influences. This may be a good thing because it insulates the organization against the influence of fads and internal political shifts, but it clearly also prevents the organization from learning from its experience.

The case of the World Bank is more complicated. It clearly does not give priority to sectors that have been performing the best over the immediate past, which is what, under the (possibly brave) assumption that past performance is a reasonable index of what we might expect in the immediate future, would have been the way to maximize immediate impact. But it does favor the sectors that have been improving the fastest. One way to rationalize this may be to assume that the World Bank sees itself as a leader in the development community. As a leader, it would make sense for it to try to promote those sectors where the potential for improvement is the highest rather than those where, on current record, the possibility of success is the highest. Sectors that have been improving fast over the past few years, but still have some distance to go, may therefore be exactly the sectors the bank would want to favor.

It is, however, possible to take a more cynical view of the same evidence. In this view, the bank is excessively influenced by shifts in current fashions in development thinking. The reason, in this view, that we see the bank reacting to improvements is that these improvements shift fashions. When something does unexpectedly well, it is easy to get excited about it, even if, on balance, it is still doing worse than better-established options.

The question, in the end, comes down to whether the projects that are being given priority are doing what they were intended to do. One way of looking at this is to examine the correlation between the fraction of planned project financing that was to come from the bank and the performance of the project according to the bank's evaluators, after controlling for fixed differences across sectors and countries, the length of the project, the year when it was approved, and the year of the evaluation. The results are shown in column 1 of table 2.3. As we have already reported (Banerjee and He 2003), there is a negative and significant correlation between the priority that the bank originally gave the project (measured by the fraction of financing that was supposed to come from the bank) and its performance. Bank-favored projects seem to do worse from an ex ante point of view relative to other projects in the same sector.

Table 2.3
On effectiveness of fund allocation

	World Bank (planned) (1)	World Bank (actual) (2)	ADB (planned) (3)	ADB (actual) (4)
% Funding	−.123** [.038]	.064 [.090]	−.585 [.54]	−.837* [.49]
Length	.0054 [.016]	.0100 [.016]	−.0705* [.038]	−.0722** [.035]
n	664	664	137	136
Adjusted R^2	.26	.24	.18	.20

Note: Dependent variable: Outcome of individual projects. Regressions include sector dummies, country dummies, year of approval dummies, and year of closing dummies.
** Significant at the 5 percent level of significance. Robust standard errors reported.
* Significant at the 10 percent level of significance. Robust standard error reported.

This negative relation goes away if we replaced the share of planned cost that the bank was supposed to pay for with the share of actual cost (column 2 of table 2.3). Basically, if projects are going really badly, the bank cancels its promised contribution to them. But even with the help of this corrective procedure, the correlation between performance and funding is nowhere near being positive and significant. Being a bank priority does not help you perform better, even after the cancellations.

We repeat this exercise for the ADB, using projects evaluated between 1997 and 2002.[13] Here percentage funding is defined as the [Loan amount approved]/[Expected project cost] in column 3 of table 2.3, and [Loan amount disbursed]/[Actual project cost] in column 4 of table 2.3. We find that the outcome rating is not significantly affected by the loan amount approved, but the amount disbursed has an effect that is negative and significant at the 10 percent level.

The lack of a positive correlation between funding and performance, in the case of the ADB, seems unsurprising, given everything else we have seen about the way they target (or rather, do not target). In the case of the World Bank, these results are consistent with the view that the bank is faddish. They can also be explained by assuming that the bank is particularly ineffective at running its projects.

But the results are also quite consistent with any view that has the World Bank playing the role of a leader and prioritizing projects that others, more focused on immediate impact, would not choose. After all, we already knew that they have not given priority to the sectors that had performed best in the past. All that this evidence really shows is that this is true within sectors as well. Of course, it is not clear that the World Bank is particularly effective as a leader, and to the extent that we take this as given, we may still want it to focus more on its rather limited direct impact.

In the end, there is little that is reliable that we can say about donor performance. The most we can say is that we found no prima facie evidence of great effectiveness.

2.4   What Limits Effectiveness?

Donor organizations are in many ways very much like other organizations, and they share many of the standard organizational constraints. Organizations like the World Bank obviously need many people to act and take decisions on their behalf, and there is nothing to guarantee that they have the right incentives. In particular, in an organization that lives by doing projects and making loans, no one achieves prominence by rejecting projects and refusing loans. For this reason alone, most people on the implementation side of the bank, in either sector departments or country missions, are probably somewhat biased in favor of making something happen. Add to this the fact that they are the ones who deal with the potential recipients, and we have a recipe for a degree of over-enthusiasm and irresponsible lending.

There is also obviously the possibility of ideological conflict within the organization. We recently saw a public example of such a conflict in the World Bank that ultimately led to the resignation of the person in charge of the 2000–2001 *World Development Report.* There must also be other fights that have less to do with ideology than with personalities and individual ambitions. All those involved in these fights must be tempted to use the power to sanction projects to help their supporters and punish their enemies.

There is also the fact that being a donor organization involved in development makes one someone that many people want to influence—ranging from the U.S. government to NGOs hostile to the U.S. government. These pressures are probably easier to resist for an organization that has an explicit ideology or an acknowledged political master, like the Salvation Army or the U.S. Agency for International Development, than a nominally apolitical organization like the United Nations Development Program (UNDP) or the bank. For such organizations, the challenge is often in maintaining their reputation for being open to many different views while continuing to make the right choices about the allocation of funds. Resisting the temptation to placate the different sides by conceding some of their less merited demands must be challenge for these organizations.

One of the biggest problems, and one that is discussed all too rarely, is the lack of an explicit scientific basis for their decision making. An eloquent exception is Lant Pritchett, a long-term bank employee:[14]

Nearly all World Bank discussions of policies and project design had the character of "ignorant armies clashing by the night"—there was heated debate amongst advocates of various activities but rarely any firm evidence presented and considered about the likely impact of the proposed actions. Certainly in my experience there was never any definitive evidence that would inform decisions of funding one broad set of activities versus another (e.g., basic education versus roads versus vaccinations versus macroeconomic reform) or even funding one instrument versus another (e.g., vaccinations versus public education about hygiene to improve health, textbook reform versus teacher training to improve health, textbook reform versus teacher training to improve educational quality). How can this combination of brilliant well-meaning people and ignorant organization be a stable equilibrium? (Pritchett 2002, 251)

A World Bank publication from a few years ago, *Empowerment and Poverty Reduction: A Sourcebook* (Narayanan 2000), provides an excellent case study of the kinds of policies that result from these deliberations. The *Sourcebook* is meant to be a catalogue of what, according to the bank, are the right strategies for poverty reduction. These are also, we presume, strategies into which the bank is prepared to put its money. It provides a long list of recommended projects, which include computer kiosks in villages, cell phones for rent in rural areas, scholarships targeted toward girls who go to secondary school, schooling voucher programs for poor children, joint forest management programs, water users' groups, citizen report cards for public services, participatory poverty assessments, Internet access for tiny firms, land titling, legal reform, microcredit based on group lending, and many others.

While many of these are surely good ideas, the book does not reveal how we know that they work. We now know that figuring out what works is not easy. There is a large literature documenting the many pitfalls of the usual intuitive approach to program evaluation. When we do something and things look as if they are getting better, it is tempting to think that it was all because of what we did. The problem is that we have no way of knowing what would have happened in the absence of the intervention. The simplest and best way to avoid this problem is to do a randomized evaluation where we assign the intervention to a randomly selected subset of the set of potential locations and compare those who got it with those who did not. This mimics the procedures used in trials of new drugs, which is the one place where, for obvious reasons, a lot of care has gone into making sure that only the things that really work are approved. In many ways, social programs are very much like drugs because they have the potential of transforming the life prospects of people. It seems appropriate that they should be held to the same high standard.[15]

Of course, even randomized trials are not perfect. Something that may work in India may fail in Indonesia. Ideally there should be multiple randomized trials in varying locations. There is also no substitute for thinking. There are often good and clear reasons why what works in Kenya will not work in Cameroon. And there are times when randomized experiments are not feasible (more on that later). However, with all that, it is hard to imagine a good reason for spending a lot of money without having done at least one successful randomized trial, assuming that a randomized trial is possible. When we talk of hard evidence, we will therefore have in mind evidence from a randomized experiment or, failing that, evidence from a true natural experiment, by which we mean an accident of history that created a setting that mimics a randomized trial.[16]

What is striking about the list of strategies offered by the *Sourcebook* is the lack of any distinction between strategies that can claim to be based on hard evidence and the rest. In fact, to the best of our knowledge, only one of these strategies—schooling vouchers for poor students in Colombia—has been subject to a randomized evaluation, and that was because it was politically necessary to allocate the vouchers by lottery. Comparing those who won the lottery with those who did not provided the perfect experiment for studying the impact of the program, and the study by Angrist et al. (2002) takes advantage of it. Yet the results from this study receive no more weight than any of the other programs.

Indeed most of these programs are recommended on the basis of very little hard evidence. Legal reform, for example, is justified by asserting that "the extent to which a society is law-bound affects its national income as well as its level of literacy and infant mortality." This may be true, but the available evidence, which comes from comparing the more law-abiding countries with the rest, confounds too many things to warrant such a confident recommendation.

And some programs, it seems, no amount of negative evidence can stop. Our favorite example is the *Gyandoot* program in Madhya Pradesh in India, which provides computer kiosks in rural areas. The *Sourcebook* acknowledges that this project was hit hard by lack of electricity and poor connectivity and that "currently only a few of the Kiosks have proved to be commercially viable." It then goes on to say, entirely without irony, "Following the success of the initiative" (p. 80).

2.5   Why Do People Resist Evidence-Based Policymaking?

Lant Pritchett (2001) goes on to argue that the resistance to hard evidence is in part a reflection of the mixed motives of those who give and receive aid. Even where there is no real corruption, as in the bank, the problem is that many of these people are true believers and see no intrinsic value in rigorously testing the policies that they are advocating. Although they recognize that good evidence might help them win friends, they also worry that it might work against them. Someone might misread the evidence, or, as chance will have it, the evidence may just refuse to cooperate. Hard evidence is simply not worth the trouble, especially if eloquence and a few carefully chosen examples can carry the day.

We do not doubt that this is a piece of what goes on, but it explains the motives of only those who have things going their way. But the bank, for example, is a contentious place. For every one person who likes where policy is currently headed, there are probably at least two who would like the tides to turn. These people have a strong incentive to look for hard evidence, since there is no other way they can upset the status quo, and it is hard to believe that they could not do a proper test of the intervention if they really wanted to. In other words, if the advocates do not provide the necessary hard evidence, we would expect their opponents to do so.

The fact that we see very little of this kind of competition by evidence suggests to us that the deeper problem is not strategic resistance to evidence, but rather a view shared by most people in the development community that basing policy on hard evidence is simply not practical. This is consistent with our experience in talking to senior officials in donor organizations, who seem to genuinely believe that there is no real alternative to the current system of decision making.

Their objections to the idea that policy should be based on evidence typically fall into one of two categories. First, there is the fear that requiring that every initiative be justified in terms of hard evidence will bias decisions in favor of what is measurable and easy to evaluate. Second, there is the conviction that at this point, there is so little that can be justified in terms of randomized trials that to rely exclusively on this evidence is tantamount to considered inaction.[17]

2.6   The Feasibility of Evidence-Based Development Policy

We feel that both of the concerns articulated in the previous paragraph are substantially exaggerated. We are certainly not saying that every policy action needs to be justified in terms of hard evidence. There are things like macropolicy that are very hard to evaluate properly. The problem is that once something is big enough ("currency boards," "democracy"), there is going to be no way to know what would have happened in its absence. And yet there are clear examples of policies that, most people would agree, make very little sense ("overvalued fixed exchange rates," "a pension plan that is headed for bankruptcy," for example). There is no question that helping governments in their efforts to get out of these indefensible policy positions is a good use of donor money.

On the other hand, there are many macro interventions that do allow for a limited micro evaluation. For example, while decentralizing political power is a macro reform, we could learn a lot about it by looking at the impact of an initial pilot, where the reform is implemented only for certain areas, chosen randomly from a larger set. Where this is not possible and the decision has to be based purely on theoretical reasoning, evidence from micro studies can still be useful because it can help us choose the right theory. Obviously how far the donor is prepared go down this evidence "quality ladder" will depend on the donor. What is key is that she has a sense of what she is giving up—the fact that there may be other projects for which we have much more reliable (and reassuring) evidence.

The other side of this same concern is that requiring evidence discriminates against projects that promote less measurable outcomes, such as female empowerment. It is true that historically the focus of economic measurement has been on concepts like consumption and income rather than empowerment, but when Chattopadhyay and Duflo (2001) needed a measure of female empowerment in the context of public action in Indian villages, they used the fraction of questions asked by women in village meetings. While this is not perfect, it is not obviously worse than using income to measure well-being, as we regularly do. We are therefore optimistic that once we commit ourselves to measurement, the interaction of the donors and the evaluators will generate a range of good measures of most things that are relevant.

To address the other main concern, that basing action on evidence will lead to paralysis, we carried out a crude but useful exercise. We began by searching for interventions that, at the time when the piece was written (2004), had been subject to an evaluation based on random assignment (though not necessarily as a part of an experiment) and appeared to work. To come up with this list, we asked researchers in the Bureau for Research in Economic Analysis of Development (BREAD) for references and used summary papers by Kremer (2003), Behrman and Knowles (2003), De Cock et al. (2000), and Working Group 5 of the Commission of Macroeconomics and Health (2001) as starting points for a literature search. In addition, a Web-based search was used. From these we deliberately left out regulations, such as tobacco taxes and bans on tobacco. The table of interventions in the appendix (table 2.A.2) lists all the papers that were eventually included in our list. It is meant to cover every category of micro intervention that we would find that has been subjected to an evaluation.

From these papers, we highlighted the subset of programs that, based on currently available evidence, look sufficiently good that it would be worth implementing them on a global scale. This cut was based on three criteria: the program must be sustainable without a strong intervention by the researchers;[18] the evidence must come from a run of the program where it was randomly placed; and finally, in that randomized trial, it must have had a significant positive impact on at least one of the initially chosen objectives. If two experiments showed different results, wherever there was a clear methodological difference, we favored the one that has the better experimental design. We also favored experiments that showed improvements in outcomes that have direct economic relevance—education, incidence of disease, weight—over outcomes that are only potentially correlated with economic outcomes—the presence of antibodies, for example. Finally, we favored experimental research by economists over experiments by clinical researchers, on the grounds that economists are more sensitive to problems relating to delivery.[19] In the end, there were few cases where we had to exercise any judgment.[20]

We left out all programs that simply gave away money but included programs (like school vouchers) that give people money that can be used only for a specific purpose. Finally, we were not quite sure of how to do deal with a program like PROGRESA in Mexico, which makes an income transfer to mothers who send their children to school. The problem is that we have no idea of how much we would need to pay to get children into schools and how much of what was paid was a pure gift. We therefore treated it as a separate category.

The goal here is purely illustrative: We want to demonstrate that one can come up with a long list of interventions that have been shown to work based on a randomized evaluation. We are not at all suggesting that the interventions listed are the only ones that work or even that they are the most efficacious among those that do work. Nor do we suggest that the programs that we list but decided not to scale up are necessarily worthless. It is entirely possible (indeed, we hope that it is true) that there are many other interventions that do work but are not included in our final list because we could not find a randomized evaluation applying to them. Other programs that were left out because there was a high degree of intervention by the researchers might have also worked with less intervention. We simply do not know. Yet others may work in some other variant but not in the form in which they were implemented during the experiment. Finally, there are probably many interventions yet to be thought of that have the potential to change the world.[21]

Given this list of successful interventions, we ask, How much will it cost to more or less mechanically scale them up to a global level? Our definition of global covers only low-income countries (LICs) unless stated otherwise. We take the population of each country to be the average of the current population and the projected 2015 population.[22]

We calculate costs by taking the point estimate of the per person cost for each program and adjust it for each country. This adjustment involves converting the expenditure on goods (vitamins, drugs) using the standard purchasing power parity conversion factor, and scaling up (or down) the expenditure on services (teachers, health workers) in proportion to the gross domestic product per capita at current exchange rates.[23] For each country, the size of the targeted population is derived from demographic information about the country. The cost spreadsheet is available online.[24] Figures are normalized to year 2000 U.S. dollars.

The results are shown in table 2.4. Our calculations show that a recurring annual expense of about $11 billion could be justified by the hard evidence we already have, without including PROGRESA. In addition, if we accept the (nonexperimental) results in Cutler and Miller (2003) showing that the health returns to improved water supply are enormous, we should consider investing in water supply infrastructure. This will cost an additional (one-time) $15 billion.

The $11 billion number was our best guess in early 2004. Since then there have been a number of randomized evaluations that have reported success. These include a program in Kenya that gives incentives to girls to do well in school and another program in Kenya that gives girls school uniforms as a way of reducing HIV infection rates (see www.povertyactionlab.org for these and other examples). As a result, if we had done this calculation today, the amount would be substantially larger.

Even $11 billion is, however, a substantial amount. It is more than the World Bank gives out as IDA loans (the main form of World Bank aid) in a given year (an average of US$6,154 million between 1996 and 2001). If we add to this what countries absolutely need to make essential macro adjustments of the kind discussed, there may be very little left from the total available donor money.

To the extent that there is still money, it can be used to provide humanitarian aid. There are people in the world who are dying because they do not have enough money to buy food or medicines. Giving them money (or food or medicines) may not promote development, but it is hard to imagine that it would not be good thing.

Indeed once we decide that we are willing to make cash gifts to people, we could make that gift conditional on the recipients' fulfilling certain conditions, such as sending their children to school. This is what PROGRESA does.

It is true that this does not deal with most of the objections against giving away money. The targeting problem was solved in Mexico by using the bureaucracy to make sure that money goes to the right person, which is part of what makes the program costly. But it is not clear that perfect targeting is worth the effort, given that most people in developing countries are actually quite poor. It may be better to set up rather lax criteria for eligibility so that only the rich are ineligible, and then to randomly check claimants and impose harsh punishments on those who are caught cheating. It is usually quite easy to identify the rich in poor countries (ownership of a car, for example, might be used). It is also true that we do not eliminate the possibility that the money may just go into consumption. But even this is less of a problem than it might appear. A number of studies, including those based on the PROGRESA experiment, have shown that more money in the hands of the female members of the family in poor countries does translate into better nutrition for children and better health care.

Ultimately, however, we should not need to argue that giving away money is without its problems. After all, it may still dominate trying to give away goods, which, as we have seen, is fraught with problems.

Clearly, being open to the idea of giving away money will make it much easier to find things to do. Just scaling up PROGRESA, by our calculations, will cost $23 billion a year, which pushes up total annual expenditure on good programs to $34 billion.

2.7 To Conclude: A New Challenge for the Millennium

We live in an age of aid pessimism. There is a strong, if rarely completely articulated, presumption that aid can at best help people survive, but it cannot promote development. The U.S. government's new initiative, the Millennium Challenge Account (MCA), is based on the idea that the whole idea of aid giving needs to be rethought. In particular, it wants to tie aid to country performance: only countries that pursue economic policies that the U.S. government approves of will be eligible for aid from this account. The premise is that aid has not been working because the policy environment is not right. While it is clear that this is a problem—there are countries where the risk of the money ending up in a government official's pocket is substantial—the thrust of our argument is that the way the money is planned to be spent is also a very big problem, but a problem whose source lies in the way the donor organizations function. Combined with the fact that many of the world's neediest live in the countries that will not make it onto the MCA list and that we expect the incentive effects of the MCA to be minimal, this suggests to us that the MCA approach amounts to abandoning a large part of the world's poorest for no fault of their own. A more effective and less unfair challenge may be to try to see if it is possible to design projects that work in the countries with the biggest problems. If we could make that work, we would not only help those who need it the most, but what is perhaps even more valuable, we will raise expectations and build hope where there is none.

Table 2.4
Program costs

Program (recurring annual expenditure)	Source and method of calculation	Randomized?	Cost (US$2000 millions)
Education			
Remedial teaching based on the Balsakhi model developed by Pratham	Source: Banerjee et al. 2003. Calculation: Unit (cost per child-year), *BalkhashiCost*, from the Pratham 2001–2002 Reports (cited on June 28, 2003). Available at www.pratham.org/reports. We use the mean of costs reported for the Dehli, Mumbai, and Pune regions. Country cost = $BalkashiPop * BalkhashiCost * GDPCorrection$	Yes	644
Universal education based on a 40:1 pupil-teacher ratio	Source: Angrist and Lavy 1999[1] Calculation: Country cost = $NotInSchool * SchoolCost$	No	1,544
School inputs (uniforms and textbooks)	Source: Kremer, Moulin, and Namunyu 2003. Calculation: Unit *InputsCost* from Kremer et al. (p. 44). Transportation costs ignored. Country cost = $InputsCost * SchoolAge * PPPCorrection$	Yes	2,268
Schooling vouchers	Source: Angrist et al. 2002. Calculation: Assumes that everyone is sufficiently motivated to achieve satisfactory performance, hence qualifying for the vouchers, and ignoring general equilibrium effects due to the resultant increase in private school fees. Unit *VoucherCost* used in our calculations is the increase in public educational expenditure per lottery winner, given in Angrist et al. (1535). This is multiplied by four because at any time, there are four cohorts in high school. Country cost = $(4/15) * VoucherCost * ChildPop * GDPCorrection$	Yes	1,478
Monetary rewards to parents for sending children to school	Source: Behrman, Segupta, and Todd 2001. Calculation: Assumes that if the subsidy is large enough, everyone will wants to send their children to school, and therefore everyone will get the subsidy. Unit *SubsidyCost* is calculated from data given in Behrman et al. (2001, 1). This is multiplied by seven because at any time there are four cohorts getting the subsidy. Country cost = $(7/15) * SubsidyCost * ChildPop * GDPCorrection$	Yes	2,3142
Nutrition supplementation			
Iron	Source: Bobonis, Miguel, and Sharma 2004. Calculation: Unit *IronCost* data from Miguel and Bobonis, private communication. The program covers five cohorts aged between ages two and six. Country cost = $(5/15) * IronCost * ChildPop * PPPCorrection$	Yes	346

Albendazole (deworming)	Yes	36	Source: Kremer and Miguel 2004. Calculation: Unit *DewormCost* data from Miguel and Bobonis, private communication. The program covers five cohorts aged between ages two and six. Country cost = (5/15) * *DewormCost* * *ChildPop* * *PPPCorrection*
Delivery of iron supplements and deworming pills through the Pratham Delhi Health Program model	Yes	270	Source: See, e.g., Bobonis et al. 2003 Calculation: Unit *TransportCost* data from Miguel and Bobonis, private communication. The program covers five cohorts aged between ages two and six. Country cost = (5/15) * *TransportCost* * *ChildPop* * *PPPCorrection*
Iodine	Yes	12	Source: Cobra et al. 1997. Calculation: Unit *IodineCost* data from International Council for the Control of Iodine Deficiency Disorders. 1998. *IDD Newsletter* 14:3. The experiment involved a once-off supplement. Country cost = (1/15) * *IodineCost* * *ChildPop* * *PPPCorrection*
Additional transportation costs			Calculation: No handle on the transportation cost for the iodine intervention. Presumably some of it can be loaded on to the EPI program.
HIV			
Condom provision	Yes	135	Source: Allen et al. 1992.
Improving STD management	Yes	428	Source: Grosskurth et al. 1995.
Voluntary counseling and testing	Yes	116	Source: Coates et al. 2000.
Prophylaxis for opportunistic infections	Yes	40	Source: Mwinga et al. 1998.
Short-course zidovudine regime	Yes	4	Source: Shaffer et al. 1999. Calculation: For all the HIV interventions: Main data source: Kumaranayake and Watts 2000. Her numbers are for sub-Saharan Africa (SSA), a group different from the low-income countries (LIC). The Commission of Macroeconomics and Health, Working Group 5 (2001, Paper 19) shows estimates of scaling up for both SSA and LIC for their set of interventions. Total Cost = *Kumaranayake SSA Cost* * *CMH LIC Cost/CMH SSA Cost*
Malaria: spraying	Yes	1,627	Source: Rowland et al. 2000. Calculation: Malaria assumed to be prevalent in all the LICs. Unit *SprayCost* data from Verlé et al. 1999. Country cost = *Population* * *SprayCost* * *PPPCorrection*

Table 2.4
(continued)

Program (recurring annual expenditure)	Source and method of calculation	Randomized?	Cost (US$2000 millions)
Fertilizer	Source: Duflo and Kremer 2003.	Yes	1,848
	Calculation: Agriculture statistics and fertilizer usage data from the 2003 World Development Indicators. We find the lowest *Fertilizer Consumption (100 grams per hectare of arable land)* and *Cereal Yield (kg per hectare)* between the four benchmark regions: [European Monetary Union], [High Income (nonOECD)], [High Income (OECD)] and the [United States]. We assume that a country is fertilizer deficient if both fertilizer consumption and the cereal yields are lower than the minimum value than the corresponding values (1045.875 and 2161.885) for the two benchmarks. For such countries we set *Deficient?* = 1, 0 otherwise. Unit *FertilizerCost* data from IFDC 2001. It does not have country-specific price estimates; hence, we are unable to correct for PPP differences. The recommended fertilizer consumption figure is also in the ballpark of the average recommendations of the net fertilizer (sum of different chemical compounds) across different countries, regions, and crops, as seen in Wichmann (n.d.).		
	*Country cost = Deficient? * (1045.875—Fertilizer Consumption) * Land Area * Land Area Arable (% of total)*		
Vaccination	Source: Hoke et al. 1988; O'Brien et al. 2003; Pérez-Schael et al. 1997.	Yes	461
	Calculation: Vaccine Fund 2002. It states that $5,069 million of additional spending is required between 2001 and 2011. We divide this number by 11.		
Total (excluding urban water provision and PROGRESA-style subsidies for school attendance)			11,257 million ≈ 11 billion
Total (excluding urban water provision)			34,399 ≈ 34 billion
Urban water provision	Source: Cutler and Miller 2003.	No	73
	Calculation: For more details, see the Water Construction section.		
Total (including urban water provision)			34,472 million ≈ 34 billion
One-off Infrastructure expenditure		R	One-time cost (US$2000 million)
Urban water construction	Source: Cutler and Miller 2003.	No	4,454

| Rural water construction | No | 10,867 |

Calculation: For each continent, the World Health Organization and United Nation's Children Fund, 2000. *Global Water and Sanitation Assessment, 2000 Report*, New York: United Nation's Children Fund, provides the unit costs (*WaterCost*) of possible interventions for rural water construction (one off), urban water construction (one off), and urban water provision (per annum). Because of South Asia's huge size, we make a special effort to find cost information for this subcontinent (details on Web site). For our estimates, we choose to use the cheapest cost option. The assessment also provides country-level statistics on the Urban (*UrbanPop*) and Rural (*RuralPop*) population, and the percentage of urban (*UNoAccess*) and rural (*RNoAccess*) people without access to water.

Urban country cost = $PopCorrect * UrbanPop * UNoAccess * UnitCost$

Rural country cost = $PopCorrect * RuralPop * RNoAccess * \underline{UnitCost}$

| Total water construction | | 15,321 million ≈ 15 billion |

Notes:

R: Randomized

1. Angrist and Lavy (1999) does not have a randomized experiment.

Assumptions behind the Table Numbers

Many bold and dubious assumptions have gone into the construction of this estimate of the cost of interventions for low-income countries. The fact that there may be economies of scale in expanding existing programs is ignored, as is the fact that the places that currently have these programs may not be randomly selected. Simplistic GDP and PPP corrections are used to correct for intercountry cost differences, and general equilibrium effects are ignored. We further assume linear population growth rates between 2000 and 2015 and that population is distributed equally among all ages between birth and fifteen years. While the time scale used here is the average annual cost between 2000 and 2015, future inflation is ignored. We try to err on the side of finding a low number.

Construction of Variables: The original data are from the 2002 Human Development Indicators in United Nations Development Program. 2002. *2002 Human Development Report*. New York: Oxford University Press (denoted in underlined italics, for example, *Total Population, 2000*), unless specified otherwise).

Country population estimate: $Population = 1,000,000 * \underline{Population\ (millions),\ 2000} + \underline{Total\ population\ (millions),\ 2000 * Population}$

Population growth factor estimate: $PopCorrect = \underline{(Total\ population\ (millions),\ 2000 + Total\ population\ (millions),\ 2015)} / (2 * \underline{Total\ population\ (millions),\ 2000})$

Child population estimate: $ChildPop = (1/100) * \underline{Population\ under\ age\ 15\ (as\ \%\ of\ total),\ 2000} * Population$

Percentage who need remedial education (method 1) (assumes that completion rates are proportional to the number of students in school. In other words, with universal education, the remedial rate will drop): $Remedial1 = 1 - \underline{Primary\ completion\ rate} / \underline{combined\ enrollment\ rate}$

Percentage that needs remedial education (method 2) (assumes that remedial rate will stay constant even with full enrollment; children do not attend school because they are unable to cope): $Remedial2 = (100 - \underline{Primary\ completion\ rate}) / 100$

Population who need the Balkashi program (a primary school length of six years is assumed): $BalkashiPop = (6/15) * ChildPop * (Remedial1 + Remedial2) / 2$

Table 2.4
(continued)

Number of school-aged population not in school: $NotInSchool = (6/15) * ChildPop * (100 - Combined\ Enrollment\ Data)/100$

Cost per child year of education (wage assumed at 3.6 times GDP per capita, at a 40:1 teacher-pupil ratio, and allowing recurrent nonteacher costs to comprise 33 percent of the expenditure): $SchoolCost = 3.6 * 1.5 * GDP\ (US\$\ billions),\ 2000/(Total\ population\ (millions),\ 2000 * 40)$

Correction for costs of different services (we expect service costs to differ across countries and assume these costs are proportional to GDP per capita. Let the country that we use for the point estimate be country X). Let the country that we want to estimate costs for be country Y. Then: $GDPperCap = \dfrac{GDP\ (US\$\ billions),\ 2000}{Total\ population\ (millions),\ 2000}$

$GDPCorrection = GDPperCap_Y/GDPperCap_X$

Correction for costs of different goods (we expect goods costs to differ across countries, and assume these costs are proportional to the country's PPP. Let the country that we use for the point estimate be country X). Let the country that we want to estimate costs for be country Y. Then: $PriceLevelrelUS = \dfrac{GDP\ (US\$\ billions),\ 2000/GDP\ (PPP\ US\$\ billions),\ 2000}{GDP\ (US\$\ billions),\ 2000/GDP\ (PPP\ US\$\ billions),\ 2000}$

$PPPCorrection = PriceLevelrelUS_Y/PriceLevelrelUS_X$

Missing countries: We do not have detailed data for seven low-income countries. Hence, to extrapolate our cost estimates to include these countries, we make the following correction: Worldwide LIC costs = [Sum of country costs calculated (for nonmissing LIC countries)] * [Sum of LIC population (2002 estimate)]/[Sum of nonmissing LIC population (2002 estimate)]

This correction ends up increasing our estimates by 3 percent.

Appendixes

Table 2.A.1
Evaluation organizations

Organization (evaluation office Web site)	Evaluation office	Year	Percentage of projects independently evaluated	Level of evaluation detail available online for independent evaluations	Rating scale for independent evaluations	Evaluation categories for independent evaluations
National Organizations						
Department for International Development (DFID) http://62.189.42.51/ DFIDstage/ policieandpriorities/ files/ev_home.htm	Evaluation Department (EVD)	1968[1] onward	Very few: An average of 9 projects were independently evaluated annually 1993–1999.[2] Only 25% of bilateral expenditure is covered by a project completion report (PCR) done by program managers.[3] "There is no system of independent verification, although one has been mooted," and "more significantly, PCRs are not used."[4]	All evaluation reports and their summaries are online or can be ordered online.	Numerical rating scales for numerous dimensions for the PCRs, but these are not independent evaluations. Independent observations are mostly prose based. Since independent evaluations are carried out by different evaluators, no standardized rating scale/category exists.	

Table 2.A.1
(continued)

Organization (evaluation office Web site)	Evaluation office	Year	Percentage of projects independently evaluated	Level of evaluation detail available online for independent evaluations	Rating scale for independent evaluations	Evaluation categories for independent evaluations
U.S. Agency for International Development (USAID) http://www.dec.org/partners/eval.cfm	Bureau for Policy and Program Coordination,[5] Center for Development Information and Evaluation (CDIE)	Before 1995[6]	All projects were evaluated,[7] but how many are independent? Regarded poorly.[8]			
		After 1995 to 2000				
		After 2000[9]	Searching through the USAID evaluation Web site shows that most project evaluations continue to be institutionally coauthored by the USAID mission to a specific country, although CDIE has some evaluations that do not involve the country mission as a coauthor.[10]	Individual project evaluations. Mostly joint authored with country mission, raising questions about independence. Annual report uses country macro-economic values as performance indicators.[11]	Qualitative measures used in its performance and accountability report.[12]	

Regional Development Banks

African Development Bank (AfDB) http://www.afdb.org/about_adb/OPEV.htm	Operations Evaluation Office Operations Evaluation Department (OPEV)[13]	1964 (est.)–2001 2001 onward[14]	Annual reviews of development effectiveness starting in 2003.[15] Annual review of results of operations evaluation apparently published, according to http://www.afdb.org/about_adb/OPEV_evaluation_guidelines.htm, however, not available online.	Project evaluations prior to 1997 are available at the DAC Web site.[16] Qualitative abstracts of project performance audit reports from 1994 to 1997 available online or by request to the webmaster. However, it is not clear if these were independent evaluations.	ARDE 2003 not currently available online.	
Asian Development Bank (ADB) http://www.adb.org/Evaluation/	Operations Evaluation Department	1974 onward[17]	40% evaluated[18]	Individual project reports (from 1995 onward).[19] Quantitative panel data grouped by sector and region available.[20] Summary tables collating evaluation details per project evaluated.[21]	Overall project rating: Highly Successful, Successful, Partly Successful, Unsuccessful[22]	Relevance, Effectiveness, Efficiency, Sustainability, Institutional Development (REESI)[23]

Table 2.A.1
(continued)

Organization (evaluation office Web site)	Evaluation office	Year	Percentage of projects independently evaluated	Level of evaluation detail available online for independent evaluations	Rating scale for independent evaluations	Evaluation categories for independent evaluations
European Bank for Reconstruction and Development (EBRD) http://www.ebrd.org/projects/eval/index.htm	Project Evaluation Department	1991 (year of establishment)[24] to 2003	44% (1991 to 1998)[25]	Examples of successful and less successful projects. Time series quantitative data of performance for all projects grouped together.[26] Forty project summaries and lessons learned (each one page long) representing "a cross-section of EBRD investment operations" published online. Previous year overview reports and all of the other project completion reports are internal documents.[27]		
		2003 onward	76% (1993 to 2002)[28]	In 2003, for the first time, Annual Evaluation Overview Report available online, giving quantitative evaluation data for each project evaluated since 1993.	Quantitative rating scales (>3 possible ratings) for each category[29]	Transition impact, Environmental performance of sponsor and bank, extent of environmental change, overall rating[30]

Inter-American Development Bank (IADB) http://www.iadb.org/cont/evo/evo_eng.htm	Evolve over time. (1) Group of Three Controllers, (2) Office of External Review and Evaluation and the Operations Evaluation Office, (3) Office of Evaluation[31]	1959–1998	Seldom undertaken, even then, only by borrower.[32] Exact figures unknown, but we find that no ex post evaluation was carried out for Mexico throughout the 1990s,[33] which gives cause for worry.		
	Office of Evaluation and Oversight[34] (OVE)	1999 onward[35]	Six to seven country programs evaluated each year (at least from 1999 to 2001). However, the lack of ex post program evaluation in the 1990s means that countries are evaluated on macro-performance. The presence of multiple donors makes assigning credit hard.[36] Very few project evaluations are done independently.[37]	Country program evaluations, each covering a ten-year period.[38] No cross-country or cross-sector comparisons. Quantitative figures, but these are based on project evaluations that were primarily self-evaluated,[39] and sometimes based on the most recent project performance monitoring reports (as opposed to the project completion reports, which were seldom done[40])	Relevance, coherence, efficiency and effectiveness[41]

Table 2.A.1
(continued)

Organization (evaluation office Web site)	Evaluation office	Year	Percentage of projects independently evaluated	Level of evaluation detail available online for independent evaluations	Rating scale for independent evaluations	Evaluation categories for independent evaluations
International Organizations						
International Monetary Fund (IMF) http://www.imf.org/external/np/ieo/index.htm	Office of Internal Audit and Inspection Evaluation Group of Executive Directors[42]	Before 1996	Insignificant numbers of external evaluation			
		Between 1996 and 2000	Trial run that covered a range of topics and were of different scale.[43]			
	Independent Evaluation Office (EVO)	After 2000	At capacity, five projects to be undertaken each year, including both country specific cases[44] and broader thematic questions.[45]	Commitment to promptly publish all reports, unless under exceptional circumstances.[46] No cross-sector (for example, comparing the performance of capital account crisis intervention versus the pro-longed use of IMF resources) or time series comparisons available yet.	While not explicit, key cross-country macroeconomic indicators are provided and implicitly used as indicators of performance. Within the two reports published thus far, there is an attempt to distinguish between different levels of success.	As of January 2004, four reports were published.[47] These looked at surveillance, program effectiveness, and IMF governance. The medium program is given in its annual report.[48]

United Nations Development Program (UNDP) http://www.undp.org/eo/	Office of Evaluation and Strategic Planning (OESP)[49]	Before 1996	For programs less than US$1 million, country managers decide if project should be evaluated. Mandatory evaluations for projects over US$1 million.[50] Even then, the compliance for mandatory evaluations was less than 80%.[51]			
	Evaluation Office (EO)	1996–1999		Individual project reports available online.[55] Quantitative time series data for each performance indicator[56] (all projects lumped together), and cross-sector (for projects evaluated from 1999 to 2000) performance impact indicators.[57]	Yes/partial/no and Significant/Satisfactory/Poor[58]	
	Evaluation Office (EO)	After 1999	Requirement that all projects over US$1 million be evaluated is abolished.[52] Decentralized evaluation process, with country managers selecting the evaluation teams and designs the term of reference.[53] The EO concentrates on independent, country-level assessment of development results (five to ten countries a year), and sector-thematic level evaluations.[54]			Typically covers relevance, performance and success (impact, sustainability, and contribution to capacity building).[59] However, this criterion is different from the previous year, which raises some questions.[60]

Table 2.A.1
(continued)

Organization (evaluation office Web site)	Evaluation office	Year	Percentage of projects independently evaluated	Level of evaluation detail available online for independent evaluations	Rating scale for independent evaluations	Evaluation categories for independent evaluations
World Bank, http://www.worldbank.org/oed/	Operations Evaluation Department	1973[61] onward	Independent evaluation at the country, sector and project levels. Project performance assessment reports for 25% of all completed projects.[62]	Individual project reports.[63] Quantitative panel data grouped by sector and region available.[64] Summary tables collating evaluation details per project evaluated.[65]	Outcome: Highly Satisfactory (Sat), Sat, Moderately Sat, Moderately UnSat, UnSat, Highly UnSat. Sustainability: Highly Likely, Likely, Unlikely, Highly Unlikely Institutional Development: Substantial, Modest, Negligible[66]	Outcome, Sustainability, Institutional Development[67]

Note: We look at only the level of evaluation detail available online for the latest incarnation of the evaluation office.

Notes for Appendix 2.A.1

1. Year of first independent evaluation as given by Department of International Development. 2003. *Catalogue of DFID Evaluation Studies.* DFID Evaluations Department. Available at http://www.dfid.gov.uk/Pubs/files/eval_studies_catalogue.pdf.

2. Flint, Michael, et al. 2002. "How Effective Is DFID? Development Effectiveness Report 2001," 2nd Draft, DFID, March 30, paragraph 118.

3. Ibid., paragraph 115.

4. Ibid., paragraph 116.

5. United States Agency for International Development. "Agency Reorganization: Generic Functional Statements." Cited 11 Feb 2004. Available http://www.usaid.gov/about/reform/functions.html.

6. Clapp-Wincek, Cynthia, and Richard Blue. 2001. "Evaluation of Recent USAID Evaluation Experience." Working Paper 320. Washington: Center for Development Information and Evaluation, p. iii.

7. Ibid.

8. Ibid., p. 37. Here we face the related problems of few evaluations done ("Of most concern is the very limited number of in-depth, program evaluations"), lack of learning even if evaluations are carried out ("Most of the evaluation work that is being done is being done by partners. The partner organizations are learning from the experience; USAID is not"), lack of independence (the USAID managers decide if they want to do the evaluations), the fly-in approach ("Scopes ask a team to come for 4–6 weeks and interview the mission, the activity staff, and 'representatives' of the local people. There isn't enough time to get any kind of representative sample. The team frequently tells the USAID manager pretty much what he already knows.")

9. Quote from ibid., p. 1, "The ADS 200 series (Sept. 2000) added a new dimension to evaluations. The 'Reform Vision' in ADS 200 states these expectations: 'Applying the lessons of successes and failure systematically and providing leadership in tackling complex problems that demand multi-agency or multi-donor responses.'"10. DuRette, Jean, and Glenn Slocum. 2001. *The Role of Transitional Assistance: The Case of East Timor.* Washington, D.C.: U.S. Agency for International Development.

11. Center for Development Information and Evaluation. 2001. *FY 2000 Performance Overview.* Washington, D.C.: U.S. Agency for International Development. See p. 29, for example.

12. U.S. Agency for International Development. 2002. *USAID Performance and Monitoring Report, FY 2002.* Washington, D.C.: United States Agency for International Development. See appendix 2.

13. African Development Bank Group. "The ADB Group—In Brief." Cited February 11, 2004. Available at http://www.afdb.org/knowledge/documents/ADB_in_brief.htm.

14. U.S. Department of the Treasury. 2003. "African Development Bank Group." Cited 11 Feb 2004. Available at http://www.ustreas.gov/offices/international-affairs/intl/fy2003/tab10_afdbg_afdb.pdf.

15. African Development Bank Group. 2002. "Strategic Plan 2003–2007." Available at http://www.afdb.org/knowledge/publications/pdf/adb_strategic_plan2003–2007e.pdf. See p. 52.

16. See http://www.dac-evaluations-cad.org/dac/.

17. Asian Development Bank. Operations Evaluation Department. 2003. *Annual Review of Evaluation Activities in 2002.* Manila: Asian Development Bank. See p. 61.

18. Asian Development Bank. "Frequently Asked Questions." Cited February 11, 2004. Available at http://www.adb.org/Evaluation/faqs.asp.

19. All reports online since 1995, at Asian Development Bank: http://www.adb.org/Evaluation/reports.asp.

20. Asian Development Bank, Operations Evaluation Department. 2003. *Annual Review of Evaluation Activities in 2002.* Manila: Asian Development Bank. See p. 67.

21. Ibid., p. 47.

22. Ibid.

23. Asian Development Bank, "PPMS Project Framework and Performance Indicators 2," Slide show. Available at http://www.adb.org/Documents/Slideshows/PPMS/4b_PPMS_Indicators.pdf.

24. Project Evaluation Department. 1999. "Project Evaluation Department." London: European Bank for Reconstruction and Development. See p. 6.

25. Ibid. See p. 6.

26. European Bank for Reconstruction and Development. 2003. *Annual Report 2002: Annual Review and Financial Report.* London: European Bank for Reconstruction and Development. See p. 70.

27. Fredrik Korfker, corporate director, evaluation, EBRD, September 9, 2003. private communication.28. European Bank for Reconstruction and Development, Project Evaluation Department. 2003. *Annual Evaluation Overview Report 2003.* London: European Bank for Reconstruction and Development. See p. 1.

Table 2.A.1
(continued)

28. European Bank for Reconstruction and Development, Project Evaluation Department. 2003. *Annual Evaluation Overview Report 2003*. London: European Bank for Reconstruction and Development. See p. 1.

29. Ibid. See appendix 2.

30. Ibid. See appendix 2.

31. Inter-American Development Bank, Office of Evaluation and Oversight, OVE. 2001. *Annual Report of the Evaluation Office 2000*. Washington, D.C.: Inter-American Development Bank. See chapter 2.1.32. Inter-American Development Bank, Office of Evaluation and Oversight, OVE. 2002. *Annual Report of the Evaluation Office 2001*. Washington, D.C.: Inter-American Development Bank. See p. 25.

33. Inter-American Development Bank, Office of Evaluation and Oversight, OVE. 2003. *Country Program Evaluation: Mexico. 1990–2000*. Washington, D.C.: Inter-American Development Bank. See p. 29.

34. See http://www.iadb.org/cont/evo/ovedocs.htm.

35. Inter-American Development Bank, Office of Evaluation and Oversight, OVE. 2001. *Annual Report of the Evaluation Office 2000*. Washington, D.C.: Inter-American Development Bank. See chapter 2.1.

36. Inter-American Development Bank, Office of Evaluation and Oversight. OVE. 2002. *Country Program Evaluation: Peru. 1990–2000*. Washington, D.C.: Inter-American Development Bank. See p. 13.

37. Inter-American Development Bank. Office of Evaluation and Oversight. OVE. 2003. *Country Program Evaluation: Costa Rica. 1990–2001*. Washington, D.C.: Inter-American Development Bank. See note 20.

38. Inter-American Development Bank. Office of Evaluation and Oversight. OVE. 2002. *Annual Report of the Evaluation Office 2001*. Washington, D.C.: Inter-American Development Bank. See note 20.

39. Inter-American Development Bank. Office of Evaluation and Oversight, OVE. 2003. *Country Program Evaluation: Costa Rica. 1990–2001*. Washington, D.C.: Inter-American Development Bank. See note 20.

40. Ibid. See p. 40. Out of the four categories of projects, only the Public Reform Sector has Project Completion Reports.

41. Inter-American Development Bank. 2002. *Annual Report of the Evaluation Office 2001*. Inter-American Development Bank. See p. 7.

42. International Monetary Fund. Evaluation Group of Executive Directors. 2000. "Review of Experience with Evaluation in the Fund." Available at http://www.imf.org/external/np/eval/2000/031400.HTM.

43. Ibid. See chapter 4.

44. Unlike the other agencies, the IMF looks after macroeconomic performance; hence, country-level evaluations make sense here.

45. International Monetary Fund. Evaluation Group. 2001. "Progress in making the independent evaluation office (IEO) operational." Available at http://www.imf.org/external/np/eval/2001/103101.htm.

46. International Monetary Fund. Executive Board. 2000. "IMF Executive Board Report to the IMFC on the Establishment of the Independent Evaluation Office (EVO) and Its Terms of Reference." Available at http://www.imf.org/external/np/eval/2000/091200.htm.

47. Independent Evaluation Office. International Monetary Fund. "Draft Issues Paper for an Evaluation of Technical Assistance Provided by the IMF." November 2003. "Fiscal Adjustment in IMF-Supported Programs." September 2003. "IMF and the Recent Capital Account Crises: Indonesia, Korea, Brazil." July 2003. "Evaluation of Prolonged Use of IMF Resources." 2002.

48. International Monetary Fund, Independent Evaluation Office. 2003. *IEO Annual Report 2003*. Washington, D.C., International Monetary Fund. See p. 10.

49. United Nations Development Program and the United Nations Population Fund. Executive Board. 2000. "Evaluation: Report of the Administrator." Available at http://www.undp.org/execbrd/pdf/dp00–34e.pdf. See p. 2.

50. United Nations Development Program, Evaluation Office. 2001. "Development Effectiveness: Review of Evaluative Evidence." New York: United Nations Development Program. See p. 15.

51. United Nations Development Program and the United Nations Population Fund, Executive Board. 2001. "Evaluation: Report of the Administrator." Available at http://www.undp.org/execbrd/pdf/dp01–26e.pdf. See table 6.

52. United Nations Development Program. Evaluation Office. 2002. "Handbook on Monitoring and Evaluating for Results." New York: United Nations Development Program. See part 1, table 3.

53. Ibid. See part 2, p. 45.

54. United Nations Development Program. Evaluation Office. 2001. See p. 15.

55. See United Nations Development Program Evaluations Database. http://www.undp.org/eo/database/index.htm.

56. United Nations Development Program, Evaluation Office. 2001. See pp. 15–19.

57. Ibid. See p. 35.

58. Ibid. See p. 19.

59. Ibid. See p. 15.

60. Ibid. See p. 10.

61. World Bank. Operations Evaluation Department. 2002. *OED: The First 30 Years.* Conference Proceedings, September 23, 2002. Available at http://www.worldbank.org/wbi/B-SPAN/docs/oed_thirty.pdf.

62. World Bank. Operations Evaluation Department. 2002. *2001 Annual Review of Development Effectiveness.* Washington, D.C.: World Bank. See annex D.

63. See http://lnweb18.worldbank.org/servlet/OEDSearchServlet?SearchType=byField&PerPage=20&DbURL=oed/oeddoclib.nsf&Series=OED%20Project%20Evaluation.

64. World Bank, Operations Evaluation Department. 2003. *2002 Annual Review of Development Effectiveness.* Washington, D.C.: World Bank. See table 5.

65. Ibid. See table 14.

66. Ibid. See table 14.

67. Ibid. See table 14.

Table 2.A.2
Table of Interventions
The following abbreviations are used in this table:
C: Intervention Category
E: Education
P: Direct poverty reduction
H: Health
O: Others
S: Is the program self-sustainable? We claim that a proposed program is not self-sustainable if the researchers ensured compliance amongst the test subjects. This is an issue for the clinical evaluations of nutritional supplements which look at the impact of a supplement assuming compliance. In real life, compliance cannot be assumed.
R: Randomized?

Intervention	C	Evaluation cited	S	R	Benefits	Including cost?
Water and Sanitation						
Clean water through a water container with a cover and a sprout	H	Roberts et al. 2001 Self-sustainable because Malawian field worker used, and "this [how to use the bucket] educational message generally took less than one minute and was never reinforced or restated during the study." Not scaled up because it was carried out in a specific instance of a refugee camp that had experienced a cholera outbreak.	Yes	Yes	Reduced diarrhea	No
Latrine provision	H	Daniels et al. 1990 Selection bias: Ownership depends on constituency, and distance to the recruiting health facility.	Yes	No	Reduced diarrhea	No. Not random
Latrine provision	H	Esrey 1996 Potential nonrandom location of latrines.	Yes	No	Reduced diarrhea, taller and heavier children	No. Not random
Education for water sanitation behavior	E H	Stanton 1987	Yes	Yes	Reduced diarrhea	Yes. (We assume that if everyone goes to school, the schools will do the education.)
Historical clean water interventions in America	H	Cutler and Miller 2003 Attempts to deal with potential endogenous placement.	Yes	No	Clean water reduces mortality	Yes (although not random)

Health care services

Summary: Gelband and Stansfield 2001

Midwife services	H	Walker et al. 2002	Yes	No	Better skills	No. Not random
		Not random due to participation selection bias.				
Midwife services	H	Frankenberg and Thomas 2001	Yes	No	Increased women Body Mass Index	No. Not random
		Actual program, but selective nonrandom midwife placement.				
Reduction in antenatal care	H	Munjanja, Lindmark, and Nystrom 1996	Yes	Yes	No effect on maternal/fetal outcomes	Cost reduction, not included
		Actual reduction in number of visits, clearly sustainable.				
Reduction in antenatal care	H	Villar et al. 2001	Yes	Yes	No effect on maternal/fetal outcomes	Cost reduction, not included
		Actual reduction in number of visits, clearly sustainable.				
Home-based neonatal care	H	Bang et al. 1999	Yes	No	Avert 1 death per 18 neonates cared for	No
		Control villages were not randomly chosen: Villages were used as controls because suitable women could not be found, or population was fewer than 300.				

Nutritional supplements

Summary: Behrman and Knowles 2003; Nemer, Gelband, and Jha 2001

Deworming drugs	E / H	Kremer and Miguel 2004	Yes	Yes	Improved health and school participation, even in neighborhood schools	Yes
		Self-sustainable because "medical treatment was delivered to schools by Kenya Ministry of Health public health nurses and ICS public health officers" and this was done within the community setting (we see some children not participating).				
Iron supplementation	E / H	Bobonis, Miguel, and Sharma 2003	Yes	Yes	Increased participation, reduced absenteeism	Yes
		Existing preschool network used.				
Zinc	H	Brown et al. 2002	No	Yes	Positive responses in health and weight	No. Not program
		Not self-sustainable because of overtly heavy fieldworker involvement—"in most cases, confirmation that the supplements were successfully delivered to the study subjects."				

Table 2.A.2
(continued)

Intervention	C	Evaluation cited	S	R	Benefits	Including cost?
Oral iodized oil supplementation	H	Claudine et al. 1997 Added to the ongoing EPI program.	Yes	Yes	Improved infant survival	Yes
Vitamin A supplementation	H	Grotto et al. 2003	No	Yes	"No consistent overall protective effect on the increase of diarrhea"	No
		Many clinical trials carried out over the years. The above meta-analysis shows that the net impact is not consistently positive.				
Supplements for lactating women	H	Tinker, Finn, and Epp 2000 Supplements were provided daily on a *volunteer* basis at a centralized location—there was no compulsion to consume it.	Yes	No	Reduced low-weight babies	No. Not random
Folate supplementation (literature review)	H	Mahomed 1997	—	—	Not enough evidence to evaluate effectiveness on clinical outcomes	No
Antiplatelet supplementation (literature review)	H	Knight et al. 2000	—	—	Timing and dosage knowledge insufficient	No
Supplemental feeding (literature review)	H	Rush 2000	—	—	Insufficient knowledge to decide if nutritional supplements are good overall.	No
Tuberculosis		Summary: Borgdorff, Floyd, and Broekmans 2001.				
Short-course chemotherapy	H	China Tuberculosis Control Collaboration. 1996.	Yes	No	Increased cure rates	No. Not random
BCG	H	Tuberculosis Research Center (ICMR), Chennai 1999.	Yes	Yes	No effect of BCG on TB	No. No effect
Preventive therapy	H	Mwinga et al. 1998	Yes	Yes	Drugs reduced TB infection for HIV-infected people in Zambia	Yes (under HIV interventions)

Vaccinations	H	Here we look for evidence for the new vaccines that the Global Alliance for Vaccines and Immunization is trying to introduce. The Vaccine Fund 2002, *Strategic Plan 2002–2006*. There is a strong evidence base for the more established basic vaccines. Here we assume that all the vaccines can be implemented as programs, due to the success of the Expanded Program for Immunization.				
Japanese encephalitis vaccine	H	Hoke et al. 1988	Yes	Yes	Reduced encephalitis attack rate	Yes
Pneumococcal vaccine	H	O'Brien et al. 2003	Yes	Yes	Prevents vaccine serotype invasive pneumococcal disease	Yes
Quadrivalent vaccine	H	Pérez-Schael et al. 1997	Yes	Yes	Protection against severe diarrhea and dehydration, and reduced hospital admissions	Yes
Malaria		Summarized in Meek, Hill, and Webster 2001				
Indoor spraying	H	Rowland et al. 2000	Yes	Yes	Reduction in anopheline porous rates	Yes
Insecticide-treated nets	H	Shulman et al. 1998	Yes	Yes	No significant impact	No. Not significant
Outdoor spraying	H	Cutler 2003	Yes	No	Increase in arable land	No. Not random
HIV		Summarized in Jha et al. 2001; Behrman and Knowles 2003				
Voluntary HIV-1 counseling and testing	H	Coates et al. 2000	Yes	Yes	Reduced intercourse with nonprimary partners	Yes
Condom provision in motel rooms	H	Egger et al. 2000	Yes	Yes	Increased condom use	Yes
Package, including drug supply, health education and STD reference clinic	H	Grosskurth et al. 1995	Yes	Yes	Reduced HIV incidence	Yes
Home-based mass antibiotic treatment	H	Wawer et al. 1999	Yes	Yes	No effect	No

Table 2.A.2
(continued)

Intervention	C	Evaluation cited	S	R	Benefits	Including cost?
Confidential HIV testing and condom promotion	H	Allen et al. 1992	Yes	Yes	Increased condom use, reduced rates of gonorrhea and HIV in urban Rwandan women	Yes
Short-course zidovudine for babies who are not breast-fed	H	Shaffer et al. 1999	Yes	Yes	Reduced risk of mother-to-child HIV transmission	Yes
Short-course zidovudine for breast-fed babies	H	Wiktor et al. 1999	Yes	Yes	Reduced risk of mother-to-child HIV transmission	Yes
Monetary transfers		Unlike the health-based interventions, all monetary transfers actually happened in a community-based context; hence, they must be self-sustainable.				
Decentralized targeting	P	Galasso and Ravallion 2001	Yes	No	Results better in more favorable conditions	No. Not program evaluation per se
Old age pension	H	Duflo 2003	Yes	No	Increased weight of girls	No. Not random
Poor-area development programs	P	Jalan and Ravallion 1998	Yes	No	Enough to prevent decline, but not enough for convergence	No. Not random
Microfinance		Unlike the health-based interventions, all micro-finance interventions actually happened in a community-based context; hence, they must be self-sustainable.				
Village-level microfinance	P	Kaboski and Townsend 2002	Yes	No	Mixed	No. Not random, not effective
Village-level microfinance	P	Morduch 1998	Yes	No	No	No. Not effective
School inputs		Unlike the health-based interventions, all school-based interventions actually happened in a community-based context; hence, they must be self-sustainable.				
School construction	E	Duflo 2001	Yes	No	Increase in education and earnings	No. Not random

Intervention	Reference	Type			Outcome	Effective
School construction	Duflo 2004	E	Yes	No	Increase labor force participation, but reduce wages of older cohorts	No. Not random
Flip charts	Glewwe et al. 2000	E	Yes	No/Yes	No evidence with prospective, positive with retrospective	No. No evidence using random evaluation
Uniforms	Kremer, Moulin, and Namunyu 2003	E	Yes	Yes	Reduce dropout rates, without reducing test scores	Yes
Teacher incentives	Glewwe, Ilias, and Kremer 2003	E	Yes	Yes	No evidence, teachers teach to test	No. Not successful
Textbook	Glewwe, Kremer, and Moulin 2003	E	Yes	Yes	Raised test scores of the highest quintile, more likely to go to secondary school	No. Very skewed results
Remedial education program	Banerjee et al. 2003	E	Yes	Yes	Increased learning	Yes
Teacher provision	Chin 2002	E	Yes	No	Increased female primary school completion and literacy	No. Not random
School incentives						
School meals	Vermeersch 2002	EH	Yes	Yes	Conditional test score improvement, higher participation, cut into instruction time	No. Questionable effectiveness
PROGRESA	Schultz 2001	E	Yes	Yes	Higher enrollments	Yes
PROGRESA	Behrman, Segupta, and Todd 2001	E	Yes	Yes	Increased educational attainment, % attending junior secondary school	
PROGRESA	Behrman and Hoddinott 2001	H	Yes	Yes	0/− effect with means, + stature with Fixed Effects	
PROGRESA	Gertler and Boyce 2003	H	Yes	Yes	Health improvements	

Table 2.A.2
(continued)

Intervention	C	S	R	Benefits	Including cost?
School vouchers	E	Yes	Yes	Higher completion, less repeating of grades	Yes
Hygiene education	EH	Yes	Yes	Reduced diarrhea	Yes (folded into other education estimates)
Fertilizer					
Fertilizer adoption through an NGO program		Yes	Yes	Increased adoption, high rate of return	Yes
Roads					
Rural road construction		Yes	No	Research in progress	Not random, research in progress

Intervention	Evaluation cited
School vouchers	Angrist et al. 2002
Hygiene education	Haggerty et al. 1994
Fertilizer	
Fertilizer adoption through an NGO program	Duflo and Kremer 2003
Roads	
Rural road construction	van de Walle 2004

Notes

1. Agriculture, Electric Power and Other Energy, Environment, Mining, Oil and Gas, PSD/ Industry, Telecommunications and Informatics, Transportation, Urban Development, and Water Supply and Sanitation.

2. Others, like USAID, just report their assessment of how well the country is doing.

3. The European Bank for Reconstructuion and Development published its results online for the first time in late 2003. Even though it provides item-by-item ratings for all projects evaluated since 1993, it does not provide the information needed to match these projects to funding information, and therefore the data are not yet usable.

4. Percentage figures from the annual reports of the World Bank: Summaries of Projects Approved for IBRD, IDA, and Trust Funds in each Fiscal year. For each project, the following information is provided: country name, sector, brief project description, World Bank contribution, and total project cost.

5. Sectors were determined by the classifications in World Bank (2000b, Annex 1), which conveniently classifies the historical performance data into the 1990–1993 and 1994–1997 periods. From these sectors, the "Social" and "Environmental" sectors were dropped because zero/one evaluation was done between 1990 and 1993. We do not have 1987–1990 data for "Mining," "Multi-sector" and "Public Sector Management" due to a change in sector classification.

6. The 1987–1990 performance data are derived by collating information from World Bank (1989, 1993). The years 1987 and 1990 here refer to the year that the project was evaluated; hence, they correspond to projects that had slightly earlier exit fiscal year groups. The 1990–1993 and 1994–1997 performance data are derived from World Bank (2000a), and correspond to projects that had exit fiscal years within the respective ranges. The 1998–2001 data are derived from collating information from World Bank (2000a, 2002a).

7. These are the four selected sectors in Morra and Thumm (1997, table 1.32).

8. The Technical Assistance category was dropped in World Bank (1994).

9. Morra and Thumm (1997, table 1.32).

10. Annual reports of the World Bank.

11. Here, unlike in the results in the previous table, we are using the gap in performance between t and $t - 1$ rather than that between $t - 1$ and $t - 2$, because of data limitations in the case of the World Bank. For the ADB we could use the gap between $t - 1$ and $t - 2$. The results are very similar.

12. For both the ADB and the World Bank, the sector dummies as a group are significant at the 1 percent level (based on their joint F-statistic), as are the country dummies, though the sector dummies become insignificant for the ADB when we drop the multisector/others category.

13. Data from World Bank (1998, 1999, 2000a, 2001, 2002a, 2003a).

14. Bill Easterly, another long-term bank employee, makes a similar point in an article in the *Journal of Economic Perspectives* (Easterly 2003).

15. Those who are interested in the argument for (and against) randomized trials as a basis for social policy may want to see Duflo (2004) and Duflo and Kremer (2004).

16. See Angrist and Lavy (1999) for an example of a very convincing natural experiment.

17. This is, in effect, how Stanley Fischer, a former chief economist of the bank, put it while commenting on our previous paper at the meetings of the American Economic Association.

18. We feel that fieldworkers ensuring that villagers comply with their daily supplement dosage constitutes overly strong intervention.

19. For example, this was the basis for choosing Miguel and Kremer's (2004) work on deworming and Bobonis, Miguel, and Sharma (2003) on iron supplementation.

20. One place where we did exercise some judgment is in including the study by Angrist and Lavy (1999), which used a natural experiment in Israel to estimate the effect of class size on learning. This

natural experiment was based on the fact that in Israel, class size is capped at forty (the so-called Maimonides rule), which generates a sharp discontinuity whenever class size hits forty. The paper exploits the fact that this discontinuity generates something very close to a pure randomization across schools.

21. We also recognize that researchers do not always have control over the experimental design and, in any case, that the research might have been done with different objectives in mind (for example, researchers might be interested in knowing the impact of supplements on growth if it could be assumed that compliance was not going to be a problem). Inclusion in the highlighted subset does not reflect any opinion of the quality of the research or the researcher. It merely reflects the suitability of the research for our purposes.

22. We chose 2015 because it is when the Millennium Development Goals are meant to be achieved and many of our programs could be ways to achieve the goals.

23. Under the plausible assumption that the PPP correction is unreliable for the salaries of skilled service providers, who tend to be scarce in developing countries.

24. http://web.mit.edu/ruimin/www/whatworks/whatworksest.xls

References

Allen, S., et al. 1992. "Confidential HIV Testing and Condom Promotion in Africa. Impact on HIV and Gonorrhea Rates." *Journal of the American Medical Association* 268, no. 23 (December): 3338–3343.

Angrist, Joshua, and Victor Lavy. 1999. "Using Maimonides' Rule to Estimate the Effect of Class Size on Children's Academic Achievement." *Quarterly Journal of Economics* 114, no. 2 (May): 533–575.

Angrist, Joshua, Eric Bettinger, Erik Bloom, Elizabeth King, and Michael Kremer. 2002. "Vouchers for Private Schooling in Columbia: Evidence from a Randomized Natural Experiment." *American Economic Review* 92, no. 5 (December): 1535–1558.

Asian Development Bank. 2003. *Annual Review of Evaluation Activities in 2002.* Available at http://www.adb.org/Documents/PERs/RPE_OTH_2003_12.pdf.

Banerjee, Abhijit, and Ruimin He. 2003. "The World Bank of the Future." *American Economic Review* 93, no. 2 (May): 39–44.

Banerjee, Abhijit, et al. 2003. "Remedying Education: Evidence from Two Randomized Experiments in India." Poverty Action Lab Paper 4.

Bang, A. T., et al. 1999. "Effect of Home-Based Neonatal Care and Management of Sepsis on Neonatal Mortality: Field Trial in Rural India." *Lancet* 354, no. 9194 (December): 1955–1961.

Behrman, Jere R., and James C. Knowles. 2003. "Assessing the Economic Returns to Investing in Youths in Developing Countries." Mimeo, University of Pennsylvania.

Behrman, Jere, and John Hoddinott. 2001. "Program Evaluation with Unobserved Heterogeneity and Selective Implementation: The Mexican PROGRESA Impact on Child Nutrition." Penn Institute for Economic Research, Working Paper 02-006.

Behrman, Jere, Pilali Segupta, and Petra Todd. 2001. "Progressing Through PROGRESA: An Impact Assessment of a School Subsidy Experiment." Penn Institute for Economic Research, Working Paper 01-033.

Bobonis, Gustavo, Edward Miguel, and Charu Sharma. 2004. "Iron Deficiency Anemia and School Participation." Mimeo, University of California, Berkeley.

Brown, K. H., et al. 2002. "Effect of Supplemental Zinc on the Growth and Serum Zinc Concentrations of Prepubertal Children: A Meta-analysis of Randomized Controlled Trials." *American Journal of Clinical Nutrition* 75, no. 6 (June): 1062–1071.

Chattopadhyay, Raghabendra, and Esther Duflo. 2001. "Women as Policy Makers: Evidence from an India Wide Randomized Experiment." Working paper 8615, December. Cambridge, Mass.: National Bureau of Economic Research.

Chin, Aimee. 2002. "The Returns to School Quality When School Quality Is Very Low: Evidence from Operation Blackboard in India." Mimeo, University of Houston.

China Tuberculosis Control Collaboration. 1996. "Results of directly observed short-course chemotherapy in 112,842 Chinese patients with smear-positive tuberculosis." *Lancet* 347, no. 8998 (February): 358–362.

Coates, et al. 2000. "Efficacy of Voluntary HIV-1 Counseling and Testing in Individuals and Couples in Kenya, Tanzania, and Trinidad: A Randomized Trial." *Lancet* 356, no. 9224 (July): 103–112.

Cobra, Claudine, et al. 1997. "Infant Survival Is Improved by Oral Iodine Supplementation." *Journal of Nutrition* 127, no. 4 (April): 574–578.

Commission of Macroeconomics and Health, Working Group 5. 2001. *Various Working Papers.* Geneva: World Health Organization. Available at http://www.cmhealth.org/cmh_papers&reports .htm.

Cutler, David, and Grant Miller. 2003. "Clean Water Measures in American History." Private communication.

Cutler, David. 2003. "The Economic Impacts of Public Health Improvements." Personal communication.

Daniels, D. L., et al. 1990. "A Case-Control Study of the Impact of Improved Sanitation on Diarrhoea Morbidity in Lesotho." *Bulletin of the World Health Organization* 68, no. 4:455–463.

De Cock, Kevin, Mary Glenn Fowler, Eric Mercier, Isabelle de Vincenzi, et al. 2000. "Prevention of Mother-to-Child HIV Transmission in Resource-Poor Countries: Translating Research into Policy and Practice." *Journal of the American Medical Association* 283, no. 9 (March): 1175–1182.

Duflo, Esther, and Michael Kremer. 2003. "Understanding Technological Choices: Fertilizers in Western Kenya." Mimeo.

Duflo, Esther, and Michael Kremer. 2005. "Use of Randomization in the Evaluation of Development Effectiveness." In *Evaluating Development Effectiveness*, ed. George Keith Pitman, Osvaldo N. Feinstein, and Gregory K. Ingram. New Brunswick, N.J.: Transaction Publishers.

Duflo, Esther. 2001. "Schooling and Labor Market Consequences of School Construction in Indonesia: Evidence from an Unusual Policy Experiment." *American Economic Review* 91, no. 4 (September): 795–813.

Duflo, Esther. 2001. "The Medium Run Effects of Educational Expansion: Evidence from a Large School Construction Program in Indonesia." Forthcoming in *Journal of Development Economics.*

Duflo, Esther. 2003. "Grandmothers and Granddaughters: Old Age Pension and Intra-household Allocation in South Africa." *World Bank Economic Review* 17, no. 1 (June): 1–25.

Duflo, Esther. 2004. "Scaling Up and Evaluation." In *Proceedings of the Annual World Bank Conference in Development Economics Conference.* Washington, D.C.: World Bank, 341–369.

Duflo, Esther, Pascaline Dupas, Michael Kremer, and Samuel Sinei. "Education and HIV/AIDS Prevention: Evidence from a Randomized Evaluation in Western Kenya." Mimeo. MIT.

Easterly, William. 2001. *The Elusive Quest for Growth: Economists' Adventures and Misadventures in the Tropics.* Cambridge, Mass.: MIT Press.

Easterly, William. 2003. "Can Foreign Aid Buy Growth." *Journal of Economic Perspectives* 17, no. 3 (Summer): 23–48.

Egger, M., et al. 2000. "Promotion of Condom Use in a High-Risk Setting in Nicaragua: A Randomized Controlled Trial." *Lancet* 355, no. 9221 (June): 2101–2105.

Esrey, S. A. 1996. "Waste, Waste, and Well-Being: A Multicountry Study." *American Journal of Epidemiology* 43, no. 6 (March): 608–623.

Frankenberg, Elizabeth, and Duncan Thomas. 2001. "Women's Health and Pregnancy Outcomes: Do Services Make a Difference?" *Demography* 38, no. 2 (May): 253–265.

Galasso, Emanuela, and Martin Ravallion. 2001. "Decentralized Targeting of an Anti-Poverty Program." Forthcoming, *Journal of Public Economics.*

Gertler, Paul, and Simone Boyce. 2003. "An Experiment in Incentive-Based Welfare: The Impact of PROGRESA on Health in Mexico." Royal Economic Society Annual Conference 2003.

Glewwe, Paul, et al. 2000. "Retrospective vs. Prospective Analyses of School Inputs: The case of Flip Charts in Kenya." NBER Working Paper 8018.

Glewwe, Paul, Michael Kremer, and Sylvie Moulin. 2003. "Textbooks and Test scores: Evidence from a Prospective Evaluation in Kenya." Mimeo, Harvard University.

Glewwe, Paul, Nauman Ilias, and Michael Kremer. 2003. "Teacher Incentives." NBER Working Paper 9671.

Grosskurth, H., et al. 1995. "Impact of Improved Treatment of Sexually Transmitted Diseases on HIV Infection in Rural Tanzania: Randomized Controlled Trial." Lancet 346, no. 8974 (August): 530–536.

Grotto, I., et al. 2003. "Vitamin A Supplementation and Childhood Morbidity from Diarrhea and Respiratory Infections: A Meta-analysis." Journal of Pediatrics 142, no. 3 (March): 297–304.

Haggerty, P. A., et al. 1994. "Community-Based Hygiene Education to Reduce Diarrhoeal Disease in Rural Zaire: Impact of the Intervention on Diarrhoeal Morbidity." International Journal of Epidemiology 23, no. 5 (October): 1050–1059.

Hoke, C. H., et al. 1988. "Protection against Japanese Encephalitis by Inactivated Vaccines." New England Journal of Medicine 319, no. 10 (September): 608–614.

IFDC. 2001. Monthly Bulletin of the International Institute of Soil Fertility Management (IFDC-Africa) 14:2 (February).

Jalan, Jyotsna, and Martin Ravallion. 1998. "Are There Dynamic Gains from a Poor-Area Development Program?" Journal of Public Economics 67:1 (January): 65–85.

Jha, P., et al. 2001. "The Evidence Base for Interventions to Prevent HIV Infection in Low and Middle-Income Countries." Commission on Macroeconomics and Health, Working Group 5, Working Paper 2.

Kaboski, Joseph, and Robert Townsend. 2002. "Policies and Impact: An Analysis of Village-Level Microfinance Institutions." Mimeo, University of Chicago.

Knight, M., et al. 2000. "Antiplatelet Agents for Preventing and Treating Pre-eclampsia (Cochrane Review)." In The Cochrane Library, February 2000:2. Oxford: Update software, 2000.

Kremer, Michael. 2003. "Randomized Evaluations of Educational Programs in Developing Countries: Some Lessons." American Economic Review 93, no. 2 (May): 102–106.

Kremer, Michael, and Edward Miguel. 2004. "Worms: Identifying Impacts on Education and Health in the Presence of Treatment Externalities." Econometrica 72, no. 1 (January): 159–217.

Kremer, Michael, Sylvie Moulin, and Robert Namunyu. 2003. "Decentralization: A Cautionary Tale." Mimeo, Harvard University.

Mahomed, K. 1997. "Folate Supplementation in Pregnancy (Cochrane Review)." In The Cochrane Library, August. Oxford: Update Software.

Meek, S., J. Hill, and J. Webster. 2001. "The Evidence Base for Interventions to Reduce Malaria in Low and Middle-Income Countries." Commission on Macroeconomics and Health, Working Group 5, Working Paper 6.

Miguel, Edward, and Michael Kremer. 2004. "Worms: Identifying Impacts on Health and Education in the Presence of Treatment Externalities." Econometrica 72, no. 1:159–217.

Morduch, Jonathan. 1998. "Does Microfinance Really Help the Poor? New Evidence from Flagship Programs in Bangladesh." Research Program in Development Studies.M mimeo, Princeton University.

Morra, Linda G., and Ulrich R. W. Thumm. 1997. 1995 Evaluation Results. Washington, D.C.: Operations Evaluation Department. World Bank.

Munjanja, S. P., G. Lindmark, and L. Nystrom. 1996. "Randomized Control of a Reduced-Visits Programme of Antenatal Care in Harare, Zimbabwe." Lancet 348, no. 9034 (August): 364–369.

Mwinga, A., et al. 1998. "Twice Weekly Tuberculosis Preventive Therapy in HIV Infection in Zambia." *AIDS* 12, no. 18 (December): 2447–2457.

Narayanan, Deepa, ed. 2000. *Empowerment and Poverty Reduction: A Sourcebook*. Washington, D.C.: World Bank.

O'Brien, Katherine L., et al. 2003. "Efficacy and Safety of Seven-Valent Conjugate Pneumococcal Vaccine in American Indian Children: Group Randomized Trial." *Lancet* 362, no. 9381 (August): 355–361.

Pérez-Schael, Irene, et al. 1997. "Efficacy of the Rhesus Rotavirus–Based Quadrivalent Vaccine in Infants and Young Children in Venezuela." *New England Journal of Medicine* 337, no. 17 (October): 1181–1189.

Pritchett, Lant. 2002. "It Pays to be Ignorant: A Simply Political Economy of Rigorous Program Evaluation." *Policy Reform* 5, no. 4:251–269.

Roberts, Les, et al. 2001. "Keeping Clean in a Malawi Refugee Camp: A Randomized Intervention Trial." *Bulletin of the World Health Organization* 79, no. 4:280–287.

Rowland, M., et al. 2000. "Indoor Residual Spraying with Alphacypermethrin Controls Malaria in Pakistan: A Community-Randomized Trial." *Tropical Medicine and International Health* 5, no. 7:472–481.

Rush, D. 2000. "Nutrition and Maternal Mortality in the Developing World." *American Journal of Clinical Nutrition* 72 (suppl): 212S–240S.

Schultz, Paul. 2001. "School Subsidies for the Poor: Evaluating the Mexican PROGRESA Poverty Program." Economic Growth Center, Center Discussion Paper 834.

Shaffer, N., et al. 1999. "Short-Course Zidovudine for Perinatal HIV-1 Transmission in Bangkok, Thailand: A Randomized Controlled Trial." *Lancet* 353, no. 9155 (March): 773–780.

Shulman, C. E., et al. 1998. "A Community Randomized Controlled Trial of Insecticide-Treated Bednets for the Prevention of Malaria and Anaemia among Primigravid Women on the Kenyan Coast." *Tropical Medicine and Internal Health* 3, no. 3 (March): 197–204.

Stanton, B. F. 1987. "An Educational Intervention for Altering Water-Sanitation Behaviors to Reduce Childhood Diarrhea in Urban Bangladesh. II. A Randomized Trial to Assess the Impact of the Intervention on Hygienic Behaviors and Rates of Diarrhea." *American Journal of Epidemiology* 125, no. 2 (February): 292–301.

Tinker, Anne, Kathleen Finn, and Joanne Epp. 2000. "Improving Women's Health: Issues and Interventions." Washington, D.C.: World Bank.

Tuberculosis Research Center (ICMR), Chennai. 1999. "Fifteen Year Follow Up of Trial of BCG Vaccines in South India for Tuberculosis Prevention." *Indian Journal of Medical Research* 110 (August): 56–69.

Vaccine Fund. 2002. *Strategic Plan 2002–2006*. Washington, D.C.: The Vaccine Fund.

van de Walle, Dominique. "Impact Evaluation of a Rural Road Rehabilitation Project in Viet Nam." Cited 11 February 2004. Available online (http://econ.worldbank.org/view.php?type=20&id=11865).

Verlé, P., et al. 1999. "Control of Malaria Vectors: Cost Analysis in a Province in Northern Vietnam." *Tropical Medicine & International Health* 4, no. 2 (February): 139–145.

Vermeersch, Christel. 2002. "School Meals, Educational Achievement and School Competition: Evidence from a Randomized Experiment." Mimeo, Harvard University.

Villar, J., et al. 2001. "WHO Antenatal Care Randomized Trial for the Evaluation of a New Model of Routine Antenatal Care." *Lancet* 357, no. 9268 (November): 1551–1564.

Walker, Damien, et al. 2002. "An Economic Analysis of Midwifery Training Programmes in South Kalimantan, Indonesia." *Bulletin of the World Health Organization* 80, no. 1:47–55.

Wawer, M. J., et al. 1999. "Control of Sexually Transmitted Diseases for AIDS Prevention in Uganda: A Randomized Community Trial." Rakai Project Study Group. *Lancet* 353, no. 9152 (February): 525–535.

Wichmann, W., eds. n.d. *World Fertilizer Use Manual*, available online at (http://www.fertilizer
.org/ifa/publicat/html/pubman/manual.htm), International Fertilizer Industry Association.

Wiktor, S. Z., et al. 1999. "Short-Course Oral Zidovudine for Prevention of Mother-to-Child
Transmission of HIV-1 in Abidjan, Côte d'Ivoire." *Lancet* 353, no. 9155 (March): 781–785.

World Bank. 1989. *Project Performance Results for 1987*. Washington, D.C.: Operations Evaluation Department, World Bank.

World Bank. 1993. *Evaluation results for 1991*. Washington, D.C.: Operations Evaluation Department, World Bank.

World Bank. 1994. *The World Bank Annual Report 1994*. Washington, D.C.: World Bank.

World Bank. 2000a. *1999 Annual Review of Development Effectiveness*. Washington, D.C.: Operations Evaluation Department, World Bank.

World Bank. 2000b. *1999 World Bank Annual Report*. Washington, D.C.: World Bank.

World Bank. 2001. 2000 *World Bank Annual Report*. Washington, D.C.: World Bank.

World Bank. 2002a. *2001 Annual Review of Development Effectiveness*. Washington, D.C.: Operations Evaluation Department, World Bank.

World Bank. 2002b. 2001 *World Bank Annual Report*. Washington, D.C.: World Bank.

World Bank. 2003a. *2002 Annual Review of Development Effectiveness*. Washington, D.C.: Operations Evaluation Department. World Bank.

World Bank. 2003b. 2002 *World Bank Annual Report*. Washington, D.C.: World Bank.

3 Use of Randomization in the Evaluation of Development Effectiveness

Esther Duflo and Michael Kremer

Historically, prospective randomized evaluations of development programs have constituted a tiny fraction of all development evaluations. In this chapter, we argue that there is scope for considerably expanding their use, although they must necessarily remain a small fraction of all evaluations.

The benefits of knowing which programs work and which do not extend far beyond any program or agency, and credible impact evaluations are global public goods in the sense that they can offer reliable guidance to international organizations, governments, donors, and nongovernmental organizations (NGOs) beyond national borders. Traditional methods of measuring program impact may be subject to serious bias due to omitted variables.

For a broad class of development programs, randomized evaluations can be used to address these problems. Of course, not all programs can be evaluated with randomized evaluations; for example, examinations of issues such as central bank independence must rely on other methods of evaluation. Programs targeted to individuals or local communities (such as sanitation, local government reforms, education, and health) are likely to be strong candidates for randomized evaluations; this chapter uses the case of educational programs in developing countries as an example.

We do not propose that all projects be subject to randomized evaluations. But we argue that there is currently a tremendous imbalance in evaluation methodology and that increasing the share of projects subject to randomized evaluation from near zero to even a small fraction could have a tremendous impact on knowledge about what works in development. All too often development policy is based on fads, and randomized evaluations could allow it to be based on evidence.

The chapter proceeds as follows. Section 3.1 discusses the methodology of randomized evaluations. We present the impact evaluation problem, review why other current evaluation methods may often be unable to adequately control for selection bias, and discuss why randomized evaluations can be useful in addressing the problems encountered by other evaluation practices. Section 3.2 reviews recent randomized evaluations of educational programs in developing countries, including programs to increase school participation, provide educational inputs, and reform education. Section 3.3 extracts lessons from these evaluations, and section 3.4 reviews an example of current practice, offers political economy explanations for why randomized evaluations are so rare, and discusses the role international agencies can play in promoting and financing rigorous evaluations, including randomized evaluations. Section 3.5 discusses the value of credible impact evaluations as international public goods.

3.1 The Methodology of Randomized Evaluations

This section discusses the selection bias problem that can arise when conducting impact evaluations and nonrandomized evaluation methods that are used in attempting to control for this bias.

3.1.1 The Evaluation Problem

Any impact evaluation attempts to answer an essentially counterfactual question: How would individuals who participated in the program have fared in the absence of the program? How would those who were not exposed to the program have fared in the presence of the program? The difficulty with these questions is immediate: at a given point in time, an individual is observed to be either exposed or not exposed to the program. Comparing the same individual over time will not, in most cases, give a reliable estimate of the impact the program had on him or her, since many other things may have changed at the same time as the program was introduced. We therefore cannot seek to obtain an estimate of the impact of the program on each individual. All we can hope for is to be able to obtain the average impact of the program on a group of individuals by comparing them to a similar group of individuals who were not exposed to the program.

The critical objective of impact evaluation is therefore to establish a credible comparison group: a group of individuals who in the absence of the program would have had outcomes similar to those who were exposed to the program. This group should give us an idea of what would have happened to the members of the program group if they had not been exposed, and thus allow us to obtain an estimate of the average impact on the group in question.

In reality, however, the individuals who participated in a program generally differ from those who did not. Programs are placed in specific areas (for example, poorer or richer areas), individuals are screened for participation in the program (for example, on the basis of poverty or on the basis of their motivation), and the decision to participate is often voluntary. For all of these reasons, those who were not exposed to a program are often a poor comparison group for those who were, and any differences between the groups can be attributed to two factors: preexisting differences (the so-called selection bias) and the impact of the program. Since we have no reliable way to estimate the size of the selection bias, we typically cannot decompose the overall difference into a treatment effect and a bias term.

To solve this problem, program evaluations typically need to be carefully planned in advance in order to determine which group is a likely control group. One situation where the selection bias disappears is when the treatment and comparison groups are selected randomly from a potential population of participants (such as individuals, communities, schools, or classrooms). In this case, on average, we can be assured that those who are exposed to the program are no different from those who are not, and thus that a statistically significant difference between the groups in the outcomes the program was planning to affect can be confidently attributed to the program.

As we will see in this chapter, the random selection of treatment and comparison groups can occur in several circumstances. Using the example of PRO-GRESA, a program designed to increase school participation in Mexico, we discuss how prospective randomized evaluations can be used and how their results can help in scaling successful programs. Using examples of school-based health programs in Kenya and India, we illustrate how prospective randomized evaluations can be used when implementing adapted replications of programs, and using the example of a school voucher program in Colombia, we illustrate how program-induced randomization can occur.

It is worth briefly outlining a few clarifications regarding the use of randomized evaluations to estimate program effects. First, a distinction can be made about what exactly the evaluation is attempting to estimate. Randomized evaluations can be used to estimate the effect of a treatment on either the entire population that was subject to the randomization or on a subset of the population defined by predetermined characteristics, whereas instrumental variable techniques estimate local average treatment effects (Imbens and Angrist 1994; Heckman et al. 1998; Heckman, James, and Todd 1997; Heckman, Lalonde, and Smith 1999). Second, randomized evaluations estimate partial equilibrium treatment effects, which may differ from general equilibrium treatment effects (Heckman, Lochner, and Taber 1998). It is possible that if some educational programs were implemented on a large scale, the programs could affect the functioning of the school system and thus have a different impact.

3.1.2   Other Techniques to Control for Selection and Other Omitted Variable Bias

Natural or organized randomized evaluations are not the only methodologies that can be used to obtain credible impact evaluations of program effects. Researchers have developed alternative techniques to control for bias as much as possible, and progress has been made, most notably by labor economists.[1] Among the techniques that are most popular with researchers are propensity score matching, difference-in-difference estimates, and regression discontinuity design.

One strategy to control for bias is to attempt to find a control group that is as comparable as possible to the treatment group, at least along observable dimensions. This can be done by collecting as many covariates as possible and then adjusting the computed differences through a regression, or by "matching" the program and the comparison group through forming a comparison group that is as similar as possible to the program group. One possibility is to predict the probability that a given individual is in the comparison or the treatment group on the basis of all available observable characteristics, and then to form a comparison group by picking people who have the same probability of being treated as those who were actually treated (propensity score matching). The challenge with this method, as with regression controls, is that it hinges on having identified all the potentially relevant differences between the treatment and control groups. In cases where the treatment is assigned on the basis of a variable that is not observed by the researcher (demand for the service, for example), this technique can lead to misleading inferences.

A second strategy is what is often called the difference-in-difference technique. When a good argument can be made that the outcome would not have had differential trends in regions that received the program if the program had not been put in place, it is possible to compare the growth in the variables of interest between program and nonprogram regions. However, it is important not to take this assumption for granted. This identification assumption cannot be tested, and even to ascertain its plausibility, one needs to have long time series of data from before the program was implemented in order to be able to compare trends over long enough periods. One also needs to make sure that no other program was implemented at the same time, which is often not the case. Finally, when drawing inferences, one must take into account that regions are often affected by time-persistent shocks that may look like program effects. Bertrand, Duflo, and Mullainathan (2002) found that difference-in-difference estimations (as commonly performed) can severely bias standard errors: the researchers randomly generated placebo laws and found that with about twenty years of data, difference-in-difference estimates found an "effect" significant at the 5 percent level of up to 45 percent of the placebo laws.

As an example of where difference-in-difference estimates can be used, Duflo (2001) took advantage of a rapid school expansion program that occurred in Indonesia in the 1970s to estimate the impact of building schools on schooling and subsequent wages. Identification was made possible by the fact that the allocation rule for the schools was known (more schools were built in places with low initial enrollment rates) and that the cohorts participating in the program were easily identified (children twelve years or older when the program started did not participate in the program). The increased growth of education across cohorts in regions that received more schools suggests that access to schools contributed to increased education. The trends were quite parallel before the program and shifted clearly for the first cohort that was exposed to the program, thus reinforcing confidence in the identification assumption. However, this identification strategy is not usually valid. Often when policy changes are used to identify the effect of a particular policy, the policy change is itself endogenous to the outcomes it was meant to affect, thus making identification impossible (Besley and Case 2000).

Finally, a third strategy, called regression discontinuity design (Campbell 1969), takes advantage of the fact that program rules sometimes generate discontinuities that can be used to identify the effect of the program by comparing those above a certain threshold to those just below it. If resources are allocated on the basis of a certain number of points, it is possible to compare those just above to those just below the threshold. Angrist and Lavy (1999) use this technique to evaluate the impact of class size in Israel, where a second teacher is allocated every time the class size grows above forty students. This policy generates discontinuities in class size when the enrollment in a grade grows from forty to forty-one (as class size changes from one class of forty students to one class each of twenty and twenty-one students). Angrist and Lavy compared test scores in classes just above and just below this threshold and found that those just above the threshold have significantly higher test scores than those just below, which can confidently be attributed to the class size, since it is very unlikely that schools on both sides of the threshold have any other systematic differences.[2] Such discontinuities in program rules, when enforced, are thus sources of identification.

In developing countries, however, it is often likely to be the case that rules are not enforced strictly enough to generate discontinuities that can be used for identification purposes. For example, researchers attempted to use as a source of identification the discontinuity in the policy of the Grameen bank (the flagship microcredit organization in Bangladesh), which is to lend only to people who own less than one acre of land (Pitt and Khandker 1998). It turns out that in practice, the Grameen bank lends to many people who own more than one acre of land and that there is no discontinuity in the probability of borrowing at the threshold (Morduch 1998).

These three techniques are subject to large biases that can lead to either overestimation or underestimation of program impact. LaLonde (1986) found that many of the econometric procedures and comparison groups used in program evaluations did not yield accurate or precise estimates and that such econometric estimates often differ significantly from experimental results.

Identification issues with nonrandomized evaluation methods must be tackled with extreme care because they are less transparent and more subject to divergence of opinion than are issues with randomized evaluations. Moreover, the differences between good and bad nonrandomized evaluations are difficult to communicate, especially to policymakers, because of all the caveats that must accompany the results. In practice, these caveats may never be provided to policymakers, and even if they are provided, they may be ignored. In either case, policymakers are likely to be radically misled. This suggests that while nonrandomized evaluations will continue to be needed, there should be a commitment to conduct randomized evaluations where possible.

3.2 Examples of Randomized Evaluations of Educational Programs

In this section, we present recent randomized evaluations of three types of educational programs in developing countries: programs designed to increase school participation, programs providing educational inputs, and educational reform programs.

3.2.1 Increasing School Participation

Education is widely considered to be critical for development: the internationally agreed-on Millennium Development Goals call for universal primary school enrollment by 2015. However, there is considerable controversy over how best to achieve this goal and how much it would cost. For example, some argue that it will be difficult to attract additional children to school since most children who are not in school are earning income their families need, while others argue that children of primary-school age are not very productive and that modest incentives or improvements in school quality would be sufficient. Some see school fees as essential for ensuring accountability in schools and as a minor barrier to participation, while others argue that eliminating fees would greatly increase school participation.

Because one obvious means of increasing school participation is to decrease or remove financial barriers, we review recent randomized evaluations of programs designed to increase school participation through reducing the cost of school, or even paying for school attendance.[3]

PROGRESA

Because positive results can help to build a consensus for a project, carefully constructed program evaluations form a sound basis for decisions on whether to scale up existing projects. The PROGRESA program in Mexico, designed to increase school participation, is a striking example of this phenomenon. PROGRESA provides cash grants to women that are conditional on children's school attendance and preventative health measures (nutrition supplementation, health care visits, and participation in health education programs). When the program was launched in 1998, officials in the Mexican government made a conscious decision to take advantage of the fact that budgetary constraints made it impossible to reach the 50,000 potential participant communities of PROGRESA immediately, and instead began with a program in 506 communities. Half of those communities were randomly selected to receive the program, and baseline and subsequent data were collected in the remaining communities (Gertler and Boyce 2001). Part of the rationale for this decision was to increase the probability that the program would be continued if there were a change in the party in power, because the proponents of the program understood that the program would require continuous political support in order to be scaled up successfully. The task of evaluating the program was given to academic researchers through the International Food Policy Research Institute (IFPRI); the data were made accessible to numerous researchers, and a number of papers have been written on PROGRESA's impact.[4]

The evaluations show that the program was effective in improving both health and education. Comparing PROGRESA participants and nonparticipants, Gertler and Boyce (2001) show that children on average had a 23 percent reduction in the incidence of illness, a 1 to 4 percent increase in height, and an 18 percent reduction in anemia. Adults experienced a reduction of 19 percent in the number of days lost due to illness. Shultz (2004) finds an average 3.4 percent increase in enrollment for all students in grades 1 through 8; the increase was largest among girls who had completed grade 6, at 14.8 percent.

In part because the randomized phase-in of the program allowed such clear documentation of the program's positive effects, PROGRESA was indeed maintained when the Mexican government changed hands: by 2000, PROGRESA was reaching 2.6 million families (10 percent of the families in Mexico) and had a budget of US$800 million, or 0.2 percent of gross domestic product (GDP) (Gertler and Boyce 2001). The program was subsequently expanded to urban communities, and with support from the World Bank, similar programs are being implemented in several neighboring Latin American countries. Mexican officials transformed a budgetary constraint into an opportunity and made evaluation the cornerstone of subsequent scaling up. They were rewarded by both the expansion of the program and the tremendous visibility that the program acquired.

School Meals, Cost of Education, and School Health in Kenya: Comparing the Cost-Effectiveness of Different Interventions

A central policy concern for developing countries is the relative cost-effectiveness of various interventions intended to increase school participation. This section discusses research on several programs to decrease the costs of education and compares the cost-effectiveness of these different interventions.

Evaluations of cost-effectiveness require knowledge of a program's costs as well as its impact, and comparability across studies requires some common environment. It is difficult to compare the impact of PROGRESA's cash transfers with that of, say, school meals in Kenya, since it is unclear whether the resulting differences are associated with the type of program or the larger environment. In general, analysts and policymakers are left with a choice between retrospective studies, which allow comparison of different factors affecting school participation, and randomized evaluations, which yield very credible estimates of the effect of single programs. One exception to our general inability to compare cost-effectiveness estimates is a recent set of studies conducted in Kenya of programs seeking to improve school participation. By evaluating a number of programs in a similar setting (a specific district in Western Kenya), it is possible to explicitly compare the cost-effectiveness of different approaches to increasing school participation. Looking at the effect of school meals on school participation, Vermeersch (2002) found that school participation was 30 percent greater in twenty-five Kenyan preschools where a free breakfast was introduced than it was in twenty-five comparison schools. However, the provision of meals cut into instruction time. Overall, test scores were .4 standard deviations greater in the program schools, but only if the teacher was well trained prior to the program.

Kremer, Moulin, and Namunyu (2002) evaluate a program in which a nongovernmental organization, Internationaal Christelijk Steunfonds Africa, provided uniforms, textbooks, and classroom construction to seven schools that were randomly selected from a pool of fourteen poorly performing candidate schools in Kenya. As in many other countries, parents face significant private costs of education for school fees and other expenses, such as uniforms. In particular, they are normally required to purchase uniforms at about $6, a substantial expense in a country with per capita income of $340. Dropout rates fell considerably in treatment schools, and after five years, pupils in treatment schools had completed about 15 percent more schooling. In addition, many students from nearby schools transferred into program schools, raising class size by 50 percent. This suggests that students and parents were willing to trade off substantially larger class sizes for the benefit of free uniforms, textbooks, and improved classrooms. Given that the combination of these extra inputs and a 50 percent increase in class size led to no measurable impact on test scores, but that the cost savings from a much smaller increase in class size would have allowed the Kenyan government to pay for the uniforms, textbooks, and other inputs provided under the program, these results suggest that existing budgets could be productively reallocated to decrease parental payments and substantially increase school participation.

Poor health may also limit school participation: for example, intestinal helminthes such as hookworm affect a quarter of the world's population and are particularly prevalent among school-age children. Miguel and Kremer (2004) evaluate a program of twice-yearly school-based mass treatment with inexpensive deworming drugs in Kenya, where the prevalence of intestinal worms among children is very high. Seventy-five schools were phased into the program in random order. Health and school participation improved not only at program schools but also at nearby schools due to reduced disease transmission. Absenteeism in treatment schools was 25 percent (or seven percentage points) lower than in comparison schools. Including the spillover effect, the program increased schooling by 0.15 years per person treated.

Because these programs were conducted in similar environments, cost-effectiveness estimates from numerous randomized evaluations can be readily compared. Deworming was found to be extraordinarily cost-effective at only $3.50 per additional year of schooling (Miguel and Kremer 2003). In contrast, even under optimistic assumptions the provision of free uniforms would cost $99 per additional year of school participation induced (Kremer, Moulin, and Namunyu 2002). The school meals program, which targeted preschoolers rather than primary school age children, cost $36 per additional year of schooling induced (Vermeersch 2003). This suggests that school health programs may be one of the most cost-effective ways of increasing school participation.

3.2.2   School Inputs

This section reviews recent randomized evaluations of programs that provide various inputs to schools in Kenya and India.

Retrospective and Prospective Studies of Inputs in Kenyan Primary Schools
Based on existing retrospective evaluations, many are skeptical about the effects of educational inputs on learning (Hanushek 1995). One potential weakness of such evaluations is that observed inputs may be correlated with omitted variables that affect educational outcomes. The evaluation could be biased upward, for example, if observed inputs are correlated with unobserved parental or community support for education, or downward if compensatory programs provide assistance to poorly performing schools.

Although retrospective studies provide at best mixed evidence on the effect of many types of school inputs, they typically suggest that the provision of additional textbooks in schools with low initial stocks can improve learning. Indeed, cross-sectional and difference-in-difference analyses of Kenyan data would suggest that textbooks have dramatic effects on test scores. Results from a randomized evaluation, however, point to a subtler picture. Provision of textbooks increased test scores by about 0.2 standard deviations, but only among students who had scored in the top one or two quintiles on pretests prior to the program. Textbook provision did not affect the scores of the bottom 60 percent of students (Glewwe, Kramer, and Moulin 2002). Many students may have failed to benefit from textbooks because they had difficulty understanding them: Kenyan textbooks are in English, the official language of instruction, but English is most pupils' third language, after their mother tongue and Swahili. More generally, the Kenyan curriculum is set at a level that, while perhaps appropriate for elite families in Nairobi, is far ahead of that typically attained by rural students, given the high rates of student and teacher absence from school.

Given the results of the textbook study, researchers tried providing flip charts, an alternative input that presumably was more accessible to weak pupils. Glewwe and others (2004) compared retrospective and prospective analyses of the effect of flip charts on test scores. Retrospective estimates using straightforward ordinary-least-squares regressions suggest that flip charts raise test scores by up to 20 percent of a standard deviation, robust to the inclusion of control variables. Difference-in-difference estimates suggest a smaller effect of about 5 percent of a standard deviation, an effect that is still significant, though sometimes only at the 10 percent level. In contrast, prospective estimates based on randomized evaluations provide no evidence that flip charts increase test scores. These results suggest that using retrospective data to compare test scores seriously overestimates the charts' effectiveness. A difference-in-difference approach reduced but did not eliminate this problem. Moreover, it is not clear that such a difference-in-difference approach has general applicability.

These examples suggest that the ordinary-least-squares estimates are biased upward rather than downward. This is plausible, since in a poor country with a substantial local role in education, inputs are likely to be correlated with favorable unobserved community characteristics. If the direction of omitted variable bias were similar in other retrospective analyses of educational inputs in developing countries, the effects of inputs may be even more modest than retrospective studies suggest.

Placing Additional Teachers in Nonformal Education Centers

Banerjee and others (2001) evaluated a program in which Seva Mandir, an Indian NGO, placed second teachers in nonformal education centers that the NGO runs in Indian villages. These nonformal schools seek to provide basic numeracy and literacy skills to children who do not attend formal school and, in the medium term, to help mainstream these children into the regular school system. The centers are plagued by high teacher and child absenteeism. A second teacher (when possible, a woman) was randomly assigned to twenty-one out of forty-two of these centers, and the hope was to increase the number of days the centers were open, increase children's participation, and increase performance by providing more individualized attention to the children. By providing a female teacher, the NGO also hoped to make school more attractive for girls. Teacher attendance and child attendance were regularly monitored throughout the duration of the project.

The project reduced the number of days a center was closed: one-teacher centers were closed 44 percent of the time, whereas two-teacher centers were closed only 39 percent of the time. Girls' attendance had increased by 50 percent. However, there were no differences in test scores. It is worth noting that careful evaluations form a sound basis for decisions of whether to scale up existing projects. In the example, the two-teacher program was not implemented on a full scale by the NGO, on the grounds that the benefits were not sufficient to outweigh the cost. The savings were used to expand other programs.

Remedial Education Programs

Pratham, an Indian NGO, implemented a remedial education program in 1994 that now reaches more than 161,000 children in twenty cities. The program hires young women from the communities to provide remedial education in government schools to children who have reached grade 2, 3, or 4 without having mastered the basic grade 1 competencies. Children who are identified as lagging are pulled out of the regular classroom for two hours a day to receive this instruction. Pratham wanted to evaluate the impact of this program, one of the NGO's flagship interventions, at the same time as it was looking to expand it; the expansion into a new city, Vadodara, provided an opportunity to conduct a randomized evaluation (Banerjee et al. 2003). In the first year (1999–2000), the program was expanded to 49 (randomly selected) of the 123 Vadodara government schools. In 2000–2001, the program was expanded to all the schools, but half the schools received a remedial teacher for grade 3 and half received one for grade 4. Grade 3 students in schools that were exposed to the program in grade 4 serve as the comparison group for grade 3 students who were directly exposed to the program. Simultaneously, a similar intervention was conducted in a district of Mumbai, where half the schools received the remedial teachers in grade 2 and half received the teachers in grade 3. The program was continued for an additional year, with the school switching groups.

The program was thus conducted in several grades, in two cities, and with all schools participating in the program. On average, after two years, the program increased student test scores by 0.39 standard deviations. Moreover, the gains were largest for children at the bottom of the distribution: children in the bottom third gained 0.6 standard deviations after two years. The impact of the program is rising over time and is very similar across cities and child gender. Hiring remedial education teachers from the community appears to be ten times more cost-effective than hiring new teachers. One can be relatively confident in recommending the scaling up of this program, at least in India, on the basis of these estimates, since the program was continued for a period of time, was evaluated in two very different contexts, and has shown its ability to be rolled out on a large scale.

3.2.3 School Reform

There is reason to believe that many school systems could benefit from considerable reform. For example, evidence from the Kenyan evaluations discussed previously suggests that budgets are misallocated and that the curriculum focuses excessively on the strongest students. Teacher incentives in Kenya, as in much of the rest of the developing world, are quite weak, and absence among teachers is quite high, at around 20 percent. Proposed school reforms range from decentralization of budget authority to strengthening links between teacher pay and performance to vouchers and school choice. As an example, a decentralization program in Kenya that provided small grants to parent-run school committees induced them to purchase textbooks, with educational consequences similar to those of the textbook program mentioned above (Glewwe, Ilias, and Kremer 2003). Providing larger grants led school committees to shift their spending toward construction, but no educational impact could be observed from this, at least in the short run.

Teacher Incentives

Some parent-run school committees in Kenya provide gifts to teachers whose students perform well. Glewwe, Ilias, and Kremer (2003) evaluate a program that provided prizes to teachers in schools that performed well on exams and had low dropout rates. In theory, this type of incentive could lead teachers to either increase effort or, alternatively, teach to the test. Empirically, teachers responded to the program by teaching to the test: they did not increase their attendance but provided more sessions to prepare students for the exams. Consistent with a model in which teachers respond by increasing their effort to manipulate test scores rather than to stimulate long-term learning, the test scores of students who had been part of the program initially increased, but by the end of the program, they had fallen back to levels similar to those of the comparison group.

School Vouchers

Angrist and others (2002) evaluate a Colombian program in which vouchers for private schools were allocated by lottery because of limitations in the program's budget. Vouchers were renewable, conditional on satisfactory academic performance. The researchers found that lottery winners were 15 to 20 percent more likely to attend private school and 10 percent more likely to complete eighth grade, and they scored 0.2 standard deviations higher on standardized tests, equivalent to a full grade level. The effects of the program were greater for girls than for boys. Winners were substantially more likely to graduate from high school, and they scored higher on high school completion and college entrance exams. The benefits of the program to participants clearly exceeded the additional cost relative to the alternative of providing places in public schools.

3.3 Lessons

The evaluations we have described offer both substantive and methodological lessons. School participation can be substantially increased through implementing inexpensive health programs, reducing the costs of school to households, or providing school meals. Given the features of the education system in Kenya, which like many other developing countries has a curriculum focused on the strongest students, limited teacher incentives, and suboptimal budget allocation, simply providing more resources may have a limited impact on school quality. A remedial education program in India suggests that it is possible to improve student test scores substantially at a very low cost. Decentralizing budgets to school committees or providing teacher incentives based on test scores had little impact in Kenya, but a school choice program in Colombia yielded dramatic benefits for participants.

We review some of the methodological lessons that can be drawn from the examples discussed.

3.3.1   Results from Randomized Evaluations Can Be Quite Different from those Drawn from Retrospective Evaluations

As seen in the studies of textbooks and flip charts in Kenya, estimates from prospective randomized evaluations can often be quite different from the effects estimated in a retrospective framework, suggesting that omitted-variable bias is a serious concern (Glewwe, Ilias, and Kremer 2003). Similar disparities between retrospective and prospective randomized estimates arise in studies of the impact of deworming in Kenya (Miguel and Kremer 2003a) and the impact of social networks on the take-up of deworming drugs (Miguel and Kremer 2003b).

Comparative studies that estimate a program's impact using experimental methods and then reestimate impact using one or several different nonexperimental methods suggest that omitted-variable bias is a significant problem beyond just the examples mentioned here. Although we are not aware of any systematic review of studies in developing countries, one recent study in developed countries suggests that omitted-variable bias is a major problem when nonexperimental methods are used (Glazerman, Levy, and Meyers 2002). This study assessed both experimental and nonexperimental methods in the context of welfare, job training, and employment service programs and found that nonexperimental estimators often produce results dramatically different from those of randomized evaluations, that the estimated bias is often large, and that no strategy seems to perform consistently well.[5]

Future research along these lines would be valuable, as such comparative studies can help to show the extent to which the biases of retrospective estimates are significant. However, when the comparison group for the nonexperimental portions of these comparative studies is decided ex post, the evaluator may be able to pick from a variety of plausible comparison groups, some of which may have results that match experimental estimates and some of which may not. (This is also an issue for retrospective studies in regard to problems with publication bias.) Possible ways of addressing these concerns in the future include conducting nonexperimental evaluations first, before the results of randomized evaluations are released, or having researchers conduct blind nonexperimental evaluations without knowledge of the results of randomized evaluations or other nonexperimental studies.

3.3.2   Randomized Evaluations Are Often Feasible

As is clear from the examples discussed in this chapter, randomized evaluations are feasible and have been conducted successfully. They are labor intensive and costly, but no more so than other data collection activities. Political economy concerns may sometimes make it difficult not to implement a program in the entire population. For example, Opportunidades, the urban version of PRO-GRESA, will not start with a randomized evaluation because of the strong opposition to delaying access to the program. Such concerns can be tackled at several levels. For example, when financial or administrative constraints necessitate phasing in programs over time, randomization may be the fairest way of determining the order of phase-in.

3.3.3   NGOs Are Well Suited to Conduct Randomized Evaluations, But Will Require Technical Assistance (for example, from Academics) and Outside Financing

Governments are not the only vehicles through which randomized evaluations can be organized. Indeed, the evidence presented in this chapter suggests that one possible model is that of evaluation of NGO projects. Unlike governments, NGOs are not expected to serve entire populations. Even small NGOs can substantially affect budgets in developing countries. Given that many NGOs exist and that they frequently seek out new projects, it is often relatively straightforward to find NGOs willing to conduct randomized evaluations; hitches are more often logistical than philosophical.

For example, the set of recent studies conducted in Kenya has been carried out through a collaboration with the Kenyan NGO Internationaal Christelijk Steunfonds (ICS) Africa. ICS was keenly interested in using randomized evaluations to see the impact its programs are having, as well in sharing credible evaluation results with other stakeholders and policymakers. A second example is the collaboration between the Indian NGO Pratham and MIT researchers, which led to the evaluations of the remedial education and computer-assisted learning programs (Banerjee et al. 2003). This collaboration was initiated when Pratham was seeking partners to evaluate its programs. Pratham understood the value of randomization and was able to convey the importance of such evaluations to the teachers involved in the project.

However, although NGOs are well placed to conduct randomized evaluations, it is less reasonable to expect them to finance these evaluations. The evaluations of the ICS deworming programs were made possible by financial support from the World Bank, the Partnership for Child Development, U.S. National Institutes of Health, and the MacArthur Foundation. In the case of the Indian educational programs, Pratham was able to find a corporate sponsor; India's second-largest bank, ICICI Bank, was keenly interested in evaluating the impact of the program and helped to finance part of the evaluation. In general, given that accurate estimates of program effects are international public goods, randomized evaluations should be financed internationally.

3.3.4   Costs Can Be Reduced and Comparability Enhanced by Conducting a Series of Evaluations in the Same Area

Once staff are trained, they can work on multiple projects. Since data collection is the most costly element of these evaluations, cross-cutting the sample can also dramatically reduce costs. For example, many of the programs seeking to increase school participation were implemented in the same area and by the same organization. The teacher incentives (Glewwe, Ilias, and Kremer 2003) and textbook (Kremer, Moulin, and Namunyu 2002) programs were evaluated in the same one hundred schools: one group had textbooks only, one had textbooks and incentives, one had incentives only, and one had neither. The effect of the incentive program should thus be interpreted as the effect of an incentive program conditional on half the schools having extra textbooks. In India, a computer-assisted learning program was implemented in Vadodara in the same set of schools as the remedial education study.

This tactic must take into account potential interactions between programs (which can be estimated if the sample is large enough) and may not be appropriate if one program makes the schools atypical.

3.3.5   Randomized Evaluations Have a Number of Limitations, But Many of These Limitations Also Apply to Other Techniques

Many of the limitations of randomized evaluations also apply to other techniques. Here we review four issues that affect both randomized and nonrandomized evaluations (sample selection bias, attrition bias, spillover effects, and behavioral responses) and argue that randomized methods often allow easier correction for these limitations than do nonrandomized methods.

Sample selection problems could arise if factors other than random assignment influence program allocation. For example, parents may move their children out of a school without the program into a school with the program. Conversely, individuals allocated to a treatment group may not receive the treatment (for example, because they decide not to take up the program). Even if randomized methods have been used and the intended allocation of the program was random, the actual allocation may not be. This problem can be addressed through intention to treat (ITT) methods or by using random assignment as an instrument of variables for actual assignment. Although the initial assignment does not guarantee in this case that someone is actually in either the program or the comparison group, in most cases it is at least more likely that someone is in the program group if he or she was initially allocated to it. The researcher can thus compare outcomes in the initially assigned group and scale up the difference by dividing it by the difference in the probability of receiving the treatment in those two groups, to obtain the local average treatment effect estimate (Imbens and Angrist 1994). Methods such as ITT estimates allow selection problems to be addressed fairly easily in the context of randomized evaluations, but it is often much more difficult to make these corrections in the case of a retrospective analysis.

A second issue affecting both randomized and nonrandomized evaluations is differential attrition in the treatment and the comparison groups: those who participate in the program may be less likely to move or otherwise drop out of the sample than those who do not. For example, the two-teacher program analyzed by Banerjee and others (2001) increased school attendance and reduced dropout rates. This means that when a test was administered in the schools, more children were present in the program schools than in the comparison schools. If children who are prevented from dropping out by the program are the weakest in the class, the comparison between the test scores of children in treatment and control schools may be biased downward. Statistical techniques can be used to bound the potential bias, but the ideal is to try to limit attrition as much as possible. For example, in the evaluation of the remedial education program in India (Banerjee et al. 2003), an attempt was made to track down all children and administer the test to them even if they had dropped out of school. Only children who had left for their home village were not tested. As a result, the attrition rate remained relatively high but did not differ between the treatment and comparison schools, increasing confidence in the estimates.

Third, programs may create spillover effects on people who have themselves not been treated. These spillovers may be physical, as found for the Kenyan deworming program by Miguel and Kremer (2003a) when deworming interferes with disease transmission and thus reduces worm infection among both children in the program schools who did not receive the medicine and children in neighboring schools. Such spillovers might also operate through prices, as when the provision of school meals leads competing local schools to reduce school fees (Vermeersch 2002).

Finally, there might also be learning and imitation effects (Duflo and Saez 2003; Miguel and Kremer 2003b).

If such spillovers are global (for example, due to changes in world prices), total program impacts will be difficult to identify with any methodology. However, if such spillovers are local, then randomization at the level of groups can allow estimation of the total program effect within groups and can generate sufficient variation in local treatment density to measure spillovers across groups. For example, the solution in the case of the deworming study was to choose the school (rather than the pupils within a school) as the unit of randomization (Miguel and Kremer 2003a) and to look at the number of treatment and comparison schools within neighborhoods. Of course, this requires a larger sample size.

One issue that may not be as easily dealt with is that the provision of inputs might temporarily increase morale among students and teachers, and hence improve performance. While this would bias randomized evaluations, it would also bias fixed-effect or difference-in-difference estimates. However, it is unclear how serious an issue this is in practice, whereas we know that selection is a serious concern.

In summary, while randomized evaluation is not a bullet-proof strategy, the potential for biases is well known and can often be corrected. This stands in contrast to biases of most other types of studies, where the bias due to the nonrandom treatment assignments often cannot be signed nor estimated.

3.3.6 Publication Bias Appears to Be Substantial with Retrospective Studies; Randomized Evaluations Can Help Address Publication Bias Problems, But Institutions Are Also Needed

Publication bias is a particularly important issue that must be addressed. Positive results naturally tend to receive a large amount of publicity: agencies that implement programs seek publicity for their successful projects, and academics are much more interested in and able to publish positive results than modest or insignificant results. However, clearly many programs fail, and publication bias will be substantial if positive results are much more likely to be published. Available evidence suggests the publication bias problem is severe (DeLong and Lang 1992) and especially significant with studies that employ nonexperimental methods.

Publication bias is likely to be a particular problem with retrospective studies. Ex post, the researchers or evaluators define their own comparison group and thus may be able to pick a variety of plausible comparison groups; in particular, researchers obtaining negative results with retrospective techniques are likely to try different approaches or not to publish. In the case of "natural experiments" and instrumental variable estimates, publication bias may actually more than compensate for the reduction in bias caused by the use of an instrumental variable, because these estimates tend to have larger standard errors and because researchers looking for significant results will select only large estimates. For example, Ashenfelter, Harmon, and Oosterbeek (1999) show that there is strong evidence of publication bias in instrumental variables-based estimates of the returns to education: on average, the estimates with larger standard errors also tend to be larger. This accounts for most of the oft-cited result that instrumental estimates of the returns to education are higher than ordinary-least-squares estimates.

In contrast, randomized evaluations commit in advance to a particular comparison group: once the work is done to conduct a prospective randomized evaluation, the results are usually documented and published even if the results suggest quite modest effects or even no effects at all.

As we will discuss in the next section, it is important to put institutions in place to ensure negative results are disseminated. Such a system is already in place for medical trial results, and creating a similar system for documenting evaluations of social programs would help to alleviate the problem of publication bias. Beyond presenting a clearer picture of which interventions have worked and which have not, this type of institution would provide the level of transparency necessary for systematic literature reviews to be less biased in their conclusions about the efficacy of particular policies and programs.

3.3.7 Although Any Given Randomized Evaluation Is Conducted within a Specific Framework with Unique Circumstances, Randomized Evaluations Can Shed Light on General Issues

Without a theory of why a program has the effect it has, generalizing from one well-executed randomized evaluation may be unwarranted. But similar issues of generalizability arise no matter what evaluation technique is being used. One way to learn about generalizability is to encourage adapted replications of randomized evaluations in key domains of interest in several different settings. It will always be possible that a program that failed in one context would have succeeded in another, but adapted replications, guided by a theory of why the program was effective, will go a long way toward alleviating this concern. This is one area where international organizations, already present in most countries, can play a key role. Such an opportunity was seized in implementing adapted replications of PROGRESA in other Latin American countries. Encouraged by the success of PROGRESA in Mexico, the World Bank encouraged (and financed) Mexico's neighbors to adopt similar programs. Some of these programs have included randomized evaluations (for example, the Programa de Asignación Familiar program in Honduras) and are being evaluated.

Often the results of the first phase of a project may be difficult to interpret because of circumstances that are unique to that phase: a project may have failed as the result of implementation problems that could be avoided later in the project, or a project may have succeeded because it received more resources than a project in a more realistic situation or less favorable context. Even if the choice of the comparison and treatment groups ensures the internal validity of estimates, any method of evaluation is subject to problems with external validity due to the specific circumstances of implementation. That is, the results may not be able to be generalized to other contexts.

One problem specific to randomized evaluations is that members of either the treatment or comparison group could potentially change their behavior, due not to the intervention but simply to the fact that they would know that they are a part of a randomized evaluation. Of course, to the extent that both groups change their behavior in the same way, this will not lead to bias. It is also perhaps less likely that this will occur immediately after the introduction of the intervention and over a long period.

One way to address questions about the external validity of any particular study, whether it is a randomized evaluation or not, is to implement adapted replications of successful (and potentially unsuccessful) programs in different contexts. Such adapted replications have two advantages: first, in the process of transplanting a program, circumstances will change and robust programs will show their effectiveness by surviving these changes; second, obtaining several estimates in different contexts will provide some information about whether the program has notably different impacts on different groups. Replication of the initial phase of a study in a new context does not imply delaying full-scale implementation of the program if that is justified on the basis of existing knowledge. More often than not, however, the introduction of the program can proceed only in stages, and the evaluation requires only that participants be phased into the program in random order. In addition, such adapted replications can be used to check whether program effects within samples vary with covariance. For example, suppose that the effect of a given program is smaller in schools with good teachers; one might consider whether in a different setting with much better teachers, the effect would be smaller.

One example is the work in India of Bobonis, Miguel, and Sharma (2002), who conducted an adapted replication of the deworming study in Kenya. The baseline revealed that although worm infection was present, the levels of infection were substantially lower than in Kenya (in the India case, "only" 27 percent of children suffered from some form of worm infection). However, 70 percent of children had moderate to severe anemia, and thus the program was modified to include iron supplementation. The program was administered through a network of preschools in urban India. After a year of providing treatment, the researchers found a nearly 50 percent reduction in moderate to severe anemia, large weight gains, and a 7 percent reduction in absenteeism among four to six year olds (though not for younger children). Their findings support the conclusion of the deworming research in Kenya (Miguel and Kremer 2003a) that school health programs may be one of the most cost-effective ways of increasing school participation and, importantly, suggest that this conclusion may be relevant in low-income countries outside Africa.

It is worth noting that the exogenous variation created by randomization can be used to help identify a structural model. Attanasio, Meghir, and Santiago (2001) and Berhman, Sengupta, and Todd (2002) are two examples of using this exercise in combination with the PROGRESA data to predict possible effects of varying the schedule of transfers. For example, Attanasio, Meghir, and Santiago (2001) found that the randomized component of the PRO-GRESA data induced extremely useful exogenous variation that helped in the identification of a richer and more flexible structural model. These studies rest on assumptions that one is free to believe or not, but at least they are freed of some assumptions by the presence of this exogenous variation.

The more general point is that randomized evaluations do not preclude the use of theory or assumptions: in fact, they generate data and variation that can be useful in identifying some aspects of these theories. For example, evaluations suggest that the Kenyan educational system is heavily geared toward top students and that reallocating budgets within primary education could lead to considerably better outcomes, pointing to perverse incentives created by Kenya's mix of local and national school finance (see Kremer, Moulin, and Namunyu 2002; Glewwe, Kremer, and Moulin 2002).

3.4 The Role International Agencies Can Play

In this section we review an example of current practice that failed to provide opportunities for rigorous evaluations due to a lack of planning, then present some political economy arguments for why randomized evaluations are so rare, and finally discuss how international agencies can support the use of credible evaluation methods, including randomized evaluations.

3.4.1 The District Primary Education Program: An Example of Lost Opportunity

The District Primary Education Program (DPEP) in India, the largest World Bank–sponsored education program, is an example of a large program with potentially interesting evaluations that have been jeopardized by lack of planning.[6] DPEP was meant to be a showcase example of the ability to go to scale with education reform (Pandey 2000). It is a comprehensive program involving teacher training, inputs, and classrooms that seeks to improve the performance of public education. Districts are generally given a high level of discretion in how to spend the additional resources.

Despite the apparent commitment to a careful evaluation of the program, several features make a convincing impact evaluation of DPEP impossible. First, the districts were selected according to two criteria: low level of achievement (as measured by low female literacy rates) and high potential for improvement. In particular, the first districts chosen to receive the program were selected "on the basis of their ability to show success in a reasonable time frame" (Pandey 2000, quoted in Case 2001). The combination of these two elements in the selection process makes clear that any comparison between the level of achievement of DPEP districts and non-DPEP districts would probably be biased downward, while any comparison between improvement of achievement between DPEP and non-DPEP districts (difference-in-difference) would probably be biased upward. This has not prevented the DPEP from putting enormous emphasis on monitoring and evaluation: large amounts of data were collected and numerous reports commissioned. However, the data collection process was conducted only in DPEP districts. These data will be useful only for before-and-after comparisons, which clearly do not make sense in an economy undergoing rapid growth and transformation. A researcher who found a credible identification strategy would have to use existing data, such as census or National Sample Survey data.

3.4.2 Why Are Randomized Evaluations So Rare? Some Political Economy Arguments

We have argued that the problems of omitted-variable bias that randomized evaluations are designed to address are real and that randomized evaluations are feasible. They are no more costly than other types of surveys and are far cheaper than pursuing ineffective policies. So why are they so rare? Cook (2001) attributes their rarity in education to the postmodern culture in American education schools, which is hostile to the traditional conception of causation that underlies statistical implementation. Pritchett (2002) argues that program advocates systematically mislead swing voters into believing exaggerated estimates of program impacts. Advocates block randomized evaluations since they would reveal programs' true impacts to voters.

A complementary explanation is that policymakers are not systematically fooled but rather have difficulty gauging the quality of evidence in part because advocates can suppress unfavorable evaluation results. Suppose retrospective regressions yield estimated program effects equal to the true effect plus measurement error plus a bias term, possibly with mean of zero. Program advocates then select the highest estimates to present to policymakers and any opponents select the most negative estimates. Knowing this, policymakers rationally discount these estimates. For example, if advocates present a study showing 100 percent rate of return, the policymaker might assume the true return is 10 percent. In this environment there is little incentive to conduct randomized evaluations. Since the resulting estimates include no bias term, they are unlikely to be high enough or low enough that advocates will present them to policymakers. Even if results are presented to policymakers, those policymakers unable to gauge the quality of particular studies will discount them. Why fund a project that a randomized evaluation suggests has a 25 percent rate of return when advocates of competing projects claim a 100 percent rate of return?

3.4.3   Evaluation in International Organizations

International organizations could play several roles in promoting and financing rigorous evaluations. It is almost certainly counterproductive to demand that all projects be subject to impact evaluations. Clearly all projects need to be monitored to make sure that they actually happen and to avoid misuse of funds. However, some programs simply cannot be evaluated with the methods discussed in this chapter. And even among projects that could potentially be evaluated, not all need impact evaluations. In fact, the value of a poorly identified impact evaluation is very low, and its cost in terms of credibility is high, especially if international organizations take a leading role in promoting quality evaluation. A first objective is thus to cut down on the number of wasteful evaluations; any proposed impact evaluation should be reviewed by a committee before any money is spent on data collection. The committee's responsibility would be to assess the ability of the evaluation to deliver reliable causal estimates of the project's impact. A second objective would be to conduct credible evaluations in key areas. In consultation with a body of researchers and practitioners, each organization should determine key areas where it will promote impact evaluations. Randomized evaluations could also be set up in other areas when the opportunity occurs.

Credible impact evaluations require a great deal of work, and their benefits extend far beyond the organization conducting the evaluation; these factors mean that incentives to conduct rigorous evaluations are less than socially optimal. One promising remedy is to embed within the institutional framework of international agencies structures that will provide sufficient incentives for evaluators. Given the current scarcity of randomized evaluations within the institutional environment of international organizations, there may be scope for setting up a specialized unit to encourage, conduct, and finance rigorous impact evaluations and disseminate the results. As we will briefly discuss, the potential for such a unit is tremendous: there exists a ready-made potential supply of evaluators within both the international agencies and academia and collaborations with NGOs, offering many opportunities for evaluating policies of wide relevance.

Such an evaluation unit would encourage data collection and the study of true natural randomized evaluations with program-induced randomization. Randomized evaluations are not the only method of conducting good impact evaluations. However, such other evaluations are conducted much more routinely, while randomized evaluations are conducted much too rarely in the light of their value and the opportunities to conduct them. Part of the problem is that no one considers conducting such evaluations to be their job, and hence no one invests sufficiently to conduct them. In addition, all evaluations have common features and thus would benefit from a specialized unit with specific expertise. Since impact evaluations generate international public goods, the unit should have a budget that would be used to finance and conduct rigorous evaluations of internal and external projects. The unit should conduct its own evaluation projects in the key areas identified by the organization.

The unit should also work with partners, especially NGOs and academics. For projects submitted from outside the unit, a committee within the unit (potentially with assisted by external reviewers) could receive proposals from within the organization or from outsiders, and from there choose projects to support. The unit could also encourage replication of important evaluations by sending out calls for specific proposals. The project could be conducted in partnership with people from the unit or other researchers (academics, in particular). The unit could provide both financial and technical support for the project, with dedicated staff and researchers. Over time, on the basis of the acquired experience, the unit could serve as a more general resource center by developing and diffusing training modules, tools, and guidelines (survey and testing instruments, as well as software that can be used for data entry and to facilitate randomization—similar in spirit to tools produced by other units in the World Bank) for randomized evaluation. The unit could also sponsor training sessions for practitioners.

Another role the unit could serve, after establishing a reputation for quality, is that of a dissemination agency (a clearinghouse of some sort). To be useful, evaluation results must be accessible to practitioners both within and outside development agencies. A key role of the unit could be to conduct systematic searches for all impact evaluations, assess their reliability, and publish the results in the form of policy briefs and in a readily accessible searchable database. The database would ideally include all information that could be useful in interpreting the results (estimates, sample size, region and time, type of project, cost, cost-benefit analysis, caveats, and so forth), as well as references to related studies. The database could include both randomized and nonrandomized impact evaluations satisfying some criteria, provided that the different types of evaluation are clearly labeled. Evaluations would need to satisfy minimum reporting requirements to be included in the database, and all projects supported by the unit would have to be included in the database, whatever their results.

Such a database would help alleviate publication bias, which may be substantial if positive results are more likely to be published. Academic journals may not be interested in publishing the results of failed programs, but from the policymakers' point of view, knowledge about negative results is just as useful as knowledge about successful projects. Comparable requirements are placed on all federally funded medical projects in the United States. Ideally, over time, the database would become a basic reference for organizations and governments, especially as they seek funding for their projects. This database could kick-start a virtuous circle, with donors demanding credible evaluations before funding or continuing projects, more evaluations being conducted, and the general quality of evaluation work rising.

3.5 Conclusion

Rigorous and systemic evaluations have the potential to leverage the impact of international organizations well beyond simply their ability to finance programs. Credible impact evaluations are international public goods: the benefits of knowing that a program works or does not work extend well beyond the organization or the country implementing the program.[7] Programs that have been shown to be successful can be adapted for use in other countries and scaled up within countries, while unsuccessful programs can be abandoned. Through promoting, encouraging, and financing rigorous evaluations (such as credible randomized evaluations) of the programs they support, as well as of programs supported by others, the international organizations can provide guidance to the international organizations themselves, as well as other donors, governments, and NGOs, in the ongoing search for successful programs. Moreover, by credibly establishing which programs work and which do not, the international agencies can counteract skepticism about the possibility of spending aid effectively and build long-term support for development. Just as randomized trials revolutionized medicine in the twentieth century, they have the potential to revolutionize social policy during the twenty-first.

Acknowledgments

This chapter draws on work that each of us has done in the field with numerous coauthors, primarily in India and Kenya, respectively, and on pieces we have written synthesizing this work and discussing issues related to randomized evaluations (Duflo 2004, Kremer 2003). Among other collaborators, we thank Josh Angrist, Abhijit Banerjee, Eric Bettinger, Erik Bloom, Raghabendra Chattopadhyay, Shawn Cole, Paul Glewwe, Nauman Ilias, Suraj Jacob, Elizabeth King, Leigh Linden, Ted Miguel, Sylvie Moulin, Robert Namunyu, Christel Vermeersch, and Eric Zitzewitz. We thank Ted Miguel for extremely detailed and useful comments. We are particularly grateful to Heidi Williams for outstanding research assistance. We are also very grateful to François Bourguignon, Anne Case, Angus Deaton, Rachel Glennerster, Emily Oster, and Paul Schultz.

Notes

1. There are numerous excellent technical and nontechnical surveys of these techniques as well as their value and limitations. See Angrist and Krueger 1999, 2001; Card 1999; Meyer 1995.

2. Angrist and Lavy (1999) note that parents who discover they received a bad draw in the "enrollment lottery" (e.g., an enrollment of thirty-eight) might then move their children out of the public school system and into private schools. However, as Angrist and Lavy discuss, private elementary schooling is rare in Israel outside the ultraorthodox community.

3. By school participation, we denote a comprehensive measure of school participation: a pupil is considered a participant if she or he is present in school on a given day and a nonparticipant if she or he is not in school on that day.

4. Most of these papers are accessible on the IFPRI Web site www.ifpri.org.

5. One recent study not included in the analysis of Glazerman, Levy, and Meyers (2002) is that of Buddlemeyer and Skoufias (2003). Buddlemeyer and Skoufias use randomized evaluation results as a benchmark to examine the performance of regression discontinuity design for evaluating the impact of the PROGRESA program on child health and school attendance and find the performance of regression discontinuity design in this case to be good.

6. Case (2001) gives an illuminating discussion of the program and the features that make its evaluation impossible.

7. In fact, the benefits of a credible evaluation are often negative for the person or organization promoting the program.

References

Angrist, Joshua, Eric Bettinger, Erik Bloom, Elizabeth King, and Michael Kremer. 2002. "Vouchers for Private Schooling in Colombia: Evidence from a Randomized Natural Experiment." *American Economic Review* 92(5):1535–1558.

Angrist, Joshua, and Alan Krueger. 1999. "Empirical Strategies in Labor Economics." In Orley Ashenfelter and David Card, eds., *Handbook of Labor Economics*, Vol. 3A. Amsterdam: North-Holland.

Angrist, Joshua, and Alan Krueger. 2001. "Instrumental Variables and the Search for Identification: From Supply and Demand to Natural Experiments." *Journal of Economic Perspectives* 15(4):69–85.

Angrist, Joshua, and Victor Lavy. 1999. "Using Maimonides' Rule to Estimate the Effect of Class Size on Scholastic Achievement." *Quarterly Journal of Economics* 114(2):533–575.

Ashenfelter, Orley, Colm Harmon, and Hessel Oosterbeek. 2000. "A Review of Estimates of Schooling/Earnings Relationship, with Tests for Publication Bias." NBER Working Paper 7457. Cambridge, Mass.: National Bureau of Economic Research.

Attanasio, Orazio, Costas Meghir, and Ana Santiago. 2001. "Education Choices in Mexico: Using a Structural Model and a Randomized Experiment to Evaluate PROGRESA." Mimeo., Inter-American Development Bank.

Banerjee, Abhijit, Shawn Cole, Esther Duflo, and Leigh Linden. 2003. "Improving the Quality of Education in India: Evidence from Three Randomized Experiments." Mimeo., Massachusetts Institute of Technology.

Banerjee, Abhijit, Suraj Jacob, and Michael Kremer, with Jenny Lanjouw and Peter Lanjouw. 2001. "Promoting School Participation in Rural Rajasthan: Results from Some Prospective Trials." Mimeo., Massachusetts Institute of Technology.

Behrman, Jere, Piyali Sengupta, and Petra Todd. 2002. "Progressing through PROGESA: An Impact Assessment of a School Subsidy Experiment in Mexico." Mimeo., University of Pennsylvania.

Bertrand, Marianne, Esther Duflo, and Sendhil Mullainathan. 2002. "How Much Should We Trust Difference in Differences Estimates?" NBER Working Paper 8841. Cambridge, Mass.: National Bureau of Economic Research.

Besley, Timothy, and Anne Case. 2000. "Unnatural Experiments? Estimating the Incidence of Endogenous Policies." *Economic Journal* 110(467):F672–F694.

Bobonis, Gustavo, Edward Miguel, and Charu Sharma. 2002. "Iron Supplementation and Early Childhood Development: A Randomized Evaluation in India." Mimeo., University of California, Berkeley.

Buddlemeyer, Hielke, and Emmanuel Skofias. 2003. "An Evaluation on the Performance of Regression Discontinuity Design on PROGRESA." Discussion Paper 827. Bonn, Germany: Institute for Study of Labor.

Campbell, Donald T. 1969. "Reforms as Experiments." *American Psychologist* 24:407–429.

Card, David. 1999. "The Causal Effect of Education on Earnings." In Orley Ashenfelter and David Card, eds., *Handbook of Labor Economics*, Vol. 3A. Amsterdam: North-Holland.

Case, Anne. 2001. "The Primacy of Education." Mimeo., Princeton University.

Cook, Thomas D. 2001. "Reappraising the Arguments Against Randomized Experiments in Education: An Analysis of the Culture of Evaluation in American Schools of Education." Mimeo., Northwestern University.

DeLong, J. Bradford, and Kevin Lang. 1992. "Are All Economic Hypotheses False?" *Journal of Political Economy* 100(6):1257–1272.

Duflo, Esther. 2001. "Schooling and Labor Market Consequences of School Construction in Indonesia: Evidence from an Unusual Policy Experiment." *American Economic Review* 91(4):795–814.

Duflo, Esther. 2004. "Scaling Up and Evaluation." In Francois Bourguignon and Bais Pleskovic, eds., *Accelerating Development*. Washington, D.C. and Oxford: World Bank and Oxford University Press.

Duflo, Esther, and Emmanuel Saez. 2003. "The Role of Information and Social Interactions in Retirement Plan Decisions: Evidence from a Randomized Experiment." *Quarterly Journal of Economics* 118(3):815–842.

Gertler, Paul J., and Simone Boyce. 2001. "An Experiment in Incentive-Based Welfare: The Impact of PROGRESA on Health in Mexico." Mimeo., University of California, Berkeley.

Glazerman, Steven, Dan Levy, and David Meyers. 2002. "Nonexperimental Replications of Social Experiments: A Systematic Review." Interim Report/Discussion Paper. Mathematica Policy Research.

Glewwe, Paul, Nauman Ilias, and Michael Kremer. 2003. "Teacher Incentives." NBER Working Paper 9671. Cambridge, Mass.: National Bureau of Economic Research.

Glewwe, Paul, Michael Kremer, and Sylvie Moulin. 2002. "Textbooks and Test Scores: Evidence from a Prospective Evaluation in Kenya." Mimeo., Harvard University.

Glewwe, Paul, Michael Kremer, Sylvie Moulin, and Eric Zitzewitz. 2004. "Retrospective vs. Prospective Analyses of School Inputs: The Case of Flip Charts in Kenya." *Journal of Development Economics* 74(1):251–268.

Hanushek, Eric A. 1995. "Interpreting Recent Research on Schooling in Developing Countries." *World Bank Research Observer* 10:227–246.

Heckman, James, Hidehiko Ichimura, Jeffrey Smith, and Petra Todd. 1998. "Characterizing Selection Bias Using Experimental Data." *Econometrica* 66(5):1017–1098.

Heckman, James, Hidehiko Ichimura, and Petra Todd. 1997. "Matching as an Econometric Evaluation Estimator: Evidence from Evaluating a Job Training Program." *Review of Economic Studies* 64(4):605–654.

Heckman, James, Robert Lalonde, and Jeffrey Smith. 1999. "The Economics and Econometrics of Active Labor Market Programs." In Orley Ashenfelter and David Card, eds., *Handbook of Labor Economics*, Vol. 3.O. Amsterdam: North-Holland.

Heckman, James, Lance Lochner, and Christopher Taber. 1998. "General Equilibrium Treatment Effects: A Study of Tuition Policy." NBER Working Paper 6426. Cambridge, Mass.: National Bureau of Economic Research.

Imbens, Guido, and Joshua Angrist. 1994. "Identification and Estimation of Local Average Treatment Effects." *Econometrica* 62(2):467–475.

Kremer, Michael. 2003. "Randomized Evaluations of Educational Programs in Developing Countries: Some Lessons." *American Economic Review Papers and Proceedings* 93(2):102–115.

Kremer, Michael, Sylvie Moulin, and Robert Namunyu. 2002. "Decentralization: a Cautionary Tale." Mimeo., Harvard University.

LaLonde, Robert. 1986. "Evaluating the Econometric Evaluations of Training with Experimental Data." *American Economic Review* 76(4):604–620.

Meyer, Bruce D. 1995. "Natural and Quasi-Experiments in Economics." *Journal of Business and Economic Statistics* 13(2):151–161.

Miguel, Edward, and Michael Kremer. 2004. "Worms: Identifying Impacts on Education and Health in the Presence of Treatment Externalities." *Econometrica* 72(1):159–217.

Miguel, Edward, and Michael Kremer. 2003. "Social Networks and Learning about Health in Kenya." Mimeo., Harvard University.

Morduch, Jonathan. 1998. "Does Microfinance Really Help the Poor? New Evidence from Flagship Programs in Bangladesh." Mimeo., Princeton University.

Narayanan, Deepa (ed.) 2000. *Empowerment and Poverty Reduction: A Sourcebook*. Washington, D.C.: World Bank.

Pandey, Raghaw Sharan. 2000. *Going to Scale with Education Reform: India's District Primary Education Program, 1995–99*. Washington, D.C.: World Bank.

Pitt, Mark, and Shahidur Khandker. 1998. "The Impact of Group-Based Credit Programs on Poor Households in Bangladesh: Does the Gender of Participants Matter?" *Journal of Political Economy* 106(5):958–996.

Pritchett, Lant. 2002. "It Pays to Be Ignorant: A Simple Political Economy of Rigorous Program Evaluation." *Journal of Policy Reform* 5(4):251–269.

Rosenbaum, Paul R. 1995. "Observational Studies." New York: Springer.

Sen, Amartya. 2002. "The Pratichi Report." New Delhi: Pratichi India Trust.

Shultz, T. Paul. 2004. "School Subsidies for the Poor: Evaluating the Mexican PROGRESA Poverty Program." *Journal of Development Economics* 74(1):199–250.

Vermeersch, Christel. 2002. "School Meals, Educational Achievement, and School Competition: Evidence from a Randomized Experiment." Mimeo., Harvard University.

4 It Pays to Be Ignorant: A Simple Political Economy of Rigorous Program Evaluation

Lant Pritchett

Nor certitude, nor peace, nor help for pain;
And here we are as on a darkling plain
Swept with confused alarms of struggle and flight
Where ignorant armies clash by night
—Matthew Arnold, "Dover Beach"

It pays to be ignorant, to be dumb, to be dense, to be ignorant.
—TV game show *It Pays to Be Ignorant* (1949) theme song

This chapter was motivated by my dozen years in the World Bank, a large, international, quasi-public, bureaucracy whose objective is "development" and whose instrument is providing loans to developing-country governments. The organization's lending activities have spanned the range: from dam construction to family planning to microcredit to steel mills to "social funds" to macroeconomic stabilization to land reform. The World Bank is for the most part staffed by internationally recruited, high-quality, highly trained, well-meaning, and experienced professionals and is arguably the premiere development institution. And yet nearly all World Bank discussions of policies or project design had the character of "ignorant armies clashing by night." There was heated debate among advocates of various activities but very rarely any firm evidence presented and considered about the likely impact of the proposed actions. Certainly in my experience, there was never any definitive evidence that would inform decisions of funding one broad set of activities versus another (e.g., basic education versus road construction or vaccinations versus macroeconomic reform) or even funding one instrument versus another (e.g., vaccinations versus public education about hygiene to improve health, textbook reform versus teacher training to improve educational quality). How can this combination of brilliant, well-meaning people and ignorant organization be a stable equilibrium?

In the United States no one can market a prescription medicine for male pattern baldness without evidence it is "safe and effective." The accepted regulatory standard evidence of safety and effectiveness is a controlled, randomized, double-blind evaluation. Yet the nonprofit market is flooded with a continual new stream of proposed programs and interventions. Few public sector actions, even those of tremendous importance, are ever evaluated to the standard required of even the most trivial medicine. To take just one example, in the United States, there is a huge and continuing debate over the importance of smaller class sizes for academic performance in primary and secondary education. One side of the debate points to the fact that per pupil expenditures in public schools have doubled while test scores have changed very little, and to many studies that find no effect of class size to argue that it is plausible that hundred of billions of dollars of educational resources have been misallocated. The other side points to evidence that smaller class sizes are associated with stronger performance. The point is not that one side is obviously right and the other obviously wrong. The point is that brilliant, well-meaning people can legitimately disagree on so fundamental a question as class size impacts on educational quality—yet there is no similar debate on the efficacy of treatments for male pattern baldness.

There is no question that estimating the impact of public activities on outcomes is harder than the science of hair loss, but it is not impossible. The key problem with evaluating the impact of any public program is that it depends not just on facts but also on a counterfactual. Even if what happened to program participants before and after the program is well documented, to know the impact of the program, one has to know what would have happened to the program participants in the absence of the program. For very good reasons, the gold standard of program evaluation is controlled experiment in which participation (or access to) the interventions is randomized.

Since this is the gold standard, the scarcity of this gold constitutes a major puzzle. That the exceptions are so well known proves the rule:

• Head Start is a program that consistently receives favorable attention, much of it based on a randomized evaluation (actually not of Head Start but of a more intensive program, the Perry Pre-School experiment) involving only 123 children (Schwienhart, Barnes, and Weikart 1993; Barnett 1996).

• In a search on the Econlit, there are twenty-nine references to the Job Training and Partnership Act (JPTA). Why? Not because it was ever a particularly large or important federal program (in the 1990s its budget was around US$1.6 billion), but Title II of the JPTA provided for the largest randomized evaluation of training, and hence analysts use the data over and over again—even though the program has ended.

• Family planning programs have existed and been promoted the world over for thirty years, motivated and supported at least in part by the belief that they lower fertility. Yet there is exactly one reliable randomized experiment (carried out in the Matlab region of Bangladesh) that plausibly demonstrates a fertility reduction impact of increased supply of contraception (Phillips et al. 1988).

• The optimal structure of insurance is an enormous policy issue, and yet there is one randomized experiment that attempted to demonstrate the impact of alternative health insurance options in the United States (Manning et al. 1987).

• "Primary health care" is a mantra widely endorsed (if not implemented) at least since the Alma Ata conference in 1978. But there is not a single rigorous evaluation demonstrating the health gains from primary health care as a public policy (Filmer, Hammer, and Pritchett 2000).[1]

• There are debates about the relative magnitude and importance of various educational inputs: Smaller class sizes? More books? Better facilities? Yet in the developing world, there are very few controlled experiments in education—and even fewer that are successfully completed and produce reliable results (Glewwe, Moulin, and Kremer 1997).

As the examples from the United States show, this is not just a development problem, but the scarcity of rigorous evaluation is particularly striking in development assistance in which donors finance discrete projects, nearly always with a monitoring and evaluation component. Yet the World Bank has lent a cumulative $100 billion, and only a handful of projects have produced compelling evidence about impacts from a reliable, randomized, evaluation.[2]

This dearth of knowledge is sufficiently striking as to deserve explanation, and common explanations casually proposed—ethical barriers, costs, and feasibility—are not sufficient. Here I construct a simple analytical model that explains both why randomized evaluations are infrequent and when evaluations can be expected.

The model focuses on the decisions faced by advocates of particular public (or nonprofit) sector activities who must mobilize funds. Advocates are the entrepreneurs of the public and nonprofit private sector. Just as with their profit-seeking counterparts in the private sector, advocates are the men and women with the passion, concern, and vision to make new things happen. Programs are typically proposed, supported, and implemented by advocates— people with strong beliefs in either the importance of a particular issue (the problem the public program addresses, such as crime, drugs, unemployment, or malnutrition) or a particular instrument (the particular solution to a problem, such as community policing, twelve-step therapy, job training, micronutrient supplementation, microcredit). Without advocates pushing to address issues and for innovative instruments—new programs, policies, treatments—the public and nonprofit sectors would be stagnant. Yet this same dynamism in the face of the intrinsic uncertainties of a complex world can lead to tensions between action and knowledge.

At the core of the model are two assumptions about evaluations and about political support for particular programs. The first assumption is that a randomized evaluation is impossible without the cooperation of the advocates responsible for program implementation so that evaluations can happen only if advocates see them in their best interest. The second is that advocates are more altruistic and care more about outcomes in their specific issue than does the general public. Given this concern for outcomes, they want to pursue the most effective instrument, and at any given level of the efficacy of the use of resources (outcome gain per dollar), they want a larger budget. If the budget is politically determined, advocates view the problem of evaluation in a dual light. On the positive side, evaluations potentially help improve program efficacy so they get more bang for the buck. But evaluations have a potential downside if they reduce political support for a larger budget for their program so they get fewer bucks.

In this model, advocates may choose ignorance over public knowledge of true program efficacy. They are better off if the true benefits are not known by the voting public even if it means they too must operate somewhat in the dark.

I build this model in three separate steps. First, I take the point of view of true believers: advocates who believe they know both the important issue and the correct instrument to address that issue. In this case, evaluations are rarely useful—and hence will be rare—because evaluations do not increase advocates' knowledge about program efficacy (as they already know) and yet they risk cutting political support.

Second, in organizations that are coalitions of advocates for the same issue (e.g., biodiversity, maternal health, basic education) but in which there is uncertainty about the efficacy of various instruments, evaluations are needed to improve efficacy of the use of organizational resources but the outcomes of these evaluations could undermine budgetary support for the organization. Third, in the most complex case, organizations are coalitions of advocates around a broad objective (e.g., development, global health) that encompass several issues and there is a problem of deciding which is the most important issue and which is the best instrument to address the issue. The political constraints imposed by the less altruistic part of the public forces this coalition of advocates into an uneasy coalition that supports ignorance in which efficacy of budget use is sacrificed to maintain budget size.

4.1 True Believers: Single-Objective, Single-Instrument Advocates

In the model I develop, there are four actors: advocates (or coalitions of advocates) and three groups of the public. In the simplest version of the model, advocates are single-objective, single-instrument advocates. That is, they know not only what is an important problem; they know the best solution. For example, population reduction is the objective and family planning is the instrument; raise welfare recipients' wages is the objective and job training is the instrument; raising the welfare of women is the objective and group microcredit is the instrument; reducing urban traffic is the objective and mass transit is the instrument; or improving child health is the objective and promotion of breast feeding is the instrument. Since these advocates believe they know the efficacy of the instrument, their only goal is to increase total expenditures on their preferred instrument.

4.1.1 Savvy Altruists

Assume that advocates:

- Believe they know the true value of program efficacy
- Believe with certainty that a rigorous evaluation will reveal that true value
- Have linear utility in program expenditures net of first-period costs[3]

Advocates take all the actions in the first period. They are the ones who initiate, administer, promote budget expansion, and perhaps evaluate programs. We assume a rigorous evaluation is impossible without advocates' cooperation. A binding requirement of rigorous evaluation is possible in this model only if it creates incentives such that advocates choose to evaluate.[4]

Advocates have only two options: "pilot and persuade" or "rigorous evaluation." If pilot and persuade is chosen, then in the first period, advocates pilot (spend just enough money on implementation to demonstrate to a reasonable person that the program is not physically impossible) and persuade (spend amount S on the dissemination of nonrigorous claims about the efficacy of the program). If "do rigorous evaluation" is chosen, the advocates implement and spend the cost of a randomized evaluation C in the first period.

In this case, the conditions for evaluation reduce to the question of whether the equilibrium chosen level of program expenditure level $E(.)$ net of costs of either persuasion or evaluation is higher with or without a rigorous evaluation:

$$Do\ evaluation\ if:\quad E^K(\alpha_{true}, \alpha_I^C) - C > E(S^*) - S^*(\alpha_I^0, \beta_I^C). \tag{4.1}$$

Which of these options is in the best interest of the advocates depends on how the level of expenditures is determined. For this, I have a simple voting model with three groups.

4.1.2 The Voting Public

After the advocates take their actions, the public votes over the level of the budget for the program. I assume the public is classified into three groups, named, for reasons that will soon be clear, core supporters hard-headed, and the middle group. The utility of these groups differs in two respects: the extent to which the program gains enter their utility (γ) and the group's belief about the program's efficacy parameter: how effective a dollar's worth of program expenditure will be in producing program gains (α).

The program efficacy parameter depends on many factors. Higher overhead costs lead to lower beneficiary impact per dollar and hence lower program efficacy. Better targeting to the poor for given dollar of benefits could raise α. Program efficacy beliefs could also reflect "specific altruism" so that group i is not indifferent between a program that delivers a dollar's worth of benefits in cash (spent as the recipient chooses) to one that delivers a dollar's worth of some good group i believes has particular merit (food for children, medical care, family planning):

$$U_i(X, E) = \gamma_i \alpha_i(.) + (1 - \gamma_i) U(X_i). \tag{4.2}$$

All three groups have exactly the same decision rule: they will vote for an additional dollar of program funding if their own utility gain from benefiting others through that program[5] exceeds the utility loss from their forgone own consumption.[6] Hence the decision rule is the same for all groups:

$$Support\ if:\quad \alpha_i > \alpha_i^{Critical} = \left(\frac{\partial U}{\partial X}\right) * \left(\frac{1 - \gamma_i}{\gamma_i}\right). \tag{4.3}$$

We assume that each group forms beliefs about program efficacy in the same way. If there has been evaluation, then all believe the efficacy is the outcome of the evaluation (this assumes the evaluation measures all the relevant dimensions of efficacy):

Table 4.1
Model structure: Key groups of the public and their distinguishing characteristics

Verbal description	Model parameter	Public		
		Core supporters	Middle	Hard-headed (economists)
Prior belief in the efficacy of the action (gain to program beneficiaries (in own group utility) per dollar expenditure)	α	High	Middle	Low
Weighting of program gains versus own consumption	γ	High	Middle	Low
Persuadability	β	High	Middle	Zero

If evaluation, beliefs are: $\alpha_i = \alpha^{RE}$. (4.4)

In the absence of an evaluation, their beliefs about program effectiveness are a combination of their initial beliefs and the amount spent by advocates on persuasion (S):[7]

If no evaluation, beliefs are: $\alpha_i = \alpha_i^0 + \beta_i * S$. (4.5)

This simple setup characterizes the three groups of the public by their weighting of program gains (γ), their initial beliefs in program efficacy (α), and how amenable their beliefs are to promotional activities of advocates, for which I use the neologism "persuadability" (table 4.1):[8]

Core supporters This groups weights program gains high relative to own consumption. There are two interpretations of this. The easier to formalize is that this is high altruism. The alternative, more cynical, perhaps more realistic, but also harder to model explanation is that core supporters are either those who consider themselves likely to be program beneficiaries or are the suppliers who will benefit from an expansion of the project. Core supporters have high initial beliefs about program efficacy and are easily swayed by persuasion.

Hard-headed This group has a relatively low prior belief about program efficacy. Economists are the prototypical hard-headed group as their models would tend to be predict low impacts of public intervention on welfare. The hard-headed are also completely unpersuadable. Their prior beliefs cannot be swayed anything less than a randomized experiment. Finally, I assume the hard-headed are also hard-hearted, so that program gains weigh less in their utility than these gains do with the other groups.

Table 4.2
Program budget outcomes under different beliefs about program efficacy

Proportion of the population supporting funding	Description of funding level	Beliefs in program efficacy
0	No program (or termination)	$\alpha_{cs} < \alpha_{CS}^C$
$F_{Core\ Supporters}$	Barebones	$\alpha_{cs} > \alpha_{CS}^C$, $\alpha_M < \alpha_M^C$
$F_{core\ supporters} + F_{middle}$	Operational	$\alpha_M > \alpha_{MS}^C$, $\alpha_{HH} < \alpha_{HH}^C$
1	Full funding	$\alpha_{HH} > \alpha_{HH}^C$

Note: α_i^C is the critical level of beliefs about program efficacy as described in equation 4.2.

Middle group   In between the core supporters and the hard-headed is the middle group, which, as the name suggests, is in between the two groups on each of the three parameters: they have modest concern for program benefits, believe public interventions can be effective, and can be swayed by evidence short of a randomized experiment.

Since we assume for simplicity the vote is over an additional dollar from each person if we express the budget in terms of dollars per person in the population, there are four possible budget outcomes (table 4.2). The outcomes depend on the proportion of each group in the population and whether for each group their beliefs about program efficacy exceed their threshold level.

4.1.3   When Will Politically Savvy Altruists Do Evaluations?

So, knowing what the voting public will do in the second period, what should the advocates do in the first? The advocate's beliefs about the findings of the level of program efficacy if a rigorous evaluation program efficacy could fall into the four ranges of the critical values for support from the various groups of the public from table 4.2:

$$p_A^0 = P\{\alpha^{RE} \leq \alpha_{CS}^C\}$$

$$p_A^{Low} = P\{\alpha_{CS}^C < \alpha^{RE} \leq \alpha_M^C\}$$

$$p_A^{Med} = P\{\alpha_M^C < \alpha^{RE} \leq \alpha_{HH}^C\}$$

$$p_A^{High} = P\{\alpha_{HH}^C < \alpha^{RE}\}$$

An advocate would favor a rigorous evaluation only if the advocate's expected utility from doing the evaluation was higher than welfare with the optimal level of spending and no evaluation:

Do evaluation if:

$$p_A^0 U_A(0 - C) + p_A^{low} U_A(E^{Barebones} - C)$$

$$+ p_A^{Med} U(E^{Operational} - C) + p_A^{High} U_A(E^{Full} - C)$$

$$> U_A(E(S^*) - S^*) \tag{4.6}$$

In the simplest case in which the advocate knows for sure the evaluation will reveal true program efficacy, this reduces to the question of whether the politically determined level of program expenditures (net of evaluation costs) if true efficacy is known exceeds the net program expenditures achievable through optimally chosen spending to persuade the various groups of the public.

The crucial decision is how much to spend on promotional activities. For a given distribution of initial beliefs, there is a level of promotional spending (possibly zero) for both the core supporters and the middle group that will just raise the group's actual belief in program efficacy to the critical level. Given the assumed simple linear assumptions about beliefs (equation 4.5) depends on the gap between initial and critical level and the persuadability for each group:

$$S_i^c = \frac{\alpha_i^c - \alpha_i^0}{\beta_i}. \tag{4.7}$$

For the hard-headed group $\beta = 0$, there is never any promotional spending (only rigorous evaluations can persuade them), but for the other groups, the optimal level of spending (conditional on spending) depends on whether the level necessary to garner their support exceeds the incremental budget (which in this simple case with the pure public good effect of promotional spending and one dollar of budget from each person is the share of the group in the population):

$$S_i^* = \frac{0 \ if \ S_i^c > F_i}{S_i^c \ if \ S_i^c \le F_i}. \tag{4.8}$$

Doing a rigorous evaluation has the drawback that it may lower the mean belief about efficacy—sufficiently to erode program support—relative to what could have been achieved by promotional activities. So the question is whether the benefits—essentially avoiding promotional costs—are worth the costs of an evaluation.

Table 4.3
Decision by single-issue, single-instrument advocates to perform rigorous evaluation depends on true value of program effectiveness, persuasion costs, and evaluation cost

Case	Configuration of advocates' (certain) beliefs about program impact and the various groups' initial beliefs about program impact	Conditions on persuadability of the public (critical values of spending for each group to attain support) and cost of randomized evaluation	Advocate chooses evaluation or pilot and promote	Resulting program expenditure level (table 4.2)
I	$\alpha^{True} \leq \alpha_{CS}^{C}$ (no support from any group if true value is known)	Ia: $S_{CS}^{C} > F_{CS}$	Pilot, zero promotion	Termination
		Ib: $S_{CS}^{C} \leq F_{CS}, S_{M}^{C} > F_{M}$	Pilot and promotion	Barebones
		Ic: $S_{M}^{C} \leq F_{M}$	Pilot and promotion	Operational
II	$\alpha_{CS}^{C} < \alpha_{CS}^{0} < \alpha^{True} \leq \alpha_{M}^{C}$ (support from core supporters at true value)	IIa: $S_{M}^{C} > F_{M}$ (persuasion costs higher than middle group gain)	Pilot, zero promotion	Barebones
		IIb: $S_{M}^{C} \leq F_{M}$ (persuasion costs low)	Pilot and promotion	Operational
III	$\alpha_{MS}^{0} < \alpha_{M}^{C} < \alpha^{True} \leq \alpha_{HH}^{C}$ (support from middle group at true value)	IIIa: $S_{M}^{C} > C, C < F_{M}$ (persuasion costs high, evaluation cost lower than middle group gain)	Evaluation	Operational
		IIIb: $S_{M}^{C} \leq C, S_{M}^{C} < F_{M}$ (persuasion costs lower than evaluation cost, middle group gain)	Pilot and promotion	Operational
IV	$\alpha_{HH}^{C} \leq \alpha^{True}$	IVa: $S_{M}^{C} > C, C < F_{M} + F_{H}$ (persuasion costs high, evaluation cost lower than gain)	Evaluation	Full funding
		IVa: $C > S_{M}^{C} + F_{H}, S_{M}^{C} < F_{M}$ (evaluation costs too high, persuasion costs for middle group less than gain)	Pilot and promotion	Operational

This depends on the allocation of groups in the population (which directly determines the differences in expenditures), the initial beliefs of the groups, and how amenable their beliefs are to promotion. Table 4.3 works through the possible configurations of true program efficacy, persuadability of the public, and cost of randomized evaluation.

Cases I and II contain subcases where politically savvy altruists may well be called cynical altruists: advocates claim program effectiveness higher than their beliefs (which is the true value) and would resist evaluations and instead prefer to pilot and persuade. In case IIb advocates believe the program is not sufficiently effective to win support if the middle group knew the true value of program effectiveness. The reason is not necessarily that efficacy is low in some absolute sense; it could also be that the middle group altruism (relative to the objectives and beneficiaries of the program) is low. Savvy advocates can plausibly reason that if the middle group cared more, as they morally should, about the issue of education/nutrition/drug abuse/homelessness/health/AIDS and/or had more humane/ethical/lofty degrees of general altruism, then the true program effectiveness would be sufficient for them to support the program (after all it is enough for us)—but they do not. Fortunately, however, the middle group is sufficiently persuadable that it is cheap enough to convince them that the program effectiveness is high. So the best approach is never to do an evaluation that would reveal the truth but rather maintain sufficient uncertainty about true program efficacy so that we can overstate program benefits sufficiently to garner middle group support.

For these advocates, the issue with evaluations is not feasibility or cost. Over some ranges of parameters, advocates would not do an evaluation even if it were free. They would be willing to pay to avoid a randomized evaluation.[9] In this case, it truly pays to be ignorant: advocates have higher utility if no one knows the truth about program efficacy.

4.1.4 Comparative Statics: What Makes Evaluations More Likely?

This is a model that explains why, given the beliefs of single-objective, single-instrument advocates about the outcome of an evaluation and the initial beliefs and persuadability of various groups advocates would prefer not to have a rigorous evaluation of the impact of their proposed intervention. In many situations, advocates prefer ignorance to knowledge. I believe that these situations are common because the gap between the altruism of advocates and the public can be large. It is hard to know how to marshal evidence, but I suspect that evaluations are rare because the middle group has low altruism and few interventions have sufficient efficacy to satisfy them relative to the level of efficacy required by advocates and core supporters (which may include providers and beneficiaries who benefit directly). In this case (essentially case IIb in table 4.3, made more likely by uncertainty), there will be many programs operating and promoted and lobbying for middle group support—but resisting evaluation. But this is not a model that predicts there will never be evaluations. Let us now examine the conditions that make an evaluation more likely. Since in cases I and II there are no conditions in which programs are evaluated, the first question is whether the state of the (model) world places us in case I and II or in II and IV.

Evaluation is less likely when altruism is small. In cases I and II advocates will never do a rigorous evaluation. The necessary condition for being in either of these cases is that true program efficacy is less than the critical value necessary for middle group support. For any given true value of program efficacy, case II is more likely than case III when the middle group's altruism is lower. That is, from equation 4.3 the middle group will support the program when the truth is known only when the marginal utility delivered to program beneficiaries is large relative to marginal utility of own consumption of the middle group, where "large" is determined by the degree of middle group altruism:

$$Support\ if:\quad \alpha_{True} > \alpha_M^{Critical} = \left(\frac{\partial U}{\partial X}\right) * \left(\frac{1 - \gamma_M}{\gamma_M}\right). \tag{4.9}$$

The derivative of the critical value of program efficacy for middle group support is

$$\frac{\partial \alpha_M^{Critical}}{\partial \gamma_M} = \left(\frac{\partial U}{\partial X}\right) * \left(-\frac{1}{\gamma_M^2}\right) \leq 0. \tag{4.10}$$

Decreases in the altruism coefficient of the middle group make it less likely that any given program really meets their criteria. Suppose, for instance, the core supporters were perfectly altruistic so that at $\gamma = .5$, they would provide support if the program were to provide exactly one unit of marginal utility to the beneficiaries per dollar of expenditures. Now suppose that the middle group's utility was such that $\gamma = .1$, so that if the marginal utility of the middle group and core supporters was equal, then they would have to believe that program efficacy was nine times as high as that of the core supporters. To me, even a value of .1 seems relatively high. Suppose that altruism was quite small and $\gamma = .01$; then program efficacy would have to be ninety-nine times their own marginal utility to justify program support.

If one believes that altruism is not in fact strong in the general public, then this would suggest that empirical conditions will nearly always be in case II. Outside of a group of core supporters program, advocates have to rely on persuasion rather than evaluation to convince the middle group. If altruism is low, very few programs will in fact be sufficiently effective to garner political support if the truth were known, so the optimal strategy will nearly always be persuasion, not rigorous evaluation.

Evaluation when the truth helps the advocates. While within case III or IV, evaluation is a possibility, it is only one possibility, and what makes program evaluation more likely within case III will be examined. In case III, true program efficacy attracts middle group support ($\alpha_{MS}^0 < \alpha_M^C < \alpha^{True}$), but this means only that advocates might choose to do an evaluation. But evaluation is still done only if (1) it is cheaper to achieve the support to expand the program through an evaluation than through the alternative and (2) achieving the additional budget is worth it. Still, in the case where the core group needs no support in the no uncertainty, linear utility model, the condition for an evaluation is that

Evaluate if:

$$C < S_M^{Critical} = \frac{\left(\frac{\partial U}{\partial X}\right) * \left(\frac{1 - \gamma_M}{\gamma_M}\right) - \alpha_M^0}{\beta_M} \quad and \quad C > E^{Op} - E^B = F_M \quad (4.11)$$

Figure 4.1 illustrates the basic comparative static exercises on the amount it takes to convince the middle group in the absence of a rigorous evaluation. A rigorous evaluation is more likely in these cases:

• *The more initially skeptical the middle group* The lower the initial belief in efficacy of the middle group (α_M^0) relative to the "truth," the more likely it will be in the interests of the advocates to carry out an evaluation rather than spend money to persuade (figure 4.1a). One has to speculate on the psychology of the middle group to say how this affects any given program, but there are some remedies that are more intuitive than others. For instance, suppose the middle group shares the objective of reducing fertility. It is plausible that public provision (or subsidization) of contraception to achieve that objective has intuitive public appeal as contraception is an obvious proximate determinant of fertility. Other actions for reducing population growth that achieve their impact through a more complex chain of causation (such as increasing female education) may have less initial credibility of program efficacy.

• *The less persuadable the middle group* If the middle group is easily persuaded (large changes in believed efficacy for a given increase in spending), then it is more likely the cost of persuasion is less than the cost of evaluation (figure 4.1b). Again, this will be program specific as it is almost certainly the case that it is easier to convince individuals of some programs' effects than others.

• *The larger the budget gain from convincing the middle group (the smaller the group of core supporters)* Even if evaluation is preferable to persuasion, it still has to be the case that the middle group is worth convincing. If the core group is very large (perhaps because of self-interest of program beneficiaries), then it may be that the advocates would do neither an evaluation nor promotional activities.

a.

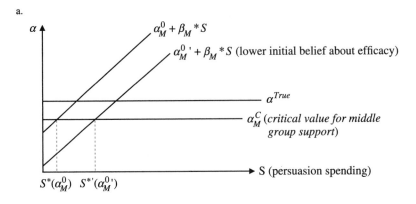

b.

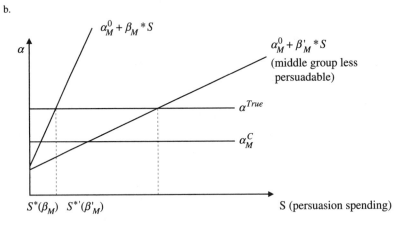

Figure 4.1
Some simple comparative statics of choosing to do a rigorous evaluation. *a.* If the middle group is initially more skeptical (lower initial belief in program efficacy), the persuasion spending necessary for middle group support (S^*) increases, making a rigorous evaluation of cost C more likely. *b.* Because the middle group is less persuadable, the spending necessary to achieve support increases, making an evaluation more likely if the true value is sufficient to attract middle group support.

4.1.5   Nervous Altruists: When Advocates Are Uncertain About Evaluation Accuracy

Uncertainty about the outcome of the randomized evaluation will create another complication: nervous altruists. One reason to fear a randomized evaluation is that the evaluation may not—for methodological reasons, complexity, mismeasurement, or just bad luck—capture the true benefits of the program. In this case, there is the risk of a bad draw. Advocates may believe that the true program efficacy is actually sufficiently high that the middle (or even hard-headed) group would support the program if the rigorous evaluation revealed the true value—but they may fear the evaluation would produce a lower value. With risk-averse advocates, the optimal decision might be not to do an evaluation even when they believe the program is effective enough relative to the middle (or high) group's levels of altruism. In this case of the nervous altruists, it pays to be ignorant even when, if they were confident the evaluation would reveal the truth, they would prefer a rigorous evaluation over pilot and persuade.

It is not worth working out all of the cases with uncertainty over outcomes and risk aversion. Instead I will work out the intuition in one case. In particular, how do outcomes change in case IIIa (the promotion to achieve middle group support was sufficiently expensive that it was preferable to evaluate) with the introduction of uncertainty and risk aversion?

The simple intuition in this subcase is that with risk aversion at the same level of evaluation cost and S^* at which advocates would have chosen evaluation, they will prefer the certain outcome under S^* to facing the uncertainty of an evaluation.[10] So unless the upside risk is large (because either the probability of a high evaluation outcome is large or the hard-headed population is large—$p_A^{High} * F_{HH}$), the advocate would prefer the certain outcome to the risk of an evaluation.

4.2 Coalitions of Single-Objective Advocates: A Pledge of Secrecy?

But, alas, ignorance is not bliss. While some advocates are convinced of both their issue and their remedy, in many other instances, advocates must form coalitions and exist in more complex institutional settings.

There are many instances in which advocates are certain about the objective they regard as important, but are not certain about the instrument that will best address that objective. By not evaluating any programs, advocates might gain funding, but they themselves are uncertain about the impact. Single-objective, multiple-instrument advocates, such as those interested in population reduction, malnutrition, and crime, for instance, want more funding but would also like more information about the relative merits of different instruments.

Suppose there are three advocates: two single-objective, single-instrument advocates named A and B (one who favors program A and one of whom favors program B) and a third advocate named C, who is passionate about the objective but agnostic between instruments A and B. Under what conditions will these advocates form a coalition and belong to the same organization, and what would such a coalition do?

One outcome is an organization that has a pledge to secrecy. Advocates A, B, and C form a coalition with the agreement that they will do a rigorous evaluation of instruments A and B and then raise monies and fund the more effective program (all of this assumes the core group support can be brought into the coalition). All of this will be done with a pledge of secrecy so that only the advocates themselves are allowed to know the actual, cardinal program efficacy. To the outside world, only the rankings of the programs are revealed. So in its money-raising efforts, the organization claims that it is funding only the most effective programs. If the middle group's persuadability is higher when the advocacy comes from a multiple-instrument organization, then there are conditions in which organizational coalitions will form around issues because this allows them to raise more funds than they would otherwise. This essentially allows them to move from case IIa, in which only a bare-bones level of funding is possible, to a case in which middle group support, and hence the operational level of funding, is available for at least one of the programs, as illustrated in figure 4.2.

The key to organizational stability is that no one cheats on the secrecy agreement. There are two obvious ways to cheat on the agreement. First is to promise a rigorous evaluation but not complete it until after the coalition partner had completed one. At that point, if the rigorous evaluation estimate of program efficacy is lower than that necessary for program support, the "cheating" partner can say, "All we can credibly promote without complete cynicism and

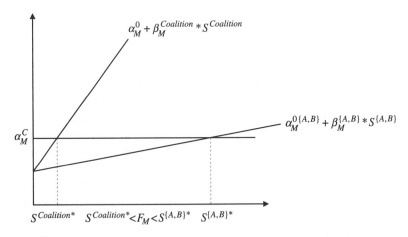

Figure 4.2
Case in which a coalition sufficiently increased middle group persuadability so that the better of intervention A or B is funded even though neither of them singly would receive middle group support.

without fear of exposure is my preferred instrument [about which we are still ignorant] and we can do that only as long as I don't complete my evaluation, so let's stop now and promote my intervention." Alternatively, suppose the evaluations reveal that program B is more effective, and hence there is no funding for instrument A. But if advocate A leaks the absolute level of program efficacy for program B, this creates a situation such that the organization can no longer raise middle group support for program B but it can still raise support for program A (as long as advocate B does not retaliate and leak the results of the evaluation of program A). Given this ex post cheating on the original agreement (to evaluate and fund only the most effective) by advocate A, it would then be in the best interests of all three (A, B, and C) to continue and advocate for program A. Of course this would make for a very unstable coalition because (1) ex ante, B and C might suspect A's sincerity, (2) if the organization requires repeated interactions, then B and C are unlikely to be fooled again, and (3) advocate B might be tempted to behave "irrationally" and quit the organization and retaliate by leaking the results of the evaluation of program A—leaving them all worse off.

4.3 Multiple Issues, Multiple Instruments: Unstable Coalitions, Naive Technocrats

It is a waste of money to add an evaluation component to nutritional programs—these evaluations never find an impact anyway—we should just move ahead with what we nutrionitsts know is right.
—Nutritional advocate in project decision meeting

It's amazing how many bad projects get support. Epistemologically, why do you think that is?
—E-mail from a colleague

While the objectives of some organizations are clear and the only question is efficacy in pursuing those objectives, in others a broad objective covers multiple issues (and within each, there are multiple possible instruments). Development banks (World Bank, Asion Development Bank) and aid agencies (U.S. Agency for International Development, Department for International Development) are examples in which the organizational mission ("development" or "poverty reduction") is sufficiently broad that a variety of issues might contribute (basic education, infrastructure, health, trade liberalization, judicial reform). Now, not only is there is a question of which instrument is best to pursue a given subobjective, but there is also the question of how any given subobjective contributes to the overall objective. Which is "more important": health or transport?

Table 4.4
Example of coalitions of advocates within an organization with a broad objective: the World Bank
and poverty reduction

	A: Education most important		
	B: Education *Classroom construction*	**C: Education** *Teacher training*	
	D: Economic growth most important		
	E: Economic growth *Trade liberalization*	**F: Economic growth** *Infrastructure investment*	
	G: Agricultural productivity most important		
	H: Agricultural production *Irrigation*	**I: Agricultural production** *Land reform*	**J: Agricultural production** *Extension*
	K: Health most important		
	L: Health *Child vaccinations*	**M: Health** **AIDS**	
		N: Health **AIDS** **Prevention**	**O: Health** **AIDS** *Treatment*
		P: Health **AIDS** **Prevention** *High-risk groups*	**Q: Health** **AIDS** **Prevention** *Mass education*

Z: Poverty reduction most important objective

Note: Each letter represents a "stakeholder" with given views about the importance for poverty reduction of various subobjectives (in bold) and the strength of their belief about particular instruments for subobjectives (in italics).

Consider the organization I happen to know best: the World Bank. Suppose the World Bank's mission really is poverty reduction, but that internally, among the staff, and externally, among the governments that are the organization's shareholders, there is a very loose coalition of general and specialized advocates that supports the mandate of poverty reduction.

Within the organization, there are advocates of all kinds: some single objective, single instrument; some single objective but with no fixed beliefs about the efficacy of specific instruments; some with no strong beliefs about either the relative importance for poverty reduction of subobjectives or the efficacy of instruments within subobjectives. Table 4.4 captures just a small fraction of this complexity, as there are layers upon layers of what might constitute subobjectives, and what with the subobjectives, groups might have strong feelings about as instruments. The categories listed in the table are obviously not mutually exclusive. In addition there are thematic concerns like gender that I cannot illustrate as they cut across all individual issues and subobjectives and instruments.

All the stakeholders in the coalition have their own agendas and specific ideas about the most effective sectors or instruments. What I mean by a loose coalition is that I assume that for many of the advocates with the organization, they would not stay within the organization (working on a different issue or instrument) if it allocated zero resources to their preferred issue or instrument. So if the World Bank devoted resources to education but zero resources to teacher training, person C would leave but not person A or B. If the World Bank were to devote zero resources to AIDS, persons M,N,O,P,Q would leave, but person P would leave even if resources were devoted to health, AIDS, and prevention but zero were allocated to prevention in high-risk groups.[11] This loose coalition nature of the organization implies that a pledge of secrecy is not possible.

In this setup, only the most naive would voluntarily undertake a rigorous evaluation of their preferred objective or instrument. An evaluation would pin down the claims the advocate could make, which makes this person a sitting duck for advocates within the organization who have not done an evaluation and would like more of the institution's resources for their preferred activity. Any evaluation will reveal weaknesses and a lower impact than could have been plausibly claimed for some other instrument. For instance, doing a rigorous evaluation of a "community driven development" project sets them up to be attacked by supporters of specific sectors (education, roads, microcredit) and vice versa.

So if there is to be any rigorous evaluation, it would have to come from agent Z in table 4.4—the stakeholder with poverty reduction as the objective who is agnostic about subobjectives and instruments—rather than emerging spontaneously. If agent Z is "management," this person would need evaluations in order to optimize the use of resources. Assume that organizational resources were fixed and there was a consensus on how to measure the objective of poverty reduction. If the magnitude of resources was fixed, then the optimum would be reached if resources were allocated to the activity with the highest poverty reduction gain, which consists of two parts: how effective program or policy A is in producing gains in the subobjective per dollar of input and how much the subobjective contributes to the overall objective of poverty reduction. So assuming a set of mutually exclusive actions A in set {A} of equivalent cost and funds for only one of them the decision rule for an organization with poverty reduction as an objective (with secure funding) should be:

$$\underset{\{A\}}{\text{Max}} \left(\frac{\partial \ Poverty \ Reduction}{\partial \ Subobjective} \right) * \alpha^A. \tag{4.12}$$

But this simple rule ignores the trade-offs. There are three elements to the trade-off faced by the management of a broad mandate organization: raising the average efficacy of actions undertaken so that resources actually do contribute to the general objective, maintaining the persuadability of the general public so that the organization is more effective in resource mobilization than the individual advocates alone would be, and sustaining the internal coalition behind the broad objective.

The only reason for the individual advocates to remain in a coalition is if they can better pursue their objectives inside than outside the organization. One reason for this is if the organization is better able to mobilize resources, in part because it is easier to mobilize middle group support for a coalition because persuadability is higher. This suggests doing sufficient evaluation activity to maintain organizational credibility.

Doing some evaluation maintains appearances of effectiveness, but doing compelling and convincing evaluations of an intervention strongly favored by an important constituency group runs a huge risk: What if, relative to other interventions, it is not in fact effective? But doing a rigorous evaluation without a pledge of secrecy implies that activities will be cut, which will undermine support for the broad objective as the advocates and core group supporters for those particular activities are lost to the broader organization.

In order to know either element of the optimal fixed budget decision rule with any degree of quantitative precision and certainty, one would have to do a rigorous evaluation. Without a rigorous evaluation, the average efficacy of the funded activities is lower than the optimal.

The solution to this general problem is going to be specific to the organization and will be a complex mix, but it almost certainly will involve a great deal of strategic ignorance. The real-world solution is likely to be one in which the organization tries to generate just enough evaluation to allow the experts and general issue advocates to push the organization toward the more effective interventions and maintain the persuadability of key stakeholders, but not so much evaluation that any sector or intervention that needs support for political reasons would be ruled out. Moreover, there would definitely not be enough evaluation to assess rigorously the overall level of efficacy of the broad organization.

4.4   Versimilitude

The model I am proposing here explains the dearth of reliable, rigorous evaluations of a variety of public and nonprofit actions as a strategic commitment to ignorance by the advocates of these programs.[12] Ironically, I cannot think of any way to rigorously test my claims about the causes of the lack of rigorous tests of claims. Why, in spite of that irony, do I think this model helps to understand reality? Partly because both less cynical and more cynical explanations fail and partly because there is a certain amount of versimilitude to the model.

4.4.1 Less and More Cynical Explanations

Perhaps there are other reasons for the lack of rigorous evaluations than the strategic behavior by advocates: cost, ethical barriers, and practical impossibility have been proposed as alternative explanations.

That evaluation is too expensive is often cited as an explanation for its scarcity, but since evaluation costs are a tiny fraction of program costs and the potential gains are enormous, it is difficult to believe this is a compelling reason for substantial areas of public intervention.[13] Ethical issues seems a poor explanation of why there are evaluations in medicine, where it is a matter of life and death, and are not evaluations of, for instance, educational innovations. Because of budget constraints, very few people have access to the intervention (e.g., small class sizes, free family planning) during the program or project in any case so the randomization does not deny anyone access to the program; budget constraints do. Finally, one would think the ethical issue of "policy malpractice" (Stigler 1974) through perpetuation of ineffective action is at least as serious an issue as structuring participation in programs of unknown efficacy in order to learn if they are effective.

That randomized evaluation is "not feasible" is usually false. Moreover, even in instances in which it would be easy to structure a randomized evaluation (for instance, where program implementation is going to be phased in due to logistical constraints and the sequence of areas receiving the intervention could be randomized), these measures are resisted.

Then there are more cynical explanations of ignorance, which is that pure political interests are at play. A more cynical explanation of the lack of rigorous evaluation of educational innovations could be built purely around the self-interest of educators than that there are altruists who honestly believe in the efficacy of their intervention. Although there is obviously some cooperation between advocates and their core groups—so that teachers' unions will fund advocacy for class size reduction—I do not believe that all advocacy is pure self-interest. Most advocates are quite sincere in their beliefs.

4.4.2 Reasons to Believe

There are several interesting facts about the evaluations that do occur, although I obviously do not have a complete sample of all evaluations, that suggest that something like the present model of strategic interest is correct.

First, a huge number of evaluations are started, but very few are finished, written up, and publicized. This evaluation attrition is too large to be consistently bad planning and is more likely strategic behavior.

Second, I do not have a complete sample, but many programs that have had randomized evaluations were in fact eliminated, and it is not clear whether this had anything to do with the evaluation. The voucher program in Colombia was eliminated before the randomized evaluation results were even available. The training program evaluated under JTPA was terminated. The fact they were eliminated ex post at least suggests these program were without solid political support and the evaluation itself was a strategy born out of weakness.

Third, randomized evaluations are often implemented by those out of the mainstream—groups with much less to lose if the outcome is adverse. For instance, the randomized evaluation of the provision of textbooks in Kenya was carried out by a small NGO, not the government (Glewwe, Moulin, and Kremer 1997). The implementation and evaluation of the Colombia voucher program was not carried out in the Ministry of Education (Angrist et al.).

Fourth, it is of interest to look at the pressures behind the evaluations that do exist, and typically one finds that the proposed intervention was either not supported by the core supporters or had strong opposition.

4.5   Conclusion

Who really wants to know? While serendipity plays some role in knowledge, most increases in knowledge about the impact of public programs or policies are the result of deliberate research. If a program can already generate sufficient support to be adequately funded, then knowledge is a danger. No advocate would want to engage in research that potentially undermines support for his or her program. Endless, but less than compelling, controversy is preferred to knowing for sure that the answer is no.

This strategic ignorance of advocates is not necessarily a bad thing. Just as Frank Knight argued that economies will have a higher growth rate when its entrepreneurs are more irrationally optimistic, it is possible that a combination of excessive subjective certainty among altruistic advocates and strategic maintained ignorance of true program effects is actually welfare improving. Rawlsian model can be developed in which people can make binding decisions from behind a prebirth position in which no one knows what their status will be, in which in some cases welfare is higher if all actors promise not to never do rigorous evaluations. Perhaps all of us quantitatively oriented public policy social scientists promoting evaluations are violating a prebirth commitment to our fellow human beings.

Acknowledgments

I would thank various people, who are not ignorant, for their comments: Alberto Ades, Julie van Domelen, Jeffrey Kling, Susan Stout, Jeffrey Hammer, Deon Filmer, and Scott Guggenheim.

Notes

1. This is about primary health care as a policy as opposed to the medical gains from specific health interventions like vaccinations. One of the persistent confusions in the literature on health policy is precisely between the effectiveness of specific actions as medical "interventions" and the impact of a public sector "intervention." It is perfectly possible that a certain therapy is medically effective and yet a policy of public provision of that therapy has no impact on the health status of the population.

2. Every World Bank loan has an "evaluation," but many of these do not involve any attempt to estimate the magnitude of impact on specific outcomes, and rarely is there any estimate of the "without the project" counterfactual. This is not a criticism of the World Bank, as other donor agencies are even less advanced in their evaluation methods.

3. I ignore discounting of the first period costs because it affects C and S equally so will not tip the decision rule.

4. This assumption can be justified in three ways. First, experience in the world suggests that far more rigorous impact evaluations are promised than begun and more begun than finished. From my observation, evaluation tends always to be low on the priority of the program initiators and advocates, and hence never gets done. Second, politically it would be almost impossible for a program evaluation finding no impact to be credible if it were undertaken by groups that were not in some sense program advocates. Third, there almost certainly could be more fundamental assumptions made about the observability of effort, in which case, it might be impossibly to credibly contract with advocates to undertake actions not in their best interest.

5. There is a more cynical, and hence more realistic, version in which core supporters benefit more or less from the program spending itself (e.g., recipients of social security, farmers lobbying for subsidized sales of food to developing nations, teachers lobbying for lower class sizes). The degree to which the voting public perceives that the program benefits them is obviously a key issue for political support of targeted programs (Gelbach and Pritchett 1997) but I want to hold that issue to one side for now.

6. I assume the three groups have equivalent income so that marginal utility is equal.

7. Note that spending is a public good in the sense that the magnitude of spending to convince each group is independent of the size of the group. Alternatively, persuasion spending could be per person, which would obviously change the role of group size in decision making.

8. I adopt an ugly new word to avoid a loaded word to describe how amenable people's beliefs are to promotional or persuasive activities. If one calls it *gullibility*, then this obviously takes one stance, while referring to it as *receptiveness* conveys an entirely different viewpoint.

9. The key word is *complete*, as there are many dollars taken to do evaluations.

10. Of course, this assumes that the only uncertainty is over the outcome of the evaluation and that all other parameters are known with certainty by the advocates. But if advocates are also uncertain about the middle group's persuadibility, then nothing can be said about the impact of uncertainty in general.

11. This is not a statement about relative magnitudes of support, as the division into issues and instruments is arbitrary and for illustration only.

12. The same is true of their private sector counterparts, and the existence of persuasive (as opposed to informative) advertising expenditures in the absence of rigorous information suggests

strategic ignorance is not limited to the private sector. I have yet to see a rigorous evaluation of the impact of breath mints.

13. In the report on the RAND Health insurance experiment (Manning et al. 1987), the authors point out that in spite of the large cost of the experiment, the savings from implementation of even one of the policy recommendations stemming from the report would pay for itself in about a week.

References

Barnett, W. S. 1996. *Lives in the Balance: Age-27 Benefit-Cost Analysis of the High/Scope Perry Preschool Program.* Ypsilanti, Mich.: High/Scope Press.

Filmer, Deon, Jeffrey Hammer, and Lant Pritchett. 2000. "Weak Links in the Chain: A Diagnosis of Health Policy in Poor Countries." *World Bank Research Observer* 15(2):199–224.

Gelbach, Jonah, and Lant Pritchett. 1997. "More for the Poor Is Less for The Poor." World Bank Policy Research Working Paper 1799.

Glewwe, Paul, Sylvie Moulin, and Michael Kremer. 1997. "Textbooks and Test Scores: Evidence from a Prospective Evaluation in Kenya." Mimeo., Harvard University.

Manning, W. G., Newhouse, J. P., Duan, N., Keeler, E. B., Leibowitz, A., and Marquis, M. S. 1987. "Health Insurance and the Demand for Medical Care: Evidence from a Randomized Experiment." *American Economic Review* 77:251–277.

Phillips, James F., Ruth Simmons, Michael Koenig, and J. Chakraborty. 1988. "Determinants of Reproductive Change in a Traditional Society: Evidence from Matlab, Bangladesh." *Studies in Family Planning* 19(6):313–334.

Schweinhart, L. J., H. V. Barnes, & D. P. Weikart. 1993. *Significant Benefits: The High/Scope Perry Preschool Study Through Age 27.* Ypsilanti, Mich.: High/Scope Press.

Stigler, George. 1975. *The Citizen and the State: Essays on Regulation.* Chicago: University of Chicago Press.

II THE PROBLEMS OF AID-FINANCED DELIVERY OF PUBLIC SERVICES: THE GORDIAN KNOT OF THE STATE

5 Solutions When the Solution Is the Problem: Arraying the Disarray in Development

Lant Pritchett and Michael Woolcock

The need for popular participation is not just sanctimonious rubbish. Indeed, the idea of development cannot be disassociated from it.
—Amartya Sen

The emphasis on empowerment is troubling [because it is, among other things,] clearly outside the [World] Bank's mandate [and promotes its] entry into domestic politics. . . . [This is an area in which] it has no experience or competence.
—T. N. Srinivasan

Impact evaluations show that social fund resources are pro-poor, and that targeting has improved over time.
—Julie van Domelen

The evidence raises questions about the effectiveness of [social funds] as a safety net for the poor and, more significantly, about the presumed greater desirability of [social funds] as an alternative to traditional government supply, or reformed versions of it.
—Judith Tendler

This chapter emerges from a puzzle among development practitioners and scholars: why so many otherwise reasonable, articulate, and experienced people arrive at such vastly different and sharply divisive interpretations of the merits of new proposals to improve public service delivery under the broad banner of participatory development. The variety of items on this new menu is broad— "participation," "social funds," "community-driven development," "empowerment," "decentralization," "NGO provision," "contracting out"—but the reviews of the new dishes vary widely. Some rave that the new menu items are the greatest thing since bread was sliced, other critics pan them as not fit for consumption, and still others deem them to be in violation of purity norms.

Our rather immodest goal in this chapter is to outline a conceptual framework that arrays the disarray in recent development initiatives, with the goal of improving policy dialogue and effectiveness and, with it, greater coherence in development research and teaching as it pertains to the provision of public services. The chapter proceeds as follows. In section 5.1, we consider the broad areas of agreement and disagreement among those proposing strategies for improving service delivery in developing countries and define the limits of what we are, and are not, going to discuss. Our primary concern is with key services in which the government has compelling interests in engagement, and how—rather than what—it should deliver. To this end, we distinguish analytically between both the degree of discretion and transaction intensiveness entailed in providing a given service, using this to frame a discussion of development policies, programs, and what we shall call practices. We then consider the five critical elements of service delivery: resources, information, decision making, delivery mechanisms, and accountability. Variations in how these responsibilities are structured are used to array traditional and current proposals for improving service delivery. In section 5.2, we lay out the basic problem of service delivery as it was originally conceived and the characteristics of the single solution that was routinely invoked to solve it; we then explain the common structures of the failure of that approach in sector after sector and the three "solutions" that were devised to address those failures. These three "solutions" also failed, however, which provides the background for section 5.3, in which we outline eight contemporary approaches to reforming public service delivery: (1) supplier autonomy, (2) single-sector participatory, (3) contracting out, (4) decentralization to states and provinces, (5) decentralization to localities and municipalities, (6) demand-side financing, (7) social funds, and (8) community-driven development. We conclude with a brief discussion of the implications of our analysis for contemporary development problems and program design, using AIDS, education, and research as examples.

5.1   Agreements and Disagreements in Public Service Delivery Debates

Despite appearances to the contrary, the factions in contemporary development debates share a fair degree of consensus (cf. Kanbur 2001). First, most agree that the debate about the Washington consensus is blown far out of proportion.[1] At times 90 percent of the ink spilled addresses 10 percent of the development battle; in the end, no matter who is right about trade policy, fiscal deficits, and the like, these policies do not add up to anything like a complete development agenda. As Rodrik (1999) and others have rightly argued, policies such as trade openness and fiscal probity need to be seen as part of, not a substitute for, a coherent development strategy. Even the augmented Washington consensus that adds the provision of some key services (like education) to the standard policy agenda leaves wide open the question of how things will actually be accomplished. In general, economists have focused their tools on the question of what governments should do, with relatively less attention given to the economics and politics of how to accomplish the "what."

Second, most agree that the (perhaps very) long-run goal is to ensure that the provision of key services such as clean water, education, sanitation, policing, safety and sanitary regulation, roads, and public health is *assured* by effective, rules-based, meritocratic, and politically accountable public agencies[2]—that is, something resembling Weberian bureaucracies.[3] We call such a world "Denmark."[4] By "Denmark" we do not, of course, mean Denmark. Rather, we mean the common core of the structure of the workings of the public sector in countries usually called developed (including new arrivals like Singapore). To be sure, there are numerous variations on the core "Denmark" ideal; indeed, remarkably similar performance outcomes can be and are delivered by different, and culturally distinctive, institutional forms—for example, Denmark, New Zealand,[5] Germany, and Japan. The historical evidence is surely that while development is likely to entail a convergence in terms of institutional performance outcomes, the precise form those institutional arrangements actually come to take in each country will continue to be as varied as the countries themselves.[6] Indeed, as we argue in detail below, the strategy of "skipping straight to Weber"—seeking to quickly reach service delivery performance goals in developing countries by simply mimicking (or adopting through colonial inheritance) the organizational forms of a particular "Denmark"—has in fact been a root cause of the deep problems that developing countries encounter as they seek to deliver key public services to their citizens.[7]

Third, most agree that while the solution of skipping straight to Weber has had some notable successes, it has also often failed—badly.[8] That is, development activities (in general, and those supported by development agencies in particular) have almost uniformly attempted to remedy problems of "inadequate services"[9] (in infrastructure, education, health, law enforcement, regulation) by calling on a centralized bureaucracy to supply a top-down and uniform public service. These decisions to skip straight to Weber were historical, social, and political processes whereby the interactions of citizens, the state, and providers were simply overlooked. *The* solution was a coherent approach to service delivery in which a universal need was met by a technical (supply) solution and then implemented by an impersonal, rules-driven provider. That is, "need as the problem, supply as the solution, civil service as the instrument" became the standard organizational algorithm for solving public services concerns.[10] This approach has had some clear successes (e.g., eradicating polio), but the more numerous and pervasive failures have caused most practitioners in developing countries to doubt its universal applicability as the sole solution.

Fourth, most agree that the new solutions to *the* solution (which has now become "the problem") will have two features: first, they will embody something like what is conveyed by terms such as *empowerment, participation, accountability, transparency,* or *good governance*; and second, how the principles are actually embodied in concrete organizational forms will involve a great deal of institutional heterogeneity. One size clearly will not fit all in countries as different as Canada, Chad, China, and Costa Rica (cf. World Bank 2003).

These broad areas of consensus (which we generously presuppose), however, still leave plenty of room for serious disagreement. Beyond a broad agreement that the proposals for reforming the institutional mechanisms of service delivery represent an attempt to move beyond the Washington consensus and find a way to make institutions work, to show that context matters and that one size does not fit all, there is tremendous disarray in the field.[11] Indeed, at times it is hard to even know who is disagreeing with whom, and why. Unlike most divides in development (and elsewhere), in which partisans line up more or less predictably along disciplinary, methodological, or political lines, participatory development seems to have exposed new schisms. For example, critics on the "left" like James Scott (1998), in *Seeing Like a State*, provide damning critiques of the impact of governments, while those on the "right," like Hernando de Soto (2000), in *The Mystery of Capital*, end a book extolling the virtues of property rights with an appeal to the power of marginalized people to overcome the established order and create new legal institutions for safeguarding their property. At the same time, the debate over the performance of social funds in Latin America (van Domolen 2002; cf. Carvalho, Perkins, and White 2002; cf. Tendler 2000a) has created sharp division among those with otherwise similar political and ideological predispositions ("pragmatic center/left"), while critics who ordinarily share none of these said dispositions (e.g., Srinivasan 2001, and Cooke and Kothari 2001) unwittingly find common cause in attacking notions such as empowerment.

"One size does not fit all" does not mean that "any size fits any" or "anything goes"; without guidance as to which size fits which, it is merely a platitude. Moreover, even if "Denmark" is the agreed-on destination, when the starting point is anywhere from Mexico to Moldova to Mozambique, it should not be all that surprising that attempts to map out the best route for getting there, and identifying the necessary provisions for the journey, generate deep differences of opinion. Is participation the new solution to improving project design, or a new form of tyranny (Cooke and Kothari 2000)? Are social funds the new instrument to promote local development, or an inconvenient but comfortable detour (van Domelen 2002)? Do services implemented through local community organizations more effectively include or marginalize the poor

(Gugerty and Kremer 2002)?[12] Is decentralization the answer to "bringing the government closer to the people," or a cynical ploy to cut deficits (Tendler 1997, 2000b)? Is social capital a potentially useful analytical tool for designing more effective services, or an attempt to avoid politics (Harriss 2002)?[13] Is the increased engagement of nongovernmental organizations (NGOs) in policy dialogue encouraging openness and accountability, or is it (as some have argued) the biggest threat to democracy the world faces? With so many alternatives on the table and the free debate of all against all, the disagreements cut across disciplinary and even ideological lines (with the "hard left" and "hard right" critiques often agreeing against the "soft left"). How can one make sense of all this confusion?

We propose that an array of the disarray can be found in an analysis that begins with the evolution of the theory and practice of public service delivery, in particular, the manner in which manifest failures were explained and the corresponding solutions justified. We argue that the variety of alternatives now on the table is a direct response to *the* solution, which itself became the problem (cf. Hirschman 1970).

5.1.1   Key, Discretionary, Transaction-Intensive Services: A Basic Framework

Our focus in this chapter is on the provision of key, discretionary, and transaction-intensive public services. Key services are those for which there is a broad consensus that some type of government action is necessary, desirable, or inevitable. This includes absolutely essential functions such as ensuring law and order and maintaining a means of payment, through to development programs that have a strong rationale for public sector involvement, like irrigation, sanitation, improved water supply, and components of education and health.[14] Even if these services are in principle able to be provided by the private sector, it is highly unlikely the government could escape assuming major responsibility for them if or when they fail (California's recent electricity crisis is an example).[15]

Services are discretionary to the extent that their delivery requires decisions by providers to be made on the basis of information that is important but inherently imperfectly specified and incomplete, thereby rendering them unable to be mechanized. As such, these decisions usually entail extensive professional (gained through training or experience) or informal context-specific knowledge.[16] In the process of service delivery, discretionary decisions are taken that are crucial to a successful outcome; the right decision depends on conditions ("states of the world") that are difficult to assess (ex ante or ex post), and hence it is very difficult to monitor whether the right decision was taken.

Table 5.1
Classifying modes of decision making in key public services

	Discretionary	Nondiscretionary
Transaction intensive	Practices	Programs
Nontransaction intensive	Policies	(Procedures, rules)

Transaction intensiveness refers simply to the extent to which the delivery of a service or an element of a service requires a large number of transactions, nearly always involving some face-to-face contact. School lunch programs, for example, require numerous cooks and cleaners to show up every day to individually prepare and distribute hundreds of meals in a hygienic environment; a small committee at a single meeting, on the other hand, can draw up the monthly menu.

Key services, then, contain elements than can be either discretionary or nondiscretionary *and* transaction intensive or nontransaction intensive. These distinctions generate a simple analytical two-by-two classification (see table 5.1) that helps distinguish between some familiar staples of contemporary development discourse: policies, programs, and what we shall call practices.[17]

We call discretionary but not transaction-intensive activities *policies*. The clearest policy examples are in macroeconomics: lowering (or raising) the interest rate, devaluing (or not) the currency, setting a fiscal deficit target. These are all actions that intrinsically involve assessing the state of the world and taking an appropriate action, but implementation itself is not transaction intensive. The politics of policy reform may (or may not) require mass support politically, but "ten smart people" can handle the actual decisions and mechanics of policy reform.[18] Their decisions require considerable professional training and judgment, and thus cannot be automated. Alan Greenspan is a maestro, not a machine.[19]

In contrast, programs require thousands or millions of individual transactions and hence thousands or tens of thousands of providers, but each transaction can be (reasonably) carried out with relatively little discretion on the part of the agent responsible for implementation. In financial matters, an example is retail banking transactions, many of which can be carried out by a junior clerk (or for the most routine transactions, a machine).[20] To implement a program, the agents of the organization need only to stick to a relatively fixed script (Leonard 2002; Dobbin 2004), in which the choices are few and judging the choice appropriate to the situation relatively easy. The primary problems with programs are technical (finding an effective and least-cost solution) and logistical (carrying out the mandated actions reliably).

Table 5.2
Examples of Discretionary and Transaction Intensive Services

Sector	Discretionary, not transaction intensive (technocratic "policies")	Discretionary and transaction intensive (idiosyncratic "practices")	Transaction intensive, not discretionary (bureaucratic "programs")
Commercial banking	Setting deposit rates	Approving loans to small businesses	Taking in deposits
Social protection	Setting eligibility criteria	Determining eligibility of marginal or special cases	Issuing checks to the eligible
Law enforcement	Law making defining criminal behavior	Handling individual conflict situations	Directing traffic
Education	Curriculum design	Classroom teaching	Providing school lunches
Health	Public information campaigns	Curative care	Vaccinations
Irrigation	Location of main canals	Allocation of water flows	Providing standpipes in every village
Central banks	Monetary policy	Banking regulation	Clearinghouse
Agricultural extension	Research priorities	Communication with farmers	Dispensing seeds

The provision of elements of services that are (more or less) discretionary and transaction intensive—practices—provide the biggest headache for even the most astute and well-intentioned practitioner,[21] because they are intrinsically incompatible with the logic and imperatives of large-scale, routinized, administrative control.[22] An analogy from private sector production is the difference between activities that can be either carried out in a large bureaucratic setting (e.g., manufacturing production) or in a franchise (e.g., fast food restaurants) versus those activities that are not amenable to large-scale routinization—witness the generally small size (relative to the national market) of most law firms, physician practices, universities, household contractors, counselors, fine restaurants, and coaches.[23]

While given sectors have relatively more or less of the three types of activity, it is not the case that education is discretionary and health is not; rather, within every sector there are examples of each in different stages of the service provision process (see table 5.2). In health, for example, providing some individualized services, such as immunization, in which the appropriate action is nearly the same for each individual of a given age (which is easily observed), can be carried out as a program. In contrast, the provision of curative medical or psychological services, in which the provider is available for and responds to the complaints presented by individuals, requires a practice.

Policies, then, are primarily technocratic, programs are primarily bureaucratic, and practices are primarily idiosyncratic. Large organizations, by nature and design, are essentially constrained to operate exclusively in terms of policies (determined by "ten smart people") or programs (implemented by "ten thousand bureaucrats"). Successful practices, when discovered and appreciated by such organizations, immediately give rise to a search for other instances, which can then be scrutinized by experts to discern their policy implications, and/or codified by rank-and-file staff into a best practices[24] handbook, CD-ROM, and training manual for standardized replication. Of course, it is entirely desirable that innovative discoveries and effective solutions to universal problems (e.g., hand-washing to avoid disease) be rapidly disseminated. As we have defined them, however, practices are by definition not able to be standardized and easily replicated. Diligent teachers might share tips about what seems to work in the classroom, and the wider dissemination of those tips may have a positive impact, but the everyday act of teaching entails making innumerable discretionary and transaction-intensive decisions, the effective execution of which are deeply embedded in the teacher's (idiosyncratic) personality and professionalism and the nature of the particular institutional context.

5.1.2   Elements of Service Delivery and the Principal-Agent Problem Revisited

We argue that effective service provision depends on the structure of incentives facing providers and recipients, which in turn are shaped by five central elements. Comparing these elements helps discriminate between *the* solution of old (need as problem, supply as solution, civil service as instrument) and the new menu of solutions. The five elements are:

• *Resources*   Where does the budget of the service providers come from? Revenue from clients? Budgetary allocations? Some mix? Who retains control of the budget flows at what level? Central allocation to functions? Discretion at the point of service?

• *Information*   Does information flow to or from the top? To whom (if anyone) is information disseminated? How accessible is that information?

• *Decision making*   What is the scope of decision making? Over what items do providers have de jure or de facto control?

• *Delivery mechanisms*   To whom is the service actually provided? Individuals? Groups? By whom? Providers in large bureaucratic organizations? Are any third-party intermediaries involved? Small groups? Staff of nongovernment organizations?

• *Accountability*   To whom are service providers accountable? What power do they have? Hire and fire? Reassignment? Compensation?

Economists (and others) will recognize these five elements as exactly the central items identified in the context of institutional and organizational solutions to the principal-agent problem, particularly with multiple tasks (e.g., Holmstrom 1999, Holmstrom and Milgrom 1991, Milgrom and Roberts 1992). This problem arises whenever one actor, called the principal (e.g., a firm), with one objective (e.g., profit maximization) contracts with another actor, called the agent (e.g., an employee), to undertake a task that affects the principal's objective function, knowing the agent may have a different objective function (e.g., leisure).[25] In this case, the problem facing the principal is how to structure the incentives for the agent so that the agent's best interest, given those incentives, leads to desirable outcomes for the principal. Even within a purely market organization, there are principal-agent problems that deal with resources (What does the agent work with?), information (How does the principal observe agent effort and outcomes?), decision making (Which decisions are made by the agent, which by the principal?), delivery mechanisms (Who does the agent interact with?), and accountability (How does the payoff to the agent depend on the agent's performance?).[26]

The provision of key, discretionary, transaction-intensive services through the public sector is the mother of all institutional and organizational design problems. Service providers with discretion over actions that are difficult to observe create contracting problems even in private sector organizations,[27] but these are much more difficult in the public sector, for three reasons. First, there are many levels of the problem, each of which can fail: the multitude of citizens (as principals) must somehow constrain the government (as an agent to the citizen) to provide services. But since the problem is in the public sector, multiple levels of interaction must be addressed simultaneously: betweens citizens and the government, between government and agencies, between agencies and its employees and contractors (the providers), and between citizens and providers and the public authorities. But then the government (as principal) must constrain the behavior of its many departments (as agents) to act in the government's best interest, and then each of these departments (e.g., water, education, police) must act as a principal to constrain the behavior of its many employees (see Wilson 1989). This necessarily complex structure of the public sector, with millions of citizens and tens of thousands of employees, requires institutional and organizational patterns that structure the interactions.

Second, many activities are in the public sector precisely because the market would fail or because it is not desirable for the citizens to bear the full cost of the service. This implies that many means of disciplining workers available to a market organization (e.g., competition for sales) or to the market as an institution (e.g., competition among alternatively structured organizations) are not available to the public sector. So while making consumers bear the full cost of educational services might improve pressures for performance of teachers, it would defeat the very objective of government involvement in education (see Pritchett 2002).

Third, we are focusing on services where discretion is a necessary part of effective service delivery, so taking discretion away from agents as a means of control, while it might have advantages in terms of reducing the abuse of discretion, also has disadvantages in terms of performance outcomes. Moreover, valuable local practices—idiosyncratic knowledge of variables crucial to the welfare of the poor (e.g., soil conditions, weather patterns, water flows)—get squeezed out, even lost completely, in large, centralized development programs designed to address these issues (cf. Ostrom 1990, Scott 1998). The myriad informal practices that indigenous communities in particular have evolved over the millennia to address these concerns may be clearly ill suited to the complexity and scale of modern economic life, but the transition from one set of mechanisms to the other cannot be made in a single bound. While not attempting the transition at all is a prescription for continued poverty, revolutionaries from Stalin to Mao to Nyerere to contemporary "shock therapists" have imagined that it was actually possible and desirable to ruthlessly "skip straight to Weber"—but with patently disastrous results. In the murky middle ground between the public services and risk management systems of "Djibouti" and "Denmark" lies the need for a much more delicate articulation of the two, an articulation that the technocrats and bureaucrats of large development and other agencies inherently and inevitably struggle to resolve.

These more graphic examples of large-scale bureaucratic disaster, however, have their counterpart in a host of smaller everyday instances of repeated failure by standardized delivery mechanisms to provide basic services to the poor. Some of these problems, of course, stem from the fact that in many instances, the state itself (for whatever reason) was unable or unwilling to provide the services that citizens wanted. Our concerns, however, apply to systemic services failures that routinely occurred even in settings where intentions and resources were reasonably good. These failures, it turns out, had a common structure.

5.2   The Common Structure of the Failure of the Solution

The basic problem with the "needs–supply–civil service" solution is that it treated all problems as amenable to the logic of policies and programs. How does *the* solution structure the key elements of resources, information, decision making, delivery mechanisms, and accountability? Resources are centralized and canalized. The center collects nearly all resources from general taxes, rents, or aid—there are few user fees or local taxes—and then allocates them into budgets of line ministries. Information, if it exists at all, is tightly controlled and flows only internally and upward (not horizontally). Decision making is done primarily by government agencies and their agents, with the discretion of local agents, at least on paper, tightly controlled by rules, regulations, and mandates from the top. Delivery mechanisms are accomplished by line agencies that reach directly from center to the service provider. Accountability of the service providers flows internally and upward, with accountability to the citizens occurring only by means of whatever political mechanisms exist for expressing discontent (which are characteristically limited in autocratic, authoritarian, and totalitarian regimes).

Consider rural water supply. At first glance this seems like a perfect case for the needs–supply–civil service delivery paradigm. After all, what could be more of a need than a biological necessity like water, especially when the health consequences from insufficient or contaminated water sources are so obviously harmful? What problem could more clearly have a supply-side solution, like developing a low-cost engineering appropriate technology such as a public standpipe that can be made available to all at virtually no cost (since, after all, no one can be denied a need)? "Safe Water for All": what agenda could be more obviously necessary and more eminently doable?

The first round of government intervention was to launch discrete (often donor-funded) projects that would create simple and inexpensive public standpipes. Sometimes it succeeded, but sometimes it failed—badly. One review of 12,000 standpipes showed that breakdown rates fell from 50 percent when maintenance was the responsibility of the national water corporation to 11 percent when it was under community control (Narayan 1995). But the importance of community input was not the conclusion reached from the first round of failures: rather, they were attributed to proximate causes and imperfect project design, and so a new round of "better of the same" solutions was launched—better training, better technology, better central funding for maintenance. Only after at least the second round of failures were the failures recognized as systemic.[28]

Three systemic failures were generic in rural water supply projects. First, decisions about the location and design of the project were made on a technocratic and expert basis almost exclusively; there was little effort to incorporate local knowledge (that was often tacit). As a result, insufficient knowledge about local conditions was taken into account, and hence technological mistakes were common. This was systemic in that improvement was not simply a matter of identifying better expert decisions; failure was inherent in the design of projects that did not allow or encourage beneficiary engagement (cf. Isham, Narayan, and Pritchett 1995).

Second, the assumption that there was a need produced a complete lack of attention to what people actually wanted from improved water supplies—that is, to the demand for improved water services. This meant that the systems often did not meet the demands of the users, and hence there was little local commitment to the projects by the beneficiaries. This low commitment led to low and improper maintenance and chronic underfunding and underprovision of recurrent inputs.

Third, providers could abuse their discretion. The difficulty of observing in detail the quality of the services rendered from either the beneficiaries themselves (who were kept in the dark about costs) or the managers above (who did not know about beneficiary satisfaction) meant that projects often had considerable slack. These monies were often siphoned off in various ways to bureaucrats and politicians. There were few pressures for cost-efficiency and actual delivery of services.

Systemic failures led to a revolution in thinking about water supply—that incorporating local knowledge was important, assessing local demand was important, and creating open, transparent conditions of supply was important. In water supply, the shorthand was that water projects had to be more participatory at every stage—involving beneficiaries in design, construction (usually with cost contributions to demonstrate commitment), and maintenance (again, usually with some cost recovery).

The same pattern of problems emerged in irrigation services—the needs–supply–civil service model led to technologically inappropriate, socially inappropriate, and economically inappropriate systems that had low political commitment (Ostrom 1990). Formal, technologically superior public systems often replaced locally developed communal systems with no impact on agricultural performance. Not surprisingly, many of these large public sector projects were often not maintained, provided low-quality services, and were even corrupt in their delivery (Wade 1988). Low farmer support for modernized systems led to little maintenance effort and major information problems in water allocation.

The same problems unfolded in education—the needs–supply–civil service approach led to schools with standardized curriculum, teachers with little training, low local commitment to the school (which was viewed as "the government's" school), excessive devotion of recurrent expenditures to wages, little real learning, and high dropout rates.

The same pattern of systemic failure is evident in agricultural extension. The needs–supply–civil service model led to extension agents with packages that were often not superior to existing practices. Few efforts were made at local adaptation in the field; extension agents arrived armed with recurrent inputs (modern technologies and techniques) to actually reach farmers, and there was a resultant low adoption of "new and improved" methods (cf. Isham 2002). The same problems emerged in the health sector. The needs–supply–civil service model ensured that some services were provided and that some health conditions did sometimes improve, but often the discretionary and transaction-intensive elements did not. The results were clinics without adequate staff and recurrent inputs—not just drugs but basic equipment like scales and medical practitioners who could listen to villagers and speak in terms they could understand. Consumers did not or could not use the facilities provided, resulting in a bypassing of public primary care services for private, traditional, and higher-level public facilities.

The same pattern was followed in family planning. The needs–supply–civil service model with a specific mode of family planning as *the* solution led to low-quality services that were not attuned to the women, underutilization of public clinics, and reliance on private sector suppliers even when they were more expensive. The same thing happened with sanitation. The same thing happened with rural road construction and maintenance (see table 5.3).

The same thing happened in all these sectors because the common structure of *the* solution created the common conditions for its failure: the lack of feedback mechanisms and modes for engagement of citizens in either controlling the state or directly controlling providers allowed systemic problems of organizational design to overwhelm logistics. But the logic of *the* solution is so seductive to governments (and donors) alike that it has taken decades of painful and expensive failures in sector after sector to see that the problem is not just a few mistakes here and there, but that as an approach to development, it can be fundamentally wrong-headed from top to bottom. Why is this approach so seductive? There are both good and bad reasons.

The first good reason is that it demonstrably works: "This is how Denmark does it *now*."[29] As development was taking off in the late 1950s and early 1960s, every country that was developed delivered the bulk of its public services through a civil service. In the United States the triumph of the Progressive era agenda was fresh—and part of the triumph was defeating the power of local political machines by making public service provision less local, less discretionary, less personalized and more rational, more scientific, and more modern (Ackerman 1999). Moreover, in many former colonies, the transferred apparatus for governing was already structured in exactly this way.

Table 5.3
Problems, solutions, and symptoms of the needs–bureaucratic supply approach

Sector	The "needs"-based problem	*The* solution	Common symptoms of the problem with *the* solution	Common deep structural problems with *the* solution
Rural water supply	Need for safe water calculated from household volume requirements and biology based safety standards.	Public provision of free water through a public works program	Lack of maintenance leads to rapid depreciation One size fits all; scientific, modern, least cost, solutions lead to mistakes and inappropriate supply	Top-down civil service organization leads accountability to flow up the organizational chart, not down to citizens Attempt at "free" provision demands little commitment from local citizens
Irrigation	Need for irrigation water calculated from increased cultivation and productivity requirements	Public provision of main works and canals	Low consultation leads to low local ownership of facilities and services	Free provision combined with low and variable governmental revenues leads to periodic or chronic recurrent input starvation
Primary health care	Need for basic preventive and curative services deduced by health experts	Public provision of primary health care at clinics provided free or at low cost	Lack of recurrent inputs and low-quality services lead to low utilization and the continued reliance on traditional community or private sector alternatives	Attempt to control service providers from the top down leads to excessive, though often ineffective, regulation and imposition of common rules to limit discretion
Roads	Need for transport services calculated from traffic flows	Public provision of roads free or low cost		
Education	Need for formal schooling to achieve enrollment targets	Public provision of basic schooling provided free or at low cost	Low local discipline leads to excessive cost, inefficiency, patronage, and corruption	

The second good reason is that it makes solutions rational, modern, scientific, technological, and controllable, while rendering more legible a host of complex problems and situations (Scott 1998). It makes development an engineering problem amenable to modern management techniques. If X thousand children are to be educated, then we need Y classrooms, Z desks, and W teachers, which can then be easily mapped into corresponding budgets, targets, goals, and plans. Today, the high-profile (and otherwise laudable) Millennium Development Goals, with their straightforward (if ambitious) numerical goals, create a fresh political impetus to build the most accurate and efficient model for identifying the resources needed for a given country to reach them.

The third good reason governments (especially in the poorest countries) adopted this approach, at least formally, is that it fit perfectly with the interests of the donor agencies, providing the latter with a powerful, coherent, and consistent agenda for action at both the macrolevel and microlevels.[30] Nothing fits the internal organization needs of an assistance agency better than an objectively quantifiable gap into which resources can be poured.

Of course, nothing becomes universal on the basis of good reasons alone. There were also bad reasons for the triumph of the needs–supply–civil service approach. This approach left the direct control over the provision of the supply in government hands, which served a variety of useful purposes. First, there was no need for consultation with, or creation of, alternative power bases among business owners, labor groups, or other civil society organizations. Second, complete government control from the top down meant the central government was able to reward supporters and punish detractors. Third, direct supply may have supplanted local power structures, but it usually did not fundamentally challenge them.

A final (though speculative) bad reason for the perpetuation of the needs approach is the blinding nature of the institutional creation myths in the countries of the developed world. De Soto's (2000) account of his investigation into the historical origin of a "good" property rights regime in the United States starts from the telling insight that no one who operates the property rights regime has any idea about its origin and that the true historical origin was exactly the opposite of how it was commonly portrayed. Donor activity often amounts to sending experts who operate institutions in "Denmark" to design institutions in "Djibouti." At best this would be like sending a cab driver to design a car. But it is worse, because institutions come with their own foundational myths that deliberately obscure the social conflict the institution was designed to solve. That is, political institutions as mediators of interactions between bodies of agents arise to solve fundamental social conflicts. Often we would argue that part of the institutional solution is to pretend the social conflict never existed, with the creation myth of the institution including a false historical account as an intrinsic component of the operational institutional and organizational vision (cf. Weick 1995). This means that those who operate currently functioning and successful Weberian bureaucracies may be sufficiently blinded by their own institutions' creation myths to lack the historical knowledge and political savvy to successfully create institutions elsewhere.

For both good reasons and bad, then, most developing countries skipped straight to Weber—that is, adopted the direct government production of public services by a civil service bureaucracy within a large political jurisdiction (e.g., nation, state, province) as *the* solution. We call this approach "skipping straight to Weber" because this form did not emerge from an internal historical process of trial and error and a political struggle (as it did in most European and North American countries). Rather it was transplanted more or less intact as a top-down decision.

While debates raged as to what governments should do—from mimimalist in neoliberal capitalist states to maximalist in socialist and Marxist states—there was very little debate about how governments should do whatever it is they were doing.[31] The formal institutional and organizational structure of delivering education or police or health looked substantially the same whether the locale was Rio or Moscow or Chicago. As we saw, however, the adoption of a uniform bureaucratic supply in response to various development needs failed in sector after sector (although it also had notable successes).

To fully understand the current intellectual and practical disarray, one needs to understand not only the common structure of failure of *the* solution but also the responses to the failure. We discuss three: intensification, amputation, and (more) policy reform.

5.2.1 Intensification

As with the water sector, in nearly all cases, the initial response to failures was to point to proximate, logistical, technical causes and attempt to remedy the failures directly, but within exactly the same institutional structure—that is, with exactly the same patterns of interactions among the agents and, hence, exactly the same incentives. If pumps are breaking down, find a technological fix—a simpler pump. If classroom pedagogy is terrible, provide teachers with more training. If maintenance expenditures are too low, find more funds for maintenance. If there is corruption, launch a program to root out corruption. If the health clinics lack drugs, create a new supply chain.

We are not criticizing these efforts per se. Intensification solutions are proposed by intelligent, motivated, well-meaning professionals trying to address the very real implementation problems that present themselves. Sometimes the problem is technical, and some of these solutions did work in some places, particularly where the systemic problems between citizen and state and between providers and citizens or the state were not overwhelming.

Intensification is a natural reaction—a much more natural reaction than considering fundamental reform—for two reasons. First, even if those involved perceived the need for more fundamental changes, they were not within the mandate of those running a particular program, and there was likely a narrow range of alternatives perceived as politically feasible. Second, a much deeper problem intellectually is that the shortest distance between two points is a straight line. That is, if existing institutional and organizational forms of service delivery are de jure isomorphic to those in "Denmark," and if "Denmark" is the desired destination, then fundamental reform is not the obvious response to failure; incremental reform is much more attractive. Even if the institutional and organizational structure is dysfunctional in "Djibouti," everyone knows that the same forms can deliver services—after all, they do deliver services in "Denmark." In many cases, proposals for more local autonomy seem a step backward in the historical sequence followed by the now-developed countries. Only after many rounds of failed intensification is it acknowledged that however well services are delivered using this structure in "Denmark," it is not going to work "here."

5.2.2   Amputation

The second failed remedy to failing public services was amputation: getting the government out of it. This was legitimized under various mottos such as "getting prices right," "scaling back the state," and "privatization" (Handler 1996). This line of reasoning was given impetus by the fact that resource pressures made fiscal retrenchment necessary in any case. But while less of a bad thing is less of a bad thing, less of a bad thing is not the same as the good thing.

The amputation strategy does not work for key discretionary and transaction-intensive services for two reasons. The first is that governments discovered there were several sectors from which they could not disassociate themselves (even if it was possible or desirable). There is a whole range of activities in which governments could feasibly sell existing assets and in doing so liquidate their entire responsibility.[32] There are other activities, however, that even the complete privatization of all assets does not absolve the government of its responsibility for continuing to play a role. We are focused on the key services where either the services are essential (e.g., policing) or the government has a difficult, if not impossible, time disassociating itself for responsibility for the service.[33] Take the example of electricity. Although this activity can be privatized in various ways, no government can pretend that it is not responsible for electrical power. If people flip the switch and nothing happens, there is almost universally a different response if the device is a car versus an electric light. If the car fails to start, no one would blame the government, but if the home owner's lights fail to come on, the government will be held responsible— whether it owns and operates any part of the system or not.[34] The latter category is what we mean by key services in the first place: the provision of these services cannot be a matter of indifference to the government.

The second reason amputation did not work is that making a weak state weaker does not solve the problems that governments need to solve. The primary strategy pursued by the central ministries (finance, economy, planning) facing macroeconomic constraints on budgets was amputation, while intensification (which usually required more money) was the primary strategy desired by all the services ministries (education, health, infrastructure). These are obviously incompatible. Not delivering services with a large budget is very possible, but delivering services with no budget is impossible. The reconciliation of fiscal protection of desirable sectors (health, education) or subsectors (primary education, public health) or components of sectors (operations and management) is a less than satisfactory alternative, as protecting resources does nothing to promote sustained improvement in services.

Amputation played out in its most extreme form in the transition from socialism. In some of the more extreme cases, creaky and ineffective institutions of communism collapsed and were replaced with ... nothing. This caricature of the transition to modern capitalism has had disastrous results. Those that have had the slowest transitions to capitalist policies or those with the most rapid transitions—but either of which have managed to maintain the basic capabilities of the state—have done much better than countries with more radical reforms that undermined the state (see Bunce 1999).

5.2.3 Policy Reform

The third response is to deepen policy reform—that is, continue with the types of reforms that can be implemented by "ten smart people." That a small(ish) cadre of high-quality technocrats made a huge difference to the success of many of the East Asian tigers and to Chile is indisputable.[35] Moreover, some argue that an important component of the success of these technocratic elites is precisely that they did not have to engage in broad, open consultative processes in deciding on policies. If they had either sufficiently strong support (and direction) from the top (e.g., Indonesia, Singapore, Taiwan), or sufficient embeddedness (e.g., Japan), or both (e.g., Korea), a small cadre of well-trained, highly committed individuals could design and implement macroeconomic and trade policies quite well (even ones that required discretion).

But precisely because the proverbial ten smart people can manage these particular development decisions, there is an almost irresistible temptation (1) for these individuals to assume or be given levels of political power and stature well beyond what they can ever actually accomplish; (2) for educators and lobbyists of all stripes to focus attention on training or influencing them, in the belief that efforts expended here are likely to have a disproportionately high impact; (3) to cast a host of complex but qualitatively different development problems as technocratic policy issues amenable to standardized responses; (4) to let an increasingly narrow set of discretionary but nontransaction-intensive policies (e.g., trade openness) replace more comprehensive (and inevitably messier) efforts at designing a broad development strategy (Rodrik 1999); and (5) to imagine that the policies adopted by successful developing countries can and should be adopted by laggards elsewhere, and that only ignorance, incompetence, or indifference prevents it from happening.

Forgotten in all five cases is that not only do discretionary, nontransaction-intensive decisions constitute one part of one development agenda, but that the very success of the decisions themselves rests on (indeed is made possible by) the viability of a vast underlying organizational infrastructure (both formal and informal). Ten smart people can make the difficult but correct decision about when to shift from first to second gear, but that matters little if they fail to note that the car's breaks, wipers, and turn signals do not work, the tires are bald, the driver does not have a license, and the road is wet, winding, steep, and full of deep potholes.[36]

This is amply demonstrated in the debate over the virtues and vices of the Washington consensus (or beyond), which is explicitly, if not implicitly, and singularly about policies. Neither side doubts that countries need effective police and effective schools, but as one moves beyond policy elements, the question is not just what to do but also how to get it done, and in transaction-intensive services such as primary school education, identifying a small cadre of elite technocrats cannot be the answer. A small cadre cannot make a difference in even a modestly sized educational system if they do not change the daily classroom behavior of thousands of teachers; a small cadre cannot create a functioning legal system if they do not change the daily behavior of the law's agents on the streets and in the courtroom.

Importantly, there is no necessary connection between the sides in a given debate about policies and their stance on the appropriate institutions and organizations for discretionary transaction-intensive services (practices). That is, some argue that policies for reducing discretion are desirable because of time inconsistency or political pressures, that a precommitment will produce better results than more active discretion with regard to monetary rules or exchange rate regimes or uniform tariffs or fiscal deficit protocols. In some circumstances, this is a powerful argument, although certainly not compelling or universal. However, we are talking about services in which local, day-to-day discretion is an intrinsic part of the service; one cannot imagine nondiscretionary education or policing or agricultural extension or health care.[37] Street-level bureaucrats, direct providers, barefoot doctors, and frontline workers all need discretion to do their jobs, but with discretion there comes the possibility of abuse of discretion. One can easily be in favor of reducing discretion of some actors in policies (e.g., independent central banks to limit discretion on monetization of deficits, uniform tariffs to limit rent seeking in trade policy, pegged exchange rates) while still favoring more community power in schooling, greater voice in local infrastructure, or higher levels of user participation in irrigation projects. Or vice versa, sometimes those advocating more policy discretion are defenders of service delivery using civil service bureaucracies that limit local flexibility and service provider discretion.

This means that any discussion about empowerment, participation, or accountability in general is bound for incoherence. A working democracy is not a series of continuous referenda but a messy collection of institutions that allocate, delegate, and limit powers. The structures will be different for each. There is nothing incoherent in choosing zero popular participation in the single most important macroeconomic decision-making body (such as the Federal Reserve) and direct community participation in schooling (such as autonomous local school boards). There is also nothing incoherent in the converse, with a civil society (in the European sense) concordat to determine wage setting (and hence inflation) and schools with nationally controlled curricula and conditions.

5.3   Where We Are Today: The (Dis)Array of Alternatives

There does seem to be a broad consensus on objectives and adjectives. Few would disagree that governments should be responsible for the provision of key services: children should learn, roads should be passable, bridges should not fall down, people should get healthier, water should arrive to crops. There is perhaps more, but still little, dispute that to accomplish these objectives, the institutions and organizations of service delivery should satisfy certain adjectives:[38] be accountable, sustainable, responsive, and transparent.

But there is tremendous controversy as to exactly how to bring about such institutions and organizations. Can participation really improve outcomes? Will decentralization really bring government closer to the people? What is the best way to get to "Denmark"? We explore the characteristics of eight different answers to these questions that can be found in the contemporary literature.

5.3.1   Eight Responses to *the* Solution

To recap, in the beginning was the problem of poverty, and the answer to the problem was *the* solution: poverty defined as a series of needs, which could best be met (supplied) through a centralized civil service bureaucracy. When *the* solution failed, the initial response was intensification, amplification, and policy reform. Now that these solutions too have failed, and thereby become the problem, a variety of new responses have emerged. These responses in fact cohere into eight alternatives (see table 5.4): (1) supplier autonomy (public sector reform II), (2) single-sector participatory, (3) contracting out, (4) decentralization to states and provinces, (5) decentralization to localities and municipalities, (6) demand-side financing, (7) social funds, and (8) community-driven development (CDD).

These eight alternatives on the contemporary development agenda are all responses to the same underlying problems in the failure of these solutions. They are alternative mechanisms for changing how resources, information, decision making, delivery mechanisms, and accountability can be changed to improve outcomes. Each of these approaches has its proponents and detractors, but the questions often boil down to whether the changes proposed will be sufficient to change outcomes.

Although these alternatives are often associated with a given sector, all of them can be (and indeed have been) applied to a single sector. Schooling, for example, is one activity that everyone agrees is a key public responsibility and is a discretionary and transaction-intensive service. How should schooling be organized? National control has been the norm, but recently nearly every one of the eight alternatives has been attempted: federalization (Brazil, Argentina), localization (Indonesia), school autonomy (Nicaragua), vouchers (Chile, Czech Republic), community control (EDUCO in El Salvador), increased parental involvement, and contracting out to NGOs (Africa) have each been touted as the new, legitimate, participatory, accountable, institutional heir to the old (failed) development solution. Are all of these right and universalizable? Are none of these right in any circumstances? Are some right in some circumstances and others in others? If so, which are which?

What is needed is a diagnostic decision tree with nodes so that one can move from a concrete problem (e.g., poor schooling quality) through a set of empirical criteria—"Is your country poor, low middle, middle, rich"? "Is your country religiously homogeneous?" "Are there important regional variations in language?"—to a specific solution. But perhaps those were the wrong set of questions, and now, with the existing state of empirical knowledge, no one even knows what the most important nodes in the decision tree are, much less

Table 5.4
The solution and the new alternatives

Alternative	How flows are structured				
	Resources	Information	Decision making	Delivery mechanisms	Accountability
The solution (national agency)	From government to agency, then within agency down to providers	Internal flows up from provider (neither horizontal, nor to "out")	All decisions centralized, little formal flexibility (but some discretion in practice)	From government provider to citizen	From providers up hierarchy
1. Supplier autonomy	Flows to point of service in a flexible way	More horizontal flows	Provider works with formal discretion	By government provider	From providers up
2. Single-sector participatory	Government to agency into programs	Greater information flows to local communities	*Process* specified centrally, decisions made locally	Local group responsible for some functions	Still mostly internal to agency, but new criteria
3. Contracting out	From center to agency to contractor	As specified in contract, usually to contracting party	Parameters specified in the contract; all decisions made by contractor	By employees of the contractor	From contractors to contracting party
4. Decentralization to states/regions	Block grants from center to states/province, then through agencies	Internal flows up from provider	By states/provinces, but subject to central control	From government provider to citizen	From providers up hierarchy
5. Decentralization to localities	(As above)				
6. Demand-side financing	Government directly to citizen	Individualized	By citizen and provider	By provider chosen	Citizens choose own provider
7. Social funds	Government to social funds to communities/groups/providers	Information about availability flows out	By social funds office in response to demand, implemented locally	Contractors working directly for local group	Social funds to government
8. Community-driven development	Straight to communities (not local government)	Localized at community level (out and in)	Community chooses project and provider has autonomy	By provider chosen by community (with government input)	Providers to communities

are able to say what the thresholds are. Today there is currently no theoretical or empirical basis for making any claims about what the right solution is for any sector in any country that has not itself tried the alternatives.

Worse, it is not clear in principle that the new consensus can provide concrete answers, in two deep senses. First, if institutional conditions really do need to be tailored to individual circumstances, then conditions for replication elsewhere may simply not exist. That is, suppose the minister of education in a poor country learns that the community control of schooling in El Salvador (EDUCO) has been empirically demonstrated to be successful. Should she adapt EDUCO? Maybe, but maybe not. Perhaps El Salvador and her country do not share the same conditions. But what are the conditions for community control to work well? Having the same political system? Common language? Colonial heritage? Ethnic homogeneity? Social capital? Low or high inequality? Levels of education? To empirically estimate each of these interactive effects would require sufficient experiences in each category, but the possible variations will rapidly and inevitably outstrip any conceivably empirical experience. So as a policymaker working in particular conditions, the minister is left to make her way forward on the basis of vacuous recommendations that "institutions matter," that she should "learn from experience," adopt "best practices," and then "adapt to individual circumstances."

5.3.2 A Pressing Example: Policies to Programs in the AIDS Pandemic

Although the efficacy of core services provision is central to development, we feel there is insufficient focus on the particular issues we have highlighted. Nowhere is this more evident than in the responses to the terrible tragedy of the AIDS pandemic in Africa. In certain influential quarters, the core problem is cast exclusively as a "mercy failure" in the provision of antiretroviral drugs to combat the symptoms of AIDS. The solution is beating a path to foundations, governments, and citizens' wallets in order to persuade them to provide funds for subsidizing the production and distribution of the necessary drugs, which will then (presumably) be made available at low cost to the masses of those infected through the national health service or private (NGO or for-profit) clinics. The implicit, if not explicit, assumption is that once the funds are available and the mercy failure has been corrected, effective drugs will be available at last, and those suffering from AIDS will flock to their local clinic to purchase the medicines they have heretofore been denied.

As with so many past and recent development problems, *the* solution is the solution. The "need" for cheap drugs is "the problem," the "supply" of the technically appropriate pharmaceuticals with subsidies to ensure they are available to the poor is "the solution," and some form of large-scale public or private bureaucratic infrastructure is "the instrument" for delivering the final product to its intended recipients. Securing this money and using it in this way doubtless has its place, but surely constitutes only part of a strategy that is likely to be effective. It is a classic twin response in which the policy technocrats first calculate the size of the gap and promote it as a need, then hand it over to bureaucrats to implement the transaction-intensive but nondiscretionary program. This type of response to AIDS is consistent with the logic of "bureaucratic high modernism" (Scott 1998), but unfortunately, as we have seen, it is one that has failed early and often whenever it has been applied to a socially complex problem not amenable to logistics.

Virtually every serious analysis of the political economy, anthropology, and epidemiology of the AIDS pandemic in Africa, however, stresses as the key elements (1) the enormous social stigma that surrounds the issue, preventing politicians and religious leaders from openly addressing the subject, (2) the overwhelming power that men exert over the frequency, diversity, and nature of sexual encounters, (3) the role of particular occupational networks in establishing disease vectors that enable rapid transmission of the disease among vulnerable populations, and (4) the onerous economic, social, and psychological toll that the prolonged illness and eventual death of young adults is having on children, surviving household members, and extended kinship systems. Whether on the prevention or cure side (both are needed), dealing systematically with stigma, identity, power, networks, and kinship systems is not something amenable to routinization and uniform administrative management, but rather entails a legion of discretionary and highly transaction-intensive decisions. If the African public health experts (and, importantly, the victims themselves) have a more accurate sense of what the problem actually is and if the corresponding solutions are ones that necessarily eschew grand standardized designs, we should be simultaneously skeptical of those promoting such designs, unsurprised that there appears to be little coherence among the various particularistic strategies that practitioners offer, and yet unrelenting in our quest to build the capacity, autonomy, and accountability of those making crucial decisions that are necessarily highly discretionary and transaction intensive.

5.4   Conclusion

The old king—that agencies of the nation-state organized through a bureaucratic (in the good sense) civil service were *the* development solution, or at least, the instrument for the development solution—is dead, wounded by disappointing experience and stabbed fatally from both the political left (Scott 1998) and political right (de Soto 2000). But there is no new king, or at least not one with the substantive coherence, to take his place. The consensus around a long series of statements—"institutions matter," "improved governance is central," "there are no magic bullets," "one size does not fit all," "development should be more participatory," "service providers need to be accountable"—do not add up to a consensus about action.

In this chapter, we have endeavored to provide an analytical and historical framework for understanding why there is—and perhaps must necessarily be—an absence of a uniform consensus regarding how to improve service delivery. Discretionary, transaction-intensive services intrinsically embody the tension between two desirable goals for public services: that they be "technocratically correct" and "locally responsive."[39] As with the tension in a musical string, going too far in either direction leads to disharmony; the right creative tension depends on particular context and requires constant tuning.

It is not the case that one of the eight items currently on the development menu is inherently better than any of the others, yet neither should we conclude that therefore anything goes. If our analysis is correct, it is the very search for a consensus amenable to technocratic policies and bureaucratic programs—a consensus driven by the powerful logic and organizational imperatives of governments, donors, and aid agencies—that must be resisted, since a sizable element of effective delivery in those services central to the well-being of the poor (schooling, health care, agricultural extension) resides in precisely that area where policies and programs alone cannot go.

It is in the tension between the interests and incentives of administrators, clients, and frontline providers that the solutions lie (cf. Lipsky 1980). These tensions—between specialists and the people, planners and citizens, authority and autonomy—cannot be escaped; rather, they need to be made creative rather than destructive. Moreover, maintaining this creative tension is crucial as historical forces (whether secular or intentional) change the balance of power between them. If the incessant quest for *the* solution is in fact the problem, development professionals need to help create the conditions under which genuine experiments to discern the most appropriate local solutions to local problems can be nurtured and sustained, while also seeing them as a necessary part of a broader and more holistic country development strategy.

Acknowledgments

For helpful comments on earlier versions of this chapter, we are grateful to Sabina Alkire, Xavier Briggs, L. David Brown, Ha-Joon Chang, William Easterly, David Ellerman, Varun Gauri, Amar Hamoudi, Michael Kremer, Asim Kwaja, Deepa Narayan, Berk Ozler, Vijayendra Rao, Natasha Sacouman,

Michael Walton, and participants at seminars held at the Institute for International Economics, the University of Cambridge, the Center for Global Development, and the World Bank. Our students have also provided constructive suggestions and feedback. The views expressed in this chapter are ours alone and should not be attributed to the organizations with which we are affiliated.

Notes

1. An exception is Fine, Lapavitsas, and Pincus (2001).

2. There are two key terminological devices in the sentence that allow us to claim consensus. First, we say that provision is ensured by a public agency. This is consistent with production being entirely in the hands of private firms. Even the most radical proposal for an entirely voucher-based system of education with no public production of schooling at all, for example, would still have some public agency that supervised and regulated the process to ensure provision. Second, we refer to key services—without specifying any particular model for determining which activities are key. We are not asserting that key services are public goods (in the economist sense) or any other technocratic definition (e.g., public health specialists designate a "key" set of services), or that any service that becomes publicly provided as the result of any political process is therefore key. We are saying that however one defines key services, public responsibility for provision is a consequence.

3. We use the term *Weberian*, though of course the West did not invent the public sector bureaucracies that Weber described; China and India have had bureaucracies for thousands of years.

4. The real Denmark, it should be noted, is presided over not by a cold all-encompassing bureaucratic state, but an interesting mixture of (latent) royalty, clean democratic government, and vibrant community input.

5. We want to stress that we are not ignoring the "new public management" literature (e.g., Moore 1996, Barzelay 2001) made famous by New Zealand's sweeping public sector reforms or the "reinventing government" (Osborne and Gaebler 1993) movement in the United States. These types of reforms, however, build on a fundamentally successful set of public services and seek to make them even better (e.g., more cost efficient, flexible), and as such do not directly address the problems associated with the dysfunctional or inadequate public services characteristic of most developing countries.

6. To be clear, we are not invoking some neomodernization theory argument that the institutions of developing countries should aspire to look like or emulate the institutional features of the West. Contra the claims of those who fret that development amounts to Westernization (or colonialism by other means), in fifty years' time, Vietnam's institutions for public service delivery will most likely just be better versions of what they are today, not pale imitations of those in Switzerland. This approach also suggests that it is vital to understand how the idea and structure of viable public service institutions evolved historically (on this, see Szreter 1997 and Chang 2002). The U.S. civil service, for example, has not always been a model of what we would now call good governance. Until the 1880s, public servants' appointments were openly familial and political (Wilson 1989).

7. An explicit historical example is the imposition of more or less common forms of governance on the Native American groups in the early twentieth century. As documented by Cornell and Kalt (1992), the extent to which the de jure institutions were compatible with social realities strongly determined their functionality.

8. We do not wish to paint an entirely bleak picture, as there have been successes. The expansion of educational access and the reduction in mortality have led to revolutionary improvements in human welfare. However, there are failures of several kinds: pure failure, in which the services do not actually function even when the physical facilities are present, and the failure to build on earlier successes in the expansion of physical access to basic services, to the qualitatively more difficult stages of providing high-quality services. The analysis that follows hopes to explain both the successes and failures.

9. As we emphasize, the idea of inadequate services generally characterized those services provided by communities or informal mechanisms (that is, not directly provided by the civil service apparatus of the state) as "inadequate" or ignored them entirely (Ostrom, Gardner, and Walker 1994).

10. Thus, the three steps: step 1 is to define the goal as a "need"—children "need" education, people "need" water, farmers "need" irrigation, citizens "need" health care. Step 2 is to find the least-cost supply solution to the need. To be "least cost," the solution will have to be standardized so that it can be replicated quickly and reliably and managed efficiently. This generates an imperative toward a standardized format for schools, primary health clinics, roads, and water supply. Step 3 is to implement this solution nationally through the public sector and thus by funding (and if necessary expanding) the civil service, a hierarchical, impersonal, rule-based organization.

11. The area we address is a subset of the larger issue of the general slow progress in second-generation reforms (Naim 1994, Navia and Velasco 2002).

12. For an extended review of the successes and limitations of community-based targeting mechanisms in development projects, see Conning and Kevane (2002).

13. On social capital's intellectual and policy career at the World Bank and the various internal and external debates it has generated, see Bebbington, Guggenheim, Olson, and Woolcock (2004).

14. We exclude a variety of services about which debate rages as to whether public sector involvement is necessary or even desirable, such as provision of finance (or microfinance) and provision of housing. We exclude these not because we have a strong view as to whether governments should or should not engage in these activities, but rather because we wish to avoid debate about this question of what governments should do in favor of the question of how services can be delivered.

15. We are self-consciously linking across long-standing literatures about organizational and institutional design in economics (Kenneth Arrow, Herbert Simon), public administration (James March), and private business organizational design (Paul Milgrom, John Roberts) to relate these to the problems in the delivery of key services. We are trying to create a minimalist vocabulary that reflects these concerns.

16. Forgive us the potential confusion as "discretionary" more appropriately refers to the mode of the arrangement of an activity (which, at some level, is an endogenous choice) while we are using the term to refer to the underlying characteristics of the activity that lead it to be provided in a discretionary manner (or suffer losses from not being provided with arrangements that provide for discretion).

17. We have chosen the term *practices* because it evokes (1) what are typically small-scale arrangements for the provision of professional services (e.g., medical and legal practices), (2) the notion of informal patterns of behavior that rely on local conditions or cultures—the local practice, and (3) the idea of repetitive action (unlike policies that might require only occasional action) but which cannot be codified into a defined algorithm. The fourth logical possibility produced by our table, procedures (nondiscretionary, nontransaction-intensive decisions) refers to invariant rules. We do not discuss them in any detail because such decisions are usually fully automated (they require minimal human involvement of any kind).

18. The classic example is the small core of three or four technocrat economists who guided macroeconomic policy in Indonesia for almost thirty years (often by holding all of the key cabinet positions simultaneously).

19. The idea of Greenspan as macroeconomic maestro comes from Woodward (2000).

20. The name *programs* has the advantage of following the usual development nomenclature (of policies versus practices) but also invoking the idea of a computer program.

21. Our rendering of *practices* should not be confused with Sunstein and Ullmann-Margalit's (1999) intriguing notion of second-order decisions, which they define as the various strategies adopted in complex environments (by key actors such as judges, politicians and administrators) to avoid having to make discretionary decisions. Our discussion is more akin to, and in some senses builds on, Heifetz's (1994) useful distinction between technical and adaptive decision making.

22. In policing, for example, "studies identified the enormous gap between the practice and the image of policing. They identified problems in policing that were not simply the product of poor management, but rather reflections of the inherent complexity of the police job: informal

arrangements... were found to be more common than was compliance with formally established procedures; individual police officers were found to be routinely exercising a great deal of discretion in deciding how to handle the tremendous variety of circumstances with which they were confronted" (Goldstein 1990, 8).

23. The exception that proves the rule in the "coaching" industry (e.g., music lessons, sports instruction) is the emergence of large organizations that provide courses to prepare students for a standardized exam.

24. Less ambitiously, it is now becoming increasingly common to talk of "good practice."

25. For an attempt to provide an interdisciplinary account of organizational behavior—one stressing game theory, leadership, and cooperation within a core principal-agent framework—see Miller (1992).

26. This is not to say, of course, that a principal-agent analysis exhausts the complexity of the service provision problem.

27. The same elements of the difficulty of observation and the need to create incentives explain why some activities are generally in large organizations while others are carried out in relatively small-scale enterprises.

28. Although we have seen donor documents where the evaluation of the second round of failed water supply projects (not just second failed project but the second generation of failed projects) concludes by proposing more of same with some minor fixes.

29. Even if, as noted above, the "Denmarks" did not do it this way then, that is, when they were "poor countries" themselves (cf. Chang 2002).

30. At the macrolevel, for example, the constraints on development were seen as the savings gap and the foreign exchange gap; therefore, having donor institutions provide loans and grants that augmented investment in the form of foreign exchange was the right and proper macro instrument. If there were more specific supply requirements to meet the "needs," especially required foreign exchange, then these could easily be bundled into discrete projects.

31. In particular, professional economists were very much absorbed in a normative framework about the scope for potential Pareto improving interventions by a hypothetical welfare-maximizing actor, with, until recently, relatively less analysis of the internal logic of the performance of public sector organizations.

32. We are taking no view on the desirability of privatization per se, as there remains a debate about activities in which nearly everyone became convinced a government role was not desirable: hotels, beer manufacturing, shoe production, textiles, and cement, for example, and another set of activities about which there was consensus that government involvement in production was not essential to economic development, but for which there was continued debate about whether government involvement was desirable: retail banking, airlines, housing.

33. This "responsibility" is not deduced from a formal model, but is rather itself a complex sociopolitical outcome. That is, we are not just referring to those goods with a well-articulated rationale for public sector involvement in the sense of an economic normative (public goods) model.

34. "Privatization" in a sector can mean three very different things: privatization/liquidation (complete disassociation from government reliability, beyond the basics for any industry or sector), privatization/contracting out (in which the government continues to provide the service in the sense of bearing direct financial responsibility but no longer produces the service, and privatization/regulation (in which the government neither provides nor produces but does have sector- or industry-specific regulation).

35. See, for example, Haggard (1990), Johnson (1990), Wade (1990), Amsden (1992), and Evans (1995).

36. The masterful book by Power (2002) on the tragedy of the U.S. failure to end genocide in (among other places) Rwanda documents powerfully the disastrous consequences of narrow technocratic (e.g., "cost-benefit") decision making by a small cadre of outsiders in situations that patently cannot be managed this way. This was also the theme of David Halberstam's (1973) classic, *The Best and the Brightest*, on how U.S. engagement in the Vietnam War was designed and carried out.

37. On the challenges of delivering discretionary and transaction-intensive services (e.g., social work, policing, welfare assistance, legal aid) in the United States, see the classic study by Lipsky (1980).

38. We rule out lots of the rhetoric as unhelpful tautologies, for example, that "governance" should be "better."

39. Hayes (1968, xiii) expressed this tension well in the 1968 preface to the paperback edition of his 1959 classic on the history of the conservation movement in early twentieth-century America: "Examination of the evolution of conservation political struggles, therefore, brings into sharp focus two competing political systems in America. On the one hand the spirit of science and technology, of rational system and organization, shifted the location of decision making continually upward so as to narrow the range of influences impinging on it and to guide that decision making with large, cosmopolitan considerations, technical expertness, and the objectives of those involved in the wider networks of a modern society. These forces tended toward a more closed system of decision making. On the other, however, were a host of political impulses, often separate and conflicting, diffuse and struggling against each other within the larger political order. Their political activities sustained a more open political system, in which the range of alternatives remained wide and always available for adoption, in which complex and esoteric facts possessed by only a few were not permitted to dominate the process of decision-making, and the satisfaction of grass-roots impulses remained a constantly viable element of the political order."

References

Ackerman, S. R. 1999. *Corruption and Government: Cause, Consequences, and Reform.* Cambridge: Cambridge University Press.

Amsden, A. 1992. *Asia's Next Giant.* New York: Oxford University Press.

Barzelay, M. 2001. *The New Public Management: Improving Research and Policy Dialogue.* Berkeley: University of California Press.

Bebbington, A., S. Guggenheim, E. Olson, and M. Woolcock. 2004. "Exploring Social Capital Debates at the World Bank." *Journal of Development Studies* 40(5):33–64.

Bunce, V. 1999. *Subversive Institutions: The Design and the Destruction of Socialism and the State.* Cambridge: Cambridge University Press.

Carvalho, S., G. Perkins, and H. White. 2002. "Social Funds, Sustainability and Institutional Development Impacts: Findings from an OED Review." *Journal of International Development* 14(5):611–625.

Chang, H.-J. 2002. *Kicking Away the Ladder: Development Strategy in Historical Perspective.* London: Anthem Press.

Conning, J., and M. Kevane. 2002. "Community-Based Targeting Mechanisms for Social Safety Nets: A Critical Review." *World Development* 30(3):375–394.

Cooke, B., and U. Kothari. 2001. *Participation: The New Tyranny?* London: Zed Books.

Cornell, S., and J. Kalt. (eds.). 1992. *What Can Tribes Do? Strategies and Institutions in American Indian Economic Development.* Los Angeles: American Indian Studies Center.

de Soto, H. 2000. *The Mystery of Capital: Why Capitalism Triumphs in the West and Fails Everywhere Else.* New York: Basic Books.

Dobbin, F. 2004. "The Sociological View of the Economy." In Frank Dobbin, ed., *The New Economic Sociology: A Reader.* Princeton, N.J.: Princeton University Press.

Evans, P. 1995. *Embedded Autonomy: States and Industrial Transformation.* Princeton, N.J.: Princeton University Press.

Fine, B., C. Lapavitsas, and J. Pincus. eds. 2001. *Development Policy in the Twenty-First Century: Beyond the Post-Washington Consensus.* London: Routledge.

Goldstein, H. 1990. *Problem Oriented Policing.* New York: McGraw-Hill.

Gugerty, M. K., and M. Kremer. 2002. "The Impact of Development Assistance on Social Capital: Evidence from Kenya." In C. Grootaert and T. van Bastelaer, eds., *The Role of Social Capital in Development: An Empirical Assessment.* Cambridge: Cambridge University Press.

Haggard, S. 1990. *Pathways from the Periphery: The Politics of Growth in the Newly Industrializing Countries.* Ithaca, N.Y.: Cornell University Press.

Halberstam, D. 1973. *The Best and the Brightest.* New York: Simon and Schuster.

Handler, J. 1996. *Down from Bureaucracy: The Ambiguity of Privatization and Empowerment.* Princeton, N.J.: Princeton University Press.

Harriss, J. 2002. *De-Politicizing Development: The World Bank and Social Capital.* London: Wimbledon Publishing Co.

Hayes, S. P. 1968. *Conservation and the Gospel of Efficiency.* Pittsburgh, Pa.: University of Pittsburgh Press.

Heifetz, R. 1994. *Leadership without Easy Answers.* Cambridge, Mass.: Harvard University Press.

Hirschman, A. 1970. "The Search for Paradigms as a Hindrance to Understanding." *World Politics* 22(3):329–343.

Holmstrom, B. 1999. "Managerial Incentive Problems: A Dynamic Perspective." *Review of Economic Studies* 66(1):169–182.

Holmstrom, B., and P. Milgrom. 1991. "Multitask Principal-Agent Analyses: Incentive Contracts, Asset Ownership, and Job Design." *Journal of Law, Economics and Organization* 7(Suppl.):25–52.

Isham, J. 2002. "The Effects of Social Capital on Fertilizer Adoption: Evidence from Rural Tanzania." *Journal of African Economies* 11(1):39–60.

Isham, J., D. Narayan, and L. Pritchett. 1995. "Does Participation Improve Performance? Establishing Causality with Subjective Data." *World Bank Economic Review* 9(2):175–200.

Johnson, C. 1990. *MITI and the Japanese Miracle.* Stanford, Calif.: Stanford University Press.

Kanbur, R. 2001. "Economic Policy, Distribution and Poverty: The Nature of Disagreements." *World Development* 29(6):1083–1094.

Leonard, D. 2002. Personal communication, March 13.

Lipsky, M. 1980. *Street-Level Bureaucracy: Dilemmas of the Individual in Public Service.* New York: Russell Sage Foundation.

Milgrom, P., and J. Roberts. 1992. *Economics, Organization, and Management.* Englewood Cliffs, N.J.: Prentice Hall.

Miller, G. 1992. *Managerial Dilemmas: The Political Economy of Hierarchy.* Cambridge: Cambridge University Press.

Moore, M. 1996. *Creating Public Value: Strategic Management in Government.* Cambridge, Mass.: Harvard University Press.

Naim, M. 1994. "Latin America: The Second Stage of Reform." *Journal of Democracy* 5(4):32–48.

Narayan, D. 1995. *The Contribution of People's Participation: Evidence from 121 Rural Water Supply Projects.* Washington, D.C.: World Bank.

Navia, P., and A. Velasco. 2002. "The Politics of Second Generation Reforms in Latin America" Mimeo., Department of Politics, New York University.

Osborne, D., and T. Gaebler. 1993. *Reinventing Government: How the Entrepreneurial Spirit Is Transforming the Public Sector.* New York: Plume Books.

Ostrom, E. 1990. *Governing the Commons: The Evolution of Institutions for Collective Action.* Cambridge: Cambridge University Press.

Ostrom, E., R. Gardner, and J. Walker. 1994. *Rules, Games, and Common-Pool Resources.* Ann Arbor: University of Michigan Press.

Power, S. 2002. *A Problem from Hell: America and the Age of Genocide.* New York: Basic Books.

Pritchett, L. 2002. "'When Will They Ever Learn?' Why All Governments Produce Education." Mimeo., Harvard University, Kennedy School of Government.

Rodrik, D. 1999. *The New Global Economy and Developing Countries: Making Openness Work.* Baltimore, Md.: Johns Hopkins University Press.

Scott, J. 1998. *Seeing Like a State: How Certain Schemes to Improve the Human Condition Have Failed.* New Haven, Conn.: Yale University Press.

Sen, A. 1999. *Development as Freedom.* New York: Norton.

Srinivasan, T. N. 2001. "Attacking Poverty—A Lost Opportunity." *South Asia Economic Journal* 2(1):123–128.

Sunstein, C., and E. Ullmann-Margalit. 1999. "Second-Order Decisions." *Ethics* 110(1):5–31.

Szreter, S. 1997. "Economic Growth, Disruption, Deprivation, Disease, and Death: On the Importance of the Politics of Public Health for Development." *Population Development Review* 23(4):693–728.

Tendler, J. 1997. *Good Government in the Tropics.* Baltimore, Md.: Johns Hopkins University Press.

Tendler, J. 2000a. "Why Are Social Funds So Popular?" In S. Yusuf, S. Evenett, and W. Wu, eds., *Local Dynamics in an Era of Globalization.* New York: Oxford University Press.

Tendler, J. 2000b. "Safety Nets and Service Delivery: What Are Social Funds Really Telling Us?" In Joseph Tulchin and Allison Garland (eds.), *Social Development in Latin America: The Politics of Reform.* Boulder, Colo.: Lynne Rienner Publishers.

van Domelen, J. 2002. "Social Funds: Evidence on Targeting, Impacts and Sustainability." *Journal of International Development* 14(5):627–642.

Wade, R. 1988. *Village Republics: Institutions for Collective Action in Rural India.* Cambridge: Cambridge University Press.

Wade, R. 1990. *Governing the Market: Economic Theory and the Role of Government in East Asian Industrialization.* Princeton, N.J.: Princeton University Press.

Weick, K. 1995. *Sensemaking in Organizations.* Thousand Oaks, Calif.: Sage.

Wilson, J. Q. 1989. *Bureaucracy.* New York: Basic Books.

Woodward, B. 2000. *Maestro: Greenspan's Fed and the American Boom.* New York: Simon and Schuster.

World Bank. 2003. *World Development Report 2004: Making Services Work for Poor People.* New York: Oxford University Press.

6 Donors and Service Delivery

Ritva Reinikka

In many developing countries, external donors support reforms to improve service delivery. In middle-income or large low-income countries, they mostly pilot innovations or implement demonstration projects. If chosen strategically and evaluated properly, these projects can be powerful. In smaller low-income countries the story is different: donors supply 20 percent or more of their public resources in more than sixty poor countries. And they supply more than 40 percent of public resources in at least thirty countries, such as Bolivia, Madagascar, Nepal, and Tanzania. For these countries, aid flows are very important for service delivery.

The donor community has come a long way in understanding what makes aid more effective, focusing on the performance and hence selection of recipient countries.[1] This chapter suggests that along with country selectivity, the way donors provide their aid matters a lot. Yet donors underestimate how difficult it is to influence institutional reform without undercutting domestic accountabilities. Too aware of failures in the existing relationships of accountability among policymakers, providers, and clients in recipient countries, donors often bypass them. This can produce good isolated projects, but it can also weaken the aid recipients' own systems and accountability relationships. Therefore, this chapter suggests that:

• Donors should strengthen the critical relationships among policymakers, providers, and clients. In circumventing those relationships, they can undermine the delivery of services.

• Donors should support recipient institutions by harmonizing and realigning their financial assistance and knowledge transfers with the recipient's service delivery (particularly where aid's share of spending is large), focusing more on outcomes and results, and by evaluating innovations systematically.

• In good country environments where there are genuine reformers, donors should integrate their support in the recipient's development strategy, budget, and service delivery.

This is all fine, but the multiple objectives of foreign aid create incentives for donors to control their interventions directly rather than to align them with the recipient's service delivery. Because of these incentives, reforming aid will not be easy. Yet for service delivery to improve, donors have to attach an even higher priority to aid effectiveness and development outcomes.

The rest of the chapter is organized as follows. Section 6.1 lays out how donors affect the three principal relationships of accountability in service delivery in recipient countries. The focus is on the countries where foreign aid represents a large share of the government budget. Section 6.2 looks at the first of these relationships: that between policymakers and provider organizations (the "compact"). In section 6.3, we focus on the effects donors can have on provider organizations and their management. Section 6.4 explores how donors can help increase weak client power over service providers, while section 6.5 examines the politics of service delivery and other voice mechanisms that donors support. Section 6.6 looks at various ways donors align their aid today according to recipients' delivery systems. Finally, section 6.7 discusses some of the underlying donor incentives that restrict this alignment and make aid delivery mechanisms hard to reform.

6.1 Donors Affect Recipients' Accountability Relationships

Aid differs in important ways from domestically financed services. The beneficiaries and financiers are not just distinct; they live in different countries, with different political constituencies.[2] This geographical and political separation—between beneficiaries in the recipient country and taxpayers in the donor country—breaks the normal performance feedback loop in service delivery (figure 6.1). For example, beneficiaries in a recipient country may be able to ob-

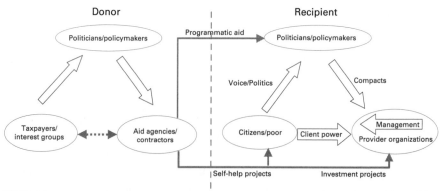

Figure 6.1

serve the performance of aid agencies. But they cannot reward or punish the policymakers responsible for this performance in donor countries. The broken feedback loop induces greater incentive biases in aid than in domestic programs. So aid effectiveness is determined not only by the performance of the recipient but also by the incentives embedded in the institutional environment of aid agencies. Understanding these incentives is central to any reform of aid to support service delivery better.

The divergence and distance between constituencies and clients may be important, but there is more. Even if donor constituencies adopted client feedback as a paramount criterion for aid, there would still be difficulties in exercising external influence without undermining local accountability relationships. To illustrate the inherent problem of external actors, consider enterprise finance. When financiers or venture capitalists want to influence an enterprise they are investing in, they become an equity holder and perhaps request a seat on the company's board. Clearly it would be politically infeasible for donors to request seats in the recipient's cabinet. Yet the influence that donors exercise on the recipient's public spending often resembles that of an equity financier.

6.2 Strengthening, Not Weakening, the Compacts

When aid flows are substantial relative to the recipient's resources, donors affect the relationship between policymakers and provider organizations, or the compact, in many ways. By influencing spending patterns and budgetary processes, donors interfere directly with the design of the compact. And by going straight to provider organizations, they sidestep the policymaker as well as the compact.

Donors affect the recipient's spending patterns and budgetary processes in the following ways:

• They may support only capital spending (construction) and expect the government to supply complementary inputs (staffing, maintenance). Governments often fail to finance the complementary inputs.

• Donors may fund projects that governments are not interested in. This contradicts ownership, though it can work where a good pilot project encourages a new approach through its demonstration effect or where a one-time intervention is needed.

• Donors may give aid to a priority sector and assume that government spending from its own resources remains unchanged. This runs into fungibility because governments attempt to smooth spending by adjusting their own allocations.[3]

• Donors may set targets for the share of spending in particular sectors as conditions for aid flows. Consider the current donor preference for social sectors, which appears to have increased both recipients' public spending on these sectors and the social sector's share of aid (from 14 percent of the aid flows in 1991 to 34 percent in 2000).[4] But strong donor preferences can leave other important areas underfunded or set perverse incentives in the privileged sector. In Zambia, protecting social spending led to deep cuts in rural infrastructure spending, possibly creating more rural poverty.[5]

To avoid such distortions, donors can discuss priorities with policymakers and work to shape public expenditure during the annual budget cycle. But the recipient has to have a budget process that functions fairly well.

Many donors see a need to align aid with the recipient's compact between policymakers and providers, but there are other tendencies as well. Global funds, which are private-public partnerships at the global level, have chosen to provide funding on a project basis directly to service providers in poor countries.[6] The new health-related global funds also develop policies for global procurement and distribution of commodities, such as mosquito nets, vaccines, and essential medicines.

In many ways, the delivery of global funds, from a global source of finance directly to the local provider, reflects the need for donors to demonstrate that the funds are additional to what otherwise would have been given. But it might also reflect dissatisfaction with the functioning of the recipient's relationships of accountability and with aid agencies. It is not clear that this is a sustainable solution to the institutional problems. Evidence from Uganda indicates that global funds can pit the recipient's policymakers, in charge of the overall spending program, against its provider organizations, who directly lobby for off-budget funds at the international level. Parallel financing mechanisms can also undermine efforts to rationalize expenditures, reform government systems, and increase transparency at the country level.

Donors interact directly with provider organizations at various levels. Some aid agencies choose to work with line ministries. Others choose to engage providers under local governments. And others go directly to frontline providers, such as health clinics or schools. Sectoral ministries independently lobby donors for funding. From the donor perspective, competition among ministries, departments, and other organizations permits a better selection process because hopeful recipients will do their best to reveal as much information as possible to attract donors. The result is that recipients' policymakers lose control of the expenditure program, because the finance is off-budget and the activities bypass the compact. Incoherent spending allocations and uneven coverage of services ensue.

Similar competition can occur among donors, making incentive problems worse. When the recipient agency knows that if one donor threatens to withdraw due to the recipient agency's poor performance other donors will step in, few incentives exist for improving its performance.[7]

Some donors, including the World Bank, even circumvent provider organizations by setting up autonomous or semiautonomous project implementation units for their interventions. Advocates of project implementation units recognize that the arrangements can undermine local capacity building, create salary distortions, and weaken the compact between the policymaker and the provider organization. But they argue that the better results outweigh the costs. A study of about a hundred World Bank projects in the Latin America and the Caribbean region shows otherwise: project implementation units have no significant positive impact on project outcomes, while the likely sustainability of results clearly suffered.[8] A parallel study in the Eastern Europe and Central Asia region produced similar findings.[9]

To staff project implementation units, donors tend to hire the most highly skilled civil servants, often at salaries many times what they could earn from the government. In Kenya a World Bank agricultural project paid eight local staff between $3,000 and $6,000 a month, many times the $250 available to a senior economist in the civil service.[10] Another study found that of twenty Kenyan government economists receiving a master's degree training in a donor-funded program between 1977 and 1985, fifteen were working for aid agencies or nongovernmental organizations (NGOs) or for their projects by 1994.[11] In countries with many donors, salaries are likely to be bid up even more as donors compete for qualified staff.

A better choice to improve aid effectiveness is to phase these units out and work with the recipient's provider organizations, building their capacity. And it should take place within the compact between the recipient's policymakers and service providers. But this requires changes in incentives in aid agencies.

6.3 Allowing Provider Organizations Manage

Donors affect the management of provider organizations in recipient countries in at least three ways: by the fragmentation of aid in a large number of donor projects, the choice of activities, and the choice of inputs.

6.3.1 The Costs of Aid Fragmentation

The problem with aid fragmentation is not that individual projects are misconceived; it is that there are too many projects for any to work efficiently. When a project's fixed costs are high and there are returns to scale, fragmented aid can be wasteful. Furthermore, when donors each have only a small share of the total aid in a recipient country, their stake in the country's development, including capacity building, may be reduced relative to their concern for the success of their own projects. Fragmentation also imposes high transactions costs on recipients, with large amounts of officials' time taken up by donor requirements.

Little systematic evidence is available on fragmentation and its effect on the management of provider organizations. One source, though limited, is the Development Gateway database, with records on about 340,000 aid projects and programs across the developing world.[12] Using the database to quantify the extent of donor fragmentation yields a mean Herfindahl index value for donor fragmentation across recipients of 0.87.[13] (Index values increase with the number of donors active in the country and with greater parity among donors. Low values indicate a smaller number of donors or that some donors dominate.[14]) For example, Tanzania has a high index value of 0.92, with more than eighty aid agencies having funded 7,000 projects over time. A similar index computed from another data set, annual aid disbursements, suggests that donor fragmentation is on the rise (figure 6.2).[15]

High fragmentation indexes could reflect donor specialization in different sectors, so that fragmentation would be low in each sector. But mean levels of the index are only slightly lower within individual sectors: 0.85 for education, 0.77 for health, and 0.78 for water projects. High fragmentation values for most recipients show that donors do not specialize very much by either sector or country. Most donors are active in many sectors in most countries: a typical recipient nation in 2000 received aid from about 15 bilaterals and 10 multilaterals (table 6.1).

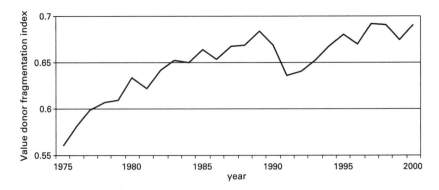

Figure 6.2
Source: Knack and Rahman, this volume.

How does donor fragmentation affect the recipient's provider organizations? Little systematic evidence is available. Knack and Rahman (chapter 11, this volume) find an association between rising fragmentation and declining bureaucratic quality in high-aid countries and in sub-Saharan Africa, controlling for changes in per capita income and other variables. This finding suggests that donors with a small share of the aid in a country may focus more on delivering successful projects, even at the expense of government capacity—for example, by hiring the most qualified government administrators to run their projects. This collective action problem may be less severe where there is a dominant donor, who has a greater incentive to take a broader and longer-term view of the country's development.

High fragmentation means high transaction costs for recipients. Tanzanian government officials had to prepare about 2,000 reports of different kinds to donors and receive more than 1,000 donor delegations each year. These requirements tax rather than build provider organizations' limited capacities, diverting efforts toward satisfying donor obligations rather than reporting to domestic policymakers. Recognizing the adverse effects, donor agencies have recently initiated measures to curb compliance costs and streamline operational policies, procedures, and practices, focusing on financial management, procurement, environmental assessment, and reporting and monitoring.

But change has been slow. The emphasis so far has been to find common international standards and principles at the aid agency level rather than to adapt donor behavior to the procedures used by the recipient's service providers in their reporting to domestic policymakers. Exceptions are beginning to emerge, including Tanzania, Bolivia, Vietnam, and Ethiopia, where donors

Table 6.1
Distribution of aid recipients according to the number and type of official donors, 2000

	Type of aid donor	
	Bilateral donors only	Bilateral and multilateral donors
Number of recipients with 1–9 donors	3	13
Number of recipients with 10–19 donors	93	27
Number of recipients with 20–29 donors	22	69
Number of recipients with 30–39 donors	0	40
Average number of donors per recipient	14	26
Median number of donors per recipient	16	23

Note: The number of donors was calculated by using figures for total official development assistance (ODA) 2000, provided by the OECD DAC. The number of recipients takes into consideration only the independent countries according to the list of member states of the United Nations. *Source*: Acharya, de Lima, and Moore (2003), from OECD DAC data.

are planning to help the government develop a harmonization program rather than limit it to the donor community.

6.3.2 Donor Influence on Choice of Activities and Inputs

Donors also influence the choice of activities within a sector. They tend to be generous with training. In Malawi, training accounts for a staggering $4.5 million, or 10 percent of donor spending on health care a year.[16] It is hard to believe that the return on this investment matches the cost or that the government would spend this much on training if it had the choice. And the real cost appears to be even higher: staff may be absent from work for long periods on training courses. Training opportunities are often a form of incentive for staff. If so, the funds would likely be better used if the sponsoring donors provided them directly to supplement salaries through the budget. The $4.5 million spent on training health workers in Malawi would translate on average to a 50 percent increase in salary for all health care staff.

The input mix in aid-financed public spending often differs from that in recipient spending. For example, donors provide far more technical assistance (and project vehicles) than the recipient would buy if it had the money. In Malawi technical assistance accounts for 24 percent of donor spending on health.[17] A major obstacle to addressing this issue is the shortage of data. Many recipient budgetary systems have much better data on the input mix for domestically financed expenditures than they do on donor projects, which are sometimes treated as single lines in the budget. Donor officials have weak incentives to provide full information to recipient governments.

6.4 Increasing Client Power

That client power—the relationship between beneficiary and service provider—tends to be weak in many developing countries has long presented donors with a dilemma. Should they help strengthen the links between users and existing providers? Or should they find a way around the recipient's service delivery system to ensure that aid-funded services reach poor people? This becomes even more complicated in heavily HIV/AIDS-affected countries, those coming out of conflict, and those with weak and corrupt public institutions. Official donor agencies have followed the example of their nongovernmental counterparts, approaching communities and user groups directly, through sharply increased funding for social funds and self-help projects. Three main problems surface in these activities: an undermining of government and other local capacity, weakened prospects of sustainability, and the capture of benefits by elites.

In principle, social funds and self-help projects could operate within the recipient's service delivery system. They could also serve as entry points for the policy dialogue with policymakers and providers and hence build local government capacity rather than undermine it. But like many other projects, they tend to be operated directly by donors with little integration.

Most assessments of social funds and self-help projects focus on poverty targeting. Overall the evidence suggests that centralized systems do better at identifying poor communities than at identifying poor households or poor individuals.[18] The effectiveness of targeting varies widely, which suggests the importance of unobserved attributes of communities. Some studies show that public service delivery, measured by access to infrastructure or outcomes, improved through community involvement,[19] while other studies found that performance could be better.[20]

Yet social funds and self-help interventions continue to face serious challenges of sustainability. One challenge arises from the cultural and social context of communities and their capacity for collective action. It is not clear that the self-help approach can benefit fractured, heterogeneous communities that have little capacity for collective action. Alternative methods of service delivery may suit such poor communities better. But there is little factual evidence on this because evaluations typically do not compare social funds and self-help projects with conventional service delivery mechanisms. Nor do they take into account the negative side effects. The sustainability of self-help projects can be in jeopardy if line ministries or local governments ignore them once they are completed. Unless communities can ensure continuing support for recurrent costs and staff, they may not be able to sustain their project.

Donors need to disburse funds fast and show visible results quickly to supporters or taxpayers. A recent study in a Sahelian country, also applicable elsewhere, shows that these needs may be incompatible with reducing poverty.[21] When donors are impatient, compete with similar agencies for good projects, or do not have the capacity to monitor activities on the ground, they may choose particular groups to work with, risking the capture of donor funds by elites. Impatient donors may even make the patient donors attach greater weight to quick results, undermining the prospects for poverty reduction. This becomes a serious problem when malevolent elites capture donor funds for private gain.

Social funds and self-help projects should be designed for each context, with best-practice templates as initial guides only. Rapid expansion of such projects by donors with little experience may not be feasible. Rather than implementing numerous enclave operations in a single recipient country, donors could pool support openly and transparently to achieve better results in scaling up and preventing elite capture, even when bypassing the policymaker-provider relationship in a failed state or low-income country under stress.[22] Where conditions are right, the pooling of aid should not stop with the donors; it should extend to national and local governments and other providers, private for profit and nonprofit.

Donors can also promote other initiatives to enhance client power. They can encourage citizen monitoring of service providers, such as report cards and public expenditure tracking surveys. They can help monitor the use of services and support benefit-incidence analyses to identify the groups missing out. However, involving providers in the design of the monitoring process is critical to ensuring buy-in for the results.

6.5 Promoting Voice

Promoting citizen voice through formal political mechanisms or through informal advocacy groups or public information campaigns is one of the most difficult endeavors for donors. Yet donors attempt to do it in many ways, a testament to the importance of voice in service reform. The attempts include imposing conditions and setting performance criteria on aid flows where voice is weak, providing direct support to democratic governance, and actively promoting transparency and participatory processes.

By imposing conditions, donors try to replace the weak voice of citizens in disciplining policymakers. Yet donor conditions are fundamentally different from citizen voice, which is diffuse, after-the-fact, and a long-term process. In the 1980s structural adjustment loans extended conditions in projects to a wide spectrum of government economic policies, processes, and public spending. There is ample evidence today that conditions based on promises do not work well because they undermine ownership of the reform program.[23]

When policymakers are not encouraged to develop their own positions on, say, privatization of water supply or other services, but rely on donor conditions in taking action, they can more easily deny responsibility for a later failure. It is not the quantity of aid that makes the recipient's policies good or institutional reforms happen. Empirical studies show that aid finance is ineffective in inducing policy reform in a bad policy environment.[24] What works better is choosing recipients more carefully, based on performance (country selectivity), and setting conditions that reward reforms completed rather than those promised.[25]

Traditional conditionality does not work well. How can donors then allocate aid so that it provides a strong incentive for the recipient to promote citizen voice and undertake service reform and thus increases aid effectiveness? In principle, there is broad agreement today that instead of conditions, the aid compact needs to contain verifiable indicators that can measure performance. But in practice, the use of performance indicators has not yet changed the incentives underpinning the relationship between recipients and donors.[26]

Few performance indicators used today measure outcomes; most still measure inputs and processes. So far the link between these operational performance indicators and the outcome targets articulated in poverty-reduction strategies remains vague. And there are few transparent mechanisms to allow donors to signal the conditions for a recipient to expect an increase or reduction in aid. Initiatives to improve the measurement of results are under way, but it will take time to establish an effective link between the volume of aid and performance.

There is also tension between the monitoring and incentive functions of performance indicators. Donors, preoccupied with fiduciary concerns, tend to keep a close watch on the programs they support—hence, the focus on short-term process undertakings rather than genuine outcome measures as triggers for performance evaluation.[27] But this can lead instead to micromanagement, exactly what the new system of performance-based conditions is intended to avoid. This tension, if unresolved, makes aid compacts incoherent.

Many bilateral donors go further and support electoral participation and democracy directly and use aid to induce and reward such reforms. For example, donors rewarded Ghana for holding free elections in 1992, despite the excessive public spending prior to the elections that resulted in poor macroeconomic performance.

Donors also support informal mechanisms to strengthen citizen voice. One is to promote participatory processes in the development of poverty-reduction strategies and budgetary processes. But aid agencies and recipient governments sometimes have different views on what form the participation should take. Aid agencies seldom hold a dialogue with parliamentarians, stressing instead the extragovernmental aspects of participation, involving a wide range of civil society. Members of parliament sometimes view the donor emphasis on civil society as undermining the legitimacy of elected representatives, particularly in emerging democracies. They also question the legitimacy of NGOs selected to speak for "the people."

Poverty-reduction strategies seek to promote stronger citizen voice, with an effective link to public spending. But they also seek to change the relationship between recipients and donors by stressing the recipient's ownership of the reform agenda. There are often trade-offs when one instrument is used to achieve multiple goals. Countries preparing the early poverty-reduction policy papers

(PRSP) faced many challenges in managing the participatory process and linking their strategy to the budget, while adhering to tight timetables for debt relief for which a PRSP was a condition. Experience in many countries suggests that when a government presents a national development strategy, supported by broad ownership and well-defined sector priorities, this contributes in no small measure to attracting broad donor support. Moreover, it also offers a framework to better align and harmonize donor support.

6.6   Aligning Aid Delivery with Service Delivery

For donors that want to align their aid delivery with service delivery in recipient countries, this chapter has three key messages. First, to reduce the costs of aid fragmentation and build capacity, it is critical for donors to harmonize and align policies, procedures, and practices around the recipient's own systems. Where country systems are weak, they need to be strengthened to meet good practice standards, not bypassed and substituted with ring-fenced donor systems and procedures. This is crucial for aid effectiveness in low-income countries that receive a substantial part of their public resources as foreign aid. But it is also relevant in middle-income countries in sectors where donors are especially active, as in social protection in Latin America and elsewhere.

Second, harmonization and realignment are best done at the country level and by strengthening the recipient's existing institutions. In countries with fairly good expenditure management and genuine service reforms—where donors and recipients trust each other—budget support may be a viable tool. Resource pooling can also be effective in scaling up service delivery and reducing transaction costs in low-income countries that are under stress—for example, due to past or current conflict.[28]

Third, it is important to evaluate interventions and aid projects for impact. More systematic evaluations of, say, an intervention's effects on student learning or health status are critical for scaling up in both middle- and low-income countries. Evaluation linked to early steps toward rebuilding state capacity is important in situations where donors are working through alternative service providers due to conflict or state failure.

6.6.1   Harmonizing Donor Support around Recipient Systems

Harmonizing is easier where the recipient has a well-functioning national development strategy and budget process that can serve as the common framework. But these are not prerequisites, for even in their absence, harmonization and pooling of aid can offer significant benefits and reduce transaction costs.[29] A common refrain is that recipients need to improve their financial management and public procurement practices before donors can align their support around the recipient's systems. But reality is more nuanced. First, donors need to ask whether relying on country systems is riskier than the alternative of ring-fencing. Currently, developing-country borrowers must produce 8,000 audit reports every year for multilateral development banks—5,500 of such reports for the World Bank. Such a fragmentation of activities cannot increase accountability. Second, even if it is riskier, this needs to be set against the more sustainable benefits of helping to build the recipient's institutions and systems. Third, donors need to avoid the trap of making a given level of capacity a condition for aligning or pooling aid, when in many cases the pooling launches efforts that can get capacity closer to where it needs to be. That said, there will still be cases in which donors judge (rather than scientifically determine) that it would be inappropriate to pool, given the fiduciary risks.

6.6.2 Sector-Wide Approaches

Since the mid-1990s, many countries have worked to integrate government and donor activities within a sector. In the ideal approach, outlined in early documents on sector-wide approaches, the government and its partners would agree on a predictable resource envelope and on a policy environment consistent with the national budget and economic strategy.[30] They would then agree on how to assign resources within this envelope. Procedures for disbursement would be harmonized, and funds would be pooled. All activities would reflect a shared view of the priorities and costs of activities. Differences would be resolved by compromises in the design of programs, not in the activities undertaken. There would be no detectable difference between the approach taken on government-funded and donor-funded activities; indeed, that distinction would wither away.

Sector-wide approaches have been established in several sectors in many low-income countries: health, education, agriculture, transport, energy, and water.[31] Efforts so far are only partial realizations of the ideal. To some extent, determining what constitutes a sector-wide approach is still an arbitrary decision. There has been progress toward pooling trust funds in recent years, however. For the twenty-four programs tracked by the Strategic Partnership with Africa in 2002, 41 percent of assistance came through projects (down from 56 percent two years earlier), 13 percent through NGOs, 11 percent as common basket, and 35 percent as budget support. In Ghana's health program, the pooling arrangements started with "one donor and minimal funding" but later reached 40 percent of program resources.[32]

Preparing and implementing sector-wide approaches can be a long, drawn-out process. It can also weaken rather than strengthen the recipient's compact between its policymakers and provider organizations by taking the sector out of the domestic decision-making process, particularly the budgetary process, financial management, and public procurement.[33] Four lessons have emerged from sector-wide approaches:

• An institutional analysis of the sector is needed beforehand, including the sector's relation to the rest of the public sector.

• If the capacity constraint is in the lead ministry rather than the country, new personnel can sometimes be found quickly, as in the Uganda education and health sectors.[34]

• Procedures need to be designed with capacity limitations in mind, particularly at decentralized levels. This will often mean encouraging public transparency and bottom-up monitoring to bolster simple but rigorously enforced upward-reporting requirements. Procurement procedures, often a major difficulty, need to balance rigor with simplicity.

• Capacity constraints are not a reason to delay a sector-wide approach. Few countries achieve the ideal, but most can benefit from some aspects of the process.

Assessments of sector-wide approaches have reached mixed findings. Ratings from the Strategic Partnership with Africa report in 2002 show an average implementation rating for programs of between 0.42 and 0.58, depending on the sector (on a scale where 0 is poor, 0.33 fair, 0.66 good, and 1.0 very good). But it is possible that these relatively poor ratings also reflect the ambitious agenda for sector-wide approaches. A tentative conclusion is that sector-wide approaches are an important part of a poverty-reduction strategy, not an alternative, and the full benefits will not be realized until financing mechanisms become more flexible.

6.6.3 Budget Support

The focus on budget support was sharpened by the debt relief for heavily indebted poor countries, allocating relief to priority sectors through the recipient's budget. Budget support restores the compact between policymakers and providers. It allows contestability in public spending. And it reduces the costs from fragmentation and separate project implementation units. Providing funds to the general budget also offers a better framework for discussing intersectoral allocations. Advocates of more funding to one sector have to show that the sector has higher returns than others at the margin. If funds go to sectors that demonstrably reduce poverty, directly or indirectly, donors should be flexible about budget allocations.

Budget support, like basket funding for a sector-wide approach, raises questions of fiduciary risk. But there is no clear evidence that the risk is greater for budget support than for project aid. Needed are transparent systems for procurement and public information to ensure that the movement of funds through the system can be publicly observed and that charges paid for services are clearly defined. Donors can contribute best by promoting these systems in the recipient country. The Utstein group of donors—the United Kingdom, the Netherlands, Norway, and Germany—has been developing monitoring arrangements along these lines. The European Union links part of its budget support to performance, using a small set of indicators.

What does all this suggest? That aid will work best where it is provided flexibly to recipients with sound overall strategies and well-designed sectoral programs. Flexible aid can catalyze processes within governments to produce sound strategies, rational spending programs, and effective services.

6.6.4 Innovate and Evaluate

Large public sector organizations in both donor and recipient countries focus on inputs and process evaluation rather than outputs and outcomes. The incentive to do this in aid agencies is even stronger because of the broken feedback loop between taxpayers in the donor country and beneficiaries in the recipient country (figure 6.1). Outcome and impact evaluations are seldom built into aid projects. Special attention is hence required to counter the tendency of aid agencies to be input oriented and to increase the share of interventions subject to rigorous impact evaluation. Outcome-oriented international targets, such as the Millennium Development Goals, can add to the incentives for aid agencies to overcome their focus on inputs.

A major difficulty in assessing the impacts of any public program is that beneficiaries are rarely selected randomly. Indeed, most programs are purposely targeted to specific groups or regions. Isolating the impacts from the circumstances that led to participation is then tortuous. Yet not doing so may produce misleading results. Schemes that select participants randomly provide the best opportunities for unbiased impact evaluation. An example is the Education, Health, and Nutrition Program of Mexico (PROGRESA), a large government transfer program. Strong evidence of its high impact led to an expansion of the program in Mexico and the adoption of similar programs elsewhere. Another example is the secondary school voucher program in Colombia, which assigned beneficiaries by lottery, making it feasible to compare those receiving vouchers with those who did not.[35] A randomly assigned pilot program for treating intestinal worms in Kenyan schoolchildren has been similarly evaluated.[36]

In many operational settings, however, randomization cannot be applied, and other methods must be found to create a matched comparison. Even when data on beneficiaries before and after implementation exist, determining the real effects of a program or policy change requires data on matched comparison groups to get at the counterfactual of what would have happened without the policy. For some schemes that do not have baseline data, it is possible to construct an adequate control group from the postintervention data. But baseline data are needed for others, such as rural roads with far-reaching impacts on poverty, health, and education outcomes.[37]

Not every program can be evaluated for impact, so governments and donors need to select programs for evaluation carefully, focusing on areas where new knowledge is needed. Interventions rolled out in phases because of budget and other constraints offer good opportunities for effective impact evaluation. Similarly, when a pilot is required before a large-scale rollout, an impact evaluation will generate important information for decision makers.

6.7 Why Rreforming Aid Is So Difficult

The unintended negative effects of donor behavior are not a recent discovery, so why has there not been more reform? Why, for instance, are donors so reluctant to channel aid as part of the recipient's budget? Simplifying donor policies, procedures, and practices and directing aid flexibly through sector-wide approaches or the budget process would lower the high transaction costs in low-income countries and allow recipients to pursue their objectives more efficiently. That could be done if donors were driven solely by the motive to reduce poverty and if recipients were perceived to be committed to the same goal. But the world is more complex. Incentives in aid agencies and the political economy of aid in donor countries work against this:

• Aid agencies want to be able to identify their own contributions, often through distinct projects, to facilitate feedback to taxpayers and sustain political support for aid flows. A new hospital is easier to showcase than the outcome of policy reform or budget support.

• Aid agencies, facing disbursement pressures, need to show quick results to taxpayers—and NGOs to their contributors. This is easier when donors are in charge of interventions.

• Politicians and policymakers in donor countries cannot dismiss the interest groups that support them—groups that may place a high priority on funding like-minded groups in developing countries.

• Many donors limit the market for aid services and supplies to their own nationals (tied aid). Foreign aid sustains a large consultancy industry in member nations of the Organization for Economic Cooperation and Development, estimated at $4 billion a year for sub-Saharan Africa, or 30 percent of aid to the continent.

• Preferences for spending differ among donors and between donors and recipients. Donors often are most comfortable with service delivery systems of the type operating in their own country. For instance, British and Nordic advisers are familiar with a clinic-based free health service and so prefer to support those systems in low-income countries too.

• Fiduciary concerns and incentives in aid agencies cause donors to focus on monitoring inputs and processes. Again, the monitoring is easier in project aid where the donor controls the design and implementation of each intervention.

• Donors may want to persuade aid recipients of the value of a different approach through a pilot project, to show success.

• Bilateral donors distribute their aid budgets across a large number of recipients and sectors, to increase the visibility of their programs or to leverage or reward diplomatic support from recipient nations.[38] More specialization among sectors or recipients, however efficient, could expose a donor to charges that it is neglecting, say, a global health crisis or a regional humanitarian crisis. Such considerations help explain why the typical bilateral donor in 2000 provided official development aid (ODA) to about 115 independent nations. Even omitting recipients that received less than $100,000, the mean number of ODA recipients for each of the twenty-two major bilateral donors was ninety-five.

These multiple objectives create incentives for donors to finance and directly control their aid interventions. That creates problems for recipient countries: donors often do not know (or do not care) what the other donors and the recipient are doing, which results in duplication, waste, and gaps in services.[39] These days, donors tend to favor social sector projects over other public expenditures. If they do not pay attention to what the others are doing, they may concentrate too much on higher-priority sectors, leaving sectors with a lower priority, such as rural roads in Zambia, short of funds. Or there may be gaps in the priority areas simply because nobody is looking at the big picture. But priorities among donors vary, and their approaches change over time.[40] So there is some scope—and hope—for improvement.

Notes

This chapter is a revised version of chapter 11 in the 2004 World Development Report *Making Services Work for Poor People*.

1. World Bank (1998), Burnside and Dollar (2000a, 2000b), Collier and Dollar (2002).

2. Martens et al. (2002) and Ostrom et al. (2001).

3. The literature on fungibility—including Devarajan and Swaroop (1998), Devarajan, Rajkumar, and Swaroop (1999), and Feyziogly, Swaroop, and Zhu (1998)—finds that only a portion of aid stays in the sector: when the government receives sector-specific aid, it shifts its own resources partially to other sectors. Fungibility suggests that donors should take a more holistic approach to recipients' public spending.

4. Development Assistance Committee (DAC) of the Organization for Economic Cooperation and Development (OECD).

5. World Bank (2001c).

6. For example, the Global Fund to Fight AIDS, Tuberculosis and Malaria; the Global Alliance for Vaccinations and Immunizations; the Global Vaccine Fund; and the Global Environment Facility.

7. Ostrom et al. (2001).

8. Boyce and Haddad (2001).

9. World Bank (2001b).

10. World Bank (1998).

11. Cohen and Wheeler (1997).

12. Data for the Development Gateway are provided by the OECD DAC and other donor sources over several decades. Unfortunately, the database has no indication of the number of projects ongoing at any given time.

13. A Herfindahl index of donor concentration is first calculated by summing the squared shares of aid over all donor agencies operating in the recipient country. This index, which ranges from 0 to 1, is then subtracted from 1 to form an index of donor fragmentation, with high values indicating greater fragmentation (Knack and Rahman 2003). See also O'Connell and Saludo (2001).

14. Index values do not necessarily rise with aid levels or number of projects; doubling each donor's aid or number of projects but keeping the number of donors and their activity shares constant leaves the index values unchanged.

15. Data are from the OECD DAC. The trend may overstate the worsening of donor fragmentation to the extent that pooling of donor funds has also increased, because the index calculated on the basis of disbursements does not distinguish pooled funds from nonpooled funds (Knack and Rahman 2003).

16. Picazo (2002).

17. Ibid.

18. Mansuri and Rao (2003).

19. Chase (2002), Newman et al. (2002), Paxson and Schady (2002), and Van Domelen (2002).

20. World Bank (2002a).

21. Platteau and Gaspart (2003).

22. World Bank (2002b).

23. Gunning (2001).

24. Collier (1997), Kapur and Webb (2000), Devarajan, Dollar, and Holmgren (2001), Dollar and Svensson (2000).

25. Svensson (2003).

26. Adam and Gunning (2002).

27. Ibid.

28. World Bank (2002b).
29. Riddel (1999).
30. Harrold and Associates (1995).
31. There have been a number of reviews of the sector-wide approach, including Brown (2000a), Conway (2000), Foster (2000), Foster, Brown, and Conway (2000), Jones (1997), Jones and Lawson (2001), and World Bank (2001a).
32. Fozzard and Foster (2001) and Kanbur and Sandler (1999).
33. Adam and Gunning (2002).
34. Brown (2000b).
35. Angrist et al. (2002).
36. Miguel and Kremer (2001).
37. van de Walle (2002) and van de Walle and Cratty (2003).
38. Most bilateral donors give more aid to countries that vote similarly to them in the United Nations General Assembly, where each nation, regardless of size, has one vote (Alesina and Dollar 2000, Wang 1999).
39. Halonen (2007).
40. See, for example, Tarp and Hjertholm (2000).

References

The word *processed* describes informally reproduced works that may not be commonly available through libraries.

Acharya, Arnab, Fuzzo de Lima, and Mick Moore. 2003. "The Proliferators: Transactions Costs and the Value of Aid." Institute of Development Studies, Sussex. Processed.

Adam, Christopher S., and Jan Willem Gunning. 2002. "Redesigning the Aid Contract: Donors' Use of Performance Indicators in Uganda." *World Development* 30(12):2045–2056.

Alesina, Alberto, and David Dollar. 2000. "Who Gives Foreign Aid and Why?" *Journal of Economic Growth* 5(1):33–63.

Angrist, Joshua, Eric Bettinger, Erik Bloom, Elizabeth M. King, and Michael Kremer. 2002. "Vouchers for Private Schooling in Colombia: Evidence from a Randomized Natural Experiment." *American Economic Review* 92(5):1535–1558.

Boyce, Daniel, and Afef Haddad. 2001. "Thematic Review on Project Implementation Units: An Analysis of Ongoing and Completed Projects in Latin America and the Caribbean." Washington, D.C.: World Bank.

Brown, Adrienne. 2000a. "Current Issues in Sector-Wide Approaches for Health Development: Mozambique Case Study." Geneva: World Health Organization.

Brown, Adrienne. 2000b. "Current Issues in Sector-Wide Approaches for Health Development: Uganda Study." Geneva: World Health Organization.

Burnside, Craig, and David Dollar. 2000a. "Aid, Growth, the Incentive Regime and Poverty Reduction." In Christopher L. Gilbert and David Vines, eds., *The World Bank Structure and Policies.* Cambridge: Cambridge University Press.

Burnside, Craig, and David Dollar. 2000b. "Aid, Policies and Growth." *American Economic Review* 90(4):847–868.

Chase, Robert. 2002. "Supporting Communities in Transition: The Impact of Armenian Social Investment Fund." *World Bank Economic Review* 16(2):219–240.

Cohen, John M., and John R. Wheeler. 1997. "Building Sustainable Professional Capacity in African Public Sectors: Retention Constraints in Kenya." *Public Administration and Development* 17:307–324.

Collier, Paul. 1997. "The Failure of Conditionality." In C. Gwin and J. M. Nelson, eds., *Perspectives on Aid and Development.* Washington, D.C.: Overseas Development Council.

Collier, Paul, and David Dollar. 2002. "Aid Allocation and Poverty Reduction." *European Economic Review* 46(8):1475–1500.

Conway, Tim. 2000. "Current Issues in Sector-Wide Approaches for Health Development: Cambodia Case Study." Geneva: World Health Organization.

Devarajan, Shantayanan, David Dollar, and Torgny Holmgren, eds. 2001. *Aid and Reform in Africa: Lessons from Ten Case Studies.* Washington, D.C.: World Bank.

Devarajan, Shantayanan, Andrew Sunil Rajkumar, and Vinaya Swaroop. 1999. "What Does Aid to Africa Finance?" World Bank Policy Research Working Paper 2092. Washington, D.C.: World Bank.

Devarajan, Shantayanan, and Vinaya Swaroop. 1998. "The Implications of Foreign Aid Fungibility for Development Assistance." World Bank Policy Research Working Paper Series 2022. Washington, D.C.: World Bank.

Dollar, David, and Jakob Svensson. 2000. "What Explains the Success or Failure of Structural Adjustment Programs?" *Economic Journal* 110(466):894–917.

Feyziogly, Tarhan, Vinaya Swaroop, and Min Zhu. 1998. "A Panel Data Analysis of the Fungibility of Foreign Aid." *World Bank Economic Review* 12(1):29–58.

Foster, Mick. 2000. "New Approaches to Development Cooperation: What Can We Learn from Experience with Implementing Sector-Wide Approaches?" London: Overseas Development Institute. Available at http://www.odi.org.uk/pppg/publications/working_papers/140.html.

Foster, Mick, Adrienne Brown, and Tim Conway. 2000. "Sector Health Approaches for Health Development: A Review of Experience." Geneva: World Health Organization.

Fozzard, Adrian, and Mick Foster. 2001. "Changing Approaches to Public Expenditure Management in Aid Dependent Low-Income Countries." World Institute for Development Economic Research Discussion Paper 107, Helsinki.

Gunning, Jan Willem. 2001. "Rethinking Aid." In Boris Pleskovic and Nicholas Stern, eds., *Annual World Bank Conference on Development Economics.* Washington, D.C.: World Bank.

Halonen-Akatwijuka, Maija. 2007. "Coordination Failure in Foreign Aid." *The B.E. Journal of Economic Analysis & Policy* 7 (1, Topics), Article 43.

Harrold, Peter, and Associates. 1995. "The Broad Sector Approach to Investment Lending: Sector Investment Programs." World Bank Discussion Paper 302. Washington, D.C.: World Bank.

Jones, Stephen. 1997. "Sector Investment Programs in Africa: Issues and Experience." World Bank Technical Paper 374, Washington, D.C.: World Bank.

Jones, Stephen, and Andrew Lawson. 2001. "Moving from Projects to Programmatic Aid." OED Working Paper Series 5. Washington, D.C.: World Bank Operation Evaluation Department.

Kanbur, Ravi, and Todd Sandler. 1999. *The Future of Development Assistance: Common Pools and International Public Goods.* Baltimore, Md.: Johns Hopkins University Press.

Kapur, Devesh, and Richard Webb. 2000. "Governance-Related Conditionalities of the International Financial Institutions." United Nations and Center for International Development Harvard University, G-24 Discussion Paper 6, New York and Boston.

Mansuri, Ghazala, and Vijayendra Rao. 2003. "Evaluating Community Driven Development: A Critical Review of the Research." World Bank, Washington, D.C. Processed.

Martens, Bertin, Uwe Mummert, Peter Murrell, and Paul Seabright. 2002. *The Institutional Economics of Foreign Aid.* Cambridge: Cambridge University Press.

Miguel, Edward, and Michael Kremer. 2001. "Worms: Education and Health Externalities in Kenya." NBER Working Paper Series 8481. Cambridge, Mass.: National Bureau of Economic Research.

Newman, John, Menno Pradhan, Laura B. Rawlings, Geert Ridder, Ramiro Coa, and José Luis Evia. 2002. "An Impact Evaluation of Education, Health and Water Supply Investments by the Bolivian Social Investment Fund." *World Bank Economic Review* 16(2):241–274.

O'Connell, Stephen A., and Charles C. Saludo. 2001. "Aid Intensity in Africa." *World Development* 29(9):1527–1552.

Ostrom, Elinor, Clark Gibson, Sujai Shivakumar, and Krister Anderson. 2001. "Aid Incentives and Sustainability: An Institutional Analysis of Development Cooperation." SIDA Studies in Evaluation 02/01. Sweden: Swedish International Development Agency.

Paxson, Christina, and Norbert A. Schady. 2002. "The Allocation and Impact of Social Funds: Spending on School Infrastructure in Peru." *World Bank Economic Review* 16(2):297–319.

Picazo, Oscar F. 2002. "Better Health Outcomes from Limited Resources: Focusing on Priority Services in Malawi." World Bank, Africa Region Human Development Working Paper Series, Washington, D.C.: World Bank.

Platteau, Jean-Philippe, and Frederic Gaspart. 2003. "The 'Elite Capture' Problem in Participatory Development." Belgium: Centre for Research on the Economics of Development, University of Namur. Processed.

Riddel, Roger C. 1999. "The End of Foreign Aid to Africa? Concerns about Donor Policies." *African Affairs* 98:309–335.

Svensson, Jakob. 2003. "Why Conditional Aid Doesn't Work and What Can Be Done about It." *Journal of Development Economics* 70(2):381–402.

Tarp, Finn, and Peter Hjertholm, eds. 2000. *Foreign Aid and Development: Lessons Learnt and Directions for the Future.* London: Routledge.

van de Walle, Dominique. 2002. "Choosing Rural Road Investments to Help Reduce Poverty." *World Development* 30(4):575–589.

van de Walle, Dominique, and Dorothyjean Cratty. 2003. "Impact Evaluation of a Rural Road Rehabilitation Project." Washington, D.C.: World Bank. Processed.

Van Domelen, Julie. 2002. "Social Funds: Evidence on Targeting, Impacts and Sustainability." *Journal of International Development* 14(5):627–642.

Wang, T. Y. 1999. "U.S. Foreign Aid and UN Voting: An Analysis of Important Issues." *International Studies Quarterly* 43:199–210.

World Bank. 1998. *Assessing Aid: What Works, What Doesn't and Why.* Washington, D.C.: Oxford University Press.

World Bank. 2001a. *Education and Health in Sub-Saharan Africa: A Review of Sector-Wide Approaches.* Washington, D.C.: World Bank.

World Bank. 2001b. "Implementation of World Bank-Finance Projects. A Note on Eastern Europe and Central Asia Experience with Projects Implementation Units." Washington, D.C.: World Bank.

World Bank. 2001c. "Zambia Public Expenditure Review: Public Expenditure, Growth and Poverty: A Synthesis." Washington, D.C.: World Bank.

World Bank. 2002a. *Social Funds: Assessing Effectiveness.* Washington, D.C.: World Bank.

World Bank. 2002b. "World Bank Group Work in Low-Income Countries Under Stress." Washington, D.C.: World Bank.

7 The Illusion of Sustainability

Michael Kremer and Edward Miguel

The history of overseas development assistance can be viewed as a series of attempts to identify and address ever more fundamental causes of global poverty. Oxfam, for example, founded in 1942 as the Oxford Committee for Famine Relief, later shifted to "support for self-help schemes whereby communities improved their own water supplies, farming practices, and health provision."[1] In the 1950s and 1960s, it was widely argued that long-run economic performance depended on capital investment, and raising savings through a "big push" (Rosenstein-Rodin 1943) would launch countries into self-sustaining growth or "take-off" (Rostow 1960). Accordingly, the World Bank largely funded infrastructure like dams and roads. By the 1980s international financial institution policymakers decided that capital accumulation and technological progress depended not so much on investment and careful engineering, but rather on a better economic policy environment (Williamson 1990, World Bank 1993a). Development assistance was extended conditionally to encourage countries to adopt economic policies associated with this "Washington consensus" view, characterized by reduced tariffs, appropriate foreign exchange rates, and low inflation. By the 1990s, this approach also became seen as inadequate by many. According to a new consensus, these policies would have only limited impact in the absence of more fundamental institutional reforms (World Bank 1998).

Part of this new consensus in overseas development assistance involved reforms to national-level institutions, but given widespread central government failures in delivering public goods, another strand emphasized encouraging local communities to sustainably provide their own public goods. Whereas orthodox public finance analysis suggests that governments or donors should indefinitely fund activities that generate positive externalities, advocates of sustainability emphasize the importance of local project ownership and promote public goods projects that require only start-up funding and can then continue without external support. These efforts typically rely on voluntary activities by community members rather than on the granting of coercive fund-raising powers to local governments.

The idea that development projects should aim at financial sustainability through voluntary local action has had tremendous influence in development thinking, in areas from microfinance to the environment.[2] In public health and water supply, sustainability advocates concentrate on cost recovery from beneficiaries, community mobilization, and health education rather than simply building wells or subsidizing medical treatments that generate externalities. The idea of replacing dependence on aid with a one-time investment that leads to long-run sustainability is certainly ideologically attractive.

Yet anecdotal evidence suggests that financial sustainability has often been an illusion, and sometimes a costly one. Morduch (1999) argues that the pursuit of sustainability by microfinance organizations has led them to move away from serving the poor. Meuwissen (2002) argues that a health cost-recovery program in Niger led to unexpectedly large drops in health care utilization and that the local health committees set up by the program failed in most of their responsibilities. In a large water project in the Kenyan area we study, 43 percent of borehole wells were useless ten years after the shift from external donor support for water well maintenance to the training of local maintenance committees (Miguel and Gugerty 2005).

While it is certainly true that in some cases, communities have developed institutions that lead individuals to contribute to local public goods (Ostrom 1990), it is less clear that external interventions, such as training sessions or the formation of user committees by donors, reliably lead to sustainable voluntary provision of local public goods. It is difficult for outsiders to understand how other societies' institutions and politics function, let alone how to influence them in a way that creates the correct incentives and does not generate unforeseen negative consequences.

In this chapter, we seek to shed light on these issues using evidence from a randomized evaluation of a deworming program in Kenya. Intestinal worms infect one in four people worldwide. They can be fought in several different ways. One approach emphasizes periodic medical treatment with low-cost drugs. Public provision of deworming medicine can likely be justified on standard public finance grounds since an estimated three-quarters of the social benefit of treatment comes through reducing disease transmission (Miguel and Kremer 2004). However, some argue that too much emphasis has been placed on just handing out deworming drugs. Since people soon become reinfected, deworming drug treatment must be continued twice per year indefinitely. In a *Lancet* article entitled "Sustainable Schistosomiasis Control—The Way Forward," Utzinger et al. (2003) argue that rather than focusing narrowly on drugs, a broader approach with greater emphasis on health education would be more sustainable. Other potential ways to make antiworm programs sustainable include requiring cost-sharing payments from those taking the drugs, promoting the diffusion of worm prevention information and behaviors through social networks, and encouraging local ownership of deworming programs.

In this study, we find that, first, the introduction of a small fee for deworming drugs (cost sharing) led to an 80 percent reduction in treatment rates, consistent with the hypothesis that people have low private valuation for deworming. Take-up dropped sharply when going from a zero price to a positive price but was not sensitive to the exact (positive) price level, suggesting that it may be particularly counterproductive to charge small positive prices for the treatment of infectious diseases. Second, an intensive school health education intervention had no impact on worm prevention behaviors. Third, a verbal commitment "mobilization" intervention—in which people were asked in advance whether they planned to take deworming drugs, exploiting a finding from social psychology that individuals strive for consistency in their statements and actions—had no impact on adoption.

We also examine peer effects in adoption, since if imitation effects in technology adoption are sufficiently strong, then a sufficiently large temporary investment to introduce deworming drugs could move society from a low-adoption to a high-adoption equilibrium. Foster and Rosenzweig (1995), Conley and Udry (2000), Burke, Fournier, and Prasad (2003), and Munshi (2004) find evidence for peer effects in technology adoption using nonexperimental data. Like Duflo and Saez (2003), we exploit experimental variation in exposure to a new technology to address the well-known econometric challenges in estimating peer effects (Manski 1993). We develop a theoretical framework that allows for peer effects from pure imitation, social learning about how to use technologies optimally, social learning about the benefits of new technologies, and epidemiological externalities. This model suggests that as long as a small fraction of the population receives subsidies sufficient to induce their adoption, further subsidies will affect steady-state take-up only in the presence of imitation effects. We collect data on the network structure of links between school communities and use this to empirically estimate the impact on adoption decisions—not only of individuals' direct social links but also of higher-order social links. Rather than imposing a preexisting definition of social links, based, for example, on geography, (Foster and Rosenzweig 1995, Burke, Fournier, and Prasad 2003), we allow survey respondents to specify their social links themselves and estimate the impact of learning through different types of links. We then simulate the impact of alternative ways of seeding the new technology given the observed network structure of links across schools in our sample.

We find that additional social links to early treatment in schools reduce the probability that children take deworming drugs and increase the probability that parents say that deworming drugs are "not effective." This negative take-up result holds for both direct social links and indirect second-order connections. We find evidence that Granovetter's (1973) weak ties are important, with individuals learning from both close and distant contacts, as measured by the frequency with which they communicate. There is also some evidence for learning through child networks, in addition to the parent networks that form the core of the analysis. In contrast, analysis of our data using nonexperimental methods would imply that individuals are more likely to take the drugs if they have greater social contact with others who have recently been exposed to deworming, suggesting substantial omitted variable bias in the nonexperimental estimates.

The lower take-up among those with more knowledge may be due to the high proportion of deworming benefits flowing not to the treated child or her family, but to others in the local community through externalities. People may have realized how much of the benefits were external only as they gained experience with the program. Negative social effects on take-up are especially large empirically for families with more schooling, a group that starts out with particularly favorable beliefs about the technology but then rapidly revises their beliefs downward as they acquire more information.

Our results are consistent with peer effects due to learning from others about the benefits of the technology and suggest that at least in this context, peer effects due to imitation, or due to learning about how to use the technology, are small. In this context, a policymaker uncertain about the benefits of a new technology might want to subsidize a small number of people to adopt in hopes of spurring a shift to a new equilibrium, but temporary subsidies beyond this level would not affect steady-state adoption.

Overall, the empirical results on cost sharing, health education, and social learning are all consistent with the hypothesis that people put limited private value on deworming. Miguel and Kremer (2004), however, suggest the social value is large. Together these results suggest that large, ongoing external subsidies may be necessary to sustain high take-up. These results may generalize to other infectious and parasitic diseases characterized by large positive treatment externalities. More generally, it is probably an illusion to think that a one-time infusion of external assistance will lead to the indefinitely sustainable voluntary provision of most local public goods. There may simply be no alternative to ongoing subsidies financed by tax revenue raised from either local or national governments or international donors.[3]

The remainder of the chapter is structured as follows. Section 7.1 provides information on worm infections and the project we study. In section 7.2, we present a simple theoretical framework for understanding the determinants of deworming take-up. Section 7.3 describes the empirical take-up impacts of direct and higher-order social links. Sections 7.4 to 7.6 describe the cost sharing, health education, and verbal commitment results, respectively. The final section discusses broader implications for public finance and development assistance in less developed countries. Readers interested primarily in social learning may wish to focus on sections 7.2 and 7.3, while those interested in development policy issues could focus mainly on sections 7.4 through 7.7.

7.1   The Primary School Deworming Project

Over 1.3 billion people worldwide are infected with hookworm, 1.3 billion with roundworm, 900 million with whipworm, and 200 million with schistosomiasis (Bundy 1994). Most have light infections, which are often asymptomatic, but more severe worm infections can lead to iron-deficiency anemia, protein energy malnutrition, stunting, wasting, listlessness, and abdominal pain. Heavy schistosomiasis infections can have even more severe consequences.[4]

Helminths do not reproduce within the human host, so high worm burdens are the result of frequent reinfection. The geohelminths (hookworm, roundworm, and whipworm) are transmitted through ingestion of, or contact with, infected fecal matter. This can occur, for example, if children defecate in the fields near their home or school, areas where they also play. Schistosomiasis is acquired through contact with infected freshwater. For example, in our Kenyan study area, people often walk to nearby Lake Victoria to bathe and fish. Medical treatment for helminth infections creates externality benefits by reducing worm deposition in the community and thus limiting reinfection among other community members (Anderson and May 1991). The geohelminths and schistosomiasis can be treated using the low-cost, single-dose oral therapies of albendazole and praziquantel, respectively. The drugs sometimes cause unpleasant and salient, but medically minor, side effects, including stomachache, diarrhea, fever, and occasionally vomiting (World Health Organization 1992), but these effects rarely last more than one day. Side effects are more severe for heavier schistosomiasis infections but can be mitigated by not consuming the drugs on an empty stomach. Private benefits of deworming may not always be particularly salient to individuals since they typically occur gradually as individual nutritional status improves in the months following treatment.

Miguel and Kremer (2004) found that deworming treatment can generate large externality benefits by interfering with disease transmission. Providing treatment to Kenyan school children led to large reductions in worm infections and increased school participation among both treated and untreated children in the treatment schools and among children in neighboring schools. Three-quarters of the social benefit of treatment was in the form of externalities. Since deworming costs only $3.50 per extra year of school participation generated, it is likely one of the most cost-effective ways to boost participation.

Both this chapter and Miguel and Kremer (2004) study the Primary School Deworming Project (PSDP), a school health program carried out by a Dutch nongovernmental organization (NGO), ICS Africa, in cooperation with the Kenyan Ministry of Health. The project took place in Busia district, a poor and densely settled farming region in western Kenya, and the seventy-five project schools include nearly all rural primary schools in the area, with over 30,000 enrolled pupils between the ages of six and eighteen, over 90 percent of whom suffer from intestinal worm infections. In January 1998, the schools were randomly divided into three groups (group 1, group 2, and group 3) of twenty-five schools each: the schools were first divided by administrative subunit (zone) and by involvement in other nongovernmental assistance programs and were then listed alphabetically, with every third school assigned to a given project group.

The intervention included both health education on worm prevention behaviors and the provision of deworming medicine. Due to administrative and financial constraints, the program was phased in over several years. Group 1 schools received assistance in 1998, 1999, 2000, and 2001 and group 2 schools in 1999, 2000 and 2001, while group 3 began receiving assistance in 2001. This design implies that in 1998, group 1 schools were treatment schools, while group 2 and 3 schools were the comparison schools; and in 1999 and 2000 group 1 and 2 schools were the treatment schools and group 3 schools were comparison schools. At each school, the project started out with a community meeting of parents and teachers organized by the NGO, which included a discussion of worm infections, the nature of medical deworming treatment, and worm prevention measures. All primary school communities in the baseline sample agreed to participate in the project. Starting in 1999, the Ministry of Health required signed individual parental consent, while in 1998 only community consent had been required, with individuals having the choice of opting out of the program if they wished. This change in 1999 may have reduced take-up in some cases if parents were reluctant to visit the school headmaster, particularly if they were late on school fee payments.

Health education efforts focused on preventing worms through hand wash-
ing, wearing shoes, and avoiding infected freshwater. This included classroom
lectures and culturally appropriate Swahili-language health education materials. This health education effort was considerably more intensive than is typical
in Kenyan primary schools, and thus the program may be more likely than
existing government programs to change child behavior. Two teachers in each
school attended a full-day training session on worm prevention lessons, as well
as on the details of the deworming program, and were instructed to impart
these lessons during school hours. These classroom lessons were supplemented
through lectures by an experienced NGO field team (the team leader was a
trained public health technician) that visited each treatment school several
times per year.

At all schools where helminth prevalence was sufficiently high, the project
provided periodic treatment with deworming drugs to be taken at the school.
The World Health Organization (WHO) has endorsed mass school-based
deworming in areas with prevalence over 50 percent, since mass treatment elim-
inates the need for costly individual screening (Warren et al. 1993, WHO
1987), and the drugs are cheap when purchased in bulk.[5]

Our best estimate is that teacher training, teacher lessons at school, the lectures delivered by the NGO field team, and the classroom wall charts and other
educational materials taken together cost at least US$0.44 per pupil per year in
the assisted schools,[6] which is comparable to the total cost of deworming drug
purchase and delivery in a nearby Tanzanian program, at US$0.49 (Partner-
ship for Child Development 1999). In our case, it is difficult to break out the
costs of health education, data collection, and drug delivery since the same field
team was responsible for all activities, so cost estimates should be seen as
approximate.

The NGO we worked with has a policy of using community cost recovery in
its projects to promote sustainability and confer project ownership on beneficiaries. In the case of deworming, the NGO temporarily waived this policy initially, and then planned to phase it in gradually. The fifty group 1 and group 2
schools were stratified by treatment group and geographic location, and then
twenty-five were randomly selected (using a computer random number generator) to pay user fees for medical treatment in 2001, while the other twenty-five
continued to receive free medical treatment that year; all group 3 schools
received free treatment in 2001. The deworming fee was set on a per family basis, like most Kenyan primary school fees at the time. This introduced within-
school variation in the per child cost of deworming since households have
different numbers of primary school children, a variation that we also use to

estimate the effect of price on drug take-up. Of the twenty-five group 1 and group 2 schools participating in cost sharing, two-thirds received albendazole at a cost of 30 Kenyan shillings per family (US$0.40 in 2001) and one-third received both albendazole and praziquantel at a cost of 100 shillings (approximately US$1.30). Whether praziquantel was given depended on the local prevalence of schistosomiasis. Since parents have 2.7 children in school on average, the average cost of deworming per child in cost-sharing schools was slightly more than US$0.30, still a heavily subsidized price, about one-fifth the cost of drug purchase and delivery through this program (at US$1.49) and 60 percent of the cost in the Tanzania program.[7]

The study area seems fertile ground for encouraging voluntary community provision of local public goods like deworming control. Kenya has a long history of community self-help programs, and indeed the national motto, *Harambee*, ("Let's Pull Together") refers to such programs. The project we examine was conducted at primary schools, one of the most widespread and firmly established institutions in rural Kenya. All primary schools have a committee composed of parents and community representatives, and historically these committees have been entrusted with raising funds locally for most nonsalary costs of running the school, including everything from chalk to classroom construction.

Cultural understandings of health, and particularly worms, in our study area also merit a brief discussion. This account draws heavily on the work of Geissler (1998a, 1998b, 2000), who studies deworming take-up in the Kenyan district that borders our study area. Medical anthropologists have long pointed out that people can simultaneously hold traditional and biomedical views of health, in a manner similar to religious syncretism, and Geissler argues that this is the case for views about worms in western Kenya. In the traditional view, worms are an integral part of the human body and necessary for digestion, and many infection symptoms are attributed to malevolent occult forces ("witchcraft") or breaking taboos (Government of Kenya 1986). Educated people are more likely to engage in the biomedical discourse and thus more likely to treat illnesses medically rather than using traditional remedies. Geissler finds that most people do not place much value on deworming treatment because worms are not seen as a pressing health problem, especially compared to malaria and HIV/ AIDS.[8] As a result, there was almost no deworming outside the school health program he studies, and most children relied on local herbal remedies to alleviate the abdominal discomfort caused by worms.

Local knowledge regarding private benefits of receiving treatment under a mass deworming program was likely very poor in our study area. The project we study was the first mass deworming treatment program in the district, to our knowledge. Albendazole and praziquantel were approved for human use only in the mid-1980s and by 1998 were still rarely used in the area. Prior to the program, fewer than 5 percent of people reported taking deworming drugs (Miguel and Kremer 2004). While many medicines, such as aspirin and antimalarials, are cheaply available in nearly all local shops, deworming was available in only a few shops and at high mark-ups, presumably due to a thin market. In fact, none of sixty-four local shops surveyed in 1999 had either albendazole (or its close substitute, mebendazole) or praziquantel in stock, though a minority carried less effective deworming drugs (levamisole hydrochloride and piperazine). Albendazole and praziquantel were available in some local health clinics. Inference about likely mass treatment impacts based on observed individual impacts was complicated for local residents by nonrandom selection into treatment, as well as the possibility of spillover effects.

7.2   A Framework for Understanding the Adoption of a New Health Technology

We model the spread of information and the evolution of take-up of a new technology in a social network. The model provides a framework for the empirical estimation of adoption peer effects and helps clarify the conditions under which a one-time subsidy can change the long-run level of adoption and thus achieve sustainability.

We develop a simple framework in which people adopt deworming if expected private benefits exceed the expected cost. They are heterogeneous in both their taste for deworming and their prior beliefs about the effectiveness of the drugs. People are linked in a social network and receive signals about adoption, drug effectiveness, and how to use the drugs. The model nests four types of peer effects proposed in the existing literature. Others' adoption can (1) influence own adoption through the disease environment, (2) directly enter the utility function through a pure imitation effect, (3) provide information about how to effectively use the technology (as in Jovanovic and Nyarko 1996 or Foster and Rosenzweig 1995), or (4) provide information on the benefits of the technology (as in Banerjee 1992 or Ellison and Fudenberg 1993).

7.2.1   Assumptions

We assume that an individual i decides to adopt a new technology (or health practice) if the expected private benefits are greater than the costs, conditional on her prior beliefs and the information received from social contacts. As noted above, the cost of deworming adoption is privately incurred, immediate, and salient, while much of the benefit is in the form of externalities and even the private benefits are delayed, so private benefits may not exceed costs, particularly for people with high discount rates.

Suppose that the total private benefit to taking the deworming drug depends on the individual's infection level γ; the effectiveness of the drug ϕ (which incorporates the percentage reduction in worm load that results from taking the drug and the rapidity of reinfection);[9] and an idiosyncratic individual specific taste for deworming μ_i, which is assumed to have a continuous distribution with no mass points and a sufficiently large support such that some individuals always take up the drug. (Note that policymakers can always guarantee that some take up the drug by heavily subsidizing a small fraction of consumers.) Individual infection γ may depend on individual characteristics X and also on others' treatment history. Because worms are transmitted through environmental contamination rather than from person to person, infection levels are likely to depend on average population treatment rather than an individual's social links.

Financial, time, or utility costs of treatment, are denoted by $C > 0$. We allow for the possibility that people may learn from their own experience and from others about how to reduce the cost of using the technology (for example, how to control side effects by taking food with the medicine), but as in Jovanovic and Nyarko (1996) and Foster and Rosenzweig (1995), we assume this learning is bounded, so that C approaches some positive C_∞. The drug subsidies, health education, and verbal commitment interventions discussed in sections 7.4 to 7.6 can be regarded as changing the adoption cost.

Finally, a desire to imitate one's social contacts may influence the decision to take up the technology. The parameter $\beta > 0$ captures the importance of this effect.

Let $\hat{\phi}_{it}$ denote the individual's beliefs in period t about drug effectiveness ϕ conditional on prior beliefs and any signals received, and let $T_{it} \in \{0, 1\}$ be an indicator variable for drug take-up in period t. Then the individual's expected private benefit from adoption can be expressed as

$$E[U(T_{it} = 1) - U(T_{it} = 0)] = \hat{\phi}_{it}h(\gamma_{it})\mu_i - C + \beta\omega_{it} \qquad (7.1)$$

where U is individual utility from deworming, conditional on the treatment choices of other individuals, and ω_{it} is the share of social contacts who took up the drug in the previous period.

We assume that individuals decide whether to adopt deworming at time t based on the current costs and benefits of adoption and do not consider the additional motive of adopting in order to learn more about the impact of the technology or how to use it in the future. This is partly to keep the model tractable, but it is also a reasonable assumption in our context. Discount rates were likely high given the temporary nature of the program and the limited foresight of schoolchildren. Moreover, deworming was introduced at the level of whole schools, so most people offered the chance to take it would have many opportunities to learn about impacts from classmates, limiting the marginal value of their own experience.

7.2.2 Information Structure

At the moment the new technology is introduced, individual i has a prior belief about the effectiveness of taking deworming medicine as part of a mass campaign, denoted ϕ_{i0}, which may be greater or less than the actual effectiveness ϕ. Priors could be less than ϕ due to traditional beliefs about worms in the study region (Geissler 1998a, 1998b). However, people could also have had overly optimistic estimates about private benefits. The enthusiasm of NGO field officers who were promoting deworming at schools may have reflected the drugs' social rather than private benefits. Although the scripts made clear that the medicine kills worms in the body but does not prevent reinfection, people may not have realized how quickly they would be reinfected. Moreover, if people estimated their expected private benefits by comparing individuals in treatment versus comparison schools, they would incorrectly assign some of the schoolwide treatment externality to private benefits, again making prior beliefs about private deworming benefits overly optimistic.

Priors about deworming effectiveness could also vary systematically with individual characteristics, such as education. This is a departure from the standard assumption of common priors but is plausible for Kenya. In the context of rural Kenya, formal schooling is considered an important predictor of favorable views about new health technologies (Akwara 1996, Kohler, Behrman, and Watkins 2001). This could reflect either the causal impact of education or simply the fact that people who are more open to "modern" or "Western" ideas and technologies obtain more education. We formalize this variation in prior beliefs by modeling the common effectiveness parameter ϕ as a draw from a distribution believed to have mean $\phi_0(X_i)$ and variance σ_0^2. While people can learn about the realization of ϕ through signals from their social links, beliefs about its distribution need not have converged to a common prior before the program intervention since mass deworming had not taken place in the area before.

All individuals who take the drug obtain a signal about effectiveness. These signals are noisy due to individual time-specific shocks to health status (e.g., malaria, typhoid, cholera) that are hard to distinguish from drug effects. Let these signals have mean ϕ and variance σ_ε^2.

We assume information diffuses through an infinite social network with a simple structure in which the network, viewed from the perspective of any node, is a proper tree. This implies that a single path connects any two nodes.[10] Each individual has m direct social links, people with whom they may exchange information, where m is a positive integer. Each of those links also has m direct links. In the special case where $m = 2$, this is equivalent to people being arrayed along an infinite line, each with direct links to two immediate neighbors.

Time is discrete. At the beginning of each period, individuals can send messages to their direct links with information from both their own signals received and others' signals. Signals are transmitted to each link with probability p each period. Later in the same period, people receive these messages from their social contacts. These lags in information diffusion are consistent with the data from Kenya.

7.2.3   Steady-State Adoption

We first solve the steady state of this model before turning to the transition path.

Note that in our model, as long as some fraction of people always adopt, information will eventually diffuse completely. This implies that in steady state, $\hat{\phi}_{it} = \phi$ and $C = C_\infty$ for all individuals i. Consider first the case in which $\beta = 0$ (no pure imitation effects). Let λ denote the share of the population taking up treatment, and let λ^* denote the steady-state share such that if a proportion λ^* of the population took the drug in the past, the same proportion will find it optimal to take the drug. An individual will adopt in the steady state if

$$\phi h(\gamma(\lambda^*, X_i))\mu_i - C_\infty > 0 \tag{7.2}$$

and forgo treatment if not. It is straightforward to show that there exists a unique equilibrium cutoff, value $\lambda^* = \iint 1\{\phi h(\gamma(\lambda^*, X))\mu - C_\infty > 0\} \cdot P(X, \mu)\, dX\, d\mu$, where $P(X, \mu)$ denotes the probability of those values occurring in the population.[11]

While λ^* is unique if $\beta = 0$, there can be multiple steady states under sufficiently strong pure imitation effects, in which others' take-up decisions directly enter the utility function in a manner complementary with own take-up. Even if parameters are such that λ^* is arbitrarily close to zero in the absence of imitation effects, if imitation effects are sufficiently strong that $\beta > C_\infty - \phi \min_i\{h(\gamma(1, X_i))\mu_i\}$, there will be another steady state in which everyone uses the technology since then, $\phi h(\gamma(1, X_i))\mu_i - C_\infty + \beta > 0$ for all i. A sufficiently large temporary subsidy in this case can lead to a switch from the partial use equilibrium to the full use equilibrium, leading to sustainable increases in take-up.

Peer effects in technology adoption are sometimes cited as a rationale for why temporary subsidies may have long-run effects. The model suggests that subsidizing a small number of people will be sufficient to ensure that those people will learn both the returns to the technology and how best to use the technology. In the absence of pure imitation effects, this will be enough to ensure widespread long-run adoption of technologies with positive private returns.[12] There is no need to subsidize a large number of people to achieve steady-state diffusion. While this result is specific to this particular model, we conjecture that similar results will apply under other Bayesian learning models. If policymakers are uncertain about the benefits of a particular technology, then providing heavy subsidies to a few people seems much more prudent than widely subsidizing what may turn out to be an unattractive technology.[13]

7.2.4 Take-Up along the Transition Path

We next turn to modeling take-up along the transition path. By time τ, the probability that a signal is transmitted from a first-order link to the receiver is $[1 - (1 - p)^{\tau}]$, the probability that a signal is transmitted from a second-order link to the receiver is $[\sum_{k=2\ldots\tau}(k-1) \cdot \{p^2(1-p)^{k-2}\}]$, and more generally the probability that a signal is transmitted from a jth-order link is

$$\sum_{k=j}^{\tau} \binom{k-1}{j-1} \cdot \{p^j(1-p)^{k-j}\}$$

for $j \leq \tau$, and 0 for $j > \tau$.

Holding fixed the take-up behavior of intermediate nodes, the direct impact of an additional signal acquired by a jth-order link on take-up is then the probability that the signal is transmitted, multiplied by an indicator for whether the receiver changes her take-up decision in response to the new signal. Let i index an individual node as above. Take-up occurs ($T_{it} = 1$) if and only if $E[U(T_{it} = 1) - U(T_{it} = 0)] > 0$, and the direct impact of an additional signal from a jth-order link by time τ is thus

$$\left[\sum_{k=j}^{\tau} \binom{k-1}{j-1} \cdot \{p^j(1-p)^{k-j}\}\right] \cdot [1\{\hat{\phi}_{it}h(\gamma_{it})\mu_i - C + \beta\omega_{it} > 0 \,|\, \text{Signal}\}$$

$$- 1\{\hat{\phi}_{it}h(\gamma_{it})\mu_i - C + \beta\omega_{it} > 0 \,|\, \text{No signal}\}]. \tag{7.3}$$

An additional signal can affect take-up behavior, so that $[(T_{it} \mid \text{Signal}) - (T_{it} \mid \text{No signal})]$ is nonzero, by changing beliefs about ϕ (or similarly by reducing the cost of take-up C, as discussed below). If a Bayesian individual has N_{it}^E total signals from early treatment school links, both direct (first order) and indirect (higher order), she then weights her prior beliefs and signals received from social links such that the posterior belief on expected effectiveness becomes

$$\hat{\phi}_{it} = \left[\left\{ \frac{\sigma_N^2}{\sigma_N^2 + \sigma_0^2} \right\} \cdot \phi_0(X_i) + \left(1 - \left\{ \frac{\sigma_N^2}{\sigma_N^2 + \sigma_0^2} \right\} \right) \cdot \phi_S \right], \tag{7.4}$$

where $\phi_0(X_i)$ is the mean of her prior distribution, ϕ_S is the sample average of signals received through the social network, and $\sigma_N^2 \equiv \sigma_\varepsilon^2 / N_{it}^E$ denotes the variance of the sample average. As individuals accumulate more signals through their social network, the variance of the sample average goes to zero, and the value of both the sample average and posterior beliefs approaches the true expected effectiveness, ϕ.

When the prior belief is greater than the true expected effectiveness ($\phi_0(X_i) > \phi$), individuals with more early treatment social links tend to have falling posterior beliefs about expected effectiveness, and thus the likelihood of adoption declines in the number of early treatment links. From equation 7.4, the decline in the expected benefit of treatment with respect to early links will be convex, as the posterior asymptotically approaches the true expected effectiveness. Similarly, when the prior is less than the true expected effectiveness, the posterior asymptotically approaches the true benefit from below. When $\phi_0(X_i) > \phi$ for all education levels (X_i) and the prior is increasing in X_i, then individuals with more education generally have higher adoption, but additional early links will lead to sharper drops in their adoption.

Similarly, the framework allows the possibility that people may learn from signals they receive, as well as from their own experience about how to use the technology, so $C(\cdot)$ is a decreasing function of the total number of signals ever received about the technology, N_{it}^E, with $C'(\cdot) < 0$, $C''(\cdot) > 0$, $C(0) > 0$, and $C(\infty) = C_\infty$.

Although epidemiological effects are likely to depend on the broader population rather than immediate social contacts, because worm infections result from contamination of water or soil rather than direct person-to-person transmission, it is worth considering the possibility that children whose families have close social interactions with households in early treatment schools may experience somewhat lower helminth infection rates and thus reductions in infection intensity. We model this by allowing the infection level to be a function of the share of direct social contacts treated.

The impact of early treatment links on the expected private benefits to adoption is thus

$$\frac{\partial E[U(T_{it} = 1) - U(T_{it} = 0)]}{\partial N_{it}^E}$$

$$= \left[\frac{-\sigma_N^2 \sigma_0^2}{(\sigma_N^2 + \sigma_0^2)^2 N_{it}^E}\right] \cdot (\phi_0(X_i) - \phi_S) \cdot h(\gamma(\omega_{it}, X_i)) \cdot \mu_i$$

$$- \frac{\partial C(N_{it}^E)}{\partial N_{it}^E} + \hat{\phi}_{it} \frac{\partial h}{\partial \gamma} \cdot \frac{\partial \gamma(\omega_{it}, X_i)}{\partial \omega_{it}} \cdot \frac{\partial \omega_{it}}{\partial N_{it}^E} \mu_i + \beta \frac{\partial \omega_{it}}{\partial N_{it}^E}. \tag{7.5}$$

The first right-hand-side term is the social effect from information on drug effectiveness and can be positive or negative depending on the difference between priors and true private adoption benefits. The second term captures the social effect from learning how to use the drugs described above and is always positive. The third term is the infection social effect, which should be negative because having more early treatment links could lead to a lower individual infection level (due to epidemiological externalities), which in turn reduces treatment benefits. The positive imitation effect is captured in the fourth term.

We conclude that to the extent that we observe negative overall social effects empirically, this is evidence that the combined effect of the information and infection externalities is larger than the learning-by-doing effect plus the pure imitation effect. Furthermore, since infection externalities appear small empirically, as we show below, we interpret negative estimated social effects as strong evidence that social effects work through the transmission of information about drug effectiveness. We find no evidence for learning-by-doing or imitation here, although we cannot rule out small effects of these types.

These formulas describe the impact of an additional signal, holding fixed the behavior of intermediate nodes in the social network. In the long run, with repeated opportunities for adoption, there will be additional effects mediated by the effect of a link's information on the take-up behavior of intermediate nodes, and thus on the subsequent number of signals that intermediate nodes possess and can send to the receiver, as well as any effects on the information and take-up of intermediate nodes mediated by imitation effects. These indirect effects would accumulate over time, but since in our experiment, people could adopt only every six months and they were able to adopt the drugs only through the program for either zero, two, or three years (depending on their treatment group), we focus on the case in which the direct effects of signals dominate the indirect effects. In section 7.3.6, though, we report results from a simulation of the transition path allowing for these indirect effects.

7.3 Empirical Results on Networks, Social Learning, and Technology Adoption

7.3.1 Data, Measurement, and Estimation

We test whether households with more social links to schools randomly chosen for early treatment were more likely to take deworming drugs, conditional on their total number of links to all project schools.

The PSDP parent questionnaire was collected in 2001 during household visits among a representative subsample of parents with children currently enrolled in group 2 and group 3 schools. A representative subsample of children (typically ten to seventeen years old) present in school on the survey day were administered a pupil questionnaire.

Parent questionnaire respondents were asked for information on their closest social links: the five friends they speak with most frequently, the five relatives they speak with most frequently, additional social contacts whose children attend local primary schools, and individuals with whom they speak specifically about child health issues. These individuals are collectively referred to as the respondent's direct social links. The survey also collected information on the deworming treatment status of social links' children and the effects of treatment on their health, how frequently the respondent speaks with each social link, which primary schools the links' children attend, the global positioning system (GPS) location of the respondent's home, and the respondent's knowledge of worm infections and attitudes toward deworming. The parent questionnaire was administered in two rounds in 2001 with households randomly allocated between the rounds. The round 2 survey collected more detailed information on the impact of deworming on links' children. Two different samples are used in the analysis. Sample 1 contains the 1,678 parents surveyed in either round 1 or 2 with complete child treatment and parent social network data.[14] Sample 2 contains the 886 parents surveyed in round 2.

On average, parent respondents have 10.2 direct (first-order) social links with children in primary school, of whom 4.4 attend the respondent's child's own school, 2.8 attend other project schools (groups 1, 2, or 3), and 1.9 attend nearby "early treatment schools" (groups 1 and 2; see table 7.1A). There is considerable variation in the number of direct early treatment links: the stan-

Table 7.1
Summary statistics

	Mean	SD	Observations
A. Parent social links (round 1 and round 2 data)			
Total direct (first-order) links	10.2	3.4	1,678
With children in own school	4.4	2.8	1,678
With children not in group 1, 2, or 3 schools	3.0	2.4	1,678
With children in group 1, 2, 3 schools—not own school	2.8	2.4	1,678
With children in group 1, 2 schools—not own school (early treatment)	1.9	2.0	1,678
With children in group 1 schools—not own school	0.9	1.4	1,678
Proportion with children in early treatment schools	0.66	0.37	1,358
With children in early treatment schools, with whom respondent speaks at least twice per week ("close links")	1.2	1.6	1,678
With children in early treatment schools, with whom respondent speaks less than twice per week ("distant links")	0.7	1.1	1,678
Second-order exposure to group 1, 2, or 3 schools (not own school), through parent links	4.5	4.1	1,678
Second-order exposure to early treatment schools (groups 1 and 2, not own school), through parent links	2.9	2.9	1,678
Third-order exposure to group 1, 2, or 3 schools (not own school), through parent links	3.9	5.3	1,678
Third-order exposure to early treatment schools (groups 1 and 2, not own school), through parent links	2.8	4.1	1,678
B. Parent social links (found 2 data)			
With children in own school who received deworming	1.5	2.2	886
With children in early treatment schools who received deworming	0.31	0.89	886
With children in early treatment schools who received deworming and had "good effects" (according to respondent)	0.21	0.76	886
With children in early treatment schools who received deworming and had "side effects" (according to respondent)	0.02	0.18	886
With children in early treatment schools who received deworming, respondent does not know effects	0.10	0.43	886
With children in early treatment schools, respondent does not know whether they received deworming	1.34	1.77	886
With children in early treatment schools who did not receive deworming	0.05	0.31	886
C. Deworming treatment take-up			
Took deworming drugs in 2001 (groups 2 and 3)	0.61	0.49	1,678
Proportion deworming drug take-up in 2001, respondent's own school	0.61	0.28	1,678
Took deworming drugs in 2001, free treatment schools	0.75	0.43	1,255
Took deworming drugs in 2001, cost-sharing schools	0.18	0.38	423
Provided parental consent for deworming drugs in 2001	0.67	0.41	1,678

Table 7.1
(continued)

	Mean	SD	Observations
D. Cost-sharing interventions			
Cost-sharing school indicator	0.25	0.43	1,678
Cost-sharing school indicator, albendazole only treatment	0.17	0.38	1,678
Cost-sharing school indicator, albendazole and praziquantel treatment	0.08	0.27	1,678
Effective price of deworming per child (Kenyan shillings)	6.3	15.7	1,678

Notes: From 2001 Parent Questionnaire and NGO administrative records. The "proportion in early treatment schools" variables exclude respondents with no links to program schools (other than their own), hence the reduced sample since the denominator is zero in that case.

dard deviation is 2.0, and approximately one-third of respondents have no social links to group 1 or 2 schools, one-third have one or two links, and one-third have three or more links.

Approximately forty parents were surveyed in each group 2 and group 3 school to construct second-order link measures. For each school we compute the average number of links that parents have to early treatment (group 1, group 2) schools and to late treatment (group 3) schools, once again excluding links to their own school. We do not have information on the social links' own social contacts at the individual level, and so rely on average school social network contacts in the higher-order analysis. In all main specifications, we exclude all self-referential links—in other words, all direct and higher-order links back to the respondent's own school.

The school average of second-order social connections is likely to be a noisy proxy for the true individual-level second-order measures, first due to idiosyncratic variation in the number of social contacts to particular schools and second due to the fact that the social network data is based on surveys with samples of group 2 and 3 parents alone rather than with all parents in all local schools. This measurement error should not be systematically correlated with the randomized deworming group assignment of social contacts' schools, preserving the identification strategy. However, it is likely to generate some attenuation bias toward zero in the estimated impact of second- (and higher-) order social contacts on deworming take-up.

In order to keep the theoretical framework tractable, we considered a network of individuals with uncorrelated signals arranged in a proper tree such that two individuals are linked by a single pathway and there are no redundant links. In practice, however, signals on the impact of deworming are likely to be correlated among individuals within the same school (due to the geographic proximity of particular local schools), and there will be cases in which school A is linked directly to school B both directly through first-order links and indirectly through second-order links to school C, which in turn has direct links to school B. In such cases, the second-order links will still convey some new information since the correlation among signals within a school is not perfect, but they are likely to convey less additional information than second-order links to a school where an individual has no direct first-order links. We focus below on specifications that exclude all such redundant higher-order links to a school, but results are similar when redundant links are included (results not shown).

Parents have 2.9 second-order social links to early treatment schools (standard deviation 2.9) and 4.5 second-order links to all program schools (excluding the respondent's own school; see table 7.1A). There remains considerable variation in these second-order link measures across individuals, and similar patterns hold for third-order social links.

We have also examined the structure of social connections among the fifty group 2 and group 3 schools with complete social network data. In our data, there is not a marked sense in which some schools are net senders and others net receivers of information. The social network is remarkably symmetric: the correlation coefficient of the average number of social links to school A named by individuals in school B, and the average number of links to school B named by individuals in school A, is high at 0.82. The pattern of connections between schools is most strongly influenced by physical distance: for every additional 10 kilometers separating two schools, the average number of named links falls by 0.06 (standard error 0.005, statistically significant at 99 percent confidence). Perhaps surprisingly, schools with the same dominant ethnic group do not have significantly more social connections, nor do schools with similar test score results. An indicator for the location of one of the schools in a market center is not statistically significantly associated with more social connections at traditional confidence levels (regressions not shown). Thus, there does not appear to be huge scope for take-up gains here by exploiting knowledge of the social network to optimally "seed" deworming interventions. We expand on this point in the simulations in section 7.3.6.

The social effect analysis with parent network data is conducted at the household level using probit estimation, and the outcome measure takes on a value of one if any child in the household was treated with deworming drugs in 2001 and zero otherwise (although results are similar if the analysis is conducted using the child as the unit of observation, results not shown).[15] T_{ij} is the main dependent variable, the 2001 treatment indicator, where i is a household in school j. The idiosyncratic deworming benefit term, e_{ij}, captures unobserved variation in parent beliefs about deworming benefits, tastes for deworming, or the costs of obtaining treatment (for instance, whether the pupil was sick on the treatment day, which increases the cost of walking to school). The individual treatment decision becomes $T_{ij} = 1(N_{ij}^{E'}a + X_{ij}'b + e_{ij} > 0)$, where N_{ij}^E is a vector of social links to early treatment schools, defined in 2001 as the group 1 and 2 schools (not including the respondent's own school). This vector may include both direct (first-order) social links and higher-order exposure to early treatment schools.

Among the explanatory variables, X_{ij}, we include total links to all program schools other than the respondent's own school (for both direct and higher-order links), as well as the number of links to nonprogram schools, represented by the vector N_{ij}. Given the randomized design of the original deworming program, the number of social links to early treatment schools is randomly assigned conditional on total links to other program schools. The interpretation of the coefficient on the total number of links is complicated by the possibility that more sociable individuals (i.e., those who name more social links) differ from less sociable people in certain unobserved dimensions. However, given the design, this does not affect the estimated impact of early treatment links since the number of early treatment links is orthogonal to the error term conditional on total named links.

The cost-sharing indicator variable, $COST_j$, takes on a value of one for schools participating in the cost-sharing project, where the financial cost of treatment was higher. Z_{ij} is a vector of additional household socioeconomic characteristics (parents' education and asset ownership), demographic characteristics (respondent fertility), and other controls (respondent membership in community groups, and a group 2 indicator) that may affect real or perceived deworming benefits and costs. Idiosyncratic disturbance terms are allowed to be correlated within each school as a result of common influences, such as headmaster efforts in promoting the program. Equation 7.6 presents the main probit specification:

$$\Pr(T_{ij} = 1) = \Phi\{N_{ij}^{E'}a + N_{ij}'b_1 + b_2 COST_j + Z_{ij}'b_3 + e_{ij}\}. \tag{7.6}$$

We include interaction terms between household characteristics and social links to estimate heterogeneous treatment effects, for example, as a function of respondent education, and also estimate effects of different types of social connections (e.g., links to relatives versus friends).

To validate the identification strategy, we first confirm that the randomization succeeded in creating program groups balanced along observable dimensions: the number of direct (first-order) social links and second- and third-order exposure to early treatment schools, as well as the group 2 indicator variable and the cost-sharing indicator, are not significantly associated with most observable household characteristics (table 7.2), including parent years of education, community group membership (e.g., women's or farming groups), or the total number of children in the household, or with household ethnic group or religious affiliation variables (ethnic and religious results not shown). The numbers of first-order and second-order early links are, however, positively and significantly associated with iron roof ownership in one speci- fication (table 7.2, regression 4), and we thus include these controls in most specifications to control for any independent effects they may have on take- up. The measure of second-order links to early treatment schools is signifi- cantly associated with moderate to heavy infection in 2001 at the 10 percent level, but the coefficient is small (and surprisingly positive). Third-order links to early treatment schools are not significantly associated with any observable characteristics.

7.3.2 Nonexperimental Social Effect Estimates

We first present nonexperimental social effect estimates. In a specification simi- lar to many existing studies, we examine the take-up rate of children in a pre- defined local social unit—here, the primary school—as the key explanatory variable. We find that the local school treatment rate (excluding the respon- dent) is strongly positively correlated with take-up, as expected, with coefficient estimate 0.852 (standard error 0.107; see table 7.3, regression 1). Take-up among children who are members of the respondent's own ethnic group in their school is somewhat more influential than take-up in other ethnic groups (re- gression not shown), a finding similar to that of Munshi and Myaux (2002), al- though in our case, we argue that this pattern is likely due to omitted variable bias rather than to actual social learning, as they claim in their context. Simi- larly, there is a positive, though not statistically significant, relationship (esti- mate 0.016, standard error 0.011, regression 2) between the number of treated first-order links named in the survey (among those attending the respondent's school) and take-up, in a specification similar to several other recent studies (Kohler, Behrman, and Watkins 2001, Bandiera and Rasul 2005).

Social links' experiences with deworming may also affect individuals' choices. In particular, we test whether take-up is higher when first-order links had good experiences with the technology, as in Conley and Udry (2000). Hav- ing more links whose children had "good effects" is not associated with higher take-up, but those who had more links with "side effects" are somewhat less

Table 7.2
Validating the randomizations: Group 2 and group 3 households

	Dependent variable					
Explanatory variables	Respondent years of education: OLS (1)	Community group member: Probit (2)	Total number of children: OLS (3)	Iron roof at home: Probit (4)	Distance home to school (km): OLS (5)	Moderate-heavy infection, 2001: Probit (6)
Number of parent links with children in early treatment schools (group 1, 2, not own school)	0.018 (0.085)	−0.004 (0.012)	−0.039 (0.067)	0.029** (0.014)	−0.178 (0.128)	−0.003 (0.018)
Number of parent links with children in group 1, 2, or 3 schools, not own school	0.086 (0.096)	0.007 (0.013)	−0.047 (0.072)	−0.016 (0.017)	0.294*** (0.101)	−0.030 (0.025)
Second-order exposure to early treatment schools (groups 1 and 2, not redundant with first-order links), parent links	−0.122 (0.083)	−0.004 (0.010)	−0.060 (0.060)	0.021* (0.012)	−0.168* (0.086)	0.044* (0.023)
Second-order exposure to group 1, 2, or 3 schools (not redundant with first order links), parent links	0.058 (0.072)	−0.000 (0.007)	0.044 (0.048)	−0.012 (0.009)	0.031 (0.096)	−0.023 (0.018)
Third-order exposure to early treatment schools (groups 1 and 2, not redundant with first- and second-order links), parent links	−0.057 (0.104)	−0.008 (0.014)	0.008 (0.055)	0.006 (0.017)	−0.103 (0.097)	−0.168*** (0.021)
Third-order exposure to group 1, 2, or 3 schools (not redundant with first- and second-order links), parent links	0.101 (0.078)	0.006 (0.011)	0.015 (0.051)	−0.003 (0.013)	0.044 (0.084)	0.024 (0.018)
Cost-sharing school indicator	0.164 (0.289)	−0.003 (0.042)	0.074 (0.231)	0.013 (0.058)	1.353 (0.849)	0.032 (0.098)
Group 2 school indicator	−0.581* (0.289)	−0.030 (0.041)	0.090 (0.203)	0.020 (0.048)	−0.089 (0.309)	−0.210*** (0.069)
Other social link controls, socioeconomic controls (excluding dependent variable)	Yes	Yes	Yes	Yes	Yes	Yes

Number of observations (parents)	1,678	1,678	1,678	1,678	1,678	745
Mean (SD) of dependent variable	4.6 (3.9)	0.58 (0.49)	5.5 (2.3)	0.61 (0.49)	1.7 (1.9)	0.31 (0.45)

Notes: Data from 2001 Parent Survey, 2001 Parasitological Survey, and 2001 administrative records. Robust standard errors in parentheses. Disturbance terms are clustered within schools. Significantly different from zero at 99 (***), 95 (**), and 90 (*) percent confidence. The socioeconomic controls are respondent years of education, community group member, total number of children, iron roof at home, and distance from home to school (but when any of these is the dependent variable, it is not included as an explanatory variable). The other social link controls include number of parent links with children not in group 1, 2, or 3 schools, and number of parent links, total.

Table 7.3
Nonexperimental social effect estimates: Groups 2 and 3

Explanatory variables	Dependent variable: Child took deworming drugs in 2001		
	(1)	(2)	(3)
Proportion deworming drug take-up in 2001, respondent's own school (not including respondent)	0.852*** (0.107)		
Number of parent links with children in respondent's own school whose children received deworming		0.016 (0.011)	
Number of parent links with children in early treatment schools whose children received deworming and had "good effects"			0.004 (0.025)
Number of parent links with children in early treatment schools whose children received deworming and had "side effects"			−0.152* (0.080)
Number of parent links with children in early treatment schools whose children received deworming and respondent does not know effects			0.003 (0.049)
Number of parent links with children in early treatment schools whose children did not receive deworming			−0.006 (0.055)
Number of parent links with children in early treatment schools, respondent does not know whether they received deworming			−0.010 (0.019)
Total social link controls, socioeconomic controls	Yes	Yes	Yes
Number of observations (parents)	1,678	886	886
Mean of dependent variable	0.61	0.56	0.56

Notes: Data from 2001 Parent Survey, and 2001 administrative records. Marginal probit coefficient estimates are presented. Robust standard errors in parentheses. Disturbance terms are clustered within schools. Significantly different from zero at 99 (***), 95 (**), and 90 (*) percent confidence. Social links controls include total number of parent links; number of parent links to group 1, 2, 3 schools (not own school); and number of links parent to nonprogram schools. Other controls are respondent years of education, community group member indicator variable, total number of children, iron roof at home indicator variable, and distance from home to school in kilometers, as well as the group 2 indicator and cost-sharing school indicator. Regression 1 presents results from round 1 and round 2 of the 2001 Parent Survey, and regressions 2 and 3 present results from round 2 alone, since only round 2 has detailed information regarding deworming treatment impacts on social links. In regression 3, the difference between the coefficient estimates on number of links with children in early treatment schools whose children received deworming and had good effects and on number of links with children in early treatment schools whose children received deworming and had side effects is marginally significant (p-value = 0.09).

likely to be treated (table 7.3, regression 3). The p-value on the hypothesis that the two estimates are equal is 0.09, but this is only suggestive.[16]

7.3.3 Experimental Social Effect Estimates

Experimental social effect estimates are markedly different from the nonexperimental estimates above, suggesting that omitted variable bias in the nonexperimental estimates is large and positive. We begin by considering direct first-order social effects to be comparable with existing work before moving on to higher-order social effect estimates.

Each additional direct parent social link to an early treatment school is associated with 3.1 percentage points lower likelihood that the respondent's children received deworming drugs in 2001, and this effect is significantly different from zero at over 95 percent confidence (table 7.4; regression 1 presents marginal probit estimates evaluated at mean values). This suggests that the respondent's small, self-defined social network has a major impact on treatment choices: having two additional early treatment links (roughly a one standard deviation increase) reduces take-up by 6 percentage points.

This result cannot simply be due to imitation or to social effects related to learning about how to use the new technology since the overall effect is negative. This implies that learning about the benefits of the technology plus the infection externality, taken together, are negative and larger in magnitude than the sum of the effect of imitation and the effect due to learning to use the technology. A quadratic term in parent social links to early treatment schools is also statistically significantly different from zero at 95 percent confidence in some specifications (see appendix 7A, regression 1). However, this quadratic term is not significant for interactions with household characteristics and the quadratic second-order early treatment exposure term is not statistically significant (regressions not shown), so we principally focus on the linear measure for simplicity in what follows.[17]

None of the demographic or socioeconomic controls is significantly associated with 2001 take-up except for distance from home to school, which is negatively related to take-up and large: take-up drops nearly 2 percentage points for each additional kilometer from home to school (using GPS measures). Distance apparently makes it costlier for parents to walk to school to provide written consent for deworming and for children to attend school, a first piece of empirical evidence that take-up is sensitive to treatment costs. Parent years of education (typically maternal education in our sample) is positively but not statistically significantly associated with higher take-up (point estimate 0.003, standard error 0.003, table 7.4, regression 1).

Table 7.4
Experimental social effect estimates: Groups 2 and 3

Explanatory variables	Dependent variable: Child took deworming drugs in 2001				
	(1)	(2)	(3)	(4)	(5)
Number of parent links with children in early treatment schools (groups 1 and 2, not own school)	−0.031** (0.014)	−0.040** (0.017)			−0.002 (0.018)
Number of parent links with children in early treatment schools * Group 2 school indicator		0.017 (0.029)			
Proportion direct (first-order) parent links with children in early treatment schools			−0.098** (0.045)		
Number of parent links with children in early treatment schools, with whom respondent speaks at least twice per week				−0.030** (0.016)	
Number of parent links with children in early treatment schools, with whom respondent speaks less than twice per week				−0.033 (0.033)	
Number of parent links with children in group 1, 2, or 3 schools, not own school, with whom respondent speaks at least twice per week				0.008 (0.012)	
Number of parent links with children in group 1, 2, or 3 schools, not own school, with whom respondent speaks less than twice per week				0.026 (0.027)	
Number of parent links with children in early treatment schools * Respondent years of education					−0.0062* (0.0032)
Number of parent links with children in group 1, 2, or 3 schools, not own school	0.013 (0.011)	0.012 (0.017)	−0.006 (0.009)		−0.014 (0.014)
Number of parent links with children not in group 1, 2, or 3 schools	−0.007 (0.007)	−0.008 (0.009)	−0.005 (0.007)	−0.007 (0.007)	−0.008 (0.011)

Table 7.4
(continued)

Explanatory variables	Dependent variable: Child took deworming drugs in 2001				
	(1)	(2)	(3)	(4)	(5)
Number of parent links, total	0.019*** (0.005)	0.029*** (0.007)	0.021*** (0.007)	0.018*** (0.005)	0.013 (0.008)
Respondent years of education	0.003 (0.003)	0.003 (0.003)	0.002 (0.004)	0.002 (0.003)	−0.016 (0.012)
Community group member	0.027 (0.026)	0.031 (0.026)	0.037 (0.029)	0.029 (0.026)	0.023 (0.026)
Total number of children	0.005 (0.006)	0.006 (0.006)	0.004 (0.007)	0.005 (0.006)	0.006 (0.006)
Iron roof at home	0.011 (0.026)	0.008 (0.027)	0.011 (0.032)	0.011 (0.026)	0.009 (0.027)
Distance home to school (km)	−0.018** (0.009)	−0.018** (0.009)	−0.0015 (0.010)	−0.018* (0.009)	−0.018** (0.009)
Group 2 school indicator	0.015 (0.045)	0.201** (0.086)	0.007 (0.046)	0.015 (0.046)	0.015 (0.045)
Cost-sharing school indicator	−0.580*** (0.054)	−0.577*** (0.054)	−0.578*** (0.058)	−0.581*** (0.054)	−0.582*** (0.054)
Number of observations (parents)	1,678	1,678	1,358	1,678	1,678
Mean of dependent variable	0.61	0.61	0.61	0.61	0.61

Notes: Data from 2001 Parent Survey, and 2001 administrative records. Marginal probit coefficient estimates are presented. Robust standard errors in parentheses. Disturbance terms are clustered within schools. Significantly different from zero at 99 (***), 95 (**), and 90 (*) percent confidence. Regression 2 also includes interaction terms (Number of parent social links with children in group 1, 2, or 3 schools, not own school) * (Group 2), (Number of parent social links with children not in group 1, 2, or 3 schools) * (Group 2), and (Number of parent social links, total) * (Group 2). Regression 3 excludes parents for which (Number of parent social links with children in group 1, 2, or 3 schools, not own school) = 0, since the proportion of links is undefined, leading to the reduction in sample size. Regression 5 also includes interaction terms (Number of parent social links with children in group 1, 2, or 3 schools, not own school) * (Respondent years of education) and (Number of parent social links with children not in Group 1, 2, or 3 schools) * (Respondent years of education), not shown.

Social effects are more negative for group 3 schools (point estimate −0.040, table 7.4, regression 2) than for group 2 (−0.023, the sum of the direct effect of early treatment links and its interaction with the group 2 indicator), although the difference is not statistically significant. This pattern of coefficient estimates is reasonable: by 2001, group 2 parents had already observed the impact of deworming treatment in their own household and community and should therefore be less influenced than group 3 parents by early links (i.e., in equation 7.5, σ_N^2 is smaller for group 2 parents than group 3 parents). Nonetheless, the persistent influence of early links on group 2 households after two years of the program is noteworthy. One possible non-Bayesian explanation is that initial pieces of information carry disproportionate weight in subsequent decision making (Rabin and Schrag 1999).[18]

The results are robust to including the proportion of links with children in early treatment schools rather than the number of such links (table 7.4, regression 3) and to controlling for the total number of parent social links nonparametrically using a set of indicator variables (results not shown). An interaction between the cost-sharing indicator and the number of early treatment links is imprecisely estimated, but it is near zero and not statistically significant (estimate -0.013, standard error 0.039—regression not shown).[19]

Several pieces of evidence suggest that learning takes place not only among individuals with strong social ties but also among those with relatively weak ties, along the lines of Granovetter (1973). When the framework is extended to include different types of parent social links—close friends, defined as those with whom the respondent speaks at least twice a week, versus relatively distant friends—each additional close link to an early treatment school is associated with 0.030 lower probability of deworming treatment in 2001 and the estimated effect of distant links is similar, although not statistically significant due to reduced precision (table 7.4, regression 4, estimate -0.033, standard error 0.033).[20] We are similarly unable to reject the hypotheses that social effects are the same for links to relatives versus nonrelatives, or for members of the respondent's own ethnic group versus other groups, conditional on being named a social link (results not shown).

Social effects are more strongly negative for respondents with more education (table 7.4, regression 5). Other studies, most notably Foster and Rosenzweig (1995), find that educated individuals learn most rapidly about new technologies and adopt first. Note that the overall impact of an additional year of schooling on deworming take-up remains positive, though not statistically significant, when all the education interaction terms, including the terms interacting education with total links, are considered (interaction term coefficient estimates not shown in regression 5).

Additional social links could have a larger impact on more educated individuals in the theoretical framework presented if they had overly optimistic prior beliefs (ϕ_{i0}) about the drugs rather than any greater receptiveness to new information. Although we cannot decisively distinguish these two explanations empirically, the relation between respondents' education and their stated belief that deworming drugs are "very effective" does provide further evidence supporting the overoptimism model. Among group 3 parents interviewed in round 1, before deworming treatment was phased into their schools, individuals who had completed primary school were 17 percentage points more likely to believe deworming drugs are "very effective" than parents who had not completed primary school. However, several months after deworming had been introduced into their schools, this falls by about half to a 9 percentage point gap between more educated and less educated group 3 parents interviewed in round 2 (recall that parents were randomly allocated between survey rounds), and there is a similar gap among group 2 parents in 2001, at 10 percentage points, two years after these schools had begun receiving treatment. Presenting the result in levels rather than differences, among group 3 parents who completed primary school, the perceived effectiveness of deworming also fell dramatically from 59 percent to 45 percent from round 1 to round 2, but fell only slightly among the less educated. To summarize, through exposure to deworming over time, views toward the drugs partially converged across parents with different educational levels and the drugs were increasingly viewed as ineffective among group 3 parents. As the medical effectiveness of the drugs is well documented, we conjecture that their disillusionment with the drugs is due to reinfection.

We also estimate social effects as a function of child social contacts in early treatment schools using the 2001 pupil questionnaire data. Average social connections across schools (for the group 2 and group 3 schools) are very similar for parents and children, with a correlation coefficient of 0.92, and this complicates the task of distinguishing between parent and child impacts. Among those children aged thirteen years and older, the estimated effect of direct child social links is negative, similar to the parent first-order early treatment estimate and statistically significant at over 95 percent confidence in a specification analogous to those in table 7.4 (point estimate -0.028, standard error 0.012). However, the point estimate is much smaller for younger children (-0.006, standard error 0.014—regressions not shown). Multiple interpretations of this pattern are possible, including that adolescents may be more influenced by peer information or pressure than younger children are, as Steinberg and Cauffman (1996) claim, or perhaps that younger children are less able to process health information from their social contacts, or that the interaction of information from parents and adolescents is particularly influential.

Unfortunately, we have only limited statistical power to disentangle parent and child impacts or to investigate possible interaction effects due to the high correlation of parent and child social networks and because matched information on both parent and child social networks exists for only a limited subset of children, reducing the sample size in the child network regressions by over half. When both parent and child first-order social links to early treatment schools are included as explanatory variables, both coefficient estimates remain negative but are no longer statistically significant due to the large increase in standard errors (regression not shown).[21]

We next consider higher-order exposure to early treatment schools through parent social networks. After reproducing the main direct first-order social link result (table 7.5, regression 1), we examine the impact of second-order exposure to early treatment schools, where second-order links are constructed using school average connections. We find that second exposure to early treatment schools is also associated with significantly lower deworming drug take-up in 2001 (estimate −0.035, standard error 0.013, regression 2), conditional on total second-order exposure to all program schools. When both first-order and second-order social networks terms are included, the estimated second-order effect is −0.047, nearly identical to the average first-order effect of −0.044, and both effects are statistically significant at high levels of confidence (regression 3). While the theoretical framework predicts that coefficients should decline monotonically for higher-order links along the transition path to steady state (since information from more distant social links is less likely to have reached the individual), we cannot reject the hypothesis that the coefficient estimates on the first-order and second-order links are equal or that first-order effects are somewhat more negative, so we do not emphasize this difference. An increase of one standard deviation in second-order early treatment school exposure is associated with a very large 19 percentage point reduction in deworming take-up. Mirroring the first-order results, more total second-order exposure to all schools (not just early treatment schools) is associated with higher take-up, which we interpret as reflecting a positive correlation between overall individual sociability and positive priors toward deworming in our sample.

The negative second-order effects we estimate suggest that higher-order links can affect behavior not only by influencing the take-up behavior of first-order links but also through changing the information of first-order links. To see this, note that theoretically, one could imagine negative imitation effects if people like to be different from their neighbors. However, a model in which higher-order links affect behavior only through changing the behavior of intermediate links (such as a pure imitation model) would imply that the impact of second-order link adoption should be equal to the square of the first-order link effect of −0.044, or 0.002. Given the results below ruling out large infection externalities at the level of individual social contacts, the large negative coefficient on second-order adoption we estimate thus provides additional evidence that diffusion works by information transmission through social networks.

This negative social learning result holds and is highly statistically significant for both first-order and second-order links when the proportion of early treatment exposure is used (table 7.5, regression 4) rather than the number of

Table 7.5
First-order and higher-order social effect estimates: Groups 2 and 3

Explanatory variables	Dependent variable: Child took deworming drugs in 2001				
	(1)	(2)	(3)	(4)	(5)
Number of parent links with children in early treatment schools (groups 1 and 2, not own school)	−0.031** (0.014)		−0.044*** (0.015)		−0.037** (0.015)
Number of parent links with children in group 1, 2, or 3 schools, not own school	0.013 (0.011)		0.021 (0.015)		0.021 (0.015)
Proportion direct (first-order) parent links with children in early treatment schools				−0.140*** (0.048)	
Second-order exposure to early treatment schools (groups 1 and 2, not own school), parent links		−0.035*** (0.013)	−0.047*** (0.013)		−0.049*** (0.013)
Second-order exposure to group 1, 2 or 3 schools (not own school), parent links		0.021** (0.012)	0.032*** (0.012)		0.032*** (0.012)
Proportion second-order parent links with children in early treatment schools				−0.231*** (0.087)	
Third-order exposure to early treatment schools (groups 1 and 2, not own school), parent links					−0.015 (0.012)
Third-order exposure to group 1, 2 or 3 schools (not own school), parent links					0.008 (0.010)
Total social link controls, socioeconomic controls	Yes	Yes	Yes	Yes	Yes
Number of observations (parents)	1,678	1,678	1,678	1,173	1,678
Mean of dependent variable	0.61	0.61	0.61	0.61	0.61

Notes: Data from 2001 Parent Survey, and 2001 administrative records. Marginal probit coefficient estimates are presented. Robust standard errors in parentheses. Disturbance terms are clustered within schools. Significantly different from zero at 99 (***), 95 (**), and 90 (*) percent confidence. Social links controls and other controls are included in all specifications. Social links controls include total number of parent links; number of parent links to group 1, 2, 3 schools (not own school); and number of parent links to non-program schools. Other controls are respondent years of education, community group member indicator variable, total number of children, iron roof at home indicator variable, and distance from home to school in kilometers, as well as the group 2 indicator and cost-sharing school indicator.

links. The interaction between second-order early treatment school exposure and respondent education remains negative, as was the case for first-order links, but the point estimate is not statistically significant (regression not shown). The second-order exposure results also hold if the first-order exposure is constructed using average school social network connections in a manner analogous to the construction of the higher-order links (coefficient estimate is -0.077, standard error 0.036, significant at 95 percent confidence—regression not shown).

Extending the analysis, we find that third-order exposure to early treatment schools, constructed analogously to the second-order links, using school averages for higher-order connections, is not statistically significantly associated with deworming take-up, although the point estimate is again negative (table 7.5, regression 5). Within the theoretical framework we outline in section 3, a possible explanation for the weaker estimated third-order effect is that insufficient time had passed for some third-order social contacts' information to reach respondents, perhaps because social contacts discuss deworming only infrequently, as suggested by our survey data.

7.3.4 Further Econometric Identification Issues

The estimated negative peer effect in technology adoption implies that social learning about the benefits of deworming and the infection externality taken together are negative and far larger in magnitude than any possible social learning about how to use the new technology plus imitation effects. Here we argue that infection effects cannot empirically explain even a small fraction of the overall direct first-order social effect of -3.1 percent (table 7.4, regression 1), since any plausible estimate of the effect of early treatment school social contacts on infection status times the effect of infection on take-up is much smaller. Thus, social learning about deworming benefits appears to be the key channel driving our results.

First, having additional direct social links to early treatment schools is associated with lower rates of moderate-heavy helminth infection, as expected (table 7.2, regression 6), but the effect is small and not statistically significant (coefficient estimate -0.3 percentage points, relative to a mean moderate-heavy infection rate of 27 percent). An additional second-order social link to early treatment schools is actually associated with a somewhat higher rate of infection, though the estimate is statistically significant only at 90 percent confidence. Note that this relatively weak relationship between early treatment school social links and child infection is not inconsistent with the strong infection externality findings in Miguel and Kremer (2004). Worm infections are not transmitted directly person to person but rather through contaminated soil and water, and a child's named social links constitute only a small fraction of all people who defecate near the child's home, school, and church or who bathe at the same points on Lake Victoria.

In terms of the second step, from infection status to take-up, prior infection status is not significantly associated with drug treatment for either group 1 in 1998 or group 2 in 1999 (Miguel and Kremer 2004) or for groups 2 and 3 in 2001 (results not shown), and the point estimates suggest that moderate-heavy worm infection is weakly negatively related to treatment rates.[22] Of course, the cross-sectional correlation between infection and treatment cannot be interpreted as causal due to omitted variables: children from unobservably low-socioeconomic-status households may have both high infection rates and low take-up, for example. However, the treated and untreated children look remarkably similar along many observable baseline socioeconomic and health characteristics (Miguel and Kremer 2004), and the relationship is similar using school-level average infection rates rather than individual data (not shown), weakening the case for strong selection into deworming treatment.

Further evidence that more infected people are not much more likely to take up the drugs is provided by the 1999 cross-school infection externality estimates, identified using exogenous program variation in the local density of early treatment schools. Although we find large average reductions in moderate-heavy worm infection rates as a result of cross-school externalities (an average reduction in infection of 0.23; Miguel and Kremer, 2004), proximity to early treatment schools leads to an average reduction in drug take-up of only 0.02, which has the expected sign but is near zero (regression not shown). Using this estimate, having a moderate-heavy infection is associated with a $0.02/0.23 = 0.09$ reduction in the likelihood of treatment, and this implies a drop in take-up due to infection first-order social effects of only $(0.09) \times (-0.3$ percent$) = 0.03$ percent, rather than the -3.1 percent overall reduction we estimate. Even if eliminating a moderate-heavy infection reduced the likelihood of drug take-up by a massive 0.5 on average (rather than the 0.09 we estimate), health externalities would account only for a $(0.5) \times (-0.3$ percent$) = -0.15$ percent reduction in take-up.

Pupil transfers among local primary schools are another potential concern, but any resulting bias would likely work against our findings. For example, parents with more health-conscious social contacts, whose children may have been more likely to transfer into early treatment schools to receive deworming, may themselves also be more health conscious and eager to have their own children receive treatment. This would bias the estimated social effect upward, in which case, our negative social effect estimate would be a bound on the true negative effect. In any case, the rate of pupil transfers between treatment and comparison schools was low and nearly symmetric in both directions (Miguel and Kremer 2004), suggesting that any transfer bias is likely to be small.

A related identification issue concerns whether social networks measured in 2001, three years after the program started, were themselves affected by the program. Any extent to which health-conscious individuals became more socially linked to individuals with children in early treatment schools would again lead to an upward bias, working against the negative effects we estimate. However, respondents were statistically no more likely to name early treatment links than links to other schools: the average number of links to early treatment schools is 1.92, while (Total number of links to PSDP schools) × (Total number of groups 1, 2 pupils/Total number of groups 1, 2, 3 pupils) is nearly identical at 1.91.

7.3.5 Parent Attitudes and Knowledge

Respondents with more direct (first-order) early treatment links are significantly more likely to claim that deworming drugs are "not effective" (respondents could choose between "not effective," "somewhat effective" and "very effective"; table 7.6, row 1).[23] This is consistent with the hypothesis that some people initially thought deworming would provide large and persistent private benefits but learned otherwise from their early treatment school contacts. We do not find a significant impact of additional early links on beliefs that deworming drugs are "very effective," although the point estimate is negative (row 2), or that the drugs have "side effects" (row 3). This last result is evidence against the possibility that drug side effect rumors were the key driver of lower take-up among those with more early treatment links.

Second-order early treatment exposure does not have a statistically significant effect on parents' belief that deworming drugs are "not effective" (regressions not shown). The discrepancy between first-order and second-order effects on deworming attitudes may be due to the deterioration of information quality with higher-order social connections: speculatively, individuals may learn from their higher-order social contacts that deworming is basically "not good" even though the precise reason is lost to them.

Although direct first-order early treatment links do affect the belief that deworming drugs are "not effective," they do not affect beliefs that "worms and schistosomiasis are very bad for child health" (table 7.6, row 4). However, some parents may report what they think the survey enumerator wants to hear regarding worms' health consequences: 92 percent of respondents claimed that helminth infections are "very bad" for child health, even though take-up is much lower than 92 percent. The number of direct early treatment links has

Table 7.6
Effects on deworming attitudes and knowledge

Dependent variable	Estimate on number of parent links with children in early treatment schools (Experimental)	Estimate on number of parent links with children in early treatment schools whose children received deworming (Nonexperimental)	Estimate on number of parent links with children in early treatment schools with whom respondent spoke about deworming (Nonexperimental)	Mean dependent variable
A. Attitudes				
1. Parent thinks deworming drugs "not effective"	0.017** (0.007)	0.009 (0.009)	0.009** (0.004)	0.12
2. Parent thinks deworming drugs "very effective"	−0.007 (0.010)	0.042** (0.013)	0.040*** (0.007)	0.43
3. Parent thinks deworming drugs have "side effects"	0.000 (0.003)	0.004 (0.003)	0.003* (0.002)	0.04
4. Parent thinks worms and schistosomiasis "very bad" for child health	−0.001 (0.006)	0.001 (0.008)	−0.006* (0.003)	0.92
B. Knowledge				
5. Parent "knows about ICS deworming program"	0.004 (0.011)	0.054*** (0.014)	0.055*** (0.011)	0.70
6. Parent "knows about the effects of worms and schistosomiasis"	−0.001 (0.013)	0.055*** (0.014)	0.039*** (0.009)	0.68
7. Number of infection symptoms parents able to name (0–10)[a]	−0.029 (0.025)	0.078*** (0.029)	0.076*** (0.015)	1.8
8. Parent able to name "fatigue" as symptom of infection	−0.004 (0.010)	0.032*** (0.008)	0.021*** (0.006)	0.20
9. Parent able to name "anemia" as symptom of infection	0.005 (0.009)	−0.001 (0.011)	0.010** (0.005)	0.22
10. Parent able to name "weight loss" as symptom of infection	0.002 (0.006)	0.002 (0.004)	−0.001 (0.004)	0.06

Notes: Data from 2001 Parent Survey, and 2001 administrative records. Marginal probit coefficient estimates are presented, and each entry is the result of a separate regression. Robust standard errors in parentheses. Disturbance terms are clustered within schools. Significantly different from zero at 99 (***), 95 (**), and 90 (*) percent confidence. Social links controls and other controls are included in all specifications. Social links controls include total number of parent links, number of parent links to group 1, 2, 3 schools (not own school), and number of parent links to nonprogram schools. Other controls are respondent years of education, community group member indicator variable, total number of children, iron roof at home indicator variable, and distance from home to school in kilometers, as well as the group 2 indicator and cost-sharing school indicator. The number of observations (parents) across regressions ranges from 1656 to 1678 depending on the extent of missing data for the dependent variable.

[a] The ten possible infection symptoms are fatigue, anemia, weight loss, stunted growth, stomach ache, bloated stomach, blood in stool, worms in stool, diarrhea, and fever. Parents were asked: "Could you name the symptoms of worm and schistosomiasis infections?" and their responses were recorded by the enumerator.

no effect on parents' self-reported knowledge of the ICS (NGO) deworming program, the effects of worms and schistosomiasis (rows 5 and 6), or the deworming treatment status of their own child (not shown). It also did not affect their objective knowledge of common worm infection symptoms (rows 7 to 10). Respondents could name only 1.8 of 10 common symptoms on average.[24] This suggests health education messages failed to spread.

Nonexperimental methods would have suggested different results. The actual number of treated social links and the number of social links with whom the respondent speaks directly about deworming are both positively and significantly related to most deworming attitudes and knowledge outcomes (table 7.6). The observed positive correlation in outcomes within social networks in the study area appears to be due to omitted variables rather than actual peer effects. Those with unobservably more interest in child health plausibly discuss worms more frequently with social links, who are themselves more likely to have their own children receive treatment.

7.3.6 Simulating Take-Up along the Transition Path

The framework in section 3 suggests that subsidies to take-up will not affect steady-state adoption under social learning about how to use new technologies or learning about their benefits, as long as at least a subset of the population uses the technology. However, subsidies could potentially have effects along the transition path to the steady state. We therefore use the empirical school-to-school social connections matrix to simulate the take-up gains along the transition path from a one-time drug subsidy for parameter values that match the estimated first-order social effects. We consider a hypothetical technology where true private benefits exceed most people's expectations, as it is of more general interest to study technologies where social learning could potentially contribute to take-up.

The simulation is based on the theoretical framework in section 7.2 with several functional form assumptions made for tractability. We assume that the health benefits of the technology times idiosyncratic utility from using the technology (the $\gamma(X_i) \cdot \mu_i$ term) is uniformly distributed on the interval $[\underline{b}, \overline{b}]$; assume that everyone in a given school starts out with the same prior belief on benefits but that priors differ across schools (and thus focus on the diffusion of information across schools rather than on heterogeneity within schools); and assume that all the social effects we observe are due to learning about the benefits of the technology.

One time period in the simulation roughly corresponds to one month. Information may diffuse between schools in each period, but individuals get an opportunity to adopt the technology only once every six months (as in the program we study). Our results are qualitatively robust to either shorter ($\tau = 1$) or longer ($\tau = 12$) lags between adoption opportunities. For tractability, we assume that information diffuses instantly within schools.

We consider parameter values for which the simulated first-order social effects fall within two standard deviations of the first-order social effect estimated empirically, though again we consider diffusion of a hypothetical technology for which actual returns exceed prior beliefs, so social learning speeds adoption.[25] While we do not explicitly match parameter values to the empirically estimated second-order social effect, the simulated second-order effect is on average close to the estimated second-order effects. As in our data, the simulated second-order effect is of a similar magnitude to the simulated first-order effect—the difference between the simulated second-order and first-order social effects is on average 0.006 (relative to an average simulated first-order effect of 0.02, a slightly smaller magnitude than the effect estimated in section 7.2).

For a wide range of parameter values, we find that beliefs about the technology and take-up rates converge quickly (within five adoption opportunities) to very close to the correct long-run value. Even in a case where signals have high variance (e.g., $\sigma_\varepsilon^2 = 9$), by the third adoption opportunity, the variance of posterior beliefs is on average less than 0.01.

Optimal seeding of a particular school with a one-time drug subsidy (in period 1) makes little difference to total discounted technology take-up. After thirty opportunities to adopt (fifteen years of a program like the one we study), the difference in total discounted take-up between seeding the single "best" school—the school that generates the highest total discounted take-up when seeded—versus the average of seeding a randomly chosen school in the sample is negligible (less than 0.01 percent) for our range of plausible parameter values. This finding of small gains to optimal seeding is consistent with the largely symmetrical observed social network structure across schools. Given that it may be costly to identify the optimal school to subsidize and that those funds could alternatively be spent on subsidizing drugs for additional schools (or subsidizing them for a longer period), efforts to target temporary drug subsidies to influential opinion leader schools appear misguided in our context.

Finally, even the take-up gains from one-time subsidies to additional schools are quite small on average. Since information diffuses rapidly, these gains primarily comprise the direct effect of the subsidy on take-up in the initial round; the impact of information spillovers is negligible. The indirect effects on take-up (through the generation of additional information) are small in magnitude and exhibit diminishing returns to additional subsidies. Total discounted take-up increases by only 0.027 percent (as a percentage of take-up in the absence of the subsidy) on average above and beyond the direct effect of the subsidy when a single school is subsidized at random. Going from subsidizing five to ten schools yields an additional marginal gain of only 0.016 percent per school.

Thus, at least in this particular context, there is little reason to think temporary subsidies will lead to a sustainable increase in technology adoption. More generally, even if a hypothetical social planner knew the returns to a particular technology were better than people expected, subsidizing even a small fraction of the population for a relatively brief period would have been sufficient to ensure long-run diffusion. In the absence of strong imitation effects, the fact that dynamic gains to subsidizing additional schools are small suggest that a "big push" is unnecessary for a technology that spreads naturally—and of course is futile in the long run for a technology where social effects are negative. To be effective in boosting adoption, ongoing subsidies appear necessary in that case.

7.4   The Impact of Subsidies on Drug Take-Up

In the remainder of the chapter, we examine the effects of three other approaches to making deworming sustainable: cost sharing through user fees (section 7.4), health education lessons (section 7.5), and a mobilization intervention (section 7.6).

Cost sharing through user fees has been advocated as necessary for the sustainability of public health services in many less developed countries (World Bank 1993b). Revenues from these fees could be used to improve the quality of health services (e.g., through expanded drug availability) or to fund other government expenditures. User fees could theoretically promote more efficient use of scarce public resources if those in greatest need of health services are willing to pay the most for them.

Several nonexperimental studies from Africa have found large drops in health care utilization after the introduction of user fees (e.g., McPake 1993, Meuwissen 2002), including in Kenya, where Mwabu et al. (1995) find utilization fell by 52 percent in 1989. Our analysis uses random assignment to estimate the effect of cost sharing.[26] The theoretical framework in section 7.2 suggests that increasing the monetary cost of deworming should lead to lower drug take-up, but the actual elasticity of demand needs to be estimated. Seventy-five percent of households in the free treatment schools received deworming drugs in 2001 (table 7.1C), while the rate was only 19 percent in cost-sharing schools (the survey data used in these regressions is described

Table 7.7
The impact of cost sharing

Explanatory variables	Dependent variable: Child took deworming drugs in 2001		
	(1)	(2)	(3)
Cost-sharing school indicator	−0.580*** (0.054)	−0.459*** (0.122)	−0.572*** (0.080)
Cost sharing × Respondent years of education		0.002 (0.007)	
Cost sharing × Community group member		0.021 (0.072)	
Cost sharing × Total number of children		−0.021 (0.016)	
Cost sharing × Iron roof at home		−0.047 (0.064)	
Effective price of deworming per child (= Cost/Number of household children in that school)			−0.001 (0.002)
1/(Number of household children in that school)			−0.348*** (0.066)
Social links, other controls	Yes	Yes	Yes
Number of observations (parents)	1,678	1,678	1,678
Mean of dependent variable	0.61	0.61	0.61

Notes: Data from 2001 Parent Survey, and 2001 administrative records. Marginal probit coefficient estimates are presented. Robust standard errors in parentheses. Disturbance terms are clustered within schools. Significantly different from zero at 99 (***), 95 (**), and 90 (*) percent confidence. Social links controls include total number of links; number of links to group 1, 2, 3 schools (not own school); and number of links to non-program schools (as in table 7.4). Other controls are respondent years of education, community group member indicator variable, total number of children in the household, iron roof at home indicator variable, and distance from home to school in kilometers, as well as the group 2 indicator (as in table 7.4).

in section 7.3). A regression analysis suggests the small fee reduced treatment by 58 percentage points (table 7.7, regression 1), with the effect similar across households with various socioeconomic characteristics (regression 2).[27] This negative effect of monetary cost is consistent with our finding (in table 7.4) of large negative effects of household distance to the school, which proxies for the time costs as parents need to walk to school to provide written consent.

The drop in take-up in cost-sharing schools cannot be attributed to the hypothesis that user fees help ensure that scarce health resources are directed to those who need them most. In fact, sicker pupils were no more likely to pay for deworming drugs: the coefficient estimate on the interaction between 2001 helminth infection status and the cost-sharing indicator is not statistically significant (not shown).

Variation in the deworming price per child was generated by the fact that cost sharing came in the form of a per family fee, so that parents with more children in the primary school in 2001 effectively faced a lower price per child. Cost sharing reduced treatment rates regardless of the per child price that the household was required to pay (table 7.7, regression 3). Ariely and Shampan'er (2004) similarly find sharp decreases in demand for goods with a small positive price relative to goods with a zero price in lab experiments. This regression specification also includes the inverse of the number of household children in primary school and the total number of household children of all ages as additional explanatory variables to control for the direct effects of household demographic structure on deworming drug demand and thus to isolate the price effect. However, we cannot explicitly control for the interaction between family size and price changes given the school-level randomization design.

The cost-sharing results suggest that introducing a small positive user fee is a particularly unattractive policy in this context, since it dramatically reduces take-up while raising little revenue and typically requires considerable administrative cost. Yet this is precisely the approach that many less developed countries, including Kenya, have adopted in the health sector (World Bank 1994, McPake 1993). The net public cost per pupil treated in our program under a full subsidy was US$1.478. Assuming a US$15.00 per school fixed cost of visiting a school (which we base on actual field costs) and a US$0.03 cost per pupil of collecting funds, the net public cost per student treated under cost sharing was US$1.374. Pupils contributed about US$0.30 additionally in cost-sharing schools. For a fixed public budget B, the difference between the total number of students treated under cost sharing versus under a full subsidy in this case will be $(B/1.374) - (B/1.478) = B * 0.0512$. The extra revenue collected from the private sector under cost sharing will be US$0.30 $* (B/1.374) = B * 0.2183$. The cost per additional student treated under cost sharing is thus $(B * 0.2183)/(B * 0.0512) = $ US$4.26. One can understand why a program administrator with a fixed public budget might institute cost sharing, but since the cost per additional student treated under a full subsidy would be only US$1.478, the deadweight cost of taxation would have to be enormous to make it rational for governments to seek to finance deworming out of user fees rather than through taxation.

It is worth bearing in mind the sequencing of the current project in interpreting the cost-sharing results. Prior to the program, fewer than 5 percent of people reported taking deworming drugs (Miguel and Kremer 2004). The schools received free treatment for two or three years, after which half the group 1 and 2 schools were assigned to cost sharing, following NGO policy. One rationale behind this sequencing was that people may be more likely to spend money on a new product if they can first try it and witness its benefits firsthand. However, some could argue that it is essential to introduce cost sharing from the outset, because after becoming accustomed to free treatment, people will develop a sense of entitlement and will refuse to pay when positive prices are later introduced. Although we are unable to directly test either hypothesis here given the study design, it is worth noting that there was no significant difference in the impact of cost sharing on take-up across group 1 and group 2 schools despite their differing lengths of exposure to free treatment (three versus two years, respectively—regression not shown), exposure that could theoretically have provided a stronger sense of entitlement among group 1 households.

The huge drop in take-up with cost sharing and the extremely low level of private deworming purchases suggest that most households in the study area place little value on deworming drugs. Even if deworming is socially beneficial, perceived private gains were smaller than private costs for most households under the cost-sharing regime. The social learning results indicate that additional information about deworming through social contacts only reinforces this view, further depressing adoption.

7.5 Impact of Health Education

There were no significant differences across treatment and comparison school pupils in early 1999 (one year into the program) on the three worm prevention behaviors that the program emphasized: pupil cleanliness (of the hands and uniform) observed by enumerators,[28] the proportion of pupils observed wearing shoes, or self-reported exposure to freshwater (table 7.8A). The results do not vary significantly by pupil age, gender, or grade (results not shown). As we found with cost sharing for deworming drugs, individuals appear unwilling to take a costly private action—here, buying shoes for their children or adopting new hygiene practices—that helps to combat worms in their local community.

One alternative explanation is that treatment school children neglected to adopt worm prevention practices precisely because they were also taking deworming drugs and thus (falsely) felt protected from reinfection. This does not seem to explain the lack of health education impacts, however, since there was no evidence of behavioral change even among older girls who did not receive the medical treatment (due to concerns about potential embryotoxicity; table 7.8B). The lack of basic knowledge about worm infections in this area makes remote the possibility that older girls in treatment schools neglected to adopt better worm prevention practices because they realized that they were benefiting from spillovers.

Table 7.8
PSDP health behavior impacts, 1999

	Group 1	Group 2	Group 1 – group 2 (SE)
A. Health behaviors, all pupils (grades 3–8)			
Clean (observed by fieldworker)	0.59	0.60	−0.01 (0.02)
Wears shoes (observed by fieldworker)	0.24	0.26	−0.02 (0.03)
Days' contact with freshwater in past week (self-reported)	2.4	2.2	0.2 (0.3)
B. Health behaviors, girls 13 years old and over			
Clean (observed by fieldworker)	0.75	0.77	−0.02 (0.02)
Wears shoes (observed by fieldworker)	0.39	0.42	−0.03 (0.06)
Days' contact with freshwater in past week (self-reported)	2.3	2.2	0.0 (0.3)

Overall cross-school externality effect for group 2

C. Health behaviors, all pupils (grades 3–8)[a]	
Clean (observed by fieldworker)	0.09 (0.21)
Wears shoes (observed by fieldworker)	−0.01 (0.08)
Days' contact with freshwater in past week (self-reported)	0.96 (0.67)

Notes: These results use data from Miguel and Kremer (2004). These are averages of individual-level data for grade 3–8 pupils; disturbance terms are clustered within schools. Robust standard errors in parentheses. Significantly different from zero at 99 (***), 95 (**), and 90 (*) percent confidence.
[a] The effects are the result of a regression in which the dependent variable is the change in the health behavior between 1998 and 1999 (school average) and the local density of group 1 pupils within 3 kilometers (per 1,000 pupils), group 1 pupils within 3 to 6 kilometers (per 1,000 pupils), total pupils within 3 kilometers (per 1,000 pupils) and total pupils within 3 to 6 kilometers (per 1,000 pupils) are the key explanatory variables. Grade indicators, school assistance controls (for other NGO programs), and the average school district mock exam score are additional explanatory variables (as in Miguel and Kremer 2004).

Moreover, there is no evidence that other children benefiting from treatment spillovers changed their prevention behavior: children attending comparison (group 2) primary schools located near deworming treatment schools in early 1999 showed large reductions in worm infection levels (Miguel and Kremer 2004), but they did not receive health education, and there was no significant change in their worm prevention behaviors either (table 7.8C), although one limitation of this analysis is that these cross-school effects are very imprecisely estimated.

Although we cannot directly measure the depreciation of knowledge, other researchers find that depreciation of health education knowledge and practices is often rapid even in settings where direct short-run program impacts were positive (Aziz et al. 1990, Haggerty et al. 1994, Hoque et al. 1996).

7.6   The Impact of Commitment

Advocates of the sustainability approach in development argue that projects should be implemented only if there is local ownership, often conveyed by beneficiaries' making an affirmative commitment to the project. In the project we study, for instance, treatment took place only after the community collectively decided to participate during a village meeting.

The notion of ownership also relates to the claim in social psychology that asking individuals whether they plan to take an action will make it more likely that they go through with it. A number of studies suggest that individuals can be motivated to take socially beneficial but individually costly actions by being asked whether they intend to perform them. Most people answer that they do, and many then feel motivated to follow through with their commitment. For example, Cioffi and Garner (1998) find large impacts of such commitments on blood donation on a U.S. university campus. (Greenwald et al. 1987 find such effects for voting behavior among university students in the United States, but in recent work, Smith, Gerber, and Orlich 2003 fail to reproduce this finding using a much larger and more representative sample of U.S. voters.)

In an application of this technique, a random subsample of pupils in PSDP schools was asked whether they would take deworming drugs in the upcoming treatment round, in an attempt to boost drug take-up without providing additional external subsidies. During 2001 pupil questionnaire administration, a random subsample of pupils was asked whether they were planning to come to school on the treatment day and whether the PSDP workers should bring pills for them on that day: 98 percent of children answered yes to both questions. All pupils interviewed—those offered the opportunity for verbal commitment and those not offered this opportunity—were provided the same information on the effects of deworming and the upcoming date of medical treatment. (All respondents were also informed that participation in data collection and treatment was voluntary.)

The verbal commitment intervention failed, reducing drug take-up by one percentage point in 2001, although this effect is not statistically significant (table 7.9, regression 1). This result is robust to controls for pupil age and gender (regression 2), and the impact of the intervention did not vary significantly with child characteristics (regression 3). The effect is somewhat more negative for pupils in cost-sharing schools and those with moderate-heavy worm infections, although in neither case are the estimates on these interactions significantly different from zero (results not shown).

These results underscore the need for further research clarifying when and where marketing techniques based on prior commitments have an impact.

Table 7.9
Impact of a verbal commitment

	Dependent variable: Child took deworming drugs in 2001		
	(1)	(2)	(3)
Verbal commitment intervention indicator	−0.014 (0.021)	−0.013 (0.021)	0.023 (0.145)
Pupil age		−0.004 (0.006)	−0.003 (0.006)
Pupil female		−0.048** (0.024)	−0.050 (0.035)
Verbal commitment intervention indicator × Age			−0.003 (0.010)
Verbal commitment intervention indicator × Female			0.005 (0.055)
Social links, other controls	Yes	Yes	Yes
Number of observations (pupils)	3,164	3,164	3,164
Mean of dependent variable	0.54	0.54	0.54

Notes: Data from 2001 parent and pupil surveys, and administrative records. Marginal probit coefficient estimates are presented, with robust standard errors in parentheses. Disturbance terms are clustered within schools. Significantly different from zero at 99 (***), 95 (**), and 90 (*) percent confidence. Social links controls are described in Miguel and Kremer (2003). Other controls include respondent years of education, community group member indicator variable, total number of children, iron roof at home indicator variable, and distance from home to school in kilometers, as well as the group 2 and cost-sharing school indicators. Summary statistics from the 2001 Pupil Questionnaire (Mean [SD]): Pupil age (12.9 [2.3]), Pupil female indicator (0.23 [0.42]) (older girls were dropped from the sample because they were not eligible for deworming due to the potential embryotoxicity of the drugs).

7.7   Conclusion

A program that provided free deworming drugs for primary school students led to high drug take-up, large reductions in moderate-heavy worm infections, and increased school participation, all at low cost. Most of the deworming program benefit was in the form of externalities due to reduced disease transmission (Miguel and Kremer 2004). Yet mass deworming treatment programs like the one we study are rare, and one in four people worldwide still suffer from these easily treated infections.

One reason for this failure is that rather than allocating funding on the basis of a standard public finance analysis, development agencies often prefer to fund "sustainable" interventions that do not require continued external funding. We examine several of these approaches to worm control in this chapter, including cost recovery from beneficiaries, health education, and individual mobilization and find all were ineffective at combating worms relative to the provision of free deworming drugs. The fact that drug take-up fell as more individuals were exposed to deworming through their social network is consistent with the idea that private valuation is low and casts doubt on the notion that a temporary intervention could lead to a sustainable long-run increase in deworming take-up through a process of social learning in this context. The analysis suggests people learned about the private benefits of deworming but provides no evidence for large pure imitation effects. Our model suggests that in the absence of such effects, expending temporary subsidies beyond a small number of people will not affect long-run take-up.

Taken together, these findings suggest that continued subsidies may be needed to control diseases characterized by large positive treatment externalities, like worms. In Africa, where half the disease burden is associated with infectious and parasitic diseases (World Health Organization 1999), this means extensive and indefinite health care subsidies may be needed to adequately address public health problems.

A broader lesson of this chapter is that it may be difficult for external interventions to promote sustainable, voluntary, local public good provision. If local public goods are to be provided, they will likely have to be paid for by tax revenue collected by local governments, national governments, or external donors. Standard theories of fiscal federalism suggest local governments might be best suited to this task, but in Kenya, as in many other developing countries, there are no locally elected bodies with taxation powers or control over revenue, perhaps because this could threaten central government primacy by creating rival power centers. National governments in Africa have not historically supplied deworming and have a poor record on local public goods provision.

Donors have sometimes provided local public goods, but typically not on a long-term basis. Rather, they often structure projects so as to be able to claim they are sustainable.

Donors may simply choose not to provide local public goods under these circumstances, or they may choose to provide them on an ongoing long-run basis, but there is little economic rationale for pursuing the illusion of sustainability. Even if donors wish to fund investment activities rather than consumption, there is little reason that they should seek projects that are sustainable on a project-by-project basis rather than taking a broader view of what constitutes a good investment. For instance, a public health project providing subsidized deworming may not be financially sustainable by itself in the short run—in the sense that communities will not voluntarily provide it—but it will help children obtain more education, and this can contribute to long-run development for society as a whole. If donors are concerned that projects such as roads or wells will go awry without regular maintenance, they could endow funds earmarked for this purpose rather than counting on potentially illusory voluntary local contributions for maintenance.

Why then do aid agencies place so much emphasis on financial sustainability? We believe that rather than reflecting an economic social welfare calculation on behalf of optimizing donors, this reflects the politics of aid and principal-agent problems between aid agencies and their ultimate funders in wealthy countries, who are generally ill informed about conditions in countries receiving aid. Aid agencies competing for limited donor funds have incentives to make bold claims about what their programs can achieve. In the short run, these claims may be useful fund-raising tools if the ultimate funders find it impossible to distinguish between, say, genuine claims regarding the temporary health benefits of providing free deworming medicine (as in the project we study) versus overstated claims about the permanent benefits of a one-time worm prevention health education intervention. Individual claims about spectacular project "bang for the buck" typically remain unchallenged, since aid agencies are not directly accountable to their programs' beneficiaries through either political mechanisms (e.g., democratic elections) or the market mechanism, and rigorous development program evaluations remain rare.

In the longer term, of course, pursuing sustainability leads to failed projects, disillusionment among donors, and the search for the next development panacea. Rather than pursue the illusion of sustainability, development organizations and developing-country governments would be better off rigorously evaluating their projects, ultimately identifying a limited number with high social returns and funding these interventions on an ongoing basis.

Appendix 7A: Robustness of Social Effect Results: Parent Networks

	Dependent variable: Child took deworming drugs in 2001			
	Probit (1)	Probit (2)	Probit (3)	Probit (4)
Number of parent links with children in early treatment schools (group 1, 2, not own school)	−0.071*** (0.023)	−0.027* (0.014)	−0.029** (0.014)	−0.016 (0.014)
{Number of parent links with children in early treatment schools (group 1, 2, not own school)}²	0.0064** (0.0029)			
Number of pupils in early treatment schools less than 3 kilometers from home (per 1,000 pupils)				−0.20*** (0.07)
Number of pupils in all schools less than 3 kilometers from home (per 1,000 pupils)				0.14** (0.07)
Parent social links controls	Yes	Yes	Yes	Yes
Other household controls	Yes	No	Yes	Yes
Ethnic, religious controls	No	No	Yes	No
Number of observations (parents)	1,678	1,678	1,678	1,678
Mean of dependent variable	0.61	0.61	0.61	0.61

Notes: Data from 2001 Parent Survey and 1999 and 2001 administrative records. Probit estimation and robust standard errors are in parentheses. Disturbance terms are clustered within schools. Significantly different from zero at 99 (***), 95 (**), and 90 (*) percent confidence. Parent social links controls include total number of parent links, number of parent links to group 1, 2, 3 schools (not own school), and number of parent links to nonprogram schools. Other household controls include respondent years of education, community group member indicator variable, total number of children, iron roof at home indicator variable, and distance from home to school in kilometers, as well as the group 2 indicator and cost-sharing school indicator.

Ethnic controls include indicators for Luhya-Samia, Luhya-Nyala, Luo, Luhya-Khayo, Luhya-Marachi, and Teso groups and an indicator for being a member of the largest ethnic group in the school (which is near zero and statistically insignificant). Religion controls include indicators for Catholic, Anglican, Pentecostal, Apostolic, Legio Mario, Roho, and Muslim faiths, and an indicator for being a member of the largest religious group in the school (which is negative and marginally statistically significant). In regression 2, no household controls are included as explanatory variables other than the standard social link controls from table 7.4.

Acknowledgments

We thank ICS Africa and the Kenya Ministry of Health for their cooperation in all stages of the project, and especially acknowledge the contributions of Alicia Bannon, Elizabeth Beasley, Laban Benaya, Simon Brooker, Lorenzo Casaburi, Pascaline Dupas, Alfred Luoba, Sylvie Moulin, Robert Namunyu, Carol Nekesa, Peter Wafula Nasokho, Polycarp Waswa, and the entire PSDP staff, without whom the project would not have been possible. John Bellows, Melissa Gonzalez-Brenes, Tina Green, Emily Oster, Avery Ouellette, and especially Jean N. Lee provided excellent research assistance. We thank Andrew Foster, Caroline Hoxby, Guido Imbens, Botond Koszegi, Kaivan Munshi, Mark Rosenzweig, John Strauss, Chris Udry, and numerous seminar participants for helpful suggestions. We are grateful for financial support from the World Bank, NIH Fogarty International Center (R01 TW05612-02), NSF (SES-0418110), and Berkeley Center for Health Research. All errors are our own.

Notes

1. Refer to the Oxfam Web site for details (http://www.oxfam.org.uk/about_us/history/history2 .htm).

2. *Sustainability* has other meanings, including an environmental meaning, but we focus on financial sustainability.

3. Lengeler (1999) reaches similar conclusions.

4. Refer to Adams et al. (1994), Corbett et al. (1992), Hotez and Pritchard (1995), and Pollitt (1990).

5. The project followed the standard practice at the time in mass deworming programs of not treating girls of reproductive age—typically aged thirteen years and older in practice—due to concern about the possibility that albendazole could cause birth defects (World Health Organization 1992, Cowden and Hotez 2000). The WHO recently called for this policy to be changed based on an accumulating record of safe use by pregnant women (see Savioli, Crompton, and Niera 2003).

6. This figure is based on an estimate that each health education teacher taught two full hours on worm prevention behaviors in each grade per school year (given an annual teacher salary and benefits of approximately US$2,000) and that the NGO team also provided two hours of health education per school per year.

7. Kenyan per capita income was US$340 (World Bank 1999); incomes may be even lower in Busia.

8. Geissler studies an ethnically Luo population (Luos speak a Nilotic language). The majority of our sample are ethnically Luhya (a Bantu-speaking group), though Luos are 4 percent of our sample. However, traditional Luo views are closely related to views found among other African groups (Green, Jurg, and Djedje 1994, Green 1997).

9. The effect of other people's treatment choices on the magnitude of private treatment benefits is unclear a priori. As a benchmark, if helminth reinfection rates are independent of own current worm load and if the health burden of infection is linear in own worm load, the private health benefits of treatment are independent of others' choices. If, instead, the health costs of infection are convex in worm load, deworming benefits will be greater in an environment that is expected to have high exposure to worms in the future. Thus, the net private benefits of treatment will be lower

if others are treated. The opposite holds with concavity. Miguel and Kremer (2004) estimate average deworming treatment spillovers and find that they are roughly linear in local treatment rates, but due to data limitations have little power to detect nonlinear higher-order terms. Here we assume the benchmark linear case.

10. As observed by Watts and Strogatz (1998), the addition of even a few links to a sparsely connected network greatly reduces the average path length between any two nodes, so in general, information will propagate more quickly in more densely connected networks than in the simple tree we consider.

11. Note that infection status in general will be a function of the entire treatment history of the network. In the steady state, however, the equilibrium take-up rate λ^* is a sufficient statistic for the entire history since the take-up rate is the same in every period.

12. We conjecture that even in the presence of peer effects, if social connections are in a tree network structure as modeled here, then subsidizing a small group of tightly socially linked people may be sufficient to ensure adoption and further diffusion of the technology, unless private returns are low enough and peer effects strong enough that people will not adopt unless a majority of contacts adopt. This is because subsidizing a small group of interconnected people will be sufficient to ensure adoption within this group, and once learning takes place within the group, adoption can then spread outward to others.

13. Of course, additional subsidies may be justified if there is learning by doing in production. Here we examine the extent to which social learning by consumers generates a case for subsidies.

14. Survey refusal rates were low, as is typical for this region. Thirteen percent of households were dropped due to missing network information, treatment information, household characteristics, or difficulty matching across the 2001 surveys and earlier PSDP data sets.

15. Treatment within a family is highly correlated, as expected, so we use the household as the unit of analysis.

16. The experiences and choices of people in social links' communities may theoretically affect respondent take-up (Munshi 2004). For each early treatment school, we computed the average difference in 1999 school participation between treated and untreated pupils and used this to classify schools into "large treated minus untreated difference" schools (those above the median difference) versus small difference schools. The treated minus untreated difference captures the average observed private benefit to deworming in that school. However, the effect of links to early treatment schools in large difference schools is not significantly different from the effect in small difference schools. Similarly, links to early treatment schools with low take-up do have a somewhat more negative effect on respondent treatment rates than links to schools with high take-up, but the difference is not significant (not shown). However, omitted variable bias concerns and limited statistical power mean these results should be interpreted cautiously.

17. Given the correlation of information among individuals in the same school, it is theoretically possible that the first signal in a particular school would be more influential than subsequent signals. We estimated these effects in our data, but due to limited statistical power cannot reject the hypothesis that the first, second, and third links to a particular early treatment school all have the same impact on take-up (regressions not shown).

18. A finding that casts some doubt on the "first impressions matter" explanation, however, is the fact that links to group 1 schools (phased in during 1998) have nearly identical impacts as links to group 2 schools (phased in during 1999, estimates not shown). Note that the persistent effects of early treatment links on take-up might be reconciled with Bayesian learning, though if individuals believed there was an important school-year specific random component to treatment effects, leading them to place extra weight on outcomes in schools other than their own.

19. The results are also robust to a specification without socioeconomic controls (Appendix Table A.1, regression 2) and to the inclusion of additional ethnic and religious controls, and indicators for whether the respondent is a member of the dominant local ethnic and religious group (regression 3); none of the six ethnic group indicator variables is significantly related to take-up. The results are similar when the local density of early treatment school pupils (located within 3 kilometers of the respondent's school) and the density of all local primary school pupils are included as controls (regression 4). However, the point estimate on early links falls by more than a third and loses

statistical significance, possibly because the local density of early treatment schools picks up part of the effect of interactions with other individuals not named in the social links roster. An F-test indicates that the early treatment social links and local density of early treatment pupils terms are jointly significant at 99 percent confidence.

20. Using another definition of link strength yields similar results. While most links were provided in response to questions about the individuals with whom the respondent speaks most frequently, others were provided in response to prompts about contacts in particular local schools. There is not a statistically significant difference in the effects of unprompted and prompted links (in fact, prompted links are somewhat more influential—not shown).

21. Refer to the working paper version (Miguel and Kremer 2003) for further discussion of child social effects.

22. The 2001 worm infection results are for a subsample of only 745 children who were randomly sampled for stool collection and were present in school on the day of the parasitological survey. Due to the relatively small sample size, we do not focus on the parasitological data in the main empirical analysis.

23. A fourth option, "effective, but the worms come back," was rarely chosen by respondents.

24. The ten symptoms are fatigue, anemia, weight loss, stunted growth, stomachache, bloated stomach, blood in stool, worms in stool, diarrhea, and fever. Parents were asked: "Could you name the symptoms of worm and schistosomiasis infections?" and their unprompted responses were recorded by the enumerator.

25. We focus on the following range of parameter values for the model: $\underline{b} = 0$, $\bar{b} = 2$, $\sigma_0^2 = 1$, $\sigma_\varepsilon^2 = 1$ to 10, $C = 0.1$ to 2, $\phi = 0.75$, $\tau = 6$, annual discount rate $\delta = 0.9$ to 1, and $p = 0.05$ to 0.2. In the simulation, we assume that all students within a school receive separate signals and exchange information. However, to compensate for making this extreme assumption, we also assume there is only a maximum of fifty possible signals that can be received per school with full take-up; with more signals per school, convergence is even faster. Given $\underline{b}$ and $\bar{b}$, varying C between 0.1 and 2, covers all of the relevant cases. Similarly, fixing σ_0^2, choosing various values for σ_ε^2, covers all of the interesting cases, since only their relative magnitudes influence weight placed on signals versus prior beliefs. The simulation code and complete results are available from the authors on request.

26. Gertler and Molyneaux (1996) find that utilization of medical care is highly sensitive to price in an experimental study in Indonesia, but since the unit of randomization in their analysis is the district and their intervention affected only eleven districts, statistical power is relatively low. In a large-scale experimental study, Manning et al. (1987) find in contrast that the price elasticity of demand for medical services in the United States is a modest -0.2.

27. Results are unchanged if group 1 households are included in the analysis (results not shown). They are excluded here since they lack the social networks data that we use as explanatory variables here and in section 7.3.

28. This also holds controlling for initial 1998 cleanliness or using differences-in-differences (regressions not shown).

References

Adams, E. J., Stephenson, L. S., Latham, M. C., and Kinoti, S. N. 1994. "Physical Activity and Growth of Kenyan School Children with Hookworm, *Trichuris trichiura* and *Ascaris lumbricoides* Infections Are Improved after Treatment with Albendazole." *Journal of Nutrition* 70:1199–1206.

Akwara, Priscilla A. 1996. "Socio-Economic Perspectives in Child Health in Kenya: A Strategy for Population Action." *African Anthropology* 3:3–43.

Anderson, R. M., and R. M. May. 1991. *Infectious Diseases of Humans.* New York: Oxford University Press.

Ariely, Dan, and Kristina Shampan'er. 2004. "Tradeoffs between Costs and Benefits: Lessons from 'the Price of 0.'" Unpublished manuscript, MIT.

Aziz, K., B. Hoque, K. Hasan, M. Patwary, S. Huttly, M. Arman, and R. Feachem. 1990. "Reduction in Diarrhoeal Diseases in Children in Rural Bangladesh by Environmental and Behavioural Modifications." *Transactions of the Royal Society of Tropical Medicine and Hygiene* 84:433–438.

Bandiera, Oriana, and Imran Rasul. 2006. "Social Networks and Technology Adoption in Northern Mozambique." *Economic Journal* 116(514):869–902.

Banerjee, Abhijit V. 1992. "A Simple Model of Herd Behavior." *Quarterly Journal of Economics* 57:797–817.

Bundy, D. A. P. 1994. "The Global Burden of Intestinal Nematode Disease." *Transactions of the Royal Society of Tropical Medicine and Hygiene* 88:259–261.

Burke, M., G. Fournier, and K. Prasad. 2003. "Physician Social Networks and Geographical Variation in Care." Unpublished working paper.

Cioffi, D., and R. Garner. 1998. "The Effect of Response Options on Decisions and Subsequent Behavior: Sometimes Inaction Is Better." *Personality and Social Psychology Bulletin* 24:463–472.

Conley, Timothy, and Christopher Udry. 2000. "Learning about a New Technology: Pineapple in Ghana." Economic Growth Center Discussion Paper 817, Yale University.

Corbett, E. L., Butterworth, A. E., Fulford, A. J. C., Ouma, J. H., and Sturock, R. F. 1992. "Nutritional Status of Children with *Schistosomiasis Mansoni* in Two Different Areas of Machakos District, Kenya." *Transactions of the Royal Society of Tropical Medicine and Hygiene* 86:266–273.

Cowden, J., and P. Hotez. 2000. "Mebendazole and Albendazole Treatment of Geohelminth Infections in Children and Pregnant Women." *Pediatric Infectious Disease Journal* 19:659–660.

Duflo, Esther, and Emmanuel Saez. 2003. "The Role of Information and Social Interactions in Retirement Plan Decisions: Evidence from a Randomized Experiment." *Quarterly Journal of Economics* 68:267–299.

Ellison, Glenn, and Drew Fudenberg. 1993. "Rules of Thumb for Social Learning." *Journal of Political Economy* 101:612–643.

Foster, Andrew, and Mark Rosenzweig. 1995. "Learning by Doing and Learning from Others: Human Capital and Technical Change in Agriculture." *Journal of Political Economy* 103:1176–1209.

Geissler, Wenzel. 1998a. "'Worms Are Our Life,' Part I: Understandings of Worms and the Body among the Luo of Western Kenya." *Anthropology and Medicine* 5:63–79.

Geissler, Wenzel. 1998b. "'Worms Are Our Life,' Part II: Luo Children's Thoughts about Worms and Illness." *Anthropology and Medicine* 5:133–144.

Geissler, Wenzel. 2000. "Children and Medicines: Self-Treatment of Common Illnesses among Luo School Children in Western Kenya." *Social Science and Medicine* 50:1771–1783.

Gertler, Paul, and Jack Molyneaux. 1996. "Pricing Public Health Services: Results from a Social Experiment in Indonesia." Mimeo., RAND.

Government of Kenya. 1986. *Kenya Socio-Cultural Profiles: Busia District.* Ed. Gideon Were. Nairobi: Ministry of Planning and National Development.

Granovetter, Mark. 1973. "The Strength of Weak Ties." *American Journal of Sociology* 68:1360–1380.

Green, E. C. 1997. "Purity, Pollution and the Invisible Snake in Southern Africa." *Medical Anthropology* 17:83–100.

Green, E. C., A. Jurg, and A. Djedje. 1994. "The Snake in the Stomach: Child Diarrhoea in Central Mozambique." *Medical Anthropology Quarterly* 8:4–24s.

Greenwald, A. G., C. G. Carnot, R. Beach, and B. Young. 1987. "Increasing Voting Behavior by Asking People If They Expect to Vote." *Journal of Applied Psychology* 72:315–318.

Haggerty, P. A., K. Muladi, B. R. Kirkwood, A. Ashworth, and M. Manunebo. 1994. "Community-Based Hygiene Education to Reduce Diarrhoeal Disease in Rural Zaire: Impact of the Intervention on Diarrhoeal Morbidity." *International Journal of Epidemiology* 23:1050–1059.

Hoque, B. A., T. Juncker, R. B. Sack, M. Ali, and K. M. Aziz. 1996. "Sustainability of a Water, Sanitation and Hygiene Education Project in Rural Bangladesh: A 5-Year Follow-Up." *Bulletin of the World Health Organization* 74:431–437.

Hotez, P. J., and D. I. Pritchard. 1995. "Hookworm Infection." *Scientific American* 272:68–74.

Jovanovic, Boyan, and Yaw Nyarko. 1996. "Learning by Doing and the Choice of Technology." *Econometrica* 64:1299–1310.

Kohler, Hans-Peter, Jere Behrman, and Susan Watkins. 2001. "The Density of Social Networks and Fertility Decisions: Evidence from South Nyanza District, Kenya." *Demography* 38:43–58.

Lengeler, C. 1999. "From Rio to Iragua: Sustainability versus Efficiency and Equity for Preventative Health Interventions." *Tropical Medicine and International Health* 4:409–411.

Manning, W. G., J. P. Newhouse, N. Duan, E. B. Keeler, A. Leibowitz, and M. S. Marquis. 1987. "Health Insurance and the Demand for Medical Care: Evidence from a Randomized Experiment." *American Economic Review* 77:251–277.

Manski, Charles. 1993. "Identification of Endogenous Social Effects: The Reflection Problem." *Review of Economics Studies* 60:531–542.

McPake, Barbara. 1993. "User Charges for Health Services in Developing Countries: A Review of the Economic Literature." *Social Science and Medicine* 36:1397–1405.

Meuwissen, Liesbeth Emm. 2002. "Problems of Cost Recovery Implementation in District Health Care: A Case Study from Niger." *Health Policy and Planning* 17:304–313.

Miguel, Edward, and Mary Kay Gugerty. 2005. "Ethnic Diversity, Social Sanctions, and Public Goods in Kenya." *Journal of Public Economics* 89:2325–2368.

Miguel, Edward, and Michael Kremer. 2003. "Networks, Social Learning, and Technology Adoption: The Case of Deworming Drugs in Kenya." Unpublished manuscript.

Miguel, Edward, and Michael Kremer. 2004. "Worms: Identifying Impacts on Education and Health in the Presence of Treatment Externalities." *Econometrica* 72:159–217.

Morduch, Jonathan. 1999. "The Microfinance Promise." *Journal of Economic Literature* 37:1569–1614.

Munshi, Kaivan. 2004. "Social Learning in a Heterogeneous Population: Technology Diffusion in the Indian Green Revolution." *Journal of Development Economics* 73:185–215.

Munshi, Kaivan, and Jacques Myaux. 2002. "Social Change and Individual Decisions: With an Application to the Demographic Transition." Unpublished working paper, University of Pennsylvania.

Mwabu, G., J. Mwanzia, and W. Liambila. 1995. "User Charges in Government Health Facilities in Kenya: Effect on Attendance and Revenue." *Health Policy and Planning* 10:164–170.

Ostrom, Elinor. 1990. *Governing the Commons: The Evolution of Institutions for Collective Action.* Cambridge: Cambridge University Press.

Partnership for Child Development. 1999. "The Cost of Large-Scale School Health Programmes Which Deliver Anthelmintics in Ghana and Tanzania." *Acta Tropica* 73:183–204.

Pollitt, E. 1990. "Infection: Schistosomiasis." In *Malnutrition and Infection in the Classroom.* Paris: Unesco.

Rabin, Matthew, and Joel Schrag. 1999. "First Impressions Matter: A Model of Confirmatory Bias." *Quarterly Journal of Economics* 114:37–82.

Rosenstein-Rodan, Paul N. 1943. "Problems of Industrialization of Eastern and South-Eastern Europe." *Economic Journal* 53:202–211.

Rostow, Walt W. 1960. *The Stages of Economic Growth.* Cambridge: Cambridge University Press.

Savioli, L., W. T. Crompton, and M. Niera. 2003. "Use of Anthelminthic Drugs During Pregnancy." *American Journal of Obstetrics and Gynecology* 188:5–6.

Smith, Jennifer K., Alan S. Gerber, and Anton Orlich. 2003. "Self-Prophecy Effects and Voter Turn-Out: An Experimental Replication." *Political Psychology* 24:593–604.

Steinberg, Laurence, and Elizabeth Cauffman. 1996. "Maturity of Judgement in Adolescence: Psychosocial Factors in Adolescent Decision Making." *Law and Human Behavior* 20:249–272.

Utzinger, J., R. Berquist, Xiao Shu-Hua, B. H. Singer, and M. Tanner. 2003. "Sustainable Schistosomiasis Control—the Way Forward." *Lancet* 362(9399):1932–1934.

Warren, K. S., et al. 1993. "Helminth infections." In Dean T. Jamison et al., eds., *Disease Control Priorities in Developing Countries.* New York: Oxford University Press and World Bank, 1993.

Watts, D. J., and S. H. Strogatz. 1998. "Collective Dynamics of 'SmallWorld' Networks." *Nature* 393(6684):440–442.

Williamson, John. 1990. "What Washington Means by Policy Reform." In John Williamson, ed., *Latin American Adjustment: How Much Has Happened?* Washington, D.C.: Institute for International Economics.

World Bank. 1993a. *The East Asian Miracle: Economic Growth and Public Policy.* New York: Oxford University Press.

World Bank. 1993b. *World Development Report: Investing in Health.* New York: Oxford University Press.

World Bank. 1994. *Better Health in Africa: Experience and Lessons Learned.* Washington, D.C.: World Bank.

World Bank. 1998. *Beyond the Washington Consensus: Institutions Matter.* New York: Oxford University Press.

World Bank. 1999. *World Development Indicators.* Retrieved from www.worldbank.org/data. November 1999.

World Bank. 2003. *School Deworming at a Glance* [Electronic version]. Washington, D.C.: World Bank.

World Health Organization. 1987. *Prevention and Control of Intestinal Parasitic Infections: Report of the WHO Scientific Group.* Geneva: World Health Organization.

World Health Organization. 1992. *Model Describing Information: Drugs Used in Parasitic Diseases.* Geneva: World Health Organization.

World Health Organization. 1999. *The World Health Report 1999.* Geneva: World Health Organization.

8 An Aid-Institutions Paradox? A Review Essay on Aid Dependency and State Building in Sub-Saharan Africa

Todd Moss, Gunilla Pettersson, and Nicolas van de Walle

The importance of public revenue to the underdeveloped countries can hardly be exaggerated if they are to achieve their hopes of accelerated progress.
—Nicolas Kaldor, *Foreign Affairs*, January 1963

I have made revenue collection a frontline institution because it is the one which can emancipate us from begging, from disturbing friends.... if we can get about 22 percent of GDP we should not need to disturb anybody by asking for aid.... Instead of coming here to bother you, give me this, give me this, I shall come here to greet you, to trade with you.
—Yoweri Museveni, President of Uganda (which collects 11 percent of GDP in taxes and receives a further 11 percent of GDP in aid). Speech delivered at Center for Global Development—Council on Foreign Relations event. Washington, D.C., September 21, 2005

After a crisis of legitimacy throughout the 1990s, aid is popular again in the policy community. Several new studies have suggested that at least a doubling of overseas development assistance (ODA) from 2000 levels is necessary as a precondition for meeting international development targets (Zedillo Panel 2001; Devarajan, Miller, and Swanson 2002). The Commission for Africa (2005), chaired by British prime minister Tony Blair, called for an immediate $25 billion increase in aid to sub-Saharan Africa, with an additional $25 billion to come by 2015. This would constitute roughly a tripling of aid to the continent. Further, the United Nations (UN) Millennium Project (2005) has estimated that global ODA will need to rise even further than the previous estimates, reaching at least $195 billion by 2015 from some $79 billion in 2004. These calls for more ODA are echoed in various parts of the UN system, the World Bank, many nongovernmental institutions, recipient countries, and even some European governments.

Many of the low-income countries targeted for substantial increases in aid already receive historically unprecedented flows. For instance, ODA to sub-Saharan Africa was the equivalent of 11.7 percent of the continent's gross national income (GNI) in 2003 (excluding Nigeria and South Africa).[1] Exactly half of the region's forty-six countries with data for 2003 received in excess of 10 percent of GNI in ODA, and 11 received more than 20 percent. Globally, there is a core set of roughly three dozen countries that have received a tenth of GNI or more in aid for at least the past two decades. This is a lengthy time period for receiving sizable aid with few historical precedents. The large flows to Europe during the Marshall Plan lasted only a few years and never exceeded 3 percent of gross domestic product (GDP) of any receiving country (De Long and Eichengreen 1991, O'Connell and Soludo 2001). While substantial U.S. support during the early cold war to allies such as Korea and Taiwan tapered off within a decade, contemporary aid ratios in these three dozen countries have tended not to recede, but to grow larger over three decades. Moreover, if the large increases in aid proposed actually materialize, aid ratios will rise substantially further and the number of countries crossing the 10 percent threshold will grow significantly (Moss and Subramanian 2005).

Skepticism about the desirability of such aid increases has tended to emphasize economic and management issues. Some observers have expressed concerns about the capacity of low-income states to absorb large new flows in addition to the flows they already receive and have pointed to the weak management capacities of governments, the dearth of good new projects and programs to fund, or the ambiguous association between aid and measurable development outcomes (White 1998, Burnside and Dollar 2000). Other observers have worried about the macroeconomic impact of large aid increases; they have pointed to "Dutch disease" effects on small economies where currency appreciation can undercut export competitiveness (see, e.g., Heller 2005, Rajan and Subramanian 2005). Relatively less critical attention has been paid to the potential effects of large increases in aid on public institutions in low-income countries.

Yet institutional issues have recently returned to the foreground in debates on economic development. The critical importance of sound public institutions to the development process has become an article of faith, not only among political scientists (e.g., Herbst 1990, Haggard 1990, Evans 1995), who could be supposed to have professional reasons to argue for the importance of institutions; it also has emerged more recently as a consensus among economists (e.g., Rodrik 2003; Ndulu and O'Connell 1999; Acemoglu, Johnson, and Robinson 2004). Sachs's (2005) view that good institutions are entirely a result of development, rather than their cause, is now a minority view.

Aid is thought to work best in environments with high-quality public institutions, presumably as part of a capable "developmental" state (among a large literature, see Burnside and Dollar 2000, World Bank 1998). Increasingly, measures of institutions are an explicit factor for aid disbursement and allocation.

Thus, institutional development is frequently an independent variable thought to affect the efficiency of aid, and thus a legitimate factor in selecting aid recipients and determining allocation strategies. This suggests that aid should be selectively focused on countries that are thought to most effectively use resources to engage in poverty reduction. Such logic underlies the International Development Association's (IDA) performance-based allocation process and the Millennium Challenge Account, a new U.S. aid program that explicitly targets assistance to countries that are thought best able to use additional resources (Radelet 2003).

In many respects, this new approach is at odds with the more traditional argument that one of the primary purposes of aid (if not its most important) should be to build effective indigenous public institutions. By this formulation, institutional development is thought to be a dependent variable, affected by targeted aid. In contrast to the selectivity philosophy, this older doctrine has been to channel aid instead to places with the greatest need for improved public institutions with the idea that aid itself will help to improve the institutional environment. This approach underlies growing donor efforts at so-called capacity building and the "big push" on aid first popular in the 1950s and 1960s and now advocated by the UN and others (Easterly 2005). The Commission for Africa report wavers back and forth between these two views of aid and institutions. It recognizes the importance of good institutions to making aid effective, in part because it argues that improved institutions will allow absorption of the much larger aid flows it advocates. But it also believes that these large increases can serve to leverage a much greater commitment on the part of African governments to improving the domestic institutions important to growth and poverty reduction.

Does aid necessarily help to develop public institutions and state capacity, or can there be an aid-institutions paradox? In this chapter, we review an emerging literature that explores the potential effects of large amounts of aid on institutional development, including some of the most basic functions of the state such as the ability to collect revenues. Given the current debates regarding large new infusions of additional aid, an analysis of the institutional effects of aid is particularly timely. Because Africa presents the greatest challenges to development and is the most aid-dependent region, we look especially at the aid-institutions relationship in that region. Many political scientists now argue that public institutions in the region are poorly suited to promote economic development because of neopatrimonial tendencies (Callaghy 1988, Sandbrook 1992, Chabal and Daloz 1999, van de Walle 2001). In the poorly integrated and fragmented states of the region, political leaders have relied on systematic clientelism and the private appropriation of state resources for political ends.

As a result, government resources have not been utilized primarily to promote economic development, as political elites have acted in a predatory fashion to maintain themselves in power.

There are other reasons for which the economies of sub-Saharan Africa have failed to gain economic development, but it is now widely conceded that these political dynamics have constituted a significant brake on growth. As a result, it is thus possible that inflows of external resources like aid could be a disincentive to state transformation. Does aid, and the manner in which it is given, encourage the transition from patrimonialism and predation to rational developmental states?

It is far from impossible that certain types of aid could undermine long-term institutional development, despite donors' sincere intentions. Such a paradox is, of course, not new to the development literature. The so-called resource curse has long posited that unearned income undermines incentives to build local institutions and perhaps a social contract with the population (see Ross 1999 for an excellent review; Karl 1997, Birdsall and Subramanian 2004). Natural resources represent an unearned rent accruing to governments; it is argued that this rent can have a negative and antidevelopmental effect on the economy, public institutions, and even the government's relationship with the citizenry. We will argue that aid can have many of the same dysfunctional effects as natural resources; that is, there can be an "aid curse" as well that might create perverse incentives and lead to antidevelopmental outcomes.

To analyze these issues, we integrate two disciplinary literatures that have too long ignored each other. On the whole, political scientists have been remarkably oblivious to the political dynamics created by foreign aid, particularly in low-income countries, where it is today the leading sector of economic activity and might thus be thought to have a significant impact on the local political economy. For their part, economists have mostly ignored a long tradition in the political science literature that establishes a historical link between the state's revenues and its political and institutional attributes.

The following section lays out the context for these questions and explains why they are particularly relevant for today's debates about aid and development. Section 8.2 reviews the well-known macroeconomic effects of large volumes of aid, and focuses on the institutional implications of these effects. Section 8.3 explores the potential negative effects of large aid flows on institution building through its effect on local bureaucratic and policymaking dynamics. Section 8.4 then examines the literature on state revenues and its relationship to foreign aid. The historical linkages between state revenue collection and state building are considered in section 8.5. A theme that emerges in the second half of the chapter is the low quality of the available data on state revenues, particularly for Africa. Data deficiencies unfortunately prevent the formal empirical testing of many of the hypotheses developed in this chapter. Nonetheless, the possibility of the existence of an aid-institutions paradox is significant, and section 8.6 discusses the policy implications of our findings before concluding.

8.1   Aid and the Development Debates

Aid clearly can be useful and has certainly contributed to economic development and improvements in quality-of-life variables in many countries. Evidence for successful aid is particularly strong in targeted programs with defined objectives (see Levine 2004 for examples in global public health). But at the same time, and especially at very high levels over a sustained period, aid could also have distorting effects on some of the very outcomes donors hope to encourage through aid, such as policy ownership, fiscal sustainability, institutional development, and, ultimately, autonomous long-term economic growth.

One way to consider this problem is to think of aid as a subsidy. As such, aid is supposed to provide temporary financial assistance in order to encourage certain long-term behaviors: revenue collection, investment in physical and human capital, and the establishment of the institutions of a developmental state. There are clearly some cases where aid-as-subsidy has played this role, for example, in South Korea and Botswana, where foreign assistance supported local efforts to do these things and the country gradually was weaned off aid. At the same time, there are many, indeed dozens of, other cases where aid is not temporary and does not seem to assist countries in fulfilling these roles. Instead, it could be argued that the subsidy has in fact discouraged revenue collection, distorted expenditure decision making, and undermined the incentives to build state capacity. In these cases, aid could be viewed as not only a crutch delaying institutional development but as potentially undercutting those efforts.

This possibility of harmful aid dynamics seems particularly acute in sub-Saharan Africa, where some countries have now entered into their third and fourth decades of receiving substantial volumes of aid. Much of this aid has also included explicit capacity-building technical assistance from donors. The World Bank alone provided Africa with seventy civil service reform projects between 1987 and 1997, for instance (Levy and Kpundeh 2005), and a recent internal World Bank evaluation estimates that over a quarter of all bank credits to the region is explicitly devoted to capacity building (Operations Evaluation Department 2005). Technical assistance to central banks seems to have been successful in building institutional capacity, but such examples appear more the exception than the rule. Many experts argue that state capacity has improved little during this period and point to specific cases of clear decline (see van de Walle 2001, 2005).

In some cases, the lack of progress on capacity building can be attributed to political instability. After all, at any given time in the past three decades, over a dozen economies in the region have been subject to violent civil conflict (see, e.g., Collier 2005) and the emergence of warlord rule in the context of the collapse of the central state (Reno 1998). Long periods of political stress, conflict, and state collapse continue to have a significant impact on state capacity, even after the return to political stability because of their long-term institutional effects, notably on the supply of trained manpower. Perhaps more striking is the slow pace of institution building in relatively stable political systems. Indeed, a substantial literature has documented the pervasive weakness of the central state in sub-Saharan Africa, which often exercises weak, if any, effective sovereignty over much of its territory and has less legitimacy than a variety of subnational and private governance structures that compete with it for popular support (Herbst 2000, Englebert 2000, Jackson and Rotberg 1982).

It has become fashionable in the donor community to blame this surprisingly slow pace of state capacity building on the nature of African bureaucracies, which are argued to be patrimonial and corrupt, and thus not particularly interested in the provision of public goods essential to development (Levy and Kpundeh 2005, Operations Evaluation Department 2005). But even if one accepts this, the question remains, Why has the large volume of aid devoted to capacity building not had a bigger impact on improving these public institutions, and transforming them into, using the Weberian terminology, more rational-legal bureaucracies?

8.2   Aid, Fiscal Policy, and Macroeconomic Outcomes

A number of potential negative effects of large aid volumes on institutional development can be identified. Much of the focus from economists has been on macroeconomic imbalances caused by large volumes of aid. One central issue has been the possibility of large official development assistance (ODA) inflows affecting the real exchange rate and undermining the competitiveness of the export sector—the so-called Dutch disease (most recently, see Rajan and Subramanian 2005). Management of the real exchange rate is arguably rendered even more difficult by ODA volatility, which also is thought to have negative effects. Dutch disease–type effects have been noted in a number of African aid recipients (see Younger 1992 on Ghana, Adam and Bevan 2003). Experiences from

Uganda (Atingi-Ego 2005, Nkusu 2004) and other countries suggest that an active central bank can manage these exchange rate appreciations and, for the most part, mitigate pernicious effects on competitiveness. Nonetheless, a number of country episodes suggest that in fact, a large volume of aid can and does undermine competitiveness.

Another set of economic concerns emphasizes the role of aid within the budget process itself, with most studies suggesting that foreign aid can undermine the ability of recipient governments to budget appropriately. Several have implicated the volatility of aid flows as the source of distortions. In a thirty-seven-country survey, Bulir and Lane (2002) found that aid is more volatile than domestic fiscal revenues and that this volatility lessens any potential positive benefits of aid on recipients. McGillivray and Morrisey (2000b) found that the volatility of aid often leads to poor budgeting and underestimation of revenues, particularly since aid commitments tend to overestimate actual disbursements. Similarly, Heller and Gupta (2002) argue that the fiscal uncertainty of dependence on external assistance makes long-term planning extremely difficult.

Beyond volatility, there have also been some questions about perverse incentives of aid on the process of economic policymaking. Bräutigam and Knack (2004), for example, found that high levels of aid serve as a "soft budget constraint": the access to foreign resources convinces decision makers that budgets are flexible and encourages fiscal indiscipline. Two case studies looking at Ghana found that as donor financing increased, so did disparities between budgeted expenditures and actual spending, suggesting that the budget process was increasingly directed toward satisfying external donors rather than reflecting actual public spending preferences. Killick (2004) thus described Ghana's "budgetary facade" and Pradhan (1996) similarly called the budget a "deceptive mirage," in which aid was distorting both the budget process itself and the government's "ownership" of the country's purported development agenda.

A number of observers have examined the impact of large volumes of aid on the mix of public expenditure and the overall spending levels. Multiple papers suggest that aid results in excessive and unsustainable levels of government consumption, also leading potentially to macro imbalances. Khan and Hoshino (1992) found aid to be generally treated as an increase in income leading to higher government consumption, but that some public investment is also financed by aid. In a broad literature review, McGillivray and Morrissey (2000a) found that aid tends to be associated with government spending increases in excess of the value of the aid, although there is no clear answer on the impact of aid on consumption versus investment. This was reinforced in McGillivray and Morrissey (2000b), where the authors concluded that aid leads to increases in expenditure not financed by the corresponding increase in revenue. More recently, Remmer (2004) found that aid leads to overall increases in government spending.

How might these possible macroeffects of aid have a negative impact public institutions? The potential loss of competitiveness means lower exports and economic growth, fewer jobs, and increased dependence on external assistance. Resource volatility contributes to macroeconomic instability, which complicates public policymaking in vital areas such as budgeting and planning and tilts public spending toward consumption rather than investment. These can exact a negative effect on the quality of the civil service, public services, and infrastructure, all indirectly undermining the ability of the state to make the transition from patrimonialism to a more developmental path.

The rest of this chapter addresses more direct and, we argue, more significant but less well-documented negative institutional effects of large volumes of aid. Much of the literature cited in this section describes dysfunctional economic outcomes but does not really explain them. To do so, we need to turn to institutional factors, which we begin examining in the next section.

8.3 Donor Practices and Institutional Change

In addition to macroeconomic and fiscal effects, there are costs of aid related to the structures, practices, and procedures of the current international aid system. These include a longstanding and well-known list of common complaints about aid: volatility and uncertainty of ODA flows, fragmentation of donor efforts, project proliferation and duplication, conflicting or dominant donor agendas, competition for staff, and high administrative and oversight costs (among many, see Cohen 1992, Berg 1993, Bräutigam and Knack 2004, Knack and Rahman 2004, van de Walle 2005). Birdsall (2004) lists many of these as the "seven deadly sins" of the aid business. Such practices are argued to have substantial costs for public administration. For instance, the proliferation of donors and projects constitutes a substantial burden for the small number of qualified public officials, who spend much of their time attending to donor concerns and managing aid activities rather than promoting the development of the country—that is, when they do not exit altogether from the civil service to go work for better wages in donor and NGO organizations. Management of donor visits ("missions") became such a problem in Tanzania that the country was forced to declare a mission holiday, a four-month period to take a break from visiting delegations in order to focus on budget preparation. Similarly, aid volatility and project proliferation complicate effective government control over budgets and development planning. Much, if not most, aid is not integrated into national budgets, thus posing real sustainability problems, and they are often implemented through parallel structures that cream the best staff from the civil service and make government coordination of policy much more difficult.

Far from helping to develop effective state bureaucracies, certain aid practices can in fact serve to reinforce the patrimonial element within recipient governments at the expense of the legal-rational. Projects provide for the allocation of all sorts of discretionary goods to be politicized and patrimonialized, including expensive four-wheel-drive cars, scholarships, decisions over where to place schools and roads, and so on. The common practice of paying cash "sitting fees" for civil servants attending donor-funded workshops, where the daily rates can exceed regular monthly salaries, turns even training into a rent to be distributed. More broadly, when donor projects are poorly integrated into national budgetary processes and not subject to much transparency or effective control, it is argued, they help sustain antidevelopmental practices within the state apparatus. Because local officials are not included in policy planning, they often come to view aid projects as little more than a set of scarce private goods to be allocated. Aid dependence thus leads to a situation in which bureaucrats are often not rewarded for focusing on their core developmental functions but rather on getting money from donors. Technocrats, who are specialized in budget management or planning, say, are less rewarded than bureaucrats, who are adept at interacting with donor organizations and accessing their resources. If these two are not part of the same skill set, the wrong kind of individual expertise may be rewarded, and real developmental capacities may atrophy over time within the administration.

Particularly pernicious for state institutions in Africa has been the combination of high aid flows and economic crisis, both sustained over a long period of time. As development policy has come to be dominated by repeated fiscal crises and driven by short-term adjustment and debt management, the patrimonial attraction of aid resources has been accentuated. In countries where power means access to state privileges and rents, and political systems are sustained by complex clientelist relationships, aid and the scarce goods it provides become all the more desirable for the political management of economic crises (van de Walle 2001). In short, states that find it difficult to meet civil service payrolls are more likely to politicize aid-funded sitting fees, per diems, and scholarships to study abroad. Indeed, they will endeavor to turn aid into a mechanism to increase government consumption rather than public investment.

It also seems reasonable to surmise that the larger the relative aid flows, the more these problems are likely to be exacerbated. In many countries of sub-Saharan Africa, aid flows are such that aid dynamics dominate local development efforts. Moss and Subramanian (2005) identify twenty-two low-income countries, sixteen of which are in sub-Saharan Africa where ODA inflows are equivalent to at least half of total government expenditures. In twelve poor countries, ten of them African, the ratio of ODA to government expenditure was 75 percent or more. Looking at a slightly earlier period, Bräutigam and Knack (2004) find roughly similar numbers of aid intensity.

Because most of the concerns listed in this section are directly related to the way in which aid is delivered and administered, in theory at least, many of these are fixable through changes on the donor side. These shortfalls have long been identified, and some efforts are underway to address them, such as donor pooling or using budget support instead of project aid (Eifert and Gelb 2005). There are also several large institutional attempts to improve the efficiency of aid delivery, such as various programs by the OECD's Development Assistance Committee or the Paris High Level Forum on Aid Harmonization and Alignment. In practice, however, these inefficiencies exist because of very real political or bureaucratic constraints, and progress in reducing them has proven to be slow and uneven. In many ways, these problems seem to be getting worse; for instance, the number of distinct projects funded by donors has nearly tripled since 1995 (Roodman 2006).

Perhaps most worrying, there appear to be few incentives for either donors or recipients to change their practices. As Bräutigam and Knack (2004) argue, "Political elites have little incentive to change a situation in which large amounts of aid provide exceptional resources for patronage and many fringe benefits" (263). Moreover, until very recently, the government's performance did not appear to affect whether it received aid, so there appeared to be little or no cost to misusing aid. Alesina and Weder (2002) find that high levels of corruption within recipient countries were positively correlated with aid flows throughout the 1990s. On the other hand, incentives to improve aid effectiveness appear less important within donor organizations than other concerns, related to bureaucratic incentives within aid agencies, and to the importance of commercial, foreign policy and ideological objectives on the part of donor governments (Easterly 2003).

8.4   The Aid-Revenue Relationship

A third institutional effect of aid posited in the literature concerns its impact on state revenues. This is an important issue since the ability of the state to collect revenues is critically linked to state capacity, while the central role of revenue collection in political development and state building has long been accepted. Schumpeter (1918/1991) was perhaps the first to argue that a country's tax system fundamentally reflects its political institutions. Reliance on citizens for raising public revenues, as opposed to unearned income by offshore extraction or external assistance, is considered an essential ingredient to establishing accountability between the state and society.

The contemporary literature suggests that taxation is a useful indicator of state capacity. Because revenues are necessary to fund the state's activities in a sustainable manner, the size and consistency of government revenues can reveal a lot about the level of capacity that exists within the state apparatus. This has long been argued in the aid literature. According to Kaldor (1963), the key determination of whether a state moves from aid dependency to economic self-sufficiency is the degree to which the state learns how to tax, thereby leading to a lessening of the need for aid. According to Bauer (1976), foreign aid displaces the processes of institutional maturation essential to development, including the capacity of the state to collect revenue. Azam, Devarajan, and O'Connell (1999) arrive at a similar conclusion, claiming that the ability of a state to remove itself from reliance on aid will depend on the degree to which the state engages in learning by doing in the public sector, a process that is greatly affected by the level of aid in relation to overall revenue and the initial institutional conditions.

Early empirical tax effort studies focused on a small set of variables considered the main determinants of tax effort, most commonly measured as tax revenue as a share of GDP (Lotz and Morss 1967; Celliah 1971; Celliah, Baas, and Kelly 1975; Tanzi 1981). The tax effort literature typically considers the level of development and the economic structure as primary determinants of tax shares: GDP per capita, the degree of openness of the economy, the agricultural or industrial share of GDP, and in some cases population growth (Tanzi 1992, Leuthold 1991, Stotsky and WoldeMariam 1997, Ghura 1998).

In the tax effort literature, foreign aid is generally expected to reduce tax shares since aid provides an alternative, nonearned source of revenue for governments in addition to tax revenue (Ghura 1998, Remmer 2004, Bräutigam and Knack 2004). Consequently, a government that receives significant amounts of aid is thought to have less incentive to tax and improve its tax administration. That is, foreign aid may be used as a substitute for domestic revenue mobilization while allowing the same level of expenditure (Heller 1975, Kimbrough 1986). Not only may aid inflows lead to lower tax effort, but they may also slow the development of domestic institutions such as the tax administration in recipient countries (Bräutigam and Knack 2004).

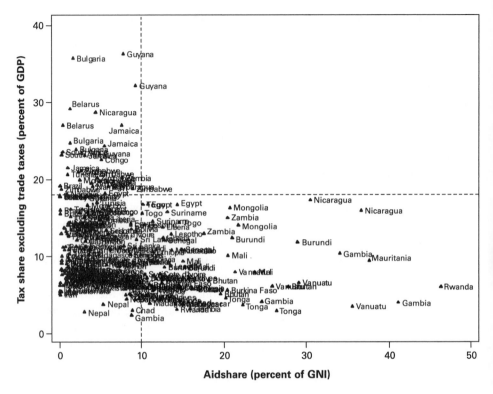

Figure 8.1
Aid and tax shares in low- and lower-middle-income countries, 1972–1999 (four-year averages, percent). *Sources*: IMF Government Finance Statistics, 2004, WDI 2005, and authors' calculations.

A negative relationship between tax revenue and aid is suggested by figure 8.1, which shows the four-year averages of tax revenue (excluding trade taxes) as a share of GDP against the four-year averages of aid as a share of GNI for fifty-five low- and lower-middle-income countries for 1972–1999, using standard International Monetary Fund (IMF) data on tax revenue. The point of this figure is merely to show the simple correlation between tax collection and aid receipts. There are many cases of low aid and low tax (those toward the bottom left). There are also a moderate number of high aid–low tax (bottom right) and low aid–high tax countries (upper left). However, there are no incidences at all of high aid (more than 10 percent of GNI) and high tax (more than 18 percent of GDP). These thresholds are, of course, arbitrary and the figure does not imply any causation, but it does indicate that based on historical experience, high levels of both do not occur at the same time.

What is the econometric evidence on behalf of this relationship? It is actually more ambiguous than one might think. Leuthold (1991) examines the effect of the standard variables, controlling for the economic structure and the level of development, and aid on tax revenue using panel data. All the standard variables are statistically significant and have the anticipated signs, whereas foreign aid has the expected negative sign but is not significant. Using data from Stotsky and WoldeMariam (1997), Bräutigam (2000) found that 71 percent of the African countries with aid/GDP above 10 percent in 1995 had lower-than-expected tax effort. Ghura (1998) examined the determinants of tax revenue for thirty-nine sub-Saharan African countries between 1985 and 1996 and found foreign aid to have a significant, negative impact on tax shares. Teera and Hudson (2004) used data for 116 developed and developing countries for 1975 to 1998, but found aid to be insignificant. A panel study of 120 middle- and low-income countries over the period 1970–1999 by Remmer (2004) finds that aid dependency is associated with lower tax revenue mobilization. The dependent variable is the change in tax revenue as a share of GDP, and the explanatory variables include the standard variables and three different measures of aid dependency (aid/GNI, aid/government expenditures, and aid/imports). All three aid dependency measures are negatively related to tax shares, although only aid as a share of imports is statistically significant. When reducing the sample to the period 1980–1999, both the aid share in imports and the aid share in government expenditures have a significant negative impact on tax effort.

One of the most recent studies focusing on the revenue response to foreign aid inflows separates total net aid into grants and loans to test if the relationship between grants and domestic government revenue is different from that of (concessional) loans (Gupta et al. 2004). This study suggests that some governments may consider grants to be a free substitute for tax revenue. By contrast, loans must be repaid, which provides incentives for governments to at least maintain tax revenues at current levels, if not to increase them (Bräutigam, 2000). Gupta et al. use the standard variables controlling for the economic structure and level of development in a panel of 107 developing countries over the period 1970–2002 and augment the model by adding grants and loans separately and a corruption variable—the International Country Risk Guide (ICRG) corruption index—to test their separate impact on the aid-revenue relationship. In their baseline regression, the overall effect of total aid (grants and loans) on domestic revenue is negative and significant. When total aid is split into grants and loans, grants have a significant, negative effect on revenue, while loans have a significant, positive impact. In their extended model, corruption is found to reduce revenue. To further test the negative effect of corruption on revenues, Gupta et al. rank countries according to their score on the ICRG corruption index and test the impact of grants versus loans on revenues in a sample consisting of the relatively corrupt countries. Their results suggest that countries with weaker institutions are likely to suffer a larger negative impact of grants on revenue than countries with better institutions.

In addition to the cross-sectional time-series studies, there are several country studies; for these, the results are more mixed. A negative relationship between aid and domestic revenue mobilization was found in Pakistan (Franco-Rodriguez, McGillivray, and Morrissey 1998), Zambia (Fagernäs and Roberts 2004a), and Cote d'Ivoire (McGillivray and Outtara 2003). By contrast, a positive relationship between aid and revenue collection was found in Indonesia (Pack and Pack 1990), Ghana (Osei, Morrissey, and Lloyd 2003), and Uganda and Malawi (Fagernäs and Roberts 2004b, 2004c).

Generally, thus, the empirical literature finds a negative relationship between aid and revenue collection, but this is not a conclusive result. For all of the studies, there are considerable concerns about the quality of the data and the sensitivity of the results to specification changes, which make firm conclusions about the aid-revenue relationship difficult. Nevertheless, the typical explanatory channels are the replacement of tax with aid in the short term and the disincentives and moral hazard faced by aid-dependent governments to build tax administration and institutional capacity over the long term.

To test the hypothesis that there is a negative causal relationship between high levels of aid and domestic tax effort, we would need reliable tax revenue data for a broad range of countries over an extended time period. Ideally, we would also have disaggregated revenue data to be able to strip out the possible differential effects of aid on trade taxes versus direct taxation and other forms of revenue. This would allow us to isolate the revenues, which require more state capacity to collect. Unfortunately, much of this information does not exist, especially for the set of countries that have been highly aid dependent (indeed, the lack of data itself suggests capacity gaps). In addition to data shortages, many of the existing fiscal data are of extremely poor quality, particularly among low-income countries. This limits our ability to empirically analyze the hypothesis with any degree of confidence and also raises caution about drawing firm conclusions from any of the data-driven assessments.[2]

To summarize this section, a bivariate relationship appears to exist between high levels of aid and low levels of taxation. Poor data quality do not, however, allow us complete confidence that this relationship is not confounded by other factors that high aid-dependent countries have in common, such as low levels of economic activity and industrialization, that are also associated with poor revenue extraction. In addition, it is very hard to establish the exact nature of the link between state capacity and levels of state revenue. Intuitively, revenue generation is so central to state survival that one would think that states would not voluntarily abstain from collecting revenues it was able to collect. However, it is not completely possible to reject the alternative hypothesis that states choose not to seek revenues they have the capacity to collect because they are able to receive the equivalent revenues from foreign aid. To gain insights into this issue, it is perhaps useful to turn to an older political science literature on state building, which explores the impact of revenue collection on regime type.

8.5 Aid, Accountability, and the Political Regime

A political regime can be defined as the set of institutions that determine the nature of political power and structure the relationship between the government and the citizenry. A third and perhaps most critical set of negative institutional effects of aid can be identified as those that influence the political regime in a way that discourages the establishment of rational developmental states. The hypothesis here is that large, sustained aid flows fundamentally alter the relationship between government elites and local citizens. Any kind of external financial flow changes the incentives faced by recipient government officials and their citizens, regardless of the precise nature of donor practices. That is, aid flows themselves, separate from particular inefficiencies in the aid system, can affect the evolution of state-society relations. If donors are providing the majority of public finance and governments are primarily accountable to those external agencies, then it may simply not be possible to expect a credible social contract to develop between the state and its citizens. Using the current terminology, aid may undercut the very principles the aid industry intends to promote: ownership, accountability, and participation.

Large aid flows can result in a reduction in governmental accountability because governing elites no longer need to ensure the support of their publics and the assent of their legislatures when they do not need to raise revenues from the local economy, as long as they keep the donors happy and willing to provide alternative sources of funding. Although governments typically complain about conditions, it is still easier to manage donor demands than the slow and politically difficult task of building or improving domestic revenue collection. A reliance on aid as a substitute for local resources means the flow of revenues to the state is not affected by government efficiency, so there will be a tendency for governments to underinvest in developmental capacity. This moral hazard effect of aid dependence is borne out empirically, as high aid is associated with decreased quality of governance (e.g., Bräutigam and Knack 2004, Knack 2000). Heller and Gupta (2002) also argue that aid creates moral hazard because it reduces the incentive to adopt good policies and reform inefficient institutions, and thus weakens the government's developmental performance and encourages rent seeking.

The link between the loss of accountability and aid is particularly striking in Africa, since the region combines sharp economic decline with a relatively high level of political stability, at least if the latter is defined as the ability of office-holders to remain in power. Thus, since 1980, the average African leader has remained in power just under twelve years, more than three times longer than democratically elected leaders in the prosperous democracies of the West (van de Walle 2001). The absence of accountability is then not a manner of speech but a practical reality: it is literally true that African governments avoid accountability for their performance.

A long-term decline in governmental accountability also appears to have a direct impact on the degree of democracy prevailing in the system. Qualitatively, Moore (1998) has argued that countries that rely on a greater proportion of "unearned" income will tend to be less democratic and have less effective institutional mechanisms and accountability. Simply put, the actions of such governments typically indicate that they do not have to worry as much about maintaining legitimacy because they do not collect revenues from their own population. Guyer (1992) and others have made exactly such an argument about Nigeria, and more recently, the negative links between aid dependency and low levels of democratic rule have been argued in a number of country case studies (see Hoffman and Gibson 2005 on Tanzania, Hanlon 1991 on Mozambique). In these dynamics, aid can be compared with a natural resource such as oil that provides unearned rents for the government. An earlier literature on rentier states in the Middle East indeed argued that oil resources have allowed governments to resist pressures to democratize (Anderson 1987, Chaudhry 1997).

Of course, it might be argued that aid comes with more strings attached than oil and that donors can affect governmental behavior by setting conditions on their aid. However imperfectly, donors do not condone government corruption, incompetence, or authoritarianism. Though inconsistently, donors have promoted democracy and better governance in Africa, at least since the end of the cold war (van de Walle 2001). Donors have also sought to explicitly promote accountability and participation, using intensified oversight of accounts and conditionality, such as the insistence on a poverty reduction strategy paper (PRSP) process, which subjects the national budget to multiple rounds of consultation with civil society groups. But the PRSPs and conditionality, and other donor processes (even if better enforced), cannot fundamentally replace government accountability toward its citizens in an equally legitimate way, no matter how well intentioned or vigilant the donors.

A large flow of aid over a sustained period also can undermine popular participation. On the one hand, the assent of the population is less important to governments that receive large amounts of external support. They will devote less time and resources to explaining and defending policy decisions to their citizens and will underfund the kinds of public institutions that encourage popular participation. On the other hand, the decline in ownership brought about by the externalization of decision making necessarily results in departicipation. If citizens believe that their leaders respond to pressures from London, Paris, or Washington, they will not devote as much time pressing demands on the local legislature and executive. More to the point, they may view the local legislature as the place to press for favors and patronage rather than for policy outcomes, and this will once again tend to reinforce the patrimonial elements in the local political economy.

The African contemporary record is certainly compatible with such an interpretation. The region is characterized by strong presidential rule, as well as weak and pliant legislatures (van de Walle 2001, Joseph 2003) and frail civil society organizations. The absence of participatory checks on the executive branch of government in the region can tentatively, at least in part, be ascribed to the high volume of aid that governments receive. Indeed, the relationship with the donors may well have served to reinforce tendencies that other structural factors were already creating. Many early observers had noted the low levels of participation in African political systems following independence (Kasfir 1971, Collier 1982), while the tendency of these countries to produce highly presidential political systems, with powerful executives and impotent legislatures, has also long been related in the literature (Schatzberg 2001, Bratton and van de Walle 1997). The weakness of civil society in the region has also been described by numerous observers (Ndegwa 1995; Harbeson, Rothchild, and Chazan 1994).

To be sure, political systems with stronger traditions of both vertical and horizontal domestic accountability might have been affected differently by a large volume of aid. But in Africa's postcolonial regimes, these aid flows inevitably enhanced an evolution already under way. Poorly integrated political communities with substantial ethnic fragmentation and a small (or nonexistent) middle class to buttress democratic rule were more likely to fall prey to authoritarian rulers relying on clientelism to remain in power. A small number of countries, such as Botswana, avoided the worst of these pitfalls (Acemoglu, Johnson, and Robertson 2003; Lewis 1993), in part thanks to unusual leadership. But for most, the postindependence period was characterized by the emergence of regimes that enjoyed little popular legitimacy and needed a combination of systematic clientelism and various repressive political instruments to remain in power. These types of regimes were comforted in these tendencies by steady increases in aid that seemed automatic throughout the 1970s and 1980s. Governments could undertake profoundly antidevelopmental actions and not threaten their relationship with Western donors. Thus, the move to authoritarian and military government in the 1960s did not reduce aid. The replacement of independent civil service commissions and merit-based promotions by politicized presidential control of the civil service was similarly condoned, not least because donors found it convenient to rely on a large number of foreign experts to palliate weaknesses in the civil service (Berg 1993). Disastrous nationalization of private firms owned by foreigners for the benefit of political cronies close to the president in countries as diverse as Nigeria and Zaire did not prevent aid from continuing its upward trajectory (see Rood 1976, Callaghy 1984 on Zaire, Biersteker 1987 on Nigeria).

A comparison with the historical experience in the West is instructive here. Much scholarly work has closely linked democratic development to the evolution of taxation (see Ross 2004 for an excellent overview). Historians of the emergence of strong democratic states in the West emphasize the link between the progressive growth of democratic and accountable government, on the one hand, and the emergence of a state apparatus that had both the capacity and the legitimacy to extract an increasing amount of revenue from society, on the other. In an influential essay, North and Weingast (1989) showed that the emergence of parliamentary sovereignty in Britain with the Glorious Revolution of 1688 dramatically increased the ability of the British government to raise taxes and ensured the country's military and economic success in the eighteenth and nineteenth centuries.

Ardant (1975) showed that the European states that were able to finance and then win wars were the states that were able to build their extractive capacity, but also to gain the assent of their populations, often by extending political rights. In Tilly's (1975) famous aphorism, "War made the state and the state made war," the need to finance wars motivated states to build their extractive capacity but also to maintain their own legitimacy (42; see also Tilly 1985). In short, taxation is important because it is essential to democratic governance, but also because it holds the key to state building and state survival. The comparison with the low-income countries in Africa is instructive, since they did not have to fight international wars to ensure their survival (Herbst 2000, Jackson and Rotberg 1982).

In the twentieth and twenty-first centuries, the basic functions of a developmental low-income state are to raise revenues and make effective expenditures in order to promote development. Successful developing countries—Korea, Taiwan, Botswana—have typically been solidly extractive states, with above-average tax effort ratios. All of these states have enjoyed democratic governance during the early phases of their development, but almost invariably, their governments enjoyed substantial political legitimacy, and none were highly repressive. Of course, most of the low–income states of Africa typically have low tax effort ratios.

In recent years, donors have financed a sharp increase in social services provision in sub-Saharan Africa, notably in health and education. Historically, such increases in provision have been the hallmark of democratic governments, or at least of governments facing substantial participatory pressures. Thus, in the West, the rise of public education coincided in general terms with the introduction of the electoral franchise. Pressures from below encouraged governments that wanted to remain in power to provide more services to its citizens. In most African countries, however, the pressures have been external. In fact, a substantial proportion of the national development effort is not integrated into the national budget and does not concern the government. It is not uncommon for donors to fund over half of the country's public investment budget, while foreign NGOs with their local partners can be providing from a third to half of the social services available to African citizens in some countries (Semboja and Therkildsen 1995). Indeed, somewhat ironically, African governments have found it politically convenient to blame the donors and NGOs for unpopular sectoral policies, poor social services, and negative economic outcomes, as if these were not among their core responsibilities.

There are similar differences in the rise of civil society. In the West, an emerging middle class sought to build a counterweight to the state and its organizations, and the result was a wide variety of membership organizations, unions, and clubs with an independent basis of power that with time were able to increase the accountability of the central state (Hall 1995). In Africa, the absence of economic growth long undermined the development of an indigenous independent civil society. In recent years, there has been a flowering of small nonstate actors, and some of them were instrumental in the emergence of democratic movements that did topple some authoritarian governments in the early 1990s (Bratton and van de Walle 1997; Harbeson, Rothchild, and Chazan 1994). Yet there remain very few membership organizations in the region, and many of the bigger NGOs that have emerged are mostly funded by the donors, typically to help undertake donor initiatives in the social sectors. Because these organizations receive funding from the donors, they are less likely to seek to build up their own memberships or autonomy. Because they help donors implement projects that governments fail to undertake, they actually help governments escape accountability for their developmental failures.

As a result of these different dynamics, governments have escaped accountability and have been allowed to focus their resources on nondevelopmental expenditures that help them remain in office. Van de Walle (2001) shows that there have been substantial increases in the size of defense expenditures in the region, for instance, and the number and size of public offices such as parliamentary bodies, ministerial cabinets, national commissions, and provincial governments have steadily risen through two decades of economic crisis, even as the share of aid in the funding of development has sharply increased. Paradoxically, as a result, in Africa, the extension of social services has often been accompanied by a decline of participation, low governance quality, and an increase in clientelistic behavior. If we agree with Fox (1994) and others that the process of democratic consolidation in low-income states requires a transition from clientelism to citizenship, in which governments engage in participatory contractual exchange relationships with the population, then donors' efforts may have paradoxically negative effects on citizen-government relations in the region.

8.6   Conclusion

Our review of the literature suggests that there are reasons to believe that a large and sustained volume of aid can have negative effects on the development of good public institutions in low-income countries. We have reviewed different bodies of literature that suggest that the current aid system may have undercut incentives for revenue collection and negatively affected public governance in Africa. In addition, we have examined a political science literature that finds both antidevelopment governance patterns across most of sub-Saharan Africa and strong historical evidence that revenue generation is central to the idea of accountability and the establishment of state institutions. Combined, they suggest that aid may undermine the development of effective state structures.

There are many gaps in the data needed to prove these tentative claims. Also, state revenues are an imperfect indicator for state capacity, since states are able to get revenues in many different ways, only some of which involve much extractive capacity. Nonetheless, the analysis does suggest that an aid-institutions paradox, whereby high levels of aid can have a negative effect on local institutions, is a potentially serious concern. Given the possibility for substantially more aid flowing to Africa in the near future, scope for such a harmful dynamic is likely to be exacerbated.

A quarter of a century ago, the World Bank issued its so-called Berg Report (World Bank 1981), which called for a doubling of aid to address developing countries' many economic and social problems. It must be particularly distressing to the development community how many of those problems persist, despite the fact that increases in aid were considerably higher than those hoped for. This fact alone should encourage skepticism about the current proposals that a sharp increase in aid volume will have the intended effects in the region. It is not at all clear that the current aid practices, with the negative effects on institutions described here, will or can be reformed. But as we have argued, there are good reasons to believe that high levels of aid over a prolonged period are likely to have negative institutional effects, at the very least, if the current aid delivery modalities are not substantially reformed.

How much is too much aid? We have studiously avoided this difficult question until the end of the chapter. Berg (1997, 2000) suggested that aid starts to have negative effects on local institutions when aid flows reach 5 percent of GDP, which would mean that the overwhelming majority of states in the region are negatively affected. A more recent and thorough review of aid absorption (Clemens and Radelet 2003) find the "saturation point" (where additional aid would produce zero economic impact) highly dependent on local conditions, but ranging from 15 to 45 percent of GDP. Surely the incentive dynamics raised by this chapter come into play well before such an extreme level is reached.

Our analysis is in no way meant to disparage the desirability of general increases in aid flows, however, or suggest that additional aid could not necessarily be spent without producing the negative institutional effects. Our findings do not cover a range of activities that might be donor financed and could have positive institutional effects, such as debt relief, peacekeeping, and regional security arrangements. Similarly, we join other analysts who have advocated substantial increases in funding for regional and global public goods, such as agricultural research or antimalaria research. All the available evidence on the likely impact of the eradication of endemic diseases in the region suggests that current funding levels are inadequate (Ferroni and Mody 2002), and a substantially larger flow of resources would be unlikely to have the kinds of negative institutional effects described here.

In sum, it seems likely that the extra public dollars now being proposed for traditional development assistance might well be better spent for other types of assistance that in the long run would have a greater impact on the development of the region. However, a historical view of the complex evolution of state institutions suggests that not only are they critical to producing developmental outcomes, but that donors should be unambiguously aware that their assistance can have perverse effects on some of the very outcomes they hope to encourage.

Acknowledgments

We thank Michael Clemens for his invaluable insights on data analysis, Scott Standley for research assistance, and John Hicklin, Stephen Nelson, Erwin Tiongson, and Adrian Wood for comments on an earlier draft. All opinions and errors are those of the authors alone.

Notes

1. Including South Africa and Nigeria, two large economies that receive very little aid, brings this proportion down to 5.7 percent of GNI (World Bank 2005).

2. Including the data used in figure 8.1.

References

Acemoglu, Daron, Simon Johnson, and James Robinson. 2003. "African Success Story: Botswana." In Dani Rodrik, ed., *Search of Prosperity: Analytical Narratives on Economic Growth.* Princeton, N.J.: Princeton University Press.

Acemoglu, Daron, Simon Johnson, and James Robinson. 2004. "Institutions as the Fundamental Cause of Long-Run Growth." NBER Working Paper 10481. Cambridge, Mass.: National Bureau of Economic Research.

Adam, Christopher S., and David L. Bevan. 2003. "Aid, Public Expenditure and Dutch Disease." CSAE Working Paper 2003–02. Oxford: Center for the Study of African Economies.

Alesina, Alberto, and Beatrice Weder. 2002. "Do Corrupt Governments Receive Less Foreign Aid?" *American Economic Review* 92(4):1126–1137.

Anderson, Lisa. 1987. "The State in the Middle East and North Africa." *Comparative Politics* 20(1):1–18.

Ardant, Gabriel. 1975. "Financial Policy and Economic Infrastructure of Modern States and Nations." In Charles Tilly, ed., *The Formation of National States in Western Europe.* Princeton, N.J.: Princeton University Press.

Atingi-Ego, Michael. 2005. "Budget Support, Aid Dependency, and Dutch Disease: The Case of Uganda." Paper presented at Practitioners' Forum on Budget Support, Cape Town, South Africa, May 5–6.

Azam, Jean-Paul, Shantayanan Devarajan, and Stephen A. O'Connell. 1999. "Aid Dependence Reconsidered." World Bank Policy Research Working Paper 2144. Washington, D.C.: World Bank.

Bauer P. T. 1976. *Dissent on Development: Studies and Debates in Development Economics.* Cambridge, Mass.: Harvard University Press.

Berg, Elliott. 1993. *Rethinking Technical Co-operation.* New York: United Nations Development Program.

Berg Elliott. 1997. "Dilemmas in Donor Aid Strategies." In Catherine Gwin and Joan M. Nelson, eds., *Perspectives on Aid and Development*. Washington, D.C.: Overseas Development Council.

Berg, Elliot. 2000. "Aid and Failed Reform: The Case of Public Sector Management." In Finn Tarp, ed., *Foreign Aid and Development: Lessons Learnt and Directions for the Future*. London: Routledge.

Biersteker, Thomas. 1987. *Multinationals, the State and Control of the Nigerian Economy*. Princeton, N.J.: Princeton University Press.

Birdsall, Nancy. 2004. "Seven Deadly Sins: Reflections on Donor Failings." CGD Working Paper 50. Washington, D.C.: Center for Global Development.

Birdsall, Nancy, and Arvind Subramanian. 2004. "Saving Iraq from Its Oil." *Foreign Affairs*, July–August.

Bratton, Michael, and Nicolas van de Walle. 1997. *Democratic Experiments in Africa: Regime Transitions in Comparative Perspective*. Cambridge: Cambridge University Press.

Bräutigam, Deborah. 2000. *Aid Dependence and Governance*. Stockholm, Sweden: Almqvist & Wiksell.

Bräutigam, Deborah, and Stephen Knack. 2004. "Foreign Aid, Institutions, and Governance in Sub-Saharan Africa." *Economic Development and Cultural Change* 52(2):255–285.

Bulir, Ales, and Timothy Lane. 2002. "Aid and Fiscal Management." In Sanjeev Gupta, Benedict Clements, and Gabriela Inchauste, eds., *Helping Countries Develop: The Role of Fiscal Policy*. Washington, D.C.: International Monetary Fund.

Burnside, Craig, and David Dollar. 2000. "Aid, Policies and Growth." *American Economic Review* 90(4):847–868.

Callaghy, Thomas M. 1984. *The State Society Struggle: Zaire in Comparative Perspective*. New York: Columbia University Press.

Callaghy, Thomas M. 1988. "The State and the Development of Capitalism in Africa: Theoretical, Historical and Comparative Reflections." In Donald Rothchild and Naomi Chazan, eds., *The Precarious Balance: State and Society in Africa*. Boulder, Colo.: Westview Press.

Celliah, Raja J. 1971. "Trends in Taxation in Developing Countries." IMF Staff Papers 18(2). Washington, D.C.: International Monetary Fund.

Celliah, Raja J., H. J. Baas, and Margaret R. Kelly. 1975. "Tax Ratios and Tax Effort in Developing Countries, 1969–1971." IMF Staff Papers 22(1). Washington, D.C.: International Monetary Fund.

Chabal, Patrick, and Jean Pierre Daloz. 1999. *Africa Works*. London: James Currey.

Chaudhry, Kiren Aziz. 1997. *The Price of Wealth: Economics and Institutions in the Middle East*. Ithaca, N.Y.: Cornell University Press.

Clemens, Michael, and Steven Radelet. 2003. "Absorptive Capacity: How Much Is Too Much?" In Steven Radelet, ed., *Challenging Foreign Aid: A Policymaker's Guide to the Millennium Challenge Account*. Washington, D.C.: Center for Global Development.

Cohen, John. 1992. "Foreign Advisors and Capacity Building: The Case of Kenya." *Public Administration and Development* 12(5):493–510.

Collier, Ruth Berins. 1982. *Regimes in Tropical Africa: Changing Forms of Supremacy, 1945–1975*. Berkeley: University of California Press.

Commission for Africa. 2005. *Our Common Interest: Report of the Commission for Africa*. Available at http://www.commissionforafrica.org/english/report/thereport/english/11-03-05_cr_report.pdf.

De Long, J. Bradford, and Barry Eichengreen. 1991. "The Marshall Plan: History's Most Successful Structural Adjustment Program." NBER Working Paper 3899. Cambridge, Mass.: National Bureau of Economic Research.

Devarajan, Shantayanan, Margaret J. Miller, and Eric V. Swanson. 2002. "Goals for Development: History, Prospects and Costs." World Bank Policy Research Working Paper 2819. Washington, D.C.: World Bank.

Easterly, William. 2003. "The Cartel of Good Intentions: The Problem of Bureaucracy in Foreign Aid." *Journal of Policy Reform* 5(4):1–28.

Easterly, William. 2005. "Reliving the '50s: The Big Push, Poverty Traps, and Takeoffs in Economic Development." CGD Working Paper 65. Washington, D.C.: Center for Global Development.

Eifert, Benn, and Alan Gelb. 2005. "Improving the Dynamics of Aid: Towards More Predictable Budget Support." Paper presented at Practitioners' Forum on Budget Support, Cape Town, South Africa, May 5–6.

Englebert, Pierre. 2000. *State Legitimacy and Development in Africa*. Boulder, Colo.: Lynne Rienner Publishers.

Evans, Peter. 1995. *Embedded Autonomy: States and Industrial Transformation*. Princeton, N.J.: Princeton University Press.

Fagernäs, Sonja, and John Roberts. 2004a. "The Fiscal Effects of Aid in Zambia." ESAU Working Paper 10. London: Economics and Statistics Analysis Unit, Overseas Development Institute.

Fagernäs, Sonja, and John Roberts. 2004b. "The Fiscal Effects of Aid in Malawi." ESAU Working Paper 7. London: Economics and Statistics Analysis Unit, Overseas Development Institute.

Fagernäs, Sonja, and John Roberts. 2004c. "The Fiscal Effects of Aid in Uganda." ESAU Working Paper 9. London: Economics and Statistics Analysis Unit, Overseas Development Institute.

Ferroni, Marco, and Ashoka Mody, eds. 2002. *International Public Goods: Incentives, Measurement and Financing*. Norwell, Mass.: Kluwer.

Fox, Jonathan. 1994. "The Difficult Transition from Clientelism to Citizenship." *World Politics* 46(2):151–184.

Franco-Rodriguez, Susana. 2000. "Recent Advances in Fiscal Response Models with an Application to Costa Rica." *Journal of International Development* 12(3):429–442.

Franco-Rodriguez, Susana, Mark McGillivray, and Oliver Morrissey. 1998. "Aid and the Public Sector in Pakistan: Evidence with Endogenous Aid." *World Development* 26(7):1241–1250.

Ghura, Dhaneshwar. 1998. "Tax Revenue in Sub-Saharan Africa: Effects of Economic Policies and Corruption." IMF Working Paper 98/135. Washington, D.C.: International Monetary Fund.

Gupta, Sanjeev, Benedict Clements, Alexander Pivovarsky, and Erwin Tiongson. 2004. "Foreign Aid and Revenue Response: Does the Composition of Foreign Aid Matter?" In Sanjeev Gupta, Benedict Clements, and Gabriela Inchauste, eds., *Helping Countries Develop: The Role of Fiscal Policy*. Washington, D.C.: International Monetary Fund.

Guyer, Jane. 1992. "Representation without Taxation: An Essay on Democracy in Rural Nigeria, 1952–1990." *African Studies Review* 35(1):41–79.

Haggard, Stephan. 1990. *Pathways from the Periphery*. Ithaca, N.Y.: Cornell University Press.

Hall, John, A., ed. 1995. *Civil Society: Theory, History and Comparison*. Cambridge: Polity Press.

Hanlon, Joseph. 1991. *Mozambique: Who Calls the Shots?* Bloomington: Indiana University Press.

Harbeson, John W., Donald Rothchild, and Naomi Chazan, eds. 1994. *Civil Society and the State in Africa*. Boulder, Colo.: Lynne Rienner Press.

Heller, Peter S. 1975. "A Model of Public Fiscal Behaviour in Developing Countries: Aid, Investment, and Taxation." *American Economic Review* 65(3):429–445.

Heller, Peter, S. 2005. " 'Pity the Finance Minister': Issues in Managing a Substantial Scaling Up of Aid Flows." IMF Working Paper 05/180. Washington, D.C.: International Monetary Fund.

Heller, Peter S., and Sanjeev Gupta. 2002. "Challenges in Expanding Development Assistance." IMF Policy Discussion Paper 02/5. Washington, D.C.: International Monetary Fund.

Herbst, Jeffrey. 1990. "The Structural Adjustment of Politics in Africa." *World Development* 18(7):949–958.

Herbst, Jeffrey. 2000. *States and Power in Africa: Comparative Lessons in Authority and Control*. Princeton, N.J.: Princeton University Press.

Hoffman, Barak, D., and Clark C. Gibson. 2005. "Fiscal Governance and Public Services: Evidence from Tanzania and Zambia." Available at http://www.polisci.ucla.edu/wgape/papers/ 9_GibsonHoffman.pdf.

Jackson, Robert H., and Carl G. Rotberg. 1982. "Why Africa's Weak States Persist: The Empirical and the Juridical in Statehood." *World Politics* 35(1):1–24.

Joseph, Richard A. 2003. "Africa: States in Crisis." *Journal of Democracy* 14(3):159–170.

Kaldor, Nicholas. 1963. "Will Underdeveloped Countries Learn to Tax?" *Foreign Affairs*, January:410–419.

Karl, Terry Lynn. 1997. *The Paradox of Plenty: Oil Booms and Petro States.* Berkeley: University of California Press.

Kasfir, Nelson. 1971. *The Shrinking Political Arena: Participation and Ethnicity in Africa Politics.* Berkeley: University of California Press.

Khan, Haider, Ali, and Eiichi Hoshino. 1992. "Impact of Foreign Aid on the Fiscal Behavior of LDC Governments." *World Development* 20(10):1481–1488.

Killick, Tony. 2004. "What Drives Change in Ghana? A Political-Economy View of Economic Prospects." Mimeo.

Kimbrough, Kent P. 1986. "Foreign Aid and Optimal Fiscal Policy." *Canadian Journal of Economics* 19(1):35–61.

Knack, Stephen. 2000. "Aid Dependence and the Quality of Governance: A Cross-Country Empirical Analysis." World Bank Policy Research Working Paper 2396. Washington, D.C.: World Bank.

Knack, Stephen, and Aminur Rahman. 2004. "Donor Fragmentation and Bureaucratic Quality in Aid Recipients." World Bank Policy Research Working 3186. Washington, D.C.: World Bank.

Leuthold, Jane H. 1991. "Tax Shares in Developing Countries: A Panel Study." *Journal of Development Economics* 35(1):173–185.

Levine, Ruth and the What Works Working Group with Molly Kinder. 2004. *Millions Saved: Proven Successes in Global Health.* Washington, D.C.: Center for Global Development.

Levy, Brian, and Sahr Kpundeh, eds. 2005. *State Capacity in Africa: New Approaches, Emerging Lessons.* Washington, D.C.: World Bank Institute.

Lewis, Stephen. 1993. "Policy Making and Economic Performance: Botswana in Comparative Perspective." In Stephen John Stedman, ed., *Botswana: The Political Economy of Democratic Development.* Boulder, Colo.: Lynne Rienner Publishers.

Lotz, Jorgen R., and Elliott R. Morss. 1967. "Measuring 'Tax Effort' in Developing Countries." IMF Staff Papers 14(3). Washington, D.C.: International Monetary Fund.

McGillivray, Mark, and Oliver Morrissey. 2000a. "A Review of Evidence on the Fiscal Effects of Aid." CREDIT Research Paper No. 01/13. Nottingham, U.K.: Centre for Research in Economic Development and International Trade, University of Nottingham.

McGillivray, Mark, and Oliver Morrissey. 2000b. "Aid Illusion and Public Sector Fiscal Behaviour." CREDIT Research Paper No. 00/9. Nottingham, U.K.: Centre for Research in Economic Development and International Trade, University of Nottingham.

McGillivray, Mark, and Bazoumana Outtara. 2003. "Aid, Debt Burden and Government Fiscal Behaviour in Cote d'Ivoire." CREDIT Research Paper 03/05. Nottingham, U.K.: Centre for Research in Economic Development and International Trade, University of Nottingham.

Moore, Mick. 1998. "Death without Taxes: Democracy, State Capacity, and Aid Dependence in the Fourth World." In Gordon White and Mark Robinson, eds., *Towards a Democratic Developmental State.* New York: Oxford University Press.

Moss, Todd, and Arvind Subramanian. 2005. "After the Big Push? Fiscal and Institutional Implications of Large Aid Increases." CGD Working Paper 71. Washington, D.C.: Center for Global Development.

Ndegwa, Stephen. 1995. *The Two Faces of Civil Society: NGOs and Politics in Africa.* West Hartford, Conn.: Kumarian Press.

Ndulu, Benno J., and Stephen A. O'Connell. 1999 "Governance and Growth in Sub-Saharan Africa." *Journal of Economic Perspectives* 13(3):41–66.

Nkusu, Mwanza. 2004. "Financing Uganda's Poverty Reduction Strategy: Is Aid Causing More Pain Than Gain?" IMF Working Paper 04/170. Washington, D.C.: International Monetary Fund.

North, Douglass, and Barry Weingast. 1989. "Constitutions and Commitment: The Evolution of Institutions Governing Public Choice in Seventeenth-Century England." *Journal of Economic History* 49(4):803–832.

O'Connell, Stephen A., and Charles C. Soludo. 2001. "Aid Intensity in Africa." *World Development* 29(9):1527–1552.

OECD-DAC database. 2005. Available at http://www.oecd.org/dataoecd/50/17/5037721.htm.

OED. 2005. *Capacity Building in Africa: An OED Evaluation of Bank Support.* Washington, D.C.: World Bank.

Osei, Robert, Oliver Morrissey, and Tim Lloyd. 2003. "Modelling the Fiscal Effects of Aid: An Impulse Response Analysis for Ghana." CREDIT Research Paper 03/10. Nottingham, U.K.: Centre for Research in Economic Development and International Trade, University of Nottingham.

Pack, Howard, and Janet Pack. 1990. "Is Foreign Aid Fungible? The Case of Indonesia." *Economic Journal* 100(399):188–194.

Pradhan, Sanjay. 1996. "Evaluating Public Spending: A Framework for Public Expenditure Reviews." World Bank Discussion Paper 323. Washington, D.C.: World Bank.

Radelet, Steven. 2003. *Challenging Foreign Aid: A Policymaker's Guide to the Millennium Challenge Account.* Washington, D.C.: Center for Global Development.

Rajan, Raghuram G., and Arvind Subramanian. 2005. "What Undermines Aid's Impact on Growth?" IMF Working Paper 05/126. Washington, D.C.: International Monetary Fund.

Remmer, Karen. 2004. "Does Foreign Aid Promote the Expansion of Government?" *American Journal of Political Science* 48(1):77–92.

Reno, William. 1998. *Warlord Politics and African States.* Boulder, Colo.: Lynne Rienner Publishers.

Rodrik, Dani (ed.). 2003. *In Search of Prosperity: Analytical Narratives on Economic Growth.* Princeton, N.J.: Princeton University Press.

Rood, Leslie L. 1976. "Nationalization and Indigenization in Africa." *Journal of Modern African Studies* 14:427–447.

Roodman, David. 2006. "Aid Project Proliferation and Absorptive Capacity." CGD Working Paper 75. Washington, D.C.: Center for Global Development.

Ross, Michael. 1999. "The Political Economy of the Resource Curse." *World Politics* 51(2):297–322.

Ross, Michael. 2004. "Does Taxation Lead to Representation?" *British Journal of Political Science* 34:229–249.

Sachs, Jeffrey. 2005. *The End of Poverty: Economic Possibilities for Our Time.* New York: Penguin Press.

Sandbrook, Richard. 1992. *The Politics of Africa's Economic Recovery.* Cambridge: Cambridge University Press.

Schatzberg, Michael. 2001. *Political Legitimacy in Middle Africa: Father, Family, Food.* Bloomington: Indiana University Press.

Schumpeter, Joseph A. 1918/1991. "The Crisis of the Tax State." In Richard A. Swedberg, ed., *Joseph A. Schumpeter: The Economics and Sociology of Capitalism.* Princeton, N.J.: Princeton University Press.

Semboja, Joseph, and Ole Therkildsen, eds. 1995. *Service Provision under Stress in East Africa.* London: James Currey.

Stotsky, Janet G., and Asegedech WoldeMariam. 1997. "Tax Effort in Sub-Saharan Africa." IMF Working Paper 97/107. Washington, D.C.: International Monetary Fund.

Tanzi, Vito. 1981. "A Statistical Evaluation of Taxation in Sub-Saharan Africa." IMF Occasional Paper 8. Washington, D.C.: International Monetary Fund.

Tanzi, Vito. 1992. "Structural Factors and Tax Revenue in Developing Countries: A Decade of Evidence." In Ian Goldin and Alan L. Winters, eds., *Open Economies: Structural Adjustment and Agriculture.* Cambridge: Cambridge University Press.

Teera, Joweria M., and John Hudson. 2004. "Tax Performance: A Comparative Study." *Journal of International Development* 16(6):785–802.

Tilly, Charles. 1975. *The Formation of National States in Western Europe.* Princeton, N.J.: Princeton University Press.

Tilly, Charles. 1985. "War Making and State-Making as Organized Crime." In Peter Evans, Dietrich Rueschemeyer, and Theda Skocpol, eds., *Bringing the State Back In.* Cambridge: Cambridge University Press.

van de Walle, Nicolas. 2001. *African Economies and the Politics of Permanent Crisis, 1979–1999.* Cambridge: Cambridge University Press.

van de Walle, Nicolas. 2005. *Overcoming Stagnation in Aid-Dependent Countries.* Washington, D.C.: Center for Global Development.

White, Howard. 1998. *Aid and Macro-Economic Performance.* Basingstoke: Macmillan.

World Bank. 1981. *Accelerated Development in Sub-Saharan Africa.* Washington, D.C.: World Bank

World Bank. 1998. *Assessing Aid—What Work, What Doesn't, and Why.* Washington, D.C.: World Bank.

World Bank. 2005. *World Development Indicators.* CD-ROM Washington, D.C.: World Bank.

Younger, Steven. 1992. "Aid and the Dutch Disease: Macroeconomic Management When Everybody Loves You." *World Development* 20(11):1587–1597.

Zedillo Panel. 2001. *Report of the High-Level Panel on Financing for Development.* New York: United Nations.

III DYSFUNCTIONAL DONORS AND HOW TO REFORM THEM

9 Why Do Aid Agencies Exist?

Bertin Martens

In his famous article, "The Nature of the Firm," Ronald Coase (1937) sought to answer the question why firms exist, why there are many firms and not just one, and why people work in firms rather than as individuals. He suggested that transaction costs could explain the boundaries of the firm, and this suggestion later gave rise to an abundant literature on vertical integration. Turning from commercial firms to aid organizations, we could ask similar questions: Why do aid agencies exist? Why are there many aid organizations and not just one? Why are there different types of aid organizations (nongovernmental organizations, bilateral and multilateral grant agencies, development banks)? Alternatively, why is foreign aid not transferred directly from a single donor to a single beneficiary rather than going through the hands of multiple persons and organizations? In other words, how can we explain the organizational setup of foreign aid delivery?

To answer these questions, we first need to determine what aid agencies actually do. At the most general level, foreign aid agencies can be defined in contrast to domestic income redistribution agencies, such as government agencies dealing with medical and unemployment benefits. While domestic aid agencies redistribute income between donors and recipients living in the same political constituency, foreign aid agencies target recipients living outside the donor's constituency, usually in developing countries. Split constituencies have major implications for the decision-making process. In domestic aid, both donors and recipients have voting rights and can influence the political decision-making process. In contrast, in foreign aid, the feedback loop between recipients and decision makers is broken; only donors have political leverage over the decision-making process. This broken feedback loop explains the origins of the ownership problem that is so frequently mentioned in connection with foreign aid, but rarely, if ever, in connection with domestic income redistribution. Ownership problems occur when donors can impose decisions on recipients, without the latter having a voice in the process.

At a more functional level, the role of aid agencies can be described in terms of the contents of their activities. One possible perception is that aid agencies deliver goods and services to developing countries, such as food, education, health services, infrastructure, and knowledge. The weakness of this point of view resides in the fact that these goods and services can be bought by developing countries on world markets; there is no specific need for aid agencies to deliver them. One could, of course, point out that developing countries are poor and cannot afford to buy these goods and services in the market. This would imply that the main function of aid agencies is to organize financial transfers. But why would that require such complicated procurement procedures, the elaboration of development strategies, and the active aid agency involvement in the minute details of the design and implementation of projects? Surely the beneficiary of the transfer could take care of all that. Sending a check from the treasury of the donor country to that of the recipient country would be sufficient in that case. Obviously foreign aid agencies are more than just a financial transfer mechanism. They are actively involved in spending decisions on both the donor and the recipient sides.

This chapter argues that the main role of aid agencies is to solve the ownership problem caused by the broken feedback loop in foreign aid. They do this through mediation between donors' and recipients' interests, or preferences. Though donors remain the main decision makers in foreign aid, mediation is necessary because virtually all aid programs require some agreement from the recipients as well, if only to authorize that the program be implemented on their sovereign territory. There is no need for mediation when donor and recipient interests are fully convergent or, in economic terminology, when their preferences are aligned. In that case, they both fully agree on how to spend the financial transfer, and there is no need to negotiate a contract; there is full joint ownership. Mediation implies that there is no full ownership by either the donor or the recipient. In most cases, ownership will be partial and shared in accordance with an agreed contract: both donor and recipient obtain a partial fulfillment of their preferences. Like every contract, aid contracts are necessarily incomplete, and some of the activities and results will be costly to verify. As a result, moral hazard and adverse selection are inherent in aid delivery. Donors will search for appropriate delivery instruments that minimize these risks, for a given cost. This chapter aims to explain the role that different types of aid agencies and aid instruments play in mediation between donors and recipients and in the management of the resulting contractual costs and risks.

A voluminous literature has emerged focusing on justifications for the existence of multilateral aid organizations, especially the Bretton Woods pair, the International Monetary Fund (IMF) and the World Bank (Gilbert and Powell 1999, Milner 2002, Hawkins et al. 2003). In general, however, research that investigates the role, incentives, and biases of donor agencies is quite scarce (Quarles, Kruyt, and Downing 1988; Carr, Eilish, and MacLachlan 1998; Ostrom et al. 2001; Martens et al. 2002). This stands in stark contrast to the growing volume of research on the (in)effectiveness of aid (e.g., Burnside and Dollar 1996, 2000; Tsikata 1998; Hansen and Tarp 2000) Why do all these aid organizations continue to exist and even flourish if they are not effective in relieving the developing world from the plight of poverty? Clearly their continued existence indicates that they are useful, though not necessarily for the reduction of poverty in the beneficiary countries. Their usefulness may well reside in the production of mediation services for which there is a demand and for which their clients (donors, recipients) are willing to pay. This would imply that an aid agency's performance should not be assessed in terms of improving welfare in beneficiary countries but rather in terms of the efficiency and effectiveness of its mediation.

One drawback of the existing literature is that there are no attempts at cross-institutional perspectives to explain the relative advantages and disadvantages of each type of agency within a single explanatory model. The role of a generic aid organization is often approached within a model of economic growth and development: how loans or grants can contribute to economic growth. That does not explain how a particular type of aid agency or aid instrument affects aid performance. This chapter aims to explain the range of diversity of aid organizations within a single approach.

The chapter starts from a simple model of direct redistribution between a donor and a beneficiary, with zero transaction costs and full alignment of preferences, and thus no moral hazard or adverse selection. It demonstrates that there is no need for an aid agency in this case. The model is then expanded to take account of positive transaction costs, nonaligned preferences, and asymmetric information. This induces the risks of moral hazard by the agent and adverse selection by the principal and the principal's need to incur transaction costs to improve information and reduce uncertainty regarding the outcome of the transaction. This is where aid agencies come into play. Various institutional arrangements (types of agencies and types of instruments) differ in their ability to reduce these risks in particular circumstances, and they affect the level of transaction costs and the benefits that donors and recipients derive from the transaction.

9.1 Private Voluntary Aid and Preference Alignment

Aid—income redistribution between humans—is a phenomenon deeply embedded in human behavior. Indeed, we could not survive without it. For instance, sharing food and other basic resources in families and kin groups is essential for the survival of human beings—as essential as it is for most other animals. What distinguishes humans from other animals, however, is our ability to redistribute and share resources within a much wider social setting, outside immediate family and kin groups, even with persons we have never met or never will meet. This chapter focuses on foreign aid—worldwide redistribution to far-away places and people.

What motivates people to redistribute part of their income voluntarily to others? Carr, Eilish, and MacLachlan (1998) explain redistribution as a cognitive process in the human mind. When a potential donor encounters individuals deprived of essential resources that the donor possesses, it may generate empathy and cognitive dissonance in his mind: the observed situation of the deprived does not correspond to his own perception of how the world should be. This may trigger a response that seeks to modify the situation in such as way as to alleviate this dissonance, in this case in an attempt to redress the relative imbalance in resource allocation. Redistribution can thus be considered as a transaction: the donor transfers resources to the recipient in return for a reduction in dissonance in the donor's mind. Dissonance reduction is a form of "consumer satisfaction." It is achieved only if the transfer does indeed change the recipient's situation in line with the donor's expectations. If the donor had incorrect expectations about the recipient's response to the gift and observes a different behavioral response, donor dissonance will not be reduced and may actually increase. An important conclusion is that donors and recipients should have identical—or at least closely aligned—preferences concerning the use of the transfer, in order to achieve a successful transfer in which both donor and recipient utility is increased.

I came across an example of this pure form of aid when, walking around on a warm evening in Key West, Florida, my wife and I encountered a person sitting on the sidewalk, holding up a begging bowl with a written statement, "Why lie? I need a beer." My wife immediately reached into her purse and contributed to the beneficiary's beer consumption. Initially I was surprised by the frankness of both the donor and the beneficiary. Thinking it over, however, I could see that this was a case of identical preferences: my wife was feeling thirsty and longing for a cold beer and fully shared the beggar's preference to allocate every penny to that purpose. Sharing her money with him reduced her cognitive dissonance about his situation. There was no need for an aid organization as an intermediary: donor and recipient met face-to-face, and the momentary exchange of information (the beggar's written statement) was sufficient to transmit a credible message to the donor about the recipient's preferences and the use he was going to make of any additional revenue that evening—and this preference turned out to be perfectly aligned with her own. There was no need for conditionality. Money was transferred in return for a reduction in the donor's cognitive dissonance and an increase in the recipient's beer consumption; it was a welfare-increasing transaction for both.

Carr, Eilish, and MacLachlan (1998) distinguish between distributional and situational responses to perceived deprivation, depending on whether the potential donor perceives the deprivation as being due to environmental factors outside the control of the deprived. Situational interpretations may cause nonalignment of preferences despite direct face-to-face meetings and exchange of (often tacit) information. If poverty is perceived as the result of the deprived's own choices, it indicates that his behavioral preferences are out of line with those of the potential donor: he could have done otherwise and avoided ending up in this situation. Consequently an income transfer to the deprived is likely to result in more wrong choices and thus be meaningless, at least from the donor's point of view. The donor may still be induced to transfer resources if he has leverage over the use of the transfer, to direct its use in line with his own preferences. Preference misalignment between donor and recipient can be corrected through tied or conditional aid—aid that puts restrictive conditions on the recipient's use of the resources and thereby reduces the discretion or ownership rights of the recipient, leaving at least some discretion to the donor. Conditionality is the price the recipient pays in order to get access to transfers in case of nonaligned preferences.

Most foreign aid is conditional. Two major types of conditionality can be distinguished. The first type, input conditionality, restricts the recipient's discretion in the spending of the resources and ties it to procurement conditions—geographical (procurement of goods and services in the donor country) or procedural (specific procurement and spending procedures agreed with the donor). The most typical form of input conditionality is traditional project aid. Projects tie income transfers to a wide range of procedures that increase donor leverage over project inputs and activities: the donor "owns" a large stake in the management of the project. Commercially tied aid is another form of input conditionality. The Organization for Economic Cooperation and Development/Development Assistance Committee (OECD/DAC) (2005, table 23) statistics show that the extent of commercially tied aid varies widely among donors, from 0.1 percent of all Norwegian aid to 48 percent of Canadian aid.

The second type of conditional aid, output conditionality, ties aid to changes in the recipient's behavior and institutions (specific policy decisions or institutional reforms, for example). However, the recipient retains most of the responsibility for management in this case. Burnside and Dollar (2000) demonstrate how aid has no noticeable impact on economic growth in the recipient country unless it is instrumental in triggering policy reforms that the country would not undertake otherwise—in other words, unless it is conditional on a change in the recipient's behavior. The Burnside and Dollar article has triggered a vast debate in the aid literature on the link between aid and growth. Since the 1980s there has been a shift away from input conditionality toward output- or result-based conditionality, mostly in the form of budget support and structural adjustment programs but also in more traditional project aid. Recently donor policy seems to be moving even further away from conditionality and toward so-called partnership and (co)ownership programs (see, e.g., Paris Declaration on Aid Effectiveness (2005)). As already noted, full ownership by both donor and recipient is possible only when their preferences are fully aligned—which is rarely the case. As such, the shift in aid semantics toward softer and less conditionality based terminology does not change the fundamental issue. Clearly, differences in preferences between donors and recipients, and the search for more efficient solutions to manage these differences in a less costly way, play an increasingly important role in aid flows. We should therefore move beyond the simple approach and allow for nonaligned preferences and nonzero transaction costs.

9.2   Ex Ante and Ex Post Transaction Costs in Aid Transfers

All transactions, including income transfers between donors and recipients, entail transaction costs (Coase 1937, North 1990, Williamson 1985). There is no single and generally accepted definition of transaction costs in the new institutional economics literature (Furubotn and Richter 1998, Masten and Williamson 1999). Two main lines of thought can be identified. North (1990) and Coase (1937) define them as the effectively realized opportunity costs of organizing a transaction: the costs of searching for a trading partner, finding the right information, measuring quantities and qualities of the traded goods and services, and negotiating a contract, plus monitoring and enforcement of that contract. Williamson (1985) starts from the assumptions of imperfect and asymmetrical information between transaction partners and opportunism, or "self-interest seeking with guile." In his view, these are the root causes of a key attribute of transactions: uncertainty. Uncertainty can be overcome through contractual arrangements or governance structures that include commitment devices to contract execution, which are costly to negotiate ex ante and to enforce ex post of contract signature. Uncertainty is thus considered to be the reason that parties in an exchange invest in finding suitable partners and products, spend time on measuring qualities and quantities, negotiate a contract, and invest in enforcement devices. In sum, this is the reason for incurring

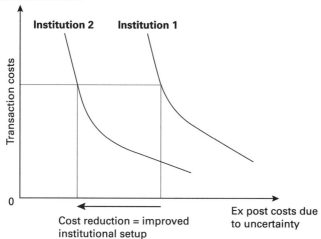

Figure 9.1
The trade-off between transaction costs and uncertainty

realized transaction costs so as to avoid potentially larger but, one hopes, un-realized transaction costs during or after contract execution. Williamson then shows how various organizational or governance arrangements entail various degrees of efficiency in the underlying commitment devices for the execution of agreements, and thereby different levels of efficiency of production. Different governance arrangements result in different cost structures with respect to ex ante (search and negotiation) and ex post (enforcement) transaction costs.

The Coase-North and Williamson definition of transaction costs can be inte-grated in a single framework. For a given institutional setting, there is a trade-off: the more we invest in ex ante realized transaction costs, the lower the potential ex post costs (figure 9.1). Improvements in institutions can be cap-tured by a shift in the trade-off curve. An improvement in institutional archi-tecture must produce lower ex post uncertainty for a given level of ex ante transaction cost or, conversely, lower transaction costs for a given level of ex ante uncertainty.

In the case of (foreign) aid transfers, ex ante and ex post transaction costs can be traced back to the various activities in the aid delivery process:

• The ex ante transaction costs for the donor to obtain information about the deprived (who and where they are, the source of their problems, and their needs) and effectively carry out the transfer (money, but also material aid and technical assistance, for instance)

• The ex post uncertainty about the recipient's intentions concerning the use he is going to make of the transfer (assessing the extent of preference alignment between donor and recipient)

In terms of figure 9.1, the one-to-one aid transfer example given above is situated close to the origin of the diagram, where both transaction costs and residual uncertainty are (nearly) zero. Geographical separation, as well as differences in preferences between donors and recipients, results in positive transaction costs and uncertainty about the outcome. It shifts the aid transfer plainly into the center of the diagram. This creates an opportunity for institutional entrepreneurs to supply institutional arrangements (aid agencies) that shift the transaction cost trade-off curve to a higher level of efficiency, that is, lower transaction costs for a given degree of uncertainty. In return, donors and recipients are willing to pay aid agencies for their services.

The concept of transaction costs has been mainstreamed in recent years in the development aid literature. It refers to the administrative and management costs of aid flows, which should be reduced through harmonization of procedures among donors. This looks like an economies-of-scale argument rather than a reference to uncertainty in transactions. As such, its current use in the development aid literature could be considered close to the original Coase (1937) interpretation. This makes it difficult to see the trade-off between the costs and benefits of transaction costs. This chapter does not stick to this simplified interpretation; it applies the combined North-Williamson interpretation.

9.3   Intermediation by NGOs

The simplest example of direct one-to-one private voluntary redistribution between a single donor and a single recipient rests on assumptions of both geographical and preference proximity. In reality, of course, transaction costs are far from negligible, especially in foreign aid, where potential donors and recipients may live thousands of miles apart, are unlikely ever to meet each other, and come from very different cultural, social, and economic backgrounds so that preference alignment between them is unlikely. Despite these formidable barriers, foreign aid has reached unprecedented historical proportions. At the dawn of the twenty-first century, it has become a full-scale multinational industry with an annual turnover estimated at nearly US$70 billion (OECD 2005). Direct contact between potential donors and recipients would not be able to achieve such massive transfers. Some sort of organizational setup is required to facilitate intermediation between them and reduce ex ante transaction costs as well as ex post uncertainty to an acceptable level.

The archetype of intermediation in foreign aid is the missionary, who mediates between potential donors in their home town and potential recipients in their mission town. Individual missionaries as well as missionary organizations may generate two types of savings in transaction costs:

• They reduce real transaction costs through economies of scale in search costs: information and appreciation of the plight of the potential recipients and transmission of information to potential donors.

• They reduce ex post uncertainty by ensuring preference alignment between donor and recipient communities. Missionaries apply the moral and religious values of their community of origin to select recipients in their missionary community.

Individual missionaries and missionary organizations are the forerunners of a more general type of private intermediation in voluntary foreign aid transfers: NGOs. NGOs constitute a first step toward a more complete answer to the intermediation problem between donors and recipients.

There is a bewildering range of types and varieties of NGOs. Some authors define them as nonprofit or voluntary organizations; others emphasize their grassroots origins as "people's" organizations; yet others insist on particular types of legal status or nongovernmental aspects (Tvedt 1998, Anheier and Seibel 1990). Some indeed are truly voluntary grassroots nonprofit organizations. Others pursue more profit-related objectives in a covert way, paying their staff handsome salaries or having some form of nonofficial linkages with government organizations. Some may actually be established by government departments and politicians.

Here I emphasize the nonprofit aspect and define NGOs as private organizations, set up by members, that pursue a single issue or a range of issues without a financial profit motive in mind (though financial constraints are obviously present). Usually the issue is of a normative nature, driven by cognitive dissonance that members experience in a particular domain: "The world is not as we would like it to be, and we want to do something about that." As such, the activities of an NGO are driven by a mission or an issue. Individuals become members of an NGO because they share a set of preferences that they would like to convey to the rest of the world. Finding an audience that is receptive to the issue and willing to adapt its behavior in line with the issue's perceived requirements is the primary concern of NGOs. NGOs may be single-issue organizations ("Save the whale") or may seek to promote a wider range of issues covering an entire policy domain such as environmental concerns, democracy, human rights, or religious causes.

The narrower an NGO's range of objectives is and the more homogeneous the preference set of its members, the more focused its actions can be. In terms of figure 9.1, this means less uncertainty in the achievement of a given objective for a given level of transaction costs, as compared with an NGO with a wider range of objectives. Broad-spectrum NGOs are more likely to encounter inconsistencies and trade-offs between various objectives (Holmstrom and Milgrom 1991, Tirole 1994). They will try to control these by investing more in transaction costs or will simply let the objectives slip into uncertainty for a given level of transaction costs. The extent of slippage may depend on the visibility or measurability of the aid objective.

Private for-profit companies seek to maximize profits, a relatively easily measurable objective (despite some evidence in recent years to the contrary). However, the achievement of an NGO's objectives is usually much harder to verify. Therefore, an NGO's best bet to enhance its credibility is to pursue vigorously activities that are perceived to be in line with its objectives. Activities, not necessarily achievements, constitute the core of an NGO's business. This vigorous drive may also be the NGO's comparative advantage. For a given budget, NGOs maximize activities in line with the issue until the budget is exhausted. Commercial companies, in contrast, when faced with a fixed budget, will minimize costs in order to maximize profits. These typical characteristics of NGOs make them well suited for the delivery of foreign aid. They are in a position to provide ex ante as well as ex post transaction cost-reducing intermediation between potential donors and beneficiaries.

Though private voluntary aid channeled through NGOs is more transaction-cost efficient than direct one-to-one aid transfers, it accounted for about US$10 billion or 14 percent only of total official development aid (ODA) flows in 2002, of which about US$1.2 billion was provided by governments, not private gifts.[1] We need to turn our attention to the largest chunk of the $70 billion annual foreign aid flow to developing countries: official bilateral aid, channeled through official foreign aid agencies. How do they come into the picture?

9.4 Official Bilateral Aid Agencies

Selecting for preference alignment between donors and recipients is one way of providing an efficient institutional arrangement for aid delivery. Often, however, donors seek to promote objectives for which it is difficult to find likeminded beneficiaries. Preferences may even differ among donors themselves. This requires more strongly leveraged intermediation—strong enough to negotiate an acceptable compromise between the preferences of various parties. At that point, NGOs become inefficient, and official bilateral aid agencies come into the picture.

In many ways, the characteristics of official aid are the very opposite of the direct voluntary private aid model we started from. Official aid is not voluntary; it is paid from enforced taxation. The taxpayer—that is, the primary donor—may actually disagree with the aid and be unwilling to give it. Official aid is not always triggered by the donor's desire to reduce cognitive dissonance in his mind, though some taxpayers may have a genuine interest in the well-being of the recipient. As a consequence, official aid may come with a lot of conditions attached to it, which the recipient may not like. Aid may be tied to the acceptance of technical assistance and commercial supplies from the donor country; it may be conditional on adopting policy changes and implementing institutional reforms that do not conform to the recipient's own preferences; it may supply goods and services that do not conform to the recipient's own standards. With official aid, we leave the rather idealized world of preference alignment between donors and recipients, for a world where transfers are used to influence the behavior of both donors and recipients alike.

9.4.1 Nonalignment of Preferences between Donors

A voluminous literature analyzes the motives and behavior of bilateral aid agencies (see Alesina and Dollar 1999 for an overview of the "who gives aid to whom and why, WWW, literature). The WWW literature looks at volumes of aid flows between donors and recipients and tries to link these to indicators of recipient needs (poverty) and the commercial, political, and other interests of donors. Most of this literature concludes that donors with former colonies allocate their aid predominantly to these countries, with a view to maintaining and deriving further benefits from this privileged historical relationship. By contrast, donors without a colonial past seem to allocate aid more readily according to recipient needs (i.e., poverty indicators). However, recent more microeconomic research casts some doubts over these conclusions. Ostrom et al. (2001) demonstrate that despite the absence of colonial ties, Swedish aid, a high-ranking "good" donor in the index of the Global Development Centre (Roodman 2004), still pursues commercial interests. Only the absence of historical ties implies that these countries care less about where to target their commercial interests. It leaves more flexibility to marry the interests of the genuine aid lobby with those of the commercial lobby. It illustrates how deceptive aid allocation judgments at country level can be when compared with within-country allocations and uses. There is obviously more going on behind the scenes of bilateral aid than the macro approach of the WWW literature is able to reveal.

Several different motives and corresponding interest groups can be identified on the donor side in a stylized way:

First, part of the electorate in a developed country may genuinely favor the use of tax revenue for wealth transfers to developing countries. Here, the overall motive could be described as poverty alleviation, which is often perceived as an extension of a more general domestic welfare programs agenda (Lumsdaine 1993). Other genuine motives are the causes that NGOs pursue: the promotion of human rights, women's empowerment, and environmental issues, or even such mundane causes as the pursuit of adequate accounting standards or establishing an industry association. In all these instances, the direct beneficiaries of the aid are the like-minded persons and organizations they work with; there is preference alignment between donors and recipients.[2]

Second, aid services suppliers or, in general, suppliers whose products and services could be valuable in developing countries, may want to use aid transfers to enhance their positions on developing-country markets (technical assistance, commercial suppliers, but also academic and research institutes, laboratories, and construction companies, among others). Here, the aid is instrumental in bringing about a preference realignment in the mind of the recipient—who gets a subsidy to do something he would otherwise not do or would do differently.

Last but not least, a donor country government may use aid flows to enhance political alliances with the recipient country government, to obtain political goodwill and changes (nonalignment in the original preferences) in the decisions and policy stance of that government. Donor governments may also wish to nurture their relationship with particular interest groups in the recipient country (preferences aligned with those of the donor government) that can be influential in political and economic decisions of interest to the donor country.

In spite of heterogeneous, and possibly conflicting, preferences, bilateral aid seems to be able to mobilize much larger aid flows than private voluntary aid. Indeed, the vast majority of all foreign aid is nonvoluntary aid, mobilized through enforced taxation in donor countries (OECD 2005, table 2). How can we explain the dominance of this type of aid, despite the fact that it takes us far from the ideal aid model with full preference alignment? What are the incentives that drive these heterogeneous interest groups to form a coalition?

The preferences of these donor interest groups are not mutually exclusive. They share a common objective: all want to maximize aid flows in order to achieve their preferences. A single aid project can benefit all three. For instance, a bilateral aid agency may approve the delivery of water pumps to a village in the recipient country. Such a project satisfies the preferences of all donor interest groups: genuine wealth transfers and empowerment of (water-carrying) women, profits for commercial water pump suppliers and consultants involved in the project, visibility for the donor government, and political goodwill from the influential village politician in support of the political interests of the donor country.

Another and possibly stronger incentive is savings in opportunity costs, or increased consumer surplus, for interest groups. If aid were to be supplied from private financial contributions only, and individual donors were to contribute up to the level of their willingness to pay for aid, the consumer surplus would be minimized to zero. On the other hand, with aid being supplied from tax revenue, the cost of contributions is probably far below the willingness to pay of interested lobby groups, especially since the opportunity cost of enforced tax money is basically zero: consumers have no choice but to pay taxes. Supplying aid from tax revenue thus greatly increases the consumer surplus of potential individual donor interest groups.

Collective action among different interest groups is easier to achieve if they jointly delegate decision making to a common agent, the official government aid agency. Joint delegation may worsen the typical problems of multiple and conflicting objectives, with poorly defined trade-offs that have a negative effect on the organization's performance (Holmstrom and Milgrom 1991). Yet while these multiple principals have different objectives and are likely to give incoherent instructions to the agency, the agency may be in a position to make its own proposals, play off different interest groups against each other, forge coalitions in support of the policies it proposes, induce collective action among members, and, in general, achieve objectives that individual members would not be able to achieve on their own (Martimort 1991). Consequently, one important task of bilateral donor agencies is to mediate between donor interest groups at home.

9.4.2 Nonalignment of Preferences between Donors and Recipients

Bilateral agencies not only seek to mobilize the largest possible coalition of donor interest groups at home. They also have to deal with the possible lack of alignment of preferences between donors at home and recipients abroad. Commercial aid services suppliers may actually be interested only in the delivery of project inputs (the sale of goods and services) rather than in the results. Donor politicians who seek visibility and goodwill abroad may also be interested mainly in visible delivery of inputs, and not so much in producing results. There is little risk of moral hazard or ex post uncertainty in such cases. However, genuine aid lobby groups in donor countries are interested in achieving results downstream of inputs delivery. In that case, bilateral agencies have at least two means to deal with preference misalignment between donors and recipients and rein in moral hazard on behalf of the recipient.

A first option for the donor, as suggested in figure 9.1, is to substantially increase investment in ex ante realized transaction costs and spend more on gathering information and monitoring recipient behavior, writing a more elaborate contract with the recipient, getting actively involved in the management of aid projects, and so on. It explains why some donor agencies maintain a strong presence in the administration of aid flows, from budgeting and programming, through contracting, implementation, supervision, and evaluation (input conditionality). The administrative costs incurred to do so are transaction costs that reduce ex post uncertainty for the donor, making sure that aid is used in line with his preferences. However, rather than citing nonalignment of preferences, donors mostly justify their involvement in aid implementation by referring to the recipient's lack of skills and expertise required for project implementation. This is not a convincing argument. Even if some projects do require exceptional skills, the recipient could buy these skills in the market. Clearly it is not the quality of the skills that is the real argument here, but control over conditionality and ex post uncertainty. Donor-hired implementation agents tend to be more loyal to donor than to recipient interests. This increases transaction costs (the additional costs of subcontracting a task to an expatriate rather than a national expert) but reduces ex post uncertainty. In terms of figure 9.1, it represents a move along the curve toward higher transaction costs in order to reduce uncertainty.

A second option for the donor is to change the disbursement arrangements for the aid and switch from input conditionality to results-based conditionality. In other words, switch from paying up front of project implementation to paying only downstream of implementation and in function of the production of the desired results. Upstream payment is used for most traditional project aid, motivated at least as much by the commercial and political interests of the donor as by the recipient's welfare. Downstream or conditional aid payment is used when donors are indeed interested in the results of an aid program (for instance, because of political and economic concerns). This is a typical arrangement in structural adjustment, budget support, and policy reform programs. The problem of moral hazard by the recipient and adverse selection by the donor is not entirely resolved, however, by this conditional approach, since information asymmetry between donor and recipient is not eliminated. There is a substantial volume of literature on the pros and cons of this approach (e.g., Killick 1995, Mosley 1997, Streeten 1998, Collier et al. 1997).

The donor agency's choice of implementation arrangements with the recipient will to a large extent be determined by the composition of the domestic coalition that supports the aid program. If commercial and domestic political interests are dominant, there is unlikely to be much results-based conditionality in aid, though there may be commercial input conditionality (tied to procurement in the donor country). But if genuine development lobbies are dominant, there may also be little conditionality since these groups often favor recipient ownership rather than externally imposed conditionality and shy away from the often painful adjustments that may be required to put policies back on track. Results-based conditionality will occur only if there are strong external policy concerns in the donor country about recipient government policies. For instance, a deep economic and political crisis may jeopardize the interests of all donor lobby groups, unleash a wave of economic and political refugees, and provide an incentive to create a coalition in favor of more conditional aid programs. Or recipient countries may actively play on the diverging interests of different donor lobbies to water down conditionality in aid programs, for instance, by threatening commercial retaliation.

In conclusion, a bilateral aid agency's margin for mediation is constrained by diverging donor and recipient interests. It has two different institutional arrangements at its disposal to manage this situation: a weakly leveraged but possibly domestically more interesting input conditionality and a more strongly leveraged results conditionality that may, however, run into domestic and recipient country opposition tactics. In terms of figure 9.1, results-based conditionality is theoretically a more efficient institutional arrangement: it lowers transaction costs for a given degree of ex post uncertainty or, alternatively, reduces ex post uncertainty for a given level of transaction costs. However, its effectiveness depends on the underlying political support.

9.5 Subcontracting by Bilateral Aid Agencies

Official aid agencies usually do not implement projects through their own staff but delegate implementation to for-profit (companies, experts) or nonprofit (NGO) subcontractors. Consequently, official bilateral aid is usually a combination of two institutional setups: the official aid agency for policy and financial decision making and the subcontractor for implementation. Different types of subcontractors have different performance incentives. NGOs will maximize activity toward achievement of their cause or the project objective for a given contractual budget constraint. Private for-profit companies will minimize costs for a given contractual budget constraint in order to maximize their profits. As a result of these differences in contractual performance incentives, the choice of type of subcontractor will also affect ex post uncertainty about the outcomes and transaction costs to establish and monitor these outcomes.

If activities and results are easily observable by the donor agency, for-profit companies have less margin to exploit their asymmetrical information advantages. For instance, the outcome of a road construction project is more easily and objectively verifiable than the outcome of an institution-building project. To the extent that projects are costly to monitor, moral hazard and adverse selection may occur (Martens et al. 2002). Increasing transaction costs to monitor the project is one solution. Another is to select for-profit subcontractors on the basis of their track record. Measurability problems are an obstacle to establishing performance track records, however.

If results are not easily observable, implementation through nonprofit NGOs may be a better solution. Selecting an NGO whose credibility—and financial resources—depend on pursuing a specific cause or objective increases the chances that all efforts and resources will be geared toward that cause. Moreover, selecting an NGO that is well embedded in a wider sociopolitical network in the donor country—for instance, NGOs affiliated with political parties, labor unions, religious groups, and other well-established social organizations—increases taxpayers' satisfaction. These affiliations reduce an NGO's margin for discretionary behavior. An NGO's financial dependence on contracts with the aid agency enables the agency to exercise some degree of control over NGO behavior.

Apart from formal subcontracting outside the aid agency, there is also subcontracting inside the agency. In fact, aid agencies, like any other large organizations, are a vast network of subcontracting of tasks from principals to their agents. The entire aid delivery chain can thus be considered a chain of subcontractors between the donor-taxpayer and the final beneficiary in the recipient country. This makes the notion of a homogeneous donor unrealistic. There are many persons involved in the delivery chain of foreign aid: private donors, taxpayers, lobby groups, officials in aid agencies, consultants and academics, politicians in donor and recipient countries, and others. It is usually assumed, implicitly or explicitly, that all of these individuals and organizations fully share a single objective: the alleviation of poverty among beneficiaries in recipient countries. In reality, however, objectives are likely to differ. Individuals pursue careers, incomes, and their own preferences; they may, but do not necessarily, have a genuine interest in alleviating poverty. Politicians pursue political objectives, agencies pursue the perpetuation and expansion of their remit and budget, consultants seek the next contract, and so on. How this chain of nonaligned preferences affects aid performance has been analyzed in detail by Martens et al. (2002). The role of aid agencies could be perceived as providing a mechanism that enables collective action to emerge from these different and often contradictory individual motives. The agency establishes explicit contracts and rules as well as implicit norms and standards that affect the behavior of individuals working with and within the organization and, consequently, the performance of aid organizations. In that sense, an aid agency could be considered the chief mediator between the preferences and interests of all persons involved in the aid delivery chain.

9.6 Multilateral Agencies

A large share of bilateral grant aid is channeled through multilateral agencies: US$18 billion out of US$58 billion in bilateral aid (OECD 2005, table 12). On top of that, multilateral development banks have their own resources (loans) to channel to developing countries. Why do bilateral aid agencies channel part of their budget and delegate decision making to multilateral agencies (Milner 2002)? How do multilateral agencies fit into the transaction cost and agency theory picture?

Just like bilateral aid, where different domestic interest groups agree to delegate the implementation of aid to a single government agency, multilateral aid is a case of joint delegation by donor countries with different interests to a single international agency. Multilateral agencies supply an institutional setting that responds to a demand from donors as well as recipients. The literature on international and multilateral organizations (Hawkins et al. 2003) identifies two clusters of factors that determine this demand.

The first cluster revolves around achieving collective action in the presence of heterogeneous preferences among donors or between donors and recipients. Donors may compete to promote their preferred projects in developing countries without diminishing their own benefits or incurring additional costs (though they may induce additional costs for the recipient). However, when the intended output of a project is a public good, collective action among donors is required. For instance, the identification of an economic reform program, a debt rescheduling agreement, or filling the external financing gap of a country requires collective action, not competition. Moreover, bilateral agencies may not be good at implementing programs that require strong conditionality because of conflicting preferences between donors and recipients or conflicting preferences in the donor country itself. Delegation to a multilateral agency avoids spillover of this conflict to donors (who may prefer to maintain a privileged relationship with the recipient) and prevents blame falling on the donor if a risky program goes wrong (Rodrik 1997). A multilateral approach, endorsed by all donors and recipients, may also strengthen the legitimacy and credibility of unpopular programs (for instance, unpopular economic stabilization and reform programs). In all of these cases, the multilateral agency acts as an intermediary between the parties. It drives a wedge between the different interest groups and uses it to design a program that may be supported by all parties.

A second (and partly related) cluster revolves around economies of scale and scope, mainly in information gathering and analysis (knowledge production). National action by individual donor countries could develop redundant capabilities—for instance, duplication of projects in similar domains or collecting information that is afterward put in the public domain. Multilateral approaches can reduce national costs and enhance the credibility of that information (Rodrik 1997). Note, however, that multilaterals do not necessarily put all the collected information in the public domain. They may use some of it to build up a comparative information advantage over their counterparts, which they can exploit to selectively promote their own policy proposals. They may specialize in specific issues for which they are the primary source of worldwide information (the IMF on fiscal monetary and balance-of-payments information; the World Bank on reform policies; the World Health Organization on health policy issues; the Food and Agriculture Organization on agricultural and food issues). This informational advantage makes their policy analysis and proposals more credible and makes it more difficult for individual member states to formulate alternative proposals. They may use these to perpetuate temporary assignments, boost their financial resources and domains of competence, and increase their leverage over a wide range of development policy issues.

We can add a third source of demand for multilateral agencies by extending the economic logic of bilateral aid agencies to multilateral development banks (MDBs). MDBs operate on the basis of loans, mobilized on international capital markets,[3] in this way enabling donor countries to supply aid to recipients at very low (close to zero) budgetary cost to themselves. This increases the "consumer surplus" for donor countries: they reap more political goodwill and economic returns from this aid than they would be willing to pay for. This argument obviously does not apply to multilateral grant aid agencies (MGAs)[4] that operate with tax money from donor countries. There the donor pays the full cost of the aid. The substantial consumer surplus that MDBs generate for donor countries may explain why they are so much more important than MGAs (in terms of volume of aid flows).

These three factors of demand for the mediation services of multilateral aid agencies benefit the donors; it looks as if there is not much in it for recipient countries (though economies of scale may also benefit them). There must be benefits for the recipient countries as well; otherwise, they would not want to participate in these institutions. A first obvious such benefit is that multilateral institutions at least partially restore the broken feedback loop that is so typical of bilateral aid. They give recipient countries a voice in decision making. How much voice they get depends on voting systems in the multilateral agency. MDBs allocate voting rights according to shares in the capital of the bank. Recipient countries usually have only very small shares. MGAs or other nonbank agencies usually operate along the one country, one vote system, treating all countries on an equal footing. This usually benefits the majority of developing countries but not the minority of developed countries, although alliances are not necessarily along these lines.

A second and probably more important and direct benefit that recipient countries can derive from multilateral institutions is access to cheap loans, which is typical for MDBs. MDBs are given relative financial autonomy: funds are mobilized on international capital markets, not from taxpayers' money. This gives them more room for discretionary decision making than grant-based aid agencies because it keeps taxpayer supervision (through their elected representatives) at arm's length.[5] It also induces a financial multiplier effect[6] that benefits both donors and recipients.

MDBs are successful to the extent that they are able to drive a wedge between the interests of donors and borrowers. Borrowing countries obtain financially advantageous interest rate conditions, far below the international financial market rates that developing countries would normally have to pay, at the cost of policy conditionalities (Rodrik 1997). Creditor countries obtain a less contentious mechanism for collective action on economic reforms. MDBs manage to marry the often conflicting objectives of donor and recipient countries, at a price to both: the relative independence of the MDB. Of course, to the extent that one or a few large shareholders dominate voting on the board of the MDB, these countries may still lean heavily on decisionmaking and reduce the MDB's independence: for instance, the position of the United States, and the G7 in general, on the boards of the World Bank and the IMF. MDBs have managed to circumvent some of the problems and exploit the advantages associated with joint delegation.

Some MDBs combine this financial advantage with an informational advantage. They gather worldwide or at least region-wide information and use their economies of scale in this process to strengthen their informational advantage over donors and recipients alike. Informational advantages are useful in presenting policies and make it harder for outsiders to verify the validity of the analysis and the policy proposals, especially when some information is not made publicly available or at least is hard to access. It also enables these MDBs to become involved in normative work and standard setting, which may include international regulatory standards as well as setting aid policy standards. Economies of scale in information gathering also put MDBs in an advantageous position for coordinating international aid. For instance, the World Bank's unique position as a worldwide MDB gives it a comparative advantage in overall information gathering and analysis, which can be exploited to its own advantage. Together with the IMF,[7] it is mostly in the lead position in the design of economic policy reform programs in developing countries, partly because of this.

MGAs have two major disadvantages compared with MDBs. First, they use taxpayers' money from donor countries, which makes it harder to keep donors' national political and economic interests at arm's length. Membership contributions are usually based on GDP, so that the industrial countries share the largest budgetary burden. Obviously donor representatives will want to keep a close eye on how that money is spent and to further their own interests through the spending process. Second, most UN agencies operate as cooperative clubs, with both donors and beneficiary countries represented in decision-making bodies that follow the one country, one vote rule. This gives recipient developing countries an overwhelming majority in decision making and creates an obvious disequilibrium between financial contributions and voting power.

However, in many cases, donor countries have various means at their disposal to reverse this disequilibrium. Obligatory membership contributions feed only into the regular budget. A considerable part of donor contributions for specific research projects and aid programs is kept off-budget and at the discretion of donors. This discretionary financing channel enables them to influence decision making. Also, most agencies take care not to approve a budget that runs counter to the interests of the major donors. This is particularly important in the realm of the so-called normative activities of various specialized UN agencies, such as WHO, FAO, and International Labor Organization, which are involved in setting worldwide standards and regulations in their domain of competence. Donor countries can use these financial levers to forge coalitions and ensure that standard setting does not operate against their interests.

This careful balancing act between financial and voting power, and between normative and development aid activities, opens a window of opportunity for the multilateral agency to exploit its position, launch proposals, and forge coalitions in their favor. It allows the agency to work itself into a key position as an agenda setter and policymaker and justify its existence as an enabling environment for collective action among its member states. This explains why donors and their bilateral aid agencies are willing to channel part of their foreign aid through multilateral specialized agencies. Multilateral agencies are uniquely placed to promote collective action in their domain of competence. It is in a donor country's interest to be a member of these organizations so as to be able to voice its interests in international policymaking. Foreign aid can be used as a lever to enhance its policy influence and reduce uncertainty, perhaps not so much in the execution of development projects but more so in normative decision making. It helps a donor country to redress its disadvantage in voting power over normative issues and other policy decisions in general.

In a way, MGAs constitute a two-sided institutional arrangement: a financial institution and a normative institution. The normative institution has high ex post uncertainty for the donors because they are usually in a minority. The financial institution has low uncertainty because of the financial leverage it gives to the donors, in return for a high transaction cost (grant contributions). Combining the two strikes a political balance acceptable to both donors and recipients. MGAs that neglect either of these sides risk losing credibility and status in the international aid community.

9.7 Conclusion

The analysis in this chapter enables us to answer the Coasian questions: (1) why aid agencies exist, (2) why there are many of them instead of just one and (3) what their distinguishing institutional features are.

Like all other institutions, aid agencies exist to reduce ex ante transaction costs and ex post uncertainties in transactions—in this case, income transfers from donors to recipients. Transaction costs exist for various reasons: the cost of collecting funds and channeling them to the recipients, the cost of collecting information on and selecting potential recipients, the cost of monitoring the implementation of aid projects, and others. Ex post uncertainties arise because both parties have different and incomplete perceptions of the other's preferences and objectives. Combined with imperfect and asymmetrical information between the parties, this may give rise to moral hazard and adverse selection. In a hypothetical world without transaction costs and contractual uncertainties, there would be no need for aid agencies; private markets would deal with aid transfers. In the real world, with positive transaction costs and uncertainties, aid agencies provide economies of scale and institutional arrangements that reduce costs and mediate between donors and recipients to reduce uncertainties due to diverging preferences. This institutional explanation for the role of aid agencies is quite different from the traditional view whereby their role is to transfer financial resources to recipients (this could be done in much simpler ways) or to supply recipients with goods, services, and know-how (no need for an aid agency since these can be bought in the market).

If all donors were fully to share a single objective—for instance, poverty reduction—then one single worldwide aid agency would be sufficient. It would maximize economies of scale in the collection of funds, selection and monitoring, policy discussions, and simplification of aid modalities. The fact that a multitude of aid agencies exists constitutes a strong indicator that a single fully shared aid objective is an unrealistic assumption. Public aid decisions are the result of a political compromise in donor countries, or between donor countries in the case of multilateral aid, that reflects a mixture of diverging preferences of different domestic lobby groups. Moreover, that domestic compromise is unlikely to fully reflect the recipient's preferences since he is not taking part in the decision-making process. Forcing donor countries and lobby groups worldwide to adhere to a single aid objective such as poverty reduction, or even a limited set of objectives such as those identified in the Millennium Development Goals, will limit the margins for political compromise around these diverging preferences and thereby reduce some groups' willingness to pay for aid. In fact, if donors and recipients were fully to share a preference for a single objective, there would be no need for any aid agency at all. Aid could be sent direct by check to the recipients, and they would take care of policies and implementation, using goods, services, and knowledge bought on international markets.

Different types of aid agencies serve different purposes, depending on their institutional architecture. Private or nongovernmental agencies can offer economies of scale and, more important, a transaction-cost-efficient mechanism to reduce ex post uncertainties in the use of private gifts. However, their financial leverage is limited: donors interested in giving aid pay the full cost of the transfer and do not enjoy a "consumer surplus." Official aid agencies have stronger financial leverage because they can increase consumer surplus for domestic interest groups, including genuine aid lobbyists and commercial suppliers of aid services. Tax money is used, sometimes as a complement to but often instead of private funds, to support the goals of these domestic interest groups. As such, these groups do not pay the full "consumer value" that aid has for them.

Similarly, multilateral development banks increase the consumer surplus or goodwill surplus for donor countries. Their funds are raised in international financial markets instead of using donor country tax money. Donor countries do not pay the cost of the aid, despite their domestic policy interest in these aid transfers. To the extent that multilateral banks use soft lending windows, subsidized by donor country grants, donors pay part of the cost, of course. At the same time, multilateral banks offer cheap loans to the borrowing countries, below the market rates they would normally have to pay, thereby increasing the borrowers' consumer surplus. The price that donors (and borrowers) pay for this increased consumer surplus is a loss of control in ex post contractual uncertainties. Monitoring contracts and uncertainties is delegated to the bilateral or multilateral agency, which may only partly satisfy the (often diverging) preferences of all parties concerned.

These conclusions cast new light on the current aid policy agenda. The aid community has apparently rallied in recent years around the single overriding objective of poverty reduction. Moreover, donors and recipients are making efforts to enhance recipient ownership, harmonize policies and procedures to reduce transaction costs, and seek convergence in objectives. The World Bank, for instance, adopted the new Development Policy Lending instrument in 2004 to replace structural adjustment lending. It explicitly seeks to strengthen recipient country institutions and enhance ownership by recipient governments and consultation with stakeholders, abandoning the prescriptive character of previous lending approaches and taking more of a long-term, programmatic approach. These policy changes have also been concretized in general aid policy documents such as the Millennium Declaration (United Nations 2000) and, recently again, in the Paris Declaration on Aid Effectiveness (2005).

Strengthening recipient countries' institutions, with or without donor aid, would certainly constitute an improvement in governance in terms of figure 9.1: it would reduce aid transaction costs for the same level of ex post uncertainty and would thus provide additional assurance to donors that aid will be used for the agreed purposes and in the agreed ways. However, it does not necessarily bring donor objectives closer to those of the recipients or bring more coherence among individual donors' objectives, for that matter. The Paris Declaration implicitly acknowledges this when it advocates linking aid to a single set of conditions and aligning it behind central government strategies "to the maximum extent possible": it leaves room for divergence among donors, between donors and the recipient government authorities, and even for bypassing national institutions when these cannot be relied on. To the extent that donors' preferences would fully converge, there would be no need to maintain a multitude of donor agencies; all donors could delegate aid delivery to a single agency, for instance, the World Bank. Fortunately, this is not a realistic policy because there is a healthy divergence of views among donors; nobody holds a monopoly on solutions to development problems. To the extent that recipient countries were to go through a fully transparent and democratic consultation process with all stakeholders, unfortunately not the case in many developing countries, donors might simply give an unconditional lump sum aid to the central government treasury to implement the recipient country's agreed policies. Even in this case, donors may still disagree with the recipient government and attempt to sponsor their preferred recipient country lobby groups and policies.

The main policy conclusion to be drawn from this chapter is that as long as donors and recipients live in different political constituencies with no overarching political institution to work out a policy compromise between them, aid agencies will fill that gap and act as mediators between donors and recipients, proposing aid delivery instruments that reduce transaction costs and ex post uncertainties in delivery. During the 1980s and early 1990s, the aid policy pendulum had swung in favor of donor-prescribed conditionality. In recent years, the pendulum has swung back toward the recipients, emphasizing ownership and donor alignment. Neither donors nor recipients can be forced into a policy straitjacket without a cost to the other party. Excessive emphasis on recipient ownership, a single aid objective, harmonization, and alignment of procedures and policies may increase benefits for the recipients but may also diminish donors' willingness to pay because it reduces their perceived consumer surplus in terms of their own domestic policy interests. It is precisely the role of aid agencies to broker a realistic compromise between the parties concerned, each according to its own institutional abilities and comparative advantages.

Notes

This chapter was originally published as a paper with the same title in the *Development Policy Review* (2005), 23(6):643–663.

1. According to Tvedt (1998), private donations account for less than 20 percent of NGO foreign aid resources in most European countries. In the United States, however, nearly all NGO development aid funds are private donations.

2. Though the target of their activities may be to change the behavior of not-so-like-minded persons and organizations.

3. Examples include the World Bank and the regional development banks such as the European Bank for Reconstruction and Development and the African, Asian and Inter-American Development Banks.

4. Examples include the United Nations Development Programme, various specialized agencies of the United Nations involved in thematic development programs (WHO, FAO, ILO, UNICEF, UNHCR, UNEP), and the European Commission's external aid programs.

5. Many MDBs have so-called soft windows that mix loans and grants into loans at a subsidized interest rate. To the extent that soft lending plays an important role in an MDB portfolio, donor supervision may come closer.

6. The combination of a gearing ratio (ratio of lending to capital) above 1 and a ratio of effectively paid-in capital below 1 results in a strong multiplier effect: for each dollar invested by donors in the capital of an MDB, many dollars can be lent by the MDB to recipient countries.

7. The IMF is not a typical MDB but shares many behavioral characteristics with MDBs.

References

Alesina, A., and D. Dollar. 1999. "Who Gives Aid to Whom and Why?" *Journal of Economic Growth* 5:33–63.

Anheier, H., and W. Seibel. 1990. *The Third Sector: Comparative Studies of Non-Profit Organisations.* Berlin: W. De Gruyter.

Burnside, C., and D. Dollar. 1996. "Aid, Policies and Growth." Policy Research Working Paper No. 1777. Washington, D.C.: World Bank.

Burnside, C., and D. Dollar. 2000. "Aid, Policies and Growth." *American Economic Review* 90(4):847–868.

Carr, S., M. Eilish, and M. MacLachlan. 1998. *Psychology of Aid.* London: Routledge.

Coase, R. 1937. "The Nature of the Firm." *Economica* 4:386–405.

Collier, P., P. Guillaumont, S. Guillaumont, and J. W. Gunning. 1997. "Redesigning Conditionality." *World Development* 25(9):1399–1407.

Furubotn, E., and R. Richter. 1998. *Institutions and Economic Theory: The Contribution of the New Institutional Economics.* Ann Arbor: University of Michigan Press.

Gilbert, C., and A. Powell. 1999. "Positioning the World Bank." *Economic Journal* 109:459.

Hansen, H., and F. Tarp. 2000. "Aid Effectiveness Disputed," *Journal of International Development* 12(3):375–398.

Hawkins, D., D. Lake, D. Nielson, and M. Tierney. 2003. "Delegation Under Anarchy: States, International Organisations and Principal-Agent Theory." Mimeo.

Holmstrom, B., and P. Milgrom. 1991. "Multitask Principal-Agent Analyses: Incentive Contracts, Asset Ownership and Job Design." *Journal of Law, Economics and Organisation* 7:24–52.

Killick, T. 1995. *A Principal-Agent Analysis of Conditionality—A Reader's Digest.* London: Overseas Development Institute.

Lumsdaine, D. 1993. *Moral Vision in International Politics: The Foreign Aid Regime.* Princeton, N.J.: Princeton University Press.

Martens, B., U. Mummert, P. Murrell, and P. Seabright. 2002. *The Institutional Economics of Foreign Aid.* Cambridge: Cambridge University Press.

Martimort, D. 1991. "Multiple Principals as a Commitment Mechanism." Mimeo., University of Toulouse.

Masten, S., and O. Williamson. 1999. *The Economics of Transaction Costs.* Cheltenham: Edward Elgar.

Milner, H. 2002. "The Rise of Multilateralism: Why Delegate the Allocation of Foreign Aid?" Mimeo., Columbia University.

Mosley, P. 1997. *Conditionality as a Bargaining Process: Structural Adjustment Lending, 1980–86.* Princeton, N.J.: Princeton University Press

North, D. 1990. *Institutions, Institutional Change and Economic Performance.* Cambridge: Cambridge University Press.

Organization for Economic Cooperation and Development. 2005. *The 2004 Development Cooperation Report.* Paris: OECD.

Ostrom, E., C. Gibson, S. Shivakumar, and K. Andersson. 2001. *Aid, Incentives and Sustainability: An Institutional Analysis of Development Cooperation.* Stockholm: Swedish International Development Agency.

Paris Declaration on Aid Effectiveness. 2005. Available at http://www1.worldbank.org/harmonization/Paris/finalparisdeclaration.pdf.

Quarles van Ufford, P., D. Kruyt, and Th. Downing. 1988. *The Hidden Crisis in Development: Development Bureaucracies.* Amsterdam: Free University Press, and Tokyo: United Nations University.

Rodrik, D. 1997. "Why Is There Multilateral Lending?" In *Proceedings of the 1995 Annual Conference on Development Economics.* Washington, D.C.: World Bank.

Roodman, D. 2004. *An Index of Donor Aid Performance.* Washington, D.C.: Center for Global Development.

Streeten, P. 1988. "Conditionality: A Double Paradox." In *North-South Co-Operation in Retrospect and Prospect.* London: Routledge.

Tirole, J. 1994. "The Internal Organisation of Government." *Oxford Economic Papers* 46:1–29.

Tsikata, T. 1998. "Aid Effectiveness: A Survey of Recent Empirical Literature." IMF PPAA/98/1. Washington, D.C.: International Monetary Fund.

Tvedt, T. 1998. *Angels of Mercy or Development Diplomats: NGOs and Foreign Aid.* Oxford: James Cassey, and Trenton, N.J.: Africa World Press.

United Nations. 2000. "Millenium Declaration," Resolution adopted by the General Assembly on 8 September 2000. See www.un.org/millenium/declaration/ares552e.htm.

Williamson, O. 1985. *The Economic Institutions of Capitalism.* New York: Free Press.

10 Absorption Capacity and Disbursement Constraints

Jakob Svensson

In many respects, foreign aid agencies are very similar to other public agencies in that they face incentive problems common in most of the public sector. These incentive constraints include multiple objectives, difficulties in measuring output and performance, and weak performance incentives. However, although common in the public sector, these institutional features are often more pronounced in the foreign aid sector. In addition, there are features in the aid business that make foreign aid particularly subject to adverse incentive effects. They include the presence of multiple principals, that is, donors, and a broken information (accountability) feedback loop between the providers and the beneficiaries.

Why do donors and recipients act the way they do? This chapter tries to answer this question partly by studying the incentive problems. The key message of the chapter is that while many other factors influence how aid is disbursed and used, to understand donor (and recipient) behavior, these incentive issues must be thoroughly studied. And to increase the effectiveness of aid, the incentive problems must be (at least partly) overcome.

The rest of the chapter is organized as follows. In section 10.1, I discuss the implications of the broken information (accountability) feedback loop. I argue that this feature, which differentiates foreign aid from domestically financed services, explains both the focus on volume of foreign aid (by both donors and recipients) rather than results and why contractors and domestic suppliers of aid-financed goods and services have a disproportionate influence on decision making. I discuss ways to mitigate the problems caused by the broken information (accountability) feedback loop and illustrate this discussion with two case studies on aid-financed public spending on primary education in Uganda and Tanzania. In section 10.2, I briefly discuss the problems caused by multiple objectives and tasks—features that are common in most of the public sector—and discuss why the incentive problems that arise from the multiplicity of tasks and objectives are likely to be more pronounced in the foreign aid sector. In section 10.3, I turn to one specific issue, the budget pressure problem, which I argue is partly a function of the incentive issues raised in sections 10.1 and 10.2. I provide some evidence of the macroeconomic implications of the budget pressure problem and discuss how the pressure to disburse can be relaxed. Section 10.4 discusses the multiple principal problem, that is, that foreign aid is handled not by one but multiple agencies. I highlight both the transaction cost implications and collective action problems that arise when multiple donors give aid to a recipient without being fully coordinated. Finally in section 10.5, I discuss the difficult trade-off facing donors today: the conflict between long-run objectives to enhance institution building and the short-run objective to minimize capture and corruption.

10.1   A Broken Information (Accountability) Feedback Loop

Foreign aid agencies, just like most other agencies in the public sector, face various incentive constraints that influence how they behave and how and why they prioritize the things they do. Three important incentive constraints that have been discussed in the agency literature on public administrations are multiple objectives, difficulties in measuring output and performance, and weak performance incentives. As discussed in more detail below, although these institutional features are common in the public sector, they are often more pronounced in donor agencies. Nevertheless, aid agencies differ from other organizations in the public sector in some important ways. Perhaps most important, the people for whose benefit aid agencies are supposed to work— poor people in the recipient countries—are not the same as those from whom their revenues are obtained: taxpayers in the donor country. As Martens et al. (2002) note, this geographical and political separation between taxpayers and beneficiaries blocks the normal performance feedback process.

In a standard model of public accountability, individuals and households have dual roles as citizens and clients. As clients, individuals hope to benefit from various public programs. As clients, individuals and households use various mechanisms to influence and control politicians and, indirectly, the performance of the public administration. When individuals and households are well informed and have mechanisms to sanction politicians—for example, the right to vote them out of office—politicians have potentially strong incentives to monitor and pressure public institutions to do what individuals and households, whom they represent, want.[1] Two key assumptions in these type of models are that individuals and households as clients are informed about programs intended for their benefit and that individuals and households as citizens can hold their representatives accountable for their action by sanctioning poor performers (politicians).

In the case of foreign aid, geographical and political separation between the beneficiaries (clients in the recipient country) and the donors (citizens in the donor country) severely constrains both mechanisms. Citizens in the donor country have no direct knowledge or experience of the programs financed by the aid agency. Moreover, it is very costly for taxpayers in the donor country to obtain reliable information on the outcomes of aid programs that they finance. The intended beneficiaries (the clients), on the other hand, are not voters in the country that pays for the aid and thus have no real political leverage over domestic politicians who approve these programs (Martens et al. 2002).

The broken information (accountability) feedback loop magnifies problems arising from multiple objectives, difficulties in measuring output and performance, and weak performance incentives. It affects both donors and recipients. It also introduces additional incentive problems. Foremost, even though many individuals in both the recipient and donor countries are responsible for ensuring the effectiveness and sustainability of aid, no one is really held accountable (Ostrom et al. 2002). This, in turn, has resulted in a number of adverse incentive effects.

For example, voters in the donor country do not derive any direct benefit from service provision funded by foreign aid or observe outcomes in the recipient country. However, they can observe the share of the government budget allocated to foreign aid. As a consequence, the volume of aid has become one of the key performance measures of aid, and political discussions and debates about aid in many donor countries center almost exclusively on the question of how much should be given in aid to poor countries. To the extent that the majority of voters are in favor of assisting poor countries, this is also a focus that benefits the aid agency. Importantly, volume of aid and outcomes are not necessarily correlated.

The political focus on volume rather than impact also influences how aid agencies work. When aid officials are not held accountable for performance, their incentives to spend time and effort seeking out information about the success and sustainability of ongoing projects will be adversely affected.

The broken information (accountability) feedback loop also explains why the interests of domestic suppliers of aid-financed goods and services play such a dominant role in the actual decision-making process (Martens et al. 2002). Consultancy companies, experts, and suppliers of goods are both direct beneficiaries of aid (through contractually agreed rewards) and have direct leverage on political decision makers in the donor country. As a result, they have a disproportionately large influence on how aid programs are designed and implemented. Cross-country work on the determinants of aid across countries provides indirect evidence of this bias. For example, Alesina and Dollar (2000) and Collier and Dollar (2002) show that almost half of the foreign aid provided by the Organization for Economic Cooperation and Development (OECD) countries have not been guided by any consideration of poverty alleviation.

Another implication of the broken information (accountability) feedback loop is that news media's influence on policy is likely to be larger for foreign aid than most domestic programs. Since voters in the donor country have little or no own experience of foreign aid, news reports are typically the sole source of information. This introduces a bias in foreign aid policy since news media tend to focus on newsworthy events. There is some empirical evidence of this effect. Eisensee and Stromberg (2005) find that to a large extent, U.S. disaster relief depends on the occurrence of other newsworthy events at the time of the disaster, which is obviously unrelated to need. They argue that the only plausible explanation is that relief decisions are driven by news coverage of disasters and that this news coverage is crowded out by newsworthy material. Since different types of disasters are more or less newsworthy, this also implies that certain disasters, such as earthquakes, receive a lot of attention, while famines receive less. Eisensee and Stromberg find that to have the same estimated probability of entering network news as an earthquake, a food shortage must have 40,000 times as many casualties.

The broken information (accountability) feedback loop also influences the recipient behavior. Most important, when projects are donor driven or financed, clients in the recipient country rationally anticipate that their influence on the financier is limited at best. In short, they cannot hold the donor accountable for performance. Public officials in the recipient country assigned to the aid project or program face similar incentives and as a result have weak incentives to exert effort.

How can the bias in foreign aid policy induced by the broken information (accountability) feedback loop be mitigated? Martens et al. (2002) argue that because of the broken natural feedback loop in foreign aid, inserting an explicit evaluation function in foreign aid programs is necessary to eliminate performance problems. However, this can at best be only a partial solution. First, to the extent that evaluations are handled by the aid agency itself, which is typically the case, it will be subject to attempts of manipulation. For example, lower-quality evaluation studies could be preferred, as it would be harder to draw firm conclusions on actual performance. Moreover, even if the evaluations are competently executed, if there is no mechanism in place to act on these evaluations, that is, no mechanism to disseminate the information to the public, the aid agency's behavior will likely not be affected. An independent foreign aid evaluation agency could mitigate these concerns.[2] Second, even if donors adopt formal evaluation as a key component in aid programs, there would still be difficulties in exercising external influence without undermining local accountability relationships (World Bank 2003).

These problems raise the need for a complementary approach of enhancing client power. For example, when possible, donors can encourage citizens to monitor projects financed by aid through report cards and public expenditure tracking surveys, as illustrated in the case study on Uganda below.

In all governments, resources earmarked for particular uses flow within legally defined institutional frameworks. Typically funds pass through several layers of government bureaucracy down to service facilities, which are charged with the responsibility of spending the funds. However, in developing countries, information on actual public spending at the frontline level or by program is seldom available. To remedy this problem, a so-called public expenditure tracking survey (PETS) was developed. A PETS is designed to follow the flow of resources through various strata of government to determine how much of the originally allocated resources reach each level. It is therefore a useful device for locating and quantifying political and bureaucratic capture, leakage of funds, and problems in the deployment of human and in-kind resources. It can also be used to evaluate impediments to the reverse flow of information needed to account for actual expenditures (Dehn, Reinikka, and Svensson 2003).

10.1.1 The Uganda Case

The first PETS was implemented in Uganda in the mid-1990s. The study was motivated by the observation that despite a substantial increase in public spending on education, the official reports showed no increase in primary enrollment. Specifically the hypothesis was that actual service delivery, proxied by primary enrollment, was worse than budgetary allocations implied because public funds were subject to capture (by local politicians and public officials) and did not reach the intended facilities (schools). To test this hypothesis, a survey was conducted of 250 randomly chosen primary schools. The survey collected five years of data on spending (including in-kind transfers), service outputs, and provider characteristics. The data were then linked to survey data from eighteen local governments (districts) and detailed disbursement data from three central government ministries (Reinikka and Svensson 2004).

The program in question—a capitation grant to cover primary schools' nonwage expenditures—is a fairly standard one in developing countries. Like many other spending programs in heavy-aid-dependent countries, it was funded to a great extent by donor funds. As part of an ongoing structural adjustment program, the World Bank was also involved in monitoring the program. Based on central government budget data, the program appeared to work well. Funds were disbursed by the ministry in charge on a regular basis, and a benefit incidence analysis carried out by the World Bank suggested that benefit incidence of public spending was neutral. However, as in many other spending programs in low-income countries, the situation on the ground was completely different from the official statistics (Reinikka and Svensson 2004).

Over the period 1991–1995, on average, only 13 percent of the total yearly capitation grant from the central government reached the schools. Eighty-seven percent either disappeared for private gain or was used to finance various political activities at the local level. A majority of schools received nothing. The picture looks slightly better when constraining the sample to the last year of the sample period. Still, only around 20 percent of the capitation grants from the central government were reaching the schools in 1995 (Reinikka and Svensson 2004).

The situation in Uganda in the mid-1990s illustrates two facts caused at least in part by the broken information (accountability) feedback loop. First, while funding the school grant program, the donor community had no idea (and had done little to find out) what impact it had: Did schools receive the funds and, if so, did this improve the learning environment? In fact, in this case, the main beneficiaries of the school grant program were local officials and politicians. As discussed in Ostrom et al. (2002), this lack of knowledge of the reality on the ground is not an exception. When donors or individual staff are not held accountable for performance, they will rationally focus their attention to other tasks. Second, the intended beneficiaries (parents) typically had no information about the school grant program—most probably did not even know about it— which made it easier for local officials and politicians to capture the funds.

The Uganda case also illustrates the power of impact evaluations in general and quantifying corruption in particular as a spark for reform. Hard evidence of corruption or capture is difficult for governments to simply brush aside, and in response to the high degree of local capture of the education fund, the central government reacted swiftly. Interestingly, the response was not the typical one: to improve the financial management system through increased monitoring by central government agencies. Instead, the central government decided to engage the citizenry. Led by the Ministries of Local Government and Finance, it began to publish data in the national newspapers on the monthly transfers of capitation grants to districts. Later, the Ministry of Education proposed extending the information campaign to all school communities. Primary schools (and district administration headquarters) were required to post notices on actual receipts of funds for all to see. In short, in this two-part campaign, information on entitlements transferred by the central government was made available through newspapers, while information on what each school actually received was posted at schools to inform parents.

In Reinikka and Svensson (2005a) we use a repeat PETS to assess the effects of the newspaper campaign. The raw data suggest a large improvement. In 2001 schools received an average of 80 percent of their annual entitlements, and the newspaper campaign can account for a large fraction of this improvement.[3]

The Uganda case also illustrates that interventions aimed at improving accountability in the public sector may be the best way, that is, the most cost-efficient way, to improve service delivery outcomes since social service delivery in developing countries is often plagued by inefficiencies and corruption. Specifically, both student enrollment and achievement increased substantially in schools that, due to the information campaign, managed to claim a higher share of their entitlements (Reinikka and Svensson 2005b).

10.1.2 The Tanzania Case

The Primary Education Development Plan (PEDP) was launched in 2002 in collaboration among the government of Tanzania, various bilateral donors, and the World Bank. The program consists of three parts: a capitation grant disbursed both in-kind (textbooks) and as a monetary grant, a development grant for investments, and a capacity grant.

A public expenditure tracking study on the PEDP was implemented in 2003–2004 (see Tungodden 2005 for details). In several respects, the findings were similar to the Uganda study. For example, just as in the Uganda case, the donor community lacked information about what impact the program had. Even more striking, the donor community was not aware that the program was run by three different ministries. The donor community was under the impression that only one of the ministries was running the program. As a result, the donors did not know how much money was being disbursed to the local administrations and if these funds actually reached the intended beneficiaries.

The results of the Tanzania PETS were alarming. First, it was unclear if all funds disbursed by the donors to finance the program had indeed been disbursed. Of the funds that had been disbursed, in one of the largest programs (the funding of school books), only around 20 percent reached the schools on average. Thus, just as in the Uganda case, the donors had little knowledge about the reality on the ground, and the intended beneficiaries had little knowledge about how the program was meant to work.

Also, the Tanzania case illustrates the power of impact evaluations, although the reaction here came from within one of the key donors. Specifically, when information about the project was discussed in the Norwegian news, the auditor general in Norway initiated an investigation on whether it was inappropriate of the Norwegian embassy to continue releasing money to the program despite information about leakage, corruption, and incomplete reporting.

10.2   Multiple Objectives and Tasks

Most donors have multiple objectives. The Swedish foreign aid agency, Sida, for example, while recently narrowing the list of main objectives to a general goal (equitable and sustainable global development), lists eight central areas for Swedish development cooperation: (1) human rights, (2) democracy and good governance, (3) gender equality, (4) sustainable use of natural resources and protection of environment, (5) economic growth, (6) social progress and security, (7) conflict management and security, and (8) global initiatives to protect the environment and combat contagious diseases. Since development is multidimensional, it is not surprising that the agencies working on development also have multiple objectives. The problem with multiple objectives is that they typically imply trade-offs, particularly in the short run. Donor agencies seldom make these trade-offs explicit, so individual managers are typically uncertain about what should be prioritized in a given situation.[4] Since it is not uncommon that managers in donor agencies shift positions at regular intervals, policy choices in a given sector or country typically shift over time, and long-term commitments become more difficult to stick to. Obviously the recipient country may act accordingly. Trying to meet short-run objectives becomes more important than reaching long-term goals. The broken information (accountability) feedback loop and the fact that in many donor organizations there are few mechanisms in place to ensure effective knowledge transfer when managers and staff change magnify the problem.

Officials in aid agencies also perform a multiplicity of tasks. While this is something that characterizes the job description in many public agencies, the broken information (accountability) feedback loop makes the incentive problem arising from the multiplicity of tasks more pronounced in donor agencies. When faced with multiple tasks that compete for their time, agents tend to focus on those that are more likely to satisfy their career concerns or require less effort. Tasks that are more easily monitorable by their supervisors (such as input activities like budget, procurement, and hiring of consultants) receive a disproportionate attention at the expense of less easily monitorable tasks (for example, effort exerted in actual implementation of a project). Thus, the disruption in the perfomance feedback loop, combined with the difficulties of measuring performance and the fact that career advancement often is unrelated to performance of past projects, results in a disproportionate focus on input activities and the expense of attention given to the quality of outputs, that is, the actual result of the aid program (Martens et al. 2002).

There is no easy way around this problem. First, with multiple objectives, it is more difficult to write or agree on output or performance contracts. This is particularly the case if some goals are more difficult to measure or operationalize than others. Second, even if this could be solved, such a contract requires that salaries or career concerns should be linked to performance of aid projects and programs—a type of payment schedule far from the traditional enumeration system of public officials in most donor countries.[5] Interventions that address the broken information (accountability) feedback loop, for example, by inserting an explicit evaluation function in foreign aid programs, could go some way in mitigating the problem.

10.3 The Budget Pressure Problem

Both donor and recipient have incentive systems which reward reaching a high volume of resource transfer, measured in relation to a predefined ceiling. . . . In many administrations, both bilateral and multilateral, the emphasis is on disbursements and country allocations. Non-disbursed amounts will be noted by executive boards or parliamentary committees and may result in reduced allocations for the next fiscal year. . . . Results are measured against volume figures, with no regards for the quality. . . . Besides, when the time has come to evaluate the actual outcome, most of those responsible for the project on both sides will have been transferred (Edgren 1996, 11—former chief economist of the Swedish aid agency).

Even in the case of a single task, there are incentive problems in the donor agency that tilt attention to committing and spending budgets rather than focusing on outcomes. In most donor organizations, it is common to separate allocation and disbursement decisions.[6] Typically the allocation process is centralized (in many countries, general guidelines and country allocations are set by the parliament), and the disbursement decision is decentralized (i.e., country or project specific). This setup also characterizes foreign aid at the project level. The planning and initiation of a project are typically coupled with a commitment of funds to that particular project. Disbursement of committed funds is a subsequent decision.

This institutional setup has resulted in a strong bias toward "always" disbursing committed funds to the ex ante designated recipient or project, regardless of the recipient government's performance or project performance and the conditions in other potential aid recipient countries (projects). Thus, resources are not shifted toward projects or countries where they can be more effectively used, and ex ante threats of not disbursing committed aid if the recipient fails to implement certain polices are not credible. The bias arises because the opportunity cost of a given aid budget (or a committed adjustment loan) for the disbursing donor agent is low.

Why is the opportunity cost low? Studies of bilateral donor organizations have emphasized that, in practice, "spending the budget" has become a key goal in itself (Paldam 1997, Edgren 1996), in large part due to the problem of multiple objectives and a broken information (accountability) feedback loop. Moreover, large unused resources are typically viewed as a sign that the country department or the specific project has a problem. Why else can it not disburse its funds? Since the allocation of the overall aid budget across country departments is partly determined by the disbursement history, a country department failing to disburse the committed funds will most likely receive a smaller allocation the following year.[7] The size of the budget in turn not only constrains the overall spending program of the country department, but also determines the status of the job (for general references to the theory of bureaucratic interests, see Wintrope 1997, Moe 1997, and Niskanen 1994). The same argument applies to project- or sector-specific aid.

Evaluations of the lending process within the World Bank have pointed toward similar incentives. Mosley, Harrington, and Toye (1995) argue that the World Bank's country loan officers are under intense pressure to meet country disbursement targets, notwithstanding how unpromising that government's subsequent implementation performance is. Apart from the maximization of the budget argument, they stress a coordination/free-rider problem; bearing in mind what other countries have gotten away with, bank staff know that it will not be financially productive to make an example of one particular recipient that defaults on conditions by refusing to disburse the committed funds. Moreover, the enforcement of conditionality might be in conflict with other goals of the bank, such as providing quick-disbursing finance so as to hinder a potential default on outstanding loans.[8]

Again donor incentives also influence how recipients behave. When assistance is given as conditional aid, it typically implies that the donors pay the recipient to do something it would otherwise not do. For this to be a credible contract, the donor agent must ex ante have incentives to halt disbursements if the conditions have not been met. However, if the true objective of the donor agent is to disburse the budget, not the actual performance of the aid project or program, such an aid contract will not be credible. That is, aid will be disbursed regardless of what actions the recipient takes. This in turn adversely influences the recipient incentives to take actions according to the specified contract ex ante.

The low opportunity cost of the committed funds hypothesis has a stark empirical implication: the disbursement decision should be independent of reform implementation. That is, the committed funds should be disbursed regardless of the recipients' actions. Svensson (2003) provides some preliminary evidence consistent with this hypothesis. Drawing on information from a recent study on the determinants of around 200 structural adjustment programs (Dollar and Svensson 2000), Svensson (2003) uses as a proxy variable of reform effort a binary variable reflecting the failure or success of World Bank–supported reform programs, as determined (ex post) by the Operations Evaluation Department (OED) of the World Bank. Using this variable has advantages and disadvantages. The advantage is that it provides a consistent measure of whether reform programs succeeded or failed. The disadvantage is that the measure of success is subjective.[9]

To assess whether the disbursement decisions depend on perceived reform outcome, Svensson (2003) uses a two-stage procedure. First, the probability of reform is estimated by means of a probit model (following Dollar and Svensson 2000). Second, the estimated probability is used as proxy for the perceived success of reform in explaining the difference between committed and disbursed funds. Formally, the two-step procedure can be stated as

$$\pi_i = \text{probit}(r_i = \beta_x \mathbf{x}_i + v_i) \tag{10.1}$$

$$sf_i = \gamma \hat{\pi}_i + \beta_z \mathbf{z}_i + \varepsilon_i, \tag{10.2}$$

where r_i is the binary reform proxy discussed above (reform); $\mathbf{x}_i$ is a vector of political determinants of reform (as identified in Dollar and Svensson 2000); sf_i is the share of committed funds disbursed during the reform period; $\hat{\pi}_i$ is the estimated probability of reform success; $\mathbf{z}_i$ is a vector of other controls influencing the disbursement decision; and v_i and ε_i are independent and identically distributed error terms.

Dollar and Svensson (2000) show that a small number of political economy variables can successfully predict the outcome of an adjustment program 75 percent of the time. Their results suggest that successful reform is associated with democratic government (demo) and political stability (stability). High degrees of ethnic fractionalization (ethnic) are bad for policy reform, and long-term incumbents (tenure) are not likely candidates for reform. The basic finding in Dollar and Svensson (2000) is replicated in table 10.1. To estimate the second-stage equation, Svensson (2003) assembles data on committed and disbursed

Table 10.1
Probit model of reform, 1980–1998

Dependent variable	c	demo	stability	ethnic	ethnic^2	tenure	tenure^2
reform	−.098	.585	−1.30	5.93	−6.51	−.089	.0033
	(.304)	(.224)	(.330)	(1.43)	(1.53)	(.043)	(.001)

Note: Standard errors in parenthesis. All variables except the constant (c) are significant at the 5 percent level. There were 220 observations (reform episodes). Predictability ($p > .05$) = .75. Log likelihood: −119.8.
Source: Svensson (2003).

funds. As additional controls in equation 10.2, Svensson includes the logarithm of initial gross domestic product (GDP) per capita (logGDPc) and the logarithm of initial population (logpop). Both variables have been shown to be highly correlated with aid flows (see, e.g., World Bank 1998). Mosley, Harrington, and Toye (1995) argue that an implicit goal of policy-based lending is to provide quick-disbursing finance so as to hinder potential default on outstanding loans. To control for this possibility, Svensson (2003) also adds the initial debt to GDP ratio (debt).

What happens with the committed funds when the recipient is perceived as failing to reform? The answer, depicted in table 10.2, is "very little." As is evident, there is no significant relationship between the share of committed funds disbursed and the estimated reform effort.[10] In fact, the estimated reform measure enters with the "wrong" sign, although close to zero. There is some evidence that smaller countries (measured by size of population) are more likely to receive committed funds and defensive lending; that is, countries with larger initial debt are less likely to experience cancellations of commitments, regardless of the reform outcome. Column 2b shows that the results are similar when considering only World Bank IDA lending.[11]

A possible objection to these results is that the dependent variable sft combines concessional and nonconcessional sources of financing. Column 2c depicts the results with the share of committed concessional funds disbursed as the dependent variable (i.e., bilateral ODA and concessional World Bank, that is, IDA, lending), sfc. The results are very similar to those reported in column 2a.

How can the donor agencies relax this pressure to disburse independent of the outcome of a project or program? One possible solution is to find ways to internalize the opportunity cost of aid at the disbursement stage. One way to achieve this is to pool projects and programs, that is, to partly centralize the disbursement decision. Thus, instead of committing a fixed amount of aid t to each recipient (or project) n ex ante and making aid conditional on reform or outcome, the donor links the allocation and disbursement decision by com-

Table 10.2
Disbursement decision, 1980–1995

	Equation (2a)	Equation (2b)	Equation (2c)
Dependent variable	*sft*	*sfwb*	*sfc*
constant	1.23***	.680***	1.94***
	(.154)	(.126)	(.255)
estimated reform	−.056	.065	−.088
	(.058)	(.045)	(.111)
logGDPc	−.010	−.003	−.065**
	(.013)	(.010)	(.027)
logpop	−.018**	.015**	−.038***
	(.008)	(.006)	(.012)
debt	.0004**	.0002*	.0003**
	(.0002)	(.0001)	(.0001)
Number	208	209	182
R^2	.12	.05	.17
SE regression	.141	.107	.208

Note: Ordinary least squares estimation with White-heteroskedasticity-consistent standard errors in parentheses. Estimated reform derived from table 10.1.
*** [**] (*) denote significance at the 1 [5] (10) percent levels.
Source: Svensson (2003).

mitting a larger amount (t^*n) to a group of recipients or projects, but where the actual amount disbursed to each individual country (or project) depends on its relative performance ex post. Linking the allocation and the disbursement decision has two important advantages as compared to the usual practices. First, it raises the opportunity cost of disbursing aid ex post, thereby giving the donor stronger incentives to use aid funds where they are most effective. Second, competition among recipients or project (in a sense, an aid tournament) allows the donor to make inferences about common shocks, which would otherwise conceal the recipients' choice of action. This enables the donor to give aid more efficiently. Both effects also raise the incentives for the recipient to exert effort (or implement reforms).

Two objections against such an institutional reform are worth stressing. First, it could be argued that competition between recipients introduces uncertainty about financial flows, which renders planning more difficult and makes fiscal spending too volatile. This may be true if making comparisons with how the aid system seems to work: commitments are always disbursed. However, this is not true if we compare it with the conditionality outcome as it is supposed to work. In fact, if the shocks facing the recipients are (highly) correlated, the uncertainties will be reduced by having the recipients compete in an aid tournament.

Second, it could be argued that the degree of reform implementation, or effort exerted by the recipient, depends on domestic political economy forces rather than on conditional aid. In fact, recent evidence suggests this to be the case (Burnside and Dollar 2000, Dollar and Svensson 2000). However, these studies analyze the impact of conditional aid (as it seems to work), not as it was meant to work. Therefore, one should not expect any significant correlation between aid flows and policy reform. More important, the institutional reform briefly discussed above deals with the incentive structure within the donor organization. Even if the degree of policy reform is solely determined by domestic political economy forces, that is, is independent of foreign assistance, linking the allocation and disbursement decisions will still be useful since this provides incentives for the donor to allocate or disburse aid to where it can be effective.

A question partly left unanswered is, Why is it that if linking of allocation and disbursement decisions improves outcome, the donor community does not explicitly link these decisions? One answer, of course, is that the potential cost of tournament-type aid schemes is perceived as being very high (for example, the cost related to the political risk of creating competition between countries or projects). However, the extent of competition among countries, and thus the potential cost, can be controlled by varying the share of aid disbursed through a tournament-type aid scheme. This also seems like a less important concern for project aid. A more plausible explanation is related to the change in the existing power structure within the donor agency–donor community implied by such a regime shift. In essence, the reform would reduce the discretionary power of many managers mainly in charge of the disbursement decisions. Moreover, by making the opportunity cost explicit in the decision process, the management would be required to make tougher choices. Recipient-specific interest groups (e.g., domestic firms, NGOs), and potentially the recipient government, may also oppose an institutional change that would imply aid flows conditional on performance rather than ex post unconditional disbursements.

10.4   Multiple Principals (Donors)

Foreign aid differs in yet another important way from domestically financed services: it is handled not by one but multiple agencies. When the donors are not fully coordinated, this can give rise to severe collective action problems. An interesting historical parallel is the success of the Marshall Plan (see Knack and Rahman 2004).

The relative success of the Marshall Plan has been attributed to the difference between the group of recipients. Unlike most recipients of foreign aid during the past decades, Western Europe had a huge advantage in putting aid to effective use. It had skilled labor, experienced managers and entrepreneurs, and reasonably efficient legal and financial institutions. The public administrations were also considered relatively competent. However, differences on the donor side may also have contributed to the great success of the Marshall Plan (Birdsall 1999). Marshall Plan recipients had to deal with only a single donor, in contrast to the large numbers of bilateral and multilateral donors and NGOs that are active in the foreign aid sector today. De Long and Eichengren (1993) further argue that the Marshall Plan assistance, "history's most successful structural adjustment program," was not disbursed in the form of a huge number of separate donor-managed projects in each recipient country. As Knack and Rahman (2004) note, aid success stories in Taiwan, Botswana, and Korea have also been attributed to the presence of a dominant donor (Brautigam 2000).

The median number of official donors in recipient countries in 2000 was twenty-three (Acharya, Fuzzo de Lima, and Moore 2003), and in the typical African recipient, aid is provided by "some thirty official donors in addition to several dozen international NGOs...through over thousand distinct projects and several hundred resident foreign experts" (van de Walle 2001, 58).

Why would the fact that multiple donors are involved with each recipient affect the efficiency in which aid is given and used? Aid involves a set of collective action problems. When there are multiple donors, each concerned partly with the development in the recipient country but also with domestic concerns, individual donors typically do not internalize the full costs of a foreign aid project, while at the same time they fully internalize the short-run benefits, or in some cases fully internalize the costs but not the social benefits. Specifically, one donor's action may, indirectly or directly, influence the efficiency of other donors' actions. This externality is typically not taken into account when a decision is made. The collective action problem may severely influence the efficiency of foreign aid and, more generally, the recipient's own financial ability and administrative capacity to govern.

The costs associated with a proliferation of donors can be grouped into three broad categories. The first is the increased transaction costs associated with numerous and diverse donor rules and procedures for managing foreign aid projects and programs (Berg 1993). The Tanzanian government, for example, has to prepare about 2,000 reports of different kinds to donors and receive more than 1,000 donor delegations each year (World Bank 2003). Duplications of analytical work such as poverty assessments, public expenditures reviews, and governance and investment client assessments are other examples of increased costs of implementation. Easterly (2003) notes that authors of these reports are frequently unaware of recent studies on the same topic in the same country funded by a different donor.

The second type of cost arises from the fact that in many cases, foreign aid projects are associated with large fixed costs and high returns to scale. If each donor works on its own individual projects, these returns to scale may go unexploited.

The third category is less direct in that it affects the recipient's financial ability and administrative capacity to govern (Knack and Rahman 2004). First, donors have tended to provide project aid—either working with individual line ministries or engaging providers under local governments and by directly funding frontline providers (schools and health clinics)—rather than budget support. Although this is slowly changing and budget support has its own limitations, this response, while officially a response to inadequate institutions and government capabilities in the recipient country, is also influenced by the fact that each individual donor fully internalizes the individual costs and benefits of a project but does not fully internalize the more diffuse notion of strengthening the recipient's own financial, budget, and service delivery systems as budget support is thought of doing.

Second, donors tend to support only capital spending (investments), expecting the recipient government to supply complementary inputs (staffing and maintenance). In this case, each individual donor in effect treats the budget for recurrent expenditures as common-pool resources (Brautigam 2000), producing a tragedy of commons in which roads are built but not repaired and schools and clinics are constructed but not staffed. Noting the widespread failure by recipient country governments to maintain infrastructure funded by foreign aid once construction is completed, donors have often reached the wrong conclusion about causes. Specifically, many observers have pointed to the lack of "ownership," not the failure to internalize the externality, that is, the reduced capacity to maintain other donor-funded projects if a new project is initiated. Advocates of financial sustainability emphasize the importance of local ownership of projects, and they promote interventions that require only start-up funding, which then can be maintained locally without external support (Kremer and Miguel 2004). When the real problem is the proliferation of donors, such a recommendation may only exaggerate the problem.[12]

Third, individual donors typically work with counterparts in the local bureaucracy and attract these local experts by paying salary supplements to the most talented local staff (Knack and Rahman 2004). Since the distinction between purely private consulting work for a donor and official work in the local bureaucracy is often blurred (Cohen and Wheeler 1997), this practice distorts incentives for civil servants to turn their attention away from their other responsibilities—even those with greater impact on development—and toward donor projects (Knack and Rahman 2004). This distortionary effect of donor behavior affects not only the division of effort for staff in the administration but also the overall allocation of talent within the recipient country. When high-level managers in the civil service can make ten times as much working directly for a donor, the most talented staff will leave the public sector to work for a donor (Knack and Rahman 2004). Similarly, in many African countries, working for a donor is much more profitable than most entrepreneurial endeavors. In short, the most talented people tend to work for donors rather in the civil service or in the private sector. Similar to the investment contra recurrent expenditures decision, donors, in deciding whether to hire the better-qualified civil servants or agents in the private sector, treat the government bureaucracy, or more generally the pool of talented people, as a common-pool resource. While the decision of an individual project manager of whom to hire may not have much effect on the recipient government's ability and administrative capacity to govern, when each individual donor manager acts in the same way, the aggregate effect may be large. The total effect may be even more detrimental, taking into account the incentive effects of the local staff working on donor projects. As the financial return of working for a donor is relatively much higher than other work, talented local staff have incentives to protect and extend aid projects from which they benefit, regardless of their merit (Knack and Rahman 2004). Performance contracts for local staff could be a way to partly overcome the latter problem.

Some cross-country evidence also suggests that the costs associated with a proliferation of donors can be substantial. Knack and Rahman (2004) show that a higher donor fragmentation (reflecting the presence of many donors with a small share of aid) is associated with a decline in bureaucratic quality. These results, however, should be interpreted as suggestive rather than providing causal evidence.

Should donors thus refrain from hiring local staff or ensure that they are paid according to what they make in their current occupations? The answer is most likely no. The resource injection from high donor-paid salaries potentially has a positive net impact on development, despite the adverse impact on the functioning of government (Knack and Rahman 2004). However, this also implies that the same benefits may be obtained without the negative effect on government's ability to implement and formulate their own policy.

The recent trend toward budget support is viewed by many as a mean of reducing transaction costs and providing both donors and recipients with incentives to focus on strengthening financial, budget, and public service delivery systems.

Institutional arrangements, such as designating a lead donor for the country or sector, as a way to get individual donors to internalize the full costs and benefits of a foreign aid project or program, would be a way forward. Efforts are underway to improve donor coordination on one aspect of this problem, although this may not be politically feasible. The efforts are to reduce transaction costs by harmonizing operational policies and procedures and establishing a Web site to disseminate information on completed and planned country work. An assessment of to what extent these initiatives have improved outcomes would be highly valuable.

10.5   The Foreign Aid Dilemma

The core problem facing the donor community is that it wants to assist poor countries to alleviate poverty. Poverty in turn is a function of both exogenous and structural features for which the recipient government can do little about, at least in the short run, and the recipient government's policy decisions. This simple fact has two stark implications.

First, good aid projects or programs typically are associated with high risk. The very reason that the recipient is in need of foreign aid is that its own institutions are weak, and this will affect the expected return to aid. Thus, to allocate aid only to recipients with well-functioning institutions and good policies typically is not optimal if poverty alleviation is the dominant criterion for foreign aid. However, because of the broken information (accountability) feedback loop, voters in the donor country face a moral hazard problem. Observing poor outcomes, they do not know to what extent this was a result of an ex ante good aid project or program with a risky return or poor design or implementation of the donor. Realizing this, the donor will tend to choose projects and programs that minimize the risk of bad publicity, not those that ex ante maximize the expected poverty alleviation.

Second, to the extent the recipient expects that the foreign aid is governed by poverty alleviation, the recipient may have little incentive to exert high effort (or channel its own resources) toward achieving this objective. It may very well be that interventions that would assist the poor are implicitly taxed if these interventions would result in less aid received in the future.[13] This "samaritan's dilemma" is made worse by moral hazard problems: the donor cannot perfectly distinguish if a poor outcome is the result of low effort (bad policies) or bad luck (Svensson 2000).

Over the past few years, several donors have argued for a shift in foreign aid practices. In part as a response to the incentive problems highlighted here and disappointment about the aggregate effects of foreign aid during the past four decades, the argument is that donors should try to harmonize their support around recipient systems (see, e.g., World Bank 2003). When the recipients have a well-functioning national development strategy, a budget process that can serve as a common framework, and institutions in place to hold both politicians and providers at least partly accountable for their actions, this recommendation makes a lot of sense. However, if foreign aid should also be primarily channeled to poor countries, there are few potential recipients that fulfill the necessary criteria. While this problem is sometimes swept under the rug, the World Bank, for example, explicitly argues that these conditions are not prerequisites for the shift in foreign aid policy. Even in their absence, harmonization and pooling of aid, typically as budget support, can offer significant benefits and reduce transaction costs (World Bank 2003). In short, the argument for an alternative way to give foreign aid is that it would reduce transaction costs but also shift the responsibility, and hence accountability, toward the recipient. This would build recipient capacity and create stronger incentives for the donors and time for monitoring and evaluating impacts and results.

The concern with such approach is the increased fiduciary risks of channeling untied funds for the recipient to use. Striking the right balance between when to pool and align their support around the recipient's system and when to basically continue with current practice while at the same time trying to minimize or at least reduce transaction costs is tricky. The political economy literature dealing with poor countries, and sub-Saharan Africa in particular, has pointed to severe and structural problems of accountability. In many African countries, power is concentrated in small elites interconnected by common schooling, marriage, friendships, shared ethnicities, or religion. Sustaining this power balance is costly, and public funds are fueling a system of patronage politics, where patrons give clients material rewards for their political loyalty and services (Reinikka and Svensson 2004). The patronage system takes different forms, including government actors' diverting public resources for their own campaigns and those of friends and family, and financing of local and private causes to neutralize voter dissatisfaction. The political parties must also supply patronage goods to their workers and members. In a rural setting, an important way of maintaining an effective political organization is through personal presence, which means a well-staffed institutional hierarchy all the way down to the village level. This model assumes substantial resources, and diversion of public resources is often the only source of funding available.

If the incentives to reform, including possibly political reforms, are too weak, channeling large, untied funds to the recipient may help the current elite to cement their position, at least in the short run. Such an outcome may be difficult to sell to the voters in the donor countries, and donors thus face a difficult pedagogic task of convincing voters in their countries that such a risk is worth taking. Promoting citizen voice is a complementary, but for donors probably the most difficult, strategy. Identifying what type of aid interventions can strengthen the relationship of accountability among politicians, service providers, and beneficiaries is probably the most important issue facing the donor community today. As the knowledge is limited and as traditional approaches to improve governance have produced weak results in most developing countries, experimentation and evaluation of new tools to enhance accountability should be high on the agenda among donors.

10.6 Conclusion

In this chapter I have highlighted some of the most important incentive constraints facing donors and recipients. Some of these incentive constraints, like multiple objectives, difficulties in measuring output or outcomes, and weak performance incentives, are problems most public agencies face, although they are often more pronounced in donor agencies. Others, like multiple agents (donors) and a weak or broken information and accountability feedback loop between beneficiaries (in the recipient country) and voters and politicians (in the donor country), are unique to the foreign aid sector. I have argued that the donors' incentives also influence the recipients' behavior and their ability to use aid productively.

This chapter is not a survey of the various incentive problems in foreign aid, and discussions of how to make foreign aid more effective need to take a much broader approach. Still, while many other factors influence how aid is disbursed and used, the incentive problems raised in this chapter are likely to be among the leading candidates for understanding donor (and recipient) behavior. Addressing these incentive constraints should therefore be high on the agenda when donors (and recipients) discuss ways to improve how aid works.

Notes

1. See Becker (1983) and Wittman (1995).

2. In Sweden an independent agency for the evaluation of foreign aid has been formed. However, domestic regional development concerns determined the location and budget for the new agency, raising concern about the political commitment to credible and independent evaluations of foreign aid.

3. Specifically, Reinikka and Svensson (2005a) show that public access to information can be a powerful deterrent to capture of funds at the local level. They show that head teachers in schools closer to a newspaper outlet are more knowledgeable of the rules governing the grant program and the timing of releases of funds by the central government. These schools also managed to claim a significantly larger part of their entitlement after the newspaper campaign was initiated.

4. The solution is not to define a very broad and general objective that encompasses almost everything. The problem goes deeper than that.

5. Ostrom et al. (2002) report that only 2 percent of the respondents interviewed at Sida indicated that promotions are based on the performance of the projects on which individuals have worked in the past.

6. This section draws from Svensson (2003).

7. Ostrom et al. (2002) provide empirical evidence of the budget pressure problem at Sida. For example, they note that in many country departments, as much as 40 percent of the year's disbursement takes place in the last two months of the budget cycle and that it is not uncommon that division chiefs come up with their own projects at the end of the budget year so as to increase the ability to disburse funds.

8. As discussed in Svensson (2003), the World Bank has a number of screening devices to counteract any pressure toward "irresponsible" lending. However, many conditions attached to bank loans are phrased in terms permitting a subjective assessment ("substantial progress," "satisfactory performance"), which facilitates the tranche release of committed funds.

9. See Svensson (2003) for details.

10. sfti is the share of the total funds committed that was actually disbursed during the reform period.

11. bi is the share of World Bank commitments disbursed during the reform period.

12. Ownership becomes an issue when donors fund projects that recipient governments are not interested in. If it is not a project that encourages a new approach through its demonstration effect or specifically designed as a one-time intervention, such an approach contradicts ownership and would not be sustainable (World Bank 2003).

13. An illustrative example is given in Fisher (2001) and quoted in Ostrom et al. (2002). Fisher tells of interviewing a Nuba rebel leader who visited an area in southern Sudan that had received considerable food aid from the United Nations. The rebel leader explains that although the people of the area are great farmers, they have not been farming because of the relief aid.

References

Acharya, A., A. Fuzzo de Lima, and M. Moore. 2003. *The Proliferators: Transactions Costs and the Value of Aid*. Institute of Development Studies. Working Paper 214, University of Sussex, U.K.

Alesina, A., and D. Dollar. 2000. "Who Gives Foreign Aid to Whom and Why?" *Journal of Economic Growth* 5:33–63.

Becker, G. 1983. "A Theory of Competition among Pressure Groups for Political Influence." *Quarterly Journal of Economics* 63:371–400.

Berg, E. 1993. *Rethinking Technical Cooperation: Reforms for Capacity Building in Africa*. New York: UNDP.

Brautigam, D. 2000. *Aid Dependence and Governance*. Stockholm: Almqvist & Wiksell.

Cohen, J. M., and J. R. Wheeler. 1997. "Training and Retention in African Public Sectors: Capacity-Building Lessons from Kenya." In Merilee S. Grindle, ed., *Getting Good Government: Capacity Building in the Public Sectors of Developing Countries*. Cambridge, Mass.: Harvard University Press.

Collier, P., and D. Dollar. 2002. "Aid Allocation and Poverty Reduction." *European Economic Review* 46:1475–1500.

Dehn, J., R. Reinikka, and J. Svensson. 2003. "Survey Tools for Assessing Performance in Service Delivery." In Luiz Pereira Da Silva and Francois Bourguignon, eds., *Evaluating the Poverty and Distributional Impact of Economic Policies*. Washington, D.C.: World Bank.

DeLong, J. B., and B. Eichengreen. 1993. "The Marshall Plan: History's Most Successful Structural Adjustment Program." In R. Dornbusch, W. Nolling, and R. Layard, eds., *Postwar Economic Reconstruction and Lessons for the East Today*. Cambridge, Mass.: MIT Press.

Dollar, D., and J. Svensson. 2000. "What Explains the Success or Failure of Structural Adjustment Programs?" *Economic Journal* 110 (October):894–917.

Easterly, W. 2003. "The Cartel of Good Intentions: The Problem of Bureaucracy in Foreign Aid." *Journal of Policy Reform* 5(4):1–28.

Edgren, G. 1996. "A Challenge to the Aid Relationship." In *Aid Dependency*. Stockholm: Swedish International Development Agency.

Eisensee, T., and D. Stromberg. 2005. "Does Disaster Relief Respond to Droughts and Floods in the Media?" Mimeo. Institute for International Economic Studies, Stockholm University.

Fisher, I. 2001. "Can International Relief Do More Harm Than Good?" *New York Times Magazine*, February 11, 72–77.

Knack, S., and A. Rahman. 2004. "Donor Fragmentation and Bureaucratic Quality in Aid Recipients." World Bank Policy Research Working Paper 3186, Washington, D.C.: World Bank.

Kremer, M., and E. Miguel. 2004. "The Illusion of Sustainability." NBER Working Paper 10324. Cambridge, Mass.: National Bureau of Economic Research.

Martens, B., U. Mummert, P. Murrell, and P. Seabright. 2002. *The Institutional Economics of Foreign Aid.* Cambridge: Cambridge University Press.

Moe, T. E. 1997. "The Positive Theory of Public Bureaucracy." In D. C. Mueller, ed., *Perspectives on Public Choice: A Handbook.* Cambridge: Cambridge University Press.

Mosley, P., J. Harrigan, and J. Toye. 1995. *Aid and Power*, vol. 1. 2nd edition. London: Routledge.

Niskanen, W. A. 1994. *Bureaucracy and Public Economics.* Oxford: Edward Elgar Publishing.

Ostrom, E., C. Gibson, S. Shivakumar, and K. Andersson. 2002. *Aid, Incentives, and Sustainability: An Institutional Analysis of Development Cooperation.* Stockholm: Sida.

Paldam, M. 1997. "The Micro Efficiency of Danish Development Aid." Working Paper 1997-13. Aarhus: Department of Economics, University of Aarhus.

Reinikka, R., and J. Svensson. 2004. "Local Capture: Evidence from a Central Government Transfer Program in Uganda." *Quarterly Journal of Economics* 119(2):679–705.

Reinikka, R., and J. Svensson. 2005a. "The Power of Information: Evidence from a Newspaper Campaign to Reduce Capture." Unpublished manuscript, Institute for International Economic Studies, Stockholm University.

Reinikka, R., and J. Svensson. 2005b. "Fighting Corruption to Improve Schooling: Evidence from a Newspaper Campaign in Uganda." *Journal of European Economic Association* 3(2–3):259–267.

Svensson, J. 2000. "When Is Foreign Aid Policy Credible? Aid Dependence and Conditionality." *Journal of Development Economics* 61(1):61–84.

Svensson, J. 2003. "Why Conditional Aid Doesn't Work and What Can Be Done About It?" *Journal of Development Economics* 70(2):381–402.

Tungodden, B. 2005. "Public Expenditure Tracking in Tanzania." Presentation given at Norad, Oslo, Norway.

Van de Walle, N. 2001. *African Economies and the Politics of Permanent Crisis.* Cambridge: Cambridge University Press.

Wintrope, R. 1997. "Modern Bureaucratic Theory." In D. C. Mueller, ed., *Perspectives on Public Choice: A Handbook.* Cambridge: Cambridge University Press.

Wittman, D. 1995. *The Myth of Democratic Failure: Why Political Institutions Are Efficient.* Chicago: University of Chicago Press.

World Bank. 2003. *World Development Report 2004: Making Services Work for Poor People.* Washington, D.C.: World Bank, and New York: Oxford University Press.

11 Donor Fragmentation

Stephen Knack and Aminur Rahman

Every few years, there are calls to launch a "new Marshall Plan," whether for Africa, Central America, or the former-Soviet bloc countries or to fight scourges such as HIV/AIDS. Most recently, Condoleezza Rice framed U.S. plans for spreading democracy in the Middle East in terms of a "new Marshall Plan."

Why is the Marshall Plan analogy so popular? Because advocates for grand new aid initiatives must go back all the way to the 1940s for an example that was widely acknowledged as a success. Performance of aid programs for less-developed nations in recent decades is generally considered to be abysmal, even by many aid industry advocates and practitioners. What accounts for the difference in performance?

Today's aid recipient nations are certainly different from Marshall Plan beneficiaries in important ways. Despite wartime death and destruction, Western Europe had skilled labor, experienced managers and entrepreneurs, and a history of reasonably effectivefinancial and judicial systems, and public administrations (Degnbol-Martinussen and Engberg-Pedersen 2003).

Donors are also different today. There are many, many more of them. Marshall Plan recipients had to deal with only a single donor, in contrast to the dozens of bilateral and multilateral agencies and hundreds of nongovernmental organizations (NGOs) in the aid business today. "The Marshall Plan worked because there was one donor, the United States, and the United States set up rules that ensured the Europeans would themselves take charge."[1] Marshall Plan aid was similar to a structural adjustment program (DeLong and Eichengreen 1993), but with conditions both fewer in number and more aligned with preferences of recipient governments than characterize many latter-day programs. Moreover, unlike much of today's aid, Marshall Plan loans were not disbursed in the form of hundreds of separate donor-managed projects in each recipient nation.

The success of aid programs in Taiwan, Botswana, and Korea is also commonly attributed in part to the presence of a single or dominant donor (Brautigam 2000, Azam, Devarajan and O'Connell 2002). In contrast, most recent recipients of large amounts of foreign aid interact with dozens of donors, each with projects in a large and increasing number of economic sectors (World Bank 2001). The UNDP resident representative in Lesotho in 1981 counted sixty-one donors financing 321 projects, in a country of only 1.4 million people (Morss 1984). In 2002, there were twenty-five bilateral and nineteen multilateral donors and about 350 international NGOs operating in Vietnam, accounting for over 8,000 development projects (Acharya, Fuzzo de Lima, and Moore 2003). In the typical African country, aid is provided by "some thirty official donors in addition to several dozen international NGOs... through over a thousand distinct projects and several hundred resident foreign experts" (van de Walle 2001, 58). Thousands of quarterly project reports are submitted to multiple oversight agencies. Hundreds of missions monitor and evaluate these projects and programs annually in many recipients, and each mission expects to meet with key government officials and to obtain comments from officials on its reports (van de Walle and Johnston 1996).[2]

Why should aid be more effective when delivered by a single (or dominant) donor? Where many donors, each responsible for only a small part of development assistance, operate, responsibility is diffused. Any single donor has little reputational stake in the success or failure of the recipient's development program (Belton 2003). From the perspective of a recipient country's welfare, incentives for any one donor to shirk on activities that maximize overall development in favor of activities that contribute to donor-specific goals strengthen as the number of donors increases.

Donors' multiple and conflicting objectives exacerbate this basic collective action problem. Donors are undoubtedly in most or all cases concerned with development of the recipient country, but must trade this objective off against other goals as well, such as commercial and security objectives. Aid agencies additionally have the objective of maximizing their budgets, requiring them to satisfy key domestic constituencies in parliament—requiring in turn that they sacrifice development objectives when those inevitably sometimes conflict with the need to maintain good relations with domestic aid contractors and advocacy groups. To build domestic support for large aid budgets, particularly in donor nations such as the United States where voters tend to be more skeptical of the value of foreign aid, the impact of aid programs must be visible, quantifiable, and directly attributable to the donor's activities. These requirements often can be met only at the expense of reducing the actual developmental benefits from aid programs.

Costs associated with a proliferation of donors can be grouped into two broad categories. Some costs are felt immediately, with the burden falling primarily on the projects or sectors in question. Tying aid to the employment of donor country contractors is a major example.[3] Also detracting from the value of aid are transactions costs associated with numerous and diverse donor rules and procedures for managing aid projects and programs, different languages, and fiscal calendars (see Berg 1993, UNDP 2003).[4]

The second category of costs is more insidious and long-lasting, involving donor practices that tend to undermine the quality of governance or retard the development of public sector capacity. A few examples of these practices are providing aid through projects rather than budget support, bypassing central government units (for example, by the use of project implementation units), relying on expatriates instead of subsidizing learning by doing by hiring local staff, and funding investment projects that in the aggregate imply unrealistically high recurrent expenditures in future years—so that roads are often built but not repaired and schools are built but not staffed (Brautigam 2000). Donors engage in these practices to increase the visibility of their efforts and the short-term appearance of success for their individual projects, at the expense of coherent policymaking and capacity building in the recipient country's public sector (World Bank 1998). It is well known in the aid business that however successful a project appears on its own terms, it will have little or no sustained impact in a poor sector-policy environment and where it is not integrated into other donor-funded or government projects (Easterly 2003, Kanbur and Sandler 1999). However, when there are numerous donors, any one of them would gain only a small share of the total benefits, in terms of project success, from devoting resources to improving administrative capacity in the country, and would be subsidizing the success mostly of other donors' projects.

Shifting this discussion from conceptual arguments and anecdotes toward systematic measurement and testing, the next section introduces measures of the degree of donor fragmentation in aid recipient countries. Using these measures, section 11.2 describes several pieces of cross-country evidence, suggesting that fragmentation may reduce quality of the public administration in aid recipients, distort public expenditure allocations, and impair progress on public budgetary management reform efforts.

11.1   Measuring Donor Fragmentation and Project Proliferation

Two data sources can be used for constructing useful measures of donor fragmentation and project proliferation. A breakdown of annual disbursements of official development assistance (ODA) by various bilateral and multilateral donor agencies, treating the various UN agencies as separate donors, is provided by the Organization for Economic Cooperation and Development (2004). From these data, an index of donor fragmentation can be calculated for each aid recipient country, for each year, by summing the squared shares of aid over all donor agencies and subtracting the resulting Herfindahl index from 1, to form an index for which higher values reflect greater fragmentation of aid.[5] Values for this index increase with the number of donors providing aid to the country and with greater equality of aid shares among donors, reflecting the absence of a dominant donor.

During the year 2000, among recipients of substantial amounts of aid, fragmentation averages about .7. Values were lowest for Jordan (.21) and Zimbabwe (.25). Many African countries had values above .9, including Mozambique (.91), Ethiopia (.92), Lesotho, and Cape Verde (.93).

Year-by-year changes in this fragmentation index, averaged over all countries, show an upward trend from 1975 onward (figure 11.1). This increase largely reflects an increase in the number of Development Assistance Committee (DAC) donors. For example, the European Bank for Reconstruction and Development (EBRD) was founded in 1991 to aid the transition economies in Eastern Europe and the former Soviet Union. Over time, some aid recipients such as Greece and Portugal became donors.[6]

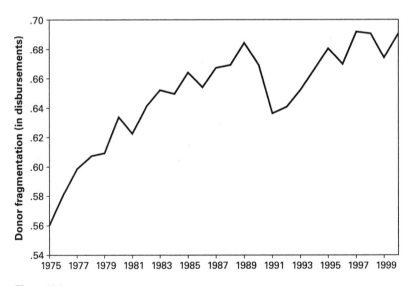

Figure 11.1
Trend in mean donor fragmentation

In addition to the DAC disbursements data, the Development Gateway's AiDA (accessible information on development activities) database is used to construct an alternative fragmentation index. This source contains records provided by the DAC and other sources on hundreds of thousands of investment projects and other activities financed by various donor agencies.[7] A count of projects sponsored by each donor can be made. From these counts, a fragmentation index is computed from donors' shares of projects. Fragmentation indexes were computed in two ways: first treating each agency or department as separate donors (e.g., the U.S. Agency for International Development and the U.S. Department of Agriculture), and second, treating each funding nation (e.g., the United States) or multilateral institution as a single donor. The mean for the first index is (by construction) somewhat higher, but the two indexes turn out to be nearly perfectly correlated. For this project-based fragmentation index for the post-1990 period, values range from .07 for Surinam to .90 for Niger and Mongolia, and .92 for Turkey.

The fragmentation indexes calculated from project counts in AiDA provide a somewhat different picture of donor fragmentation across countries than does the index calculated from DAC aid volumes. The latter, averaged for the 1990s, is correlated at only .44 with indexes based on projects with start dates in the 1990s. The two types of indexes are not directly comparable, however. First, the DAC data used include only ODA, while the AiDA database also includes some nonconcessional loans. Second, it is more difficult to pin down relevant dates for the projects data. About 60 percent of all activities included in AiDA lack project start and end dates. Indexes computed for any given subperiod, such as the post-1990 period, require dropping all projects without start dates. Particularly for years prior to 1987, such indexes will therefore be based on very incomplete project data.[8] Unlike the case using the DAC disbursements data, AiDA cannot be used to generate annual fragmentation values at all. However, it is likely that fragmentation is fairly stable across countries over time; for example, the fragmentation indexes for 1982 and 1997 based on DAC aid volumes are correlated at .87. An index based on all AiDA records (some dating to the late 1940s) is correlated with one based on activities with start dates of 1990 or later at .81.

Certain caveats apply equally to interpretation of both sets of fragmentation measures. Most notably, a donor's expenditure share or project count share will not always accurately reflect its level of involvement and influence on a recipient's development program. Both the DAC- and AiDA-based indexes measure only donors' "market shares." One donor may undertake its activities in ways that are less intrusive and less institutionally corrosive than another donor with a similar share of aid.

Table 11.1
Project counts: Start date of 1990 or later

India	3,013
South Africa	2,393
Tanzania	2,382
Mozambique	2,147
Bangladesh	1,972
Russia	1,911
Indonesia	1,909
Zimbabwe	1,867
Kenya	1,833
Ethiopia	1,762

Source: AiDA, 2007 (Development Gateway).

Fragmentation can be computed for different aid sectors, such as education, health, and water, because projects (in AiDA) and aid commitments (but not disbursements in the DAC data) are coded by sector. A high level of fragmentation overall is in principal consistent with donor specialization and hence low fragmentation in individual sectors. Mean levels of fragmentation in fact are somewhat, but not dramatically, lower within individual sectors. However, in countries where fragmentation overall is high, fragmentation within sectors also tends to be high.

The AiDA database can also be used to construct a project proliferation measure from the total count of projects recorded in a period (with or without adjusting for size of the recipient country), subject to the limitations noted above. Table 11.1 lists the ten countries with the largest number of projects with start dates after 1990.[9] Larger countries, unsurprisingly, tend to have more projects. The correlation between (log of) 1990 population and (the log of) projects is .62. Also not surprising, fragmented aid tends to be associated with project proliferation: the DAC-based and AiDA-based fragmentation indexes for the 1990s are each correlated at about .51 with (the log of) the number of projects with start dates of 1990 or later. This relationship remains very strong controlling for population.

11.2 Where Is Aid More Fragmented?

Table 11.2 reports mean levels of fragmentation and project counts (for 1990 and later) for various country groups. Donor fragmentation and project proliferation tend to be more extreme in low-income than in middle-income aid

Table 11.2
Fragmentation and proliferation by income and region groupings

	AiDA (agency)	AiDA (donor)	DAC	Projects (AiDA)
Low income	.79	.78	.80	606
Middle income	.68	.67	.68	325
Sub-Saharan Africa (45)	.79	.78	.80	606
East Europe/Central Asia (10)	.86	.85	.66	537
South Asia (6)	.81	.80	.85	809
Middle East/North Africa (8)	.80	.79	.75	242
Latin America/Caribbean (18)	.58	.57	.64	361
East Asia/Pacific (22)	.57	.56	.57	269

Note: Numbers in parentheses indicate number of countries represented.

recipients. By region, Latin America and East Asia/Pacific stand out for having lower rates of fragmentation. Both project counts and fragmentation measures are highest in South Asia; an obvious hypothesis is that this has something to do with the average size of countries and low average incomes in this region, which includes India, Bangladesh, and Pakistan.

Table 11.3 reports regressions of country-level fragmentation and project counts on aid/gross national income (GNI), per capita income, country size, and a set of regional dummies (with sub-Saharan Africa as the reference category). The partial effect of aid levels on the AiDA-based fragmentation variables is insignificant (equations 11.1 and 11.2 in table 11.3). Aid is actually negatively related to fragmentation averaged over 1990–2001 as measured by DAC disbursements (equation 11.3). As expected, aid is positively and significantly associated with project counts (equation 11.4).

Per capita income is significantly related only to the disbursements-based fragmentation measure, with higher incomes associated with lower fragmentation (equation 11.3). Some, but not all, fragmentation measures are positively and significantly associated with country size (equations 11.1 to 11.3). Other things (including aid/GNI) equal, larger countries have more projects (equation 11.4).

Even with the control variables, the same two regions—Latin America/ Caribbean and East Asia/Pacific—stand out for their lower rates of fragmentation. Latin America, however, has significantly more projects than otherwise predicted by country size and levels of aid and income (equation 11.4). East Europe/Central Asia stands out for its high fragmentation values (equations 11.1 and 11.2). The South Asia dummy is insignificant in every case: the high average rates of fragmentation and project proliferation for these countries in

Table 11.3
Correlates of donor fragmentation

	Equation 11.1	Equation 11.2	Equation 11.3	Equation 11.4
Dependent variable	AIDA (agency)	AIDA (donor)	DAC	Project count
Constant	14.60 (44.27)	12.87 (43.97)	201.71 (40.31)	−3.50 (1.52)
Aid/GNI	0.11 (0.12)	0.12 (0.12)	−0.20* (0.10)	0.02** (0.01)
Log GDP per capita, 1990	−0.85 (3.53)	−0.68 (3.52)	−13.21* (3.52)	0.04 (0.12)
Log population, 1990	4.48** (1.56)	4.46** (1.54)	−2.36 (1.31)	0.58** (0.06)
Latin America/Caribbean	−13.01* (6.36)	−12.84* (6.32)	1.26 (5.61)	0.59** (0.21)
East Europe/Central Asia	8.79** (3.28)	8.08* (3.29)	−7.04 (4.75)	−0.26 (0.27)
Middle East/North Africa	−0.66 (7.84)	−1.09 (7.45)	4.46 (5.59)	−0.66 (0.34)
South Asia	0.83 (5.83)	1.04 (5.83)	1.61 (2.60)	0.22 (0.18)
East Asia/Pacific	−12.70* (4.99)	−12.32* (4.94)	−12.27* (5.15)	0.19 (0.20)
R^2	.50	.49	.52	.69
SE of estimate	13.9	13.7	12.8	0.65
Mean, dependent variable	73.6	72.9	75.6	5.63

Note: Sample includes countries with aid's share of GDP exceeding 2 percent. Sample size is 89 in equations 11.1, 11.2, and 11.4 and 90 in equation 11.3. Robust standard errors are in parentheses. A * (**) indicates significance at .05 (.01) for two-tailed tests. Dependent variable is fragmentation index in equations 11.1 to 11.3 (multiplied by 100) and log of projects count in equation 11.4. Dependent variables are based on AiDA projects with start dates of 1990 or later in equations 11.1, 11.2, and 11.4 and for equation 11.3 is the average over 1990–2001 of annual values constructed from DAC disbursements data.

table 11.2 are explained very well in table 11.3 by their large populations and, to a lesser extent, their relatively low incomes and aid/GNI levels.

11.3   Does Fragmentation Matter? Cross-Country Evidence

11.3.1   Poaching

Pressures to show tangible results for their projects commonly lead donors to pay salary supplements to the more talented local staff. This practice distorts incentives for civil servants to turn their attention away from their other responsibilities—even those with greater impact on development—and toward the donor's projects (Arndt 2000).[10] It also creates incentives for officials to protect and extend aid projects from which they benefit, regardless of their merit, and to help perpetuate the practice of spending aid funds in the form of independent projects rather than in the form of coordinated, sector-wide programs or budget support (Acharya, Fuzzo de Lima, and Moore 2003). Examples of these problems are prevalent in Africa.

In Niger, for instance, the majority of NGOs appear to be operated by moonlighting civil servants and former cabinet ministers. In several cases, high-level officials left government to create NGOs in order to receive donor support that had once gone to the official's ministry (van de Walle 2001).

In Malawi and other southern African countries, doctors and nurses are leaving public hospitals and clinics in droves "to take more lucrative positions in foreign-funded HIV-AIDS programmes" (Burkhalter 2004). Fallon and da Silva (1994, 98) write of Mozambique: "Donor-driven competition for skilled personnel is creating immense problems for government. The preoccupation of many donors with ensuring that their local administrations have a full complement of qualified staff and with securing, at all costs, the manpower required to implement their projects is depriving the government of the capacity to effectively manage its administration."

In this spirit, Knack and Rahman (2007) write a simple formal model of donors' choices regarding whether to "poach" the better-qualified civil servants to run their own projects. A competent government bureaucracy increases the returns to all donor-run projects, but in maximizing the likelihood of success in their respective projects, each donor treats the government bureaucracy as a common-pool resource. Where there are fewer donors, each with a larger share of projects adversely affected by deteriorating administrative capacity, the external costs from poaching may be sufficiently high for an individual donor to influence its decision.

The model predicts that bureaucratic quality will erode more in recipients with greater donor fragmentation, that is, with a larger number of donors, each with a smaller share of the project market. Bureaucratic quality can be measured by a subjective index available for most countries from the International Country Risk Guide (ICRG) over the 1982–2001 period. Controlling for aid/GNI, the initial level of bureaucratic quality, the length of the interval over which ICRG data are available for each country, population growth, and per capita income growth, Knack and Rahman (2004) find that donor fragmentation is associated with larger declines (or smaller improvements) in bureaucratic quality. Figure 11.2 depicts the partial relationship between fragmentation (measured by the AiDA project counts) and changes in bureaucratic quality for sub-Saharan Africa, the most aid-intensive region.

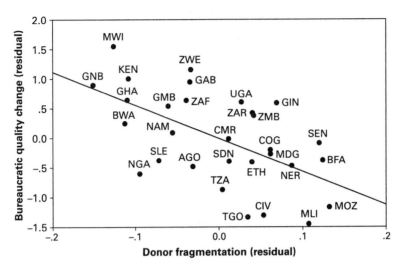

Figure 11.2
Donor fragmentation and bureaucratic quality (partial plot, sub-Saharan Africa). *Note*: AGO Angola, BFA Burkina Faso, BWA Botswana, CIV Ivory Coast, CMR Cameroon, COG Republic of Congo, ETH Ethiopia, GAB Gabon, GHA Ghana, GIN Guinea, GMB Gambia, GNB Guinea Bissan, KEN Kenya, MDG Madagascar, MLI Mali, MOZ Mozambique, MWI Malawi, NAM Namibia, NER Niger, NGA Nigeria, SDN Sudan, SEN Senegal, SLE Sierra Leone, TGO Togo, TZA Tanzania, UGA Uganda, ZAF South Africa, ZAR Democratic Republic of Congo, ZMB Zambia, ZWE Zimbabwe.

11.3.2   Public Expenditures

Greater donor fragmentation, implying reduced donor accountability, can increase the risk of uncontrolled investment spending. A donor with a small share of the aid market in a country is less likely to be concerned about whether future recurrent spending implied by today's investment projects is sustainable and about whether the projects are mutually consistent. It is more likely to bypass the central finance and planning ministries to work directly with line ministries or local governments, which view future budgets as a common resource pool (Brautigam 2000).

Unless aid is fully fungible, more aid can be expected to raise capital expenditure as a share of total public spending. The arguments here imply that this tendency should be stronger where donor fragmentation is greater. Equations 11.5 and 11.6 of table 11.4 test this proposition using cross-country annual data for the period 1975–2001. Control variables are per capita income, population, and a time trend.[11] In both random (equation 11.5) and fixed (equation 11.6) effects, estimation, the interaction term aid x fragmentation has a positive and significant coefficient, as expected. The mean value for capital expenditure in the sample is about 22 percent of central government spending. The insignif-

Table 11.4
Donor fragmentation and distortion of public expenditures

	Equation 11.5	Equation 11.6	Equation 11.7	Equation 11.8
Dependent variable	Capital expenditure as share of total		Social sector share of aid	
Method	Random effects	Fixed effects	Random effects	Fixed effects
Year	−0.396** (0.035)	−0.666** (0.056)	0.461** (0.037)	0.576** (0.082)
Log GDP per capita	3.796** (0.898)	10.809** (1.163)	−0.449 (0.512)	1.196 (1.502)
Log population	0.081 (0.586)	8.684** (2.014)	−0.854** (0.221)	−6.078* (3.009)
Aid/GNI (%)	−0.045 (0.153)	−0.040 (0.153)	−0.136** (0.039)	−0.165** (0.047)
Fragmentation (DAC)	0.368 (1.734)	0.211 (1.717)	4.583** (1.745)	0.620 (2.328)
Aid * fragmentation	0.393* (0.185)	0.368* (0.186)		
N	1338		2867	
R^2 (within group)	.13	.16	.05	.05
Mean, dependent variable	21.8		11.5	

Note: Dependent variable in equations 11.5 and 11.6 is capital expenditure as a percentage of all central government expenditure (capital and current). Dependent variable in equations 11.7 and 11.8 is health and education sector aid as a percentage of all official development assistance. * (**) Significance at .05 (.01) for two-tailed tests.

icant coefficient on the fragmentation term indicates that when aid/GNI is near 0, the level of fragmentation, unsurprisingly, has no significant effect on capital spending. This effect increases significantly as aid increases, however. For aid/GNI of about 10 percent (a threshold exceeded in about one-sixth of the observations), an increase in fragmentation from .4 to .9 is associated with an increase of about 2 percentage points to the capital spending share.

Fragmentation can also free donors to target their aid to more fashionable sectors that appeal to home-country constituencies. In recent years, education and health have emerged as the clear fashionable sectors among most donors, in part because of their more apparently direct impacts on poverty reduction, which has displaced growth and other objectives as the primary motive of aid for most major donors.[12]

Equations 11.7 and 11.8 test the hypothesis that the share of aid targeted to the fashionable sectors, education and health, is higher where fragmentation is higher. The hypothesis is supported in the random effects test in equation 11.7. Each .1 increment in fragmentation is associated with an increase of nearly 0.5

percentage points in the share of aid targeted at health and education. This is a fairly large effect, relative to the sample mean of 11.5 percent of aid going to those sectors. Fragmentation is not significant in the more demanding fixed effects test of equation 11.8, however, in which estimates are influenced only by within-country variation over time.

11.3.3   Public Budgetary Management Reform

Even where recipient countries are committed to public sector reform programs advocated by donors, fragmentation can impair progress if donors' ideas of best practice vary at all or if each donor is responsible for only a small part of the overall reform program. As part of the heavily indebted poor countries (HIPC) debt relief initiative, twenty-four HIPC countries agreed to participate in an IMF–World Bank assessment of their public budgetary systems. With assistance from these institutions, countries agreed to action plans to address various weaknesses that were diagnosed in these systems, with the goal of improving donors' confidence that debt relief would be used by recipient governments for worthy poverty-fighting purposes. In some countries, a very small number of donor agencies were involved in these budgetary reform efforts, while in other countries numerous donors provided technical support and advice. A systematic review found that, controlling for other factors, more progress was made on budgetary reform in countries with fewer donors "helping" them (IMF/World Bank, 2004).

11.4   Conclusion

If fragmentation has damaging consequences, why aren't more recipients more selective about the aid they accept? In principal, aid recipient governments can take measures to prevent the inefficiencies associated with competitive donor practices by refusing some aid[13] or attempting to reduce the number of donors active in the country (or, at least, the number active in each sector). In practice, principal-agent problems within the recipient country, between either a government with short time horizons and its citizens or between line ministries and central ministries (Wuyts 1996, van de Walle 2001), often reduce the government's ability or willingness to curtail donor activities that are destructive for the long-run development of the country overall. For political leaders without sufficiently lengthy time horizons, the short-term personal benefits of corruption and patronage practices often outweigh the long-term costs of subverting administrative capacity (and judicial systems); insecure leaders treat the rational-legal order essential for development as a common-pool resource (van de Walle 2001).

At least in some cases, therefore, poor people in recipient countries could be made better off if donors organized to undertake measures aimed at reducing fragmentation. This does not mean that a donor cartel should decide on a sole or lead donor to be matched with each recipient. Each recipient could be encouraged to select for itself a lead donor, at least for each sector receiving significant volumes of aid. Presumably recipients would normally choose as its lead donor the one with the most relevant expertise (based on region or sector) or which comes with the least commercial or security objective baggage.

Strong political forces and other interests work against further increases in donor specialization by country or by sector, however. Leaving certain problems or countries for other donors to deal with exposes an aid agency to charges by NGOs or the media that it is irresponsibly underfunding critically important development problems.[14] Arcane justifications based on efficiency benefits of donor harmonization and comparative advantage are unlikely to be an effective public relations response. Interagency funding could be a partial solution to this problem. Norway and Sweden both fund education and health sector programs in Ethiopia, but Sweden is arranging to channel its health funding through Norway, while Norway will channel its education funding through Sweden (Organization for Economic Cooperation and Development 2003).

Competition at the global level among aid agencies also tends to inhibit specialization; for example, the World Bank attempts to establish intellectual leadership in as many development themes and sectors as possible. Despite the ongoing high-level harmonization initiatives by aid agencies, there remain grounds for skepticism that political and bureaucratic exigencies of donors will be trumped by demands for improved aid effectiveness (van de Walle 2001, Organization for Economic Cooperation and Development 2003).

Publicizing various measures of donor performance, by the OECD DAC or by independent organizations such as the Center for Global Development, could marginally improve the incentives faced by aid agencies. Performance measures could include not only the share of aid that is tied but also measures of how each donor proliferates aid across recipients and sectors (Acharya, Fuzzo de Lima, and Moore 2003), the share of aid channeled through multilateral organizations, the number of missions and reports required relative to aid levels, and frequency of delegation to lead donors.

Acknowledgments

We are grateful to Virginia Yee for information on and assistance with the AiDA database and to Claudio Montenegro and Denis Nikitin for assistance with the OECD-DAC aid data. The conclusions of this work are not intended to represent the views of the World Bank, its executive directors, or the countries they represent.

Notes

1. From Nancy Birdsall's foreword to Kanbur and Sandler (1999).

2. Tanzania in desperation recently imposed a temporary moratorium on donor missions.

3. This practice is estimated to reduce aid's real value by between 15 and 30 percent (Jepma 1991).

4. In Vietnam, it took eighteen months and the involvement of 150 government workers to purchase five vehicles for a project funded by several donors with diverse procurement policies (World Bank 2003). In Bolivia, five donors sponsoring a single poverty survey each required separate financial and technical reporting, leading the government official assigned to the project to spend nearly as much of her time meeting these requirements as in undertaking the actual survey (World Bank 2003). "Country analytical work" (e.g., poverty assessments, public expenditure reviews, governance and investment climate assessments), sponsored by donors is often duplicated, with authors of these reports often unaware of each other's work (Organization for Economic Cooperation and Development 2003, Easterly 2003).

5. O'Connell and Saludo (2001) compute Herfindahl indexes of donor concentration for aid recipients in Africa in the 1990s using the DAC data.

6. The trend in this measure may overstate the increase in donor uncoordination, however, as budget support and the prevalence of sector-wide approaches have increased somewhat in recent years.

7. See http://aida.developmentgateway.org/AidaHome.do.

8. The number of projects with start dates for 1987 is five times the number for 1986, and the number doubled from 1994 to 1995, suggesting that some donors failed to report start dates until recently.

9. These counts of projects with post-1990 start dates were obtained from Virginia Yee of the Development Gateway in 2002. Updated counts presumably would be substantially higher.

10. In Malawi some years ago, thirty-three of the thirty-six permanent secretaries attended a week-long meeting to discuss the European Union's aid program. This level of participation was achieved by paying them the same daily rate as Brussels staff on mission. "The EU had bought the government for a week—doubtless on the agenda was the government's inability to implement its policies" (private correspondence with World Bank specialist on African civil services).

11. Results on fragmentation are unchanged when year dummies are substituted for the linear time trend variable.

12. The positive and significant coefficients on the time trend variable in equations 11.3 and 11.4 reflect the increased popularity of social sector aid over time among donors.

13. Uganda's stated policy is to decline all offers of stand-alone donor projects (Organization for Economic Cooperation and Development 2003). Eritrea also has a reputation for being highly selective about accepting aid offers.

14. For example, a *Washington Post* editorial ("Action for AIDS," December 6, 2003) complained that "Australia has not given a cent" to the Global Fund to Fight AIDS, Tuberculosis and Malaria.

References

Acharya, Arnab, Ana Fuzzo de Lima, and Mick Moore. 2006. "Proliferation and Fragmentation: Transactions Costs and the Value of Aid." *Journal of Development Studies* 42(1):1–21.

Arndt, Channing. 2000. "Technical Cooperation." In F. Tarp, ed., *Foreign Aid and Development: Lessons Learnt and Directions for the Future*. London: Routledge.

AiDA. 2007. "Accessible Information on Development Activities." Development Gateway ⟨http://aida.developmentgateway.org⟩. Accessed July 12, 2007.

Azam, Jean-Paul, Shantayanan Devarajan, and Stephen A. O'Connell. 2002. "Equilibrium Aid Dependence." Unpublished manuscript, University of Toulouse.

Belton, Rachel. 2003. "Rebuilding Iraq: No Job for a Coalition." *Washington Post*, April 28.

Brautigam, Deborah. 2000. *Aid Dependence and Governance*. Stockholm: Almqvist & Wiksell.

Burkhalter, Holly. 2004. "Misplaced Help in the AIDS Fight." *Washington Post*, May 25, A17.

Degnbol-Martinussen, John, and Poul Engberg-Pedersen. 2003. *Aid: Understanding International Development Cooperation*. London: Zed Books.

DeLong, J. Bradford, and Barry Eichengreen. 1993. "The Marshall Plan: History's Most Successful Structural Adjustment Program." In Rudiger Dornbusch, Wilhelm Nolling, and Richard Layard, eds., *Postwar Economic Reconstruction and Lessons for the East Today*. Cambridge, Mass.: MIT Press.

Easterly, William. 2003. "The Cartel of Good Intentions: The Problem of Bureaucracy in Foreign Aid." *Journal of Policy Reform* 5(4):1–28.

Fallon, Peter R., and Luiz A. Pereira da Silva. 1994. "Recognizing Labor Market Constraints: Government-Donor Competition for Manpower in Mozambique." In D. L. Lindauer and Barbara Nunberg, eds., *Rehabilitating Government: Pay and Employment Reform in Africa*. Washington, D.C.: World Bank.

IMF/World Bank. 2004. *Update on Implementation of Action Plans to Strengthen Capacity of HIPCS to Track Poverty-Reducing Public Spending*. Washington, D.C.: IMF/World Bank.

Jepma, Catrinus J. 1991. *The Tying of Aid*. Paris: OECD Development Center.

Kanbur, Ravi, and Todd Sandler. 1999. *The Future of Development Assistance: Common Pools and International Public Goods*. Washington, D.C.: Overseas Development Council.

Knack, Stephen, and Aminur Rahman. 2007. "Donor Fragmentation and Bureaucratic Quality in Aid Recipients." *Journal of Development Economics* 83(1):176–197.

Morss, Elliott R. 1984. "Institutional Destruction Resulting from Donor and Project Proliferation in Sub-Saharan African Countries." *World Development* 12(4):465–470.

Organization for Economic Cooperation and Development. 2003. *Harmonizing Donor Practices for Effective Aid Delivery*. Paris: OECD.

Organization for Economic Cooperation and Development. 2004. *Geographical Distribution of Financial Flows to Aid Recipients 1998–2002*. Paris: OECD Development Assistance Committee. CD-ROM.

O'Connell, Stephen A., and Charles C. Soludo. 2001. "Aid Intensity in Africa." *World Development* 29(9):1527–1552.

UNDP. 2003. *Human Development Report 2003*. New York: Oxford University Press.

Van de Walle, Nicolas. 2001. *African Economies and the Politics of Permanent Crisis*. Cambridge: Cambridge University Press.

Van de Walle, Nicolas, and Timothy Johnston. 1996. *Improving Aid to Africa*. ODC Policy Essay no. 21. Washington, D.C.: Overseas Development Council.

World Bank. 2003. "Cutting the Red Tape: Better Aid Delivery through Better Donor Coordination." Press release, February 21.

World Bank. 2001. *The Drive to Partnership: Aid Coordination and the World Bank*. Washington, D.C.: Operations Evaluation Department.

World Bank. 1998. *Assessing Aid: What Works, What Doesn't, and Why*. New York: Oxford University Press.

Wuyts, Marc. 1996. "Foreign Aid, Structural Adjustment, and Public Management: The Mozambican Experience." *Development and Change* 27:717–749.

IV THE IMF AND WORLD BANK

12 The IMF and Economic Development

James Raymond Vreeland

Originally intended to address short-term balance-of-payments problems, the lending activities of the International Monetary Fund (IMF) have gradually become enmeshed in the economic policies of the vast majority of developing countries around the world. More than 140 countries have entered into about one thousand separate arrangements with the IMF, arrangements commonly called IMF programs. Many programs have lasted two, three, and even four years, and most of them have been arranged consecutively. Haiti, for example, was participating in IMF arrangements during thirty-six of the past fifty years. Argentina participated during twenty-nine years, Pakistan during twenty-eight years, and even East Asian Tiger South Korea participated during twenty-two years. Cumulatively, IMF programs have affected the lives of billions of people. The primary goal of these economic programs has become economic growth.

When a country borrows from the IMF, the borrowing government is usually required to adopt economic policies intended to improve its country's economic situation. These policies typically entail fiscal austerity, tight monetary policy, and sometimes currency devaluation. Such an economic program presumably addresses the balance-of-payments shortfall that led the country to the IMF in the first place and sets the stage for economic prosperity.

Evidence of program effectiveness with respect to economic growth is, however, murky at best. From an anecdotal point of view, there have been both spectacular successes and failures. Yet economic growth depends on many factors besides the presence of an IMF program, making it difficult to discern what effect, if any, is due to the program. Many evaluations of these programs have thus been statistical. By drawing on the wealth of data generated from over fifty years of IMF programs, researchers attempt to control for other factors that affect economic growth to isolate the IMF effect.

Some studies have found a positive effect, such as Killick, Malik and Manuel (1992), Conway (1994),[1] and Dicks-Mireaux, Mecagni, and Schadler (2000).

Other studies report a positive but statistically insignificant effect, among them, Reichman and Stillson (1978) and Schadler (1995). Still others report no discernable effect of IMF programs on economic growth: Connors (1979), Gylfason (1987), and Pastor (1987a, 1987b). And some studies report a negative, although statistically insignificant, effect on economic growth (e.g., Khan and Knight 1981). My own research shows that the effects of IMF programs on growth are negative and statistically significant (Przeworski and Vreeland 2000, Vreeland 2003).

Why do we find such contradictory results across the board? Evaluating the effects of IMF programs is not straightforward. The circumstances of countries that participate in these programs differ systematically from the circumstances of countries that do not. Governments turn to the IMF when economic conditions are bad. There may be other factors, perhaps even factors that are difficult or impossible to observe, that are also systematically related to IMF participation. To evaluate the effectiveness of IMF programs, one must be able to identify what part of the outcome is due to the circumstances that lead countries to enter into IMF programs and what part is due to the IMF programs.

Various statistical techniques have been applied to disentangle the effects of nonrandom selection and the actual effects of IMF programs. The estimated effect of IMF programs depends on the statistical technique that is employed. For example, Goldstein and Montiel (1986) found a negative effect when comparing growth before programs to growth after programs, but they detected a positive effect when they compared the experience of countries participating in IMF programs to a control group. They found a negative effect again, however, when they employed a simulation technique called generalized evaluation. Khan (1990) also employed the generalized evaluation estimator and found a similar negative effect in the short run but with an improving long-run effect.

This chapter presents a method to evaluate the effects of IMF programs that accounts for both observable and unobserved factors that influence why governments participate in IMF programs. Most studies ignore selection effects from unobserved factors that might drive why countries enter into IMF programs and persevere throughout them. Yet unobserved factors may confound the effects of selection and the inherent effects of IMF programs. Consider political will as an example.

When a country fails to persevere in a program, the IMF often claims that the government lacks the "political will" to continue. Graham Bird, one of the most prominent IMF scholars, observes, "The IMF has frequently blamed the poor record of the programs that it supports on a lack of 'political will' to carry them through" (1998, 90). Note that by blaming a lack of political will when programs fall apart, one implies that countries persevering throughout a program do have political will. Despite constant references to a failure of political will, however, the IMF is notoriously bad at defining exactly what the term means (see Bird 1998 for a discussion; also see Nelson 1990). Humphreys (1999) indicates that it is related to a government's timing of program implementation. Bird (1998) conjectures that it may have something to do with the government's commitment to the program. Perhaps IMF officials are referring to the competence of the government and its advisers, or to the government's reputation, or its publicly unobserved negotiation posture with international creditors. Alternatively, it may refer to other, as yet unnamed, factors. The bottom line is that there is some factor that observers close to IMF programs—the IMF officials themselves—claim systematically determines both participation in programs (perseverance) and their outcomes (program success).

This has important implications for the evaluation of the effects of IMF programs. Suppose the IMF continues signing arrangements only with countries that have high levels of political will. If political will also affects economic growth, then one will overstate the effectiveness of IMF programs if one fails to control for this unobserved determinant of participation and performance. Simply that we do not observe all factors affecting selection and performance does not imply that we should ignore them.

How can we account for unobserved factors in statistical analyses of IMF effectiveness? This chapter addresses this question in technical detail, but the intuition is presented here. Two steps are involved in the statistical analysis. First is the selection question—why governments participate in IMF programs. Next is the economic growth question—what effect IMF programs have on growth. Nonrandom selection is addressed by adjusting for the degree of correlation between the determinants of the selection question and the economic growth question. Unobserved factors, like a government's political will, are addressed by looking at the correlations of the error terms associated with the selection question and the economic growth question. Using this technique, I find that IMF programs hurt economic growth: the typical effect is negative.

This disturbing finding begs at least two questions: Why do IMF programs hurt growth? and Why do governments participate in programs that hurt growth? My answer is controversial. I argue that governments use the IMF as political leverage to implement policies that protect elite interests. These policies, which are bad for economic growth, place the burden of economic problems on labor and the poor, exacerbating income inequality.

This chapter proceeds as follows. After presenting a brief background of the IMF, it addresses the questions of why governments turn to the IMF and with what effects. The chapter then discusses how IMF programs may negatively affect growth and suggests different policy implications from various interpretations of the finding.

12.1   The IMF

In 1944, forty-four countries signed the Bretton Woods Agreements founding the International Bank for Reconstruction and Development (now commonly known as the World Bank) and the IMF. Both institutions were intended to promote national prosperity, but the World Bank was originally assigned the task of promoting economic growth, while the IMF was assigned that of promoting international financial stability. Over time, however, the IMF became more and more concerned with growth.

The founders of the IMF believed that an international lender could prevent the beggar-thy-neighbor policies, such as trade barriers and competitive currency devaluations, which led to the Great Depression. Countries facing temporary shortfalls in foreign currency reserves due to the normal course of trading could turn to the IMF for a loan. This would facilitate trade and obviate the closing of borders to trade in the face of a balance-of-payments deficit. Members of the IMF would hold a given amount of currency (based on the member's economic size and involvement in international trade) on reserve at the IMF. The IMF could lend this currency to specific members to ensure them against the risk of international trade.

The problem, as with any other form of insurance, is that this may reduce the incentives of governments to avoid balance-of-payments crises in the first place. To mitigate this form of moral hazard, the IMF may attach policy conditions to its loans. A member can obtain small loans of up to 25 percent of its subscription to the IMF—or "quota"—with no conditions attached. If a government needs to draw more than the somewhat arbitrary 25 percent, however, it is assumed that the country has bad policies, and the IMF imposes "conditionality"—required policy conditions in return for continued installments of the line of credit.[2]

Early on, the policy conditions attached to IMF loans were merely intended to correct balance-of-payments problems, but the IMF had also been given the mandate to promote national prosperity. Over time, the IMF has become more concerned with promoting economic development with program conditions. A concern for growth was always present to a degree, but certain events pushed the IMF to become more focused on development.

At first, IMF lending programs were intended to last only about eighteen months. Currency would "stand by" during the course of the arrangement and would be available as long as governments complied with the prescribed conditions. The first Standby Arrangement was concluded in 1952. IMF officials recognized that some countries would require more than temporary programs. In 1974, they developed the Extended Fund Facility (EFF), where programs would last up to four years.

In the early 1970s, the world abandoned the Bretton Woods system where currency was ultimately backed up by actual gold held on reserve. Governments then had less need for IMF lending for the strict purpose of maintaining exchange rates. The IMF faced a crisis of purpose but began to focus on lending for the purpose of promoting development, and became deeply involved in the development strategies of its clients.[3]

In the 1980s, after the Latin American debt crisis, the IMF began to promote structural adjustment through conditionality. Fixing the economic problems of the developing world was no longer viewed as merely a question of stabilization. Rather, the fundamental structure and management of the economy was now seen to be at fault. In the long run, stabilization was a futile task as long as the underlying problems in the economy remained. The IMF opened the Structural Adjustment Facility (SAF) in 1986 and then, for particularly poor countries, the Enhanced Structural Adjustment Facility (ESAF) in 1987, which provided concessional interest rate loans as opposed to the market rate loans available through the three other facilities.[4]

By 1990, the head of the IMF, Managing Director Michel Camdessus, announced, "Our primary objective is growth.... It is toward growth that our programs and their conditionality are aimed" (IMF Survey 1990, 235).

In the aftermath of the East Asian financial crisis, the IMF reemphasized its focus on economic growth, renaming the ESAF the Poverty Reduction and Growth Facility (PRGF), which is designed to allow more input in policy conditions from the government of the country in question, to promote greater "ownership" of programs and emphasize the importance of government accountability.

This shift in emphasis toward ownership is indicative of the politics behind why governments have chosen to enter into IMF programs. Historically, some governments, it has been noted by the IMF, have not "owned" their IMF economic program; the program was imposed by the IMF and accepted by the government only because of a desperate need for a loan. But this is not always the case. Domestically, there are winners and losers from the policy changes supported by the IMF. Winners may actually seek out the IMF as an ally to promote policy change. The official stance of the IMF is not to interfere in the domestic politics of program countries, but IMF policy conditions obviously have a domestic impact. As the following section shows, IMF conditionality has been used by governments to push through unpopular policies. IMF economic programs are inherently political.

12.2 Why Governments Enter into IMF Programs and with What Effects

Emphasis on country ownership of IMF programs acknowledges that governments may not necessarily agree with the policy conditions that the IMF requires in return for a loan. Of course, if a government is strongly enough opposed, it may choose not to enter into an arrangement with the IMF, even if it has a desperate need for a loan of foreign currency. Such was the case of President Nyerere in the early 1980s. As reported in the *New York Times* on December 20, 1979, Nyerere announced in the context of IMF negotiations, "People who think Tanzania will change her cherished policies of socialism because of the current economic difficulties are wasting their time." Sometimes governments choose not to participate in IMF programs even though they need a loan.

Most developing countries, however, do participate in IMF programs when they face an economic crisis, and standard economic explanations of why governments turn to the IMF are supported by statistical evidence. Bird (1996) reports that there is consensus regarding low development, low foreign reserves, an overvalued exchange rate, and low gross domestic product (GDP) growth as determinants of IMF program participation. High debt is also associated with arrangements (Santaella 1996, Knight and Santaella 1997, Conway 1994). A country's need for an IMF loan is a good predictor of IMF program participation.

Economic variables do not always predict arrangements, however, and some key variables are surprisingly poor predictors. The IMF Articles of Agreement stipulate that member countries are entitled to take out loans from the IMF provided "the member represents that it has a need to make the purchase because of its balance of payments or its reserve position or developments in its reserves." Yet Knight and Santaella (1997), Conway (1994), and Edwards and Santaella (1993) do not find that the balance of payments matters in determining selection into IMF programs. In my own research, I have never found the current account, which measures credits minus the debits of goods, services, income, and current transfers, to be a robustly significant predictor of IMF programs. Sometimes the key to understanding IMF participation is as much political as economic.

Governments may actually want conditions imposed—for domestic political reasons—when they turn to the IMF. Many have argued that a reform-oriented executive can use IMF arrangements to push through unpopular policies (Spaventa 1983, Vaubel 1986, Remmer 1986, Putnam 1988, Edwards and Santaella 1993, Dixit 1996). Drazen (2006) provides a mechanism. He shows that when a government faces domestic opposition to economic reform, the presence of an IMF loan can help the government persuade actors in a position to block reforms to approve them, lest they forgo the next installment of the IMF loan. In my work, I note that failing to comply with IMF programs has other costs in addition to not receiving the loan installment, since creditors and investors follow signals from the IMF.

How does an IMF arrangement help an executive push through unpopular policies? Unlike other international agreements, executives enter into IMF arrangements unilaterally. The approval of veto players, such as the legislature in a presidential system or a coalition partner in a parliamentary system, may be required for policy change, but their approval is not required for the executive to enter into an IMF arrangement (Gold 1970). IMF arrangements are spelled out in a letter of intent written by IMF staff and government officials and formally sent from the country's executive branch—recognized by the IMF as the country's "proper authority"—to the IMF managing director. The managing director subsequently brings it before the IMF executive board for approval. Once the board approves the letter of intent, the country is under an IMF program. The approval of veto players is bypassed.

After the government executive has entered into an IMF arrangement, failure to enact policy change becomes more costly, because rejection of reform is not merely a rejection of the executive but also a rejection of the IMF. Rejecting the IMF is costly to all domestic actors, including veto players: the IMF may restrict access to loans, it may preclude debt rescheduling with creditors that require an IMF arrangement to be in good standing, and it may result in decreased investment if investors take cues from the IMF.[5] These increased costs may lead veto players to approve of policy changes that they otherwise would have opposed.

Such a strategy is available to executives in different types of regimes, democracies and dictatorships alike, and the best way to test how often governments use this strategy would be to get inside their heads and measure their true preferences. This, of course, is impossible, as true preferences or political will are unobserved. But there are other observable implications of this strategy that one can test.

Using the IMF to help push through unpopular policy is most likely to be pursued when there is greater institutional resistance to policy change. I follow Tsebelis (1995), who argues that policy stability (or resistance to change) is a function of the number of veto players in a political system. Executives facing more veto players are more likely to face opposition to their policies and are therefore more likely to find useful the outside pressure of the IMF to push through their agenda. As the number of veto players increases, governments should be more likely to participate in IMF programs, all else being equal.

When there is too much resistance to change, however, even the outside pressure of the IMF may not be enough. Executives hindered by a system with many checks and balances may require the most assistance to push through unpopular reforms, but they are also the least able to commit to large policy shifts. The IMF prefers to enter into arrangements with countries that can bring about the most reform, so they may be more likely to enter into arrangements with countries with lower numbers of veto players. As Putnam (1988, 449) explains, "diplomats representing an entrenched dictatorship are less able than representatives of a democracy to claim credibly that domestic pressures preclude some disadvantageous deal."

Because countries with fewer veto players are less constrained, they have the ability to agree to greater reform and may be preferred by the IMF. So my argument is not that the IMF has an intrinsic preference for dictatorships, or any other political system with a low number of veto players. The IMF actually has had a reputation for not paying attention to politics or political regimes (Polak 1991, Tanzi 1989, Denoon 1986). Rather, the IMF has a preference for countries that promise a high degree of economic reform. Countries with fewer veto players, on average, will be able to accept a greater degree of policy change, so the IMF may prefer to enter into arrangements with them. Countries with a high number of veto players are unable to make the same commitments. Because the IMF faces a budget constraint,[6] it may prefer to sign arrangements with countries that commit to the most reform and thus tend to avoid countries with many veto players.

The arguments about the effect of the number of veto players should hold only on average. The actual determinant of the desire for conditions to be imposed is not something we can directly measure. Yet this discussion highlights that in addition to controlling for standard economic determinants of participation in IMF programs, it is also important to account for the systematic effects that political institutions may have. I hypothesize that as the number of veto players in a political system increases, the probability that a government will seek out the political pressure of the IMF increases, but the probability that the IMF will actually want to enter into an arrangements with such a government decreases.

12.3 The Statistical Model

The fact that some governments seek out IMF conditionality has important implications for evaluating the effectiveness of IMF programs. Suppose that governments that seek out IMF assistance are also more likely to experience economic growth. If one fails to account for this, one may mistakenly attribute the effects of this "political will" to the IMF program. Yet, the true intentions of governments are not something we can easily observe, much less code systematically for data analysis.

How can we account for such unobserved factors in an analysis of IMF program effectiveness? The intuition is straightforward: participation and performance are modeled statistically; to the extent that the error terms from these estimations are correlated, unobserved factors driving one process are associated with those driving the other process. Once such a correlation is detected, one can correct for selection bias. The technical details follow, but those readers who prefer can skim these details, skipping ahead to section 12.4, on results.[7]

Suppose that the government (G) and the IMF (F) want an IMF arrangement when the values of their underlying decision functions are positive. Let these decision functions, subscripted i for each country and t for each year, be

$$d_{i,t}^{G*} = \gamma' \mathbf{x}_{i,t-1}^{G} + \kappa' \mathbf{x}_{i,t-1}^{G} d_{i,t-1} + v_{i,t}^{G}, \tag{12.1}$$

and

$$d_{i,t}^{F*} = \mu' \mathbf{x}_{i,t-1}^{F} + \eta' \mathbf{x}_{i,t-1}^{F} d_{i,t-1} + v_{i,t}^{F}, \tag{12.2}$$

where $\mathbf{x}_{i,t-1}^{G}$ is the vector of variables that determine the decision of the government, and $\mathbf{x}_{i,t-1}^{F}$ is the vector of variables that determine the decision of the IMF. Unobserved factors are captured by $v_{i,t}^{G}$ and $v_{i,t}^{F}$, which are assumed to be uncorrelated to one another[8] and distributed according to the standard normal distribution. Note that $d_{i,t-1}$ is a dummy variable indicating whether country i was participating at time $t - 1$. Thus, the effects of $\mathbf{x}_{i,t-1}^{G}$ for the government to enter into an IMF arrangement are captured by γ, and the effects of $\mathbf{x}_{i,t-1}^{G}$ for the government to continue participating in an IMF arrangement are captured by $\gamma + \kappa$. Similarly, the effects of $\mathbf{x}_{i,t-1}^{F}$ for the IMF to enter into an arrangement are captured by μ, and the effects of $\mathbf{x}_{i,t-1}^{F}$ for the IMF to continue an arrangement are captured by $\mu + \eta$.

Participation in IMF programs $(d_{i,t} = 1)$ can thus be estimated as

$$\Pr(d_{i,t} = 1 \mid \mathbf{x}_{i,t-1}^{G}, \mathbf{x}_{i,t-1}^{F}, d_{i,t-1})$$

$$= \Phi(\gamma' \mathbf{x}_{i,t-1}^{G} + \kappa' \mathbf{x}_{i,t-1}^{G} d_{i,t-1}) \Phi(\mu' \mathbf{x}_{i,t-1}^{F} + \eta' \mathbf{x}_{i,t-1}^{F} d_{i,t-1}), \tag{12.3}$$

where $\Phi(\cdot)$ represents the cumulative distribution function of the standard normal distribution. One caveat of the bivariate approach is that $\mathbf{x}^{G}$ cannot include exactly the same set variables as $\mathbf{x}^{F}$, or the model will not be identified. One must therefore have prior beliefs about the variables that matter to the executive and those that matter to the IMF. At least one of these variables must not be in common between the two actors. The variable I use to distinguish the IMF is the overall balance-of-payments deficit weighted by the economic size of a country. I use this variable because the mandate of the IMF includes maintaining global financial stability. The IMF may give special attention to countries with large balance-of-payments problems in absolute terms, while governments care about the relative size of a foreign exchange crisis.

This, then, describes a statistical model of the dynamics of participation in IMF programs.

Now consider economic growth. Suppose the underlying production function is $Y = AK^{\alpha}L^{\beta}$, where Y is output, A represents the current level of technology, K is stock of capital, L is the size of the labor force, α captures the efficiency of capital, and β the efficiency of labor, with $\alpha + \beta = 1$. A statistical model of growth is thus

$$\frac{\dot{Y}_{i,t}}{Y_{i,t}} = \frac{\dot{A}}{A} + \alpha \frac{\dot{K}_{i,t}}{K_{i,t}} + \beta \frac{\dot{L}_{i,t}}{L_{i,t}} + e_{i,t},$$

where overdot $(\cdot)$ denotes "change in," and $e_{i,t}$ captures the effects of any unobserved factors.

When countries participate in IMF programs (indicated by the subscript 1 in the following equation), their expected rate of growth can be described as

$$E\left(\frac{\dot{Y}_{i,t}}{Y_{i,t_1}}\right) = \frac{\dot{A}}{A_1} + \alpha_1 \frac{\dot{K}_{i,t}}{K_{i,t}} + \beta_1 \frac{\dot{L}_{i,t}}{L_{i,t}} + E(e_{1,i,t} \mid d^{G^*} > 0, d^{F^*} > 0), \tag{12.4}$$

where $E(e_{1,i,t} \mid d^{G^*} > 0, d^{F^*} > 0)$ is the conditional expectation of $e_{1,i,t}$, given that the country is participating. Recall that d^{G^*} and d^{F^*} are the decisions of the government and the IMF to participate in IMF programs from equations 12.1 and 12.2. Following from equations 12.1 to 12.3, this term can be estimated as $E(e_{1,i,t} \mid d^{G^*} > 0, d^{F^*} > 0) = \theta_1^G \lambda_{1,i,t}^G + \theta_1^F \lambda_{1,i,t}^F$, where the λ's are simply hazard rates, measuring the marginal probability of misclassifying an observation given the probability of observing it in one state or the other:

$$\lambda_{1,i,t}^G = E(v_{i,t}^G \mid d_{i,t}^{G^*} > 0) = \frac{\phi[(\gamma + \kappa)'x_{i,t-1}^G]}{\Phi[(\gamma + \kappa)'x_{i,t-1}^G]}$$

and

$$\lambda_{1,i,t}^F = E(v_{i,t}^F \mid d_{i,t}^{F^*} > 0) = \frac{\phi[(\mu + \eta)'x_{i,t-1}^F]}{\Phi[(\mu + \eta)'x_{i,t-1}^F]}.$$

The θ coefficients are straightforward regression coefficients and can thus be described as:

$$\theta_1^G = \frac{\text{cov}(e_{1,i,t}, v_{i,t}^G)}{\text{var}(e_{1,i,t})} \quad \text{and} \quad \theta_1^F = \frac{\text{cov}(e_{1,i,t}, v_{i,t}^F)}{\text{var}(e_{1,i,t})}.$$

It is easy to see from these coefficients why controlling for selection only on observed variables does not correct for selection on unobserved factors, and indeed can even increase selection bias. Including additional observed variables can decrease the variance of the error term, $\text{var}(e_{1,i,t})$, but may not decrease its covariance with the errors from selection, $\text{cov}(e_{1,i,t}, v_{i,t}^G)$ and $\text{cov}(e_{1,i,t}, v_{i,t}^F)$. The impact of the omitted θ coefficients could thus be exacerbated.

The corresponding expected growth when the government and the IMF do not want an arrangement (subscripted 0) is[9]

$$E\left(\frac{\dot{Y}_{i,t}}{Y_{i,t_0}}\right) = \frac{\dot{A}}{A_0} + \alpha_0 \frac{\dot{K}_{i,t}}{K_{i,t}} + \beta_0 \frac{\dot{L}_{i,t}}{L_{i,t}} + \theta_0^G \lambda_{0,i,t}^G + \theta_0^F \lambda_{0,i,t}^F.$$

12.4 Results

I employ the above statistical model to estimate the effect of IMF programs on growth. The data are in country-year format covering seventy-nine countries from 1976 to 1990. The panel is unbalanced due to missing data on both political and economic variables, so the total number of observations is 879. Larger samples with many different specifications are available in Vreeland (2003). The results presented here are used to demonstrate some empirical support for the political story of IMF participation presented above and to show how selection processes can be incorporated in an estimation of economic growth. The particular findings on growth presented here are strongly negative. Other samples and specifications reported in Vreeland (2003) produce findings that are weaker, but all come to the same qualitative conclusion: IMF programs lower economic growth.

I begin with the selection stage. The economic variables I use to estimate the decision of the government to participate are foreign reserves in terms of monthly imports, fiscal budget balance as a percentage of GDP, debt service as a percentage of GNP, and investment (private and public) as a percentage of GDP. I also include a variable measuring the number of veto players. For presidential systems, this variable is the sum of the following: 1 for the executive, 1 if multiple parties are legal and compete in executive elections, and 1 for each legislative chamber. For parliamentary systems, this variable is the sum of

1 for the prime minister and the number of parties in the coalition. Dictatorships have a score of 1.[10]

For the IMF, in addition to controlling for the absolute size of a country's balance of payments, I include the number of other countries participating. I expect this variable to proxy a budget constraint and have a negative effect. Also included is the veto player's measure for the IMF, although I expect it to have a negative effect here.

Complete descriptions of these variables, along with several other model specifications where different variables are included for the government and the IMF, are available in Vreeland (2003). I present just this one specification to demonstrate how the IMF program selection process can be accounted for when estimating the effects on economic growth.[11] Results are presented in table 12.1.

The results indicate that predicting why countries enter into IMF programs is more straightforward than why they continue. Governments with low foreign reserves, large budget deficits, high debt service, and low investment are more likely to enter into IMF programs. By and large, these variables have the same effects on the decision to continue participation, but the effects are not statistically significant. As predicted, governments are also more likely to participate in IMF programs when there are more veto players in the political system.

The IMF is more likely to enter into and continue arrangements with countries with a large balance-of-payments deficit. They are less likely to sign with an additional country when many other countries are already participating (or conversely, they are more likely to sign with a country when few others are participating). Again, as predicted, the IMF is more likely to sign arrangements with countries that have few veto players. This may be driven in part by a de facto preference for dictatorships, which can have only one veto player by definition. Historically, "the IMF has rarely met a dictatorship that it didn't like" (Bandow 1992, 26). Other work confirms the IMF preference for dictatorships (Przeworski and Vreeland 2000).

Note the importance of the economic variables. The effects of foreign reserves, debt service, and investment indicate that the need for an IMF loan is a strong predictor of IMF arrangements. Governments typically turn to the IMF because they need a loan of foreign exchange. What is surprising is that even after one controls for these economic factors, domestic political institutions also play a role. Governments may also turn to the IMF when they want specific IMF conditions to be imposed on them. They may require international political assistance to push policy change past veto players. When there are too many veto players in the political system, however, not enough change

Table 12.1
Effect of the number of veto players

	Variable	Decision to enter	Decision to remain
Government	Constant	−0.01 (0.43)	2.06** (0.85)
	Reserves	−2.23** (0.84)	−1.53 (1.41)
	Budget balance	−0.48** (0.20)	0.59 (0.46)
	Debt service	1.57** (0.57)	0.96 (1.71)
	Investment	−7.30** (2.38)	6.30 (5.65)
	Log(Number of veto players)	0.81** (0.38)	−0.61 (0.73)
IMF	Constant	1.71* (0.94)	0.79* (0.45)
	BOP × Size	−1.21** (0.43)	−0.29 (0.20)
	Number Under	−0.43** (0.18)	0.12 (0.11)
	Log(Number of veto players)	−0.88** (0.36)	−0.08 (0.24)

Number of observations: 879
Correctly predicted: 79%
Log-likelihood function: −307.75
Restricted log likelihood: −608.41
Chi squared: 601.32

Note: Standard errors in parentheses. All variables are lagged one year.
*Significance at the 90 percent level. **Significance at the 95 percent level.

is possible to win IMF approval. Hence, there is a combined nonlinear effect: increasing the number of veto players first increases the probability of IMF participation and then decreases the probability.

Many other political factors may also influence participation in IMF programs that are difficult to measure, particularly in a large n setting. The IMF has noted level of political will, for example, as an influence on whether a country will persevere through programs. The domestic level of trust in government may also determine whether governments will continue programs or whether they will face too much domestic unrest to continue. These unobserved factors may also have an impact on economic growth. Many have argued the trust can reduce transaction costs and contribute to economic growth (see Dasgupta 1988; Coleman 1988, 1990; Putnam 1993; Hardin 1993; Fukuyama 1995;

Table 12.2
Growth regression by participation status

	Not Under		Under		Variable Mean
	Biased	Selection	Biased	Selection	
Constant	−0.23	0.06	−0.36	−2.54	1.00
	(0.24)	(0.44)	(0.18)	(0.57)	
Capital stock growth	0.43**	0.43**	0.49	0.49**	4.20
	(0.02)	(0.02)	(0.02)	(0.02)	
Labor force growth	0.57**	0.57**	0.51	0.51**	2.73
	(0.02)	(0.02)	(0.02)	(0.02)	
λ^G		0.23		2.27	−0.32
		(0.34)		(2.36)	
λ^F		0.18		10.61**	−0.27
		(0.39)		(2.77)	
Number of observations	459	459	420	420	
D-W	1.91	1.91	1.70	1.71	
Adjusted R^2	0.54	0.54	0.69	0.70	

Selection-biased estimated effect of IMF programs: −0.05
Selection-corrected estimated effect of IMF programs: −2.52

Note: Standard errors are in parentheses.

Levi 1998). Political will may translate into a stronger negotiation posture with creditors and the respect of investors, or these governments may be advised by the most prestigious and trusted economists. If unobserved factors drive both selection and performance, they should be accounted for when estimating the effects of IMF programs.

Thus, the estimates from table 12.1 are employed to correct for selection bias in the analysis of economic growth in table 12.2. Table 12.2 presents four sets of results: growth estimated using observations of countries under and not under IMF programs without correcting for selection bias and growth estimated using observations of countries under and not under programs, including the correction for selection bias, as described in the statistical model above. The specification presented here is barebones, including just capital stock growth and labor force growth, but several other specifications are discussed at length in Vreeland (2003). For the selection-corrected specifications, the hazard rates described above are included. Note the strong selection effect indicated by the positive significant coefficient for λ_1^F, the hazard rate for countries participating in IMF programs. This indicates a strong correlation between unobserved factors driving the IMF decision to continue arrangements with a country and the unobserved factors that drive growth. Perhaps the IMF cuts off countries that are performing poorly.

The overall estimated effect of IMF programs using this specification is −2.52 percent per year. Tests indicate that this finding is statistically significant. This indicates that countries participating in IMF programs had output growth reduced by more than 2 percent each year they participated. However, this particularly high estimate may be due to this specific sample, which is limited because of missing observations on the economic and political variables. Using a larger sample, I have found the effect to be much smaller, −0.67, but still a statistically significant negative effect. The difference between the results could be due to omitted variable bias in the larger sample, since several statistically significant variables with missing data are not used in the selection stage. Or the difference could be due to the sample bias.[12] Either way, these analyses rule out the story that IMF programs improve growth or have benign effects in the short run. Furthermore, in my analyses of long-run growth, I have found no evidence of a positive trend (Przeworski and Vreeland 2000, Vreeland 2003).

Recent studies broadly confirm what is presented here. Hutchison and Noy (2003) use a general evaluation estimator, which essentially controls for selection on observed variables, and find a negative effect of IMF programs on growth, though the result is driven almost entirely by the Latin American experience with IMF programs. Barro and Lee (2005) use an instrumental variables approach to control for selection bias and find a nonsignificant negative effect of IMF programs on economic growth in the short run and a significant negative effect in the long run. Dreher (2006) also uses an instrumental variables approach to account for nonrandom selection and finds a negative effect of IMF programs on economic growth.

12.5   Discussion

I argue above that some governments seek out IMF programs to help push through unpopular policies. The growth results beg the question: Why do governments seek to push through programs that hurt growth? The ostensible goals of IMF programs are to promote economic stability and growth, yet for nearly twenty years, every study has found that IMF programs have no effect on economic growth (Reichmann and Stillson 1978; Pastor 1987a, 1987b; Killick 1995). Recent studies such as this one even show that the immediate impact on growth is negative. Regarding economic stability, Bird (1996) contends, "While IMF-backed packages seem to nudge countries toward better overall balance-of-payments performance, their impact is rather muted" (502). If IMF programs do not consistently improve growth or stability, what effects do they have that would lead executives to enter into them?

Perhaps governments care about income distribution. Pastor found that "the single most consistent effect the IMF seems to have is the redistribution of income away from workers" (1987a, 89). Garuda (2000) confirmed this finding, showing that typically income inequality is exacerbated for most countries participating in IMF programs. In other research (Vreeland 2002a, 2003), I have found that even if IMF programs have overall contractionary effects, the favorable shift in income toward some groups is large enough to mitigate lower growth. The income of the owners of capital can actually increase in the short run.

Hence, this study depicts the following picture of participation in IMF programs: governments enter into IMF programs under bad economic circumstances. Their choice is not usually between good and bad economic performance, but between bad performance on their own—without the IMF—or worse performance under a program sponsored by the IMF. Why would governments agree to programs that hurt economic growth? The reason is that by bringing in the IMF, governments gain political leverage, via conditionality, to help push through unpopular policies. For some constituencies, these policies dampen the effects of bad economic performance by redistributing income upward and thus rewarding elites. If the distributional consequences are strong enough, key groups can be made better off even though growth is hurt. But IMF programs doubly hurt the less well-off in society: total output growth is lowered, and income is shifted away from them.

If the most consistent effect that IMF programs have is on the distribution of resources in a society, it should not be surprising to find that political institutions play a role in the decisions of governments to bring in the IMF. Some groups stand to gain by pushing through the policies supported by the IMF, while others stand to lose. When there are more veto players, there is greater potential that at least one of them will represent the potential losers. The evidence presented in this chapter suggests that where there are more of these potential opponents with veto power, a government is more likely to bring in the IMF. Executives find IMF conditionality useful where institutional resistance to policy change is high.

This finding adds impetus to the debate over reform of IMF conditionality. Some argue, for example, that seeking out and assisting reform-oriented governments should become the explicit policy of the IMF (Dollar and Svensson 2000). This would essentially make my argument—that governments enter into IMF programs to force their own reform agendas—the explicit policy of the IMF. Instead of "making" reformers, the IMF should look for reformers and extend financial and political assistance to them.

Others might argue that this approach will exacerbate problems already present in the imposition of IMF programs by increasing the animosity of groups within a country that are left out. If governments use IMF programs as leverage to push through policies that increase income inequality, labor and the poor have grounds for concern. This does not mean that without IMF programs, governments would not or should not undertake reform, but as Remmer (1986, 7) argues, "The politics of stabilization are likely to be rather different where an outside villain [the IMF] cannot be identified so readily."

This point of view supports a recent IMF staff suggestion that "subject to the guidance of the authorities, the Fund staff can ... play a role ... by holding substantive discussions with other groups, including other ministries, trade unions, industry representatives, and local non-governmental organizations, especially at a stage at which the design of the program is still under consideration" (IMF 2001, 42). The goal of such meetings is to "help groups within the country to participate meaningfully in the process" (42). In terms of this chapter, this suggestion would have veto players included in the initial negotiations of an IMF arrangement instead of bypassing them at that stage.

Regardless of the direction that the IMF takes, it should make explicit the role it plays in domestic politics. Historically, the IMF has shied away from domestic issues, claiming it should not get involved. Yet the moment it demands that deficits be cut and interest rates raised, the IMF has entered into domestic politics. Its influence can be used as leverage to push through policies that favor some at the expense of others.

What is still unknown, however, is exactly what policies IMF programs help governments to push through. Consider the observation of Joseph Stiglitz (2000, 551), Nobel Prize laureate and former chief economist at the World Bank: "There is ... a process of self-selection of reforms: the ruling elite has taken advantage of the reform process and the asymmetries of information—both between themselves and the citizenry and between the international aid community and themselves—to push those reforms that would benefit them." From the work in this chapter, it is not obvious that the policies pursued by governments under IMF programs are in fact the policies that have been prescribed by the IMF. What is at stake here is the question of compliance.[13]

Like most of the other studies evaluating the effects of IMF programs, this one has employed a simple dummy variable for IMF program participation, coded 1 when countries participate and 0 when they do not. What does 1 really indicate? Participation in an IMF program entails two broad components: the loan and the conditions attached to the loan. Without a measure of compliance with IMF programs, it is difficult to interpret exactly how the IMF affects growth. This has important implications on the debate over the reform of the IMF.

Consider the critique from the political economy left: the negative effect of the IMF on economic growth could be due to the austere economic policies the Fund imposes. Rather than allow governments to prime the pump during an economic crisis, the IMF attacks excess demand by encouraging governments to cut public spending, raise taxes, place a ceiling on credit creation, raise interest rates, and perhaps devalue currency. All of these policies may curtail economic growth, which may exacerbate the economic problems that led to the economic crisis in the first place.

Note that this critique assumes that governments actually comply with IMF programs. Yet this may not be the case. This opens the door to the political economy right critique: the problem with IMF programs is not the policy conditions but the loans. The policy conditions are the correct ones. If a country has gotten itself into a balance-of-payments or excessive debt problem, demand should indeed be curtailed by bringing about fiscal responsibility. But because governments do not comply with all of the policy conditions, IMF programs do not help make the necessary adjustments. They may engage in only partially completed economic reform programs because of income distribution issues. In some cases, economic reform may not be forthcoming at all. Most important, according to this line of thinking, the IMF loans that governments receive act as a subsidy for the bad policies that got them into the crisis in the first place. The mechanism by which IMF programs hurt economic growth may be through the IMF loan itself.

Neither the far left nor the far right paints a complete picture, but both have valid points, and there is no way to settle this debate with a dummy variable. What may be required is careful analysis of the impact of the actual policies prescribed by the IMF and the degree of compliance with them.

Researchers in universities and at the IMF have long grappled with the question of compliance, and it is no accident that most have focused on the simple dummy variable to measure IMF participation. The study of compliance with IMF programs was originally fraught with difficulties because—until the aftermath of the East Asian financial crisis of the late 1990s—the details of most IMF programs were confidential. To get around this obstacle, researchers employed various proxies for compliance, but they are not fully satisfactory.

It is interesting to note that recent studies by Dreher (2006) and Hutchison and Noy (2003) incorporating a proxy for compliance show that compliance does not mitigate the negative impact of IMF programs on growth. These are important studies suggesting that IMF conditions may be at fault for the poor economic performance of IMF program countries. Yet this research invokes the percentage of the IMF loan that was released to the country as a proxy for compliance. This may be the best proxy yet available, but it is somewhat problematic. Stone (2002) shows that the degree of punishment by the IMF may be a function of international political forces rather than strictly compliance: countries favored by the United States can get out of punishment easier than other countries. The influence of the United States over the implementation of IMF programs is also supported by the work of Thacker (1999) and Broz and Hawes (2006). So some countries may get larger use of the IMF loan than they deserve. Stone finds that at least with respect to postcommunist eastern European countries, once one controls for the likelihood of punishment by the IMF, its programs reduce inflation, at least in countries where the threat of IMF punishment is credible. Mercer-Blackman and Unigovskaya (2000) use an IMF internal database of the number of conditions imposed versus the number of conditions completed as a different proxy for compliance. They find a positive relationship between their index of compliance and economic growth, although they note that this may simply be because the countries experienced growth for exogenous reasons and found it easier to implement the IMF-prescribed polices.

Stone's (2002) work reveals that IMF decisions are not entirely objective with respect to economic variables and that international politics may also play a role. So we may not be able to rely on IMF assessments of compliance as an actual measure of whether countries followed the policies initially prescribed.

To settle the debate, it would be nice to have some experimental evidence. Field experimentation would be a powerful method for drawing inferences about the effect of IMF programs. If treatment and control groups were randomly assigned, we could more readily compare the two groups. Any difference between the outcomes of the two groups would be due to the treatment. The advantage of an experimental design is that even rudimentary data analysis would reveal the effect of IMF programs and their policies.

Of course, IMF officials would object to such experimentation. Advocates of experimental approaches acknowledge that policymakers may be willing to engage in experimental design only if they are indifferent between alternative approaches. The decision makers at the IMF do not, of course, believe they operate according to arbitrary rules. They are trained economists who have a canon of theories with which they approach the world. If there were some arbitrary rule of thumb not based on theory, however, perhaps there would be room for experimentation. Green and Gerber (2002) suggest that policymakers are likely to be willing to engage in experimental design when they are indifferent between different ways of proceeding. If decision rules are arbitrary, policymakers may be willing to experiment. "In such cases," they argue, "decision makers may as well randomize... since they could then derive some useful information about the consequences of their actions."

This begs the question: Does the IMF follow any obviously arbitrary decision rule where there is room for experimental design? Indeed it does. Recall that each member contributes a specified sum of currency held on deposit at the IMF called a "quota." A member can obtain small loans up to 25 percent of its quota with no conditions attached. If a government needs to draw on more than 25 percent, however, it is assumed that the country has bad policies, and the IMF imposes conditionality. There is no obvious reason, however, that 25 percent is the appropriate cut-off between what constitutes bad luck and bad policy. The decision rule is arbitrary.

Given that this 25 percent rule is arbitrary, it is instructive to imagine what one could learn from experimenting with it. Suppose the IMF could randomly assign all countries in the world into two groups: a control group, which would maintain the 25 percent rule, and an experimental group, where the 25 percent rule would be relaxed to some higher level. The IMF would continue to operate as usual, providing small loans whenever requested and large loans subject to conditionality. All that would change is that "small" and "large" would be defined differently for the two groups.

What would we learn from such an experiment? If IMF conditions hurt growth, the group of countries required to submit to conditions under the strict 25 percent rule of thumb would have lower growth than the experimental group because the experimental group would receive conditions less often. If the IMF conditions prescribed are good for growth, the group required to submit to conditions under the strict 25 percent rule would have higher average growth than the experimental group. If conditionality has no effect, the average rates of growth between the two groups would be about the same.

This thought experiment highlights a sad situation: assuming conditionality has an effect on growth, millions—even billions—of people might suffer under this experiment. Some lucky countries would be assigned the decision rule that produces better results. But unlucky countries would be assigned to the group that produces worse results. The unlucky group would suffer lower rates of economic growth, which could result in a plethora of negative outcomes associated with lower income: lower standards of living, less stable democracy, more civil unrest, less education, more wars, more children dying. The detrimental consequences of policies that hurt economic growth should not be understated. The particularly sad part is that we do not know which group would be the lucky one.

This kind of experimentation would probably meet with political resistance. Governments might object to being randomly assigned to one group or the other, even though, a priori, it is unknown which group would fare better. So this experiment might not be feasible. Perhaps, however, there are other creative and less politically sensitive experiments that can be designed to help shed light on the ways in which IMF loans and IMF conditions affect economic growth.

In the meantime, the best way to proceed is to take advantage of newly available data on the details of IMF conditions. Since the late 1990s and the East Asian financial crisis, the IMF has placed increased emphasis on the importance of transparency. It has been argued that the dissemination of regular and accurate information lowers transaction costs and increases investor confidence. Governments have thus been encouraged to make economic data more readily available. In this vein, the IMF has also made available more information about its operations. Formerly, the details of an IMF program were made publicly available only at the behest of governments. Technically governments still have the right to keep letters of intent private, but the IMF encourages them to be made public and even posts recent letters of intent on its Web site. This makes it possible to directly study compliance with the commitments that governments make through IMF arrangements.

Even with the ability to observe the details of IMF arrangements, however, measuring compliance is not straightforward. IMF arrangements span many dimensions. Governments may comply with several of the commitments they make and fail to comply with others. Also, the dimensions vary from arrangement to arrangement. Some governments commit to devaluing the national currency, while others are required to make drastic fiscal adjustments. And even along one dimension, governments are not held to the same standard. Some governments commit to a balanced budget or even a surplus, while others commit to a reduction of the deficit. The systematic study of the details of IMF policy prescriptions is a daunting task indeed.

Such study can provide important insights, however, as Gould (2003) has demonstrated. Gould has studied "bank-friendly" conditions as a component of IMF arrangements. She has found that sometimes the IMF requests the assistance of private financial institutions to provide "supplemental" loans to go along with an IMF loan to facilitate an economic reform program. When such supplemental financing is present, Gould finds that the IMF is likely to include a specific bank-friendly condition in the IMF arrangement, requiring, for example, the government to repay the private financial institution before other forms of debt are addressed. This work reveals the importance of studying the assignment of specific conditions under different situations. It also shows that the systematic study of specific conditions, and their effects, is possible.

Another policy-specific study looks at the impact of IMF programs on social spending. Nooruddin and Simmons (2006) show that the effects depend on political institutions. Under dictatorships, where spending on health and education is low, the IMF has a positive effect. Social spending increases, although spending levels remain well below democracy levels. For democracies, however, the effect is the opposite. IMF programs have a negative effect on health and education expenditures. Taken together, IMF programs make the two regime types look similar. IMF programs make democracies look more like dictatorships when it comes to health and education. Nooruddin and Simmons conclude that any optimism about the IMF successfully helping the poor "is out of place."

The frontier of research on the IMF should be pushed toward the further study of compliance. Only with detailed policy analysis will we be able to settle the debate about whether the IMF should be engaged in lending to countries in crisis and whether its policies have helped. We know that as they stand, IMF programs have failed to promote economic growth. More and more studies confirm what critics have argued for decades: IMF programs actually hurt economic growth. Yet the question of why IMF programs fail is still open. We should thus be willing to experiment and entertain various suggestions for reform. The IMF is staffed by some of the world's best, brightest, and well-intentioned economists who dedicate their lives to improving the conditions of people in the developing world. Unfortunately, the track record is, at best, mixed—partly because of political problems in recipient countries. It is important to scrutinize evidence of program performance so that we can better understand how to improve the institution. My research supports reform of the international institution. The IMF has the potential to do much good.

Acknowledgments

I acknowledge the research assistance of and helpful comments by Leanna Sudhof. This research was supported in part through a grant from Carnegie Corporation of New York and a one-year residence at the UCLA International Institute as part of the UCLA Global Fellows Program.

Notes

1. Conway (1994) finds a short-run negative effect, but a significant positive effect in the long run.

2. The 25 percent rule is not entirely arbitrary. Up to 25 percent of a country's quota must be paid in a widely accepted currency (the U.S. dollar, the euro, the yen, or the pound sterling), but this threshold is itself arbitrary. See Vreeland (2007) for a discussion.

3. For a more detailed discussion, see Vreeland (2007).

4. These four facilities differ in their time horizons, but not in their fundamental policy goals. Thus, like many other authors, I do not distinguish among them in my empirical work here.

5. This does not mean that enforcement of IMF conditions is perfect. Indeed, there are many anecdotes of the IMF relaxing conditions or continuing to extend credit to a country that has not fully complied with an IMF arrangement. But as others have shown, noncompliance is often sanctioned (Schadler 1995; Callaghy 1997, 2002; Stone 2002; Edwards 2000).

6. Like most other bureaucracies, this budget has grown over the years, but at any given point in time, the resources of the IMF are limited.

7. The following statistical model is presented in full detail in Vreeland (2003) and Przeworski and Vreeland (2000). The model builds off the work of Heckman (1978, 1979, 1988), Poirier (1980), Abowd and Farber (1982), Amemiya (1985), and Przeworski and Vreeland (2002).

8. In the work I have done, presented below, statistical tests indicate that this is a valid assumption.

9. For robustness, I have also tested specifications where one of the actors does not want the arrangement but the other does. The qualitative results presented below obtain. See Vreeland (2003) for details.

10. The source is Beck et al. (1999), where the variable appears as CHECK1A. Results hold when CHECK2A is used as well.

11. Extensive robustness tests are also provided in Vreeland (2002b).

12. In other work, I have found that data are not missing at random (Rosendorff and Vreeland 2005).

13. For a detailed discussion of the compliance question, see Vreeland (2006).

References

Abowd, John M., and Henry S. Farber. 1982. "Job Queues and the Union Status of Workers." *Industrial and Labor Relations Review* 35:354–367.

Amemiya, Takeshi. 1985. *Advanced Econometrics*. Cambridge, Mass.: Harvard University Press.

Bandow, Doug. 1994. "The IMF: A Record of Addiction and Failure." In Doug Bandow and Ian Vasquez, eds., *Perpetuating Poverty: The World Bank, the IMF, and the Developing World*. Washington, DC: The Cato Institute.

Barro, Robert J., and Jong-Wha Lee. 2005. "IMF Programs: Who Is Chosen and What Are the Effects?" *Journal of Monetary Economics* 52:1245–1269.

Beck, Thorsten, George Clarke, Alberto Groff, Philip Keefer, and Patrick Walsh. 1999. New tools and new tests in comparative political economy: The Database of Political Institutions. Development Research Group, The World Bank. Groff: Federal Department of Foreign Affairs (Switzerland).

Bird, Graham. 1996. "Borrowing from the IMF: The Policy Implications of Recent Empirical Research." *World Development* 24:1753–1760.

Bird, G. 1998. "The Effectiveness of Conditionality and the Political Economy of Policy Reform: Is It Simply a Matter of Political Will?" *Journal of Policy Reform* 1:89–113.

Broz, J. Lawrence, and Michael Brewster Hawes. 2006. "Congressional Politics of Financing the IMF." *International Organization* 60:367–399.

Callaghy, Thomas. 1997. "Globalization and Marginalization: Debt and the International Underclass." *Current History* 96:392–396.

Callaghy, Thomas. 2002. "Networks and Governance in Africa: Innovation in the Debt Regime." In Thomas M. Callaghy, Ronald Kassimir, and Robert Latham, eds., *Intervention and Transnationalism in Africa: Global-Local Networks of Power*. Cambridge: Cambridge University Press.

Coleman James S. 1988. "Social Capital in the Creation of Human Capital." *American Journal of Sociology* 94:S95–S120.

Coleman, James S. 1990. *Foundations of Social Theory*. Cambridge, MA: Harvard University Press.

Connors, Thomas A. 1979. "The Apparent Effects of Recent IMF Stabilization Programs." International Finance Discussion Papers 135. Washington, D.C.: Board of Governors of the Federal Reserve System.

Conway, Patrick. 1994. "IMF Lending Programs: Participation and Impact." *Journal of Development Economics* 45:365–391.

Dasgupta, Partha. 1988. "Trust as a Commodity." In Diego Gambetta, ed., *Trust: Making and Breaking Cooperative Relations*. New York: Basil Blackwell.

Denoon, David B. H. 1986. *Devaluation Under Pressure*. Cambridge, MA: MIT Press.

Dicks-Mireaux, Louis, Mauro Mecagni, and Susan Schadler. 2000. "Evaluating the Effect of IMF Lending to Low-Income Countries." *Journal of Development Economics* 61:495–526.

Dixit, Avinash K. 1996. *The Making of Economic Policy: A Transaction-Cost Politics Perspective*. Cambridge, Mass.: MIT Press.

Dollar, David, and Jakob Svensson. 2000. "What Explains the Success or Failure of Structural Adjustment Programs." *Economic Journal* 110:894–917.

Drazen, Allen. 2006. "Conditionality and Ownership in IMF Lending: A Political Economy Approach." In Gustav Ranis, James Vreeland, and Stephen Kosack, eds., *Globalization and the Nation State: The Impact of the IMF and the World Bank*. New York: Routledge.

Dreher, Axel. 2004. "IMF and Economic Growth: The Effects of Programs, Loans, and Compliance with Conditionality." *World Development* 34:769–788.

Dreher, Axel. 2006. "IMF and Economic Growth: The Effects of Programs, Loans, and Compliance with Conditionality." *World Development* 34:769–788.

Edwards, Martin S. 2000. "Reevaluating the 'Catalytic' Effect of IMF Programs." Paper presented at the annual meeting of the American Political Science Association, August 31–September 3, Washington, D.C.

Edwards, Sebastian, and Julio A. Santaella. 1993. "Devaluation Controversies in the Developing Countries: Lessons from the Bretton Woods Era." In Michael D. Bordo and Barry Eichengreen, eds., *A Retrospective on the Bretton Woods System*. Chicago: University of Chicago Press.

Fukuyama, Francis. 1995. *Trust: The Social Virtues and the Creation of Prosperity*. New York: Free Press.

Garuda, Gopal. 2000. "The Distributional Effects of IMF Programs: A Cross-Country Analysis." *World Development* 28:1031–1051.

Gold, Joseph. 1970. *The Stand-by Arrangements of the International Monetary Fund: A Commentary on Their Formal, Legal, and Financial Aspects*. Washington, D.C.: International Monetary Fund.

Goldstein, Morris, and Peter J. Montiel. 1986. "Evaluating Fund Stabilization Programs with Multicountry Data: Some Methodological Pitfalls." *IMF Staff Papers* 33:304–344.

Gould, Erica. 2003. "Money Talks: Supplementary Financiers and International Monetary Fund Conditionality." *International Organization* 57(3):551–586.

Green, Donald P., and Alan S. Gerber. 2002. "Reclaiming the Experimental Tradition in Political Science." In Helen V. Milner and Ira Katznelson, eds., *Political Science: The State of the Discipline*, 3rd ed. New York: Norton.

Gylfason, Thorvaldur. 1987. *Credit Policy and Economic Activity in Developing Countries with IMF Stabilization Programs*. Princeton, NJ: International Finance Section, Department of Economics, Princeton University.

Hardin, Russell. 1993. "The Street Level Epistemology of Trust." *Politics and Society* 21:505–529.

Heckman, James J. 1978. "Dummy Endogenous Variables in a Simultaneous Equation System." *Econometrica* 46:931–959.

Heckman, James J. 1979. "Sample Selection Bias as a Specification Error." *Econometrica* 47:153–161.

Heckman, James J. 1988. *The Microeconomic Evaluation of Social Programs and Economic Institutions*. Taipei: Institute of Economics, Academia Sinica.

Humphreys, Norman K. 1999. *Historical Dictionary of the International Monetary Fund, Second Edition*. Lanham, MD: Scarecrow Press, Inc.

Hutchison, Michael, and Ilan Noy. 2003. "Macroeconomic effects of IMF-sponsored programs in Latin America: Output costs, program recidivism and the vicious cycle of failed stabilization." *Journal of International Money and Finance* 22:91–1014.

IMF Survey. 1990. "Statement before the United Nations Economic and Social Council in Geneva, July 11." *IMF Survey* 19:235–236.

IMF. 2001. "Conditionality in Fund-Supported Programs—Policy Issues." Prepared by the Policy Development and Review Department (in consultation with other departments). Approved by Jack Boorman.

Khan, Mohsin S. 1990. "The Macroeconomic Effects of Fund-Supported Adjustment Programs." *IMF Staff Papers* 37:195–234.

Khan, Mohsin S., and Malcolm D. Knight. 1981. "Stabilization Programs in Developing Countries: A Formal Framework." IMF Staff Papers 28. Washington, D.C.: International Monetary Fund.

Killick, Tony. 1995. *IMF Programs in Developing Countries: Design and Impact*. London: Routledge.

Killick, Tony, Moazzam Malik, and Manuel Marcus. 1992. "What Can We Know about the Effects of IMF Programmes?" *World Economy* 15:575–597.

Knight, Malcolm, and Julio A. Santaella. 1997. "Economic Determinants of Fund Financial Arrangements." *Journal of Development Economics* 54:405–436.

Levi, Margaret. 1998. "A State of Trust." In Valerie Braithwaite and Margaret Levi, eds., *Trust and Governance*. New York: Russell Sage Foundation.

Mercer-Blackman, Valerie, and Anna Unigovskaya. 2000. "Compliance with IMF Indicators and Growth in Transition Economies." IMF Working Paper (00/47).

Nelson, Joan, ed. 1990. *Economic Crisis and Policy Choice*. Princeton, N.J.: Princeton University Press.

Nooruddin, Irfan, and Joel W. Simmons. 2006. "The Politics of Hard Choices: IMF Programs and Government Spending." *International Organization* 60:1001–1033.

Pastor, Manuel. 1987a. *The International Monetary Fund and Latin America: Economic Stabilization and Class Conflict*. Boulder, Colo.: Westview Press.

Pastor, Manuel. 1987b. "The Effects of IMF Programs in the Third World: Debate and Evidence from Latin America." *World Development* 15:365–391.

Polak, Jacques. 1991. *The Changing Nature of IMF Conditionality*. Princeton, NJ: International Finance Section, Department of Economics, Princeton University.

Poirier, Dale J. 1980. "Partial Observability in Bivariate Probit Models." *Journal of Econometrics* 12:209–217.

Przeworski, Adam, and James Raymond Vreeland. 2000. "The Effect of IMF Programs on Economic Growth." *Journal of Development Economics* 62:385–421.

Putnam, Robert D. 1988. "Diplomacy and Domestic Politics: The Logic of Two-Level Games." *International Organization* 42:427–460.

Putnam, Robert. 1993. *Making Democracy Work: Civic Traditions in Modern Italy*. Princeton, N.J.: Princeton University Press.

Reichmann, Thomas M., and Richard T. Stillson. 1978. "Experience with Programs of Balance of Payments Adjustment: Stand-By Arrangements in the Highest Tranches, 1963–72." IMF Staff Papers 25. Washington, D.C.: International Monetary Fund.

Remmer, Karen L. 1986. "The Politics of Economic Stabilization, IMF Standby Programs in Latin America, 1954–1984." Comparative Politics 19:1–24.

Rosendorff, B. Peter, and James Raymond Vreeland. 2005. "Democracy and Data Dissemination: The Effect of Political Regime on Transparency." Paper presented at the annual meeting of the Midwest Political Science Association, April 7–10, Chicago.

Santaella, Julio A. 1996. "Stylized Facts Before IMF-Supported Adjustment." IMF Staff Papers 43:502–544.

Schadler, Susan, ed. 1995. "Experience under Stand-by and Extended Arrangements. Part II: Background Papers." Occasional Paper 129. Washington, D.C.: International Monetary Fund.

Spaventa, Luigi. 1983. "Two Letters of Intent: External Crises and Stabilization Policy, Italy, 1973–77." In John Williamson, ed., IMF Conditionality. Washington, D.C.: Institute for International Economics.

Stiglitz, Joseph. 2000. "Reflections on the Theory and Practice of Reform." In Anne O. Krueger, ed., Economic Policy Reform: The Second Stage. Chicago: University of Chicago Press.

Stone, Randall W. 2002. Lending Credibility: The International Monetary Fund and the Post-Communist Transition. Princeton, N.J.: Princeton University Press.

Tanzi, Vito. 1989. "Fiscal Policy, Growth, and the Design of Stabilization Programs." In Mario I. Blejer and Ke-young Chu, eds., Fiscal Policy, Stabilization, and Growth in Developing Countries. Washington, D.C.: IMF.

Thacker, Strom. 1999. "The High Politics of IMF Lending." World Politics 52:38–75.

Tsebelis, George. 1995. "Decision Making in Political Systems." British Journal of Political Science 25:289–326.

Vaubel, Roland. 1986. "A Public Choice Approach to International Organization." Public Choice 51:39–57.

Vreeland, James. 2002a. "The Effect of IMF Programs on Labor." World Development 30:121–139.

Vreeland, James Raymond. 2002b. "Institutional Determinants of IMF Agreements." Unpublished manuscript, Department of Political Science, Yale University. Available at http://pantheon.yale.edu/~jrv9/Veto.pdf.

Vreeland, James Raymond. 2003. The IMF and Economic Development. Cambridge: Cambridge University Press.

Vreeland, James Raymond. 2006. "IMF Program Compliance: Aggregate Index versus Policy Specific Research Strategies." Review of International Organizations 1:359–378.

Vreeland, James Raymond. 2007. The International Monetary Fund: Politics of Conditional Lending. New York: Routledge.

13 The Knowledge Bank

Jonathan Morduch

The late Hollis Chenery, Cabot Professor of Economics at Harvard and chief economist at the World Bank under Robert McNamara, was asked to write the entry on foreign aid for *The New Palgrave: A Dictionary of Economics* when the original 1894 edition was updated in 1987. After recounting the litany of incentive problems with the existing aid system, Chenery concluded with a thought on knowledge: "Finally, the most enduring aspect of aid is likely to be the discovery and dissemination of knowledge to fit the development needs of poor countries. A notable success has been the joint sponsorship of agricultural research by multilateral and bilateral aid agencies over the past fifteen years. Knowledge is a classic case of the economist's 'public good', and the expansion of this aspect of the international aid system should command wide support" (1989, 144).

Chenery's paragraph is an optimistic note appended to an essay on foreign aid that is mainly resigned and pessimistic. A decade later, James Wolfensohn, president of the World Bank at that time, echoed the same optimistic tone in announcing the transformation of his institution into a "Knowledge Bank."[1] The bank's chief economist at the time, Joseph Stiglitz, reiterated that the principle of public goods justifies a leading role for international agencies like the World Bank in spreading global knowledge (Stiglitz 1999).

Organizations like the World Bank are thus reimagining themselves as packagers and providers of knowledge, no longer mainly distributors of grants and loans, and the change is pushing their reach far beyond the limits of their purses. The World Bank's Development Gateway, a Web-based repository of development data, opinion, and experience, is built on this hope.[2] A computer search can now reveal in seconds how to build household solar energy systems, incorporate gender concerns into sanitation policy, fight local corruption, train teachers, and myriad other lessons and suggested development strategies.[3] The bank's external Web site reaches 700,000 users per month, and in 2004, the World Bank was named one of the top twenty "Most Admired Knowledge

Enterepries" for the fifth year in a row, joining, among others, IBM, Toyota, and Siemens.[4]

In principle, the knowledge bank should improve the making of development policy by fostering better data collection, independent analyses, and more extensive evaluations. The needs are great. A 2002 report of the General Accounting Office, the investigative arm of the U.S. Congress, for example, put its message in its title: "Foreign Assistance: USAID Relies Heavily on Nongovernmental Organizations, But Better Data Needed to Evaluate Approaches" (General Accounting Office 2002). A July 2004 *New York Times* article expanded on the theme: "Wealthy nations and international organizations, including the World Bank, spend more than $55 billion annually to better the lot of the world's 2.7 poor people," Celia Dugger reported. "Yet they have scant evidence that the myriad projects they finance have made any real difference, many economists say" (Dugger 2004, A4). As these examples suggest, the need is not just for better dissemination of existing information but also for generation of new data.

Becoming a knowledge bank has been a natural turn for the World Bank, but the past decade of experience suggests there are additional steps to take before being able to command wide support. This chapter lays out issues and identifies central tensions with knowledge provision—those likely to arise through conflicts with ideological agendas and with the professional, career objectives of staff at development agencies. Drawing on Matsui and Morduch (2004), I argue that the deployment of the standard theory of public goods is more complicated (and often less appropriate) than the initial applications suggest. As a result, effective knowledge strategies cannot rely solely on synthesizing existing experience. Optimal strategies also require mandated data collection and systematic experimentation with competing models and contrarian views. Next steps will require both humility and activism. The ideas are illustrated with a discussion of knowledge dissemination about microcredit, an important antipoverty strategy of the past decade.

13.1 The Knowledge Bank Experience

Chenery's thoughts provide a sharp contrast to President Harry Truman's inaugural address of 1949, which famously highlighted four points, the fourth of which focused on foreign aid. "We must embark on a bold new program for making the benefits of our scientific advances and industrial progress available for the improvement and growth of underdeveloped areas," Truman had proclaimed from the East Portico of the Capitol.[5] Highways were to be built, rivers to be dammed, and electricity to be wired. The U.S. Congress met this challenge with the Foreign Economic Assistance Act of 1950, hoping to do for the rest of the world what the Marshall Plan was doing for the war-ravaged countries of Europe. State Department officials set about promoting industry, technology, and infrastructure overseas, aiming to reshape economies that were only then throwing off the yoke of a colonial past.

For Truman, the task was to share the fruits of existing knowledge by exporting and building capital goods and infrastructure abroad without necessarily transferring the knowledge itself. We now know how difficult (and perhaps wrong-headed) that task turned out to be (Easterly 2001). For Chenery, as for Wolfensohn, the aim was instead to create new, relevant bodies of knowledge and to export the knowledge directly.

The increasingly easy traffic in information, made far cheaper and faster through new communications technologies, makes this possible. Sending messages and posting data have become nearly costless as more and more people and organizations gain access to the Internet. In 1970, transmitting a trillion bits of information across the United States would have cost $150,000; by 1999 the cost was just 12 cents. And while there were just 200 Web sites in mid-1993, there were 20 million Web sites and 400 million users by late 2000; by the end of 2004, over 800 million users were logging on.[6]

The World Bank's knowledge bank strategy combines the new technological possibilities with a rethinking of staff deployment. The knowledge strategy built on a prior reorganization of bank staff that in part confronted the tendency to confine conversations about regional issues to regional operations units. The reorganization linked staff by cross-cutting "families" and "networks" that created explicit ties between a sanitation expert working in North Africa, say, and her counterpart working in Eastern Europe. Reinforcing these connective tissues is the development of communities of practice within units (and sometimes with outside experts as well) to share experiences and distill lessons. Within the bank, these communities are called thematic groups, and there are roughly eighty, ranging in size from 25 to 200 people, with voluntary participation and leadership (Gwin 2003). The vision thus goes beyond simply transferring knowledge by sending individual staff around the world to dispense expertise (Fukuda-Parr, Lopes, and Malik 2002). Instead, in principle, it seeks to foster ongoing conversations within practitioner and academic communities, creating "open access" facilities for outsiders to retrieve information (notably from the Web), and encouraging partners abroad to participate in the knowledge generation process on an equal footing.[7] In the six years since announcing the knowledge bank strategy, the World Bank has founded 37 distance learning centers, hosted 875 distance learning conferences, created 80 new practitioner networks, and run over 4,700 video conferences.[8]

These changes have happened as the policy environment has shifted in ways that create demand for new perspectives and ways to quickly share and retrieve information. Among the most important changes is that nongovernmental organizations (NGOs) are growing in number and clout. Leading international organizations like the World Bank, which used to work only with governments, are now working directly with NGOs and representatives of civil society—sometimes in opposition to elected governments. Between 1996 and April 2003, for example, the involvement of civil society in bank projects grew from under half to over 70 percent, and the value of community-driven elements of projects grew from $700 million to $2 billion.[9] These turns have reinforced the shift in policy agendas toward greater concern with poverty alleviation, human rights, environmental degradation, and civic participation—all of which push toward involving many actors engaged in local, bottom-up interventions rather than a few actors pursuing centralized, top-down measures (Einhorn 2001). A second, concurrent change is that decentralization is occurring throughout the world, with central governments yielding greater powers of taxation and policymaking to regional authorities, many of which are learning on the job.[10] Activists may criticize specifics of bank policies, but they find it increasingly difficult to make the case that the bank has been ignoring key economic and social sectors.

The knowledge bank effort to date has been impressive in scope and ambition, but the World Bank's efforts have nevertheless received mixed reviews. Critics accept the energy and ambition of the bank's knowledge efforts and have fired instead at the nature of the information disseminated. The loudest criticisms come from those who also assert that bank staff have at times dragged their feet on environmental concerns, corruption, gender roles, human rights, and a host of other concerns.[11] Activists withdrew from a collaborative arrangement for knowledge dissemination, for example, and publicly scolded the bank in an "open letter" that argues that the bank's "Internet gateway" overly privileges narrow probusiness interests over broader social concerns (Wilks 2002). Other dissenting views have been collected by the Panos Institute (1998), Gmelin, King, and McGrath (2001), and Jha, Semour, and Sims (2004). In 2003, the World bank's own Operations Evaluation Department (OED) issued a comprehensive review that echoed many of the outside complaints (Gwin 2003).

While finding much to celebrate in the main text of the OED review, Appendix G contains the results of a survey of Development Gateway users in Bangladesh, Brazil, Poland, Senegal, and Tanzania. As noted above, the Web site has 700,000 users per month, but only 10 to 20 percent live in developing countries and much of the site remains in English only (Gwin 2003). Among the main findings of the survey were (Gwin 2003, 60):

• While finding the analysis technically sophisticated, "respondents were often critical of the Bank's ability to provide information that is realistic in light of local circumstances and responsive to local needs."

• "Frustration with the Bank's failure to consider alternatives. The majority of respondents complained that the Bank is too narrowly focused in the analyses and 'best practices' that it presents, with little or no attention to alternative perspectives."

• "Poor record in dissemination," caused by too great a focus on governments and "top-down" approaches.

• "Mixed reviews on collaboration." Some were very happy with the way that the bank collaborated and used local experties, but an equal number noted "condescension toward their own knowledge and experience."

Despite the sharp criticisms, most noted improvements and were impressed by the scope of the vision, especially for such a new initiative.

13.2 Contested Knowledge

Doing better begins with respect for the contested nature of much knowledge about development. The protests of the World Bank have not always been fair or accurate, but one does not need to be fully sympathetic to each particular claim to recognize that much about development remains contested. Debates rage about whether and how trade barriers should be dropped. Should controls be placed on international capital flows? Is improving education quality likely to generate large returns? Can microcredit make a large dent in poverty rates? Will aggregate income growth quickly reach the poor? As Ravi Kanbur, the former World Bank chief economist for Africa, writes, "The central issue is that frameworks for understanding and interpreting information and knowledge in the development process are contested" (Kanbur 2002, 16).

The knowledge bank can be helpful here. Several years ago, a World Bank mission went to Ethiopia to discuss privatization. They laid out their views to the Ethiopian counterparts but were rebuffed. The Ethiopians had gone to the World Bank Web site and seen that there were competing views on privatization even within the bank, and they determined they were more interested in the alternatives. Based on this knowledge, the Ethiopians sent the World Bank team back to Washington empty-handed.[12] The result may have been judged a failure by the bank team, but it can be seen as a positive example of how a knowledge bank broadens discourse when there are competing views.

Outcomes are not always positive. In other cases, the knowledge that is shared may be incomplete, not generalizable, or inappropriate. One respondent to the World Bank OED survey, a government worker in Tanzania, noted that "some Bank experts are biased, based on their experiences of what has worked elsewhere in the world, with little attention to local needs or ideas" (Gwin 2003, 69). A government worker in Bangladesh similarly noted, "My general impression is that the Bank presents information and perspectives that support its own policy agenda" (Gwin 2003, 65). And a journalist from Senegal asserted that "the Bank often ignores potentially useful solutions from other parts of the world which were not sponsored or supported by the Bank (for example, rural electrification in Morocco)" (Gwin 2003, 65). Other respondents were more positive, but the overall tone of responses quoted in the OED report is both wariness and an eagerness for more information.

Analyses of knowledge banking cannot be divorced from a reckoning of the broader incentives, constraints, and opportunities experienced by the staff of international organizations. William Easterly (2001), for example, suggests that poorly designed incentives push recipients and donors to put their private gain ahead of improving social welfare, a reading that echoes the public choice analysis of Niskanen (1971) and, as applied to international organizations, Frey (1984), Vaubel and Willet (1991), and others. Part of the problem according to Easterly is that World Bank staff have been rewarded professionally according to the quantity of loans rather than their quality, a problem noted widely since the Wapenhans Report (World Bank 1992) but which, Easterly argues, remains a problem a decade later.

Others point to problems created by cultural divides—due to professional training, upbringing, or social class—that may open the eyes of staff members to some phenomena but make it harder to see others. Stern and Ferreira (1997), for example, report on a survey of 465 World Bank staff members completed in 1992. Of these, 55 percent had graduate degrees in either economics or finance, and although Bank staff are drawn from many nations, nearly 80 percent had attended either British (74 respondents) or American (290 respondents) graduate schools. This creates potential biases, as Stern and Ferreira note (587–588): "U.S. graduate schools, not surprisingly, tend to focus on U.S. examples, and the United States is in many ways a peculiar country. For example, it has a tax system and a constitution that are very different from those found in other countries, and a strand in political philosophy oriented toward individualism and against the state that is much more dominant than is the case in other countries. U.S. graduate schools, for example, have shown less interest in applied welfare economics, poverty, and income distribution than their counterparts elsewhere."[13]

The World Bank has set about trying to hire more sociologists, anthropologists, and other social scientists, but it remains an institution whose intellectual work is dominated by economists. Since much of the bank's business is economics, this seems sensible, but it has implications for how development issues are discussed—and how they are not discussed.

James Ferguson (1994) tells a cautionary tale in *The Anti-Politics Machine*. He describes a World Bank-CIDA agricultural project in Lesotho, analyzing it memo by memo. Ferguson argues that the project failed for lack of attention to the political ambitions of the Lesotho government, as well as due to a mischaracterization of the economy as being based on traditional subsistence agriculture—despite the existence of an active cash crop sector and extensive labor flows to the South African mining sector. The bank reports and memos Ferguson cited, however, are full of data on technical aspects of agriculture, hardly breathing a word about politics or the broader dynamics of the economy. Ferguson's book is a reminder of the blinders that can descend as experts focus sharply on their field of expertise.[14]

A related example is given by Stephen Denning (2001), quoting a report by the World Bank Operations Evaluation Department on the Zambia Structural Adjustment Credit of 1990:

Projects and programs of technical cooperation are developed within the governing sets of assumptions or paradigms, and must comply with them, even in situations where the staff and the client know that the prevailing paradigm is highly unreliable, if not downright wrong. The phenomenon is quite striking in the field of economic adjustment where an operation containing a few important measures is expected to return an entire economy to a strong growth path within a miraculously short timeframe, despite a backlog of decades of economic mismanagement. When, as might be expected, the operation by itself fails to achieve the promised economic growth, reports are written assigning reasons for the shortfall. Ironically, the one cause that such evaluation reports are not allowed to discover is frequently the real reason—namely a faulty paradigm. (p. 13)

Ideology will inevitably color knowledge sharing, not necessarily in a self-conscious way but as a matter of course. Expecting experts to get beyond their ideological frames is a tall task, and an unreasonable one. A more practical solution must thus rest with greater transparency and data availability, so that ideas can be put to empirical tests and debated by others in the light of relevant evidence.

13.3   Where Are the Numbers?

Issues of ideology play out in basic data collection efforts as well—in particular, in whether data are collected in the first place. Simple theories of the policy process suggest that where ideas are most strongly contested, they should also be most subject to empirical scrutiny. Studies will be mandated, data will be collected, and researchers will try to get to the bottom of debates. It is also natural to assume that where data are weak or absent, analysts will be most circumspect.[15]

But the opposite is very often the case, with clear consequences for knowledge creation. Jeffrey Hammer puts forward the following "law" based on two decades of work as a research economist at the World Bank: "The intensity of people's views on a topic is inversely proportional to the amount of evidence available on the topic."[16] Hammer's law suggests two different interpretations. First, without being confronted with convincing data, observers can maintain strong positions without challenge. But there is another reading of Hammer's law. Instead, people with strong positions (for either careerist or ideological reasons) may actively work to discourage data collection that could undermine their credibility. If their views have initial currency, data collection yields a large downside risk with little compensating upside benefit. In contrast, if one's position is already on the outs, there will be more support for data collection since the downside risk is more limited while the upside potential is greater.

The example of microcredit below illustrates the incentives that work against data collection, and Lant Pritchett (2002) raises similar issues when wondering why so few randomized evaluations of education and health get done. Prichett asks whether "it pays to be ignorant" for advocates of social programs. The essential problem is one identified by Aaron Wildavsky (1972) with regard to the paucity of "self-evaluating organizations." As Van Evera (2002, 2) writes in his parallel analysis of why governments fail to self-evaluate: "Aaron Wildavsky contends that organizations poorly evaluate their own policies and beliefs because they often turn against their own evaluative units, attacking or destroying them. Evaluation promotes innovation and change. This threatens the jobs and status of incumbent members of the organization. Hence incumbents often seek to hamper or prevent evaluation and to punish evaluators. These incumbents tend to dominate the organization's decision making, so evaluation finds itself with stronger enemies than friends within the organization. Hence self-evaluation is often timid and ineffective." The spirit of the analysis also helps to explain why organizations are generally difficult to reform from within. Less cynically, the antievaluation bent may emerge when staff members have strong and true beliefs in the worth of the project—and fear that formal statistical evaluations may fail to adequately measure the project's direct and indirect benefits.

Bertin Martens (2002) frames the issues in terms of the expected precision of evaluations of foreign aid projects. In Martens's analysis, "woolly" reporting will arise when it is in the interest of politicians, NGOs, or other interested parties to ensure that measured performance appears to fall close to expected targets. In statistical terms, it becomes difficult to reject that targets have been met when standard deviations around the estimated coefficients are larger, and the political outcome will often be one that guarantees large standard errors.

But this is only one part of the story. It is clear why program managers typically eschew evaluations—they are time-consuming and carry the risk of bad news—but why don't advocates of health programs, say, push for better studies of competing education programs? Or why can't other groups provide the required pressure? Martens (2002) argues that one important pressure group, taxpayers, are in no position to evaluate performance for themselves: "Contrary to domestic aid programs, where taxpayers can experience the performance of programs themselves and obtain first-hand information, in foreign aid programs taxpayers pay for the program but do not get the benefits" (170). Pritchett argues that log-rolling (we will not evaluate you if you do not evaluate us) explains an equilibrium where practitioners in different sectors agree not to evaluate anyone seriously. These lines of argument suggest that the lack of data is not a temporary deficit; it is a systemic feature of development work. The analysis of Matsui and Morduch (2003), described below, suggests that the problem is inherent in the nature of knowledge as a public good.

13.4   Knowledge As a Public Good

As Chenery and Stiglitz asserted, international agencies like the World Bank can claim responsibility for providing information because information is a public good; it will thus be underprovided unless the public sector steps in (Stiglitz 1999). The logic reflects a core principle of economics, drawing on Adam Smith and formalized as a basis of public economics by Paul Samuelson (1954).

Like a lighthouse, the classic example of a public good, information is nonrivalrous (use by one individual does not diminish use by another) and nonexcludable (no one can be easily excluded from using the product or service). The result is that incentives to voluntarily pay a firm for the services of lighthouses are severely reduced, providing the government with a rationale to step in to improve matters. The same holds for much information: it crosses boundaries freely, and it too will be insufficiently supplied unless international agencies step in to improve matters (Stiglitz 1999). Yes, there may be important independent information providers, but, the logic goes, their contributions will typically be insufficient. Thus, it is asserted, there is an important role for international agencies to collect data, conduct research, and disseminate understandings—or at least to support those activities.[17]

The tension is not with the theory, which is sound. It is with the assumption that there will be agreement on which information to collect and disseminate. When ideas are contested, the role of knowledge banks becomes far less clear. One general set of incentive problems is raised by Anupam Khanna (2000, 9), writing from within the World Bank:

> Much of the knowledge and information generated at the World Bank also has the character of a public good, especially when it is disembodied and codified. This of course sits well with the cooperative multilateral status of the institution whereby it has a legitimate role in filling gaps in the provision of public goods caused by market failures. However, this does attenuate internal incentives for efficiency due to diffuse accountability and soft budget constraints typically encountered in the public sector. More important than cost inefficiencies, however, is the concern that the lack of adequate market tests may also lead to poor quality, for example through inadequate customization of knowledge transfers.

Khanna suggests that inadequate customization of knowledge may be a product of lack of effort on the part of bank staff, produced by inadequate incentives to do better.[18] But the critique can go further. Rather than generically poor-quality knowledge sharing, could incentive systems lead to the promotion of certain kinds of knowledge that are deliberately shaded to further the bureaucratic objectives of bank staff? Or as in the discussion of (lack of) data collection below, might generically poor-quality knowledge transmission be a mechanism to encourage particular decisions on the part of recipients?[19] Theoretical work on information transmission in macroeconomic contexts, for example, suggests that policy advice may at times be deliberately shaded to such a degree that it is difficult to ignore. In a more general theoretical setting, Crawford and Sobel (1982) argue that advisers have incentives to limit the richness of information they provide when they perceive potential conflicts with recipients.[20]

Take the issue of quality shading, for example. Under the incentive system criticized by Wapenhans, the bank operations staff were rewarded for getting loans out the door. Thus, projects that involved large loans and little spadework were especially attractive. A cynical view suggests that this helps to explain the positive attention given to financial deregulation in the World Bank's knowledge sharing during the 1990s.[21]

Another, related problem Ferguson identified was a culture that exhibited low tolerance for project failure, even though, as Ferguson (1984, 8) suggests from his experience, "Again and again development projects in Lesotho are launched, and again and again they fail; but no matter how many times this happens there always seems to be someone ready to try again with yet another project." The World Bank's failure rates in 1991 were about one-third, with failure rates over 80 percent in some African countries (World Bank 1992). In 1996, 31 percent of projects were still "unsatisfactory," falling to 22 percent by April 2003.[22] These numbers are much higher than casual readers of World Bank publications would suspect. The problem for the knowledge bank is not so much that projects fail "again and again" but that the level of discussion of failure is inadequate. What results are lists of generic best practices but seldom careful renderings of mistaken approaches from which recipients and other bank staff might more fruitfully learn.[23]

The shading and partial reporting may not be an explicit strategy; it may arise instead by not bending over backward to provide alternative views and specific caveats. Where it is unreasonable for bank staff to do the bending over backward themselves, matters could be improved by providing links and funding to outside organizations that can fill in the knowledge gaps and alternative views, steps that in some cases are already being taken by providing outside organizations that have been allocated space on the bank's Development Gateway.

Giving more credence to alternative views may help the bank's ability to make its own case. Kanbur (2002), for example, suggests that the appearance of one-sidedness can make knowledge provided by the bank seem less than fully credible. Thus, to Kanbur (17–18),

The central question is whether research in institutions like the Bank, who have to take stances and views on policy in their operations, can ever command wide enough trust to be a [global public good]. This is no way to impugn the motives of the many fine individuals who do research in these institutions. But they do face constraints, and this is entirely to be expected in an operational organization. The point is not whether there should or should not be a research organization in an operational institution—any such institution will need a group dedicated to specific analysis and to interacting with outside analysis. The point rather, is whether [international financial institution] research can claim the mantle of [a global public good]. . . . Our conclusion on this is a skeptical one, at least where there is a widespread perception that the research is in the service of a particular line or policy stance to the exclusion of others.

So Kanbur argues that while information in the abstract may be a global public good, World Bank information may be too tainted to be so.

A different approach is to accept World Bank information as a package of content that may be relevant or shaded (whether the shading is deliberate or not). Having greater access to more information, even if it is not wholly relevant, can still be useful. The question is whether recipients will be able to sort out the relevant content from the rest. To take matters further, imagine that analysts at the U.S. Agency for International Development (USAID) were convinced that rapid economic reform is the surest means for success, while others

believe that slow, careful reform often works better (as many Japanese economists have argued; Stiglitz 2000). Because analysts at USAID are well endowed
with resources to complete analyses and disseminate results widely, they spread
the word on the merits of rapid reform. It would be hoped that helpful aspects
of their advice can be embraced and any unhelpful parts could be ignored.

But the very nature of knowledge as a global public good can create difficulties in distinguishing helpful from unhelpful advice. This is because, just as individual users of policy advice lack incentives to generate comprehensive
knowledge bases on their own, they also lack incentives to build the capacity
to independently assess the relevance of contested claims.[24] The dilemma is
that the kinds of information required to verify, balance, and extend information provided by knowledge banks are often themselves public goods. The typical knowledge bank, though, is not set up to provide evidence that contradicts
and questions the very information it seeks to disseminate as being most useful.
Thus, independent users of the information, limited by their own resources and
analytical capabilities, have little way to carefully judge World Bank (or other)
studies for themselves.

Matsui and Morduch (2003) describe a theoretical context in which knowledge is ultimately a product of inputs provided by organizations like the World
Bank and by local users. It is a context consistent, for example, with Stiglitz's
(2001) dictum to "scan globally and reinvent locally." The World Bank can
complement local efforts or possibly supplant them, and information content
may be shaded.

The framework takes as given that World Bank knowledge inputs may be a
substitute for or a complement (in the traditional economic senses of those
terms) to local knowledge inputs. When the overall objective is to maximize
the coproduction of the final knowledge outcome that arises when all inputs
are combined, optimal strategies will be conditioned on the nature of the complementarities and possibilities for substitution.

In the case of complements, the bank can provide information inputs and
help to build local analytical capacity in ways that reinforce the possibility of
"crowding in" local knowledge, a vision highlighted by King and McGrath's
(2004) survey of knowledge banking efforts by development agencies. The idea
is already part of the Bank's Global Development Learning Network initiative,
for example, as well as efforts to ensure that the bank's well-regarded Living
Standards Measurement Surveys are comparable and publicly accessible.

Alternatively, restricting data access and providing information of limited
usefulness (so local efforts also bring lower returns) can crowd out local efforts.
This much should be obvious. In the case of substitutes, though, the bank
might crowd out local efforts by taking what had been the favorable path

above—providing information that appears to be so useful that local efforts are not worth making.[25] Crowding out local efforts is not inherently bad, but in principle there will be cases in which overall welfare is reduced, even though local efforts are voluntarily restricted.

The idea that knowledge is a public good thus does not in itself justify the bank's actions at all times. Since local knowledge inputs may be public goods themselves, the theoretical justification for the knowledge bank is conditional on the nature of the coproduction of knowledge: the way that global and local knowledge inputs combine to produce relevant understandings by end users. As King and McGrath (2004) argue, effective knowledge banking efforts should thus be built from the bottom up.

13.5   Lessons From Microcredit: Are "Best Practices" Always Best?

Microcredit (or microfinance) involves the expansion of banking services in poor and low-income communities, made possible by combining lessons from both formal and informal financial institutions (see, e.g., Armendariz de Aghion and Morduch 2005). Microbanking is in many ways a perfect match for knowledge banking: it is a well-defined intervention that can take many forms and can be started at a variety of scales. The "microfinance gateway" launched on the Internet by the Consultative Group to Assist the Poor, a donor consortium based at the World Bank, is an impressive effort to share knowledge and spread current thinking, paralleling the larger and broader development gateway.

There is a range of approaches to providing microcredit, but the major donors have settled on a particular set of ideas about the right approaches. The microfinance gateway contains a spectrum of views, but most support the donor consensus. Those ideas hinge on the argument that poor customers are able to profit handsomely from small loans and thus should be able to pay high enough interest rates to support microbanks operating on a commercial basis (Gonzalez-Vega 1994). The role for donors in this new world of finance for the poor, it is argued, should be limited to aiding new institutions during their initial start-up years.[26] Behind this vision is the assumption that these new commercial microbanks, with boards seeking profits, will not drift toward richer clients at the expense of the poor. It is also argued that customers should look elsewhere for support if they cannot pay full price for financial services. They should turn to traditional charities, for example, or health and education programs. And it has been argued by those pushing this line that providing financial services is sufficient: there are no real gains (and considerable complications) to also providing health or skills-training services alongside finance. In sum, the push toward commercialization is viewed as the most effective path toward poverty reduction on a large scale.[27]

These are cogent arguments built on particular assumptions about household behavior and the nature of returns to capital. They are not universal truths, though, and are likely to vary with the contexts in which microcredit operates. All the same, the major donors' list of microcredit "best practices" follows the single-minded orthodoxy above. In keeping with that particular thought chain, the best practices list is long on ways to improve the financial success of the new institutions and short on other ways to effect meaningful social change in communities—perhaps most striking, short on ways of considering trade-offs between the two.[28] Moroever, the "best practices" put forward as consensus guidelines are notably devoid of context, implying that there may be many paths but a single direction to follow in achieving economic and social goals.

The debates over the applicability of the vision—over the pros and cons of commercialization and subsidization—are neither mystical nor metaphysical; to the contrary, they involve largely straightforward technical questions. The underlying empirical questions (How great are returns to capital for different groups below poverty lines? How high are household impacts?) are answerable with the right data, but getting comprehensive data is complicated enough that independent researchers have had difficulty making headway on their own.

Donors have not helped as much as they might have. Financial data on microcredit have been collected, posted, and analyzed with much greater energy than is the case for rigorous data on social outcomes.[29] Just a scattering of reliable control-treatment impact studies has been completed in the past fifteen years. Few programs have completed even basic, comparable surveys of their clients. Thus, they cannot easily communicate to outsiders exactly how poor their clients are (e.g., the percentage below national poverty lines). Donors have instead relied on average loan size as the rough-and-ready metric of the depth of outreach, a data point that is calculated by microbanks in the course of their financial accounting. Since poorer customers tend to take smaller loans than richer countries, the average loan size granted by a microbank gives an indication of how poor its clients are, but the measure is widely known to be noisy and often misleading (Dunford 2002). The situation became so problematic that in 2004, the U.S. Congress felt compelled to force the USAID to develop practical methods for surveying the living standards of microcredit customers, a stipulation at the heart of the Microenterprise Results and Accountability Act of 2004.[30]

Why are we missing exactly the data that practitioners and policymakers need to contextualize best practices, explore assumptions, and draw specific lessons for the wide variety of microcredit contexts? One explanation is that data collection is expensive and that incentives work against funding public goods. Another explanation for the muddiness is that the lack of clarity has yielded important benefits: it has helped microcredit to become popular quickly, riding a crest of success stories unchecked by hard numbers. It has also fostered a remarkable degree of consensus and goodwill for the movement, built on fuzzy measures of inputs and outcomes. Most microcredit institutions themselves have not been eager to collect sharper data for reasons described above, but it is likely that they would have with donor pressure and support.

Now that the microcredit movement has matured, the time is opportune for deploying that pressure and support. USAID has advanced several model impact studies, and the Consultative Group to Assist the Poor has developed tools to gauge poverty levels. The World Bank's research committee is also sponsoring novel studies on microcredit impacts and mechanisms. These are good starts, and they reflect shifts in leadership that have brought ideological loosenings, coupled with new understandings about microcredit and external pressures (from the U.S. Congress, for example, and from increasingly active social investors in the private sector).[31] While the trends are positive, the earlier experience of selective data collection and analysis is a reminder that knowledge distribution is partly a political outcome, determined in large part by who is at the helm of knowledge banks and the constraints under which they operate.

13.6 What Next?

Hollis Chenery, in the quote at the start of this chapter, highlighted the successful "joint sponsorship of agricultural research by multilateral and bilateral aid agencies." Evenson, Pray, and Rosengrant (1999) bear this out for India, calculating that the marginal internal rates of return to agricultural research between 1956 and 1987 were over 50 percent for public research—higher than the marginal returns for extension, imported high-yielding varieties (HYVs), or private research and development. It is a vision of knowledge banking that goes beyond "knowledge sharing," the preferred term of the World Bank (see, e.g., www.worldbank.org/ks/).

The bank's own Global Development Learning Network initiative, Living Standards Measurement Surveys, and research efforts provide models for more active knowledge creation efforts (Squire 2000). As noted, above, though, both knowledge creation and knowledge sharing are likely to be driven in part by bureaucratic and professional incentives, not just by the pure pursuit of relevant information. The essential problem highlighted above is that knowledge about development is contested and that learning often arises by synthesizing viewpoints and experience from multiple angles. While it is often said that the knowledge collected by development agencies has the property of a public good, dissent and contrarian evidence are often public goods as well. Strategies that build on this recognition cannot rely just on synthesizing existing experience as seen from the vantage of development agencies; optimal strategies will also require active support for systematic experimentation with competing models and activist data collection efforts. Creating more favorable incentives can be done only in a culture that tolerates failure and seeks to learn from it; judges performance by outcomes, not inputs; and respects alternative positions and seeks open debate.

The World Bank is arguably the world's most important creator of data on development, but the lack of relevant data, particularly on project impacts and household behavior, continues to be a constraint. There will always be arguments against collecting data and completing high-quality empirical evaluations, so a strong hand may be required to encourage and coordinate efforts. One challenge will be to secure funding and find mechanisms to ensure voluntary participation by households in the surveys. In principle, there will be times when compensation is necessary to encourage voluntary participation in experiments—on the principle that the knowledge gained is, after all, a public good to be shared globally. Ultimately the data collected should be publicly accessible.

Implementing high-quality independent impact evaluations for all bank projects would be burdensome, though, and one option is to evaluate project impacts on a random basis—just as tax authorities regularly complete random audits of tax returns. In this case, an independent evaluation team would enter the picture from the start of the project and would be given the authority and funding to modify the project as needed for the evaluation, possibly introducing randomized elements or staggering the program rollout in ways that foster evaluation. The possibility of being chosen would have to be recognized from the start and accepted as part of the standard operational protocols. As with tax audits, the probability of evaluation could be increased by specific features of the project deemed of particular importance to learning efforts. If implemented, the approach would take the development community closer toward sorting through current debates and would take the knowledge bank closer to meeting its potential.

Acknowledgments

I have benefited from conversations with Stephen Denning, Bill Easterly, Garance Genicot, Debraj Ray, Hari Srinivas, Alex Wilks, and participants in a meeting at the Japan International Cooperation Agency in Tokyo in June 2003 and at a meeting on "Reinventing Foreign Aid" held at the Center for Global Development, Washington, D.C., August 19, 2002. John Gershman provided particularly helpful comments on an early draft. I appreciate financial support under an Abe Fellowship of the Social Science Research Council and Japan Center for Global Partnership. All views and any errors are my own.

Notes

1. See Wolfensohn (1996), Gilbert, Powell, and Vines (2000), and World Bank (1998). I focus on the World Bank disproportionately here since it has been the leader in knowledge-sharing efforts to date, but the general issues pertain to the United Nations and other international organizations. See King and McGrath (2004) for a discussion of knowledge banking by the Swedish, British, and Japanese development agencies, as well as the World Bank.

2. For critical views see King (2002), Wilks (2002), and Fukuda-Parr and Hill (2002).

3. See, for example, www.bestpractices.org and www.worldbank.org.

4. The award was made by Teleos, an independent research firm. The World Bank was the only nonprofit or government institution to join the list in 2004.

5. U.S. Congress (1989).

6. Data on transcontinental information transmission are from Fukuda-Parr and Hill (2002, 187). Data on Internet use are from Fukuda-Parr and Hill (2002, figures 3.1.2 and 3.1.3). The December 2004 figure is from http://www.internetworldstats.com/stats.htm. The number of users can be compared to a projected population of 6.45 billion in 2005 according to the Population Division of the Department of Economic and Social Affairs of the United Nations Secretariat, *World Population Prospects: The 2002 Revision* and *World Urbanization Prospects: The 2001 Revision*, http://esa.un .org/unpp.

7. For a comprehensive view, see Gilbert, Powell, and Vines (2000) and, especially, King (2002).

8. Data are from April 2003 from "A Changing World Bank," posted on DevNews Media Briefs on the World Bank Web site.

9. Ibid.

10. The knowledge bank strategy also has appealing political spins. While foreign aid is taken to task (e.g., Easterly 2001, 2002), providing information is hard to criticize as a source of weak incentives and inefficiencies. Funneling billions of dollars to Mobuto's Zaire fueled a kleptocracy. Funneling ideas and data to trouble spots is a safer bet.

11. The UK-based Bretton Woods project is one source for critical perspectives (www .brettonwoodsproject.org). Another is the 50 Years Is Enough movement (www.50years.org).

12. Steve Denning related this story to me, interview, July 19, 2002, Washington, D.C.

13. These views are very much inside views. At the time of writing the chapter, Ferreira was a member of the World Bank staff and Stern was a professor at the London School of Economics and the chief economist of the European Bank for Reconstruction and Development. He became World Bank chief economist and senior vice president of development economics in July 2000.

14. Seers (1962) has further speculations on "why visiting economists fail."

15. See, for example, MacRae and Whittington (1997).

16. Conversation with Jeffrey Hammer, July 19, 2002, World Bank. Counterexamples exist, but the broad observation remains striking.

17. Theory says only that international agencies may have a role in financing the provision of global public goods. Theory does not say that international agencies should provide the goods themselves; see, e.g., Jayaraman and Kanbur (1999). Stiglitz (1999) makes a slightly less bold claim

with regard to public goods, arguing that the hallmark of nonrivalry is that the marginal cost of provision to another user is zero. This, he claims, is true for knowledge provision, so social optimality implies public distribution. At the same time, though, he notes that people may often be excluded from access from information, making it an impure public good in those cases—and making it possible to charge for receipt of information (a fact that the consulting industry—and universities—understand well).

18. Low quality need not be a function of lack of overall effort. It may be the opposite: overburdened staff with too many tasks to manage may not be able to be as attentive to any given task as they would like.

19. Martine Haas (2001) suggests the opposite possibility based on her study of the internal efficiency of World Bank operations. She suggests that too much information can undermine projects where absorptive capacity is low. She does not suggest that this is strategic, but one might imagine that in some cases, it could be. Just as with lawyers who sometimes dump too much information on opposing counsel, it may be strategic sometimes to provide too much information when trying to shape the actions of recipients.

20. The observation that knowledge may be controlled and regulated by powerful institutions in society to foster particular conversations and ways of thinking (and to dissuade others) is not new (Haas 1990). Both postmodern social critics and Marxist scholars have argued the point forcefully, and they been widely influential, although not, notably, within mainstream economics (Foucault 1981, Lyotard 1984). Even staying within a strictly neoclassical economic frame, though, questions of the strategic generation and sharing of information and knowledge—and implications for efficiency and equity—can be unpacked fruitfully (e.g., Dewatripont and Tirole 1999). The kinds of questions this could raise are suggested below.

21. Bill Easterly suggested this example based on conversations with colleagues working on financial reform. Nancy Birdsall, a former senior staff member of the World Bank, has countered (in comments on an earlier draft of this chapter) that the Wapenhans Report diagnosis may be overplayed.

22. Data are from April 2003, from "A Changing World Bank," posted on DevNews Media Briefs on the World Bank Web site, www.worldbank.org.

23. Students of public policy will note a change from a time when teaching focused mainly on intensive case studies of efforts that went awry. One difficulty is that that kind of pedagogy is harder to accomplish through distance-learning and Web-based methods.

24. So unlike, for example, assumptions maintained in the seminal theoretical work of Milgrom and Roberts (1986), information is not verifiable.

25. A different case in which too much knowledge can be problematic emerges when there is "herding." Consider the case of a favored new idea like microcredit. It is one of many possible solutions, but it has generated particular attention in the past decade. With each new program and each replication, the microcredit community learns more about the practice. Over time, prospective microlenders have richer stories and more reliable data by which to judge whether to join the movement. And with those data, they are more likely to jump aboard. In turn, another example is created, adding more stories and more data—and a stronger push toward microcredit. The trouble is not that microcredit is a bad idea; it is that there are other ideas that do not get adequately tested simply because they lack an initial impetus. In recent theoretical work, Burguet and Vives (2000) show that there are cases when keeping quiet about new ideas—taking the opposite approach from the knowledge bank—can improve welfare. This is because keeping quiet limits the chances that an "inefficient" fad will emerge and gives a wider variety of ideas a fighting chance. As Burguet and Vives conclude, "More public information may hurt." The policy conclusion is not to stay mum but to be aware that providing information can sometimes unintentionally lead to disproportionate focuses on particular interventions at the expense of others.

26. That it is a "new world" is a characterization taken from Otero, Rhyne, and Houghton (1994). See also Robinson (2001).

27. Thus, the public position of USAID and the World Bank's Consultative Group to Assist the Poor is against ongoing subsidies for these new poverty alleviation efforts, although basic economic principles dictate that if the subsidies are effective in delivering important social changes to the

poor, then the subsidies should be taken seriously as a policy tool. CGAP positions are succinctly summarized in its "focus notes" and "donor briefs" available at www.cgap.org. For a broader view, see Morduch (2000).

28. In practice, there is not a single official list but instead a series of partial lists that recur in reports and policy notes of key donors and advocates. The donor community is a large and ever-changing group, and microcredit conversations are not static. While there are important counter-tendencies on the margins, the observations here capture general tendencies within the movement.

29. See, for example, the *Microbanking Bulletin* at www.mixmbb.org.

30. Microenterprise Results and Accountability Act of 2004, 108th Congress, 2nd session, H. R. 3818, February 24, 2004.

31. While best practices get circulated, failures tend to be papered over and forgotten (unless it serves a useful objective of donors). A nice exception is Elisabeth Rhyne's (2001) book on financial and institutional problems that competition brought to commercialized microcredit in Bolivia and Jean Steege's (1998) anatomy of the boom and bust of Colombia's Corposol. Discussions of financially sound institutions that fail to achieve social missions are far harder to find.

References

Armendariz de Aghion, Beatriz, and Jonathan Morduch. 2005. *The Economics of Microfinance*. Cambridge, Mass.: MIT Press.

Burguet, Roberto, and Xavier Vives. 2000. "Social Learning and Costly Information Acquisition." *Economic Theory* 15:185–205.

Chenery, Hollis. 1989. "Foreign Aid." In John Eatwell, Murray Milgate, and Peter Newman, eds., *The New Palgrave: Economic Development*. London: Macmillan.

Crawford, Vincent, and Joel Sobel. 1982. "Strategic Information Transmission." *Econometrica* 50(6):1431–1451.

Denning, Stephen. 2001. "Technical Cooperation and Knowledge Networks." Unpublished draft manuscript. December 2, 2001.

Dewatripont, Mathias, and Jean Tirole. 1999. "Advocates." *Journal of Political Economy* 107(1):1–39.

Dugger, Celia. 2004. "World Bank Challenged: Are the Poor Really Helped?" *New York Times*, July 28, 2004, A4.

Dunford, Christopher. 2002. "What's Wrong with Loan Size?" Freedom from Hunger, Davis, CA. Available at http://www.ffhtechnical.org/publications/summary/loansize0302.html.

Easterly, William. 2001. *The Elusive Quest for Growth: Economists Adventures and Misadventures in the Tropics*. Cambridge, Mass.: MIT Press.

Easterly, William. 2002. "The Cartel of Good Intentions: Bureaucracy versus Markets in Foreign Aid." Center for Global Development Working Paper 4. Washington, D.C.: Center for Global Development.

Einhorn, Jessica. 2001. "The World Bank's Mission Creep." *Foreign Affairs*, September/October: 22–31.

Evenson, Robert, Carl Pray, and Mark Rosengrant. 1999. *Agricultural Research and Productivity Growth in India*. Washington, D.C.: International Food Policy Research Institute.

Ferguson, James. 1994. *The Anti-Politics Machine: Development, Depoliticization, and Bureaucratic Power in Lesotho*. Minneapolis: University of Minnesota Press.

Foucault, Michel. 1981. *Power/Knowledge: Selected Interviews and Other Writings, 1972–1977*. New York: Pantheon.

Frey, Bruno S. 1984. "The Public Choice View of International Political Economy." *International Organization* 38(1):199–223.

Fukuda-Parr, Sakiko, and Ruth Hill. 2002. "The Network Age: Creating New Models of Technical Cooperation," In Sakiko Fukuda-Parr, Carlos Lopes, and Khalid Malik, eds., *Capacity for Development: New Solutions to Old Problems*. London: Earthscan Publications.

Fukuda-Parr, Sakiko, Carlos Lopes, and Khalid Malik, eds. 2002. *Capacity for Development: New Solutions to Old Problems*. London: Earthscan Publications.

Gilbert, Christopher, L., Andrew Powell, and David Vines. 2000. "Positioning the World Bank." In Christopher L. Gilbert and David Vines, eds., *The World Bank: Structure and Policies*. Cambridge: Cambridge University Press.

Gmelin, Wolfgang, Kenneth King, and Simon McGrath. 2001. *Development Knowledge, National Research, and International Cooperation*. Edinburgh, Bonn, and Geneva: Centre for African Studies—Deutsche Stiftung fur Internationale Entwicklung—Northern Research Review and Analysis Group.

Gonzalez-Vega, Claudio. 1994. "Do Financial Institutions Have a Role in Assisting the Poor?" Economics and Sociology Occasional Paper no. 2169, Rural Finance Program, Department of Agricultural Economics, Ohio State University.

Gwin, Catherine. 2003. *Sharing Knowledge: Innovations and Remaining Challenges*. Washington, D.C.: World Bank, Operations Evaluation Department, Available at http://www.worldbank.org/oed/knowledge_evaluation/.

Haas, Ernst B. 1990. *When Knowledge Is Power: Three Models of Change in International Organizations*. Berkeley and Los Angeles: University of California Press.

Haas, Martine. 2001. "Acting On What Others Know: Distributed Knowledge And Team Performance." Working paper, Hauser Center, Kennedy School of Government, Harvard University.

Jayaraman, Rajshri, and Ravi Kanbur. 1999. "International Public Goods and the Case for Foreign Aid." In Inge Kaul et al., eds. *Global Public Goods: International Cooperation in the 21st Century*. New York: Oxford University Press.

Jha, Aditya, Vicky Semour, and Sean Sims. 2004. *Evaluation of the Development Gateway, Final Report*. Prepared for Bretton Woods Project, London, July.

Kanbur, Ravi. 2002. "IFI's and IPG's: Operational Implications for the World Bank." Cornell University working paper. Ithaca, N.Y.: Cornell University.

Khanna, Anupam. 2000. "Knowledge Creation and Management in Global Enterprises: Some Issues for Discussion." Washington, D.C.: World Bank, Office of the Vice President for Development Economics.

King, Kenneth. 2002. "Banking on Knowledge: The New Knowledge Projects of the World Bank." *Compare* 32(3):314–326.

King, Kenneth, and Simon McGrath. 2004. *Knowledge for Development? Comparing British, Japanese, Swedish and World Bank Aid*. London: Zed Books.

Lyotard, Jean-François. 1984. *The Postmodern Condition: A Report on Knowledge*. Minneapolis: University of Minnesota Press.

MacRae, Duncan, and Dale Whittington. 1997. *Expert Advice for Policy Choice*. Washington, D.C.: Georgetown University Press.

Martens, Bertin. 2002. "The Role of Evaluation in Foreign Aid Programs." In Bertin Martens, Uwe Mummert, Peter Murrell, and Paul Seabright, *The Institutional Economics of Foreign Aid*. Cambridge: Cambridge University Press.

Matsui, Akihiko, and Jonathan Morduch. 2003. "The Strategy of Global Public Goods." Unpublished manuscript, University of Tokyo and New York University.

Milgrom, Paul, and John Roberts. 1986. "Relying on the Information of Interested Parties." *Rand Journal of Economics* 17(1):18–32.

Morduch, Jonathan. 2000. "The Microfinance Schism." *World Development* 28(4):607–629.

Niskanen, William. 1971. *Bureaucracy and Representative Government*. Chicago: Aldine-Atherton.

Otero, Maria, Elisabeth Rhyne, and Mary Houghton. 1994. *The New World of Microenterprise Finance: Building Healthy Institutions for the Poor*. Bloomfield, Conn.: Kumarian Press.

Panos Institute. 1998. "Information, Knowledge, and Development." London: Panos Institute.

Pritchett, Lant. 2002. "It Pays to Be Ignorant: A Simple Political Economy of Rigorous Program Evaluation." *Journal of Policy Reform* 5(4):251–269.

Rhyne, Elisabeth. 2001. *Mainstreaming Microfinance: How Lending to the Poor Began, Grew, and Came of Age in Bolivia*. Bloomfield, Conn.: Kumarian Press.

Robinson, Marguerite. 2001. *The Microfinance Revolution*. Washington, D.C.: World Bank.

Samuelson, Paul. 1954. *Foundations of Economic Analysis*. Cambridge, MA: Harvard University Press.

Seers, Dudley. 1962. "Why Visiting Economists Fail." *Journal of Political Economy* 70(4):325–338.

Squire, Lyn. 2000. "Why the World Bank Should Be Involved in Development Research." In Christopher L. Gilbert and David Vines, eds., *The World Bank: Structure and Policies*. Cambridge: Cambridge University Press.

Steege, Jean. 1998. *The Rise and Fall of Corposol: Lessons from the Challenges of Managing Growth*. Microfinance Best Practices Report: 1–134.

Stern, Nicholas, and Francisco Ferreira. 1997. "The World Bank as 'Intellectual Actor.'" In Devesh Kapur, John P. Lewis, and Richard Webb, eds., *The World Bank: Its First Half Century*. Washington, D.C.: Brookings Institution Press.

Stiglitz, Joseph. 1999. "Knowledge as a Global Public Good." In Inge Kaul et al., eds., *Global Public Goods: International Cooperation in the 21st Century*. New York: Oxford University Press.

Stiglitz, Joseph. 2000. "Reflections on the Theory and Practice of Reform." In Anne Krueger, ed., *Economic Policy Reform: The Second Stage*. Chicago: University of Chicago Press.

Stiglitz, Joseph. 2001. "Scan Globally, Reinvent Locally: Knowledge Infrastructure and the Localization of Knowledge." In Ha-Joon Change, ed., *Joseph Stiglitz and the World Bank: The Rebel Within*. London: Anthem Press.

U.S. Congress. 1989. *Inaugural Addresses of the Presidents of the United States*. Washington, D.C.: U.S. Government Printing Office.

U.S. General Accounting Office. 2002. "Foreign Assistance: USAID Relies Heavily on Nongovernmental Organizations, But Better Data Needed to Evaluate Approaches." Report to the Chairman, Subcommittee on National Security, Veterans Affairs, and International Relations, Committee on Government Reform, House of Representatives.

Van Evera, Stephen. 2002. "Why States Believe Foolish Ideas: Non-Self-Evaluation in States and Societies." Unpublished manuscript, Department of Political Science, MIT.

Vaubel, Roland, and Thomas D. Willet, eds. 1991. *The Political Economy of International Organizations: A Public Choice Approach*. Boulder, Colo.: Westview Press.

Wildavsky, Aaron. 1972. "The Self-Evaluating Organization." *Public Administration Review* 32(5):509–520.

Wilks, Alex. 2002. "From the Adam Smith Institute to the Zapatistas: An Internet Gateway to All Development Knowledge." *Compare* 32(3):327–337.

Wolfensohn, James, D. 1996. "People and Development." Speech at 1996 Annual Meetings of the World Bank and International Monetary Fund. Available at http://www.worldbank.org/html/extdr/extme/jdwams96.htm.

World Bank. 1992. "Effective Implementation: Key to Development Impact." World Bank Working Paper R92-195, Washington, D.C., November 3.

World Bank. 1998. *World Development Report 1998/1999: Knowledge for Development*. New York: Oxford University Press.

14 Debt Relief and Fiscal Sustainability for Heavily Indebted Poor Countries

Craig Burnside and Domenico Fanizza

Debt relief under the HIPC initiative differs from previous major debt relief initiatives, such as the Baker and Brady plans, in that it concerns official rather than commercial debt. It also differs from previous Paris Club debt reduction and rescheduling agreements in that it imposes well-defined conditionality on government spending in the debtor country. In particular, it requires that budgetary resources no longer needed for debt service be used for poverty reduction purposes.[1]

In this chapter we argue that the conditionality of HIPC debt relief implies that it provides no net relaxation of the government's lifetime budget constraint. To the extent that the resources freed from debt service are used to increase government spending, any initial budgetary shortfall faced by the government remains in place.

We also argue that central banks in countries receiving debt relief may face a monetary policy dilemma. An increase in government spending on domestic goods, services, or transfers will naturally lead to a monetary injection into the economy. If the central bank responds passively to this inflow, inflation will be destabilized, rising during the implementation of debt relief and falling during the postdebt relief period. If the central bank acts to sterilize this monetary injection, inflation will be stable, but the stock of debt will rise to its predebt relief level.

In section 14.1 we illustrate the short-term impact of debt relief with HIPC conditionality using a simple one-period model. We use a standard specification of the government budget constraint to establish that any shortfall the government faces is invariant to its receiving debt relief with conditionality that requires it to increase spending.

We then use standard textbook T-accounts to illustrate the central bank's monetary policy dilemma. We show that a natural consequence of the government's increased spending on poverty reduction is a monetary injection equal in value to the amount of debt relief the government receives. To the extent that the central bank sterilizes this injection, it must sell government debt or reduce its foreign reserves by the same amount. This leaves its debt unchanged relative to its predebt relief level. Thus, debt relief replaces existing official foreign currency–denominated public debt with only domestic debt or new external debt.

In section 14.2 we extend our analysis to a simple multiperiod model of the government's budget and money demand. Within this framework, our results are robust. Debt relief with HIPC conditionality provides no net relaxation of the government's lifetime budget constraint. Absent other changes in its benchmark fiscal policy, the increase in government spending over the lifetime of the initiative and implied by its conditionality offsets the value of the forgiven debt service. To the extent that the government had difficulty satisfying its lifetime budget constraint, it still does.

We also extend our results on the monetary policy dilemma using a simple monetary model based on the quantity theory of money. With this model, we can fully characterize the equilibrium dynamics of prices, inflation, debt, and seigniorage during and after the implementation of a debt relief initiative. We describe the central bank as passive if it does not sterilize the monetary injection associated with the increase in government spending that follows from HIPC conditionality. Passive policy causes a short-term increase in inflation, which is reversed in the postdebt relief period. An active central bank can stabilize inflation at its initial level, but to do so, it must sterilize the monetary injection. If it does, we show that the government's net debt level will be equal to its predebt relief level by the terminal date of the initiative.

In section 14.3, we provide concluding remarks as well as caveats to our analysis. Importantly, our analysis says nothing about the welfare implications of the HIPC initiative. It is clear that regardless of fiscal sustainability issues, the initiative represents a resource transfer from creditors to debtors. So absent strategic issues, this transfer should be welfare increasing for the debtor countries. An important strategic issue that we ignore is the possibility that donors will treat debt relief as a substitute for other forms of aid. To the extent that they do this, of course, the extent to which the HIPC benefits from debt relief is reduced. We also ignore concerns that debt relief reduces the incentive for HIPC governments to introduce economic reforms. Finally, we discuss whether there are indirect benefits to fiscal sustainability stemming from HIPC debt relief. If the government's increased spending spurs development, this may increase government revenue. We argue, however, that the magnitude of such effects is likely to be modest.

14.1   A One-Period Model

In this section we outline a one-period model that allows us to derive our main results within the simplest possible framework. We begin by discussing the implications of debt relief with HIPC conditionality for fiscal sustainability. Then, within a framework familiar to students of monetary theory and policy, we discuss a possible monetary policy dilemma faced by a recipient government.

14.1.1   Fiscal Sustainability in a One-Period Model

Imagine a model of a single period in which a government enters the period with some outstanding amount of debt, D. Since the world lasts for only a single period, this debt must be retired at the end of the period. Therefore, the government's budget constraint is simply:

$$\text{Outstanding debt} = \text{Budget balance} + \text{seigniorage} \tag{14.1}$$

or

$$D = BB + \Delta M, \tag{14.2}$$

where D is the level of net debt, BB is the budget balance, and ΔM is seigniorage revenue. Within the budget balance, we may distinguish between interest on the debt, rD, primary government expenditure, G, government revenue, T, and foreign aid, A. So equation 14.2 becomes

$$D = T + A - G - rD + \Delta M$$

or

$$(1 + r)D = T + A - G + \Delta M. \tag{14.3}$$

Since the HIPC initiative is targeted at countries that among their characteristics have difficulty servicing their debt, we interpret these countries' initial condition as one in which D is very large. By "very large" we mean that the government must either raise an implausibly, or punitively, high level of tax revenue (T), seek extraordinary amounts of aid (A), slash its spending (G), or print a large amount of money (ΔM), to avoid default.

To highlight the role of debt relief in determining the government's financial state, we rearrange equation 14.3 as follows:

$$(1 + r)D - A = T - G + \Delta M. \tag{14.4}$$

Let us imagine that given the government's benchmark budget plans and the likely amounts of aid it will receive, there is a shortfall in its budget. That is, suppose $(1 + r)D - A > T - G + \Delta M$, so that equation 14.4 does not hold. This would require the government to default on a portion of its debt with the same value as the shortfall

$$S = (1 + r)D - A - (T - G + \Delta M). \tag{14.5}$$

We think of countries that need debt relief as those with large values of S given reasonable benchmarks for their budgetary plans.

Suppose the government obtains debt cancellation or, equivalently, additional outside aid with a value of R. Let $A' = A + R$ be the new level of aid being received by the government. This implies that the government's budget shortfall is reduced by the amount of this relief:

$$S' = (1 + r)D - A' - (T - G + \Delta M) = S - R. \tag{14.6}$$

If $R \geq S$, the government will be able to finance its benchmark budget plans without default. If the government still faces a budget shortfall, there is a sense in which the sustainability of its finances has been improved. The amount by which $T - G + \Delta M$ would have to adjust upward relative to the benchmark budget would be smaller.

Now suppose that the government receives debt relief, as under the HIPC initiative, which commits it to increased expenditures on goods and services equal to the value of the aid it receives. In other words, relative to its benchmark level of spending, the government must increase G to the level $G' = G + R$. Now

$$S'' = (1 + r)D - A' - (T - G' + \Delta M) = S. \tag{14.7}$$

This simple example illustrates that aid with HIPC conditionality leaves the government in the same fiscal situation it was in before. To the extent that the government faced a budget shortfall before, it still faces one now. There is no change in the sustainability of the government's budget plans.[2] One caveat to our analysis is that the HIPC initiative includes a top-up clause through which countries can receive additional debt relief on reaching the completion point. However, as originally envisaged, this top-up would have been rare and relatively small compared to the size of the baseline debt reduction.

14.1.2 The Monetary Policy Dilemma

To illustrate the monetary policy dilemma that arises with debt relief and HIPC conditionality, we use a simple accounting framework. Imagine a scenario in which the central bank and government simplified balance sheets at the beginning of the period are as described as in table 14.1a.

Table 14.1
Public sector balance sheets before debt relief

Central Bank		Government	
Assets	Liabilities	Assets	Liabilities
a. Initial balance sheets of the public sector			
FX reserves	Monetary base	Government deposits	Gross debt
Government bonds	Government deposits		
Net nonmonetary debt of the public sector: Gross debt − government bonds held by the central bank − FX reserves			
b. Changes in balance sheets after revenue inflows and expenditure outflows			
FX reserves $+A$	Monetary base $+(G-T)$	Government deposits $+(A+T-G)$	Gross debt n.c.
Government bonds n.c.	Government deposits $+(A+T-G)$		
Net nonmonetary debt of the public sector: $-A$			
c. Changes in balance sheets after government pays off debt			
FX reserves $+A$	Monetary base $+A$	Government deposits n.c.	Gross debt $-(A+T-G)$
Government bonds n.c.	Government deposits n.c.		
Net nonmonetary debt of the public sector: $-(2A+T-G)$			
d. Changes in balance sheets after central bank manages the public sector debt			
FX reserves n.c.	Monetary base $+\Delta M$	Government deposits n.c.	Gross debt $-(A+T-G)$
Government bonds $+\Delta M$	Government deposits n.c.		
Net nonmonetary debt of the public sector: $-(A+T-G+\Delta M)$			

Note: n.c.: No change.

In the absence of debt relief, as above, we assume that the government receives revenue in the form of aid, A, and taxes, T. These inflows affect the balance sheet in the manner indicated in table 14.1b. Aid arrives in the form of a grant of additional foreign exchange reserves, A, which the central bank credits to the government's deposit account. Taxes, T, flow into the government's account at the central bank in either the form of cash or checks drawn on the banking system, so the increase in the government's deposits at the central bank is matched one for one by a decrease in the monetary base. In table 14.1b we also see the result of the government's expenditure on goods and services, G. These draw down the government's deposits at the central bank by G and, at the same time, increase the stock of base money.[3]

At the end of the period, the government's deposits at the central bank have increased by the amount $A + T - G$, so the government consolidates its finances at the end of the period by writing a check on its deposit account to pay down its debt by the amount $A + T - G$ (see table 14.1c). Its deposit account at the central bank is thus reduced to zero.

Notice that if the period were to end as described by table 14.1c, the public sector's nonmonetary debt would have changed by the amount $-(2A + T - G)$, while the monetary base would have increased by the amount A. If we consolidated monetary and nonmonetary debt, this would imply a net change in debt equal to $-(A + T - G)$. We like to think of the central bank as a debt manager who chooses the allocation of this change in debt between monetary and nonmonetary debt. We assume that the central bank conducts open market sales of foreign exchange (with a total value of A), and open market purchases of government bonds (with a total value of ΔM), so that the end-of-period balance sheets appear as in table 14.1d. Notice that since the change in nonmonetary debt is now $-(A + T - G + \Delta M)$ and the change in the monetary base is ΔM, the overall change in debt is still $-(A + T - G)$.

Now suppose the government obtains debt relief with value R from a foreign donor. In table 14.2, we ask how the public sector balance sheets change as a result of this debt relief, relative to their state in table 14.1d. Of course, debt relief directly reduces the government's debt and public sector net debt by an amount R, as in table 14.2a.

Suppose, however, that in order to receive debt relief, the government must commit itself to an increase in government purchases of domestic goods and services, or transfers to domestic residents, with value R. Assuming that the government does not raise new taxes or cut other government expenditure in order to finance this increased spending, the central bank must create money. In fact, this money creation is the natural result of the government's increasing its spending in the absence of any additional taxation. The public sector accounts end up looking like table 14.2b.

The effect on the money supply of the government's increased spending can be sterilized by the central bank. It can sell government bonds in an open market operation, as in table 14.2c. Notice, however, that as a result of the central bank's decision, the public sector's net debt position rises back to its predebt relief level.[4]

Suppose that rather than increasing domestic purchases or transfers, as in table 14.2b, the government increases its spending on imported goods and services. Then, instead of there being an increase in the monetary base, as in table 14.2b, the central bank's foreign exchange reserves are drawn down by the amount R (see table 14.2d). Notice, however, that the final outcome is equivalent to table 14.2c in terms of the public sector's net debt. It is unchanged relative to the predebt relief level.

Table 14.2
Public sector balance sheets after debt relief

Central Bank		Government	
Assets	Liabilities	Assets	Liabilities
a. Changes in balance sheets after debt relief is provided			
FX reserves n.c.	Monetary base n.c.	Government deposits n.c.	Gross debt $-R$
Government bonds n.c.	Government deposits n.c.		
Net nonmonetary debt of the public sector: $-R$			
b. Changes in balance sheets after HIPC conditionality is imposed			
FX reserves n.c.	Monetary base $+R$	Government deposits $-R$	Gross debt $-R$
Government bonds n.c.	Government deposits $-R$		
Net nonmonetary debt of the public sector: $-R$			
c. Changes in balance sheets after central bank sterilizes the monetary injection			
FX reserves n.c.	Monetary base n.c.	Government deposits $-R$	Gross debt $-R$
Government bonds $-R$	Government deposits $-R$		
Net nonmonetary debt of the public sector: n.c.			
d. Changes in balance sheets after increased government purchases are directed toward imported goods			
FX reserves $-R$	Monetary base n.c.	Government deposits $-R$	Gross debt $-R$
Government bonds	Government deposits $-R$		
Net nonmonetary debt of the public sector: n.c.			

Note: n.c.: No change.

14.2   A Multiperiod Analysis

In this section we extend the results we obtained with the one-period model to a dynamic model. Once again we show that debt relief with HIPC conditionality has no impact on a government's fiscal sustainability. In the dynamic model, this means that there is no relaxation of the government's lifetime budget constraint implied by debt relief. Similarly, we show that the central bank faces a monetary policy dilemma. The natural consequence of the government's increased spending for poverty reduction is a monetary injection that occurs over the life of the debt relief initiative. To the extent that the central bank sterilizes this injection, inflation can be stabilized, but this implies no long-run reduction in the government's level of debt.

14.2.1   The Government's Intertemporal Budget Constraint

We now present a standard model of the government's intertemporal budget constraint in continuous time. In our simple model, there is only one good, whose price is P_t. The government issues only one type of debt, D_t, whose value is indexed in terms of that good. We assume, for simplicity, that the net real interest rate on government debt is some constant r. The government finances its interest payments, rD_t, and its spending on goods, services, and transfers, G_t, in four ways: by raising tax revenue, T_t; through the issuance of base money, M_t; by receiving aid, A_t; or through the issuance of new debt. The government raises funds by issuing base money using seigniorage revenue, $\dot{M}_t/P_t$, where P_t is the price level and $\dot{M}_t$ is the time derivative of the money stock.[5] Hence, the government's flow budget constraint is given by

$$\dot{D}_t = rD_t + G_t - T_t - A_t - \dot{M}_t/P_t, \tag{14.8}$$

where all variables are measured in units of the single good.

The solution to the differential equation 14.8 is

$$D_t = e^{rt}D_0 - \int_0^t (T_s - G_s + A_s + \dot{M}_s/P_s)e^{r(t-s)}\,ds. \tag{14.9}$$

If we take the limit as $t \to \infty$ and impose the no-Ponzi scheme condition that $\lim_{t \to \infty} e^{-rt}D_t = 0$, we obtain

$$D_0 = \int_0^\infty (T_t - G_t + A_t + \dot{M}_t/P_t)e^{-rt}\,dt. \tag{14.10}$$

Our interpretation of a highly indebted government at time t is as follows: given the likely paths of $\{T_t\}_{t \in [0,\infty)}$, $\{G_t\}_{t \in [0,\infty)}$, $\{A_t\}_{t \in [0,\infty)}$, and $\{\dot{M}_t/P_t\}_{t \in [0,\infty)}$, the government's lifetime budget constraint, equation 14.10, is violated. In other words, without (1) fiscal reforms that would increase future values of T_t or decrease future values of G_t, (2) a substantial increased in anticipated aid inflows, A_t, or (3) higher rates of money growth and seigniorage revenue, the government will be unable to service its debt while avoiding default. The lifetime budget constraint holds only if a government does not default.

To measure the degree to which a highly indebted government has a fiscal sustainability problem, we define

$$V_0 \equiv \int_0^\infty (T_t - G_t + A_t + \dot{M}_t/P_t)e^{-rt}\,dt. \tag{14.11}$$

Here V_0 represents the present value of the government's future primary surpluses and seigniorage revenue given benchmark values for its future revenue, spending, aid, and seigniorage flows. The government's lifetime budget shortfall is given by $S_0 = D_0 - V_0$, the difference between the value of the government's initial debt and the extent to which it will be able to service it based on its benchmark budget.

The design of the HIPC debt relief program can be interpreted as follows. A country that receives debt forgiveness under the program is one that finds its debt level at date 0 reduced to $D_0' = (1 - \theta)D_0$, with $0 < \theta < 1$. Formally, the initiative reduces debt by forgiving a substantial portion of future debt service payments. Here θD_0 represents the present value of these forgiven payments.

Clearly if debt relief were given unconditionally, this would reduce the government's budget shortfall since we would have $S_0' = D_0' - V_0 = S_0 - \theta D_0$. Debt relief under the HIPC initiative, however, comes with conditionality attached. This conditionality is equivalent to a simultaneous increase in the present value of the future path of $\{G_t\}_{t \in [0, \infty)}$ equal in value to θD_0. This is because the forgiven debt service payments are targeted toward increased spending on poverty reduction initiatives. So the present value of future government spending will rise by an equivalent amount to the present value of the forgiven debt service absent some independent fiscal reform. Hence, the present value of the government's future primary surpluses plus seigniorage revenue falls by the amount θD_0: $V_0' = V_0 - \theta D_0$. There is no change in the size of the government's lifetime budget shortfall, which equals $S_0' = D_0' - V_0' = S_0$. Thus, in a well-defined sense, the design of the debt relief initiative does not make the government's debt position more sustainable.

14.2.2   A Simple Monetary Framework

In this section, we examine a simple model of price determination. Together with the government budget constraint, this model allows us to discuss the dynamic inflationary implications of different policy responses to debt relief.

We assume that money demand takes the form implied by the quantity theory of money,

$$M_t^d = v^{-1} P_t Y_t, \tag{14.12}$$

where $v > 0$ is some constant, Y_t represents the level of output, and P_t continues to denote the price level. Although some of the specific implications of the quantity theory do not hold for more general money demand specifications, our qualitative results are robust to different models of money demand.[6] We will assume that the level of output is constant, and we will normalize it to equal 1. Hence, in money market equilibrium, our solution for the price level is just

$$P_t = vM_t, \tag{14.13}$$

where M_t is the supply of money. If the money growth rate is $\mu_t = \dot{M}_t/M_t$, this means that seigniorage revenue is

$$\dot{M}_t/P_t = v^{-1}\mu_t. \tag{14.14}$$

To analyze the impact of debt relief on the price level, we will situate the economy in an initial steady state at time 0. Since we wish to abstract from issues of default and have shown that the initiative has no net impact on long-run sustainability, we assume that with or without debt relief, the government will, with difficulty, adjust its benchmark fiscal plans so that its lifetime budget constraint, equation 14.10, holds.

In the initial predebt relief steady state, we assume that G_t, T_t, A_t, and μ_t are given by constant values G, T, A, and μ. Using these assumptions, the government's lifetime budget constraint, equation 14.10, can be rewritten as

$$rD_0 = T - G + A + v^{-1}\mu. \tag{14.15}$$

The government must set its fiscal plans so that its primary balance plus seigniorage is equal to its flow of debt service. Furthermore, from the flow budget constraint, equation 14.8, we get the implication that the government's debt stock is constant at the level D_0. Given that money grows at a constant rate, the inflation rate is simply $\pi_t = \mu$ for all t.

To make our example as simple as possible, we will assume that the government issues debt in the form of perpetuities. So in the initial steady state, the government has a stock of perpetuities that will pay out interest equal to rD_0 in each period into the infinite future.

The HIPC initiative typically forgives some fraction of a country's existing debt service obligations out to some finite horizon in the future. To capture this aspect of the initiative, we will assume that at time 0, the holders of the government's perpetuities announce that between date 0 and date $\bar{t}$, they will forgive some fraction ψ of the interest payments on the existing stock of perpetuities. For this to amount to a reduction of the government's debt by the amount θD_0, we can see that the parameter ψ must be such that $\theta D_0 = \int_0^{\bar{t}} \psi r D_0 e^{-rt}\, dt = \psi(1 - e^{-r\bar{t}})D_0$. Hence, $\psi = \theta/(1 - e^{-r\bar{t}})$.

Our interpretation of the HIPC initiative is that at time 0, the country receives previously unanticipated debt relief of the form described above. We interpret the conditionality of the HIPC initiative as requiring that government expenditure increase by as much as the aid flow until date $\bar{t}$:

$$G_t = \begin{cases} G + \psi r D_0 & \text{for } 0 \leq t < \bar{t} \\ G & \text{for } t \geq \bar{t}. \end{cases} \tag{14.16}$$

We assume that taxes and aid remain unchanged, so that $T_t = T$ and $A_t = A$ for all t. Together these assumptions imply that the present value of the government's primary surpluses goes down by the amount θD_0, which is precisely the same as the reduction in the value of the government's debt at time 0.

So far we have said nothing about the path of the money supply under the debt relief initiative. We now explore monetary policy by considering two alternative paths for the money supply in the postdebt relief world.

Notice that under the HIPC initiative, as described in the previous section, the government increases its primary expenditure by the amount $\psi r D_0$ for $0 \leq t < \bar{t}$. As we saw in the simple T-account examples, increased government spending requires an instantaneous injection of money into the domestic economy. In response to this monetary injection, the central bank could be passive, in the sense that it could take no action. Alternatively, the central bank could sterilize the monetary injection through an offsetting sale of domestic government debt or foreign reserves. In what follows, we explore these two possibilities, keeping in mind, of course, that there are many others.

Passive Monetary Policy

We first describe a passive central bank that does not respond to the injection of liquidity created by the government's increased spending. The real value of government spending is higher by the amount $\psi r D_0$ in the period $0 \leq t < \bar{t}$. So if the central bank acts passively, the real value of seigniorage revenue, $\dot{M}_t/P_t = v^{-1}\mu_t$, will be higher by the same amount. Hence, $\dot{M}_t/P_t = v^{-1}\mu_t = v^{-1}\mu + \psi r D_0$, and the money growth rate (and the inflation rate) will rise to the level

$$\mu_t = \bar{\mu} = \mu + v\psi r D_0 \quad \text{for } 0 \leq t \leq \bar{t}. \tag{14.17}$$

To get some sense of the quantitative magnitudes implied, imagine that the country's initial debt level is 70 percent of GDP ($D_0 = 0.7$), the real interest rate is 2 percent ($r = 0.02$), the monetary base is 10 percent of GDP ($v^{-1} = 0.1$), 50 percent of the debt is forgiven ($\theta = 0.5$), and the life of the initiative is 20 years ($\bar{t} = 20$). Together these assumptions imply that $\psi = 1.52$ and $\bar{\mu} - \mu = 0.21$; the inflation rate would rise by roughly 21 percentage points.

An interesting consequence of passive policy is that the government's debt level is reduced by the terminal date of the initiative, despite our result that there is no net relaxation of the government's lifetime budget constraint at time 0. From equation 14.9, we can see that

$$D_{\bar{t}} = e^{r\bar{t}}(1 - \theta)D_0 - \int_0^{\bar{t}} (T - G + A + v^{-1}\mu)e^{r(\bar{t}-s)}\, ds$$

$$= (1 - \theta e^{r\bar{t}})D_0. \tag{14.18}$$

The first line follows from the fact that $G_t = G + \psi r D_0$, while seigniorage revenue is $v^{-1}\mu + \psi r D_0$. The second line follows from equation 14.15. The reason that the debt level is permanently reduced is that with passive policy, the increased government spending is financed by seigniorage revenue and debt relief provides additional financing.

Given the previous result, notice that the government would satisfy its lifetime budget constraint at date $\bar{t}$ if, for $t > \bar{t}$, it set $\dot{M}_t/P_t$ consistent with

$$D_{\bar{t}} = \frac{1}{r}(T - G + A) + \int_{\bar{t}}^{\infty} (\dot{M}_t/P_t)e^{-r(t-\bar{t})}\, dt. \tag{14.19}$$

If the government sets the money growth rate equal to a constant μ for $t > \bar{t}$, equation 14.18, combined with equations 14.19 and 14.15, implies

$$\underline{\mu} - \mu = -vr\theta e^{r\bar{t}}D_0.$$

So the long-run inflation rate, $\underline{\mu}$, is lower than the initial inflation rate. In our numerical example, we would have $\underline{\mu} - \mu = -0.10$: the inflation rate is lower in the long run by 10 percentage points.

Active Monetary Policy

By an active central bank, we mean one that sterilizes the monetary injection associated with the government's increased spending in the period $0 \leq t < \bar{t}$. As money flows into the economy, the central bank buys in back from the private sector through an offsetting sale of domestic government debt or foreign reserves.

Under this policy, the money supply continues to grow at the rate μ, and the inflation rate stays the same as in the predebt relief steady state. From equation 14.9, we can see that

$$D_{\bar{t}} = e^{r\bar{t}}(1 - \theta)D_0 - \int_0^{\bar{t}} (T - G - \psi r D + A + v^{-1}\mu)e^{r(\bar{t}-s)}\, ds$$

$$= D_0. \tag{14.20}$$

By the time the terminal date of the initiative is reached, the country's debt level is once again equal to its initial debt level. This is the cumulative result of the central bank's policy of sterilization.

Of course, once the initiative is over, the government's debt level remains at D_0, and money growth and inflation continue at the rate μ.

Discussion

We summarize our findings as follows. Under active monetary policy, (1) the government's debt level is not permanently reduced but (2) inflation is stable. Under passive monetary policy, (1) the government's debt level is permanently reduced, but (2) inflation is unstable, rising during the period of increased government spending and falling after the initiative ends.

We should note that under either type of policy, we kept $T_t = T$ and $A_t = A$ for all t. The path of government purchases was described by equation 14.16 in both cases. Since the initial debt level was $(1 - \theta)D_0$ in both cases, it is clear that the present value of seigniorage revenue is identical across the two examples. The distinction between the two is that the timing of seigniorage revenue is different. Under passive policy, bigger monetary injections during the life of the initiative are followed by smaller ones in the postinitiative period. Under active policy, monetary financing is stable over time.[7]

14.3 Caveats and Conclusions

We conclude by first pointing out several important caveats to our analysis. Most important, our analysis is not a negative statement about the welfare implications of the HIPC initiative. Although we argue that fiscal sustainability is not enhanced, it is clear that the initiative represents a resource transfer from creditor countries to debtor countries. Therefore, other things equal, it is welfare enhancing to the debtor countries.[8]

We abstract from the possibility, raised by Cohen (2001), that donors will decrease their nondebt relief aid once the HIPC initiative is under way. Of course, any decline in other forms of aid would offset the value of the debt relief provided by the donors and would imply a net worsening of the government's fiscal position.

We have also ignored incentives effects that stem from aid and debt relief.[9] For example, we do not take into account the possibility that with preferences unchanged, HIPC governments may undo the effects of debt relief (see Easterly 2002, Burnside and Fanizza 2004).

Undoubtedly there may be some indirect benefits to fiscal sustainability stemming from the impact of HIPC debt relief on domestic income. We explore the likely magnitude of these effects in Burnside and Fanizza (2004) and conclude that they are relatively modest, perhaps amounting to at most about one-quarter of the country's initial debt stock under generous assumptions about the returns to foreign aid.[10]

Our main focus has been on two simple points. First, debt relief conditioned on increased government spending does not relax the government's lifetime budget constraint. Second, monetary policymakers face a policy dilemma. If they act passively in the face of monetary inflows stemming from increased government spending, this can have a destabilizing effect on inflation. But if they active sterilize these inflows, the government stock of debt returns to its predebt relief level.

Notes

1. For a simple description of the HIPC initiative, see Van Trotsenburg and MacArthur (1999) and the World Bank's HIPC Web site: www.worldbank.org/hipc.

2. Later, we show that this result extends to a multiperiod model. In the context of that model, debt relief with HIPC conditionality has no impact on the government lifetime budget constraint.

3. We are implicitly assuming that the government's purchases of goods and services are made in the domestic goods market.

4. Later, in a dynamic context, we obtain a similar result. The government can postpone the monetary implications of debt relief with HIPC conditionality through sterilization. However, it must eventually face the reality of its intertemporal budget constraint: absent cuts in future spending or rises in future taxes, the present value of future seigniorage revenue must rise in order for the level of debt to fall.

5. We generically indicate time derivatives, $\partial Z_t / \partial t$, as $\dot{Z}_t$.

6. In Burnside and Fanizza (2004), we use a Cagan money demand framework. When money demand is interest elastic, future values of the quantity of money influence the current price level, whereas under the quantity theory, all that is relevant is the current quantity. With interest-elastic money demand, this means that the precise timing of inflation may be different than it is under the quantity theory.

7. Our results are the mirror image of Sargent and Wallace's (1981) unpleasant monetarist arithmetic: without a change in the primary surplus, low inflation now means more inflation later. In our case, lower inflation in the future means higher inflation now.

8. Our analysis has also omitted the possible welfare consequences of destabilized inflation under passive monetary policy.

9. See, for example, Corden (1989), Bulow and Rogoff (1990), Casella and Eichengreen (1996), and Svensson (2000).

10. The results in Burnside and Fanizza (2004) are based on the assumption that the returns to foreign aid are quite high, of a magnitude consistent with what Burnside and Dollar (2000) suggest is consistent with a good policy country. Implicit in the analysis is the notion that government investment in capital leads to growth. Easterly and Levine (2001), and Devarajan, Easterly, and Pack (2003) provide independent evidence that there is good reason to think that our assumptions are, if anything, overly generous.

References

Bulow, Jeremy, and Kenneth Rogoff. 1990. "Cleaning Up Third World Debt without Getting Taken to the Cleaners." *Journal of Economic Perspectives* 4:31–42.

Burnside, Craig, and David Dollar. 2000. "Aid, Policies, and Growth." *American Economic Review* 90:847–868.

Burnside, Craig, and Domenico Fanizza. 2004. "Hiccups for HIPCs?" NBER Working Paper 10903. Cambridge, Mass.: National Bureau of Economic Research.

Casella, Alessandra, and Barry Eichengreen. 1996. "Can Foreign Aid Accelerate Stabilization?" *Economic Journal* 106:605–619.

Cohen, Daniel. 2001. "The HIPC Initiative: True and False Promises." *International Finance* 4:363–380.

Corden, W. Max. 1989. "Debt Relief and Adjustment Incentives." In Jacob A. Frenkel, Michael P. Dooley, and Peter Wickham, eds., *Analytical Issues in Debt*. Washington, D.C.: International Monetary Fund.

Devarajan, Shanta, William Easterly, and Howard Pack. 2003. "Low Investment Is Not the Constraint on African Development." *Economic Development and Cultural Change* 51:547–571.

Easterly, William. 2002. "How Did the Heavily Indebted Poor Countries Become Heavily Indebted? Reviewing Two Decades of Debt Relief." *World Development* 30:1677–1696.

Easterly, William, and Ross Levine. 2001. "What Have We Learned from a Decade of Empirical Research on Growth? It's Not Factor Accumulation: Stylized Facts and Growth Models." *World Bank Economic Review* 15:177–219.

Sargent, Thomas, and Wallace, Neil. 1981. "Some Unpleasant Monetarist Arithmetic." *Federal Reserve Bank of Minneapolis Quarterly Review* 5(Fall):1–17.

Svensson, Jakob. 2000. "Foreign Aid and Rent-Seeking." *Journal of International Economics* 51:437–461.

Van Trotsenburg, Axel, and Alan MacArthur. 1999. "The HIPC Initiative: Delivering Debt Relief to Poor Countries." Washington, D.C.: International Monetary Fund and World Bank.

V IMAGINING NEW FORMS OF FOREIGN AID

15 Making Vaccines Pay

Michael Kremer

Malaria, tuberculosis, and the strains of HIV common in Africa kill 5 million people each year, overwhelmingly in poor countries. Vaccines offer the best hope for conquering these diseases, yet research on such vaccines remains minimal, largely because prospective developers fear that they will not be able to sell sufficient quantities to recoup their investments.

This underinvestment reflects not only the concentration of these diseases in poor countries but also market distortions that limit research on treatments for these diseases, particularly on vaccines. Prices for vaccines for developing countries have historically been low because, once pharmaceutical companies have sunk investments in R&D to develop them, governments often use their powers as regulators, major purchasers, and arbiters of intellectual property rights to keep prices down.

Research on vaccines is an international public good; hence, none of the many countries that would benefit from a malaria, tuberculosis, or HIV vaccine has sufficient incentive to encourage research by unilaterally offering to pay higher prices. Property rights in pharmaceuticals have therefore historically been weak in poor countries. Most vaccines sold in those countries are priced at pennies per dose—a tiny fraction of their social value. More expensive on-patent vaccines have typically not been purchased by the poorest countries. Thus, private developers lack incentives to pursue research on diseases that primarily affect poor countries.

Programs to encourage development of new products can be classified in two broad categories: "push" programs, which subsidize research, and "pull" programs, which reward developers for producing the desired product. Government-directed push programs have proved well suited for basic research, but for the later stages of research, the pull approach has important advantages.

With pull programs, the public pays only if a successful product is developed. This feature gives pharmaceutical firms and scientists strong incentives to select projects that they believe have a reasonable chance of leading to useful products and to focus on creating viable vaccines or drugs rather than pursuing other goals.

Moreover, pull programs can help to ensure that if new products are indeed developed, they will reach those who need them. For example, a pull program's sponsor might guarantee that for an effective malaria vaccine, it would pay the developer $20 for each of the first 250 million people immunized, subject to a 10 percent copayment by the recipient country or other donors.

This type of policy initiative has recently been gathering momentum. In February 2007, five country governments (Canada, Italy, Norway, Russia, and the United Kingdom) together with the Bill and Melinda Gates Foundation committed $1.5 billion to launch an "advance market commitment" (a type of pull mechanism) for a pneumococcal vaccine, a disease that kills more than 1.5 million individuals annually.

If a vaccine commitment failed to stimulate the development of an effective vaccine, no funds would be spent; if it succeeded, tens of millions of lives would be saved.

15.1   Vaccines and Health in Poor Countries

Infectious and parasitic diseases account for one-third of the disease burden in low-income countries and nearly half of Africa's disease burden. In contrast, infectious and parasitic diseases account for only 3 percent of the burden in high-income countries (World Health Organization 2002). Burdens can be compared across countries using the concept of disability-adjusted life-years (DALYs), which takes into account not only the lives lost through disease but also the number of years of disability caused.

Differences in environment contribute to this gap. Poor countries are generally in the tropics, and the high biodiversity of the tropics gives rise to more numerous and more virulent infectious diseases. They also have more effective disease vectors, like African mosquitoes that spread malaria. Poverty leads to poor nutrition, sanitation, and education, all of which contribute to the spread of diseases. Dysfunctional or desperately poor governments fail to provide clean water, sanitation, and public health programs like antituberculosis campaigns.

Another key reason for the spread of infection is the reality of weak health care systems in poor countries: budgets are low, government health care workers are vulnerable to corruption, and the ranks of private health providers are filled with quacks, making it difficult to deliver all but the simplest health care. Low-income sub-Saharan African nations spend only 6 percent of their

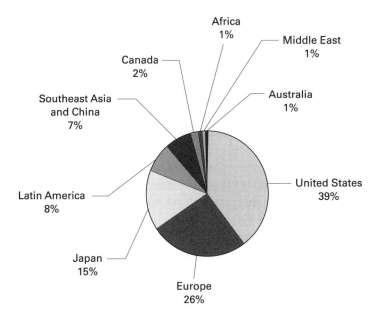

Figure 15.1
World pharmaceutical market, sales by region, 1998

average $300 per capita GDP on health—around $18 per person. Connecticut spends more on health than the thirty-eight low-income countries of sub-Saharan Africa combined. Whereas the United States has 2.7 trained physicians per thousand people and Europe has 3.9, sub-Saharan Africa has only 0.1 (World Bank 2001).

Still, health in developing countries has improved tremendously over the past fifty years, due largely to the adoption of cheap, easy-to-use technologies. Vaccines are the paradigmatic example. They do not require diagnosis for use, can be taken in a few doses instead of long-term regimens, and rarely have major side effects. Hence, compared to drugs, they can be delivered more easily by health care workers with limited training. Seventy-four percent of the world's children receive a standard package of cheap, off-patent vaccines through the World Health Organization's Expanded Program on Immunization, and these vaccines save 3 million lives per year at a cost of pennies per dose (Kim-Farley et al. 1992). The vaccine-driven eradication of smallpox more than two decades ago averted 40 million deaths.

In contrast, despite dramatic price reductions, only 50,000 people in Africa are taking antiretroviral medicines for HIV/AIDS, while 25 million are estimated to have the disease and 4.1 million have reached the stage of the disease where treatment would be considered appropriate (World Health Organization 2003).

Expenditures on vaccines save more lives for a given budget than almost any other health measure, largely because of the low cost of delivery. Thus, vaccines are the best hope for a long-run sustainable solution to the problem of infectious diseases in the developing world.

15.2   R&D and Poor Countries

Very little R&D is done on vaccines or drugs oriented primarily to the developing world. Of the 1,233 drugs licensed worldwide between 1975 and 1997, only 13 were directed at tropical diseases. Of these, 5 came from veterinary research, 2 were modifications of existing medicines, and 2 were produced for the U.S. military. Only 4 were developed by pharmaceutical firms specifically for tropical diseases in humans (Pecoul et al. 1999).

In 1992, half of global health R&D was undertaken by private industry. But according to the World Health Organization, less than 5 percent of that was spent on diseases specific to poor countries (World Health Organization 1996).

While diseases like schistosomiasis and malaria that almost exclusively affect low-income countries are particularly starved of research funds, even HIV/AIDS research, which is more active, has not been oriented toward the needs of the countries where the disease is most prevalent. Most research has been on drugs rather than vaccines. Most candidate vaccines for HIV tested worldwide are based on what researchers call clade B, the strain widespread in the United States, Europe, Australia, and Latin America, rather than clade C, the most common strain in Africa, where two-thirds of new infections occur.

A possible reason that research on vaccines for malaria, tuberculosis, and HIV is so limited, despite the pressing need, is that developing vaccines for each represents a formidable scientific challenge. Nonetheless, many scientists are optimistic. Recent advances in immunology, biochemistry, and biotechnology have created tools for understanding the immune response to these diseases, as well as for testing the potential efficacy of candidate vaccines, in both the lab and animals. Genetic sequencing of HIV and the organisms causing tuberculosis and malaria is either complete or advanced. This progress may help scientists create vaccines that aim at many different antigens and will be more effective in the face of genetic diversity.

Thus, although the nature of the challenge may have slowed research, it is probably not the main reason for the disappointing pace of development. As noted above, there is an extraordinary divergence between the extent of R&D devoted to rich-country and poor-country diseases. The more plausible explanation for the dearth of research on diseases of low-income countries is that their markets for advanced drugs are very small. Indeed, all of Africa constitutes just 1 percent of the global pharmaceuticals market (PhRMA 2000).

Drug developers often do not even bother to take out patents in small, poor countries. Most of the key intellectual property underlying AIDS drugs is not patented in many African countries, presumably because the manufacturers did not consider protecting the local market worth the filing fee.

15.3 Why Markets Do Not Work for Developing-Country Vaccines

The small market for vaccines is due not only to low incomes in developing nations, but also to inefficiency in the markets for vaccines and in vaccine R&D. As a result, the rewards to a private developer would be far lower than the value people in poor countries would place on a vaccine, even given their low incomes. Thus, government aid aimed at vaccine research for neglected diseases would be highly cost-effective—even more so than aid for food, shelter, and other desperately needed goods.

Economists often argue against aiming foreign aid at specific goods because in most cases, recipients are the best judges of what they need most. If we were thinking only about goods like eggs, that would make sense. Where people place a high value on having more protein in their diet, they might spend their additional money on eggs. Farmers would start raising more chickens and selling the eggs, thus supplying people with protein. A key assumption driving this conclusion is that if people put a higher value on a product than it costs to produce, businesses will spring up to serve the need. However, that is not likely to happen with new pharmaceuticals. There are two critical differences between eggs and pharmaceuticals. First, people who buy eggs enjoy all the benefits themselves, while people who buy vaccines benefit others by reducing the spread of disease. Second, the main cost of producing new pharmaceuticals is R&D. The key output of biotechnology and pharmaceutical firms is not a physical product but knowledge, and it is hard for firms to capture the full benefits. In particular, once invented, pharmaceuticals can usually be manufactured relatively cheaply, so firms that have not invested in R&D may end up as beneficiaries.

Vaccines may also be underproduced for other reasons. Consumers may be myopic in the sense that they are more willing to pay for treatment than for prevention. Many potential consumers in poor countries place limited credence in official pronouncements about vaccination benefits, and they may wait to observe the effects on neighbors before getting vaccinations themselves. The chief beneficiaries of vaccines are often children, and some parents who make decisions on their children's behalf may not take their welfare into account in spending decisions.

All of these factors suggest that the benefits to society of R&D on vaccines are typically many times greater than the benefits that accrue to the developer. A malaria vaccine would produce social benefits conservatively valued at $4 billion per year, while the total developing-country outlay for childhood vaccines is just $200 million annually (World Bank AIDS Vaccine Task Force 2000).

Back-of-the-envelope calculations imply that a twenty–fold gap between private and social value is likely. Thus, pharmaceutical developers lack incentives to pursue research projects that would be worthwhile from the point of view of society as a whole. And by the same token, assistance from governments or nonprofit agencies that encourages vaccine research potentially has a much higher payoff than other forms of economic or medical aid.

15.4   Where Government Fits In

Patent protection can help developers secure a greater portion of the benefits of R&D. But the monopoly associated with patents has a big downside: by allowing producers to charge far more than the incremental cost of manufacture, it prevents millions of people from benefiting from products that are relatively cheap to produce at the margin. As a result, many poor countries have historically limited patent protection for pharmaceuticals. And, not surprisingly, drug companies have been reluctant to create products for their needs. This is particularly true for vaccines, which are nearly always purchased by governments or by agencies like UNICEF, which use their market power as very large buyers to push down prices.

Governments have historically not paid vaccine developers anything near the societal value of vaccines for two main reasons. First, once pharmaceutical developers have made their R&D investments, governments have every incentive to force prices down to a level that covers only the manufacturing costs. This is true even if before developers have made their investment, the government sees the need to provide greater incentives (the time-inconsistency or sunk-cost problem). Second, because vaccine development is a global public good, each country has an incentive to free-ride off research financed elsewhere or induced by other countries' intellectual property protection. Each country benefits—but each prefers some other country to pay the costs of development.

The dearth of vaccine research for malaria, tuberculosis, and variants of the HIV virus prevalent in Africa thus stems not only from abject poverty but also from free-rider problems that plague the production of all global public goods.

Large countries like the United States know they risk stemming future research if they free-ride. But small, poor countries like Uganda know their policies barely affect research incentives.

The free-rider problem is particularly severe for countries that constitute only modest fractions of the world market for pharmaceuticals and reap proportionately small fractions of worldwide research benefits. For example, in European Union countries, pharmaceutical prices are regulated by governments to force down the prices to levels roughly half those in the United States. And in Japan, with its even smaller population, drug prices are one-quarter their U.S. equivalents. Malaria, tuberculosis, and AIDS affect many poor countries that have even less reason to pay a proportional share of development costs than do Europe and Japan.

Aside from these sunk-cost and global public-good problems, some governments do not put much priority on obtaining and distributing vaccines for political reasons. Because vaccines have widely distributed benefits, they receive less political support than expenditures benefiting more concentrated, well-organized groups. For example, building a hospital largely benefits those living nearby, so residents will lobby for the hospital.

The debate over pricing of antiretroviral drugs to treat AIDS illustrates the conflict between the goals of promoting R&D and treating a large share of the afflicted—a conflict that exists when intellectual property rights provide the only form of incentives for R&D. These issues came to a head when South Africa and Brazil fought for the right to license production of AIDS drugs without consent from the patent holders. As a result of public outcry, Washington, Dropped its efforts to champion drug company rights in these two countries (see, e.g., Lewis 1999 and BBC News 2001). Pharmaceutical firms, faced with a public relations nightmare, eventually cut prices in least-developed countries to zero- or negative-profit levels.

Whatever the overall benefits of decisions regarding compulsory licensing of generic versions of AIDS drugs, it seems clear that pharmaceutical developers will see this as setting a precedent that poor countries may use to obtain vaccines and drugs at low prices in the future. In these circumstances, pharmaceutical companies may be reluctant to invest heavily in drug or vaccine research for diseases that primarily affect developing countries.

The world needs new institutions that both encourage new pharmaceutical development and provide the poor with access to these new drugs. Such institutions would ideally address both time-consistency (sunk-cost) and free-riding problems.

The world cannot wait until a vaccine is almost ready for production to address these issues. Rather, it is necessary to put in place incentives for R&D up front in order to motivate vaccine developers. The free-riding problem suggests that individual countries acting in narrow self-interest will not solve the problem. Solutions will have to come from entities addressing disease problems in the developing world as a whole.

15.5 Push and Pull

Analyses of research incentives distinguish between push programs, which subsidize research inputs, and pull programs, which reward developers for research outputs. Examples of push programs are grants to academics, public equity investments in product development, R&D tax credits, and work in government laboratories. Pull programs could commit themselves in advance to finance the purchase of new vaccines and make them available to the people who need them.

The R&D system for developed countries, which has been successful in generating new products, involves a combination of push and pull. Government organizations like the National Institutes for Health support basic research, and the private sector is stimulated to turn these into usable products by the promise of the market.

Applying the principle to vaccines and drugs for developing countries would suggest using push programs for basic research and pull programs to encourage applied research. A number of push programs are currently supporting research on diseases of the poor, including the International AIDS Vaccine Initiative, the Medicines for Malaria Venture, and the Malaria Vaccine Initiative. In contrast, there are no programs in place to reward developers of effective malaria, tuberculosis, or HIV vaccines.

Used on their own, push programs have a mixed record. Some programs, like the development of a vaccine for meningococcal meningitis, have been successful, but there have also been some notable failures. For example, in the 1980s, the U.S. Agency for International Development invested considerable effort and millions of dollars in research for a malaria vaccine. Instead of a vaccine, the program yielded only a dramatic illustration of the problems with the push approach.

The U.S. Agency for International Development (USAID) initially funded one research team that developed a candidate vaccine. Tests found that only two of nine recipients were actually protected from malaria and suggested that the vaccine had serious side effects. Yet these mixed results led USAID to claim a "major breakthrough in the development of a vaccine against the most deadly form of malaria in human beings. The vaccine should be ready for use around the world, especially in developing countries, within five years" (Desowitz 1991). That was in 1984.

Early work by a second team yielded even more disappointing results. But the project was funded despite the recommendations of expert reviewers. Once the grant came through, the principal investigator transferred funds to his personal account. He was later indicted for theft.

The independent evaluations of a third proposal found it both mediocre and unrealistic. However, the USAID project director ignored the report and arranged for the project to be fully funded. The principal investigator and his administrative assistant were later indicted for diverting money from the grant to their personal accounts. Just before his arrest, the Rockefeller Foundation provided the principal investigator with a $750,000 research grant, and USAID announced it was giving him an additional $1.65 million. By 1986, USAID had spent more than $60 million on its malaria vaccine efforts, with little to show for it (Desowitz 1991).

The USAID malaria example is extreme, but it illustrates a number of general problems with push programs. Because they pay for research rather than results, decisions must be made about where to commit funds before a product is developed. Moreover, these decisions must be made by people who either do not have full information or must rely on information from those with vested interests in the decisions.

In general, researchers funded on the basis of an outsider's assessment of potential, rather than for actual product delivery, have incentives to report overly optimistic assessments, and even to divert resources from the search for the desired product. Normally, this would not take the form of theft. But push-funded researchers may devote effort to other projects rather than toward the sometimes tedious work in developing a usable vaccine. Similar incentive problems arise if push funds come in other forms—for example, R&D tax credits for research or government investments in private research programs in exchange for a commitment to price the product at a low level.

By contrast, other historical examples suggest that pull programs in which public policies increase the value of markets for pharmaceuticals can spur effective R&D. Consider America's Orphan Drug Act, which went into effect in 1983. It created a variety of financial incentives for companies to develop drugs for orphan diseases with limited markets like Huntington's, ALS (Lou Gehrig's disease), and muscular dystrophy, each of which affects fewer than 200,000 Americans.

The act provides grants and tax credits for clinical development and testing of orphan drugs. But its primary draw for pharmaceutical companies is a promise of seven years of market exclusivity. Since the act was passed, more than 200 orphan drugs have been developed. In the preceding decade, fewer than 10 were introduced (Lichtenberg and Waldfogel 2003).

Consider also the effect of the 1993 decision under which Medicare covers the full cost of flu vaccinations, a decision that substantially enlarged the expected market for such vaccines. The best flu vaccines in existence at the time the policy was implemented had an efficacy rate of 58 percent. Since then, more effective vaccines have been introduced, including the first intranasal vaccine, which has an 85 percent efficacy rate in healthy adults. The resulting reduction in flu since 1993 is expected to produce annual health benefits of close to $6 billion (Finkelstein 2004).

From the perspective of the funders, a key benefit of pull programs is that they pay only for results. This means government officials or foundations do not have to worry that they are investing millions in projects that fail. Indeed, they do not even need to decide which scientists are most capable of developing the vaccines, which scientific approaches are most promising, or even for which diseases the science is most ready for vaccine development. Pull programs efficiently align incentives, with governments and nonprofit funders defining the problem as commercial developers compete to design the best solution.

Another advantage of pull programs is that they encourage researchers to focus on the job at hand. Many academic and government researchers have career goals and intellectual interests that drive them away from the nuts and bolts of innovation. The later stages of product development include activities that are not particularly interesting but require considerable time and effort. Techniques for manufacturing sufficient quantities of candidate vaccines at a sufficient level of purity must be developed, animal models for the disease must be created, and product trials must be conducted. Nobody wins a Nobel Prize for these critical steps. But by linking payment to results, pull programs provide strong incentives to researchers to concentrate their efforts on developing workable technology suitable for commercialization rather than on publishing academic articles or preparing the next grant application.

Yet another advantage of pull programs is that they would help avoid budgetary conflicts between current health measures and the R&D needed to develop long-term solutions. Because no expenditure is incurred until the vaccine is available, governments can concentrate current spending on immediate needs while committing themselves to spend future budgets on vaccines.

15.6 Designing a Pull Program

Legally binding commitments to finance vaccine purchases for poor countries may be the most attractive form of pull programs. Alternative pull-type incentives can introduce their own distortions or are less efficient. Extending patents on other pharmaceuticals to reward developers of new products, for example, would place the entire burden of financing new products on the people who need the old pharmaceuticals. Increasing prices for current vaccines without explicit incentives for developing new vaccines would be an expensive and potentially ineffective way to spur new research.

The higher the price offered and the larger the market, the more research will be undertaken, and the sooner a vaccine is likely to be developed. However, guaranteeing $20 per person for the first 250 million people vaccinated, subject to a 10 percent copayment by developing countries or other donors, would provide a market that would attract the attention of biotechnology and pharmaceutical companies. Purchasing a malaria vaccine at this price would be one of the most cost-effective health interventions available, saving more lives than virtually any other use of the funds. The manufacturer could be required to make the vaccine available at much lower prices after the first 250 million people were immunized. The guarantee should be structured as a legally binding contract and should be limited to vaccines judged safe and efficacious by existing regulatory agencies, like the U.S. Food and Drug Administration or its counterparts overseas.

15.7 Moving Forward

The idea of pull-based incentives for vaccines has broad appeal across a wide ideological spectrum because it adopts a market-based approach to deliver benefits to some of the world's poorest people. A working group convened by the Center for Global Development in Washington, D.C., with financial support from the Bill and Melinda Gates Foundation, released in 2005 a report exploring the details of how such a vaccine commitment could be implemented.

This type of initiative has recently seen movement in the political sphere. In February 2007, five country governments (Canada, Italy, Norway, Russia, and the United Kingdom) together with the Bill and Melinda Gates Foundation committed $1.5 billion to launch an "advance market commitment" (a type of pull mechanism) for a pneumococcal vaccine, a disease which kills more than 1.5 million individuals annually.

Future commitments to purchase vaccines for other diseases could be undertaken by credible entities like the governments of rich countries, international institutions like the World Bank, private foundations like the Bill and Melinda Gates Foundation, or by some combination of these. For example, the World Bank could commit to provide subsidized loans to any member country that wanted to purchase the vaccine, as long as prespecified terms were met. The bank could also sweeten the standard terms of such loans for vaccine-purchase commitments by providing part of the purchase price through grants. Alternatively, other donors—private foundations or governments—could provide subsidies by committing themselves to buy down loans. In other words, they would give the member the money to repay the loan, as was done in Nigeria's polio eradication campaign.

The process of creating large, credible commitments to a market for vaccines will not be easy, and it certainly will not lack risks. But the alternative—a status quo in which millions die annually from malaria, tuberculosis, and HIV, and vaccines against these diseases remain a low priority for most pharmaceutical firms—is unacceptable. By offering to help buy vaccines against these diseases if they are developed, a program sponsor could harness the inventiveness the private sector has shown in confronting diseases common in developed countries and direct it toward addressing the health needs of the world's poor. If such a commitment fails to induce the development of the needed products, no funds will be spent and no harm done. If it succeeds, millions of lives will be saved each year.

Note

The ideas in this chapter are presented in greater detail in *Strong Medicine: Creating Incentives for Pharmaceutical Research on Neglected Diseases*, joint with Rachel Glennerster, published by Princeton University Press in 2004.

References

BBC News. 2001. "U.S. drops Brazil Aids drugs case." June 25.

Desowitz, Robert. 1991. *The Malaria Capers: Tales of Parasites and People*. New York, NY: W. W. Norton.

Finkelstein, Amy. 2004. "Static and dynamic effects of health policy: Evidence from the vaccine industry." *Quarterly Journal of Economics* 119(2):527–564.

Kim-Farley, Robert and the Expanded Programme on Immunization Team. 1992. "Global Immunization." *Annual Review of Public Health* 13:223–237.

Lewis, Neil. 1999. "U.S. industry to drop AIDS drug lawsuit against South Africa." *New York Times*, September 10.

Lichtenberg, Frank, and Joel Waldfogel. 2003. "Does misery love company? Evidence from pharmaceutical markets before and after the Orphan Drug Act." NBER Working Paper 9750. Cambridge, MA: National Bureau of Economic Research.

Pecoul, Bernard, Pierre Chirac, Patrice Trouiller, and Jacques Pinel. 1999. "Access to Essential Drugs in Poor Countries: A Lost Battle?" *Journal of the American Medical Association* 281(4):361–367.

PhRMA. 2000. *PhRMA Industry Profile 2000*. [Online]. Available: http://www.phrma.org/publications/publications/profile00/.

U.S. Census Bureau. 2000. "Federal, State, and Local Governments: 2000 State Government Finance Data." [Online]. Available: http://www.census.gov/govs/www/state00.html.

World Bank. 2001. *World Development Indicators.* Washington, DC: Oxford University Press.

World Bank AIDS Vaccine Task Force. 2000. "Accelerating an AIDS Vaccine for Developing Countries: Recommendations for the World Bank." February 28. Washington, DC: World Bank.

World Health Organization (WHO). 1996. *Investing in Health Research and Development: Report of the Ad Hoc Committee on Health Research Relating to Future Intervention Options.* Geneva: WHO.

World Health Organization (WHO). 2002. *World Health Report 2002.* Geneva: WHO.

World Health Organization (WHO). 2003. "The 3 by 5 Initiative" [Fact Sheet 274]. Geneva: WHO.

16 Can We Build a Better Mousetrap? Three New Institutions Designed to Improve Aid Effectiveness

Steven Radelet and Ruth Levine

When the cold war ended in the early 1990s, many foreign aid programs lost their raison d'être and much of their political support. Criticisms of aid grew sharply, with detractors from left and right arguing that aid programs were heavily bureaucratic, unfocused, poorly managed, and ineffective in supporting development. While a growing body of evidence suggests that aid by and large has been modestly effective in helping achieve development outcomes, even the most ardent supporters recognize the weaknesses of aid programs and the validity of many of the criticisms.

In response to these criticisms, donors have begun to experiment with changes in how they deliver aid. Some changes are modest, such as donors changing how they allocate aid across countries. Some are more significant, such as donors providing aid directly to villages through community-driven development programs rather than to central governments. But perhaps the most dramatic are cases in which donors have established entirely new institutions designed to deliver aid in fundamentally different ways than have traditional aid agencies. In this regard, three new institutions created in the last few years stand out: the Global Fund to Fight AIDS, Tuberculosis, and Malaria (the Global Fund), the United States' Millennium Challenge Corporation (MCC), and the Global Alliance for Vaccines and Immunizations (GAVI).

Why have these new institutions all been created in recent years? Can they build on lessons from the past and make aid more effective in spurring development? Or perhaps after a few years and a burst of new energy and resources, are they ultimately destined to operate little differently from their predecessors? This chapter examines why these new mechanisms arose in the context of the debates about aid and how they differ in several important ways from other donor agencies. While it is too early to tell whether these institutions' performance actually will improve on the past, we identify some of the key questions on which their success or failure may turn and explore the implications for aid institutions more broadly.

We begin by reviewing the views on aid effectiveness emerging from the academic literature that influenced the reform debates. Although much of the evidence shows a positive impact of aid, the balance of the evidence is far from overwhelming. It leaves little doubt that there is ample room for making aid more effective. We then explore the specific criticisms leveled against aid since the 1990s. We compare and contrast how the new agencies responded to these critiques, sometimes similarly and sometimes very differently, and the key issues that may determine their success or failure in the future.

16.1 The Impetus for Reform

Controversies about foreign aid go back decades. In 1947 U.S. Congressman (later Senator) Everett Dirksen labeled the Marshall Plan "Operation Rat-Hole." Milton Friedman (1958), Peter Bauer (1972), William Easterly (2001), and other economists have leveled stinging critiques at aid, charging that it has enlarged government bureaucracies, perpetuated bad governments, enriched the elite in poor countries, or just been wasted. Critics from both left and right see aid as a political tool that distorts incentives, invites corruption, and entrenches corrupt dictators.

Supporters counter that although these arguments are partially correct, they are overstated. Jeffrey Sachs and others (2004), Joseph Stiglitz (2002), Nicholas Stern (2002), and others have argued that although aid has sometimes failed, it has supported poverty reduction and growth in some countries and prevented even worse performance in others. Advocates argue that many of the weaknesses of aid have more to do with donors than recipients, especially because much aid is given to support political allies rather than to development. This provides the basis for attempts to reform the way donors provide aid.

16.1.1 Three Broad Views on Aid Effectiveness

Most of the academic debate on aid effectiveness has centered on the relationship between aid and growth (even though a substantial portion of aid is not primarily aimed at growth). This research has helped define the contours of the debates on reforming aid and provide the foundation for many of the recommendations that led to the formation of the MCC, the Global Fund and GAVI.[1] Three broad strands have emerged in the empirical literature on aid.

The first strand is that aid has no effect on growth and may actually undermine it. Peter Bauer was perhaps the most outspoken proponent of this view (e.g., Bauer 1972), although he did not offer empirical support for his argument. Griffen and Enos (1970) were among the first to publish empirical research questioning aid effectiveness, finding negative simple correlations between aid and growth in twenty-seven countries. Many other studies similarly concluded that aid undermines incentives for saving and investment, generates Dutch disease, perpetuates corrupt governments, enlarges the public sector, encourages corruption, creates incompetent aid bureaucracies, or produces aid dependency.[2] These studies have been influential and gird the widely held view that aid has been ineffective in supporting growth. However, very few empirical studies published in the past decade have reached this conclusion.

Most of the studies in this strand of the literature share two characteristics. First, they assume and test only a linear relationship between aid and growth, basing their model on a Harrod-Domar-type production function. Second, they examine the relationship between aggregate aid and growth, in effect imposing the restriction that different types of aid aimed at different purposes all must have the same relationship with growth.

A recent study by Rajan and Subramanian (2005) is the most prominent recent study of this type. The authors find no relationship between aid and growth when they restrict their model to a linear relationship, which they do in the vast majority of their tests, verifying the result of no linear relationship between aid and growth. However, when they relax the linearity assumption, they consistently find a positive relationship (albeit not always statistically significant); when they further relax the assumption that all aid is alike, they find a strong positive and significant relationship between "economic aid" and growth, with diminishing returns.[3]

The second strand is that aid has a positive relationship with growth on average across countries (although not in every country), but with diminishing returns as the volume of aid increases. Several early studies found a positive relationship between aid and growth (e.g., Papenek 1973, Levy 1988). This strand of the literature took a significant turn in the mid-1990s when researchers began to investigate whether aid might spur growth with diminishing returns. Oddly—given Solow's response to the Harrod-Domar model in the 1950s— research on aid and growth until the mid-1990s tested only a linear relationship. Most newer studies that allow for diminishing returns have found a positive relationship covering different countries and time periods (Hajimichael et al. 1995; Durbarry, Gemmell, and Greenaway 1998; Dalgaard and Hansen 2000; Hansen and Tarp 2000, 2001; Lensink and White 2001; Dalgaard, Hansen, and Tarp 2004). Most of these studies do not conclude that aid has always worked, but rather that on average, higher aid flows have been associated with more rapid growth. Roodman (2004) conducts sensitivity analyses on three of these studies and finds two of the three (Dalgaard 2004 and the GMM results of Hansen and Tarp 2001) to be reasonably robust.

Some researchers have begun to go further and relax the assumption that all aid is alike, initially in several country-specific studies (Owens and Hoddinott 1999, Mavrotas 2002, Mavrotas 2003). Clemens, Radelet, and Bhavnani (2004) relax both the usual linearity assumption and the aid homogeneity assumption, and find a strong positive relationship between growth and aid aimed at growth (e.g., to, build roads, ports, and electricity generators, or support agriculture), leaving aside other types of aid not directly aimed at growth (such as humanitarian and emergency assistance, which typically should be expected to have a negative relationship with growth). They subjected the results to all the robustness checks used by Easterly, Levine, and Roodman (2004) and Roodman (2004), along with several others, and the results remained robust. As mentioned, Rajan and Subramanian (2004) confirm the result that economic aid has a positive relationship with growth with diminishing returns.

Aside from growth, some project-level analysis suggests aid has supported certain activities aimed at nongrowth outcomes with very high rates of return, especially in health. Levine and the What Works Group (2004) document more than a dozen cases of large-scale health interventions supported by aid that have been very successful, including the campaigns against river blindness, smallpox, and polio. Duflo (2001) finds substantial increases in educational attainment and higher wages for graduates resulting from aid-financed primary school expansion in Indonesia.

Finally, the third strand finds that aid has a conditional relationship with growth, helping to accelerate growth only under certain circumstances. This view is based on the idea that aid has supported growth in some circumstances but not others and searches for key characteristics associated with the difference. This "conditional" strand of the literature has two broad subcategories: aid effectiveness depends on either the characteristics of the recipient country or the practices and procedures of the donors.

• *Recipient country characteristics* Isham, Kaufmann, and Pritchett (1995) found that World Bank projects had higher rates of returns in countries with stronger civil liberties than in countries with weaker civil liberties. Burnside and Dollar (2000), in an influential study, concluded that aid stimulated growth in countries with good policies but not otherwise. Other researchers have proposed different country characteristics that might affect the aid-growth relationship, including export price shocks (Collier and Dehn 2001), climatic shocks and the terms of trade (Guillaumont and Chauvet 2001, Chauvet and Guillaumont 2002), policy and institutional quality (Collier and Dollar 2002), institutional quality alone (Burnside and Dollar 2004), policy and warfare (Collier and Hoeffler 2002), "totalitarian" government (Islam 2003), and location in the tropics (Dalgaard, 2004).

All of these studies assume a linear relationship and rely on an interaction term between aid and the variable in question. Not surprisingly, many of the interaction terms are fragile, as they tend to be in econometric studies. Easterly, Levine, and Roodman (2004) find that the original Burnside and Dollar results do not hold up to modest robustness checks. Roodman (2004) tests several other "conditional" studies and finds most of them to be relatively fragile, although the conclusions of Dalgaard (2004) are more robust. Clemens, Radelet, and Bhavnani (2004) show that in the original Burnside and Dollar study, if the interaction term is dropped and the model instead allows for diminishing returns, there is a positive and significant relationship between aid and growth.

• *Donor practices*   Many analysts have argued that donor practices strongly influence aid effectiveness. For example, multilateral aid might be more effective than bilateral aid, and untied aid is thought to have higher returns than tied aid. Many observers argue that donors that have large bureaucracies, do not coordinate or harmonize with other donors, or have ineffective monitoring and evaluation systems undermine the effectiveness of their own programs. Two influential and overlapping views argue that aid would be more effective if there were greater "country ownership" or broader "participation" among government and community groups in recipient countries in setting priorities and designing programs. To date very little systematic research has connected specific donor practices to aid effectiveness.

In sum, research that assumes a linear relationship and that all aid is alike tends to find little or no relationship between aid and growth. Conditional studies that hypothesize that aid works better in countries with stronger policies and institutions have gained much popular support, suggesting that aid allocation can make a substantial difference, but the interaction terms that underlie this research tend to be fragile. Studies that incorporate diminishing returns and allow for heterogeneity of aid tend to find a positive and significant relationship. But even in these studies, the aid-growth relationship is modest, suggesting that there is ample room to strengthen the effectiveness of aid transfers.

16.1.2 Specific Criticisms of Aid

The academic literature is the starting point for the criticisms of aid and reflects the widespread views that either aid had not worked at all or that even if it had produced some success, there was plenty of potential for improvement. No one argues that aid has always worked or been as effective as it could have been, and over the past few years, almost everyone has argued for some type of reform. Among the most common criticisms of aid are the following:[4]

• *Poor allocation* Critics charge that donors are insufficiently selective and give too much aid to countries that do not have policies and institutions conducive to using aid effectively or enhancing development more broadly. This idea is simple: give more aid to countries that can use it well. It is consistent with the Burnside and Dollar (2000) findings discussed earlier but also reflects a view widely held by aid practitioners that aid is much more likely to be effective in countries with a decent policy and institutional environment than in poorly run countries. Aid agencies are also criticized for providing too much aid to middle-income countries and to political allies. Collier and Dollar (2002) propose a "poverty-efficient" allocation rule for distributing aid based on the quality of policies and the extent of poverty to maximize its effectiveness in fighting poverty.

• *Lack of ownership or participation* Some argue that aid programs do not sufficiently reflect local priorities and do not involve recipients (government and nongovernment entities) in their design and because they earmark significant funds for their own priorities. In this view, more ownership by the government or greater participation by government and nongovernment groups could strengthen the commitment to and effectiveness of donor-financed programs. Birdsall (2004), however, points out that country ownership and participation are not equivalent.

• *Too bureaucratic* Virtually all observers agree that aid programs are too bureaucratic, and as a result significant amounts of aid dollars never reach their intended recipients (Easterly 2002). Donors impose high costs on recipients who must review countless documents, fill out myriad forms, and host hundreds of donor missions per year. According to the World Bank, recipient countries typically work with thirty or more aid agencies, each sending an average of five missions a year to oversee their projects. Governments can find themselves hosting three or more aid missions a week.[5] The government of Tanzania, which hosts several hundred aid missions each year, has introduced a "quiet time" from April to August of each year during which it asks donors to minimize meetings and missions so that the government has time to adequately prepare its annual budget.

• *Too many objectives* Taxpayers, advocacy groups, parliamentarians, executive branch officials, and aid agency managers impose multiple and often conflicting goals on aid agencies, encompassing supporting political allies, encouraging growth, improving health and education, strengthening the environment, responding to humanitarian emergencies, and distributing surplus agricultural production as food aid, along with many other goals.

• *Lack of coordination and harmonization* Donor activities are not well harmonized, with multiple donors financing similar projects, each with its own independent design, implementation, monitoring, and evaluation systems. Critics charge that the lack of harmonization leads to duplication, higher administrative costs for the recipients, and less effective aid flows. For example, in Tanzania in the early 1990s, donors were simultaneously implementing fifteen separate health projects (van de Walle 2001). There are really two issues here. First, each donor demands that recipients use separate systems for project design, monitoring, reporting, and evaluation and sends an endless progression of missions to the country. These multiple systems add to bureaucratic costs and can be extremely time-consuming for what might be poor countries' scarcest resource: their skilled senior officials. Second, each donor works on its own, implementing many small projects that match the donor's own priorities but are not always well coordinated with each other or the government's programs. As David Roodman (2006) has pointed out, although smaller projects can be easier to manage, the overall costs of many small projects can be significant.

• *Results do not matter* Monitoring and evaluation systems are badly flawed, and aid disbursements bear little relationship to performance. Donors rarely measure results, so there is little historical systematic information about what works and what does not. This lack of information makes it harder to allocate new funds efficiently, and increases the perception that aid is ineffective. It also weakens incentives for performance: donors continue to provide money even when things are not working, and recipients have little incentive to improve performance.

• *Too little funding and too little sustainability in funding* Many advocates argue that aid amounts are too small to make a significant difference. Jeffrey Sachs regularly uses the analogy of throwing a twenty-foot lifeline to a person drowning forty feet away, watching it fail, and then concluding that lifelines do not work. In a related argument, some analysts argue that aid flows are erratic, making planning and implementation much less predictable for the recipient, adding to bureaucratic costs through regular renegotiations, and generally increasing the risks for the recipient (Birdsall 2004). In particular, some programs do not build in plans for sustainability. Roads are not maintained, immunization programs shrink when donor attention turns elsewhere, and new schools are built without attention to the costs of books, teachers, and supplies.

These criticisms have led to long debates, countless conferences and workshops, and much talk about how to improve aid. But they have also led to some changes in how donors provide aid. Some of the changes are superficial and will make little difference. Others are modest and might make some difference, and some of the changes are more fundamental. The World Bank and International Monetary Fund (IMF) introduced poverty reduction strategy papers, which in theory are based on country-led participatory processes that enhance country ownership. In some countries these have been pro forma, with countries simply going through the motions, but in others, they have triggered a valuable process. The IMF moved to streamline its conditions, especially following the East Asian financial crises, a shift that carried over to the World Bank and the regional multilateral development banks. The World Bank and regional development banks started using performance-based allocation systems to distribute aid based on county need and policy and institutional performance. The UK's Department of International Development (DfID) and some other European programs began to finance sector-wide approaches and broader budget support for a select group of well-performing countries aimed at reducing bureaucratic costs, increasing donor coordination, and reducing project proliferation.

16.3 New Aid Mechanisms

By far the biggest change on the aid landscape in recent years has been the establishment of entire new agencies: the MCC, Global Fund, and GAVI.[6] These agencies were created in direct reaction to the major critiques of foreign aid, although each responded in different ways.

Why new agencies? In effect, donors decided it would be easier and more effective to create new mechanisms with different operating principles than to reform existing ones. Those who spearheaded the new initiatives clearly believed that aid could be made more effective, but only if donor agencies were organized in fundamentally different ways, with different operating procedures, incentives, and structures. They also clearly felt that trying to reorganize and reform existing agencies would be much more difficult than to create new agencies with different mandates, objectives, and operating principles.

16.3.1 The Millennium Challenge Corporation

In February 2004 the United States established the new Millennium Challenge Corporation (MCC) to provide substantial funding to a select group of low-income countries that are "ruling justly, investing in their people, and establishing economic freedom." The MCC has gained widespread attention both because of its size (proposed to grow to $5 billion per year, although it is unlikely that it will ever reach that amount, as its current annual budget is just under $2 billion) and because it is supposed to deliver aid very differently from other U.S. programs. The basic idea is to select countries based on their demonstrated commitment to sound policies and good governance, give them more voice in designing programs, focus the programs more clearly on supporting economic growth, provide recipients with larger sums of money, and hold them accountable for achieving results. As such the MCA is meant to respond to some but not all of the seven criticisms of aid listed earlier.[7]

Selectivity

The MCC chooses countries to be eligible to apply for funding primarily on the basis of sixteen quantitative indicators drawn from publicly available sources (table 16.1). To qualify, a country must score above the median for its peer group of countries (either low income or lower middle income) on half the indicators in each of the three categories—ruling justly, investing in people, establishing economic freedom—and it must score above the median on corruption. The MCC board has some discretion to select countries that do not meet these tests or not select some that do, but to date, it has used that discretion relatively

Table 16.1*
Eligibility criteria for the Millennium Challenge Account

Indicator	Source
Ruling justly	
1. Control of corruption	World Bank Institute
2. Rule of law	World Bank Institute
3. Voice and accountability	World Bank Institute
4. Government effectiveness	World Bank Institute
5. Civil liberties	Freedom House
6. Political rights	Freedom House
Investing in people	
7. Immunization rate (DPT and measles)	World Health Organization/World Bank
8. Primary education completion rate	World Bank/United Nations Educational, Scientific, and Cultural Organization
9. Public primary education spending/GDP	National sources
10. Public expenditure on health/GDP	National sources
Ensuring economic freedom	
11. Costs to start a business	World Bank
12. Inflation	International Monetary Fund
13. Regulatory quality	World Bank Institute
14. Budget deficit/GDP	National sources
15. Trade policy	Heritage Foundation
16. Days to start a business	World Bank

Note: To qualify, countries must be above the median for countries in their income group on half the indicators in each of the three categories and above the median on corruption.
Source: http://www.mcc.gov/selection/indicators/index.php.
*This table has changed since the time of writing in 2005. Please view the source link for an updated version.

sparingly. As of fiscal year 2006 the MCC had selected twenty-three countries to be eligible to apply for funding.[8]

Many details of the selection process have been extensively debated, including the sixteen indicators, the use of the median cutoff, the focus on the level rather than changes, and the insistence on achieving a corruption score above the median (Radelet 2003a, Brainard et al. 2003). Without repeating these debates, three key points are worth emphasizing:

1. By using a public, transparent (albeit imperfect) methodology, the MCC was designed to reduce (although not eliminate) political considerations in selecting countries, basing the choice on development criteria.

2. The process is essentially a very strong version of the Burnside and Dollar selectivity argument: only a small number of countries qualify. Most developing countries will be excluded, although many would continue to receive U.S. foreign aid through other channels.

3. Qualification is based on changes that a country has already made, not on promises of future reforms. Thus, the MCC differs from traditional conditionality in which disbursements are tied to specific promised policy reforms. In this way, the MCA acts more like a pull mechanism in which countries must achieve certain basic standards to become eligible, rather than traditional aid push mechanisms in which donors try to "buy" reforms by promising aid in return for specific policy reforms (Radelet 2006). The extent to which this change will shift incentives remains to be seen.

Country Ownership and Participation

The MCA is intended to give recipients the lead in setting priorities and designing programs. This approach is integrally linked to the country selection process: the United States is willing to grant extensive flexibility only to countries that it believes have good governance and not to countries with weak governance, high levels of corruption, or poor policies. The MCC does not send out teams to design programs, but instead expects recipients to design programs based on an open consultative process. Recipient countries have substantial latitude in deciding which activities to fund (say, for rural roads, water systems, or worker training), as long as the activity is related to economic growth and has buy-in from citizens. To date nine countries have designed programs and signed agreements with the MCC.[9]

As in other aid programs, however, "country ownership" and "participation" are difficult to define clearly and to achieve in practice. With respect to ownership, as with any other funder, the MCC will not simply give countries carte blanche in designing programs and will implicitly favor (if not explicitly push for) activities that are consistent with what it believes to be the highest priorities and the best program design. Moreover, the MCC has found that allowing countries to take ownership cannot mean a total hands-off approach, because (as with any foundation) it wants the proposals to follow a certain format and answer specific questions. Too much hands-off can lead to confusion.

Creating a more participatory process is fraught with difficulties because even under the best of circumstances, issues of representation and delegation are far from clear, and not every group can have a seat at the table. And it is not clear under what circumstances the MCC should accept or build on previous participatory processes (such as in poverty reduction strategies) or determine that a separate process is necessary. There is a danger that instituting a process intended to give recipients more voice could in the end just create more bureaucratic hurdles. It is still early in the MCA's experience. Important challenges have emerged from the first round of compacts: the need for balancing efficiency and speed with thorough consultation, the need for gathering baseline information and assessing the extent of consultation in related programs, and the need for more formal and more timely opportunities for civil society to weigh in on specific program designs (not just sectoral priority setting).[10]

Smaller Bureaucracy
The MCC currently has a staff of 230 and has authority to grow to 300. It will place one or two residents in each recipient country. Its small staff size reflects the intention to stay removed from design and implementation. Because it will be providing funds directly to recipient countries it will not procure consulting and implementation services as the U.S. Agency for International Development (USAID) does. It is outsourcing some of its activities, including some of its monitoring and evaluation services, as discussed below. Its original legislation does not include many of the rules and regulations that burden USAID. For example, none of the funding is earmarked for specific purposes, and funds are not explicitly tied to purchases from U.S. contractors and suppliers.

Focused Objectives
The MCC has a moderate focus of activities—narrower than for many other aid agencies but much wider than for GAVI or the Global Fund. According to the MCC Web site, "The MCC will focus specifically on promoting sustainable economic growth that reduces poverty through investments in areas such as agriculture, education, private sector development, and capacity building." It thus has a somewhat clearer mandate than other agencies that are involved in disaster relief, refugee assistance, reacting to financial crises, and building democracies. The clearer focus should help management set priorities and

make decisions and (at least in theory) could help better judge the MCC's success or failure. Nevertheless, the MCC faces two major challenges. First, a wide range of activities can be connected with growth, so the scope of activities is likely to become fairly expansive over time. Second, and perhaps more important, the MCC will find that it is nearly impossible to directly tie any particular activity to a country's rate of economic growth. Establishing the appropriate counterfactual and establishing cause and effect in a convincing manner will be daunting problems. We discuss these evaluation difficulties more below.

Harmonization and Coordination with Other Donors
The MCC concept ignores this critique of aid. It is a completely bilateral program, formed with little discussion with other donors and implemented with little coordination. The MCC argues that because governments are designing the programs, it is up to them to coordinate MCC programs with other activities. As for harmonizing reporting procedures, far from reducing the administrative burden on recipient countries, the MCA is likely to add to it by establishing its own set of procedures and reporting requirements.

Performance-Based Management
The United States claims that the MCA will be performance based and that it will generously fund initiatives that achieve their goals and reduce or eliminate funding for those that do not. Of course, many donors make the same pledge, but few implement it. For the MCA, this will require collecting good baseline data, establishing measurable and appropriate benchmarks, thinking clearly through counterfactuals, and implementing a strong monitoring and evaluation (M&E) program, none of them easy. As Duflo and Kremer (2003) and others have pointed out, donors can never be certain of the impact of aid-financed program in the absence of controlled programs.

Getting the M&E process right will be absolutely crucial to the success of the MCC. The MCC is still building its M&E process, and it is not yet clear what it will ultimately look like. It appears that it will establish clear ex ante targets, a major improvement over most aid agencies. It is considering, but has not yet committed to, establishing controlled programs in some circumstances, which would be a major step forward. It will outsource some activities, require recipients to undertake some internal M&E activities, and undertake others itself. Although these steps may improve the process, they do not resolve one of the basic problems confronting many agencies: the obvious conflict of interest in evaluating one's own programs. Unfortunately, it does not appear that the MCC will establish a truly independent M&E process, in which an outside independent entity takes on the evaluation role. This is a missed opportunity.

In addition, it is unclear how the MCC will use the information it generates from its M&E process. Ideally, such information can be used for midcourse corrections, inform the design of new activities about what works and what does not, create incentives for stronger performance by recipients, and provide the MCC board with the information it needs to cut back or eliminate some programs and expand others. It remains to be seen whether the right information is both collected and disseminated to serve these multiple purposes. The acid test will be if the board actually suspends programs for nonperformance or finds excuses to keep the money flowing.

Scaled-Up and Sustainable Funding

The MCA was expected to bring substantial new funding for qualifying countries. President Bush originally proposed $5 billion in funding by 2006, which for twenty to twenty-five countries would imply $200 million to $250 million in funding each year (depending on the country), the equivalent of up to 6 percent of recipient income (Radelet 2003a). In practice, the MCC's budget is currently $1.77 billion, and it seems unlikely to ever reach much more than $2 billion per year. This would imply figures closer to $80 million to $100 million per recipient per year, or about 1.5 percent of income. Although not as large as originally envisaged, this is still substantial new funding in many countries.

The sustainability of MCC programs is open to question. Some in the U.S. administration argued that after one five-year program, recipients should be able to graduate to private flows. Perhaps more important, many of the early projects are roads and other infrastructure, and the MCC appears to be repeating the same mistake that many other donors have made by assuming that recipients will fully finance maintenance and repair costs over time and not building in realistic long-term financing plans.

The MCC deserves credit for being innovative and nonpolitical in its country selection process and for going much further than other U.S. programs in giving recipients control over priorities and content. These are major steps forward. But the MCC faces huge tests in the next two years in program implementation and in ensuring effective oversight, monitoring, and evaluation systems. Its future success will depend on its ability to implement programs without adding unnecessary bureaucratic procedures for the recipients, reasonably measure the results of its programs, keep politics out of allocation and evaluation decisions, and, perhaps most important, be willing to end funding for programs that do not show results.

16.3.2   The Global Fund to Fight AIDS, Tuberculosis, and Malaria

The Global Fund was founded in early 2002 as a result of growing belief that the international response to the three diseases had been too slow and small and that existing agencies were responding ineffectively. In April 2001, UN Secretary General Kofi Annan called for a new fund, and in July 2001 the G-7 heads of state agreed to the concept and provided an initial commitment of $1.3 billion.[11] The United States and some other donors were willing to support the idea, but only if it were not part of existing agencies such as the World Bank or the World Health Organization. As with the MCC and GAVI, donors chose to launch a new mechanism with different operating principles rather than try to reform existing institutions. The Global Fund is neither a UN nor multilateral agency, but a foundation whose funding comes from voluntary contributions from governments and the private sector (e.g., the Bill and Melinda Gates Foundation). It is governed by a twenty-four-member board designed with a deliberately inclusive structure, with representatives from donor countries, recipient countries, NGOs, affected communities, foundations, and private companies. As of the end of 2005, Global Fund grants had provided antiretroviral treatment for 384,000 people living with HIV, HIV testing and counseling for 3.9 million people, TB treatment for 1 million people, and 7.7 million malaria bed nets.[12]

The Global Fund was designed to bring about two key changes. First, by having a very clear focus, it was meant to stimulate a substantial increase in financing for programs to fight the three diseases. The fund grew quickly in its first three years: as of mid-2006, it had approved funding for 363 programs in 132 countries—a larger set of countries than almost any other donor—with signed two-year grants agreements totaling $3.4 billion. Second, it was designed to provide aid through a very different model: a narrow substantive focus on the three diseases, operating exclusively as a financing instrument (it does not implement programs or provide technical assistance), an open and participatory approach with wide representation on its board and other structures, a focus on recipient-driven strategies, a small bureaucracy, and a (promised) focus on performance. The fund is far more open and transparent than other donors, with every approved proposal on its Web site, along with progress reports and full data (updated daily) on funds raised and disbursed by project. Whether this different model will achieve stronger results remains to be seen, but the fund clearly was designed to respond to some, but not all, of the criticisms of aid programs outlined above.

Selectivity

The Global Fund eschews the idea of country selectivity. Any country can submit a proposal. Instead of ex ante selectivity, the fund is designed to be performance based and claims that over time, its funding will follow performance rather than relying on broader measures of governance and policy performance. Nevertheless, in its third year, the Global Fund began to treat some countries differently. It has introduced "additional safeguards procedures" for a small number of countries that the board feels are governed particularly poorly, including North Korea, Myanmar, Cuba, Iran, and Sudan. It has considered, but has not yet introduced, a proposal to begin to rate each country based on its early progress and procedures, with a view toward providing streamlined procedures for more highly rated programs and greater oversight for countries with weaker performance (Radelet 2004b).

Country Ownership and Participation

The Global Fund goes beyond other donors in incorporating country ownership and broad participation. It takes an unusually hands-off approach, leaving much of the responsibility for program design and implementation to country representatives and local groups. It has no staff resident in any recipient country. To apply for funding, a country must first establish a country coordinating mechanism (CCM) consisting of government, NGO, civil society, faith-based organizations, and others to prepare and submit a proposal. Each proposal is reviewed by the Global Fund's technical review panel, an independent group of experts (none of whom work for the fund) that assesses proposals for technical rigor and makes recommendations to the board. Approval is far from automatic, with the board accepting just 40 to 50 percent of proposals. The CCMs nominate one or more of their members as principal recipients (PRs) to receive funds and take the lead in implementing programs.

These procedures have generated significant debate. Interestingly, the more the Global Fund invites broader participation, the more debate it generates about whether it does so extensively enough. Concerns have been raised about whether participation is sufficiently representative, the role of consultants in designing programs, and the slow pace of program design and implementation that is partly due to the participatory approach. These issues create significant challenges for the Global Fund, because "ownership" and "participation" are matters of degree rather than absolutes. Moreover, these approaches are experimental rather than based on evidence; no research links different participation and ownership mechanisms to results.

The Global Fund deserves credit for attempting to be bold and innovative in this respect. But it faces a risk in the extensive focus and debate on process. A critical issue is balancing its focus on process—in the belief that process matters for results—and the focus on the ultimate results themselves. What is clear is that the Global Fund is taking a radically different approach in these areas compared to almost all other donors.

Smaller Bureaucracy

The Global Fund has an unusually small structure, with only about 200 staff for 363 programs in 132 countries. (The World Bank, with more than 11,000 staff working in about 130 countries, has more than 80 staff members per country.) The secretariat's work is augmented by the technical review panel and by local fund agents (LFAs)—usually local affiliates of international accounting firms—that the secretariat contracts with in each country to carry out assessment and monitoring activities. Some have raised concerns that the Global Fund's staff may be too small. Too large a staff can make aid bureaucratic, but too small a staff could undermine effectiveness, because the secretariat may not be able to effectively support programs in all countries (Radelet 2004b). Although the fund has increased its staff size in the past two years (from a tiny staff of eighty), it is still not clear whether it is the right size or has the right mix of skills to adequately manage programs in so many countries.

Focused Objectives
The Global Fund's activities are centered on just the three diseases. It was specifically designed to have a narrow focus to help minimize mission creep and strengthen management by clarifying objectives and goals. The sharper focus helps concentrate proposals, streamline the technical review process, and establish measurable objectives. It also helps in communicating to donors (and taxpayers in donor countries) the purpose of the fund. But it rules out other pressing health problems, and by focusing narrowly, it may overlook the importance of broader health systems and institutions. The Global Fund has experienced pressure to expand its purposes, as some advocates believe that sustained progress in health is possible only through broader horizontal approaches that encompass health systems reform rather than vertical approaches that focus intensively on a narrow set of diseases. There is some truth to these critiques: HIV/AIDS programs cannot be sustained in many countries if the broader public health system is in disarray. But there also is a risk that if the Global Fund broadens its remit to institution building, it will lose its focus and some of its support. It has tried to balance this tension by funding broader institutional building when proposals link it directly to programs fighting the three diseases.

Harmonization and Coordination with Other Donors
The Global Fund is much more like a traditional foundation rather than a development agency, as it was explicitly designed as a financing agent only, providing funds to fill gaps not covered by others. It does not design or implement programs, nor does it provide technical assistance (TA). The clear view of the designers was that there were plenty of other agencies that already provided those roles, that the critical shortage was funding, and that the fund should concentrate on raising money and delivering it where it could be used well. But for this model to work, the Global Fund has to work in tandem with other

actors (what it refers to as the "network"), all with specialized roles in fighting the three diseases. On paper, countries design activities that are supposed to be fully integrated and coordinated with other activities and that fit into national strategies. The Global Fund then provides financing, and other agencies provide TA and other support as needed.

In practice, this vision is difficult to carry out. For many programs, TA is not always available, and other donors complain of the "unfunded mandate" of providing TA to support Global Fund programs. Moreover, in many countries, the Global Fund has begun to look like one more donor with its own requirements (the CCM, its proposal process, its own monitoring and evaluation system, and others) rather than one part of an integrated approach. However, there are some steps underway toward greater coordination. The Global Fund agreed with several other donors on a uniform monitoring and evaluation toolkit and is taking steps to integrate CCMs with existing bodies (e.g., National AIDS Councils) rather than stand as separate bodies. The jury is still out about whether the Global Fund will add to the burden on recipients by adding its own independent requirements or will be a force toward a more streamlined approach.

Performance-Based Management

The Global Fund is supposed to be strongly performance based. Programs are designed with a five-year time horizon, but the board initially approves two years of funding, with a three-year extension dependent on performance. Grant recipients report interim data on a quarterly basis, some of which are verified by the local fund agents (LFAs), which are independent organizations (usually local affiliates of international accounting firms) contracted by the secretariat to provide assessments and ongoing oversight and verification of reported data.

At this writing in mid-2006, it is too early to judge the extent to which the Global Fund will be performance based in practice, although some evidence is beginning to trickle in. In four cases, the Global Fund has quickly acted to suspend programs when they went dramatically off-track: the Ukraine, Burma, Chad, and Uganda. By December-2006 215 programs had completed their first two years and been reviewed: 106 were continued as designed, 104 were continued pending some changes, and 5 were terminated. But the terminations have been difficult, and some programs with weak performance have been continued. The board faces enormous challenges in balancing its commitment to be performance based with pressures to continue programs even when performance is substandard. Although all donors face a Samaritan's challenge of being reluctant to cut funding for humanitarian programs, the challenge is especially acute for HIV/AIDS programs. Board decisions are complicated by the board's composition of donors, recipient countries, and people living with the diseases. But there is a growing danger that programs with poor performance will be allowed to continue, which could weaken the incentives for countries to achieve specified goals, and undermine the support for the fund from some donors that place a high priority on performance-based funding.

Scaled-Up and Sustainable Funding
The fund was meant to dramatically scale up financing for the three diseases, although a target size was never officially stated. At the upper end, the World Health Organization (WHO) Commission on Macroeconomics and Health suggested Global Fund disbursements of $8 billion per year by 2007 (WHO 2001). Currently, the fund is disbursing at a rate equivalent to about $1.5 billion per year. Many advocates are pushing for greater funding more in line with huge (and growing) global needs, but it is uncertain how much larger the fund will grow. As an independent foundation, the Global Fund relies on voluntary contributions from governments and the private sector, and does not operate on the basis of fixed shares like the World Bank and other multilaterals. The United States has provided about 30 percent of the funding so far. The Bush administration originally was very supportive of the fund, but its support waned after it announced its own large bilateral HIV/AIDS initiative, so large increases from the United States are uncertain at best. The Bill and Melinda Gates Foundation recently announced an unprecedented private sector contribution of $500 million.

The uncertainty of future funding has created a major dilemma for the Global Fund. Its board has announced its strong commitment to continuing to fund existing programs, which is sensible in particular for HIV/AIDS programs in which patients require treatment for life (but GAVI takes a different approach for immunizations, as we discuss below). However, without an increase in overall funding, the Global Fund will be able to continue funding only existing programs, not new ones. This is a particular problem since all projections point to a worsening of the global HIV/AIDS pandemic over the next decade, even under best-case scenarios. Because of a shortage of funds, the Global Fund initially decided not to accept new proposals in 2006, although it later reversed the decision when some funds became available. As funding becomes limited and the global disease burden continues to grow, the Global Fund will be facing difficult trade-offs in the near future.

16.3.3   The Global Alliance for Vaccines and Immunizations

At its inception, GAVI and its funding arm, the Vaccine Fund,[13] were designed to respond to both the shortcomings of traditional aid mechanisms and a serious public health problem: the erosion of many of the gains made during the 1980s in childhood immunization coverage, particularly in sub-Saharan Africa. Public health professionals were painfully aware that traditional childhood immunization, a proven intervention capable of saving millions of children's lives at very low cost, was losing ground. In part, this was attributed to diminished interest and lack of a coordinated approach among donors and technical agencies, along with disintegration in African health systems as the AIDS pandemic and lack of national resources for health took their toll. International public health experts also recognized that newer vaccines, for example, against hepatitis B and haemophilus influenza B, would likely not be affordable for developing countries for decades without a major new subsidy. Public health advocates found a receptive audience for their concerns in Bill Gates, who in the late 1990s was seeking ways to invigorate major gains in global health and was attracted to the promise of immunization, which is as close as public health gets to a magic bullet.

Recognizing the challenges of working within the fractious international institutions and seeking to take advantage (but not get bogged down in the bureaucracies) of the WHO, the World Bank, bilateral donor agencies, and UNICEF, the GAVI designers envisioned an alliance of leading agencies working in immunization, along with representatives of technical agencies such as the U.S. Centers for Disease Control and Prevention, and the private sector, including both multinational and developing-country vaccine suppliers. The alliance is intended to coordinate actions and policies among various actors in global immunization—for example, by working to align the advice given by WHO and UNICEF to ministries of health about priorities for their immunization programs. Importantly, it has the sometimes conflicting aims of strengthening routine immunization programs, expanding the number and type of vaccines delivered by national government's immunization programs, accelerating movement to a "mature" (low) price for vaccines that have been licensed relatively recently, and promoting sustainable immunization program financing.

The main function of GAVI, beyond coordination, is to be a vehicle for new funding to improve immunization programs in low-income countries. And bring money it has done. GAVI was launched at the World Economic Forum in January 2000 with a five-year start-up grant of $750 million from the Bill and Melinda Gates Foundation, later supplemented with almost $800 million from the governments of Canada, the United States, the United Kingdom, and several other European nations. In 2005, the Gates Foundation replenished the Vaccine Fund with $750 million committed over ten years; another $900 million has been pledged by governments over that period. In addition, the governments of Brazil, France, Italy, Norway, South Africa, Spain, Sweden, and the United Kingdom have committed almost $4 billion through the new International Finance Facility for Immunization, which will channel funds through GAVI over a ten-year period. In short, GAVI is a large source of long-term funding, targeted at improving and expanding immunization programs in developing countries.

The funding, provided to countries in the form of five-year grants (typically extended to seven or eight years), often doubles the existing immunization support at the national level. The monies are used to strengthen delivery systems for basic childhood vaccines and the in-kind provision of newer vaccines, including those against hepatitis B, hemophilus influenza B (Hib), and yellow fever. In the future, it is expected that GAVI funds will be used to support the widespread introduction of still newer products, including rotavirus and pneumococcal conjugate vaccine.

In its design, explicit efforts were made to make GAVI different from other global health efforts, and certainly distinct from traditional aid transfers. Over the six-year track record of the program, some of those ambitions have been shown to be overly optimistic; others have endured.

Selectivity

GAVI does not select countries or allocate funds based on Burnside and Dollar types of policy and institutional quality measures, but it is selective on the basis of both income and immunization program performance and adheres to clear criteria for funding. Grants are offered only to countries with per capita income less than $1,000. Funds are made available for immunization system strengthening for countries with less than 80 percent coverage of traditional childhood vaccines; these are the countries whose relatively weak immunization performance reflects a need for greater investment. Funds are available for the introduction of new vaccines only for countries that have achieved at least 50 percent coverage. Countries whose immunization programs are below that standard are encouraged to focus first on strengthening the core aspects of their delivery system rather than being distracted by the introduction of newer products. For the most part, this basic concept has been maintained, although a greater recognition—and funding—than originally anticipated has gone to strengthening immunization systems within countries at all coverage levels.

Country Ownership and Participation

In concept, grants are intended to support the government's priorities for its immunization program—that is, for expansion of coverage, improvement of quality, or introduction of newer vaccines. Countries can apply for distinct types of support, depending on their preferences and aims for their program.

For example, a country may select among several different vaccine presentations, each with implications for recurrent costs and delivery requirements. In practice, however, those choices may be driven in part by the larger global agenda of accelerating the introduction of new vaccines, even where that may not have been what national immunization programs value the most. Anecdotal reports of the earlier rounds of the GAVI grant application process note that representatives of technical agencies and the expatriate technical personnel providing assistance to countries to prepare the submission tended to advocate for the introduction of combination vaccines (tetravalent and pentavalent), sometimes over the questions (and even mild objections) of country officials. And in the early days of the program, tetravalent vaccine was in short supply, so countries were encouraged to apply for the much more costly pentavalent product.

Smaller Bureaucracy

In its initial design, GAVI was relatively light on bureaucratic requirements. The application for grants demanded a much smaller amount of documentation than for many externally funded projects, and most of the required information could be derived from standard multiyear and annual plans that national immunization programs are, in the main, accustomed to preparing for their own operational purposes. GAVI applications must be endorsed by the InterAgency Coordinating Committee (ICC) within each country, a body that is supposed to include both domestic public sector and donor representatives who are active in immunization. Applications to GAVI are reviewed by the independent review committee, comprising international experts on immunization programs.

As the program has evolved, however, donor requirements have increased. First, so-called data quality audits (DQAs), expert reviews of the quality of information on program coverage, were required before governments could receive performance-based awards. DQAs are relatively costly, averaging US$45,000 per country, and have created controversy when they have challenged the validity of government statistical data. Second, financial sustainability plans (FSPs) or analyses of the income and expenditures of the national immunization program must be prepared by grant recipients two to three years after the start of funding. In the plans, governments estimate the financial requirements associated with program priorities and targets and calculate the recurrent cost burden of expanded coverage and a broadened immunization schedule. Governments also are asked to document current program financing and project secure and probable funding in the postgrant period. While undertaking this data collection and analysis has been burdensome for program officials, it also has revealed essential information about financing challenges, serving as an early warning system for the GAVI partners, who became aware that many national governments are unlikely to be able to assume full program financing after the first grant ends.

Focused Objectives

Compared with broad development programs, GAVI is narrowly focused on childhood immunization. While the tight focus of GAVI permits it to act in a relatively efficient and uncomplicated manner, it has also left the alliance vulnerable to critiques that it distorts national priorities by skewing attention toward one health intervention. Defenders argue that childhood immunization is a core government responsibility and represents one of the most cost-effective interventions, and thus should be privileged in any allocation of resources. Critics, however, note that the cost-effectiveness of the newer products, and particularly the vaccines against Hib, has not been fully established, and their introduction has greatly increased the overall cost of the program—in some cases, increasing from 4 percent of total health spending to close to 12 percent. Concerns also have been expressed that health system strengthening took a backseat within GAVI to the introduction of newer vaccines. In response, GAVI has increased its commitment to system strengthening.

Harmonization and Coordination with Other Donors

GAVI is a mechanism for coordinating disparate donor and technical agency efforts to support improved immunization. Its aims, in fact, cannot be achieved with its own money alone. The technical assistance, financial transfers, and procurement expertise of GAVI partners are also necessary.

GAVI has been relatively successful in providing a means for coordination among partners, but it has faced some significant obstacles. Each of the GAVI agencies has its own governance, priorities, and internal incentives, and significant effort is required to overcome institutional jealousies and cultural differences across agencies. In addition, most GAVI partners have both global and country-level offices and decision makers. While coordination has been relatively good at the global level, headquarters'-led initiatives are not always welcomed within country offices. Agreements among the GAVI partners at board meetings in Geneva, Washington, and elsewhere do not automatically translate to staff working in particular countries.

Performance-Based Allocations

A special feature of GAVI is the reward for performance embedded within the rules for funding the strengthening of immunization delivery systems. Under its system support, GAVI provides an incentive for expanded coverage in two ways. First is a stick: GAVI ceases funding if and when coverage declines or fails to increase at an acceptable rate. Then, using a carrot, GAVI rewards countries that succeed in increasing coverage with a one-time transfer of $20 per additional fully immunized child.[14] The $20 comes without conditions, so countries can use it for whatever they wish. GAVI is not the first to implement cash transfers based on specific results, but it is one of the small minority.

GAVI has shown that it can and will cut off funding for poor performers. In late 2003, three years after funding was first offered, the GAVI board terminated grants to ten countries that were underperforming relative to what they had promised. This places GAVI in a small minority of aid mechanisms that have enforced performance conditionalities. GAVI has also shown that it will reward countries for good performance. ISS support has been increased for twenty-three countries that have demonstrated increases in immunization coverage.

Scaled-Up and Sustainable Funding

The catalytic nature of GAVI support for the introduction of newer vaccines depends on mobilizing non-GAVI financing to sustain the gains made under the initial grant. GAVI partners have taken the question of sustainability seriously and have applied a definition of sustainability that takes into consideration real-world conditions in very poor countries. At the same time, they have been at least partially stymied in their efforts to affect the market for vaccines as they had hoped.

The GAVI definition of sustainability attempts to recognize that many poor countries are not going to be able to be self-sufficient in financing their immunization programs for a very long time and thus must depend on a combination of government and donor resources. Therefore, in discussions of sustaining the program, the financing prospects of both government and donors are brought to the light and expectations have been raised about the extent to which donors will pick up where GAVI leaves off.

At the outset, GAVI's designers expected that prices of the newer products would decline quickly—more quickly than had been the case for products in the past—and other funders would increase immunization program funding to a higher level than had been witnessed in the past. This assumption was a surprising one, given that through its funding GAVI was increasing demand, which could be expected to increase, not decrease, prices, all else equal. Now, more than five years later, it is clear that reality does not measure up to expectations. In the case of tetravalent vaccine, the price increased from about US$1 per dose in 2000 to almost US$1.32 in 2005; for pentavalent vaccine, the price increased from slightly less than US$3.40 per dose in 2000 to about US$3.80 per dose in 2005, in part due to the fall of the dollar. (The only supplier of pentavalent vaccine that is prequalified by WHO is a European manufacturer, Glaxo-Smith-Kline, which sets prices in euros.) And while both government and donor funding for immunization (other than the Vaccine Fund contributions) have increased slightly, this is insufficient to offset the much larger program costs. Consequently, many countries that introduced combination vaccines with GAVI resources are unlikely to be able to continue to obtain the products once the grant ends. Responding to this, the GAVI partners are actively exploring ways to extend financing while still maintaining the original conception of a time-limited and catalytic function for grants.

In sum, GAVI has several features that distinguish it from both traditional aid mechanisms and either the Global Fund or the MCC. It provides financial support to poor countries with immunization programs that are not yet performing at the level required to achieve the maximum public health benefit. It provides material incentives for expanded coverage and disincentives for slipping performance. And it sees financial sustainability as a partnership between poor countries and donors rather than through the traditional—but often futile—lens of near-term self-sufficiency in social sector financing by very low-income countries.

16.4 Will the Changes Matter? Three Issues to Watch

It is too early too tell whether these new agencies will be any more effective than traditional donor mechanisms or whether over time their innovations will fade, until they do not appear much different. These new programs are not the first attempt by donors to establish new, effective agencies. The United Nations is replete with specialized agencies that began with the promise of a narrow focus, clear objectives, a smaller bureaucracy, and more effective support for development (recall that UNICEF won the Nobel Peace Prize in 1965). President John F. Kennedy established USAID in an attempt to reorganize and streamline U.S. foreign aid programs and make them more effective in fighting poverty. Starting fresh does not guarantee success. Going forward, three key issues will go a long way toward determining success or failure.

16.4.1 Will the Programs Be Performance Based?

At the end of the day, funders, the taxpayers behind the funders, and the people living in recipient countries all want results. But there are two large challenges in making programs performance based. The first is technical: actually measuring the results, and connecting them to development outcomes, is difficult. Some things are comparatively easy to measure, like how many kilometers of roads were built and how many children were immunized. But other things are much more difficult, like building capacity and strengthening institutions. And there is always the temptation to measure what is easy to measure rather than what matters. But even when outputs can be measured, connecting them to development outcomes like economic growth or poverty reduction is fraught with difficulties.

The second challenge has more to do with institutional and political incentives. Even if results can be measured, do the institutions really want to know when their programs do not work? Will they be willing to terminate programs to friends and allies, or terminate programs that are aimed at saving lives, even if the evidence shows they are not working?

One way out of this dilemma is to introduce a truly independent entity to monitor and evaluate aid programs, addressing some of the enduring questions about what works. While the idea of strengthening evaluation is a perennial topic within discussions of aid effectiveness, recent efforts have provided momentum for better evaluation, and have offered specifics about how to do it, by confronting institutional constraints. In mid-2006, the Center for Global Development's Evaluation Gap Working Group issued a report calling for the creation of an international council that would fund the design and implementation of independent, external impact evaluations of development programs, particularly those in the social sectors; the council would also set quality standards for impact evaluations and disseminate evaluation findings (Savedoff, Levine, and Birdsall 2006). The working group noted that such an arrangement would overcome the multiple structural impediments to good evaluation: the public goods nature of the knowledge generated, the tension between using resources for operational versus research or evaluation purposes, and the potential censoring of unfavorable findings within development agencies. The idea of an independent fund for good-quality evaluation has attracted interest from both governments and private foundations and may become a reality within a year or so.

16.4.2   Will the Programs and Their Impact Be Sustainable?

If programs that initially achieve important results are not sustained, the gains will erode. GAVI is the clearest case in point. It was designed with the assumption that once programs were established and benefits were clear, recipient countries would take over the funding. But in low-income countries with very constrained financing, this assumption has proved to be optimistic in many cases. Faced with pressures to continue funding the new vaccines whose introduction it supported, and yet committed to the notion that it wants funding to support expansion of immunization programs to include even newer vaccines, GAVI is struggling to sort out a sensible approach to financing. The current strategy appears to be to lengthen the period of support to up to ten years and to ask for modest copayments that, it is hoped, set the stage for countries' funding vaccine purchase after prices decline. GAVI leaders now understand that prices will likely decline only with concerted efforts—for example, to negotiate long-term binding contracts with manufacturers.

The Global Fund followed a different path and decided that its top priority would be to continue funding programs as long as necessary, provided that they achieved results. But a concern is that this approach will simply create dependency and that it does not create the incentives for recipients to eventually fund programs.

The MCC is financing significant amounts of infrastructure, and there is a long history of problems in financing the recurrent costs of aid-financed infrastructure problems. The extent to which the MCC recognizes this problem is not clear. To date, it has taken the traditional approach of asking recipients to commit to financing maintenance and repairs and proceeding on that basis. It may need to try more innovative ideas such as sinking funds or committing to providing matching funds for maintenance, perhaps with a declining share over time depending on the investment. But without coming to grips with this issue, the MCC may find that its new roads show great promise and bring significant benefits for a few years, but the benefits decline quickly over time.

16.4.3 Will They Be Too Bureaucratic?

Ensuring strong benefits and sustaining them is just half the equation; the other half is ensuring that the costs of the programs and projects, including bureaucratic costs, are not too high. The focus in each institution in showing its own results creates incentives for each to establish its own procedures for designing, managing, monitoring, and evaluation. The results can be duplication of activities and a huge burden on recipients to meet with mission teams, send quarterly reports, establish separate monitoring processes, and so on. This tendency puts the burden on the skilled personnel in recipient countries, which may be their scarcest resource. As a result, these programs can have significant unmeasured costs through the opportunity costs of time and attention of skilled personnel, who spend all of their time dealing with donors rather than on more pressing issues. The right balance between, one the one hand, many donors, each with its own programs but creating some competition and innovation, and on the other hand putting all funds into one basket is not clear. GAVI and the Global Fund seem to be very aware of the danger of too much bureaucracy stemming from too many donors and are taking steps to minimize bureaucratic costs and coordinate processes with other donors. This is less evident with the MCC, at least at this writing.

16.4.4   The Ultimate Impact

The success or failure of these three new programs has strong implications for other aid agencies. Each is being watched closely to see if it can keep its administrative structures small, maintain focused objectives, and create the incentives that will lead to stronger results that can be sustained over time. With either success or failure, they will have a significant impact on how donors structure and deliver foreign assistance in the future. Each has significant promise to deliver assistance more effectively; whether they will succeed remains an open question.

Acknowledgments

We thank Sheila Herrling and Kaysie Brown for value input and advice, and Carol Lancaster and Nancy Birdsall for comments on an earlier draft. We also thank the William and Flora Hewlett Foundation for its support of our work on aid effectiveness.

Notes

The text and data in this chapter reflect the situation at the time of writing in 2005.

1. This summary draws heavily from the review in Clemens, Radelet, and Bhavnani (2004).

2. Dutch disease refers to a situation in which a large inflow of foreign exchange (perhaps from an export commodity boom or aid inflows) causes the exchange rate to appreciate and undermines the incentives for exports, thus reducing growth. See, e.g., Mosley (1980), Mosley, Hudson, and Horrell (1987), Dowling and Hiemenz (1982), Singh (1985), and Boone (1984).

3. The authors dismiss this result as a special case, when in fact it is the more general since it relaxes the assumptions about linearity and homogeneity of aid. They take the position that aid-growth results are robust and convincing only if they find positive and significant results in both cases of a linear and nonlinear relationship.

4. This list is drawn from Radelet (2004a). Birdsall (2004) provides a list of "seven deadly sins" that afflict donors.

5. "Cutting the Red Tape" (2003).

6. Officially these take a variety of institutional forms—foundations, corporations, alliances—but we will refer to them as agencies.

7. For earlier analyses of the MCA see Radelet (2003a, 2003b, 2004a), and Brainard et al. (2003). For ongoing analysis of MCA issues, see http://www.cgdev.org/section/initiatives/_active/mcamonitor.

8. Armenia, Benin, Bolivia, Burkina Faso, Cape Verde, East Timor, El Salvador, The Gambia, Georgia, Ghana, Honduras, Lesotho, Madagascar, Mali, Mongolia, Morocco, Mozambique, Namibia, Nicaragua, Senegal, Sri Lanka, Tanzania, and Vanuatu.

9. Ghana, Armenia, Benin, Cape Verde, Madagascar, Honduras, Georgia, Nicaragua, and Vanuatu. Mali and El Salvador are likely to be approved by the end of 2006. Disbursements, however, have been slow, with only Madagascar showing much progress.

10. For individual country assessments on consultation and donor coordination, see CGD's MCA Monitor Field Reports: http://www.cgdev.org/section/initiatives/_active/mcamonitor/fieldreports.

11. See the secretary general's remarks at www.un.org/News/Press/docs/2001/SGSM7779R1 .doc.htm. The G-7 agreement can be found at "G8 Communique Genoa 2001," paragraph 15, www.library.utoronto.ca/g7/summit/2001genoa/finalcommunique.html.

12. "Global Fund Grants Deliver Substantial New Results." Global Fund press release, November 30, 2005, http://www.theglobalfund.org/en/media_center/press/pr_051130.asp

13. Although GAVI and the Vaccine Fund were separate entities, for the simplicity we refer only to GAVI. The Vaccine Fund was originally conceived of as being responsible for funding the decisions taken by the GAVI board. In 2005, the two parts of the organizations merged.

14. Although accounts vary about the source of the $20 per child figure, it is approximately equivalent to the cost to fully immunize a child under typical developing country conditions.

References

Bauer, Peter. 1972. *Dissent on Development*. Cambridge, Mass.: Harvard University Press.

Birdsall, Nancy. 2004. "Seven Deadly Sins: Reflections on Donor Failings." Center for Global Development Working Paper 50. Washington, D.C.: Center for Global Development.

Boone, Peter. 1994. "The Impact of Foreign Aid on Savings and Growth." Centre for Economic Performance Working Paper 677. London: London School of Economics.

Brainard, Lael, Carol Graham, Nigel Purvis, Steven Radelet, and Gayle Smith. 2003. *The Other War: Global Poverty and the Millennium Challenge Account*. Washington, D.C.: Brookings Institution Press and the Center for Global Development.

Burnside, Craig, and David Dollar. 2000. "Aid, Policies, and Growth." *American Economic Review* 90(4):847–868.

Clemens, Michael, Steven Radelet, and Rikhil Bhavnani. 2004. "Counting Chickens When They Hatch: The Short-Term Effect of Aid on Growth." Center for Global Development Working Paper 44. Washington, D.C.: Center for Global Development.

Collier, Paul, and Jan Dehn. 2001. "Aid, Shocks, and Growth." World Bank Policy Research Working Paper 2688. Washington, D.C.: World Bank.

Collier, Paul, and David Dollar. 2002. "Aid Allocation and Poverty Reduction." *European Economic Review* 45(1):1–26.

"Cutting the Red Tape." 2003. World Bank Development News Media, February 21.

Dowling, Malcolm, and Ulrich Hiemenz. 1982. "Aid, Savings, and Growth in the Asian Region." Manila: Economic Office, Asian Development Bank.

Dalgaard, Carl-Johan, and Henrik Hansen. 2000. "On aid, Growth, and Good Policies." CREDIT Research Paper 00/17. Nottingham: Centre for Research in Economic Development and International Trade, University of Nottingham.

Dalgaard, Carl-Johan, Henrik Hansen, and Finn Tarp. 2004. "On the Empirics of Foreign Aid and Growth." *Economic Journal* 114(496):191–216.

Duflo, Esther. 2001. "Schooling and Labor Market Consequences of School Construction in Indonesia: Evidence from an Unusual Policy Experiment." *American Economic Review* 91(4):795–813.

Duflo, Esther, and Michael Kremer. 2003. "Use of Randomization in the Evaluation of Development Effectiveness." Paper prepared for the World Bank Operations Evaluation Department, July.

Durbarry, Ramesh, Norman Gemmell, and David Greenaway. 1998. "New Evidence on the Impact of Foreign Aid on Economic Growth." CREDIT Research Paper 98/8. Nottingham: Centre for Research in Economic Development and International Trade, University of Nottingham.

Easterly, William. 2001. *The Elusive Quest for Growth: An Economist's Adventures and Misadventures in the Tropics*. Cambridge, Mass.: MIT Press.

Easterly, William. 2002. "The Cartel of Good Intentions: The Problem of Bureaucracy in Foreign Aid." *Journal of Policy Reform* 5(4):223–250.

Easterly, William, Ross Levine, and David Roodman. 2004. "New Data, New Doubts: A Comment on Burnside and Dollar's "Aid, Policies, and Growth."" *American Economic Review* 94(3):774–780.

Friedman, Milton. 1958. "Foreign Economic Aid." *Yale Review* 47(4):501–516.

Griffen, Keith B., and J. L. Enos. 1970. "Foreign Assistance: Objectives and Consequences." Economic Development and Cultural Change 18(2):313–27.

Hadjimichael, Michael T., Dhaneshwar Ghura, Martin Muhleisen, Roger Nord, and E. Murat Ucer. 1995. "Sub-Saharan Africa: Growth, Savings, and Investment 1986–93." Occasional Paper 118. Washington, D.C.: International Monetary Fund.

Hansen, Henrik, and Finn Tarp. 2000. "Aid Effectiveness Disputed." *Journal of International Development* 12:375–398.

Hansen, Henrik, and Finn Tarp. 2001. "Aid and Growth Regressions." *Journal of Development Economics* 64:547–570.

Isham, Jonathan, Daniel Kaufmann, and Lant Pritchett. 1995. "Governance and Returns on Investment: An Empirical Investigation." World Bank Policy Research Working Paper 1550. Washington, D.C.: World Bank.

Lensink, Robert, and Howard White. 2001. "Are There Negative Returns to Aid?" *Journal of Development Studies* 37(6):42–65.

Levine, Ruth, and the What Works Working Group, with Molly Kinder. 2004. *Millions Saved: Proven Success in Global Health.* Washington, D.C.: Center for Global Development.

Levy, Victor. 1988. "Aid and Growth in Sub-Saharan Africa: The Recent Experience." *European Economic Review* 32(9):1777–1795.

Mavrotas, George. 2002. "Aid and Growth in India: Some Evidence from Disaggregated Aid Data." *South Asia Economic Journal* 3(1):19–49.

Mavrotas, George. 2003. "Assessing Aid Effectiveness in Uganda: An Aid-Disaggregation Approach." Oxford: Oxford Policy Management.

Mosley, Paul. 1980. "Aid, Savings, and Growth Revisited." *Oxford Bulletin of Economics and Statistics* 42(2):79–96.

Mosley, Paul, John Hudson, and Sara Horrell. 1987. "Aid, the Public Sector and the Market in Less Developed Countries." *Economic Journal* 97(387):616–641.

Owens, Trudy, and John Hoddinott. 1999. "Investing in Development or Investing in Relief: Quantifying the Poverty Tradeoffs Using Zimbabwe Household Panel Data." Working Paper 99-4. Oxford: Centre for the Study of African Economies, Department of Economics, Oxford University.

Papenek, Gustav F. 1973. "Aid, Foreign Private Investment, Savings, and Growth in Less Developed Countries." *Journal of Political Economy* 81(1):120–130.

Radelet, Steven. 2003a. *Challenging Foreign Aid: A Policymaker's Guide to the Millennium Challenge Account.* Washington, D.C.: Center for Global Development.

Radelet, Steven. 2003b. "Bush and Foreign Aid." *Foreign Affairs* 82:104–117.

Radelet, Steven. 2004a. "The Millennium Challenge Account: Transforming U.S. Foreign Assistance Policy?" *Agenda* 11(1):53–70.

Radelet, Steven. 2004b. "The Global Fund to Fight AIDS, Tuberculosis, and Malaria: Progress, Potential, and Challenges for the Future." Available at http://www.cgdev.org/Publications/ ?PubID=127.

Radelet, Steven. 2006. "From Pushing Reforms to Pulling Reforms: The Role of Challenge Programs in Foreign Aid Policy." In Inge Kaul and Pedro Conceição eds., *The New Public Finance: Responding to Global Challenges.* Oxford University Press.

Rajan, Raghuram, and Arvind Subramanian. 2005. "Aid and Growth: What Does the Cross-Country Evidence Really Show?" IMF Working Paper 05/127. Washington, D.C.: International Monetary Fund.

Roodman, David. 2004. "The Anarchy of Numbers: Aid, Development, and Cross Country Empirics." Center for Global Development Working Paper 32. Washington, D.C.: Center for Global Development.

Roodman, David. 2006. "Competitive Proliferation of Aid Projects: A Model." Center for Global Development Working Paper 89. Washington, D.C.: Center for Global Development.

Sachs, Jeffrey, John McArthur, Guido Schmidt-Traub, Margaret Kruk, Chandrika Bahadur, Michael Faye, and Gordon McCord. 2004. "Ending Africa's Poverty Trap." *Brookings Papers on Economic Activity* 1. Washington, D.C.: Brookings Institution.

Savedoff, William D., Ruth Levine, Nancy Birdsall, and the Evaluation Gap Working Group. 2006. "When Will We Ever Learn? Improving Lives Through Impact Evaluation." Washington, D.C.: Center for Global Development.

Singh, Ram D. 1985. "State Intervention, Foreign Economic Aid, Savings and Growth in LDCs: Some recent Evidence." *Kyklos* 38(2):216–232.

Stern, Nicholas. 2002. "Making the Case for Aid." In World Bank, *A Case for Aid: Building a Consensus for Development Assistance*. Washington, D.C.: World Bank.

Stiglitz, Joseph. 2002. "Overseas Aid Is Money Well Spent." *Financial Times*, April 14.

Svensson, Jakob. 2003. "Why Conditional Aid Does Not Work and What Can Be Done about It." *Journal of Development Economics* 70(2):381–402.

van de Walle, Nicolas. 2001. *African Economies and the Politics of Permanent Crisis, 1979–1999*. Cambridge: Cambridge University Press.

World Health Organization. 2001. *Macroeconomics and Health: Investing in Health for Economic Development. Report of the Commission on Macroeconomics and Health*. Geneva: World Health Organization.

17 Competing with Central Planning: Marketplaces for International Aid

Dennis Whittle and Mari Kuraishi

It has been nineteen years since the Berlin Wall came down, and in its collapse, economists and government officials alike have learned a few things about the differences between what market economies and centrally planned ones can achieve. The evidence is clear: market economies have succeeded where centrally planned ones collapsed. Markets, a form of economic democracy in which many small and large individual actors make choices for their businesses and communities, generally produce better results than a few distant elite thinkers planning for the needs of a society.

While this lesson has been learned and absorbed in many facets of economics, it has been largely ignored in the structure of the foreign aid regime. Efforts in international development are conducted largely by unwieldy bureaucracies that centrally plan economies of developing countries, by making large-scale choices. If the international aid regime were a national economy, one thing is clear: the World Bank and International Monetary Fund (IMF) would be after it to reform.

Where are the results from fifty years of foreign aid? The current international aid regime structure needs a fundamental rethinking to better meet the needs of the many local actors who want to improve their communities, as well as the distant planners. While some aid agencies are experimenting with progressive new approaches, the paradigm has still not shifted.

Many would argue that the over $1 trillion given in aid to developing countries over the past half-century has failed—or at best has produced disappointing results. Development challenges are daunting and vast. Although there certainly have been successes, traditional approaches to foreign aid are not having the impact needed to cause hoped-for economic growth in the global South or to meet social objectives such as the Millennium Development goals. For instance, between 1980 and 2000, per capita gross domestic product (GDP) in Africa actually shrank 16 percent.[1] On the social side, consider that 2 billion people do not have access to electricity. Half the world's population lives on less than \$2 per day. One billion people cannot even sign their own name. More than a third of the world's children are malnourished. By the year 2010, 42 million children will be without parents, orphaned by HIV/AIDS.[2]

This chapter examines some of the problems with foreign aid and discusses proposed solutions. As part of that effort, we make an analogy between the failures of centrally planned economies and the troubles of foreign aid. We argue that bringing a few market elements into traditional structures of foreign aid might remedy some of the shortcomings of today's bureaucratic and sluggish aid system. We make the case that creating a marketplace for development can lead to much greater innovation, efficiency, and resource flows, and we discuss some of the challenges to the emergence of such a market.

We are not claiming that markets are the solution to everything. Clearly there are many examples of market failures as well as government failures. Well-functioning markets require an appropriate policy and regulatory environment, along with a degree of public investment in infrastructure and public goods. The same would hold true for a well-functioning market in aid.

We first demonstrate a few nonmarket features of the current system and show why they are so problematic. Then we discuss, briefly, what such a market would involve. Finally, we elaborate on a framework for thinking about how to catalyze a market for one segment of the aid industry.

17.1 Aid Is Centrally Planned

Clearly the economic development and aid regimes today do not resemble the synergistic networks of Silicon Valley or the free interaction of many competing donors and social entrepreneurs. Many of the reasons that centrally planned economies fail are reflected in international aid structures (both the official aid sector as well as the private aid sector), such as domination by a few large players, a top-down system in which projects are driven more by donor initiatives than by recipient needs, no feedback loops and insufficient accountability, little entry and exit of aid givers or receivers, sluggish innovation, and low efficiency.

We argue that there is a parallel between why markets work so well in economies and why market mechanisms would improve the allocation and impact of development aid. A full-length discussion of all aid's problems is beyond the scope of this chapter, but we offer a summary of the main nonmarket features of the system that we see as the keys to its shortcomings. Put simply, the aid system more closely resembles central planning than a market-based economy.

Note that while the official aid sector displays these attributes most clearly, the international nongovernmental organization (NGO) sector is also characterized by many of the same features. To be fair, some change is underway. But there has not yet been a paradigm shift.

17.1.1 Dominated by a Few Large Players and Large Projects

First, international aid is dominated by a few large players, while a vast number of smaller players lead a market. Much of foreign aid is in the form of bilateral or multilateral agencies contributing to other large actors such as governments. For instance, the World Bank and the U.S. government together account for most official development assistance. Furthermore, projects are planned on a grand scale by elites of the international aid community and elites in recipient countries rather than by many local actors on the ground. While such macroprojects and big sources of capital are important, a thriving network of many smaller projects is also essential to growth and social welfare. The current international development efforts have the emphasis wrong, with the development scene dominated by the big, with less emphasis on large numbers of the small. A more effective aid regime would facilitate more small and innovative projects.

To illustrate by way of analogy, it is the millions of small businesses that provide the lion's share of the impetus for the U.S. economy rather than the large corporations for which the United States is renowned. The 2000 U.S. census found that 99.7 percent of all establishments were small businesses, defined as having fewer than 500 employees. These small businesses accounted for about 75 percent of the U.S. payroll.[3] And no single company or group of companies dominates. In 2002, General Electric had the greatest market value of any other American company and yet represented less than 2 percent of the total market.[4]

17.1.2 Top-Down

The nature of this system driven by large players tends to be top-down rather than bottom up. Such top-down and agency-driven approaches translate into projects that are not responsive to the needs of local communities, tend to serve the priorities and perspectives of so-called aid experts rather than the aid recipients, and lead to inefficient results.

Much of the failure of decades of aid to the poorest parts of the world, in particular to Africa, arguably stems from bureaucratic central planning and its inefficiencies.[5] First, bilateral aid often is a political reward rather than given for sound development efforts. It is often conferred to political allies, even if their governments are poorly run or corrupt. Such aid is not good development policy, as it is often mismanaged or disappears into the pockets of political elites. Next, projects are often poorly designed by distant bureaucrats with little knowledge of the needs of local people. Projects are thus donor driven rather than recipient driven. Countries often do not feel ownership of the projects that are done for them, and governments often stop maintaining projects once donors have left. Next, tied bilateral aid comes with strings attached, often requiring aid recipients to hire companies or purchase products from the donor country. This practice can force project managers to make inefficient choices and purchase lower-quality or more expensive services. Finally, donor bureaucrats often have incentives to keep poorly run projects afloat in order not to lose their programmatic budgets. These are just a few of the problems with the bureaucratic aid regime, limited for the sake of space. William Easterly, in Chapter 1, more fully addresses the top-down bureaucratic problems of aid.

Imagine a private bank run with these standards, with loans given for political reasons or cronyism. Such banks often feature in corrupt societies rather than in industrialized, well-functioning economies, and they generally fail.

A market in a strong economy functions differently, with the bulk of the contribution to the economy bottom up rather than top down. Many smaller actors choose their projects and business ventures without a central bureaucracy hierarchy coordinating or dictating what will be produced, built, or sold. Of course, in the United States, the federal government provides regulation and a financial and physical infrastructure, and it directs certain infrastructure projects. But the government sector accounts for only about one-third of the economy, and the bulk of economic growth and organization comes from individuals working to make their businesses or organizations better. And most social services are run by local and state actors, not the distant federal government.

17.1.3 No Feedback Loops and Little Accountability

Another feature of the current international aid regime is the absence of feedback loops, or systematic ratings and learning processes of both aid providers and recipients. This lack of feedback loops leads to a deficiency of accountability by both aid givers and recipients. In sum, there are too few donors and too few recipients, leading to a concentration of each aid recipient's sources of aid. This concentration means a lack of competition among both donors and recipients, and the resultant improvement and accountability that would appear in a market. A market has many buyers and many sellers.

Aid providers are few and dominate recipients eager for funding. They call the shots for what programs will happen and how they will be managed. Recipients of international aid tend to be dependent on the will of often foreign organizations. In this donor's market, the donors dictate the terms. Recipients, eager for funding, often accept inefficient terms, such as tied aid, aid with strings attached, or aid for programs that are not interoperable with their other programs.[6] Such recipients are often too intimidated to give useful or forceful feedback to their donors.[7]

Aid agencies are not accountable to the poor whom they are trying to serve, but more often accountable to a distant bureaucracy. One former official of the U.S. Agency for International Development (USAID) writes, "In contrast to many government agencies in Western countries, the intended beneficiaries of aid agencies—the poor of other countries—have very little say over how aid agencies are organized and run because those agencies are not accountable to those beneficiaries."[8] Aid projects thus often reflect the priorities of foreign governments rather than those of locals themselves. Joseph Stiglitz points out that the IMF and World Bank do not feel accountable to the masses of poor they serve. Most contributors to these organizations are democracies that demand transparency and accountability at home. It should follow that these organizations then practice the same transparency and accountability. Instead, they generally report to the ministries of finance and central banks of governments around the world.[9] And while disclosure of information is improving, far too many decisions are taken behind closed doors.

Very few channels for feedback, ratings, and improvement of recipients exist either. There is no systematic way of rating aid receivers to weed out the good ones from the bad. Recipients cannot create a far-reaching reputation that might either prevent corrupt ones from receiving aid again or allow strong ones to attract additional capital for their projects.[10]

A market features ratings of both lenders and borrowers, by analogy the aid funders and recipients. Banks compete through customer service and by choosing credible projects. Poorly performing financial institutions receive lower bond ratings, and insoluble banks are put out of business by regulators. Consumers also have credit ratings that lead to reputation building; they know that not repaying loans or not paying bills will lead to a poor credit rating and a loss or decrease in access to credit. Lenders can check consumers' credit ratings to determine whether they are a safe bet for credit. Consumers with good credit can have access to additional services or preferential treatment. Such ratings also lead to branding, indirect indicators of quality that producers want to protect over the long haul. Both lenders and borrowers can benefit from these ratings.

17.1.4 Little Entry and Exit

Next, international development efforts see very little entry and exit of donors and recipients. The international aid scene remains dominated by the same players, usually large-scale donors such as governments, multilateral organizations, and large foundations. The largest recipients remain governments. The long-term efforts of these organizations provide stability. It is clear that at the government level, the market equivalent of entry and exit is not desirable.

But this also means that there is very little competition among either donors or recipients, as in a market, that would provide pressure to shape up or ship out. On the smaller project level, we argue that competition and accountability should lead to shutting down poorly run and poorly performing projects and opening the way for more innovative or better-managed projects. However, competition on merit does not always govern who gets projects.

Most official aid goes to governments, meaning inherently little entry. Outside smaller actors have difficulty tapping into traditional sources of aid, regardless of the merits of their proposals. The dominance of the few large players diminishes the ability of smaller players to compete and enter with new ideas, or fail and go out of business. The same phenomenon also holds true in the nonprofit world, where about 6 percent of nonprofits attract four-fifths of the resources. And during the 1990s, seven of the top ten largest NGOs at the beginning of the decade either maintained or grew relative to the rest of the NGO sector.[11]

Well-functioning markets, on the other hand, demonstrate significant entry and exit from the market, as companies with innovative ideas enter to compete and companies that have lost their edge go out of business. To illustrate, from 1990 to 1999, only three of the top ten companies (ranked by market capitalization) at the beginning of the decade remained in the top ten list by the end of the decade. All of those three companies had lost market share. The other seven companies in the top ten in 1999 had not been on the list at the beginning of the decade.[12]

17.1.5 Sluggish Innovation

The international aid regime is characterized by little innovation in techniques and development methods, as many of the same theories are recycled and retried for decades, regardless of mediocre results. The application of development theories that have proven ineffective, harsh on the poorest continues, or behind current thinking in the World Bank and other development organizations as bureaucracies remains entrenched in rigid procedures.[13] More evaluation of what works and what does not, and innovation based on the results, are needed in development efforts.

MIT's "Poverty Action Lab" advocates systematic evaluation and randomized trials of the effects of development aid programs on people's lives, health, and prosperity rather than just measures of how many roads built, schools constructed, or microcredit loans approved. This entails randomly assigning people to receive an antipoverty program or not and then comparing the people who have had the intervention to those who have not. The World Bank now reports that it plans to follow suit in its own efforts at randomized evaluation, since previously only 2 percent of World Bank projects underwent an evaluation for their effectiveness.

One former USAID official writes, "The bottom line is that aid agencies, probably more than any other government agencies, need to be flexible, 'learning' agencies with the ability to say no. . . . In reality, aid agencies tend to be highly centralized, with most decisions made at headquarters, to have elaborate, standardized, and at times rigid programming systems, to use the quantity of funds spent as a measure of the effectiveness of projects and programs while having weak and underused evaluation systems."[14]

While international development strategies and methods change relatively slowly, compare this with the rate of technological change or innovations with management practices. During the past half-century, we have seen countless small innovations by numerous actors in the business setting, each trying to make its own business a bit more efficient. Interestingly, we see more innovation flowing from the numerous small actors than from the few larger players. A particularly telling example of the disproportionate innovation flowing from small businesses is that small businesses produce thirteen to fourteen times more patents per employee than large patenting firms. And these patents from small businesses are about twice as likely as those from large businesses to be among the 1 percent most cited.[15]

17.1.6   Low Efficiency

The aid industry has often been categorized as well by waste and inefficiency. Much of the inefficiency stems from some of the reasons discussed above, including bureaucracy with adverse incentives. We look at just a few egregious examples.

The aid industry abounds with red tape and inefficiency. For instance, much of foreign aid is tied, meaning that recipients must purchase products or services from the government that gave the aid instead of choosing the best value or most fitting. Some have estimated conservatively that tied aid reduces aid's value by up to 30 percent.[16] In Guinea, new primary school facilities cost anywhere from $130 to $878 per square meter, depending on the donor country leading the project. If the less efficient donors instead hired the more efficient donors, they could give Guinea up to an extra $748 per square meter of classroom to devote to teachers or textbooks.[17]

In addition to official development assistance, philanthropic assistance could greatly improve on its efficiency. A McKinsey study, spearheaded by former New Jersey senator Bill Bradley, makes the case that by relatively minor administrative changes and coordination, philanthropic and nonprofit institutions could save in the aggregate of $100 billion per year. For instance, in 1999, the nonprofit sector spent about 18 percent of its revenue on fund-raising; businesses often spend about 10 percent in sales and marketing, the roughly private sector equivalent of fund raising. And costs of raising money by phone or mail can be steep, at about a dollar or more per solicitation as opposed to about 20 cents by the Internet.[18]

Aid is often wasted on corrupt governments as well. One study found that an increase in aid increases corruption and that corruption is positively correlated with aid received from the United States. There was no evidence that donors chose to fund less corrupt governments over more corrupt ones.[19]

Economic growth, on the other hand, is characterized by increasing efficiency, as societies are able to produce more per person than previously, because of increases in technology, skill, or more efficient management practices. The aid industry, both official and philanthropic, should increase its speed and efficient use of money. A market in aid could greatly enhance efficiency through competition and transparency.[20]

17.2   What Would a Marketplace for Aid Look Like?

What would a market in development aid look like? How would one work? A market for development aid would be a dense network of (1) people and institutions carrying out development projects and programs connected to (2) institutions and people with financial resources and (3) institutions and people with relevant know-how. A market for development would facilitate many-to-many interactions among these agents. In practice, project managers, donors, and advisers would communicate and interact frequently through Internet platforms, telecommunication, or personal meetings. There would be many sources of funding and many projects competing for that funding. Such a many-to-many marketplace would dramatically change how ideas for development projects are generated, how they are funded, and how they are implemented.

17.2.1   All Revved Up and No Place to Go

A market needs buyers and sellers, along with a place for them to interact and compete (as well as appropriate regulation and public infrastructure, which we discuss at the end of this section). Traditionally such a place has not existed. This is highly unfortunate, because the number of potential participants on the project design, funding, and implementation sides have all dramatically risen over the past decades. Official agencies, foundations, and even private companies that want to combat poverty abroad, assist with HIV/AIDS projects, or invest in schools in developing countries all have no place to "shop," so to speak, for projects. On the other side of the equation, people with projects cannot find donors. Many cannot find each other to collaborate; the heads of local health projects in Zimbabwe are not in easy contact with the heads of local health projects in Sri Lanka or Guatemala.

The potential for such an approach was revealed in an experimental new approach to soliciting ideas at the World Bank called the Development Marketplace (see box 17.1). This marketplace led to the creation outside the bank of an Internet-based platform called GlobalGiving. GlobalGiving has been supported by a number of innovative actors in the field of aid and philanthropy, including the Skoll Foundation, the Omidyar Foundation, and USAID's Global Development Alliance initiative. GlobalGiving is the first functioning platform that treats foreign aid and philanthropy like a marketplace, where donors and recipients come together to exchange information and resources. On an eBay-like Web site, hundreds of project leaders have posted initiatives that need funding, and millions of dollars have been provided by individuals and institutional donors to the projects they find most worthy.

In addition to the general public, major corporations such as HP, VISA International, Applied Materials, the Gap, and the North Face have been using GlobalGiving to connect directly with development projects in countries where they do business. These companies consider it in their own interests to invest in the communities that make their products and will eventually become consumers of their products as well. In addition, they make GlobalGiving funding opportunities available (often on a matching basis) to their employees and customers as a way of demonstrating their social awareness and creating a sense of community.

Of course, a full marketplace for development would include much more than the GlobalGiving Web site, much as the American economy is made up of much more than eBay. Below is a description of some of the benefits that such a full marketplace in aid would confer.

17.2.3 Networks and Emergence

A dense network of people interconnected through the Internet, telephone, or in-person meetings could greatly enhance knowledge sharing, funding, and ultimately effectiveness. For development to take off, we need professors in Iowa to be in communication with officials at the World Bank, who are in collaboration with project managers in Afghanistan, who speak regularly about their

Box 17.1
Microinnovation Can Produce Macroresults

In a market for goods and services, buyers and sellers find one another without much intervening bureaucracy. Surely it must be possible to build a market for antipoverty ideas where innovators and funding sources can network.
—*Harvard Business Review* on the World Bank's Development Marketplace

The World Bank's first Development Marketplace set out to do just that. On February 9, 2000, 270 teams set up booths to demonstrate their ideas on alleviating poverty in a competitive market setting: 1,138 proposals from around the world had initially poured in for the competition. The Development Marketplace created a forum in which individuals or small organizations could pitch their innovative proposals for development ideas to World Bank officials, who funded forty-four of these teams with innovation grants from a pot of $5 million.

The program traces its roots to 1998, when World Bank president James Wolfensohn proposed a new-products initiative. The new-products team found that there were too many ideas for new approaches but not an efficient way to sort through them. In a brainstorming session, the idea of making a marketplace for development ideas came to them.

The first round, called the Innovation Marketplace, involved only World Bank employees and gave eleven grants for a total of $3 million. It was so successful that it spawned the second round, open to anyone from around the world with innovative ideas.

The marketplace approach enabled the World Bank team to make small commitments fast without the long bureaucratic review processes of the bank. It gave staffers permission to look beyond established hierarchies and practices and innovate with their own approaches. Through such small projects, the bank could develop rapid and repeated experimentation with development techniques. It could make seed investments in the tens of thousands rather than in the millions, and use market competition to refine half-baked ideas. Instead of large projects with rigorous reviews, the Development Marketplace created an experimental forum for small projects. The program emphasized experimentation over traditional slow decision making and small projects instead of multimillion-dollar investments.

The Innovation and Development Marketplaces have initiated funding of several new and effective approaches to combat poverty, such as a project to overcome market barriers to the production of vaccines for tropical diseases and insurance for postdisaster construction. It also showed the World Bank new ways to harness the potential of its staff and small-scale social entrepreneurs around the world.

The competitions also created demand for a secondary market in which those who did not win in the competition could also gain from connections and exposure. This demand led the original creators of the Development Marketplace concept at the bank to spin off a separate initiative called GlobalGiving.com.

The *Harvard Business Review* concluded, "Systemic problems are not solved by a few smart people (whether World Bank bureaucrats or corporate planners) thinking really, really deep thoughts abut really, really important things. They are solved when a vibrant and competitive marketplace first tests and then confirms or disproves an array of possible approaches."

Adapted from Robert Chapman Wood and Gary Hamel, "The World Bank's Innovation Market," *Harvard Business Review*, November 2002.

experiences with counterparts in Cambodia, who in turn are funded by civic groups in Milwaukee.

We see the potential for the emergence of a marketplace in which social entrepreneurs compete for well-managed and worthy projects, and individual donors have information about these projects and a basis for comparison for where to vote with their dollars. Recent scholarship on topics as diverse as ant colonies, city formation, embryo development, and the business cycle has examined the phenomenon of emergence, in which many individual elements, each acting separately according to simple rules, demonstrate remarkable ability to act in a coordinated, efficient manner. One author writes, "We see emergent behavior in systems like ant colonies when the individual agents in the system pay attention to their immediate neighbors rather than wait for orders from above. They think locally and act locally, but their collective action produces global behavior."[21] Micromotives can mean macrobehavior.

Growth often comes from networks and economies of scale, or what William Easterly would call leaks, matches, and traps.[22] Growth happens when groups of people cooperate, coordinate, and build a synergy of their work together. Dense networks of people cause knowledge, skills, and experience to spread from one to another. They allow people to find others who are doing similar things and then communicate, collaborate, and share lessons learned.

Such international networks have proven vital to international movements such as human rights, the environment, and violence against women. Margaret E. Keck and Kathryn Sikkink in *Activists Beyond Borders* have shown how networks of people connected around the world, overcoming obstacles of time, space, and language, have come together to promote causes they believe in.[23] It is the interconnectivity of the network, in which people from around the globe mutually supported each other in combating local problems, that empowered local actors. The networks created a synergy.

On the private sector side, the dramatic success of Silicon Valley has shown a strong connection between the success of firms and the broader structure of the region in which they are embedded.[24] Dense networks of firms that interact in hierarchy-free interaction led to dramatic growth in knowledge, technology, and technology in a tiny geographical area. A network or marketplace for development clearly would not rely so heavily on physical proximity and geography, but such a dense network could come about through ways made possible through telecommunication and Internet technology.

17.2.4 Private Aid May Eclipse Public Aid

Aid has often been thought of as a public sector function. But the existing size and future potential of private giving overseas is immense. And a system of aid based on both private and public funding interactions offers much more potential for dense networks than does a system based mainly on government-to-government and international agency interactions. For instance, U.S. official development assistance was about $10 billion in 2000 and total bilateral official development aid (ODA) was $29 billion. Net multilateral aid flows averaged around $11 billion from 1999 to 2001. By contrast, in 2000, U.S. private assistance abroad was estimated at $33.6 billion, of which about $18 billion was remittances and $15 billion was from foundations, nonprofits, and corporations. Furthermore, over half of the nonremittance funding came from individuals.[25]

17.2.5   Public Aid Agencies Must Evolve in This Marketplace

Markets alone are obviously not a panacea. The current aid system does bear the hallmarks of central planning, and we have learned that central planning works poorly. But the experience of post-Soviet economies in transition shows that strong public institutions are critical underpinnings of a thriving economy. Elements of the current aid system can be refashioned to play a role in delivering the public goods often provided by public institutions.

Information
Some types of information are essential public goods. The World Bank, UN, bilateral agencies, and large foundations have a critical role to play in the analysis and dissemination of best practices and policies. Rapid dissemination of information and adoption of innovation are key drivers in a thriving market economy, and large public agencies and foundations can play and have played—a role in both exploring and implementing the public policies that support these information flows. Arguably, the knowledge generated by these institutions has had a greater positive influence on growth and development than all the financial commitments made over the years.

Global Public Goods
The second area where public institutions must play a role is in global public goods. These good are defined as those where the costs and benefits of programs cross national boundaries. Examples are trade, contagious diseases, and global warming. These types of issues are increasingly central to the development agenda, and transnational mechanisms are needed to coordinate policies, regulatory environments, and investments.

Infrastructure
The third area where public institutions have a role is in large investments in infrastructure. Although the private provision of infrastructure has grown in re-

cent years, there will be a role for public investments for the foreseeable future. Private financial flows to developing countries have been generally increasing, but public sector borrowing by developing-country governments is subject to wide fluctuations in cost, maturities, and other terms. Official institutions such as the World Bank will be called on to provide financing for infrastructure, especially in countries that have restricted access to capital markets.

17.2.6   Where from Here?

The next section draws on these observations to discuss some of the challenges that must be tackled to catalyze the emergence of such a marketplace. Given the potential of private aid, we give particular emphasis to the emergence of the marketplace intermediating private flows with relatively grassroots, bottom-up project ideas and the social entrepreneurs who drive them. As with any market structure, there will be many submarkets that specialize in different types of financing, investment size, risk, and other attributes. But there is no reason that the same basic principles would not apply to most of these submarkets. And the best outcomes will be achieved if these submarkets share standards and are interoperable to the extent possible, which would allow the most successful projects and ideas to migrate smoothly from the high-risk start-up phase through the scale-up replication phase.

17.3   Toward a Framework for Thinking about a Marketplace

Does anyone know how to build markets where none existed before? It has been fifteen years since the Berlin Wall came down, but there are as yet few pretenders to the title of market czar in the transition countries. Many, if not most, formerly centrally planned economies have had a tough time making a swift transition to a market-based economy. The lessons in how to make an effective transition in these countries have filled many books. With this in mind, how can we create a market for foreign aid?

In this chapter, we look to a different source for inspiration. One example of a wildly successful built market is eBay. Unlike countries of the former Soviet bloc, it started from scratch with few legacy problems and has been implemented largely in cyberspace, which has made it extremely efficient. Nonetheless, eBay reveals some of the key institutional and community underpinnings in market formation.

The challenges in building a market for international development are many. Along the lines of reinventing aid, they include getting better outcomes, getting additional resources, and dramatically changing the context in which economic and social entrepreneurs operate in the developing world. Each of these goals is mind-numbingly ambitious; the hubris of tackling all three together seems insane—unless they mutually reinforce one another, which, arguably, they do. More resources, especially from nontraditional sources, are unlikely to flow unless we can point to better outcomes. Better outcomes may seem like the most ambitious of them all, but are unlikely to be achieved until the environment and context in which local initiative is rewarded and supported is changed dramatically.

What follows is an attempt to slice up the challenges into separate objectives and a discussion of some approaches to catalyzing the emergence of a market for aid. They do not as yet add up to a comprehensive solution. But they do point in the right direction and provide the basis for some expanded experiments.

This section of the chapter looks to eBay, Silicon Valley, and a few other successful cases to support our framework for thinking about the creation of one part of a potential marketplace for international aid: that subsector based on private aid, and specifically private philanthropy in the United States. Although we do not explicitly extend this framework to the official aid sector, there are obvious lessons to be drawn.

We will discuss four factors involved in creating a model for a network-based marketplace for development: interest, aggregation (the freewheeling coming together of disparate actors engaged in similar pursuits), agglomeration (the coordination and organization of many individual choices, as per Surowiecki),[26] and rules of interaction. This discussion addresses some of the implied actions stemming from the previous section on nonmarket elements in development.

17.3.1 Interest

The challenge that is unique to this particular attempt to redefine foreign assistance revolves around U.S. donors' willingness to consider overseas or global projects or causes to be as important as the local community in which they live. Why would American individuals, corporations, or foundations choose to donate abroad instead of in their own communities? There are interesting pointers about what mechanisms or triggers may be used to encourage this, but essentially the question is unsolvable by analysis. It simply has to be tried with the most promising tools at our disposal. A promising starting point is outlined below.

First, observe in the United States a very strong self-organizing community spirit. Scholars and observers of American culture back to Tocqueville at the creation of the United States have commented on the American propensity for local, grassroots self-organization to solve the needs of communities.[27] Americans like to organize themselves at the grassroots level to solve problems that they see. It is that very impulse which leads Americans to be so active in coming together to refurbish their local library or support their local Boy or Girl Scout troop.

Next, many Americans are viewing international problems as closer to home. There are many areas of life where the maximum size of the functioning social group is now at the global, rather than national or local, level. Both technology and knowledge have supported a progressive amplification of the way individuals think and communicate and share what they know. Interest becomes global as communication technology makes many people feel that the world has shrunk.[28]

Finally, individual choices to join a movement such as a network for development are triggered by the proportion of other people who join; small acts of cooperation, including the choice to come together to support a small-scale project in the developing world, will not require massive forms of collaboration.[29] This has been facilitated by technological advances in the transfer of goods, funds, and information. It is hard to believe that fifty-plus years ago, the staff of the World Bank were taking ocean liners to work in developing countries and the most urgent communications were handled by telegrams.

In fact, private giving to international causes has been on an upward trend since 1987. For example, in 2003, giving to international affairs organizations was up 14.8 percent from the previous year.[30]

So what has prevented U.S. philanthropy from embracing globalism even more? First, the nonprofit sector has been slower in embracing technology in all its forms, mostly because of the cost (especially the recurring cost of maintaining pace with technological advances) and the attendant difficulty in showing the return on such a big-ticket investment. Such arguments are easier to make in the context of the for-profit sector, which typically has deeper pockets and a clearer metric. Second, precisely because the United States has such a strong tradition of taking care of local issues, ties to physical communities are quite strong. Finally, another specifically U.S. characteristic gets in the way— what Tocqueville called "habits of inattention attendant on the democratic spirit," which makes it harder for complex global issues (media errs on the side of presenting issues holistically, in all their complexity) to come to the fore. The challenge is finding a way of introducing technology into this process while presenting the more concrete, specific perspectives on global concerns.

Whatever effort is made in this area, whether by mobilizing the religious or more local affiliations that already bind U.S. donors together, the key to both agglomeration and aggregation discussed in the following sections is the interest in doing so.

17.3.2   Aggregation: Making Better Choices

For the creation of a market in development and philanthropy, the aggregation of individuals and actions must occur. We define aggregation as many individuals coming together to make many separate choices that, in a combined way, would cause a synergetic market to emerge. Local actions of competitive supply and demand would combine to create the whole—a competitive market for development projects and philanthropy. Decentralized choices can be more powerful than centralized decisions.

James Surowiecki points out in his book *The Wisdom of Crowds* that large groups of people are unexpectedly smarter at solving problems of cognition, coordination, and cooperation than individual experts. So whether the problem is, "Where is the best place in town to build an AIDS orphanage?" or "How do groups of donors work together to support a project that requires their combined resources?" Surowiecki makes the case that society is better off when these choices are left to a large number of people. Surowiecki's examples range from simple exercises like guessing the weight of an ox at a fair (the average of people's guesses is consistently closer than the best guess in numerous iterations) to more complicated, predictive exercises like the Iowa Electronic Markets in predicting presidential races. Conveniently, these people do not have to be experts on grassroots development or philanthropy. They just need to have access to lots of different information, they need to be independent, and they need to work in the context of an aggregating mechanism.[31]

Paul Krugman offers a good example of how economies can often aggregate, or organize themselves, in a bottom-up approach rather than a top-down approach. In *The Self-Organizing Economy*, he describes how city centers develop on their own, without a hierarchical central planner calling the shots and telling businesses where to locate. Following the simple rules of wanting to be right next to other businesses while not wanting to be only a little bit away, businesses organize themselves into business districts.[32] This idea of bottom-up self-organization harks back to Adam Smith's "invisible hand" directing many individuals to make choices in self-interest that lead to the greater good.

Currently, most of the choices about where money goes in international development are made by an elite group of experts. Whether they sit in official aid agencies or established foundations, they have earned their seats at the table by demonstrating a particular interest and expertise in development or good works. In the case of official aid agencies, although there are multilateral organizations that insist on national diversity, these same organizations tend to recruit from a few schools considered to turn out the best development experts, so that diversity in national origin masks a remarkable homogeneity in educational and professional background. For aggregation, more diversity in actors and perspectives is needed.

The situation is very different in domestic philanthropy in the United States; the bulk of the donors are individuals from many different walks of life. The numbers in private philanthropy are very telling. Out of $295 billion in contributions for private philanthropy, over $246 billion came from individuals and households (including bequests); only $49 billion came from foundations and corporations.[33] That reflects a particularly American culture of private philanthropy that dates back to the founding of the United States, but it makes for a highly decentralized decision-making process when it comes to support for programs and activities for public benefit.

So at least among U.S. donors, two of the preconditions for better choices through aggregation as defined by Surowiecki already exist: many diverse donors making choices independently. Arguably, no good aggregation mechanism exists as yet. Choices are soaked up into individual localities and organizations without transparent clearing mechanisms that exist on the for-profit side of life.

Once the interest is there, how do we promote agglomeration in international aid and philanthropy? In other words, how do we bring together a network of people in development and philanthropy circles?

17.3.3 Agglomeration

Scholars and casual observers alike have observed the remarkable growth, creativity, and innovation of Silicon Valley. This small geographical area led the world in computer and technological business innovation for well over a decade during the dot-com boom. The rise of such a hot spot has been attributed to the agglomeration effect: the explosive tendency for successful enterprises to spin off from other ones. Firms or individuals learn rapidly from their neighbors and form tight networks that lead to booms of creativity. One author defines the agglomeration effect as involving "the spin-off of other enterprises within an innovative community, the effects that accrue to firms from close proximity to others engaged in related activities in these rapidly evolving industries." The agglomeration effect is thus the effect of proximity and large numbers.[34]

The next step in a marketplace for development is agglomeration. That is, tight networks of people aggregated together learn from one another about best practices. This could provide a useful parallel to agglomeration in global philanthropy. Social entrepreneurs and project leaders similarly would want to be where other project leaders are, but currently geography gets in the way.

However, a virtual marketplace could bring them together and facilitate the agglomeration of social entrepreneurs. If many social entrepreneurs cluster together in a virtual marketplace, the buyers will come.

Another way to look at this issue of agglomeration is to think about the differences between capital and consumer markets. There is a school of thought in the philanthropic community that holds that social capital markets are fundamentally unlike regular financial markets. The thinking is that the traditional inverse relationship between risk and return does not hold when thinking about allocating money into social ventures. It may well be empirically true that you can find high-social-return investments with relatively low risk (in other words, in the social capital market universe, you *can* find $100 bills on the sidewalk). What that implies, though, is that the social capital market is immature. These anomalous "deals" exist because there are as yet few actors in this capital market, and information is sorely lacking. In normal markets, the high return–low risk examples were gobbled up a long time ago, and the high risk–low return cases are pointedly ignored. The reason they exist in the social capital markets is that not enough people are looking into the issue to surface the information about each of these deals, or that even with a lot people looking into them there is not enough agreement on the definition of social value. Financial value has a common metric that can be used for inputs, income, and growth of capital, but social value on the outcomes and outputs ends is hard to define.

Another way to parse this issue of how comparable social capital markets are to financial markets is to consider whether decisions about philanthropy are undertaken as if they were consumption or investment decisions. It is arguable that they are treated more like consumption. Ironically this may be key to understanding how a market could function and how one might be designed. Investment decisions at least in theory are driven by expected net present value of returns and are often based on profit-to-earnings ratios, analysts' ratings, personal calculations about one's need for income versus growth, and risk aversion. As such, these decisions require much data and information.

By contrast, the value of the must-have Hermés bag is seemingly ineffable, but the price tag on the bag is definitely knowable. Yet thousands of people look at such bags and know with a certainty that it is "worth" the price on the tag. They frequently know it is worth that price because they make complicated decisions that have to do with the cachet such a bag might confer on the user in certain circles of society; about the signaling value it might have to potential employers, partners, and friends; and the extent to which it resonates with the purchaser's values. In many cases, that is how philanthropy decisions are made as well. Philanthropy is undertaken for many reasons, and some of them include standing in society; signaling value to potential partners, friends, and sometimes even employers; and resonance with one's values. Take, for example, the charity balls that crowd the New York City social calendar; the whole point is to draw attention to one's affinity to a cause and to spend time with other acknowledged members of the group. Church- or temple-inspired philanthropy is not seemingly that different. Perhaps it is less opulent, but it is equally based in affirming one's credentials as part of a social group.

Hence, any market for international aid or philanthropy will need trust and aggregation mechanisms that conform to the social frameworks surrounding these decisions. That might include, for instance, less advice from experts and more transparency about what others are doing.

Finally, the question as to whether one should enable and make more powerful existing ways of doing things, such as work with church groups to bring their international philanthropy online, or to try to serve new entrants to the aid marketplace is a hard one. The two top examples of the dot-com boom and bust (Amazon and eBay) point in two different directions. Amazon took existing book buyers and made their experience more social and more convenient. eBay began by creating a brand-new market for the smallest sellers (a national market for virtually anything) and eventually won over the bigger existing players that already had access to a national market through their own distribution channels but found the eBay market too lucrative to resist. Many of the business-to-business marketplaces that tried to structure and make more transparent existing supplier-purchaser relationships did not succeed, even with the buy-in of some or all of the players. The latter point to existing ways of doing things and infrastructure that supports it. Without overwhelming pressure to show different results, those existing patterns and relationships could end up being roadblocks.

17.3.4   Rules of Interaction: Building Trust

One great obstacle to American philanthropy abroad has been the issue of trust. How would someone who wants to give abroad know that a project or social entrepreneur is trustworthy? How will she know that her money is spent on social causes rather than disappearing into someone's pocket? How can she monitor how the project is going if she is not in close proximity or contact with the project?

Let us look at eBay's experience in overcoming problems of trust and monitoring as an example. eBay defied the prediction of every formal model about trust in markets. Extrapolating from arguments that "lemons" drive out good cars in used-car markets to the seemingly vast potential for fraud in cyberspace where you cannot meet the buyer to ascertain she exists, let alone physically inspect the car for quality, should it exist, the academic arguments against eBay's becoming successful were many.[35] In response to extremely clear evidence to the contrary, there is now an emerging body of literature about why eBay works. But it points only to the mechanisms that eBay has in place to overcome the predicted problems of trust and monitoring (through feedback mechanisms and prompt action when fraud is detected, for example). It still does not answer how—if you determine that it is important to try building a market to try and deal with some of the myriad problems discussed in this book—you should go about it.

Two dimensions of trust need to be addressed in the market for international aid. The first sets the base level of trust in the system and builds trust in the market brand. This dimension of trust, which we might call legitimation, is built on compliance and enforcement of compliance with the laws and regulations surrounding international grant making (including various antiterrorism and anti-money-laundering provisions). Legitimation relies heavily on being able to verify that individuals and organizations are who they say they are and on being able to ascertain the reputations and track records that accompany those identities. This level of trust is almost implicit to the potential buyer; it would become an issue if it is ever violated, but is unlikely to be an issue that the buyer would participate in. Instead, the marketplace itself deals with the problem. Checks and balances that are built into systems like eBay or PayPal or Amazon include verifying physical addresses and identities with financial information on file (credit cards or bank accounts). The system is not foolproof, since fake accounts can be set up, but it piggybacks on long-established and vast networks and databases that exist. The equivalent in international aid is the collective intelligence and knowledge of the public and private players in international philanthropy today.

The second level of trust, which we could call confidence building, is where buyers could take a far more active role; it revolves around experiential track records and reviews. In e-commerce, brand name and reputation have a strong effect on price. For instance, Amazon consistently can charge higher prices than Barnes & Noble. And negative customer-written reviews have a much stronger impact on purchases than positive reviews, since prospective shoppers suspect that positive reviews are perhaps an untrustworthy marketing pitch for the author.[36] On eBay, sellers with higher reputation points can command a higher price for the same product. Here the challenge is about the tangibility of the experience and the time cycle for completion or "consumption." The transaction experience (i.e., receiving, examining, and using the physical good bought) on eBay is almost immediate, and reading a book or using a new vacuum cleaner from Amazon is only slightly less so. Funding a project in the developing world is slower—in some cases by years—than either of those experiences, and often the funder will have no firsthand knowledge of the project's output or impact. So the challenge here is to find proxies for the immediate experience to build up a donor's confidence in a project.[37]

At the level of legitimation, the challenge is to build systems that allow verification that social entrepreneurs are whom they say they are, that their project exists, that their reported activities are carried out, and that ultimately they have a certain impact. Systems like eBay and PayPal began with strong systems for credit card verification or bank account information—all of them already primed for extremely compatible information transfers and secure information transmission along every step of the way. There are systems of legitimation, even those that go further into confidence building, at the base of microlending or savings circles, but to date, most of these systems remain extremely localized and not always interoperable with regional or global systems, enforceable, or even expressible in written legal contracts. In some respects, the challenge is steepest at the beginning and less so as the system begins to acquire its own momentum; as flows increase, the inflow of projects will increase, providing greater competition for funds among social entrepreneurs and incentives for proven better performance, and allowing for quicker turnaround begins to shorten the transaction, if not the project cycles. Other challenges emerge as these dynamics take hold, but the public policy challenges of a dynamic market are much simpler than the challenge of how to jump-start them.

One last point that relates to trust and deserves mention is the role of formal state authority. In most countries, the ultimate arbiter of legitimacy is the state. The state establishes who you are by issuing you a voter registration card, passport, or social benefits card. In many developing countries, the allocation of legitimacy, let alone other resources, is neither transparent nor equitable—or perceived as such, which is of course the stuff that leads to civil wars. One can imagine that in highly polarized countries, the power to confirm that someone is who he says he is becomes a means of control and coercion. So decentralized means of identity and legitimation are particularly desirable in those contexts, yet there are very few, and perhaps no, examples of reliable, decentralized, and scalable means of legitimation in the developing world. And as you edge into these issues that fundamentally challenge state authority, the question of a global order that can fill in the gaps or transcend unsatisfactory sovereign legitimation comes to the fore. The reader might want to ponder this issue by turning to the foremost thinkers in this field, including Anne-Marie Slaughter (*A New World Order*) and Wolfgang Reinecke (*Global Public Policy*).[38]

17.4   Conclusion

The aid system as conceived today is dominated by the public sector and operates in a fashion that resembles central planning more than it does a well-functioning market. Few mechanisms exist for facilitating the flow of resources to ideas and investments that have the highest returns. While public aid agencies will continue to play an important role, these agencies must evolve to perform more of a policy, regulatory, and knowledge-sharing role. In some instances these agencies will also be needed to fund large public (and global public) infrastructure projects. But private aid will begin to play a much larger role. Public and private aid should increasingly be allocated through market-based mechanisms. It is not trivial to create such market mechanisms, but their efficiency and network effects hold promise to stimulate innovation, generate more aid resources, and increase impact substantially.

Acknowledgments

We thank Shelly Culbertson for her major contribution to this chapter. Elizabeth Stefanski provided key analytical insights. Meredith Landis provided production and research assistance.

Notes

1. U.S. Agency for International Development, *Foreign Aid in the National Interest: Promoting Freedom, Security, and Opportunity* (Washington, D.C.: U.S. Government Printing Office, 2002).

2. Center for Global Development, *Campaign 2004—A Guide to Global Development* (Washington, D.C., Center for Global Development 2004).

3. *Statistical Abstract of the United States: 2003*, 123rd ed. nos. 744 and 747 (Washington, D.C.: U.S. Department of Commerce, 2003).

4. Disclosure SEC [CD-ROM], December 2002. Available from Disclosure, Inc.

5. Steven Radelet, *Challenging Foreign Aid: A Policymaker's Guide to the Millennium Challenge Account* (Washington, D.C.: Center for Global Development, 2003), and Carol Lancaster, *Aid to Africa: So Much to Do, So Little Done* (Chicago: University of Chicago Press, 1999).

6. Ibid.

7. One bright exception is the Center for Effective Philanthropy, which has begun polling its recipients on the performance of the foundation as a donor.

8. Lancaster, *Aid to Africa*.

9. Joseph E. Stiglitz, *Globalization and Its Discontents* (New York: Norton, 2002), 12–22.

10. A number of standards and reporting initiatives are starting in this area, including the Keystone Reporting initiative led by David Bonbright, formerly of the Aga Khan Foundation. GlobalGiving.com is phasing in an eBay-style rating system.

11. Jed Emerson and Paul Carttar, "Money Matters: The Structure, Operations and Challenges of Nonprofit Funding" (Bridgespan Group, January 2003), 63.

12. Ibid.

13. For a discussion of outdated development methods and disastrous results, see William Easterly, *The Elusive Quest for Growth: Economists' Adventures and Misadventures in the Tropics* (Cambridge, Mass.: MIT Press, 2002), and Stiglitz, *Globalization and Its Discontents*.

14. Lancaster, *Aid to Africa*, 226.

15. Small Business Association Office of Advocacy, "Small Business by the Numbers: Answers to Frequently Asked Questions" (Washington, D.C.: U.S. Government Printing Office, May 2003).

16. Nancy Birdsall and Brian Deese, "Hard Currency," *Washington Monthly* 36 (March 2004): 39.

17. Ibid.

18. Bill Bradley, Paul Jansen, and Les Silverman, "The Nonprofit Sector's $100 Billion Opportunity," *Harvard Business Review* 81 (May 2003): 94–103.

19. Alberto Alesina and Beatrice Weder, "Do Corrupt Governments Receive Less Foreign Aid?" *American Economic Review* 92 (September 2002): 1126. The U.S. government is experimenting with a new approach to foreign aid in the Millennium Challenge Corporation, an organization parallel to USAID that gives to governments that rank well in terms of good policies.

20. One example of improved efficiency is a project posted on the GlobalGiving Web site to raise money for toilets for a school in India. All the money necessary was raised within two weeks—what the *Washington Post* characterized as the "foreign aid equivalent of the speed of light." The market format allowed for the much more rapid meeting of recipient needs in comparison with slow bureaucracy. From Jacqueline L. Salmon, "Given to Skepticism: With Charity Scandals in the News and Less Money to Give, Donors Are Asking More Questions," *Washington Post*, November 3, 2002, H.01.

21. Steven Johnson, *Emergence: The Connected Lives of Ants, Brains, Cities and Software* (New York: Scribner, 2001), 79.

22. Easterly, *Elusive Quest for Growth*, 145–170.

23. Margaret E. Keck and Kathryn Sikkink, *Activists beyond Borders: Advocacy Networks in International Politics* (Ithaca, N.Y.: Cornell University Press, 1998).

24. Meric S. Gertler, Paivi Oinas, Michael Storper, and Phillip Scranton, "Discussion of Regional Advantage," *Economic Geography* 71 (April 1995): 199.

25. See USAID, http://www.usaid.gov/fani/ch06/objectives02.htm and World Bank, *Global Development Finance 2004*. Note that total worker remittances to developing countries was $68 billion in 2000.

26. James Surowiecki, *The Wisdom of Crowds* (New York: Doubleday, 2004), 66–84.

27. Alexis deTocqueville, *Democracy in America*, ed. J. P. Mayer, trans. George Lawrence (Garden City, N.Y.: Anchor Books, 1835), 513–517.

28. Howard Rheingold, *Smart Mobs* (New York: Basic Books, 2002), 180–181.

29. Mark Granovetter, "Threshold Models of Collective Behavior," *American Journal of Sociology* 83(1978):1420–1443.

30. *Giving USA 2003: The Annual Report on Philanthropy for the Year 2003*, 49th annual issue (Indianapolis: Center on Philanthropy at Indiana University, 2004).

31. Surowiecki, *Wisdom of Crowds*.

32. Paul Krugman, *The Self-Organizing Economy* (Cambridge, Mass.: Blackwell, 1996).

33. Holly Hall, "A Record High," *The Chronicle of Philanthropy*, June 28, 2007.

34. Paul A. Herbig and James E. Golden. "The Rise of Innovative Hot Spots: Silicon Valley and Route 128," *International Marketing Review*, 10:35 (1993).

35. John H. Huston and Roger W. Spencer, "Quality, Uncertainty and the Internet: The Market for Cyber Lemons," *American Economist* 46 (Spring 2002): 55–61.

36. Lee Gomes, "E-Commerce Sites Make Great Laboratory for Today's Economists." *Wall Street Journal*, October 11, 2004.

37. One interesting anecdote from our experience is that a social entrepreneur on the GlobalGiving site was recently awarded the Nobel Peace Prize. Her project received over $12,000 in funding in just two weeks after the prize committee's announcement. This is a prime example of how reputations can lead to confidence building.

38. Anne-Marie Slaughter, *A New World Order* (Princeton, N.J.: Princeton University Press, 2004), and Wolfgang Reinecke, *Global Public Policy* (Washington, D.C.: Brookings Institute, 1998).

18 Placing Enterprise and Business Thinking at the Heart of the War on Poverty

Kurt Hoffman

The modern world has always encompassed extremes of affluence and poverty. But in 2005 the confluence of advocacy, political serendipity, and natural disaster rapidly pushed the plight of the impoverished up the agenda of the wealthy as never before. The sharpness of the challenge thrown down on behalf of the poor and the pressure on the rich to take action in response is unprecedented, as is the level of debate on a topic previously all but ignored by the public and mainstream media.

Most important, the campaign to "Make Poverty History" by doubling aid, securing new debt relief commitments, and reforming the trading regime has apparently borne fruit with major commitments already made at the G-8 Gleneagles Summit in July 2005 by the rich countries at least on the campaign's aid and debt agenda.[1] This is a significant accomplishment and should be applauded. However, the biggest challenge now facing the international aid community will be how to take advantage of the new opportunities to open up viable, sustainable routes out of poverty for all poor people.[2]

These challenges are the focus of this chapter. I take two things as givens, both of which I have documented elsewhere:

• Economic growth is key for poor countries and poor people to escape poverty.

• Equitable economic growth must be driven by the growth of private sector economic activity carried out by enterprises of all kinds, but especially for the poorest countries, by the small and medium-sized enterprises (SMEs).

In the first section, we look at why the promotion of enterprise is of so little interest to the aid community.

18.1 Not Enough Attention Is Given to Promoting the Growth of Enterprise in the Fight Against Poverty

Helping poor countries to achieve sustainable, enterprise-led economic growth is the overarching objective for the efforts of virtually all players in the development community. Yet curiously enough, aid-financed initiatives in enterprise creation, always limited, have become almost invisible in recent years as the aid community has spread its money and effort across an ever widening array of urgent poverty (especially health and environmental-related) issues. At least that is what appears to be the case by looking at the relative amount of expert attention and financial resources devoted over the past decade directly to catalyzing enterprise growth.

These admittedly rough calculations suggest that enterprise has attracted much less than 10 percent of all official and private aid flows of the past decade.[3] And of the attention that was given by the aid community to enterprise, an informed assessment of the effectiveness of SME development programs and the efforts of many agencies with an enterprise orientation in the UN system would be that they have made little real contribution to the creation of a viable "pro-poor" enterprise sector[4] in most poor countries.[5] This is not, however, an omission of only the aid community. Even multinational corporations (MNCs), whose very existence is enterprise based, use only a fraction of their corporate social responsibility (CSR) spending to help poor communities through pro-poor enterprise creation.

So historically, the priority given by the aid community and large private enterprise operating in poor developing countries to the specifics of catalyzing pro-poor enterprise on the ground, as it were, bears no relation to the proven importance of enterprise growth for the permanent elimination of poverty.

18.1.1 Enterprise Is There, But Not There in Current Poverty Debate

If we look at the current context, many of the lead players in the Make Poverty History campaign offer both analytical and practical support to the importance of enterprise as manifets on their Web sites and even in the field. And the recent reports of the influential and high-profile UN Millennium Project (2005) and even more so that of the UK Commission for Africa are laced with references to the role of the private sector and the need to improve the enabling environment for the market economy to flourish.

But despite these nods in the direction of enterprise, the issue actually received very little real airtime during the Make Poverty History campaign and ensuing public debate in 2005. Increasing aid and debt relief were the main messages, though trade featured quite a bit (but mainly at the high policy level). But enterprise and what to do about it was rarely mentioned in press releases, sound bites, or speeches by poverty campaigners; it also hardly featured on the agendas of the many pro-poverty conferences and talkfests taking place and in the many recommendations being made by mainstream aid actors.[6]

I suggest that this omission is a reflection that those in the aid community doing the poverty talking during 2005, as well as advising on and implementing aid spending plans, have a mind-set overwhelmingly focused on what local government, donors, or the other battalions of aid actors and nongovernmental organizations (NGOs) need to do first to achieve the Millennium Development Gs and their debt, aid and trade targets.

"What to do" about enterprise usually comes way down the list, while there is an axiomatic, unrealistic, even naive feel about what is proposed about enterprise, expected of the private sector, and to be done in the name of the private sector in the aid community–led fight against poverty. This is borne out by the money proposals. Traditional aid issues get the lion's share of the proposed spending. Witness the UK Commission on Africa—which among all the pro-poverty initiatives underway has in fact paid the most explicit attention to enterprise—via the efforts and input of its Business Action for Africa (BAA) Group supported by some sixty companies, most of them large multinationals.

The problem is that despite the high profile given the BAA, when it came down to it, the Africa Commission's only practical spending recommendation related to enterprise was for a $550 million "investment climate facility." Not only is this a tiny fraction of the many billions of dollars of extra aid that the Africa Commission recommended be channeled to Africa, but the fund is meant to be spent over seven years and spread over two countries, which comes to about only US$2.9 million a year per country.

This general lack of attention by the aid community to catalyzing enterprise as a key element in the war on poverty is curious (to put it mildly) given the importance we all attach to economic growth and the role of the private sector. It is understandable, however, given that the aid community is largely composed of professionals who are expert in one aspect or another of development and poverty but usually have little competence and much less real-life experience of the private sector, "markets," or the reality of enterprise, especially the small variety. Private sector, enterprise-led solutions to poverty are not on their radar screen. They look first to the state as the vehicle through which to deliver development and are more inclined to view the private sector with suspicion or, at best, as just one of a number of stakeholders that need to be consulted in the process of putting together aid agency or state lead antipoverty initiatives.

Matters are not helped much by the fact that the challenge of how to tackle poverty directly is rarely a top business issue or even a public engagement agenda item for most firms. This is despite patient drum beating of a few groups,[7] the prominence of the private sector at the World Summit on Sustainable Development (WSSD), and in the UN Global Compact and the recent excitement given the nascent bottom-of-the-pyramid phenomenon.[8] Plenty of attention is also devoted to traditional CSR matters to be sure, but business overall has not exactly forced its way onto center stage in the poverty debate.

As a result of the aid community's not paying attention and the business community's not shouting loud enough, there is far less effective communication than there should be between them over how best to tackle the millennium development goals (MDGs), for example. But more important, this analysis suggests that neither enterprise issues nor the business sector, nor people with enterprise experience, are as near to or as influential in the process of deciding how the international community will conduct its latest assault on poverty as the importance of enterprise-led economic growth to the whole business dictates they should be.

This means that, at least from our perspective, the most important, but as yet not properly addressed, questions for the aid community going forward after the (hoped for) fund-raising successes of 2005 are three fold:

• How to increase the scale and effectiveness of pro-poor enterprise interventions[9]

• How to make the objective of pro-poor enterprise growth an integral part of poverty reduction strategies advanced by the aid community and pursued by developing countries

• How to more effectively engage the private sector, but especially big business, in aid community efforts to tackle poverty through enterprise both directly and as a source of insight, advice, and skills transfer

In short, my proposition is that whatever other poverty priorities are addressed, more effective attention must be given to catalyzing enterprise in the poorest countries. If this does not happen, there is a real possibility we will need to launch yet more Make Poverty History campaigns at the beginning of each century in this millennium just to stay in the same place as we are now in the fight against poverty.

18.2   How to Better Bring Enterprise and Business Thinking to Bear on the Challenges of Overcoming Poverty

In an earlier publication, I used the experience and the approach of the Shell Foundation to explore two routes to catalyzing the emergence and growth of what I called pro-poor enterprise: enterprises owned by, employing, or providing goods and service to poor people.[10] The first was with the application of business thinking and business principles to the design, selection, and management of pro-poor enterprise interventions. The second showed how these enterprise development efforts can benefit from the exploitation of value-creating assets belonging to international businesses.

Shell Foundation's experience to date is still far too limited to generalize. But there are others operating in the same space as we are, all trying to harness the power of business thinking and finance to the challenge of overcoming poverty, whose experiences reinforce our own.[11] So I offer some propositions for wider debate by the aid and international business communities around the specific challenge of catalyzing pro-poor enterprise development—and with the expectation that these may have broader relevance in the battle to overcome poverty.

18.2.1   Propositions for the International Development Community

The first set relates primarily to the role of donors who, because they control the money, are critically important influences on what issues aid actors focus on and how they work. The community of donors I have in mind spreads from the treasuries of rich country governments that approve aid budgets, through the bilateral and multilateral aid organizations, private foundations and philanthropists, the charitable grant-making arms of big business, and the larger international NGOs that act like donors by redistributing charitable funds to others to carry out poverty projects in developing countries.

Give Less, Invest More

The core proposition is that donors should act less like charities and more like investors. In part, this means allocating more of available resources (such as might be forthcoming from the ICF) toward investment vehicles targeting the pro-poor enterprise sector. But I also mean that when donors spend aid money through their normal partners, such as government agencies and NGOs, the principal bottom-line return they should be after is measurable growth in the pro-poor enterprise sector.

Thus, all seeking support should demonstrate precisely how their program, project, policy, or initiative will advance this objective. I now think the best mechanism to do this is provided by incorporating into proposals of all kinds the thinking behind business plans. Typically these emphasize risk assessment, knowing what the target "customer" wants,[12] setting out precisely how the project is going to help meet those wants at lowest cost and how many customers (in our case, pro-poor enterprises or poor people) are going to be measurably better off at the end of the project.

Moreover, donors might consider requiring grantees to make real financial contributions from their own funds. Grant payments could be phased against meeting performance targets. Financial incentives could be built in to reward the funding recipient if the project exceeds its targets (including awarding bonuses or retaining any surplus). And the grantee should face sanctions and be held accountable if it does not deliver on what is promised—perhaps, for example, by having to return a percentage of the grant to the donor.

And just to demonstrate commitment, the donors themselves could use their own internal incentive structures to ensure staff and managers are rewarded or held accountable for the performance of their projects against the only bottom line that should matter in the fight against poverty: measurable growth among pro-poor enterprises and increased benefits flowing to poor people as a result.

These are clearly extreme propositions for the donor community, and to be sure, even the Shell Foundation does not operate entirely along these lines. Many objections could be raised, not least of which is that some elements might contravene charity law and others could introduce the more negative aspects of profit-seeking behavior.

Respond to the "Customer," Not the Paymaster

I offer this up in such stark terms to encourage debate. My proposition is that by striving toward the ideal of measurable contributions to pro-poor enterprise as the principle, accountable targets for allocation and use of aid, donors, and grantees will be catalyzed into becoming more enterprising, innovative, and efficient in their search for solutions to poverty. That is because this approach tackles a costly (for the poor) contradiction at the heart of the aid-poverty equation: it is actually the donors who constitute the real "market" for aid actors, not the ultimate customers these actors want to serve—the poor and pro-poor enterprise.

The "failure" of projects in the Shell Foundation portfolio and elsewhere can often be traced directly to the fact that the project partners were not focused on best meeting the needs of their real customers but were responding to other incentives, including donor agendas and their own professional interests.[13]

Businesspeople will recognize the logic. To paraphrase Easterly, aid actors respond to incentives like everyone else.[14] So setting them incentives linked to customer satisfaction (i.e., measurable success or failure in pro-poor enterprise creation) should ensure maximum effort is focused on delivering results that matter.[15]

The logic of the approach I am proposing is simple. The challenges in actually implementing it are obviously not. It requires donors and recipients of aid funding to think very differently about how they do what they do. More important, it would lead them to work within a risk-return relationship and consequence accountability structure similar to that which exists between an investor and a start-up business and between shareholders and management—cultures that are both foreign and an anathema to many donors and grantees.

Nevertheless, my experience and that of others suggest it is possible to structure interventions and incentives that powerfully and successfully focus everyone's attention on the end game of pro-poor enterprise creation, and I suggest the topic is worthy of wider debate and consideration.

It's Not the Money That Matters

This proposition harks back to my arguments about the importance of getting local capital into a lead role in financing pro-poor enterprise development. As argued earlier, using softer money from abroad to invest in pro-poor enterprise can play an important starter or demonstration role. And clearly, in regions such as sub-Saharan Africa, it is very important to do everything possible to enhance investor confidence.

But there will never be enough foreign soft money to allow pro-poor enterprise financing to go to scale. And too much exposure to money from overseas can rob the local enterprise finance and support sector of hugely valuable learning-by-doing opportunities.

So the introduction of pro-poor enterprise aid funding should from the outset complement and catalyze the increasing involvement of local capital and local suppliers of business development services—not substitute for them. It is possible to do this, and it can work as the efforts of Shell Foundation and others to set up small enterprise investment funds in Uganda, South Africa, and India have shown.

Link MDG Interventions, Debt Relief, and Other Macrointerventions to Pro-Poor Enterprise Creation

The share of available resources and effort going to pro-poor enterprise creation will always be limited. However pro-poor interventions in other areas can be calibrated to help contribute to the enterprise objective without detracting from their core objectives. Debt relief conditions, the way aid financing is delivered and various MDG programs, including the provision of education, health care, and clean water, can relatively easily incorporate pro-poor enterprise objectives that do not have negative impacts elsewhere. In the case of MDGs, this would range from ensuring money spent on pro-poor service delivery catalyzed local enterprise growth through to the application of enterprise or business thinking to better ensure MDG plans delivered specific measurable outcomes benefiting the most poor people at least cost.

The same logic applies in relation to interventions designed to tackle corruption or strengthening the management capacities of local government. These are very big problems in most poor countries, and the resources do not exist to tackle them everywhere at once. Interventions in these problems areas must be prioritized.

Select and Focus

Why not focus on those aspects of the generic problems of corruption or capacity that most inhibit the growth of enterprise? Entrepreneurs and business-people can help governments and the major donors map out the "value chain" of activities and stages where corruption or lack of government capacities impinges on enterprise creation. Then, provided the political commitment is present, intervention could focus on tackling the most important blockages.

These are not back-door strategies for the privatization of the delivery of poverty services or the imposition of user fees. They are simply suggestions that those designing MDG policies and programs be aware, competent, and incentivized to apply enterprise thinking to what they are doing and leverage their resources to aid pro-poor enterprise creation.

There are probably some good examples of this happening, but as aid flows targeting MDGs increase, many more opportunities will arise. My concern is that if enterprise thinking and objectives are not mainstreamed now, these opportunities will be ignored—at great long-term cost to poor people.

Reengineer the International Development Supply Chain

I have argued elsewhere that the presence of business DNA in partners, whether nonprofit or for-profit, is an important ingredient in the success of pro-poor enterprise interventions. This experience underpins my proposition that donors should be considering three options.

Transfer Business DNA The first option is how they can best use their position and resources to promote the transfusion of business DNA and enterprise behavior all along the international development supply chain. Some of the best examples of this process at work relate mostly to frontline NGOs that are traditionally donor funded and typically operate in development project mode insulated from market forces.

Other parts of the development supply chain could probably do with an injection of business DNA as well. Most academics, policymakers, and development agency professionals endeavoring to catalyze pro-poor enterprise do not have real business-based experience to draw on. Their knowledge of how markets operate and the problems businesses of all kinds face is largely theoretical or conceptual. This mismatch is obviously not the sole reason that many enterprise- (and growth-) oriented policies and interventions in poor countries have not worked as well as intended.

But there is a certain logic in the argument that if we want policies and interventions that really do help pro-poor enterprise grow, it would be useful to be able to inject more experience-based business DNA into the project and policy design process. It is not easy,[16] but it can be done, and donors are perfectly positioned to drive this process—perhaps even using new forms of partnership with big business that would facilitate the transfer of their business DNA into the development supply chain.[17]

Develop Alternative Sources of Supply   The second option is to construct an alternative development supply chain by working more extensively and more directly with the for-profit sector on devising and delivering pro-poor enterprise interventions. My experience is that the efficiency of resource use is higher, the transaction and learning costs lower, and the going-to-scale opportunities much greater than when trying to accomplish the same thing with the nonprofit sector.

Promote Hybrids   A third route could be to use market principles to encourage the emergence of financially viable, hybrid network business models capable of delivering pro-poor services on a large scale. Donors could facilitate the coming together of private and nonprofit entities into a new form of hybrid "enterprise" that could use smart subsidies and commercial capital and best-practice business and developmental skills to deliver differentially priced services to different segments of the poverty market.

This is an approach Shell Foundation is piloting in the scale-up phase of its program to tackle indoor air pollution (IAP). IAP refers to the tragic situation whereby up to 2 million women and young children die annually in Africa, Asia, and Central America from the health-related impacts of inhaling smoke coming from leaky wood stoves and open-wood-fueled cooking used internally. The aid community has tried and failed for decades to address this problem. But these efforts have been handicapped by only having limited resources available and by trying to foist Western-designed solutions on poor households.

In India and elsewhere, we at the Shell Foundation have been working with NGOs that have already developed links to poor communities as conduits through which they channeled donor-funded technical solutions to IAP. Because of limited funding, these links could be used to distribute only relatively few stoves and other devices. Through long and sometimes painful interactions with these NGOs, involving the transfer of a great deal of business DNA, the NGOs have gradually developed a business-like approach to their concerns and developed market-based schemes for securing finance, distributing, and "selling" cleaner stoves and fuels to these extremely poor households in volumes that dwarf anything they were able to achieve previously. In India, one pilot has successfully sold at least 65,000 unsubsidized stoves and now has plans to raise this number to 2 million within three years. In Guatemala, a NGO that was previously marketing only hundreds of clean stoves per year, after a long engagement involving transfer of business DNA has financed plans to reach millions of poor household customers on a commercial basis.

Beyond our efforts, the reengineering of the development supply chain along business lines is happening to a certain extent as some donors and nonprofits try to apply business thinking to what they do.[18] But these business-like development entities and experiments are still in the minority and largely peripheral to the way most of the aid community is organized and incentivized. We suggest therefore that whether and how to introduce business principles and business DNA into the mainstream aid community is a topic worthy of further urgent debate.

18.2.2 Propositions for the International Business Community

This second set of propositions relates to the role of large businesses, especially multinational corporations, in tackling poverty. My core position is that through harnessing its value-creating assets, big business is especially well equipped to add enormous value to pro-poor enterprise initiatives and elsewhere in the poverty war.

I acknowledge that business of all kinds can do the most for poverty reduction by simply being profitable and responsible businesses. By extension, this means that the greatest contribution host governments and the aid community can make is to create the policy framework and other enabling conditions under which this will happen.

But progress in this direction is very slow in most poor countries for many reasons. I believe big business can accelerate this process by bringing its value-creating assets into play, in partnership with others, specifically to advance the development of enterprise in poor countries. In doing this, significant short-term poverty benefits will be generated, and business will contribute directly to creating conditions under which it can grow and be profitable in the future.[19]

The interaction I am calling for is already happening, particularly in the way big business now frequently works with its fence-line and stakeholder communities not just to mitigate impact but to maximize benefit from its presence.[20] There is also great pro-poor potential inherent in the few examples of the bottom-of-the-pyramid logic that business and social value can be created by selling appropriate products profitably into poverty markets. But these efforts are still relatively limited compared to the size of the poverty problem. So the challenge to big business as well as aid actors and host governments is going to scale by getting more big businesses to invest more of their value-creating assets in tackling poverty in a business-like way.

My propositions below focus on how to make this happen—not only through direct enterprise development initiatives but also by business working with others to grapple with the many capacity, policy, and governance obstacles to pro-poor enterprise development that currently exist in the "enabling environment."[21]

A Case of Mutual Myopia: Nobody Asks, Nobody Offers

There are some understandable reasons that not enough of the "right" kind of business engagement with poverty is taking place. Some are internal to business and linked to its natural, and appropriate, tendency toward cost and risk minimization. Frequently this orientation is reinforced by a traditional corporate philanthropic mind-set that dictates tackling poverty as a business by giving money away to the neediest.[22] So business in effect doesn't think or know how to deploy its value-creating assets when tackling poverty. It mainly offers money.

These internal drivers are reinforced by external expectations. The traditional CSR community largely wants business to concentrate on obeying the law, doing less that bad and mitigating or remedying operational harm, rather than creating value.[23]

At the same time, those closer to the problem, such as host governments, donors, NGOs, and local communities do not appreciate where in businesses these value-creating assets can be found or indeed even what these are.

But primarily they have other expectations and agendas when they approach business about tackling poverty, most of which boil down to requests for money. So in my view, governments and civil society do not make the right "ask" when they approach business for help in tackling poverty.

No doubt some behavior change can be brought about through education and exhortation directed at both sides so that the big business poverty "ask and offer" focuses on promoting pro-poor enterprise and the conditions for enterprise development.

But I think something more fundamental has to occur in order to break through the self-reinforcing, mutual myopia that leads to the suboptimal involvement of business in the fight against poverty.

Make Poverty Partnerships More Like Business Partnerships

This "something" has to do with recasting the "risk-return profile" of the poverty projects and public-private partnerships that business is asked to join or sets out to create.

Commercial partnerships between businesses are formed because they offer each partner specific value they cannot secure by acting alone. The partners first work together to define the project and specify its concrete outputs and returns and the inputs to be exclusively provided by each side. This is wrapped up in a legal contract setting out roles and responsibilities and the penalties to be imposed if any partner fails to deliver what is expected of it.

The contrast could not be greater with the typical poverty project or public private partnership (PPP) in which business is asked to participate. Business is not usually consulted in its design. Money is usually the main input asked of business.[24] PPP objectives, though worthy, are frequently so generally specified that the outcomes, even if achieved, will have little real social or business relevance.

Moreover, these partners are not really at risk in any meaningful sense because they rely on aid or public money to fund their involvement, and the individuals involved are not likely suffer any consequences if the project fails.[25] And most important, the lead civil society partners, whilst knowledgeable and articulate, usually do not have influence or are not empowered to deliver change where it is needed in order to help achieve the PPPs objectives.

Not surprisingly, big business turns down most invitations to join PPPs because of this sort of risk-return profile—and it is quite right to do so from a social as well as a shareholder's perspective. And when business does join up, the inputs, sincerely offered, are appropriate to the circumstances but are rarely the value-creating assets where I believe real social value lies.

So my proposition is that if the PPPs and poverty projects involving business are set up and run along the same principles as commercial partnerships, business will bring more of its value-creating assets to bear on the problem. Everyone will benefit, especially poor people.

There are examples already where some of these principles have been applied and recommendations have already been made in print about the principles of effective public-private partnership.[26] So again I offer only a few observations by way of a contribution to the debate.

• *Ensure the right parties are at the PPP table, or do not bother issuing the invitations* Big business is often appropriately criticized for not involving key stakeholders in discussions and decision making about actions by the business that directly affect them. But its also the case that for a variety of reasons, many of those who set up or participate in PPPs are well informed and intentioned but have no real power or influence in doing anything about it. The net result is PPPs (and meetings, workshops, and roundtables) that look good and sound good but do not accomplish much and represent a real waste of scarce resources.

Successfully tackling specific poverty problems using PPPs means overcoming in a fixed time frame a number of specific obstacles along the chain of cause and effect. Only parties that add real value to this effort, are empowered and able to deliver changes where they are needed, and, most important, have something to lose if they fail should participate in PPPs. The Extractive Industries Transparency Initiative (EITI) is a good example of a PPP where the right parties are now involved and there are good prospects for significant advances on the governance and transparency front that will ultimately benefit poor people.[27]

• *Set goals that make a difference to poor people, but ensure that the partners also secure returns they value* Any pro-poor project or PPP of value must have achievable goals that deliver measurable and wanted benefits to poor people. This is pretty obvious, though many PPPs and projects do not start out with well-defined, attainable goals.

But my main point here is not about the poverty outcomes of PPPs but about the benefits that devolve to the partners as a result of participating in the initiative. It seems to me that to get big business to invest value-creating assets in PPPs, these need to generate returns to all partners in "currencies" they value and at a scale commensurate to the risk they are taking.

This is precisely the logic deployed in the design of the Shell Foundation's SME funds in South Africa and Uganda. The local banks felt that the SMEs helped initially would eventually become customers for larger commercial loans, and Shell Foundation got involved to demonstrate to other banks that investing in SMEs was good business.

The logic at work in this example is pretty linear and in the banks' case clearly linked to future profits. Other risk-return relationships are possible. For example, big businesses operating in the same country could pool their input needs and thus create a market for local SMEs in return for government efforts to introduce level-playing-field policies with regard to adherence to standards or the removal of differential pricing structure.

Get the Risk and Return Balance Right

There are many dimensions that could be explored coming out of the proposition that PPPs should be structured like commercial partnerships. But they all essentially stem from the fact that the parties involved would have to deal with the implications of a very new set of risk-return relationships.

NGOs might be faced with the challenge of having to work exclusively with specific business brands on a long-term basis or be asked to put themselves, their management, and their resources at real joint risk with business in order to secure the highest social returns possible. Would this be worth the risk or even legally possible under current rules and perceptions governing the behavior of nonprofits?

If society believes that access to the business DNA possessed by MNCs could lead to significant pro-poor benefits, perhaps donors should be prepared to find ways to buy down the early risks incurred by MNCs in making these assets available.

Host governments may have to shoulder the political risk of being perceived as using tax revenues, business expertise, and donor money in effect to do better for enterprise (both the big business partners and the small business beneficiaries) at the expense of meeting the urgent needs of the poor.

And finally, big business will be taking the risk of incurring shareholder, NGO, media, and regulator wrath and the high learning costs associated with deploying their core value-creating assets in entirely new ways and with new partners with little guarantee of real benefit.

18.3   Coming Together: An Invitation to Redefine the Role of Enterprise in Tackling Poverty

Society is clearly in an era of renewed commitment to explore new ways of tackling the scourge of poverty with the aspiration of banishing it to the history books. This is a moment to be seized. Already there is much creative and bold experimentation going on within the aid community by developing-country governments, leading politicians and actors in the industrialized countries, and big business. So the propositions put forward in this chapter that encourage focus and experimentation around the issue of enterprise and poverty reduction do not necessarily break new ground. This is very positive because it means there is already much to talk about and much to learn from each other.

Some of the right kind of talking and learning is taking place, but not enough, especially since the sales pitches are already being made and plans are already being laid to deploy the new pro-poor political and resource commitments that were secured in 2005.

Given the scale of the problem to be tackled and the encouraging signs that results can be delivered, the aid community, developing-country governments, and the big business community need to explore the enterprise-poverty territory together, robustly and urgently.

Notes

1. The slogan "Make Poverty History" was coined by the rock star Bono and adopted as a headline soundbite by the Global Call for Action Against Poverty coalition, a group composed largely of poverty-oriented NGOs that sometimes combine advocacy and fieldwork. See www .makepovertyhistory.org. The work of this coalition is most visible in the United Kingdom, where it has triggered an intense and broad-ranging public debate. Elsewhere, the push for more help to poor countries is less high profile but just as earnest and is being carried forward by politicians and officials from the UK and other European countries and by the senior hierarchy of the international development community.

2. The aid community I refer to in this chapter includes private and corporate foundations, individual philanthropists, multilateral and bilateral development agencies and departments, and nonprofit groups concerned with poverty and development, including academic institutions and professional NGOs. Unless specifically mentioned, not included are donors, academics, and agencies concerned with humanitarian and disaster relief, developing-country governments, or private sector actors who work on publicly funded development and poverty projects.

3. Based on a simple analysis of DAC aid allocations between 1990 and 2000 at the three- and six-digit SIC level and of the grant allocation of the ten major private U.S.-based donors with international programs.

4. By which we mean enterprises employing, owned by, or providing such goods and services to poor people.

5. See K. Hallberg and Y. Konishi, "Bringing SMEs into Global Market" in G. Fields and G. Pfefferman, eds., *Pathways out of Poverty: Private Firms and Economic Mobility in Developing Countries* (Norwell, Mass.: Kluwer, 2003), for a review of the failure of government and donor-funded SME interventions and policies. For the donor's response to their failures in this area, see Committee of Donor Agencies for Small Enterprise Development, *Business Development Services for Small Enterprises: Guiding Principles for Donor Intervention* (Washington, D.C.: SME Donor Committee Secretariat, World Bank, 2001). With reference to agency performance, development financing institutions such as the International Finance Corporation (IFC) and Dutch Development Financial Agency (FMO) have contributed directly to enterprise creation (though SME finance forms too small a part of their portfolio). But while other agencies have done their best to draw attention to the importance of enterprise through myriad conferences, commissions, studies, workshops, expert meetings, and expert missions, this is not the same as having a direct role in generating real firms employing real people.

6. For example, enterprise does not feature in any of twenty-four recommendations given in Oxfam, *Paying the Price: Why Rich Countries Must Invest Now in a War on Poverty* (London: Oxfam, 2004) on aid reform. Issues linked to growth and poverty—the core intellectual challenge that has been troubling economists for 300 hundred years—are addressed and dismissed in only in few paragraphs. The report of the distinguished UN Millennium Project addresses the need for enterprise and the role of the private sector much more comprehensively. The problem is that it also addresses every other aspect of poverty comprehensively, thus reducing the implementation prospects for all of its recommendations. See UN Millennium Project, *Investing in Development: A Practical Plan to Achieve the Millennium Development Goals* (New York: United Nations, 2005).

7. I can mention the World Business Commissions for Sustainable Development, UN Global Compact , Prince of Wales International Business Leaders Forum, Business for Social Responsibility in the United States, and entities such as the Resource Centre for the Social Dimensions of Poverty in the UK and individual actors such as TechnoServe and Development Alternatives International in the United States and many NGOs in developing countries such as TERI in India and ApproTec in Kenya. There is as well a wide range of relatively new and small players that could be subsumed under the heading of blended value or double bottom-line investors such as Acumen Fund, the Provenex Fund of the Rockefeller Foundation, the Gatsby Charitable Foundation, the Skoll Foundation, Schwab Foundation for Social Entrepreneurship, and the Lemelson Foundation.

8. See C. K. Pralahad, *The Fortune at the Bottom of the Pyramid: Enabling Dignity and Choice through Markets* (Philadelphia: Wharton School Publishing, 2004) for a discussion and the agendas of recent conferences held in San Francisco. See WRI.org for details on its December 2004 "Eradicating Poverty through Profit" conference and see "Eradicating Poverty Through Profit: A dialogue meeting convened by University of Cambridge Programme for Industry and the Chatham House Sustainable Development Programme, December 3, 2004, Chatham House, London, UK.

9. And though I will be discussing mostly enterprise-level interventions, my concept of enterprise interventions encompasses actions to improve the "enabling environment" or, in Porter's terms, the competitive context and relating to governance, standards and regulations, tariffs, training, infrastructure, finance, and so on.

10. See Shell Foundation (2005).

11. See, for example, the various initiatives of the participants at a meeting in London in early 2004 on financing the SME sector in developing countries and organized by the Shell Foundation and Forum of the Future and those attending a slightly broader focused meeting in late 2004 hosted by the World Economic Forum and convened by the IFC and the Rockefeller Corporation. See Forum of the Future, *Sustainable Investment in Africa: Pipedream or Possibility? Innovative Financing Mechanism for SMEs in Africa* (London: Forum of the Future, 2004), and "Private Investment with Social Goals: Workshop on Building the Blended Value Capital Market," WEF Headquarters, Geneva, September 21–22, 2004, sponsored by IFC, the Rockefeller Foundation, and the World Economic Forum.

12. On the basis of real market research, not literature reviews.

13. For example, in one Shell Foundation project intended to test the commercialization possibilities of village-scale biomass gasifiers, our partner, a team from a university engineering department who had developed the technology, spent most their time and our money on R&D issues close to their hearts as engineers. But they did not pay attention to the main developmental challenge (and objective of the project) of commercializing the technology and so carried out no market research and as result were unable to secure the local investor interest that the plan called for. In another example, the social entrepreneur we supported, again in an effort to commercialize a technically viable village power production system, had a strong developmental aim, which was bringing electricity to unserved villages and creating microenterprises able to use the power provided. Much donor money was raised and used to subsidize the pilots, thus eliminating the "need" to charge poor customers the full cost of the power provided. This confounded our efforts to assess whether commercial finance could be used to scale up to meet the needs of thousands of unelectrified villages. And this means the NGO partner is now continually having to raise ever more "soft" money just to keep the few pilots operational.

Those familiar with the history and current status of the famous multifunctional platform (MFP) in West Africa may recognize a similar conundrum. See UNIDO/UN Development Programme (UNDP) regional *Multi-Functional Platform Programme*, at www.un.org/special-rep/ohrlls/ UN_system/unido.htm. The MFP is a diesel-powered generator that drives a set of agroprocessing equipment for productive use at the village level and managed by women's associations. Its development has been completely donor funded with a social objective: to empower the women who operate the platform. As a consequence, not much business thinking is applied to the management of the platform (for example, capital costs are never factored into user fees) or to the challenge of going to scale. Intriguingly, there is evidence that the MFP, emphatically a pro-poor piece of technology, is in fact commercially viable. This means that at least some of the costs of a rollout could be financed commercially, and as long the operators are women's groups, the original empowerment objectives could be met as well. However, significant donor and public money is now being used to finance rollout in some West African countries.

14. See William Easterly, *The Elusive Quest for Growth* (Cambridge, Mass.: MIT Press, 2002).

15. This is illustrated by the evolution of Shell Foundation's engagement with Integra, a Romanian NGO involved in microfinance, as part of the work of its Market Access program. Integra realized its clients were producing products for which there was no market. We at Shell engaged with them around this problem and pushed them to understand that they could offer much greater value to their clients if they started by identifying market opportunities rather than just rushing to set up production and then looking for somewhere to sell. This engagement catalyzed Integra into educating itself, with the help of expert consultants, about how markets work and the most appropriate routes to market for their clients. This kicked off a process whereby their clients started to produce more marketable products. Integra also realized that this new knowledge itself had commercial value and opened up a business opportunity for it that will produce more income for the NGO and benefits for its clients.

16. Many development agencies report that when experienced business people do wind up working with them on development issues, they often become "softer" than the development professionals.

17. Shell Foundation is partnering with the IUCN and UNESCO to do precisely this in a slightly different context by using the business and site management skills and techniques available in the Shell Group to upgrade the local management of UNESCO's World Heritage sites throughout Africa and get these on a more financially viable footing for the longer term. There are obviously other examples of this kind of skill transfer taking place between big business and the aid community.

18. In some cases, quite innovative experiments are being attempted, such as the emergence of development marketplaces on the Web and under the aegis of some multilateral agencies such as the World Bank.

19. See M. Porter and M. Kramer, "The Competitive Advantages of Corporate Philanthropy," *Harvard Business Review*, December 2002, for a business school perspective on this issue and how this approach can also deliver significant long-term business benefits—not by boosting short-term profit but through improving the competitive context in which businesses operate.

20. See, for example, Michael Winner, "Levers and Pulleys: Extractive Industries and Local Economic Development in Poor Regions—Incentivising Innovation by Lead Contractors through Contract Tendering," Briefing Note no. 3, in the *Enhancing Social Performance in the Engineering Services Sector Programme*, *Overseas Development Institute*, London, 2005, and the case studies cited in IFC, "Addressing the Social Dimensions of Private Sector Projects," Good Practice Note no. 3 (Washington, D.C.: World Bank Group, 2003), and Titus Moser, "Social Performance: Key Lessons from Recent Experiences within Shell" (London: Social Performance Management Group, Shell International, 2004), available at http://www.shell.com/static/royal-en/downloads/society_environment/SPinShell_0304%20_ss.pdf. See also the examples cited in Alison Maitland, "From a Handout to a Hand Up," *Financial Times*, February 3, 2005.

21. These start with microproblems such lack of property rights, enterprise financing, or appropriate skills run through all manner of regulatory and other issues at the level of the market and into the big governance concerns of corruption, stakeholder engagement, and the rule of law. Big business operating in poor countries faces and overcomes these issues daily. In so doing, they generate specific pools of practical knowledge that, deployed properly, could help unblock huge obstacles to enterprise development in poor countries.

22. I am simplifying, of course, to make a point. Many corporates have very professional charitable donation programs that work closely with recipient charities to deliver significant social benefits in imaginative ways. But typically these good causes are not connected to their business, and the skills deployed by the company in support of this are those associated with giving money away rather than creating value. See Porter and Kramer, "Competitive Advantages."

23. There are many other weaknesses in the thinking underpinning the intellectual cul-de-sac represented by traditional CSR reasoning. See Clive Crook, "The Good Company: A Survey of Corporate Social Responsibility," *Economist*, January 22, 2005.

24. Though speaking opportunities at high-profile tables or in working groups are often attached to the modern versions of PPP.

25. This is certainly the case in our different but still analogous experience as a donor where we have provided financial support to grantees from the nonprofit sector to allow them to develop commercial initiatives where they failed to even come close to delivering what they promised but never took any action against the project managers who presided over the failures.

26. See, for example, Michael Winner, *The New Broker: Brokering Partnerships for Development* (London: Overseas Development Institute, 2003), and Jane Nelson, *Partnering for Success* (Geneva: World Economic Forum, 2004). There are fortunately already some good examples of what we are after. See also George C. Lodge, "The Corporate Key: Using Big Business to Fight Poverty," *Foreign Affairs* 81(4), 2002, who proposes a world development corporation with some of the features we are calling for in PPPs. For a nonenterprise example see UNAIDS, *Aids in Africa: Three Scenarios* (New York: Joint UN Programme on HIV/AIDS, 2004), for a case where a core value-creating asset of the Shell Group—its scenarios methodologies—is being used in partnership with the United Nations to tackle HIV/AIDS in Africa. We know of other current examples where large MNCs are deploying core skills and assets working in PPPS to tackle the problems of child malnutrition and community health.

27. EITI has only begun to make progress toward its ultimate goal of getting more state revenues from energy and mineral exports flowing to help poor people once host governments joined the international energy industry at the negotiating table See www2.dfid.gov.uk/news/files/extractiveindustries.asp.

VI IN CONCLUSION: THE BIG PICTURE

19 Avoid Hubris: And Other Lessons for Reformers

John McMillan

Should development aid be made conditional on institutional reform? Should the West offer aid only to countries that are cleaning up corruption, adhering to the rule of law, educating their children, removing inefficient regulations, and lowering their trade barriers? The United States's Millennium Challenge Account (MCA) represents, in the words of President George W. Bush, "a new compact for global development, defined by new accountability for both rich and poor nations alike. Greater contributions from developed nations must be linked to greater responsibility from developing nations." Countries are to be ranked according to sixteen quantitative indicators, and their aid levels are to reflect their scores. The UK's proposal for an international finance facility (IFF) envisages a doubling of aid levels while making the aid "subject to the recipient countries meeting a fundamental condition of good governance."[1]

While the idea of using aid to create incentives for developing-country governments to enact needed economic reforms doubtless has merit, it has danger as well. There is a risk of being overprescriptive. What exactly does "good governance" mean in a country with weak institutions? What reforms are most needed? It is hard to specify in the abstract which reforms are urgent and which can be postponed. The West does not have a good track record of offering economic advice. Sometimes the advice offered has been overambitious and, as a result, counterproductive.

Reform is hard to do because we cannot predict its effects. Reform advice often seems be based on the presumption that we know where we are going and we know how to get there. Perhaps we know where we want to go, but often we do not know how to get there. There is no recipe for success. Since we do not know for sure what will work or how long it will take to work, all we can do is trial and error. Acknowledging our ignorance means moving step by step rather than betting everything on a comprehensive blueprint.

This should not come as a revelation. The whole point of the market economy, after all, is that it handles, better than any more centralized alternative, the unforeseen and the unforeseeable. If we could plan the reforms, we could have planned the economy.

The experience of reform in various developing and former communist countries over the past two decades or so, from Uganda to the Czech Republic, holds lessons for reformers. Market-oriented reforms like privatization and trade opening, the data show, have usually brought their intended benefits. But the gains have been spotty: often slow in coming and relatively small. The effectiveness of any one policy depends on other policies, in ways that are usually unforeseeable. The chief lesson is: avoid hubris.

19.1 Experience with Reform

The past two decades have seen a worldwide shift to markets. Globalization has opened domestic markets to international competition. The former communist countries have converted themselves, to varying degrees, into market economies. In the low-income countries, privatization has reduced the share of state production in gross domestic product (GDP) from 16 percent, on average, to 5 percent. The results of this expansion of markets have been mixed.

The Asian financial crisis of 1997–1998 caused severe hardship to millions of ordinary Indonesians, Koreans, and Thais. Russia's 1991 market reforms were followed by a decade of disaster. In Latin America, privatization was often so corrupt that in polls, a clear majority now say it was not beneficial.

Not all is gloom, however. The good news, though less dramatic, arguably outweighs the bad. India and China have grown. The average Chinese is three times as well off now as in 1980, and the average Indian is more than twice as well off. It is impossible to exaggerate the significance of the switch to rapid growth of two of the world's poorest countries, containing a third of the world's population.

The good news goes beyond China and India. Economists studying the reforms find that mostly they have yielded gains in the direction their proponents expected. However, the gains have been moderate in size. Trade opening and privatization have brought efficiency gains, but the gains have not been large enough to be conspicuous. You have to look hard at the data to see them.

Studies of countries lowering their trade barriers have found that while the consequences have varied widely from country to country, trade reform has usually improved economic performance. Consumers benefit from the lower prices. Reacting to the new competition from imports, firms raise their productivity. An econometric analysis of 141 countries in the 1980s and 1990s (Wacziarg and Welch 2003) estimated that a substantial trade opening boosts economic growth by an average of 1.5 percentage points. An increase in growth from, say, 4 percent per annum to 5.5 percent would mean that instead of taking eighteen years for national income to double, it would take thirteen years. The measured benefits from trade opening are not trivial, but they are not huge.

With privatization the story is similar: it has brought genuine but unspectacular improvements. After being privatized, the typical firm boosts its labor productivity, increases its investment, and lowers its prices to consumers (Megginson and Netter 2001, Sheshinski and López-Calva 2003). If we aggregate the results of three studies, of a total of 211 firms in more than 50 countries, that compare each firm's performance for the three years before privatization with the three years after it (Megginson, Nash, and van Randenborgh 1994; Boubakri and Cosset 1998; D'Souza and Megginson 1999), we find that investment as a percentage of sales rose an average of 36 percent and output per worker rose an average of 18 percent.

In the United States, per capita income is $35,000; in Tanzania it is $550 (World Bank 2002). The gap in living standards is sixty-four to one. The measured gains from trade opening and privatization, raising annual growth rates by a percentage point or two, do not go far in shrinking that gap.

19.2 Transforming the System

Why haven't the gains from market building been larger? Reform means transforming the entire economic system. The various parts of a reform package reinforce each other. A pair of reforms may be complementary in a precise sense: unless one is already in place, the other is ineffective (Gates, Milgrom, and Roberts 1996). A potentially worthwhile reform could even be harmful if its complementary reforms are missing.

"Trade is the most certain path to lasting prosperity," President Bush told the leaders of Latin American nations at the 2004 Summit of the Americas. It is ironic that Bush happened to be in Mexico when he spoke these words, for Mexico's own experience contradicted him. After Mexico lowered its trade barriers in 1986, its economic growth averaged 2.2 percentage points less than it had been before.

Mexico illustrates that trade provides no guarantees, no certain path. For some countries, trade opening did not bring its intended benefits. In a sample of twenty-four countries that substantially liberalized their trade (Wacziarg and Horn 2003), about half achieved faster growth following liberalization. For example, Chile grew 2.8 percentage points faster and Uganda 2.2 percentage points faster. However, others (about a quarter of them, for example, the Philippines) obtained no improvement in growth. Still others (the remaining quarter, for example, Mexico) actually grew more slowly than before.

The effects of trade reforms have varied widely from country to country. There is a lot of variation around the average 1.5 percent boost to economic growth. It is widely agreed among those who have studied economic reform that opening the economy to trade is good policy—but only if the economy is ready for it.

Trade opening might not have beneficial effects if the labor market is distorted. The gains from a trade reform come, in principle, from reallocating labor. Workers move within a given industry from the less efficient firms to the more efficient ones. Workers also move across industries, from those that had been protected into those in which the nation has a comparative advantage.

After Brazil lowered its tariff and nontariff barriers in the early 1990s, for example, firms revamped their operations, and workers moved from the less productive firms to the more productive. However, most of the efficiency gains came from reallocations within each industry. This was unexpected. Contrary to the trade theory textbooks, there was little movement of workers across industries (Muendler 2003). Moreover, many of those thrown out of work when the unproductive firms went out of business were not rehired elsewhere but experienced a long period of unemployment; many left the formal sector and scraped by in the informal sector. The workers bore high transitional costs.

In other countries, the pattern was similar. A study of twenty-five countries that significantly opened their trade found that surprisingly little intersectoral labor mobility occurred and surprisingly small structural change (Wacziarg and Wallack 2004). Part of the explanation presumably is that the movement of workers from declining industries into the industries of the future is held back if the labor market is not up to the task. Labor market reforms complement trade reforms.

Similarly, whether privatizing a state-owned firm improves its performance depends on its economic environment. Ownership incentives are not enough by themselves to induce large firms to be run efficiently. Also needed are the oversights that come from well-functioning (and well-regulated) financial markets. As Enron illustrates, these oversights sometimes fail even where sophisticated financial markets exist. Enron-type problems are pervasive where financial markets are underdeveloped.

The Russian natural gas giant Gazprom, for example, in 2002 had a market value far below the sum of its assets (which amounted to one-third of the world's proven gas reserves). Its low valuation reflected stockholders' skepticism about asset stripping. Gazprom's managers had sold off gas deposits for a fraction of their value. Assets worth least US$7 billion had vanished (McMillan and Twiss 2002). The insider dealing was well known, but nothing was done to correct it.

After Mexico's banks were privatized, their managers engaged in related lending, meaning they made loans on generous terms to themselves. In the mid-1990s, related lending amounted to 20 percent of all commercial lending in Mexico. Related borrowers paid interest rates that averaged 3 percentage points lower than arm's-length borrowers and defaulted 30 percent more often (La Porta, Lopes de Silanes, and Zamarippa 2003). Related lending was simply a way for the managers to seize the resources of the banks' depositors and shareholders. Knowing they would not be sanctioned, they did this quite blatantly.

Privatization can backfire if financial market oversights are missing. Asset stripping is not universal; on the contrary, the data show that privatization usually brought improved firm performance. But asset stripping may occur if privatization policies are pursued in isolation of other reforms. Financial market reforms complement privatization.

Is tackling corruption the solution to underdevelopment? The evidence says it helps, but no more than that. Econometric analyses show that, as anyone would expect, countries hampered by corruption grow slowly. Indexes of countries' overall levels of corruption on a 0 to 10 scale, with 10 meaning the country is absolutely free of corruption and 0 meaning highly corrupt, are constructed from questionnaires administered to foreign businesspeople. A two-point improvement in the corruption index, it is estimated, raises investment by four percentage points, which in turn raises economic growth by about half a percentage point. India's corruption index, for example, is calculated to be 3.3 and Italy's 7.3. Extrapolating, we can predict that if India were to cut its corruption level to that of Italy, it would boost its annual growth rate by one percentage point (Mauro 1995, Wei 1998). Cracking down on corruption would improve economic performance, but as with any other single policy, it is no panacea.

Wide-ranging reform is what is needed, but it is hard to do. When New Zealand radically deregulated in the mid-1980s—slashing trade barriers, removing agricultural price supports, flattening taxes, trimming financial market regulation, corporatizing and privatizing state-owned firms—it suffered a major recession, with negative growth and high unemployment. It took more than a decade for any beneficial effects to start to show. The setting for the reforms was favorable. New Zealand, an industrialized country, had started with a full set of market-supporting institutions like laws of contract, and its labor and financial markets had been operating reasonably effectively. The reform process can be expected to be more painful in a country like Mexico or Turkey, where the legal system is creaky and the labor and financial markets suffer from high transaction costs, and even more painful in a country like Tanzania or Bangladesh, where market mechanisms are stunted.

19.3 Piecemeal Social Engineering

The need for a package of reforms could be a reason, on the face of it, for doing everything at once. But here is the rub. The systemic interactions are hard to predict. We know little about how the pieces of the market system fit together. Some interactions may be complex and indirect, and so we may not even be able to anticipate their existence. Others are straightforward, like trade reform plus the labor market or privatization plus the equity market, but we have few data on their magnitude.

Within each individual market, there are also systemic complexities. Building a smoothly functioning labor or financial market is a far harder task, and more time-consuming, than freeing up trade or privatizing firms. Imagine being charged with creating an equity market in a country that lacks one, like Burma. The equity market relies on trust: investors hand over their money to managers with little direct assurance that it will not be misused. To sustain that trust, it is necessary to build a mix of private sector and government-based mechanisms (Black 2000). The firms that oversee the market—accountants, investment banks, law firms—must have, and want to keep, a reputation for trustworthiness; such a reputation is developed only over time. Self-regulating organizations—the stock exchange, with its rules on financial reporting and its sanction of delisting, and various voluntary industry associations—help keep the players honest. A vigorous business press is needed to scrutinize companies' dealings. To prevent managers from expropriating the investors' funds, the government must write laws and train judges. To ensure investors receive accurate information, the government must set up a regulator like the U.S. Securities and Exchange Commission to bolster the courts. The workability of each of these equity-market mechanisms is contingent, in ways we cannot fully anticipate, on the presence of the others.

Karl Popper recognized this half a century ago. In *The Open Society and Its Enemies* (1971), he contrasted two modes of reform. Utopian social engineering involves a grand blueprint for society: "it pursues its aim consciously and consistently," and "it determines its means according to this end." Piecemeal social engineering, by contrast, involves tinkering with parts of the system, with no overall plan. Whereas piecemeal reform entails "searching for, and fighting against, the greatest and most urgent evils of society," utopian reform entails "searching for, and fighting for, its greatest ultimate good."

With its appeal to rational thought, the utopian approach is "convincing and attractive." However, Popper argued that it was folly. The utopian method, "using a blueprint of society as a whole, is one which demands a strong centralized rule of a few." By contrast, piecemeal social engineering can succeed. It recognizes that "perfection, if at all attainable, is far distant." For this reason, it is "the only method of improving matters which has so far been really successful, at any time, and in any place" (Popper 1971, 157–159). Popper's beliefs were tested in the late twentieth century's move away from communism. China tried piecemeal reform, Russia utopian.

Shock therapy was characterized by its architect Jeffrey Sachs as "a rapid, comprehensive and far-reaching program of reforms to implement 'normal' capitalism" (1994). This fits Popper's definition of utopian social engineering, in being "comprehensive" and in having a stated end point, "'normal' capitalism." Following Russia's reforms, national income fell rapidly. By 1999, national income was 61 percent of what it had been in 1990, just before the reforms. This overestimates the drop in living standards, as there was growth in the unmeasured underground economy. If retail sales (in real terms) and electricity consumption are used as indicators of economic activity, Russia's 1999 economy was operating at about 80 percent of its 1990 level (Shleifer and Treisman 2003). Whatever the size of the drop in per capita income, it was a drop. The consequences of Russia's shock therapy corroborated Popper's dismissal of grandiose schemes.

China's reforms, which brought world-record growth of around 8 percent per capita for thirty years, were piecemeal. Each reform was tried out on a small scale and expanded if it worked. In Deng Xiaoping's folksy formulation, China was "crossing the river by feeling each stone." When pressed on where China was headed, its leaders said they wanted a "social market economy with Chinese characteristics." This phrase is empty of meaning, and presumably intentionally so. The end point was undefined.

Where should reformers start? The modest prescription is to start with something that is feasible and seems sensible. In 1980s China, for example, early success came in agriculture. When the collective farms were abolished and replaced with individual plots, China's supply of food doubled. The collectives were an extremely inefficient way of organizing farming, as the farmers themselves were well aware, so easy gains were to be had. China's other early reform success was in the creation of village enterprises: small manufacturing firms owned and run by village governments. The reformers failed to anticipate the village enterprises' rapid growth. Deng later said it "took us by surprise completely." With hindsight, though, these firms' success is explicable: they found a ready market for their products by filling empty market niches; they created rural employment; they obtained finance, otherwise unobtainable, via the villages' powers of taxation; and they were induced to operate efficiently by the intense competition to sell their outputs that quickly developed among themselves (McMillan 2002).

In reform, one size does not fit all. That village-owned firms were an initial source of China's success is the clearest possible illustration of that. In any other country, creating village-owned firms is unlikely to be the solution. What works will vary with the country's initial conditions. In general, if the reforms start where the distortions are biggest and a few changes could make a difference, momentum is built to sustain the harder reforms.

19.4   Lesson for Reformers

Market-oriented reforms have usually brought benefits, but the gains have tended to be slow and relatively small. Reforms interact with each other. Whether any one policy is effective depends in complex ways on other policies.

The honest approach to economic reform is to be deliberately experimental and empirical (as was argued by McMillan and Naughton 1992). To claim we are able to do something more premeditated than trial and error is to exaggerate our knowledge of reform processes. Avoid hubris.

Note

1. The MCA conditions are: governing justly (civil liberties, political rights, voice and accountability, government effectiveness, rule of law, control of corruption); investing in people (public primary education spending as a percentage of GDP, primary education completion rate, public expenditures on health as a percentage of GDP, immunization rates for DPT and measles); and promoting economic freedom (country credit rating, inflation, three-year budget deficit, trade policy, regulatory quality, days to start a business). See http://www.whitehouse.gov/infocus/ developingnations/millennium.html. On the IFF, see http://www.hm-treasury.gov.uk/media// CA634/ACF6FB.pdf.

References

Black, Bernard. 2000. "The Legal and Institutional Preconditions for Strong Stock Markets." *UCLA Law Review* 48:781–855. Available at http://ssrn.com/abstract=182169.

Boubakri, Narjess, and Jean-Claude Cosset. 1998. "The Financial and Operating Performance of Newly Privatized Firms: Evidence from Developing Countries." *Journal of Finance* 53:1081–1110.

D'Souza, Juliet, and William L. Megginson. 1999. "The Financial and Operating Performance of Newly Privatized Firms in the 1990s." *Journal of Finance* 54:1397–1438.

Gates, Susan, Paul Milgrom, and John Roberts. 1996. "Complementarities in the Transition from Socialism." In J. McMillan and B. Naughton eds., *Reforming Asian Socialism*. Ann Arbor: University of Michigan Press.

"Iraq's Economic Liberalisation: Let's All Go to the Yard Sale." 2003. *Economist*, September 27.

La Porta, Rafael, Florencio Lopes de Silanes, and Guillermo Zamarippa. 2003. "Related Lending." *Quarterly Journal of Economics* 118(1):231–268.

Mauro, Paolo. 1995. "Corruption and Growth." *Quarterly Journal of Economics* 110(3):681–712.

McMillan, John. 2002. *Reinventing the Bazaar: A Natural History of Markets*. New York: Norton.

McMillan, John, and Barry Naughton. 1992. "How to Reform a Planned Economy: Lessons from China." *Oxford Review of Economic Policy* 8:130–143.

McMillan, John, and Jim Twiss. 2002. "Gazprom and Hermitage Capital: Shareholder Activism in Russia." Stanford GSB Case IB-36, Stanford University.

Megginson, William L., Robert Nash, and Matthias van Randenborgh. 1994. "The Financial and Operating Performance of Newly Privatized Firms: An International Empirical Analysis." *Journal of Finance* 49:403–452.

Megginson, William L., and Jeffry M. Netter. 2001. "From State to Market: A Survey of Empirical Studies on Privatization." *Journal of Economic Literature* 39:321–389.

Muendler, Marc. 2003. "Trade and Growth: The Case of Brazil." Department of Economics, University of California, San Diego. Available at http://econ.ucsd.edu/seminars/muendler_brazil.pdf.

Popper, Karl. 1971. *The Open Society and Its Enemies*, vol. 1. Princeton, N.J.: Princeton University Press.

Sachs, Jeffrey. 1994. "Shock Therapy in Poland: Perspectives of Five Years." Tanner Lectures on Human Values, University of Utah. Available at http://www.tannerlectures.utah.edu/lectures/sachs95.pdf.

Sheshinski, Eytan, and Luis Filipe López-Calva. 2003. "Privatization and Its Benefits: Theory and Evidence." *CESIfo Economic Studies* 49(3):429–459.

Shleifer, Andrei, and Daniel Treisman. 2003. "A Normal Country." NBER Working Paper 10057. Cambridge, Mass.: National Bureau of Economic Research.

Wacziarg, Romain, and Jessica Seddon Wallack. 2004. "Trade Liberalization and Intersectoral Labor Movements." *Journal of International Economics* 64(2):223–568.

Wacziarg, Romain, and Karen Horn Welch. 2003. "Trade Liberalization and Growth: New Evidence." Stanford Graduate School of Business. Available at www.stanford.edu/~wacziarg/downloads/integration.pdf.

Wei, Shang Jin. 1998. "Corruption in Economic Development: Beneficial Grease, Minor Annoyance, or Major Obstacle?" Harvard University. Available at http://www.worldbank.org/wbi/gac/gac_pdfs/wei.pdf.

World Bank. 2002. "GNI Per Capita 2002." Available at http://www.worldbank.org/data/databytopic/GNIPC.pdf.

20 Seven Deadly Sins: Reflections on Donor Failings

Nancy Birdsall

The donor community may look back on the 1990s as a watershed. In that decade, some developing countries took off in growth terms, apparently benefiting from and effectively exploiting the increasing integration of the global market. But others, in sub-Saharan Africa, Latin America, and much of Central Asia, seemed stuck. Many of the countries where growth faltered had been major recipients of development assistance over several decades, and under the tutelage of the donors had implemented structural reforms and thousands of projects. In doing so, some had accumulated substantial debt to multilateral and bilateral creditors, to the point where the donors were engaged in a major effort to write down those debts. For many of the world's poorest countries, the record of development and of development assistance seemed dismal.

As a community, donors responded in the past decade with new efforts to assess their own policies and practices. The end of the cold war made it possible to imagine ensuring that foreign aid could more directly address fundamental development problems. As a result, there have been not only new calls to increase the volume of development assistance, but new resolutions to reform the process by which assistance is designed and delivered.

In this chapter I focus on the "sins" of donors as a community in the hope it will enrich the ongoing discussion of reform of what might be called the "business" of development assistance. I deal with the shortcomings of the donor countries as providers of development assistance, leaving aside here their shortcomings in such other areas as trade, security, and international migration that also affect the developing countries. In referring to donors and the donor community, I refer both to bilateral donors and the World Bank, the International Monetary Fund (IMF), and other international institutions that provide credit at below-market rates to developing countries and whose policies and practices are heavily influenced by the rich countries.

After more than a decade of declines in total foreign aid, commitments on amounts of aid have increased in both the United States and Europe, so I refer only briefly to the inadequate quantity of aid. Instead I concentrate on problems with the quality of aid. The problems with aid quality matter tremendously because research indicates that they reduce considerably the effective value of the aid that is transferred, and in the most aid-dependent countries may well mean that the way the "business of aid" is conducted actually undermines those countries' long-term development prospects. The sins I discuss are, in the order in which I address them:

1. Impatience (with institution building)
2. Envy (collusion and coordination failure)
3. Ignorance (failure to evaluate)
4. Pride (failure to exit)
5. Sloth (pretending participation is sufficient for ownership)
6. Greed (unreliable as well as stingy transfers)
7. Foolishness (underfunding of global and regional public goods)

My purpose is not to condemn the donor "sins" but, by being frank and clear about them, to generate a broader conversation among donors, recipients, and the concerned nonofficial development community, about how they might be addressed. In that spirit, I suggest "fixes" for the sins of donors.

20.1 Deadly Sin 1: Impatience with Institution Building

Increasingly development theorists are emphasizing the importance of the "software" of an economy: the institutions, customs, laws, and social cohesion that help to create and sustain markets for growth and poverty reduction.[1] Good software can come in many forms, ranging from the European Union's independent central bank to the ingenious Chinese experiment with the village enterprise system.[2] In some societies, it can take less tangible forms, such as the longstanding trust that exists between private contracting Chinese parties that fueled growth in Malaysia. In other societies, it takes the form of legally enforceable property titles and contracts and an uncorrupted court system. Conversely, it is becoming increasingly clear that economies without the right institutions will falter. Poor supervision of banks can lead to financial crises, civil service systems without performance standards and rewards undermine public services, and abuses of property rights discourage the creation of small businesses.

So development can be thought of as a process of creating and sustaining the economic and political institutions that support equitable and sustainable growth. But what about the great majority of developing countries, where political and economic institutions are by definition (as they are developing countries) weak, yet where the poverty and lack of opportunity of millions of people cannot easily be ignored? These include not only the recently failed states such as Somalia, Afghanistan, Sierra Leone, and Liberia, but another fifty or more states that are "weak," "poorly performing" or "under stress."[3] Most of these are low-income (as opposed to middle-income) countries with large proportions of poor people—not surprising, since by definition, they lack the institutions critical to ensuring sustainable growth.

In the case of failed states, the donors have not generally had patience for the long-term challenge of building new institutions. The example of Haiti, where the donors entered in the mid-1990s with the return of Jean-Bertrand Aristide, only to exit within a few years, and have now reentered, is not encouraging.[4] Nor is the current situation in Afghanistan, where donors are not meeting their pledges of assistance. The evidence is that external financing surges in the first year or two after resolution of a conflict, but then tails off just when it might better be absorbed as institutions begin to take hold.[5] One problem is that aid is budgeted annually in the donor countries, while nation building takes predictable and continuous support over many years. In addition, nation building requires spending on high-risk programs such as police and security assistance, the immediate benefits of which are less visible and less attractive politically than humanitarian assistance or reconstruction of infrastructure.[6]

Even less defensible is the limited success of donors over the past three and more decades in supporting institutional development in the many more countries that are not or have not "failed" but are now variously labeled as weak or poorly performing. They are in what might be called the gray zone, with functioning governments but gaps in their legitimacy, their capacity, or their ability to maintain security.[7] In these generally aid-dependent countries (where aid constitutes more than 5 percent of GDP and finances as much as 50 percent of all government spending), donors face the dilemma that aid inflows, including through nongovernmental organizations (NGOs), drive up the demand for local skilled people, often competing with the beleaguered government itself; in these settings, aid may be counterproductive, undermining rather than strengthening public institutions.[8]

Consider examples of how donor impatience avoids and even undermines the challenge of building institutions.

Impatience for "results" has led to programs and projects in which monitoring focuses on visible short-run inputs (such as purchase of goods and issuing of contracts) and sometimes intermediate outcomes (such as an increase in government spending on social programs). In the best but rare cases, the emphasis is on actual results that can be attributed to new programs or inputs financed or inspired by a donor, such as a reduction in infant mortality, an increase in what students are learning in school, or a decline in the cost of transportation due to an adequately maintained road. In general, however, impatience for results leads to reluctance to invest over the long term (and outside the confines of donor-sponsored programs and projects) in local capacity to do budgeting, personnel management, auditing, accounting, and other nuts-and-bolts functions—which require and reinforce institutions but do not yield obvious immediate results.

Impatience to disburse money and see something happen precludes attention to the fundamental institutional problems, such as political patronage influencing teacher placement in the case of education programs or vested interests preventing banking sector or judicial sector reforms.[9] Part of the problem is that bilateral donors work from annual budgeted amounts by their legislatures and fear that their inability to spend down authorized amounts will be judged as their own ineffectiveness or poor planning. Even the World Bank and the other multilaterals face pressures to meet annual disbursement goals.

Consider the persistence of project implementation units (PIUs). In their impatience to implement "their" projects, donors continue to constitute special units outside the recipient country governments as a mechanism to bypass the bureaucratic, salary, and other constraints of recipient governments. Research shows that hoped-for better (or faster) results do not outweigh salary distortions and the opportunity cost of failing to ensure that projects and programs are ultimately incorporated into the government's own budgeting, staffing, and other institutional arrangement that provide for continuity.[10]

Impatience for policy change leads donors and official creditors to abstract from the political constraints reformers face in their own governments, sometimes undermining the efforts of reformers rather than supporting them. Willful naiveté about political reality may help explain why many structural adjustment programs supported by the IMF and the World Bank, and endorsed by the larger donor community, have failed to generate growth (Easterly 2002a).[11] In the worst cases, impatience leads to waivers of conditionality altogether, eliding the problem of institutions; the repeated waivers of conditionality regarding taxation of agricultural land (resisted fiercely by large landholders) in World Bank and IMF adjustment loans to Pakistan throughout the 1980s and 1990s are a good illustration.[12]

Institution building has to be local to respond creatively to local constraints and opportunities. Donors can provide financial encouragement for countries to address what Rodrik calls "first-order economic principles" or "functions" such as protection of property rights, appropriate incentives, and sound money.[13] But they have generally failed when they have pushed specific institutional packages for carrying out those functions. The judicial system, the parliamentary rules, the financing of health care that work in one country may not work in another. The failures have inspired the new emphasis of donors on recipient country ownership of their own reform programs, an issue I return to below.

20.1.1 Some Donor Efforts

In principle, the more "selective" approach to country support embodied in the Millennium Challenge Account (MCA), and the Country Policy and Institutional Assessment (CPIA) of the World Bank creates an incentive for countries in the gray zone to climb the ladder toward first-order economic and political principles without dictating the institutional form for doing so.[14] If fully transparent, these measures would catalyze local civil society or legislative or private business pressures for the changes needed to bring greater external assistance, which may be also key to creating or strengthening critical institutions. But in neither case is it clear that countries have much leverage on use of resources, nor are the measures as transparent as they could be (tables 20.1, 20.2).[15]

Also on the positive side, donors are moving in the direction of providing large inflows of budget support (including in the form of debt relief) and sector-wide support for relatively good performers. Time will tell whether donors remain patient with the risk that countries' "performance" will not be sustained or that "results" will be limited in the short run.

20.1.2 A Real Donor Fix?

But the challenge remains how to help the many developing countries with limited institutional capacity and thus limited ability to absorb large infusions of external aid.

In today's good performers, the use of new delivery mechanisms that are more accordion-like would make sense. These would allow small initial transfers but build in predictable and automatic increases tied to transparent indicators of increasing absorption capacity. The current seven-year and longer projects supported by the development banks are reasonably good examples. But the banks want to meet disbursement schedules and disburse "on time," when patience to wait out periods of poor performance would ultimately be more effective and less wasteful. Grants to nongovernment groups also make sense, particularly to support the advocacy and training that might create healthy pressure on government to adhere to first principles. An example would be support for groups demanding election reform or campaigning for freedom of the press. And grants to individuals for long-term education and training at

Table 20.1
Qualifying (or not) for the MCA

	Countries eligible to apply for MCA assistance for FY2004	CPIA ranking by quintile, 2002
Countries eliminated from the MCA by the corruption criteria		
Albania	—	2
Bangladesh	—	2
Malawi	—	3
Moldova	—	3
Mozambique	Mozambique	3
Missed MCA by one indicator (out of 16)		
Benin	Benin	2
Burkina Faso	—	2
Georgia	Georgia	4
India	—	1
Mali	Mali	2
Mauritania	—	1
São Tome and Principe	—	5
Togo	—	5
	Cape Verde	1
	Vanuatu	4

Note: The countries listed under each gap are a selection from a larger set of countries.
Sources: Radelet (2003) and International Development Association (2004).

Table 20.2
Inconsistency in country rankings

Countries in top two quintiles of the CPIA and with a security gap	Countries in top two quintiles of the CPIA and with a legitimacy gap	Countries in top two quintiles of the CPIA and with a capacity gap
Senegal	Vietnam	Bhutan
Sri Lanka	Pakistan	India
Uganda	Rwanda	Mauritania
Indonesia		Senegal
Nepal		Burkina Faso
Rwanda		Indonesia
		Mali
		Pakistan

Note: The security gap measures conflict in low-income countries, 1998–2003, and the level of conflict is used as a proxy for how effectively governments can preserve internal security.
Sources: International Development Association (2004); and "On the Brink. Weak States and U.S. National Security." A report of the Commission on Weak States and U.S. National Security. Sponsored by the Center for Global Development 2004.

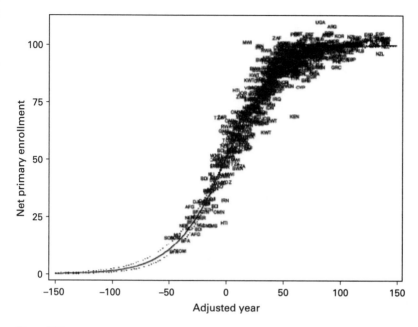

Figure 20.1
Transition in net primary enrollment, all countries, 1960–2000. *Notes*: "Adjusted years" are the elapsed time since 50 percent enrollment. Data points show country years, spaced quinquennially. *Source*: Clemens (2004).

home or abroad ought to be resuscitated; after the 1960s, they were abandoned by the U.S. and other aid programs.

Nevertheless, the real fix will come only when the donor community admits how fundamental the challenge is. If institution building in weak states is at the heart of development, then development assistance has to support the creation and strengthening of institutions—a long-term project that requires more predictable aid budgets (discussed below), patience, and the stomach for programs inherently lacking observable short-term performance indicators.

20.1.3 A Related Reflection on Donor Impatience and the Millennium Development Goals

On the positive side, the Millennium Development Goals allow for and invite a relatively long planning horizon. On the negative side, countries that by historical standards are succeeding beyond measure, such as Burkina Faso, Mali, and Uganda (see figure 20.1),[16] are currently characterized as "off-track" on such measures as education and infant mortality in UN reports (e.g., the Human Development Report of 2003, which uses a simple linear measure of

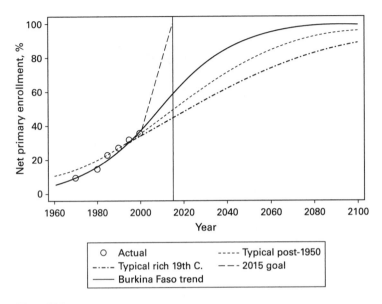

Figure 20.2
Burkina Faso: Unlikely to meet the school enrollment MDGs but performing strongly by historical standards. *Source*: Clemens, Kenny, and Moss (2004).

trends), and unless they can accelerate progress even more dramatically will not meet certain of the goals by 2015. For example, Burkina Faso is off-track from meeting the goal of universal primary schooling by 2015. The net primary enrollment rate was just 35 percent in 2000, and by one estimate (extrapolating from historical experience of more than 100 countries which takes the form of a logistics curve; see Clemens 2004) would reach "only" 59 percent by 2015. However, compared to the historical performance of today's rich countries, that rate of progress would be impressive. It would roughly match South Korea's rate of progress in the two decades prior to the Korean war, the fastest such increase on record,[17] but far outpace the progress of the United States, which, starting at Burkina Faso's current enrollment rate of 42 percent, took thirty years to increase its rate to 57 percent (figure 20.2).

Given our limited understanding of how to create and sustain the institutional setting that must complement additional donor transfers to achieve the goals in those countries, the MDGs create the risk that the donor community will succumb (even more) to the distortions that impatience creates. The MDGs should not become a lightning rod around which countries that have been unusually successful (compared to historical trends and given their income and institutional capacity) are, in 2015, characterized as "failures." Better that the MDGs become a lightning rod for ending donor impatience, so that additional donor transfers to the poorest countries can be more explicitly attuned to institution building. Under that arrangement, donors would have to exhibit patience when there are setbacks, and in some cases a willingness to hold back funds. That brings us to the second sin.

20.2 Deadly Sin 2: Envy (Collusion and Coordination Failure)

In contrast to the early days of development assistance, when, for example, the United States was the dominant donor (the only donor in the case of the Marshall Plan), recipient countries now cope with dozens of official creditors, bilateral donors, UN and other public agencies, and international NGOs. All of these in turn operate in dozens of countries (more than 100 in the case of Germany, the Netherlands, the United States, France, Japan, and the United Kingdom—see figure 20.3). In each country, donors also typically operate in many sectors with many projects. Managing their "own" projects increases donor visibility, and doing so in many countries maximizes donor countries' ability to leverage the diplomatic support of small countries for their objectives (and sometimes their candidates for high posts) in the United Nations and other international settings.

Over 2000–2002, the United States disbursed about $100 million of aid in Tanzania, financing fifty different projects at an average of just $2 million apiece (figure 20.4). With more than 1,300 projects altogether in that period, and an estimated 1,000 donor meetings a year and 2,400 reports to donors every quarter, Tanzania several years ago announced a four-month holiday during which it would not accept donor visits.[18]

The donors are neither competing nor collaborating. They are in effect colluding—something easy to do for suppliers in the absence of a competitive market.[19] The proliferation of colluding donors (i.e., the tendency of donors to operate in many countries and in many sectors within countries) creates what is now called fragmentation at the recipient country level, with the measure of fragmentation rising for each recipient country with the number of donors and the smaller these donors' aid shares. Donors are aware of the resulting high transactions costs recipients face (with many different missions, reporting requirements, and procurement rules, for example), and the associated managerial costs for the government (lack of focus and accountability and competition among sector ministries for external financing independent of overall government priorities).

The donor response has been to work on harmonizing procurement and reporting rules among themselves, which is certainly a step in the right direction. But the cost to recipients of donor fragmentation goes well beyond the

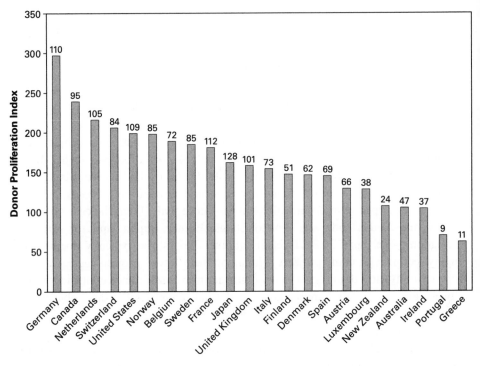

Figure 20.3
Index of donor proliferation, 1999–2000 average. *Note*: The donor proliferation index is the inverse of a Theil index, multiplied by 100 to avoid decimals. There is more donor proliferation (aid dispersion) when a donor's aid is allocated to a larger share of the total number of potential aid recipients and when each aid recipient gets a relatively equal share of the donor's total aid. A higher score indicates higher donor proliferation. The figures above the bars indicate the number of countries that received aid from each donor. *Source*: Acharya, de Lima and Moore (2004).

reduction in the monetary value of donor transfers of high transactions and managerial costs. With many donors competing with each other for visibility and quick success, donors are treating the limited public sector capacity (and the limited recurrent budget) of recipient countries as a common pool resource (Brautigam 2000), in effect undermining that resource rather than building it up. Donor proliferation and fragmentation (like impatience) are thus bad for recipient country institutions in the broadest sense of the word. Knack and Rahman (2004) cite "poaching" of local qualified staff by donors as an example and find that recipients suffering higher donor fragmentation show greater declines in a measure of bureaucratic quality over the period 1982–2001. Their finding is alarming; it suggests that not only do donors not know how to encourage building institutions in the low-income countries, they may actually have contributed to undermining those institutions.

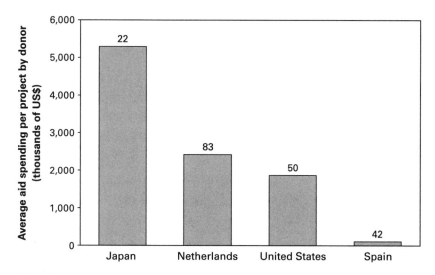

Figure 20.4
Tanzania: Average aid spending per project by donor, 2000–2002 average (thousands of US$).
Note: Numbers in columns indicate the number of projects each donor has in Tanzania. *Source*:
Center for Global Development and Foreign Policy (2005).

Ideally donors would form a common pool of funds[20] and then would compete with each other to finance the best proposals submitted by recipient countries, regions, and other entities. Contributions of donors to multilateral funds such as the World Bank are a step in that direction since they reduce fragmentation at the recipient country level. But they do not create the healthy competition among donors in "buying" good programs and projects that would put recipients in the driver's seat. Another option would be for donors to create market competition in the provision of aid. In a recent note prepared by the private sector group in the World Bank, the authors make the point that aid agencies can finance aid without providing aid.[21] Donors could "buy aid services" in a competitive market, generating competition among service delivery organizations, including in-country civil society and for-profit groups. To the extent some donors now do buy services, their purchases tend to be tied to home contractors, even if not officially, and that contracting rarely implies less of a presence of the aid bureaucracy itself in countries.

Regarding contributions to multilateral programs (figure 20.5), it is notable that the United States, the United Kingdom, and Japan, among the largest bilateral donors in absolute spending, give less as a proportion of their own total aid budgets, presumably because their ability to spread greater absolute resources across multilateral and their own bilateral programs secures them influence in both settings.

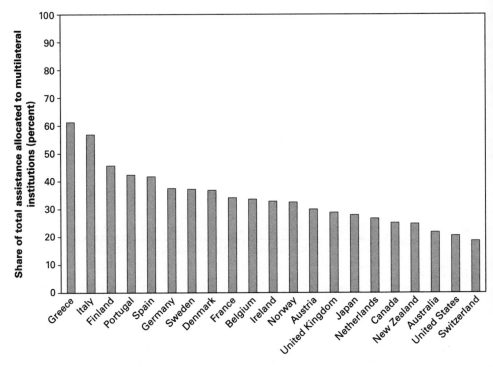

Figure 20.5
Share of each donor's total assistance allocated to multilateral institutions in 2002 (percent).
Source: OECD/DAC database (2004).

Donors are well aware of their collective sin of "envy." The Development Assistance Committee (DAC) of the Organization for Economic Cooperation and Development (OECD) is sponsoring pilot programs of donor harmonization in eight countries, in which many of the donors operating locally have agreed to pool their financing for general budget support or for major support to large sector programs such as education. The idea is to minimize the burden on recipient governments of multiple and different negotiations, procurement and reporting rules, and disbursement procedures. The heavily indebted poor countries (HIPC) initiative is by accident, if not by initial intention, an excellent example of donor collaboration in which donors as a group agreed on rules for eligibility and arrangements for implementation.[22] Donors have also recently sponsored and supported such "global" programs as the Global Fund to Fight AIDS, TB and Malaria, and the Fast Track Program for basic education.

Though the spirit is right behind these efforts, the jury is still out on whether they reduce the costs of donor fragmentation for recipients, including the poaching of qualified local staff and the insidious distraction of local officials from managing their own resources and priorities to coping with donors.

20.2.1 A Donor (Partial) Fix

Bilateral donors could contribute higher shares of their aid to multilateral programs; a gradual increase to 50 percent seems reasonable. More donors could try to concentrate their resources in fewer countries (the Nordics and the UK have announced countries where they will "concentrate" resources). Donors could agree on no more than one or two bilateral "lead" donors in recipient countries, with the others providing financing but leaving (say, over a five-year period) management of the dialogue, monitoring, reporting, and so on to one or the other lead donor.

Donors could make themselves accountable as a group for their commitments on coordination by giving recipient countries access to some of the commonly financed independent evaluation funds (see section 20.3), for periodic assessment and public reporting of each donor's cooperative behavior in their country. Until the evaluation fund is set up, the OECD DAC could make grants to policy groups in poor countries where many donors are active for this purpose, putting a priority on providing a high-level and public forum for reporting and discussion. Just as recipient countries have their behavior scrutinized and discussed in the boards of the IMF, the World Bank, and other international organizations, so might the behavior of donors be discussed.

Ultimately, however, the idea of solving the problem by greater coordination would ideally yield to much more fundamental change. The donors as a group should commission work on how they might, in practical ways, test the waters of a common pool and of "buying" execution of programs instead of direct provision with their own bureaucracies.

20.3 Deadly Sin 3: Ignorance (Failure to Evaluate)

Official and private agencies that develop and manage development assistance programs hesitate, with some justification, to advertise the limits of their craft. In the donor countries that finance assistance, suspicion that much such assistance is wasted runs high, and exposure of a program's current shortcomings could reduce its future funding.[23] Even if only a cover for lack of generosity, such suspicions are politically important. It is easier to limit than to expand foreign aid budgets, and in the interests of the latter, those who see and work with the urgent needs of people in poor countries have no obvious incentive to invest in long-term evaluation of what they do.

Moreover, rigorous evaluation of the impact of an intervention is costly. It is likely to seem a distraction for donor officials wanting to be sure programs get implemented and add to the burdens of the limited number of experienced local staff. For many development assistance programs, there is also the attribution problem. Without baseline information and a controlled experiment, it is difficult to attribute program success or failure to the programs themselves, as opposed to the environment in which they operate and the unpredictable shocks, positive and negative, that influence their effectiveness. Those who develop and manage assistance programs are cursed with their own intimate knowledge of this particular complication and are understandably wary of subjecting their work to the crude political criticism and limits on new resources for aid programs that transparent evaluation might trigger.[24]

That may explain why, in fifty years of postwar foreign aid, systematic evaluation of aid projects has been so rare.[25] Though the donors have financed billions of dollars worth of projects, few have had built into them the ingredients for a systematic evaluation. The exception is in the field of public health, where the tradition of epidemiological studies using controlled experiments led to such programs as that in Matlab Thana, Bangladesh, and the evaluations of bed nets to prevent malaria in Tanzania and of the onchocerciasis program in West Africa. But even these are exceptions that prove the apparent rule that it is more convenient and less risky politically to minimize serious evaluation.[26]

The multilateral banks do fund internal ex post assessments of the projects and programs they finance. But they face tremendous attribution problems, and their results and implications are rarely immediately internalized in new decisions, especially if they challenge conventional wisdom or raise awkward questions regarding donors' strategies.[27] Examples include the HIPC program of debt relief, in which even the second "enhanced" funding was (predictably, given the optimism of the original projections) not adequate to ensure debt sustainability of the recipient countries;[28] the continuing failure of the PRSP (Poverty Reduction Strategy Papers) approach to deliver donor coordination and country ownership;[29] and the structural adjustment programs of the IMF, the World Bank, and other donors discussed above. For all of these, it has generally been independent studies that have created the pressure for enhancements and adjustments.

The lack of emphasis on good evaluation has been immensely costly. In the absence of timely, credible, and independent evaluation, many aid dollars have been misdirected. It took more than a decade, for example, before the IMF "discovered" the repeatedly waived conditionality of its often failed adjustment programs in poor countries—and only then when the multilateral debt of the poorest countries had become so high that the IMF and World Bank were pressed into what appeared to be "defensive lending."[30]

20.3.1 A Donor Fix: An Independent Evaluation Fund

Evaluation is critical to the effective use of hoped-for increased donor transfers to help poor countries meet the Millennium Development Goals.[31] The critical ingredients for evaluation of development assistance are that it be independent, collectively agreed, and financed by a minimum set of the large multilateral creditors and bilateral donors.

Independent evaluation of the effectiveness of the World Bank and other multilaterals has been called for by groups on the left, right, and center, including in the past few years a commission of the Overseas Development Council, the Meltzer Commission, and a commission of the Carnegie Endowment.[32] Donors could finance an independent entity, which would in turn finance evaluation of selected donor-financed programs. Financing could be provided in the form of a small tax on each donor's total annual disbursements. A tax of 0.05 percent on $60 billion a year would generate $30 million for evaluation— a large amount given that spending would complement, not substitute for, existing internal evaluation programs.

A collective decision, once agreed, would help lock in donor agencies to the good behavior of more and better evaluation, perhaps partly insulating specific programs from the political pressures associated with initial negative evaluation findings, which the agencies justifiably fear. It would allow much more rapid and less costly adjustment when findings are negative, minimizing the risk of prolonging misguided approaches, which in the end may come back anyway to harm development assistance efforts politically and have high opportunity costs in forgone well-being of the poor. In addition, the visible independence of evaluation results that are good would build the political case for increased financing.

To minimize the risk of creating another bureaucracy, an ex ante "fee" or "tax" on disbursements could be channeled to an entity that would periodically commission third-party independent studies. A minimum set of the large donors—at least four or five—would have to participate to insulate the entity from the natural pressures that funding from only one or two donors or agencies would create and to allow studies across countries and types of programs and donor modalities.

20.4 Deadly Sin 4: Pride (Failure to Exit)

The impatience of donors is accompanied, ironically, by an inability and unwillingness to exit from programs and countries where their aid is not helping. By "exit" in this context, I do not mean withdrawing from continuing engagement through dialogue, technical advice, and even small transfers for training and technical assistance. I mean stopping large financial transfers, the benefits of which are reliant on adequate local conditions. (Education abroad could be continued, for example.)

Impatience and inability to exit are not inconsistent. Impatience to spend money, even badly, is unfortunately fully consistent with an inability to stop big spending while remaining engaged. Pride (and bureaucratic politics, including the coordination failures among donors discussed above) has generally precluded exit as a way to minimize waste.[33] In recipient countries in the gray zone, where there is a reasonable but not high expectation of adequate performance, the donors, once committed, tend to let misguided optimism (and an enlightened commitment to "do something" for the reform-minded minister of agriculture or health or finance struggling in a weak or corrupt system) trump good judgment.

A telling example of the reluctance to exit is the repeated rounds of unsuccessful adjustment loans of the IMF, the World Bank, and in most countries a regional development bank to the twenty countries with the most adjustment loans over the twenty-year period 1980 to 1999. Over that period, Côte d'Ivoire, Ghana, and Argentina had twenty-six to thirty adjustment loans each, and Senegal, Uganda, Mexico, Morocco, and Pakistan had twenty to twenty-five each (table 20.3).[34] Perhaps some of those countries would have reformed even less or grown even less without the loans. But Easterly (2002a) finds no evidence of any effects of the programs these loans supported on policy change or on growth. The implication, as he notes, is that "new loans had to be given because earlier loans were not effective." That is also the unpleasant implication of the accumulated debt to the multilateral creditors of low-income countries that failed to grow yet continued to receive loans in the 1990s that they were unable to service; these eventually entered the HIPC program.[35] Other evidence on failure of the creditors to exit is summarized in the 2002 report of the IMF's Independent Evaluation Office on prolonged lending, defined

Table 20.3
Number of adjustment loans to the twenty countries with most adjustment loans, 1980–1999

14–19 loans	Niger, Zambia, Madagascar, Togo, Malawi, Mali, Mauritania, Kenya, Bolivia, Philippines, Jamaica, Bangladesh
20–25 loans	Senegal, Uganda, Mexico, Morocco, Pakistan
26–30 loans	Côte d'Ivoire, Ghana, Argentina

Notes: These are IMF and World Bank adjustment loans. The average number of adjustment loans for these countries over the period is nineteen compared to the average of seven for all developing countries. Of these countries, only Bangladesh, Pakistan, and Uganda achieved annual per capita growth rates above 2 percent over the period from their first adjustment loan to 1999.
Source: Easterly (2002a).

as lending to countries that have been under IMF arrangements for at least seven years out of any ten. Along the same lines is evidence on repeated waivers of conditionality with cancellation and new loans with new promises, reported in Bird, Hussain, and Joyce (2004) and Joyce (2005).

20.4.1 A Donor Fix

Engagement is possible without large flows of assistance. The threat of exit need not imply an unwillingness to finance small programs that focus on institutional support over the long haul and to continue engaging through external training programs and policy dialogue. Donors ought to be prepared more often to exit from support to governments that fail to meet commitments on structural reforms and on projects needed to ensure that growth is pro-poor. At the same time, withdrawal of financial support need not be seen as punishment for bad behavior, but as a reasonable decision to limit the extent to which donor aid is not generating any reasonable return. It makes sense even when governments are willing but unable to use money well, because of internal political constraints or temporarily insufficient absorptive capacity.

Work in the development assistance demands a can-do attitude. That leads structurally to enlightened but misguided optimism that success is always just around the corner. A structural shift is needed. Many more programs that involve large transfers could build in exit as the natural default, setting conditions for continuing support, for example, that the recipient is meeting preagreed benchmarks. In some cases, that might mean more emphasis on monitoring government performance in such areas as press freedom, protection of property, and microreforms to reduce patronage.[36] In other cases, it might simply mean halting disbursements to a particular sector or project unless and until agreed performance benchmarks are met.

20.5 Deadly Sin 5: Sloth (Pretending "Participation" Is Sufficient for "Ownership")

It took too long, but experience and empirical analysis led to the recognition in the 1990s that the conditionality typically included in World Bank and IMF loans (and often implicitly or explicitly followed by other official creditors and donors) was ineffective.[37] Good policy apparently cannot be imposed or even encouraged by bribelike transfers. Good policy, as the discussion of institutions above suggests, seems to be the outcome, at least partially, of the "software" of a society, which in turn is a function of history, geography, customs, and other factors that, though malleable in the long run, are difficult to change in the short run. Apparently a country's "ownership" of a reform agenda is the key to implementation of reforms, and not the apparent enforcement of implementation through loan conditions.

But that discovery led to a new kind of simplification (in practice, if not in conception): that "participation" of citizens through civil society groups is sufficient to secure "ownership." The misguided imposition of policy conditions morphed into the misguided imposition of "participation." In principle, the logic of widespread participation in setting a reform agenda makes sense. The theory is that reforms that are not politically feasible will not endure, even if they are implemented (itself unlikely). The expectation of economic actors that reforms will not endure in turn undermines the credibility of promised reforms and thus their potentially positive effects on investment and growth.

But the prevailing approach to participation, as demanded by donors, has been narrow and apolitical. In practical terms, it has relied mostly on engagement of civil society groups in discussions of proposed government programs (including the PRSPs). In this form, it overlooks the deeper challenge of creating or strengthening durable political mechanisms for resolving disputes and trade-offs. Members of minority groups and the truly poor are often excluded from apparently open discussions, reflecting the reality that participatory efforts alone are unlikely to alter the prevailing distribution of power and influence.[38] Democratic governments, particularly in Latin America, argue that emphasis on civil society, especially where large inflows of external funds were concerned, undermines the role of their own legislatures and local governments in the give and take of political decision making about economic issues.

It would be wrong to condemn the idea of greater participation in itself. But equally it would be wrong to delude oneself that participation creates or indicates political and social ownership of major reforms.

Moreover, in the case of the IMF and the World Bank, the initial and principal purveyors of conditionality, ownership of country reforms at the country level is made more difficult by the lack of real ownership of the institutions' own policies and practices. Dervis (2005) explains the difficulty of pushing through IMF-supported reforms during Turkey's financial crisis of 2000–2001 because reforms "demanded" by the IMF were seen as representing the interests of foreign banks and businesses. The problem is obvious and analogous to that at the country level: though developing countries "participate" in the governance of these institutions, they cannot be assumed to "own" the institutions' overall policy approach, given their limited voting shares and limited influence in choosing the leadership of these institutions. Budget decisions and decisions regarding use of net income are different in the Inter-American Development Bank, where borrowers have more votes, more influence, and more ownership (see table 20.4).[39]

Table 20.4
Who "owns" IFI policies?

| | Voting share (%) | | | | Directors | | | | | |
	United States	Other G-7	Other non-borrowers	Developing-country borrowers	United States	Other G-7	Other non-borrowers	Developing-country borrowers	Total	President
IMF	17.1	28.2	16.7	38	1	6	6	11	24	Nonborrower
WB	16.4	26.6	18.2	38.8	1	6	7	10	24	Nonborrower
IADB	30	15.7	4.3	50	1	4	0	9	14	Borrower
AFDB	6.6	21	12.4	60	1	4	1	12	18	Borrower
ASDB	13	27.4	14.6	45	1	4	1	6	12	Nonborrower
EBRD	10.1	46.5	30.2	13.2	1	6	12	4	23	Nonborrower

Note: IMF is the International Monetary Fund. WB is the World Bank. IADB is the Inter-American Development Bank. AFDB is the African Development Bank. ASDB is the Asian Development Bank. EBRD is the European Bank for Reconstruction and Development.
Source: Birdsall (2006).

Table 20.5
One option: Assess the politics and institutions of pro-poor growth

	Stakeholder Analysis	Institutional Analysis
Trend Extrapolation	Reforms under way Decision-making style Attribution of agency	Institutional mapping Veto point analysis Capacity assessment
Impact Analysis	Impact on balance of power	Impact on institutional setup

Source: IEO (2002).

20.5.1   A Donor Fix

Donors could experiment with the "foundation" approach,[40] under which the donor and financier would respond to proposals from governments (and non-government groups) rather than themselves proposing and shaping programs. This passive stance assumes the proposer "owns" the program to be financed; it is one currently used by the Global Fund to Fight Aids, TB and Malaria and is to be used by the U.S. Millennium Challenge Corporation (at least that is the idea). It is probably not, however, a full solution to a complex problem.

What is more fundamental is for donors, and particularly the IMF and the multilateral banks, to acknowledge that the reforms they advocate are hard to do precisely because they violate the interests of powerful groups and have no active political constituency. Pro-poor reforms are politically tough to implement. That is the bottom line. Even those that are "owned" by reform-minded ministers or have been discussed with civil society groups will not necessarily get implemented. That implies that donors need to engage, before committing resources, in assessment of the interests of politically powerful stakeholders, the record of existing governments on difficult reforms, and its vulnerability to an ouster if it takes certain steps (see table 20.5). Promises and participation are not an adequate substitute for political ownership and are no better than traditional conditionality as guarantees of change.

Ultimately developing countries are more likely to be pushed along internally in the direction of pro-poor reforms and complementary market policies only when their own domestic political imperatives support it and when some of the global institutions in which they "participate" are also more fully "owned" by them.

20.6   Deadly Sin 6: Greed (Unreliable as Well as Stingy Transfers)

It is odd to accuse donors of stinginess, since by definition they are providing resources voluntarily and any amount might be viewed as generous. Yet given the claims of "partnership" (for example, in the context of the Millennium Development Goals), the donors as a group can be called "stingy," at least relative to their commitments.[41] Only Denmark, Norway, Sweden, and the Netherlands have met the goal of aid as a share of GDP of 0.7 percent to which all committed at Monterrey, Mexico (confirming even earlier commitments), in 2002.[42]

At an average of about 0.3 percent of donor GDP, development assistance spending by the rich countries is extraordinarily low compared to internal transfers. Most of the OECD countries spend at least 20 percent of GDP on transfers for investments in education, health, and other quasi–public goods meant to ensure reasonably equal opportunities for their own citizens independent of citizens' income, and for money and in-kind transfers of food, housing, and other goods and services as social insurance for families and to alleviate poverty. On the one hand, it is not surprising that internal assistance budgets are much larger than external ones. On the other hand, given increasing global interdependence, rising concern about failing states since the 9/11 attack, and the huge (hundred-fold) gap between average income in the richest compared to the poorest countries, a hundred-fold difference between domestic and overseas transfers suggests a stunning failure to adjust to a changed world.

Donors also tend to portray actual transfers as higher than they are. Of an estimated $20 billion reported by bilateral donors as disbursements to the low-income countries in 2002, after subtracting about $7 billion for emergency aid and technical cooperation funds (spent mostly on donor contractors) and almost $3 billion in repayments of loans and interest, only 50 percent, or $10 billion, actually went to the low-income countries for direct support.[43]

From the point of view of those managing the economies of low-income countries, as problematic as low absolute amounts is that donors as a group are unreliable. At the country level, donor financing has been volatile, unpredictable, and, in the more aid-dependent countries, procyclical—declining at times when countries need the external infusion most, for example, because of a commodity prices shock (and increasing procyclically when a country's own tax revenues are growing).[44]

Lack of reliability for the recipient country is the result of two factors. First, changes in the foreign aid totals of different donors and in the objectives of the donors as a group affect financing for particular countries and programs. The diversion of funds of large donors for political purposes to one or another country reduces amounts available to other countries and programs. Financing for Iraq (in the case of the United States) and for AIDS prevention and treatment are almost certainly reducing aggregate financing now for some countries and for other health and nonhealth programs. Changes in donor strategy also affect flows. Killick (2004) reports evidence that non-HIPC countries saw a reduction in their share of total donor assistance from 56 to 24 percent between 1998 and 2000, implying a virtually certain reduction in absolute flows for those countries when donors decided to provide debt relief for the most highly indebted countries. There is also evidence that the new aid initiatives of the United States, for the MCA program and for AIDS, are associated with reductions in absolute spending on long-standing programs managed by the U.S. Agency for International Development (USAID).[45]

Aside from these large shifts, aid inflows at the country level are uncertain because of the way the aid business operates, with actual disbursements at varying levels year-to-year below commitments and highly volatile. In the case of Malawi in the 1990s, aid inflows bounced dramatically up and down in the 1990s between 8 and 20 percent of GDP (Bulír and Hamann 2001). This would be the equivalent in the United States of quintupling the deficit in one year and then a year later absorbing a huge recession-like effect on jobs and incomes. In many countries in Africa, aid inflows exceed 10 percent of GDP, 50 percent of total revenues, and as much as 60 percent of total new investments.[46] In these settings, the volatility of aid is systematically greater than the volatility of tax revenues and clearly exacerbates the problem of economic instability— ironically creating challenges for economic management in the countries least able to cope financially because they are unable to borrow internally and because their fiscal and monetary institutions are beleaguered already.

The unreliability and lack of predictability of future donor flows reduces the value of current flows because responsible managers in developing countries cannot make the highest-return immediate use of external resources for new investment without assurance of continuing flows to finance the resulting recurrent costs. In many low-income countries, a decision to scale up teacher training or institute large new programs for treatment of AIDS cannot be made in the absence of predictable and reliable future donor financing of the resultant higher stream of salary and other costs over many years. Similarly the decision to build new rural roads will not be rational if the medium-term financing for maintenance, agricultural extension, and other services needed to allow farmers to exploit the resulting larger market cannot be ensured.

The cost of unreliability is not only in the volatility of existing flows and the effects on existing programs. The higher cost may be the complete absence of otherwise highly effective programs. An example is financing of research on vaccines against malaria and other tropical diseases. In the absence of an apparently profitable market since the victims of these diseases are mostly poor and reside in poor countries, pharmaceutical firms have no incentive to produce them. Even where pharmaceutical products exist, if they are used primarily in developing countries, they will be more expensive and less reliably available because of the absence of guaranteed donor financing for long-term purchase contracts.[47]

20.6.1 Donor Fixes?

On the amount of aid, there is some hope that the Monterrey promises will yield gradual increases—though still below what a truly global system demands not only to respond to the moral and humanitarian challenge of the poor but in the enlightened interests of the rich in an increasingly interdependent system. Atkinson (2003) discusses many other ideas that have been on the table in one form or another for some years, such as a Tobin tax on currency transactions and a global lottery. Gordon Brown, chancellor of the exchequer of the UK, has proposed creating a facility that could borrow on private markets now to ramp up available financing. A tiny tax on carbon emissions would raise billions for foreign assistance and have the additional benefit of possibly reducing those emissions. Birdsall and Williamson (2002) propose sale or revaluation of IMF gold to provide insurance-like coverage to HIPC countries subject to external shocks. Soros (2002) proposes the creation of new special drawing rights (SDRs) at the IMF with the resulting finances targeted to the poor countries.

Addressing the problem of unpredictable and volatile flows requires a bigger step away from business as usual. The proposal of Gordon Brown of the UK for an international financing facility, to borrow from private markets and fund the resulting debt using future donor allocations, is meant to double the annual amount of financing immediately. Its greater benefit may be that it creates a mechanism that could also make future flows more reliable and predictable, since donors could borrow in the near term and commit to maintain flows to particular countries or programs independent of subsequent uncertain legislative approvals.[48] Essentially the donor community needs to develop new trust or endowment-type instruments for longer-term, more patient, and more predictable funding of development assistance. The real fix to the lack of predictability almost certainly has to come as the result of this sort of larger breakthrough in the overall aid architecture.

20.7 Deadly Sin 7: Foolishness (Underfunding of Global and Regional Public Goods)

Donors direct almost all of their resources to individual recipient countries, as opposed to regional groupings and global public goods.[49] Financing for global public goods has grown in the past decade, primarily in response to the pressures of environmental groups in the rich countries. In the case of global public goods, rich countries have an evident self-interest, though much of the spending benefits developing countries as well. But global public goods that would primarily benefit developing countries are almost surely underfunded. That includes tropical agricultural research given its extraordinarily high past returns relative to most country programs and projects, and research on malaria and AIDS vaccines.[50]

Regional public goods have received even less attention. Of the approximately $60 billion in development aid disbursed in 2002, a rough guess would be that at most $1 billion to $2 billion was spent on multicountry programs and projects in the developing world, such as harmonization of stock markets in Africa, or development of a shared electricity grid in Central America, or multi-country roads and watersheds in Asia (table 20.6).[51] The rest was channeled through agreements with national governments of individual countries in what might be called conventional country-focused assistance. The World Bank and the regional banks, as well as the UN agencies, operate mostly at the country recipient level—in the case of the banks, in part because their principal instrument is the country loan.

There has been virtually no analysis of the potential returns to greater investments in regional and transnational or multicountry public and quasi-public goods. I argue elsewhere, however, that as is the case with all public goods (the benefits of which cannot be confined to those who finance them), regional public and quasi-public goods are underfunded—by countries that would potentially benefit from them and by donors concerned with increasing growth and poverty reduction in those countries and their neighbors.[52] Lost opportunities for high-return investments are most obvious for sub-Saharan Africa, where the "internal" market (all of sub-Saharan Africa, including South Africa) is only about the size of the economy of Chicago. That is sufficient to support specialization and scale investments were it fully integrated into a single market. But of course it is not. Poor roads and other infrastructure, bureaucratic delays and corruption in customs, and absence of network externalities in sea and air transport all contribute to high border costs. And the large number of countries ensures that there are many of these costly borders.

If the returns to regional investments are potentially high, why are those investments not made? Regional investments are likely to be underfunded (compared to some unknown optimum, which we do not know, given the difficulty of estimating benefits of investments in public goods in general) by developing-country governments for two reasons: recipient countries' own domestic political systems will be more responsive to social demands for country-specific public goods such as universal primary education, roads, and public

Table 20.6
Donor commitments to regional programs and projects for selected multilateral and bilateral donors, 2002

	Regional public goods commitments	
	By each donor (millions of US$)	As share of total ODA commitments by each donor (percent)
World Bank[a]	n/a	n/a
African Development Bank	30	1.2
Inter-American Development Bank[b]	20	0.4
Asian Development Bank[c]	45	0.7
European Bank for Reconstruction and Development[d]	99	2.7
UNDP[e]	55	2.1
WHO[f]	138	7.1
United States[g]	303	2.4
United Kingdom[g]	98	2.6
Total	788	2.1

Notes: To the extent possible, commitments shown are for programs and projects that were managed by a regional organization such as the West African Monetary Union or the Central American Development Bank, regardless of the source. Commitments are from sources where they are probably shown in nominal terms.
[a] The annual reports of the Inter-American Development Bank (Table IV. Yearly and Cumulative Loans and Guarantees), The African Development Bank (Annex II-7 Bank Group Loan and Grant Approvals by Country), the European Bank for Reconstruction and Development (Projects signed in 2002 section), and the Asian Development Bank (Public and Private Sector Loan Approvals by Country) all include a line item showing annual commitments to regional programs and projects. The World Bank Annual Report does not seem to provide a comparable line item.
[b] The Inter-American Development Bank also reports regional disbursements in addition to regional commitments. In 2002, regional disbursements were $67 million. In the past, IDB has also made concessional loans to the Central American Bank for Economic Integration and to other subregional development banks.
[c] The Asian Development Bank's regional commitments reflect one project only: the Trade Finance Facilitation Program.
[d] This is the capital of six private equity or debt funds established to invest in or lend to private firms across two or more countries; whether these funds should be counted as multicountry programs as defined here is not entirely clear.
[e] The UNDP figure is for 2001. The UNDP also granted an additional $9.5 million for interregional and global projects that year and $16 million total for intercountry programs in 2000.
[f] The WHO figure is for 1998–1999. The same amount was spent in 1996–1997.
[g] These figures are probably inflated since they are figures for all "unspecified funds" going to a region and are likely to include funds that in fact went to individual countries.
Source: Birdsall (2004).

health, and there are substantial coordination problems associated with co-operating with other governments. Donors, in turn, face two problems. To the extent donors respond to the explicit immediate interests of recipient governments, they will see a trade-off between encouraging investment in regional public goods and institutions and recipient "ownership," though this may just underline the risks of too narrow a concept of country "ownership." The donor focus on ownership and greater harmonization does not address the institutional problem that recipient countries face in coordinating among themselves.

Second, the funding of regional programs is complicated for donors. Some of the fault lies with developing countries that have limited political incentives to cooperate. For the multilateral banks, there is the additional problem of lack of grant funds. Loan commitments to groups of recipient countries are difficult to make since they would require a clear allocation of repayment and other legal obligations to each borrower, which is difficult to negotiate. (Thus, for the banks, the country loan as an instrument has dictated the logic of organizing operational staff and budgets into country teams with country-based allocations for lending.) Bilateral donors have grant resources but need a single interlocutor who can be held accountable—and their aid recipients would rather put grants they can get into their own country programs. Bilateral donors also face the risk of a weak link country in the chain of effectiveness. For example, a major program with SADC (the Southern African Development Community) could be hurt if donors felt the need to cut off all aid to Zimbabwe.

In short, global public goods that would primarily benefit developing countries are almost surely underfunded by donors. The case is even stronger for regional public goods given the absence of any self-interest on the part of donors and the additional costs and risks compared with country-focused assistance.

20.7.1 A Donor Fix?

The donor community should put the challenge of greater support for global and regional programs on the table for discussion.[53] As a start, the Development Assistance Committee of the OECD could establish common reporting requirements for the bilateral donors and multilateral creditors on their support for regional programs and projects. This would establish the minimum of information needed for even cursory assessment of the relative cost-effectiveness of regional institutions and programs.

Some donors could take responsibility for special emphasis on the strengthening of regional institutions; this seems particularly important for sub-Saharan Africa, where France and the UK might take a greater lead. The increasing presence of the Economic Commission for Africa and the formation of Nepad are good signs of progress with African ownership of its development challenges as a region; donors ought to be unusually receptive to these African initiatives. Multicountry physical infrastructure projects should be a priority, despite the fact they may take longer to design and organize and may not seem to have the immediate ownership or easily measurable effects in relation to the Millennium Development Goals. The incipient demand is huge, yet not reflected in the rhetoric of donors or much considered in PRSPs, which tend to focus heavily on increased social spending. In the trade area, where so much could be done to reduce the high costs of borders, there seems little question that African policymakers would benefit from clear incentives to consolidate what are now at least a dozen trade agreements within the region, all but three of which have no more than two or three members.

Finally, the constraint that the multilateral development banks face in actively supporting global and regional programs needs attention. What financing they have done has come from trust funds and from their highly limited grant funding. The donors could encourage more use of net income to finance these initiatives by giving the middle-income countries whose borrowing costs would be affected more influence in setting priorities for use of net income. This would make particular sense in the regional development banks. South Africa might push for such a pilot program of this type at the African Development Bank (except that it borrows so little from the hard window that its membership does not generate net income). Bilateral donors could also develop facilities that would finance guarantees for regional groups that were borrowing from the multilateral banks or the private market, or could subsidize the borrowing costs to individual countries participating in regional borrowings.

For donors, the fundamental challenge is not actually in the details of what or how to address support for regional and global public goods in the developing world. It is how to address their own lack of incentives to work actively in these areas.

20.8   A Summary of Donor Fixes

20.8.1   Deadly Sin 1: Impatience (with Institution Building)

This is the most central and fundamental challenge. A first step would be for the donor community to acknowledge its overall past failure and undertake a collective assessment of how to address that failure, in close and constant consultation with wise people from the developing countries. If it cannot be done collectively (for example, at the Development Assistance Committee of the OECD), leadership will have to be taken by a single large bilateral donor such as the United States or the United Kingdom.[54]

20.8.2   Deadly Sin 2: Envy (Collusion and Coordination Failures)

Minor fixes could include agreement of the bilateral donor governments to increase the portion of their total assistance spending that goes to multilateral institutions and programs, agreement to the concept of lead donors in highly aid-dependent countries, and the financing through DAC of grants to developing-country policy groups to report on in-country performance of the individual donors. Like impatience, however, this challenge is fundamental and may not yield to minor fixes. The major fix would be establishment of a true common pool of donor funds.

20.8.3   Deadly Sin 3: Ignorance (Failure to Evaluate)

A minimum number of major donors could make a collective agreement to self-finance a fully independent evaluation entity, which would in turn contract third-party evaluations of selected donor-financed projects and programs and of donor behaviors and modalities.

20.8.4   Deadly Sin 4: Pride (Failure to Exit)

New longer-term, more accordion-like instruments are needed that make exit (defined as stopping the flow of large transfers not as abandoning engagement through dialogue and advisory services) the default. Exit should be established as the norm, not as punishment or judgment, but as a natural response to signs that investments being financed will not yield adequate returns.

20.8.5   Deadly Sin 5: Sloth (Pretending Participation Is Sufficient for Ownership)

Donors need to end their apolitical approach to ownership and engage instead in assessment of the interests of politically powerful stakeholders, the record of existing governments on difficult reforms, and governments' vulnerability to an ouster if it takes certain steps. This is particularly critical in the case of pro-poor reforms, since they usually undermine powerful interests and have weak domestic constituencies. Ultimately it may be that only when developing-country recipients have more voice (and votes) in the major institutions will they assume real "ownership" of pro-poor economic and political reforms donors wish to support.

20.8.6   Deadly Sin 6: Greed (Unreliable as Well as Stingy Transfers)

Instruments that build in less volatile and more predictable financing are needed, as well as larger aid budgets. New ideas are on the table, in part impelled by the commitments rich countries made in the context of the MDGs.

But they are more visible with respect to the amount of aid than with respect to its predictability; the latter requires more radical rethinking of current instruments and practices.

20.8.7 Deadly Sin 7: Foolishness (Underfunding of Global and Regional Public Goods)

Financing of global and regional public goods needs a big push. The case for regional programs in Africa is especially obvious; a donor champion—probably the British or the French who could push for a revamping of the singular country focus that now prevails—is needed. Grant funds at the multilateral banks would create internal incentives for supporting global and regional investments; they could be supported in part by transfers of net income from the hard windows of the banks, where the middle-income countries whose borrowing costs were affected given more control over the use of those resources.

20.9 Conclusion

Perhaps it is worth concluding with a rephrasing of some of my introductory language. My purpose has not been to condemn the donor "sins" (since in this area shame and blame are not likely to work anyway) but to generate a broader, more ambitious conversation among all interested parties. Some "sins," such as the tying of aid to a donor's own services and goods, are already on the reform agenda of the official community, and I have not discussed them here. Instead I have tried to focus on shortcomings of the business of aid on which new research has or could shed light and which have not yet been adequately or explicitly incorporated into the donor community's reform agenda. These shortcomings of the business matter tremendously, especially in the context that the focus on achieving the MDGs by 2015 has brought. That is because research shows that they reduce considerably the effective value of the aid that is transferred, and in the most aid-dependent countries may even mean that the business of aid actually undermines those countries' long-term development prospects.

Acknowledgments

I am enormously grateful to Gunilla Pettersson for her many suggestions on content and concepts and for timely and cheerful research assistance. I thank Owen Barder, Stijn Claessens, Peter Isard, Charles Kenny, Steven Knack,

Maureen Lewis, Mick Moore, David Roodman, and participants in seminars at the Operations Evaluation Department at the World Bank and at the Bangladesh Economics Association for their comments on an earlier draft.

Notes

1. A good example is Acemoglu, Johnson, and Robinson (2004). See also North (1990).

2. Rodrik (2003) cites other examples from China to help explain its success outside the boundaries of conventional wisdom.

3. The terms are used in, respectively, Commission on Weak and Failing States, 2004; DAC (2001), and World Bank (2002).

4. Weinstein (2004) argues that in some cases, it may be better for the international community to hold off on intervening before countries in conflict have struggled politically toward a new internal equilibrium. Here I am discussing impatience, however, not with an initial intervention, where the trade-off with saving lives may be particularly difficult, but with postconflict development assistance.

5. Collier and Hoeffler (2002).

6. Greater support for police and other forms of security assistance is included among the recommendations in the report of the Commission on Weak States and U.S. National Security (2004). See Center for Global Development (2004).

7. See note 3 above.

8. See Moss, Pettersson, and van de Walle (2005); Rajan and Subramanian (2005); and Birdsall (2007).

9. For all its value, even the recent emphasis of the World Bank and its partners on expenditure monitoring in the context of PRSP programs does not in itself go to the heart of the problem.

10. See World Bank (2004, 205–206) for examples from Bangladesh and elsewhere and citations to relevant research.

11. See also chart 20.2 from Easterly (2002a).

12. For an excellent if depressing analysis of prolonged lending by the IMF, including the story in Pakistan, see Internal Evaluations Office (2002).

13. See, for example, Rodrik (2003, 2004). See also Hausmann and Rodrik (2002).

14. Radelet (2004a) describes the MCA criteria and analyzes their implications for country eligibility.

15. The MCA criteria are transparent, though not the final country choices of the U.S. government (see Radelet, Lucas, and Bhavnani 2004). The CPIA is not transparent; the exact quantitative basis for countries' scores is not published, only the quintile in which each country falls. The CPIA incorporates a partial measure of "institutions." The difficulty of measuring "institutions" may explain why there is some inconsistency in the ranking of developing countries across different measures. For example, several countries eliminated from the MCA due to the corruption criterion or insufficiently high rankings on other criteria are in the first or second highest quintile of the CPIA measure (Bangladesh, Albania, Burkina Faso, Mauritania). And of countries ranking in the top two quintiles of the CPIA measure, Vietnam and Pakistan are in the bottom two quintiles of "legitimacy." Senegal, Mauritania, Burkina Faso, and Mali, among others, are in the bottom two quintiles of "capacity" (see tables 20.1 and 20.2). In its report on weak states and U.S. national security, the Center for Global Development (2004) put countries into quintiles of "legitimacy" based on the Kaufman, Kraay, and Zoido-Lobaton (2002) measure of "voice and accountability," and quintiles of "capacity" based on the immunization rate.

16. See Clemens (2004) on education and Clemens, Kenny, and Moss (2004) on education, infant mortality and other goals.

17. Personal correspondence with Michael Clemens, July 31, 2007, and based on the assumption that the rate of increase in net enrollment in Korea (data for which are not available) tracked roughly the apparent rate of increase in gross enrollment in that decade.

18. Birdsall and Deese (2004) use this example to introduce an essay on the current U.S. foreign aid program, which is largely unilateral in conception and implementation.

19. Thus, Easterly (2002b) labels the system a cartel of good intentions. "Once a collusive agreement (among donors) is in place, bureaucracies will not cheat on the agreement by supplying a larger quantity of foreign aid services at a lower price" (10). Collusion also allows sharing the blame of failures, which dictates minimal effort at evaluation.

20. Kanbur and Sandler with Morrison (1999) define and elaborate on the idea of a common pool.

21. Harford, Hadjimichael, and Klein (2004).

22. Birdsall and Deese (2004) point out that one benefit of donor collaboration on the HIPC program is that the rules and transfers are somewhat less vulnerable to changes in the political environment within individual donor countries.

23. It is true that such suspicions seem less powerful in Western Europe than in the United States, Australia, and Canada. Various theories have been suggested to explain the persistent differences across donor countries in the amounts of public foreign aid. One is that where tolerance for income inequality varies across countries and that where such inequality is higher, it is associated with the view that people get what they deserve, and if they are poor in faraway places, perhaps that is all they deserve. The other is that the form of government in the United States, in which it is possible to have an opposition party controlling the legislative branch, is particularly unfriendly to foreign aid. See Lancaster (2007).

24. The official agencies do sponsor internal ex post assessment of the interventions they finance. The World Bank has, for example, its Independent Evaluation Group (formerly Operations Evaluations Department), as do the other multilateral banks and the bilateral aid agencies. The International Monetary Fund recently established the Independent Evaluation Office (IEO), though it took over fifty years before it felt the need to do so, finally responding to the pressure of civil society groups. These offices do a creditable job (the first studies of the IEO are impressive). However, their studies are subject to the review and comment not only of staff in the institutions but of the countries whose programs are often the subject of the evaluations. There is a natural process of minimizing the harshness of language, the awareness of which rebounds back to those undertaking these "evaluations."

25. As Pritchett (2002) suggests, sometimes it seems to "pay to be ignorant."

26. See Levine and the What Works Working Group, with Kinder (2004). This study, sponsored by the Health Policy Research Network of the Center for Global Development, was based on the seventeen (of many more) scaled-up health interventions in the past several decades that had adequate evaluations to be judged successful.

27. For an example, see Birdsall, Vaishnav, and Malik (2005) on the World Bank's decade of lending for poverty reduction in Pakistan.

28. Birdsall and Williamson (2002), Birdsall and Vaishnav (2004). For discussion and definitions, see Birdsall and Williamson (2002). For the conclusion that the HIPC II financing was not additional, see Killick (2004).

29. World Bank Operations Evaluation Department (2004). The OED report does not use the term *failure*, but the evidence it presents can be so interpreted.

30. Birdsall, Claessens, and Diwan (2004).

31. Following recommendations of a Center for Global Development Working Group (Levine et al. 2006), a new entity for evaluation of donor, foundation, and developing country-financed programs, the International Initiative for Independent Evaluation is being formed. Information available at www.cgdev.org/section/initiatives/_active/evalgap

32. Meltzer (2000); Sewell, Birdsall, and Morrison (2000); CEIP and IAD (2001).

33. The design of the MCA indirectly reflects the difficulty of exit; it limits the risk of failure by restricting large transfers to recipient countries where there is minimal risk of failure.

34. See Easterly (2002a).

35. Birdsall, Claessens, and Diwan (2003) show that low-income countries with high indebtedness to the multilateral creditors received new loans even if they scored poorly on the IDA measure of performance.

36. Using five-year contracts, exit as the default after five years is in effect being adopted by the Millennium Challenge Corporation in managing the MCA.

37. For example, see Collier et al. (1997) and Gunning (2000).

38. Christian Aid (2002).

39. See Birdsall 2005.

40. Van de Walle (2005) recommends this approach, while recognizing its dangers and its limits.

41. See Center for Global Development and Foreign Policy (2006) for information on how twenty-one rich countries ranked in 2004 on the "quantity" (as well as the quality) of aid.

42. In the 1969 Pearson report, official development assistance of 0.7 percent of GDP was agreed to as the objective. See Moss and Clemens (2005) for details.

43. United Nations Millennium Project (2004).

44. Bulír and Hamann (2003).

45. Bhavnani, Birdsall, and Shapiro (2004).

46. O'Connell and Soludo (1998).

47. Birdsall and Moss (2004).

48. In late November 2004, the UK announced it would support a scheme of guaranteed purchases of malaria and AIDS vaccines. For discussion of this kind of advanced market or pull mechanism, see Levine, Kremer, and Albright (2005) and Kremer and Glennerster (2004).

49. This section is taken mostly from Birdsall (2004) which includes sources and citations for the points made here.

50. The case for more donor spending on global public goods is especially compelling given the short-term problems of absorption capacity, which limits effective, institution-friendly donor spending in many poor countries. On agriculture see Evenson (1987). On vaccines see Levine, Kremer, and Albright (2005) and Levine, the What Works Working Group, with Kinder (2004).

51. Some private foundations such as Gates and Rockefeller put large portions of their total grant making into global programs that sometimes operate at the "regional" level, but even in these cases, the focus is global.

52. Birdsall (2004).

53. A working group at the Center for Global Development has proposed that the shareholders of the World Bank and the Inter-American Development Bank consider a much stronger mandate with adequate financing to substantially expand their financial, strategic, and technical support for respectively, global and regional public goods. See Birdsall and Kapur (2005) and CLAAF and CGD (2006).

54. The World Bank could be asked to do technical work; much is already set out in World Bank (2004). It is a matter of turning analysis into ideas for new instruments, procedures, and practices.

References

Acemoglu, Daron, Simon Johnson, and James Robinson. 2004. "Institutions as the Fundamental Cause of Long-Run Growth." NBER Working Paper 10481. Cambridge, Mass.: National Bureau of Economic Research.

Acharya, Arnab, Ana Fuzzo de Lima, and Mick Moore. 2003. "The Proliferators: Transactions Costs and the Value of Aid." IDS Working Paper. Sussex, UK: Institute of Development Studies.

Atkinson, Tony. 2003. "Innovative Sources for Development Finance—Global Public Economics." Paper presented at Annual Bank Conference on Development Economics in Europe, May 15–16. Available at http://wbln0018.worldbank.org/eurvp/web.nsf/Pages/Paper+by+Atkinson/$File/ATKINSON.PDF.

Bhavnani, Rikhil, Nancy Birdsall, and Isaac Shapiro. 2004. "Whither Development Assistance? An Analysis of the President's 2005 Budget Request." Washington, D.C.: Center for Global Development and Center on Budget and Policy Priorities.

Bird, Graham, Mumtaz Hussain, and Joseph P. Joyce. 2004. "Many Happy Returns? Recidivism and the IMF." *Journal of International Money and Finance* 23(2):231–252.

Birdsall, Nancy. 2005. "Why It Matters Who Runs the IMF and the World Bank." In Gustav Ranis, James Raymond Vreeland, and Stephen Kosack, eds., *Globalization and the Nation State: The Impact of the IMF and the World Bank*. London: Routledge.

Birdsall, Nancy. 2006. "Underfunded Regionalism in the Developing World." In Inge Kaul and Pedro Conceição, eds., *The New Public Finance: Responding to Global Challenges*. New York: Oxford University Press.

Birdsall, Nancy. 2007. "Do No Harm: Aid, Weak Institutions and the Missing Middle in Africa." *Development Policy Review* 25(5):575–598.

Birdsall, Nancy, Stijn Claessens, and Ishac Diwan. 2004. "Policy Selectivity Foregone: Debt and Donor Behavior in Africa." *World Bank Economic Review* 17(3):409–435.

Birdsall, Nancy, and Michael Clemens. 2003. "From Promise to Performance: How Rich Countries Can Help Poor Countries Help Themselves." CGD Brief Vol. 2(1). Washington, D.C.: Center for Global Development.

Birdsall, Nancy, and Brian Deese. 2004. "Hard Currency Unilateralism Doesn't Work for Foreign Aid Either." *Washington Monthly*, March. Available at http://www.washingtonmonthly.com/features/2004/0403.birdsall.html.

Birdsall, Nancy, and Devesh Kapur. 2005. *The Hardest Job in the World: Five Crucial Tasks for the New President of the World Bank*. Washington, D.C.: Center for Global Development World Bank Working Group. Available at http://www.cgdev.org/content/publications/detail/2868/.

Birdsall, Nancy, and Todd Moss. 2004. "How Wall Street Can Aid the Poor of the World." *Financial Times*, April 30.

Birdsall, Nancy, and Arvind Subramanian. 2004. "Saving Iraq from Its Oil." *Foreign Affairs* 83(4):77–89.

Birdsall, Nancy, and Milan Vaishnav. 2004. "Getting to Home Plate: Why *Smarter* Debt Relief Matters for the Millennium Development Goals." Prepared for the Helsinki Process on Globalisation and Democracy, March 26–28. Available at http://www.cgdev.org/docs/Debt%20Relief%20and%20the%20MDGs.pdf.

Birdsall, Nancy, Milan Vaishnav, and Adeel Malik. 2005. "Poverty and the Social Sectors: The World Bank in Pakistan." Washington, D.C.: Operations Evaluations Department, World Bank.

Birdsall, Nancy, and John Williamson. 2002. *Delivering on Debt Relief: From IMF Gold to a New Aid Architecture*. Washington, D.C.: Center for Global Development.

Brautigam, Deborah. 2000. *Aid Dependence and Governance*. Stockholm: Almquist & Wiksell International.

Brautigam, Deborah A., and Stephen Knack. "Aid Dependence, Institutions and Governance in Sub-Saharan Africa." *Economic Development and Cultural Change* 52(2):255–285.

Bulír, Aleš, and Timothy D. Lane. 2004. "Aid and Fiscal Management." In Sanjeev Gupta, Benedict Clements, and Gabriela Inchauste, eds., *Helping Countries Develop: The Role of Fiscal Policy*. Washington, D.C.: International Monetary Fund.

Bulír, Aleš, and A. Javier Hamann. 2001. "How Volatile and Predictable Are Aid Flows, and What Are the Policy Implications?" IMF Working Paper no. 01/167. Washington, D.C.: International Monetary Fund.

Bulír, Aleš, and A. Javier Hamann. 2003. "Aid Volatility: An Empirical Assessment." *IMF Staff Papers* 50(1):64–89.

Burnside, Craig, and David Dollar. 2000. "Aid, Policies and Growth." *American Economic Review* 90(4):847–868.

Burnside, Craig, and David Dollar. 2004. "Aid, Policies and Growth: Revisiting the Evidence." World Bank Policy Research Paper no. O-2834. Washington, D.C.: World Bank.

CEIP and IAD. 2001. "The Role of the Multilateral Development Banks in Emerging Markets." Washington, D.C.: Carnegie Endowment for International Peace and the Inter-American Dialogue.

Center for Global Development and Foreign Policy. 2006. "Ranking the Rich 2004." *Foreign Policy*, May–June.

Christian Aid. 2002. "Quality Participation in Poverty Reduction Strategies: Experiences from Malawi, Bolivia and Rwanda." Available at http://www.christianaid.org.uk/iindepth/0208qual/quality .htm.

CLAAF and CGD. 2006. *Priorities and Challenges for the New Era of the Inter-American Development Bank.* Comité Latinoamericano de Asuntos Financieros and Center for Global Development.

Clemens, Michael. 2004. "The Long Walk to School: International Education Goals in Historical Perspective." CGD Working Paper 39. Washington, D.C.: Center for Global Development.

Clemens, Michael, Charles J. Kenny, and Todd Moss. 2004. "The Trouble with the MGDs: Confronting Expectations of Aid and Development Success." CGD Working Paper 40. Washington, D.C.: Center for Global Development.

Clemens, Michael, Steve Radelet, and Rikhil Bhavnani. 2004. "Counting Chickens When They Hatch: The Short-Term Effect of Aid on Growth." CGD Working Paper 44. Washington, D.C.: Center for Global Development.

Cline, William. 2003. "HIPC Debt Sustainability and Post-Relief Lending Policy." Washington, D.C.: HIPC Unit, World Bank.

Cline, William. 2004. *Trade Policy and Global Poverty.* Washington, D.C.: Center for Global Development.

Collier, Paul, and David Dollar. 2000. "Can the World Cut Poverty in Half? How Policy Reform and Effective Aid Can Meet the International Development Goals." World Bank Policy Research Working Paper 2403. Washington, D.C.: World Bank.

Collier, Paul, and David Dollar. 2002. "Aid Allocation and Poverty Reduction." *European Economic Review* 46(8):1475–1500.

Collier, Paul, Patrick Guillaumont, Sylviane Guillaumont, and Jan Willem Gunning. 1997. "Redesigning Conditionality." *World Development* 25(9):1399–1407.

Collier, Paul, and Anke Hoeffler. 2002. "Aid, Policy, and Growth in Post-Conflict Societies." Washington, D.C.: World Bank Development Research Group.

Commission on Weak States and U.S. National Security. 2004. *On the Brink: Weak States and U.S. National Security.* Washington, D.C.: Center for Global Development.

DAC. 2001. "Poor Performers: Basic Approaches for Supporting Development in Difficult Partnerships." Note by the Secretariat, DCD/DAC(2001)26/REV1. Paris: Organization for Economic Cooperation Development.

Dervis, Kemal. 2005. *A Better Globalization: Perspectives on Legitimacy Reform and Global Governance.* Washington, D.C.: Center for Global Development.

Easterly, William. 2002a. "What Did Structural Adjustment Adjust? The Association of Policies and Growth with Repeated IMF and World Bank Adjustment Loans." CGD Working Paper 11. Washington, D.C.: Center for Global Development.

Easterly, William. 2002b. "The Cartel of Good Intentions: Bureaucracy versus Markets in Foreign Aid." CGD Working Paper 4. Washington, D.C.: Center for Global Development.

Easterly, William, and David Dollar. 1999. "The Search for the Key: Aid, Investment, and Policies in Africa." *Journal of African Economies* 8(4):546–577.

Easterly, William, Ross Levine, and David Roodman. 2003. "New Data. New Doubts: A Comment on Burnside and Dollar's 'Aid, Policies, and Growth (2000).'" NBER Working Paper 9846. Cambridge, Mass.: National Bureau of Economic Research.

Evenson, Robert E. 1987. "The International Agricultural Research Centers: Their Impact on Spending for National Agricultural Research and Extension." CGIAR Study Paper 22. Washington, D.C.: Consultative Group on International Agricultural Research, World Bank.

Gunning, Jan Willem. 2000. "The Reform of Aid: Conditionality, Selectivity and Ownership." Paper presented at Aid and Development Conference, Stockholm, January 21–22. Available at http://www.sida.se/Sida/articles/3600–3699/3676/papgun.pdf.

Gupta, Sanjeev, Benedict Clements, Alexander Pivovarsky, and Erwin R. Tiongson. 2004. "Foreign Aid and Revenue Response: Does the Composition of Aid Matter?" In Sanjeev Gupta, Benedict Clements, and Gabriela Inchauste, eds., Helping Countries Develop: The Role of Fiscal Policy. Washington, D.C.: International Monetary Fund.

Hansen, Henrik, and Finn Tarp. 2001. "Aid and Growth Regressions." Journal of Development Economics 64(2):547–570.

Harford, Tim, Bita Hadjimichael, and Michael Klein. 2004. "Aid Agency Competition." World Bank Private Sector Development Presidency, Note 277. Washington, D.C.: World Bank.

Hausmann, Ricardo, and Rodrik, Dani. 2002. "Economic Development as Self-Discovery." NBER Working Paper 8952. Cambridge, Mass.: National Bureau of Economic Research.

Hibbs, Douglas A., Jr., and Ola Olsson. 2004. "Geography, Biogeography and Why Some Countries are Rich and Others Poor." Proceedings of the National Academy of Sciences of the United States 101:3715–3720.

IDA. 2003. "IDA's Commitments, Disbursements and Funding in FY03." International Development Association Board Report 27081. Washington, D.C.: World Bank.

IDA. 2004. "Allocating IDA Funds Based on Performance. Fourth Annual Report on IDA's Country Assessment and Allocation Process." Washington, D.C.: International Development Association.

IEO. 2002. "Evaluation of Prolonged Use of IMF Resources." Internal Evaluations Office of the International Monetary Fund. Evaluation Report. Washington, D.C.: International Monetary Fund.

IMF and IDA. 2004. "Debt Sustainability in Low-Income Countries: Further Considerations on an Operational Framework and Policy Implications." Available at http://siteresources.worldbank.org/INTDEBTDEPT/PolicyPapers/20279458/DSfullpapersept.pdf.

Inter-American Development Bank. 2003. "Annual Report." Washington, D.C.: Inter-American Development Bank.

Joyce, Joseph P. 2003. "Promises Made, Promises Broken: A Model of IMF Program Implementation." Wellesley College Department of Economics Working Paper 2003-04. Wellesley, Mass.: Wellesley College.

Joyce, Joseph P. 2005. "Time Present and Time Past: A Duration Analysis of IMF Program Spells." Review of International Economics 13(2):283–297.

Kanbur, Ravi, and Todd Sandler with Kevin Morrison. 1999. "The Future of Development Assistance: Common Pools and International Public Goods." Overseas Development Council Policy Essay 25. Washington, D.C.: Overseas Development Council.

Kaufmann, Daniel, Aart Kraay, and Pablo Zoido-Lobaton. 2002. "Governance Matters II: Updated Indicators for 2000/01." World Bank Policy Research Working Paper 2772. Washington, D.C.: World Bank.

Killick, Tony. 2004. "Politics, Evidence and the New Aid Agenda." Development Policy Review 22(1):5–29.

Knack, Stephen. "Aid Dependence and the Quality of Governance: A Cross-Country Empirical Analysis." Southern Economic Journal 68(2):310–329.

Knack, Stephen, and Aminur Rahman. 2004. "Donor Fragmentation and Bureaucratic Quality in Aid Recipients." World Bank Policy Research Working Paper 3186. Washington, D.C.: World Bank.

Kremer, Michael, and Rachel Glennerster. 2004. *Strong Medicine: Creating Incentives for Pharmaceutical Research on Neglected Diseases.* Princeton, N.J.: Princeton University Press.

Lancaster, Carol. 2007. *Foreign Aid: Diplomacy, Development, Domestic Politics.* Chicago, IL: University of Chicago Press.

Levine, Ruth, Michael Kremer, and Alice Albright. 2005. *Making Markets for Vaccines: Ideas to Action.* Washington, D.C.: Center for Global Development.

Levine, Ruth, and the What Works Working Group with Molly Kinder. 2004. *Millions Saved: Proven Successes in Global Health.* Washington, D.C.: Center for Global Development.

Meltzer, Allan H. 2000. "Report of the International Financial Institution Advisory Commission." Available at http://www.house.gov/jec/imf/meltzer.pdf.

Moss, Todd, and Michael Clemens. 2005. "Ghost of 0.7%: Origins and Relevance of the International Aid Target." CGD Working Paper 68. Washington, D.C.: Center for Global Development.

Moss, Todd, Gunilla Pettersson, and Nicolas van de Walle. 2005. "An Aid-Institutions Paradox? A Review Essay on Aid Dependency and State Building in Sub-Saharan Africa." Mario Einaudi Center for International Studies Working Paper 11-05. Ithaca, N.Y.

North, Douglass C. 1990. *Institutions, Institutional Change, and Economic Performance.* Cambridge: Cambridge University Press.

O'Connell, Stephen A., and Charles C. Soludo. 1998. "Aid Intensity in Africa." CSAE Working Paper 88. Oxford: Centre for the Study of African Economies.

ODC. 2000. "The Right Role for the IMF in Development." Overseas Development Council Task Force Report. Washington, D.C.: Overseas Development Council.

OECD/DAC Database. 2004. Available at http://222.oecd.org/dataoecd/50/17/5037721.htm.

Pearson, Lester B. 1969. *Partners in Development: Report of the Commission on International Development.* New York: Praeger.

Picciotto, Robert. 2004. "Aid and Conflict: The Policy Coherence Challenge." Paper presented at the Security and Development Workshop, New Delhi, January 25–26, organized by the Global Policy Project. Available at http://www.wider.unu.edu/conference/conference-2004–1/conference%202004–1–papers/Picciotto-2505.pdf.

Pritchett, Lant. 2002. "It Pays to Be Ignorant: A Simple Political Economy of Rigorous Program Evaluation." *Journal of Policy Reform* 5(4):251–269.

Radelet, Steven. 2003. *Challenging Foreign Aid: A Policymaker's Guide to the Millennium Challenge Account.* Washington, D.C.: Center for Global Development.

Radelet, Steve. 2004a. *Challenging Foreign Aid. A Policymaker's Guide to the Millennium Challenge Account.* Washington, D.C.: Center for Global Development.

Radelet, Steve. 2004b. "Aid Effectiveness and the Millennium Development Goals." CGD Working Paper 30. Washington, D.C.: Center for Global Development.

Radelet, Steve, Sarah Lucas, and Rikhil Bhavnani. 2004. "2004 MCA Threshold Program: A Comment on Country Selection." Washington, D.C.: Center for Global Development.

Rajan, Raghuram G., and Arvind Subramanian. 2005. "Aid and Growth: What Does the Cross-Country Evidence Really Show?" NBER Working Paper W11513. Cambridge, Mass.: National Bureau of Economic Research.

Reisen, Helmut, Marcelo Soto, and Thomas Weithöner. 2004. "Financing Global and Regional Public Goods through ODA: Analysis and Evidence from the OECD Creditor Reporting System." OECD Working Paper 232. Paris: Organization for Economic Cooperation and Development.

Rigobon, Roberto, and Dani Rodrik. 2004. "Rule of Law, Openness, and Income: Estimating the Interrelationships." NBER Working Paper W10750. Cambridge, Mass.: National Bureau of Economic Research.

Rodrik, Dani. 2000. "Institutions for High-Quality Growth: What They Are and How to Acquire Them." NBER Working Paper 7540. Cambridge, Mass.: National Bureau of Economic Research.

Rodrik, Dani. 2003. "Growth Strategies." CEPR Discussion Paper 4100. London: Centre for Economic Policy Research.

Rodrik, Dani. 2004. "Getting Institutions Right." Available at http://ksghome.harvard.edu/~drodrik/ifo-institutions%20article%20_April%202004_.pdf.

Roodman, David. 2003. "The Anarchy of Numbers: Aid, Development, and Cross-Country Empirics." CGD Working Paper 32. Washington, D.C.: Center for Global Development.

Sewell, John, Nancy Birdsall, and Kevin Morrison. 2000. "The Right Role for the IMF in Development." ODC Task Force on the Future Role of the IMF in Development. Washington, D.C.: Overseas Development Council.

Soros, George. 2002. *George Soros on Globalization.* Oxford: Public Affairs.

Stewart, Frances. 2004. "Development and security." CRISE Working Paper 3. Oxford: Centre for Research on Inequality, Human Security and Ethnicity.

United Nations Millennium Project. 2004. "Global Plan to Reach the Millennium Development Goals." Draft. November 12.

Van de Walle, Nicolas. 2005. *Stagnation, Power and Politics in Aid-Dependent Countries.* Washington, D.C.: Center for Global Development.

Weinstein, Jeremy. 2004. "Which Path to Peace? Autonomous Recovery and International Intervention in Comparative Perspective." Mimeo., Stanford University.

World Bank. 2002. "World Bank Group Work in Low-Income Countries Under Stress: A Task Force Report." Washington, D.C.: World Bank.

World Bank. 2003. *Annual Report.* Washington, D.C.: World Bank.

World Bank. 2004. *World Development Report 2004: Making Services Work for the Poor.* Washington, D.C.: World Bank.

World Bank Operations Evaluation Department. 2005. *2004 Annual Report on Operations Evaluation.* Washington, D.C.: World Bank.

Contributors

Abhijit Banerjee
Massachusetts Institute of
Technology

Nancy Birdsall
Center for Global Development

Esther Duflo
Massachusetts Institute of
Technology

William Easterly
New York University

Ruimin He
Massachusetts Institute of
Technology

Kurt Hoffman
Shell Foundation

Stephen Knack
The World Bank

Michael Kremer
Harvard University

Mari Kuraishi
GlobalGiving Foundation

Ruth Levine
Center for Global Development

Bertin Martens
Vrije Universiteit Brussel

John McMillan
Stanford University

Edward Miguel
University of California, Berkeley

Jonathan Morduch
New York University

Todd Moss
Center for Global Development

Gunilla Pettersson
Mid Sweden University

Lant Pritchett
The World Bank

Steven Radelet
Center for Global Development

Aminur Rahman
University College London

Ritva Reinikka
The World Bank

Jakob Svensson
Stockholm University

Nicolas van de Walle
Mario Einaudi Center for
International Studies

James Raymond Vreeland
Yale University

Dennis Whittle
GlobalGiving Foundation

Michael Woolcock
The World Bank and Kennedy
School of Government, Harvard
University

Index